Ashley
Seville

Did you
picture?

Scholastic Children's Encyclopedia

Scholastic
Children's
Encyclopedia

Library of Congress Cataloging-in-Publication Data

Scholastic children's encyclopedia.

p. cm.

Includes index.

Summary: Presents brief articles on a wide variety of topics from Abolition Movement and Earthquakes to Prehistoric Peoples and Zoology.

ISBN 0-439-43816-0

1. Children's encyclopedias and dictionaries. [1. Encyclopedias and
    dictionaries.] I. Scholastic Inc.

AG5.S36 2004

031–dc21   2003045591

10 9 8 7 6 5 4 3 2 1   04 05 06 07 08

Printed in the U.S.A.   56

First printing, August 2004

CONTENTS

STAFF AND ADVISORY BOARD

Encyclopedia Staff

SCHOLASTIC INC.

Editorial Director	Kenneth Wright
Editors	Virginia Koeth
	Danielle Denega
	Paula Manzanero
Art Director	Nancy Sabato
Managing Editor	Karyn Browne
Production Editor	Karen Capria
Manufacturing	Heidi Robinson
Coordinators	Ann Goff

THE BROWN REFERENCE GROUP PLC

Project Editor	Claire Chandler
Designer	Wayne Humphries
Picture Researcher	Sharon Southren
Editors	Clive Carpenter
	Tim Footman
	Fiona Plowman
	Gillian Sutton
	Matt Turner
Maps	Mark Walker
Illustration	Darren Awuah
Index	Kay Ollerenshaw
Art Director	Dave Goodman
Production Director	Alastair Gourlay
Managing Editor	Tim Cooke
Editorial Director	Lindsey Lowe

Advisory Board

General Consultant	Robert Stremme, NBCT, Longstreth School, Centennial School District, Warminster, PA, and Eastern University, St. Davids, PA
Library Advisors	Ellen Fader, Youth Services Coordinator, Multnomah County Library, Oregon Kathleen T. Horning, Special Collections Coordinator, Cooperative Children's Book Center, School of Education, University of Wisconsin-Madison
Language Arts Advisor	Beverly Ann Chin, Professor of English, University of Montana
Science Advisor	Stephen M. Tomecek, Executive Director, Science Plus Inc., Bellerose, New York

TIMELINE OF HISTORIC PERIODS

A NOTE ON DATES

In this encyclopedia, phrases such as "in the 19th century" often appear. A century is a period of 100 years. But "in the 19th century" does not mean the same as the phrase "in the 1900s." It actually refers to the years 1801–1900. "In the 1900s" refers to the years 1900–99. A decade is a period of 10 years. The phrase "the 1920s" refers to the years 1920–29.

About 1,500 years ago, a monk named Dionysius Exiguus suggested that the system of counting years be reset to honor the birth of Jesus Christ. He called the first year of the Christian Era *Anno Domini* (abbreviated as A.D.), meaning "in the year of our Lord." Dionysius believed that Christ was born on December 25 of the year preceding A.D. 1. This year is known as 1 B.C. (before Christ). (In fact, the birth of Christ is now placed several years before the date adopted by Dionysius.) There is no "year 0" between 1 B.C. and A.D. 1. Therefore, the first century of the Christian Era began in A.D. 1 and finished at the end of the year A.D. 100. This means that the 21st century officially began on January 1, 2001, although the beginning of the new century and the new millennium (a period of 1,000 years) was widely celebrated at the start of the year 2000.

The timeline on this page shows the approximate dates of some major historic periods. When we study the history of entire civilizations or regions, it is useful to divide the subject into periods. However, history is not an exact science, and it is impossible to give precise dates, especially because periods are often identified and named many years after the events took place. There is seldom a single event that "opens" or "closes" a particular period, and periods frequently overlap. In particular, the early periods of this timeline occurred at different times in different parts of the world.

2,500,000 B.C.	**Paleolithic Period** (Old Stone Age)	STONE AGE
9000 B.C.	**Mesolithic Period** (Middle Stone Age)	STONE AGE
6000 B.C.	**Neolithic Period** (New Stone Age)	STONE AGE
3300 B.C.	**Bronze Age**	
1500 B.C.	**Iron Age**	
800 B.C.	**Classical Age**	
A.D. 476	**Early Middle Ages**	MIDDLE AGES
1000	**High Middle Ages**	MIDDLE AGES
1300	**Late Middle Ages**	MIDDLE AGES
1375	**Renaissance**	
1500	**Reformation**	
1650	**Age of Enlightenment**	
1789	**Age of Revolution**	MODERN AGE
1848	**Age of Liberalism**	MODERN AGE
1914	**Age of World Wars**	MODERN AGE
1945	**Nuclear Age**	MODERN AGE
1980	**Digital Age**	MODERN AGE

HOW TO USE THIS ENCYCLOPEDIA

The entries in this all-new general encyclopedia are arranged alphabetically, letter by letter. Entries are illustrated with photographs, diagrams, timelines, and maps. The maps show the key geographical features, capitals, and major cities for continents, regions, and countries. On the country maps, capital cities are indicated by black squares; other cities are indicated by black dots. Population figures for the United States and Canada are based on the 2000 U.S. Census and the 2001 Canadian Census. Population figures for other countries are based on mid-2000 estimates provided by the United Nations. Biography boxes introduce some of the people who have made important contributions to many subject areas.

"Did You Know?" boxes provide detailed information on a wide range of topics.

"See also" boxes refer you to entries on closely related topics for each entry.

The section called **For Further Reference** at the end of the book contains maps, tables, and diagrams on key topics. There is also a detailed index of the encyclopedia's contents.

This guide explains the other features of the encyclopedia.

Entry headings are marked with an asterisk.

K

* KORAN

The Koran (also called the Qur'an) is the sacred book of Islam, the world's second-largest religion. It is one of the most important books in history.

The followers of Islam—Muslims—believe that the Koran contains the actual words, or revelations, of God (Allah) that were delivered to the prophet Muhammad (about A.D. 570–632) by the archangel Gabriel in Arabia. Muhammad recited these words to his followers, and they became the basis of Islam.

Contents

The Koran focuses on the importance of submitting to Allah's will, correct moral behavior, and the coming Day of Judgment. It promises rewards for good and punishment for evil—Paradise and Hell, which are both described in detail.

The Koran also includes many biblical stories, such as those featuring Adam and Eve, Noah and the flood, and Moses. But some of the details of the stories are different from those found in the Bible.

Organization

Unlike the Bible, the Koran is not organized chronologically (in the order in which events happened). It has 114 chapters, called surahs. These are divided into more than 6,000 verses, or ayahs. The chapters are ordered according to length, from the longest to the shortest. Each chapter is designed to stand alone.

Certain themes appear more than once: people's relationship with Allah; politics; and family matters. Although the Koran is seen as the ultimate source of divine instruction, it contains very few laws.

The Koran is written in beautiful, poetic language. Muslims show great respect for their holy book. It must never be laid on the ground or allowed to get dirty. It has been translated into many different languages, but only the original Arabic text is believed to be the true Koran.

DID YOU KNOW?

Many Muslims memorize the whole of the Koran, and Muslim children study it in school. If a person memorizes the Koran perfectly, they become a *Hafiz*, which means "preserver." To achieve this is seen as a sign of spiritual excellence.

Many Muslims around the world learn Arabic so that they can study the Koran in its original form.

SEE ALSO:
Bible; Islam; Religions

346

Cross-references direct you from a term not used as an entry to the entry where information will be found.

Informative captions clarify illustrations and photographs.

Dougl... first b... to hol... gover... positi...

184

KOREA
The divided country of Korea lies on a peninsula n East Asia situated between China and Japan.

orea was liberated from 35 years of panese rule in 1945. In 1948 the country as divided into two states—the Republic Korea (South Korea) and the Democratic ople's Republic of Korea (North Korea).

and and climate
though Korea has wide, fertile valleys in e south and west that produce rice and her crops, the rest of the countryside is ountainous. Only about one-fifth of the nd is suitable for farming.

the northern inland areas, winter mperatures remain below freezing five months. Along the coasts in the uth, warm ocean currents moderate mperatures so that they rarely fall below eezing. All of Korea has hot summers.

ople and economy
though North Korea is the larger state in ea, South Korea has nearly twice as any people. Most of the population is sed in lowland areas in the west and uth. The main religions are Buddhism, ristianity, and a native Korean religion lled Chondokyo, or "religion of the avenly way." In North Korea, where a mmunist government holds power, all rms of religion are strongly discouraged.

e economy of North Korea is controlled the state. It aims to meet all its own eeds for goods and has little foreign de. By contrast, South Korea produces any goods for export and is the world's th-largest trading country.

istory
orea's history dates back thousands of ars. China and Japan have been strong fluences on Korea throughout its history.

Both North and South Korea were admitted to the United Nations in 1991. Later that year they signed a treaty of reconciliation and nonaggression.

North Korea's national flag

South Korea's national flag

SEE ALSO: Buddhism; China; Communism; Japan; Korean War

KEY FACTS

OFFICIAL NAME:
Democratic People's Republic of Korea (North Korea)

AREA:
46,540 sq. mi. (120,539 sq. km)

POPULATION:
24,039,000

CAPITAL & LARGEST CITY:
Pyongyang

MAJOR RELIGION:
None

MAJOR LANGUAGE:
Korean

CURRENCY:
Won

OFFICIAL NAME:
Republic of Korea (South Korea)

AREA:
38,025 sq. mi. (98,485 sq. km)

POPULATION:
46,844,000

CAPITAL & LARGEST CITY:
Seoul

MAJOR RELIGIONS:
Buddhism, Christianity, Chondokyo

MAJOR LANGUAGE:
Korean

CURRENCY:
Won

347

many to chase badgers. Hunters on rseback often follow a pack of

hundreds, sometimes thousands, of years and are especially popular as show dogs.

OLPHINS SEE ⋆WHALES AND DOLPHINS

OUGLASS, FREDERICK (1817–95)
rederick Douglass was one of the most dynamic aders of the abolition movement, which worked get rid of slavery.

derick Douglass was born Frederick gustus Washington Bailey in Maryland. was the son of a white father and a ve mother. He learned to read and te while working as a house slave. 1838 he escaped to the North and anged his name.

1841 Douglass addressed a meeting the Massachusetts Anti-Slavery ciety. He spoke so well that some ople doubted he could ever have en a slave. In response, he wrote an tobiography entitled Narrative of the e of Frederick Douglass.

In 1845 Douglass went on a lecture tour of England, earning the money to buy his freedom. In 1847 he founded North Star, an antislavery newspaper. During the Civil War (1861–65) he organized regiments of black soldiers. After the war, he became a leader of the Republican Party. From 1889 to 1891, he was U.S. minister to Haiti.

SEE ALSO: Abolition Movement; African Americans; Civil Rights; Civil War; Emancipation Proclamation; Slavery

E

S AND HEARING
ing is the sense that receives sound. Ears ive sound waves and change them into signals the brain translates into the sensation of sound.

described by volume—how loud d by frequency—how high or low lume is measured in decibels. A conversation is about 65 decibels. cy is measured in hertz. Most can hear frequencies between about 16 and 20,000 hertz.

People hear sounds when they pick up vibrations called sound waves. The waves enter the ear and strike the eardrum, causing a vibration that moves tiny bones inside the skull. This sends a message along the auditory nerves to the brain.

The brain does not just register the volume and frequency of sounds. It also makes sense of them. A loud rock band

and a pneumatic drill might sound similar, but the human brain can tell them apart.

Many animals need more sensitive hearing than humans so they can hear their prey. Dolphins and bats make ultrasonic sounds that are too high-pitched to be heard by the human ear.

When a person cannot hear the normal range of volume or frequency, he or she has a hearing impairment. If someone cannot hear sounds below 90 decibels, the condition is identified as deafness.

SEE ALSO:
Bats; Brain and Nervous System; Human Body; Sound; Whales and Dolphins

AMAZING FACTS!

The Beatles' album Sergeant Pepper's Lonely Hearts Club Band (1967) ends with a sound so high-pitched that humans cannot hear it—but dogs can.
A blue whale can make low-frequency noises with a volume of 188 decibels. By comparison, a jumbo jet on takeoff only makes a sound of 120 decibels.

INSIDE THE EAR

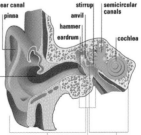

ear canal | pinna | stirrup | anvil | hammer | eardrum | semicircular canals | cochlea

outer ear | middle ear | inner ear

The outer ear is made up of the pinna, which is the part that you can see, and the ear canal. The middle ear contains three tiny bones that connect the inner and the outer ear. The inner ear has sensory receptors for hearing, and it controls balance.

185

ix

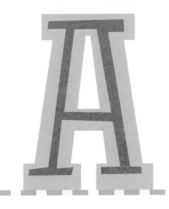

✳ ABOLITION MOVEMENT
The abolition movement was a campaign to free American blacks from slavery. The word *abolition* comes from *abolish*, which means to "get rid of."

The first slaves in America were black Africans who arrived in the 1600s. White European settlers put them to work on plantations, in mines, or in their homes. Many slave owners did not see their slaves as people with rights and feelings. Instead, they bought and sold them like goods. Late in the 17th century, some groups argued that slavery was wrong and should be abolished.

Many Americans agreed. They pressed the government to abolish slavery. It was a long fight, but by 1804 slavery was prohibited in many Northern states. In 1808 it became illegal to import slaves to the United States, though slaves and their children remained slaves.

Slavery remained important in the South. The South depended on cotton, and slaves did most of the work in the cotton fields. The campaign against slavery in the South united black and white Americans. They made speeches and wrote books against slavery. In 1833 the American Anti-Slavery Society was founded. Still, the situation in the South did not change.

War over slavery
As America expanded westward in the 19th century, settlers in new states could choose whether or not to allow slavery. In 1854 Nebraskans voted against slavery,

but Kansans voted for it. In response, John Brown, an abolitionist, attacked and killed Kansas slaveholders.

Meanwhile, other abolitionists secretly helped slaves escape to the North in spite of an 1850 law against doing so. Some people believed that all abolitionists were encouraging people to break the law.

Attitudes toward slavery divided the North and South. The Southern states tried to leave the Union, sparking the Civil War in April 1861. On September 22, 1862, President Abraham Lincoln issued the Emancipation Proclamation. It promised that any slave in the United States would be "forever free."

The Civil War ended in a victory for the North in April 1865. Later that year, the 13th Amendment to the Constitution made slavery illegal in the United States.

Sojourner Truth was born a slave in about 1797. In 1843 she began traveling around the United States, speaking out against slavery. She died in 1883.

SEE ALSO: African Americans; Civil Rights; Civil War; Constitution, United States; Douglass, Frederick; Emancipation Proclamation; Slavery; Tubman, Harriet

✳ ABORIGINES

The word *aborigine* describes the earliest known people to live in a land. It is mostly used to describe the first inhabitants of Australia.

The first journey
The Aborigines of Australia left Southeast Asia more than 40,000 years ago. They probably crossed the ocean to Australia by raft or dugout canoe.

Life in Australia
The Aborigines formed about 500 tribal groups. Each had its own language. Every tribe had a territory (area of land) where they hunted, fished, and gathered food.

Tribes were like large families, made up of several clans, or groups, of 30 to 40 people. Each clan had a symbol, or totem—usually an animal or a plant.

The Aborigines believed that all things on Earth—people, animals, plants, and even rocks—were important parts of nature and of the unseen spirit world.

The Aborigines used spears and several types of curved throwing sticks called boomerangs—some for sport, others for hunting or fighting. They also created rock carvings and painted pictures on cave walls and strips of tree bark.

In 1788, when the first European settlers came to Australia, there were perhaps more than 300,000 Aborigines. As the Europeans spread out, they drove Aborigines from their lands into remote areas. Many died from foreign diseases.

Modern Aborigines
Today there are about 352,000 Aboriginal people in Australia, or about 1.5 percent of the national population. Roughly one-third of them are wholly Aborigine. The rest have some European ancestry.

Most Aborigines live in cities or towns. In the past few decades the Australian government has run programs to help the Aborigines get jobs and houses.

Land ownership
The Aborigines of today want to live freely on their ancestral lands. In 1992 the Australian High Court ruled that the Aborigines had owned Australia before European settlers arrived. Since 1993, the Aborigines have been allowed to claim land as "natives." They now own parts of the Northern Territory, South Australia, and Western Australia.

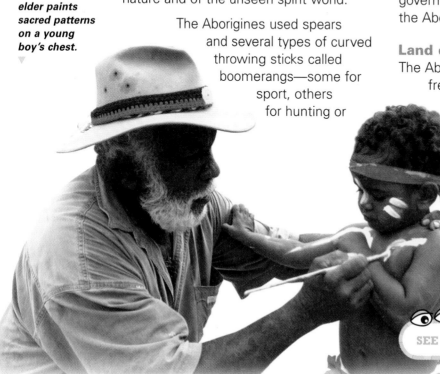

An Aboriginal elder paints sacred patterns on a young boy's chest.

SEE ALSO: **Australia and New Zealand**

✳ ADDAMS, JANE (1860–1935)

Jane Addams worked to make life better for women and for poor people. She founded Hull House, a center that offered help and education.

Born on September 6, 1860, in Cedarville, Illinois, Jane Addams came from a wealthy family. She attended Rockford College and then went to medical school, but poor health forced her to leave.

While traveling in England, Addams became impressed with Toynbee Hall. Founded in 1884, it was a settlement house—a place offering help to the poor.

In 1889, with the help of Ellen Gates Starr, Addams founded Hull House in Chicago. She opened its doors to city people from poor neighborhoods. Many of them had come from other countries to seek a better life. Some had not been to school and spoke no English.

By 1907 Hull House had grown to 13 buildings. It offered help with child care, adult education, and other services. Meanwhile, Addams fought for new labor laws to protect children from being forced to work, and women from working more than eight hours a day. She tried hard to win women the right to vote. She also published many books and articles, including *Twenty Years at Hull House*.

Jane Addams worked hard for world peace. In 1931 she won the Nobel Peace Prize.

SEE ALSO: Education; Nobel Prize; Women's Rights

✳AFRICA

Africa is the world's second-largest continent in area after Asia. It also has the highest population after Asia.

Land and climate

Africa is made up of 53 countries, 6 of which are islands. The continent lies across the equator, and much of it is extremely hot. In the north is the world's largest desert, the Sahara, which is almost the same size as the United States. The world's longest river, the Nile, flows through Egypt. Across Central Africa, near the equator, rainfall is high, and tropical rain forests grow. Between the forests and the deserts lie savannas—grassy plains dotted with trees.

Much of Africa is made up of plateaus (flat areas of high land). The eastern plateau is cut by the Great Rift Valley, a crack in the earth's crust that was created by volcanic activity. Some of Africa's largest lakes lie in the Rift's long valleys.

Plants and animals

The plants and animals of the deserts are adapted to the harsh, dry conditions. The equatorial rain forests are home to gorillas, forest elephants, and tropical birds. On the savannas live some of the world's most

(continued on page 5)

3

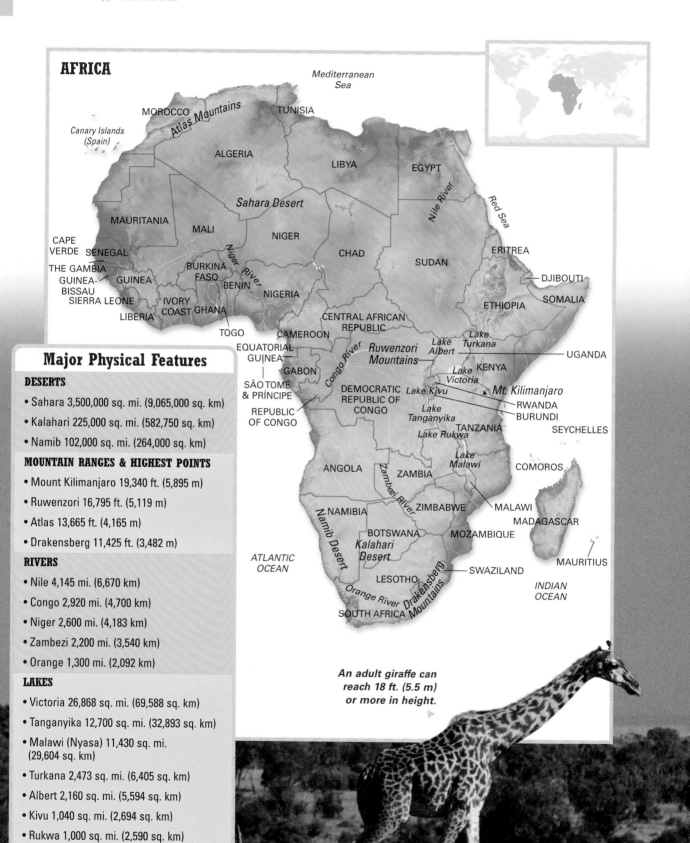

AFRICA

Mediterranean Sea

MOROCCO
Atlas Mountains
TUNISIA
Canary Islands (Spain)
ALGERIA
LIBYA
EGYPT
Nile River
Red Sea
Sahara Desert
MAURITANIA
MALI
NIGER
CHAD
SUDAN
ERITREA
CAPE VERDE
SENEGAL
BURKINA FASO
Niger River
DJIBOUTI
THE GAMBIA
GUINEA-BISSAU
GUINEA
BENIN
NIGERIA
SIERRA LEONE
IVORY COAST
GHANA
LIBERIA
TOGO
CAMEROON
CENTRAL AFRICAN REPUBLIC
ETHIOPIA
SOMALIA
EQUATORIAL GUINEA
Congo River
Ruwenzori Mountains
Lake Albert
Lake Turkana
UGANDA
SÃO TOMÉ & PRÍNCIPE
GABON
KENYA
Lake Victoria
Mt. Kilimanjaro
REPUBLIC OF CONGO
DEMOCRATIC REPUBLIC OF CONGO
Lake Kivu
RWANDA
BURUNDI
Lake Tanganyika
TANZANIA
Lake Rukwa
SEYCHELLES
ANGOLA
Lake Malawi
COMOROS
Zambezi River
ZAMBIA
NAMIBIA
ZIMBABWE
MALAWI
MADAGASCAR
Namib Desert
BOTSWANA
MOZAMBIQUE
ATLANTIC OCEAN
Kalahari Desert
MAURITIUS
LESOTHO
Drakensberg Mountains
SWAZILAND
INDIAN OCEAN
Orange River
SOUTH AFRICA

Major Physical Features

DESERTS
• Sahara 3,500,000 sq. mi. (9,065,000 sq. km)
• Kalahari 225,000 sq. mi. (582,750 sq. km)
• Namib 102,000 sq. mi. (264,000 sq. km)

MOUNTAIN RANGES & HIGHEST POINTS
• Mount Kilimanjaro 19,340 ft. (5,895 m)
• Ruwenzori 16,795 ft. (5,119 m)
• Atlas 13,665 ft. (4,165 m)
• Drakensberg 11,425 ft. (3,482 m)

RIVERS
• Nile 4,145 mi. (6,670 km)
• Congo 2,920 mi. (4,700 km)
• Niger 2,600 mi. (4,183 km)
• Zambezi 2,200 mi. (3,540 km)
• Orange 1,300 mi. (2,092 km)

LAKES
• Victoria 26,868 sq. mi. (69,588 sq. km)
• Tanganyika 12,700 sq. mi. (32,893 sq. km)
• Malawi (Nyasa) 11,430 sq. mi. (29,604 sq. km)
• Turkana 2,473 sq. mi. (6,405 sq. km)
• Albert 2,160 sq. mi. (5,594 sq. km)
• Kivu 1,040 sq. mi. (2,694 sq. km)
• Rukwa 1,000 sq. mi. (2,590 sq. km)

An adult giraffe can reach 18 ft. (5.5 m) or more in height.
▶

varied wildlife, including lions, cheetahs, and hyenas that prey on antelope and zebras. Across Africa, expanding human settlements are steadily invading wildlife habitats. Many animals are now kept in national parks to protect them.

People

Africa is home to many races and tribes. More than 1,000 languages are spoken south of the Sahara alone. The people of northern Africa are mostly Arabs and Berbers, who speak Arabic and are Muslims. The countries in southern Africa are largely populated by black Africans. Most Africans are Muslim or Christian, but more than a quarter still follow ancient local beliefs.

Nomadic peoples, such as the Tuareg, wander the Sahara on camels. They live in tents and trade goods such as salt and dates, as they have done for many centuries. Elsewhere, most Africans live in villages and farm the land.

Minerals, such as diamonds, gold, iron ore, and copper, are mined for export. Several countries, including Algeria and Angola, produce oil. However, war,

disease, famine, and drought mean that Africa is home to two-thirds of the world's poorest countries.

Early civilizations

Fossils indicate that humans first evolved in Africa as early as seven million years ago. Nearly 5,000 years ago ancient Egypt, one of the world's first great civilizations, arose in northern Africa. It thrived until 30 B.C., when it became part of the Roman Empire. Beginning about 1000 B.C., black peoples who spoke Bantu languages began to spread from their homes in West Africa, displacing other peoples and gradually dominating central and southern Africa. In the seventh century the Arabs conquered and converted the North African peoples to Islam.

European exploration

Between A.D. 1100 and 1500, Arab traders brought news to Europe of great empires in West Africa, such

▲ *Craftsmen in the West African kingdom of Benin created many beautiful bronze statues.*

The cheetah is the fastest land animal. It can reach speeds of almost 70 mph (113 kph) as it hunts prey.
▼

as Mali, Songhai, and Benin. The continent's wealth attracted the interest of many Europeans. The Portuguese began mapping the African coastline in the 15th century. They were first to export slaves from West Africa, a trade that continued into the 1800s. The Portuguese set up colonies there in Guinea-Bissau and the Cape Verde Islands. Angola and Mozambique in southern Africa were Portuguese colonies until 1975.

The Tuareg people follow the Islamic faith. Unlike other Muslims, Tuareg men, not women, wear veils.
▼

AREA:
11,667,000 sq. mi.
(30,316,000 sq. km)

POPULATION:
784,445,000

COUNTRIES:
53

LARGEST COUNTRY:
Sudan

SMALLEST COUNTRY:
Seychelles

RELIGIONS:
Islam, Christianity, folk religions, animism

LANGUAGES:
Over 1,000, including Arabic, Fulani, Hausa, Swahili, Xhosa

The colonial era
Many Europeans settled in Africa during the 19th century. Some came to put an end to slave trading, some to bring the Christian gospel, and others simply to seize land for colonies.

By the late 19th century most of Africa was ruled by Europe. France took control of Algeria and Tunisia, and Great Britain, Spain, and Italy claimed other parts of North Africa. King Leopold of Belgium set up the Congo Free State in Central Africa and profited greatly from its rubber, ivory, and minerals. In 1908 the Belgian government took the colony from the king to protect its people from cruel treatment. In East Africa only Ethiopia remained independent, although the Italians occupied the country from 1936 to 1941 during World War II.

The road to independence
After the end of World War II in 1945 African nationalism began to grow. The majority of African peoples wanted their independence from European rule, and by the 1950s the process had begun. In 1960 alone 17 nations gained their independence. By 1970 most African countries were free of colonial rule.

Generally independence was won peacefully, but in some countries there was fighting before it was achieved.

South Africa
In the 17th century Dutch settlers (Afrikaners) arrived in South Africa. In 1948 the whites set up the apartheid system (*apartheid* means "separateness"). It denied basic rights to blacks until 1994, when South Africa became a democracy under black president Nelson Mandela.

◄

Horses are an essential mode of transport in the mountains of Lesotho in southern Africa.

👀

SEE ALSO:
Central Africa;
Continents;
East Africa;
Egypt; Egypt,
Ancient;
Ghana; Kenya;
Nigeria; North
Africa; Slavery;
South Africa;
Southern
Africa; West
Africa

✳ AFRICAN AMERICANS
African Americans are U.S. citizens who are descended, at least partly, from Africans. For many African Americans this ancestry is linked with the slave trade, which started in the early 1600s.

For nearly 300 years Europeans brought Africans to America to work the land, mostly in the South. Many white Americans spoke out against slavery. The Civil War (1861–65) was fought between the states of the North, which opposed slavery, and the slave states in the South. The North won, and slaves gained freedom and citizenship. Although they were now free, African Americans were still treated unfairly. They were often attacked by racist groups such as the Ku Klux Klan. The Supreme Court allowed states to pass "Jim Crow" laws that forced blacks to live separately from whites. The Southern states passed laws that made it hard for blacks to vote.

Northward bound
In the late 1800s and early 1900s, many black people headed north in search of a better life. Most found poor housing and

dead-end jobs. Various organizations were set up to help them: The National Association for the Advancement of Colored People (NAACP) started in 1909, and the National Urban League (NUL) was founded in 1911.

In the two world wars of 1914–18 and 1939–45, more than one million African Americans served their country.

▲
African American soldiers of the Black Regiment, based at Camp William Penn in Philadelphia, fought for the Northern states in the Civil War.

➡

General conditions improved for blacks. The government ordered companies to hire blacks and whites on equal terms, and by the late 1940s more than one million blacks were registered to vote.

The civil rights movement

In 1954 the Supreme Court decided that racial segregation (separation) in public schools was unlawful. Beginning in 1960, blacks and whites joined protests and campaigned for change. This was the civil rights movement.

On August 28, 1963, more than 200,000 civil rights supporters gathered in Washington, D.C. Dr. Martin Luther King Jr. delivered a stirring speech in which he imagined a world without social injustice.

In 1964 Congress passed the Civil Rights Act. It made all racial discrimination in public life illegal, but it could not stop people from being racists. Many African Americans grew impatient and demanded action. Groups such as the Black Panthers urged blacks to fight whites. Riots

Astronaut Mae Jemison, seen here on the space shuttle Endeavour, was the first African American woman in space.

broke out in Los Angeles, New York City, and Newark, New Jersey. Then, on April 4, 1968, Dr. King was shot and killed by a white man in Memphis, Tennessee.

Beyond civil rights

Since the 1960s there have been both setbacks and successes for African Americans. Louis Farrakhan, leader of the Nation of

In this demonstration in 1934, NAACP members protested lynching, a practice in which people take the law into their own hands and kill someone, by hanging, without a trial.

Islam, called for blacks and whites to live separately. More positively, the Reverend Jesse Jackson's Rainbow Coalition was founded in 1984 to improve the lives of African Americans and others.

Today African Americans number about 34.6 million, or 12.3 percent of the total U.S. population. Although circumstances do not always allow them to enjoy the same successes as whites, they have achieved much. In 1992 Mae C. Jemison was the first African American woman in space. In 2001 General Colin L. Powell was the first African American to be named secretary of state. These accomplishments, along with many others, have enriched American culture and made the nation what it is today.

Colin Powell became leader of the Joint Chiefs of Staff in 1989, making him the highest-ranking African American in the military.

SEE ALSO:
Abolition Movement;
Civil Rights;
Civil War;
King, Martin Luther, Jr.;
Slavery

✳ AGRICULTURE
Agriculture is the process of growing crops and rearing animals to provide food, clothing, and other important products.

Today people take it for granted that they can walk into a store and buy a can of beans or a carton of milk. But there is a huge industry behind the food that we buy in supermarkets, and a long history that goes back over 10,000 years.

The first farmers
The first farmers were Stone Age people who lived in Africa, Asia, and Europe around 11,000 B.C. They started to herd the wild animals that provided them with their food and clothing, instead of hunting them. By about 7000 B.C. people had learned to grow crops by clearing land and sowing the wild plant seeds that they had gathered for their food. These early farmers probably grew grains, such as wheat and barley. They soon discovered that if they broke up the soil with hoes and sticks (cultivated) and added animal dung (fertilized), the plants produced better crops. ➡

This Egyptian wall painting, from a 3,500-year-old tomb, shows farmers working the land. Water from the Nile River helped them raise crops and livestock.

9

A farmer uses a tractor and a cultivator to dig up weeds between rows of soybean plants.

Corn is harvested and prepared for storage on a farm in rural Iowa.

Around 4000 B.C. the Sumerian people of Mesopotamia (modern Iraq) and the Egyptians along the Nile River in North Africa came up with the idea of irrigating their land. They diverted water from the rivers to flood the land or created channels and watering devices so that they could grow crops in very dry places. Once these farmers produced a surplus—grew more than they could eat themselves—other people were able to stop working the land and move away. Early cities and civilizations sprang up.

Modern agriculture

Although farming has changed a lot over the centuries with the introduction of new tools and machines, today's farmers still have to consider many of the same things as their distant ancestors. The climate (temperature, rainfall, and wind) and the fertility of the soil affect the types of crops they can grow. They must also decide where they are going to sell their produce.

Most modern farms specialize in one or two products so that they can concentrate on the crops and livestock best suited to the land and they will need only a limited range of machinery. For example, wheat grows in the High Plains region, from Montana and North Dakota to Oklahoma; corn grows in the wetter region of the Midwest, from Nebraska to Ohio; and California and Florida specialize in fruit and vegetables, which are easy to grow in sunny, well-watered, fertile areas. Dairy farming tends to be concentrated close to major cities, such as Los Angeles, so that the milk can be transported quickly to the people who live there.

Following advances in the 20th century in chemistry, breeding, and technology, modern agriculture has become a science. Agricultural experts have to decide how much fertilizer and which pest-control chemicals to use to improve crops and livestock. Corn now grows faster, with bigger heads on each plant. Fruit is sweeter and easier to transport. Cows produce more milk, and pigs have longer backs to provide more bacon. Some of these changes have led to debates about forcing changes on nature—whether such food is as good for people as it used to be, and whether animals are suffering as a result of modern farming practices.

AMAZING FACTS !

The state of Florida is the world's second-largest producer of oranges, after Brazil. It produces over 250 million boxes of oranges a year. About 90 percent of the oranges are squeezed to make juice—over 1.5 billion gallons (5.7 billion liters) a year, which is enough to fill around three million Olympic-size swimming pools.

SEE ALSO: Ancient Civilizations; Climate; Fruit; Prehistoric Peoples; Soil; Vegetables; Weather

✳ AIRCRAFT
Airplanes have had a great impact on our lives. They are a convenient, speedy method of travel and transport. They have also changed the nature of war.

Before the beginning of the 20th century, people had flown only in balloons and gliders. But the development of the gasoline engine and a reliable propeller system enabled Orville and Wilbur Wright to make the first powered, controlled flight in December 1903.

Forces in action
An airplane is heavier than air, so it can fly only if air flows over its wings fast enough to produce an upward force called lift. This force must be stronger than the force of gravity (the force that pulls objects toward the ground).

A third force, called thrust, produced by a plane's engines, moves the plane forward through the air. Thrust must be stronger

The B-2 Spirit is a bomber that can carry both conventional and nuclear bombs. It has a crew of two pilots.

than drag (the resistance of the air to anything moving through it) for the aircraft to stay in the air.

The force of lift can be explained by looking at the pressure of air particles on the wings. A wing has a curved top surface and a relatively flat lower surface. As the wing moves through the air, the air particles flow either over or under the wing and meet again behind it. The air passing over the top of the wing has a longer distance to travel than the air passing under the wing, so it moves faster. This means that there is less pressure acting on the top of the wing than underneath, and that pulls the wing up. This upward force is lift. As an airplane moves faster along a runway, the lift increases until it can pull the airplane up.

More lift—up to one-quarter of the total—is created as the result of air pushing up on the underside of the wing. In normal flight the wing is tilted, so the front is slightly higher than the back. When the air strikes the underside of the wing, it is deflected, or turned, downward. The force of this deflected air exerts an equal force in the opposite direction, upward against the bottom of the wing.

An F/A-18 Hornet jet fighter breaks the sound barrier in the sky over the Pacific Ocean. The photograph was taken as the jet flew past the aircraft carrier USS **Constellation.**

FORCES ON AIRPLANES

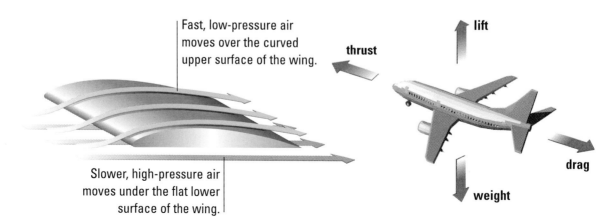

Fast, low-pressure air moves over the curved upper surface of the wing.

Slower, high-pressure air moves under the flat lower surface of the wing.

lift

thrust

drag

weight

AMAZING FACTS !

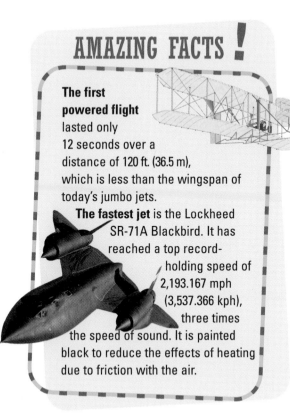

The first powered flight lasted only 12 seconds over a distance of 120 ft. (36.5 m), which is less than the wingspan of today's jumbo jets.

The fastest jet is the Lockheed SR-71A Blackbird. It has reached a top record-holding speed of 2,193.167 mph (3,537.366 kph), three times the speed of sound. It is painted black to reduce the effects of heating due to friction with the air.

Thrust

At first planes had engines that drove propellers. The rapidly rotating blades of the propellers scooped their way through the air, converting engine power into thrust. Modern planes have jet engines, which work on a similar principle but have fans inside the engine to suck the air through them. As the air is forced out of the back of the engine, it pushes the aircraft forward.

Supersonic flight

In the early days of airplane flight, the top speed of planes was about 50 mph (80 kph). Today some airplanes exceed the speed of sound by two or three times. Flight at speeds greater than the speed of sound is called supersonic flight. *Supersonic* means "above sound."

At sea level the speed of sound is about 760 mph (1,225 kph). At higher altitudes the speed of sound is less because the particles of air are farther apart. As it reaches the speed of sound, an airplane is said to meet the sound barrier. When this happens, the plane's wings produce a shock wave, which increases drag, destroys lift, and violently shakes the plane. A plane must be specially designed to go through the sound barrier safely.

A shock wave spreads out behind the plane like the wave formed by the bow of a ship. As it sweeps along the ground, it produces a thunderlike noise called a sonic boom. The boom is caused by

Concorde, the only supersonic passenger airplane, flies from Europe to New York in less than three and a half hours.
▼

pressure differences between the air in the shock wave and the air near the ground. It is mainly military aircraft that travel this fast, but there is one supersonic passenger jet, the Concorde, that can break the sound barrier, too. The Concorde flies smoothly at more than twice the speed of sound. The sonic boom it creates at low altitude is strong enough to shake houses. For this reason, the Concorde is permitted to fly at supersonic speeds only when over the ocean.

The speeds of fast-moving planes are measured in units called Mach numbers, named after Ernst Mach, an Austrian scientist. A plane traveling at the speed of sound is said to fly at Mach 1. For a plane flying at twice that speed, the Mach number is 2. A spacecraft reentering Earth's atmosphere may travel at Mach 20 or higher. Flight at speeds above Mach 4 or 5 is called hypersonic flight.

SEE ALSO: Airports; Balloons and Airships; Engines; Helicopters; Wright, Orville and Wilbur

✳ AIRPORTS

Airports are places where planes take off and land. Some are huge, busy, and complex; others are no more than a flat strip of grass.

The simplest airport is no more than a landing strip—a runway consisting of a few hundred acres of level ground along which planes can take off and land. But most airports also have hangars (garages for planes), refueling equipment, waiting areas for passengers, and storage buildings for freight.

Modern airports have a control tower, a tall building with large windows near the center of the complex, from which controllers watch all plane movements. Pilots are not allowed to move their aircraft on the ground or in the air around the airport without permission from the air traffic controllers. In the same building as the control tower there is usually a meteorological office that provides up-to-date information about local weather conditions.

Departures and arrivals

The waiting areas at an airport are called terminals. It is there that passengers go to register for their flights, or check in. At the check-in desk, they show their tickets to the airline staff and hand over (check) the baggage that they want to store in the aircraft's hold during the flight. Passengers then go through a security check in which both they and their hand luggage are screened for weapons and explosives. (The hold luggage is also screened before it is loaded onto the plane.)

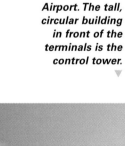

Hong Kong Airport. The tall, circular building in front of the terminals is the control tower.

After that, passengers go to the departure gate, sometimes pausing to have their passports checked if they are taking an international flight. The departure gate is in a part of the airport called airside that cannot be entered by anyone who has not gone through the security procedures.

Passengers board the planes through covered walkways attached to the aircraft or by walking to them across the apron (the area where planes are parked).

In another part of the terminal building is an arrivals area. Here passengers collect their baggage. Travelers arriving from abroad also go through passport control to get permission to come into the country, and then through customs, where inspectors make sure they are not carrying items such as illegal drugs, or food or plants that could spread diseases.

Ready for takeoff

Once the plane is loaded and the pilot has permission from the control tower to leave the gate, the aircraft will drive, or taxi, to the end of the runway. Then, after having been granted permission to do so, the plane will accelerate down the runway and take off.

SEE ALSO:
Aircraft

✳AIRSHIPS 👀 ✳BALLOONS AND AIRSHIPS

✳ ALEXANDER THE GREAT (356–323 B.C.)

Alexander III of Macedon, known as Alexander the Great, was a superb military commander who became the ruler of a powerful empire.

Alexander was born in 356 B.C. in Pella, Macedon (or Macedonia), in what is now part of northern Greece but was then a separate kingdom. His father, Philip II, made Macedon into a major power and conquered the cities of Greece. Philip's assassination in 336 B.C. put Alexander on the throne of Macedon.

In 334 B.C. Alexander declared war on the vast Persian Empire. He led an army of Macedonian and Greek soldiers across the Dardanelles, the strip of water dividing Europe and Asia. Egypt, which was then a Persian territory, fell to him, and he founded the city of Alexandria on the Nile River. Alexander defeated King Darius III of Persia in 331 B.C., and he later became Lord of Asia.

▲
A Greek coin bearing the head of Alexander III of Macedon.

Conquest and exploration

From 329 to 326 B.C. Alexander led his army through Central Asia to the border of India. There he gave his soldiers permission to go home. Alexander went to Babylon (in modern Iraq), where he died in 323 B.C. at age 32 of malaria and war wounds.

Alexander introduced Greek thought and culture to Egypt and western Asia. His conquests and captivating personality established him as a legend.

SEE ALSO:
Egypt, Ancient;
Greece, Ancient

✳ ALGEBRA

Algebra is a branch of mathematics that uses letters and symbols to solve problems with unknown quantities. Engineers, scientists, and people who work with money all use algebra.

Equations

Arithmetic uses numbers to solve problems—for example, **1 + 2 = 3**. Algebra uses numbers, too, but it also uses symbols. Most often these are letters, such as **x**, **y**, and **z**. Because the letter **x** looks so similar to the multiplication sign, mathematicians write **xy**, or **x · y**, or **(x) · (y)** for "**x** times **y**" to avoid confusion.

1 + 2 = 3 is an equation. The value of numbers and symbols on one side of an equal sign is the same as those on the other side. Algebra also uses equations to solve problems.

For example: A boy and a girl have **$29** between them. The girl has **$3** more than the boy. How much does the boy have?

We can call the boy's amount **x**. So the amount the girl has is **x + 3**. We know the total is **29**, so we can write the equation **x + x + 3 = 29**, or **2x + 3 = 29**.

We can then simplify the equation, or make it shorter. We can add, subtract, multiply, or divide one side of the equation, provided we do exactly the same to the other.

If we subtract **3** from each side, we have **2x + 3 - 3 = 29 - 3**, or **2x = 26**. So we know that **x = 13**. The boy has **$13**, so the girl must have **$16**.

Formulas

We can use some algebraic equations to solve problems in practical situations. These equations are called formulas.

For example, the formula for the area of a rectangle is **a = lw**. In other words, **area = length times width**. If you want to buy new carpet for a room in your house, you measure the length and width of the room and multiply them. So a room **10** feet long and **12** feet wide has an area of **120** square feet (**10 · 12 = 120**).

History

Almost 4,000 years ago, the Egyptians and Babylonians were using algebraic equations. But it was the Greek mathematician Diphantus who first used letters in equations to solve problems, in about A.D. 250.

The word *algebra* comes from the Arabic word *al-jabr*, which was used in the title of Al-Khwarizmi's book of mathematics, written in about A.D. 825.

An Egyptian document known as the Rhind papyrus, written around 1700 B.C., contains algebra problems such as, "What number plus one-seventh of that number equals 19?" (The answer is 16.625.)

SEE ALSO:
Einstein, Albert; Geometry; Mathematics

AMAZING FACTS !

The world's most famous algebraic equation is $E=mc^2$. Renowned physicist Albert Einstein (1879–1955) came up with this formula to explain the relationship between matter and energy. *E* stands for energy, *m* stands for mass, and c^2 is the speed of light squared (multiplied by itself). This simple equation revolutionized the world of physics.

$$E=mc^2$$

✳ ALLIGATORS AND CROCODILES

Alligators and crocodiles are reptiles. They belong to a group of 25 species called the crocodilians, which also include caimans and gavials.

Crocodilians

All crocodilians have long tails and large jaws. Their skin consists of bony plates and scales. They live on or near water, and are good swimmers. On land, they can run only for short distances.

Crocodilians lay 20 to 90 eggs at a time. The eggs are usually long and white, with hard shells. A mother crocodilian lays her eggs in a hole that she scoops out of a riverbank, or builds a nest out of grass or other plant materials.

When they hatch, young crocodilians eat fishes, insects, and shellfish. When they are adults, they will eat any animals, including their own species. They can grab an animal and pull it into the water, or knock it in with their tails. They then hold it underwater with their jaws until it drowns.

Crocodilians are dangerous—they have killed and eaten people. You should never go near a crocodile or an alligator.

Alligators

Except for one species in China, all alligators live in the warm parts of the Americas. They are most often found in the coastal areas of the southern United States, the Caribbean, Central America, Colombia, and Ecuador. An adult American alligator weighs about 500 lb. (227 kg).

The best way to tell an alligator from a crocodile is by looking at its head. The alligator has a broad, rounded snout. The smaller caiman, from South America, has a similarly shaped head.

Crocodiles

Crocodiles live in warm parts of North and South America, Australia, Africa, and Asia. They have long, tapering snouts and triangular-shaped heads. American crocodiles can weigh over 1,300 lb. (590 kg). When a crocodile closes its mouth, it looks as if it is grinning. The gavial, found in India, also has a long, thin snout.

Like many other reptiles, crocodiles lay eggs. When the mother hears the eggs hatching, she comes back to the nest to guard the babies.

SEE ALSO: Animals; Reptiles; Rivers

✳ ALPHABET

An alphabet is a list of signs that are used to record a language. The signs, called letters, usually represent the sounds of the language.

The earliest writing was made up of simple pictures that represented words. The first writing systems were developed about 3000 B.C. by the Sumerians, who lived in Mesopotamia (modern Iraq), and the Egyptians. The Sumerian writing was called cuneiform, and the Egyptian writing was called hieroglyphics.

Having a picture for every word meant that a huge number of signs were needed. The Egyptians and Sumerians soon simplified their writing by choosing a symbol for each syllable (part of a word) and combining symbols to write words.

The first alphabet

The Phoenicians, who lived on the coast of modern Syria and Lebanon, developed the first alphabet in about 1100 B.C. It had 22 symbols for consonant sounds—readers had to guess the vowel sounds. Each symbol had a name. The first two symbols, or letters,

◀

This stone monument shows capital letters carved by the Romans.

were *aleph*, the Phoenician word for bull, and *beth*, the word for house. From these names came our word *alphabet*.

In about the eighth century B.C., the Greeks took over the Phoenician alphabet but used some of the symbols as vowel signs. For the first time each sound in a language had its own sign.

Later, the Etruscans of northern Italy introduced more changes. The Romans adapted the Etruscan alphabet, and by the third century B.C. they used much the same alphabet we know today, but without a *j*, *u*, *w*, *y*, or *z*. When the Romans conquered Greece in the first century B.C., many Greek words were taken into Latin, the Roman language, and *y* and *z* were added to the alphabet. The remaining letters came much later.

AMAZING FACTS !

The letter *j* was not introduced into the alphabet used in most of Europe and in English-speaking countries until the 17th century.

The Romans used only capital letters (which were easier to carve in stone). Small letters were introduced when people started to use pens and brushes and wanted to write more speedily.

SEE ALSO: Ancient Civilizations; Egypt, Ancient; Roman Empire; Writing

✳ AMERICAN REVOLUTION

In the Revolutionary War of 1775–81, the 13 British colonies in America fought for the right to govern themselves. Their victory led to the birth of the United States.

The road to war

In the mid-1700s, Britain's American colonies were lands of opportunity, far from the conflicts of Europe. They had little interference from their mother country, which was busy fighting France. This suddenly changed in 1763.

In that year Britain defeated the French in Canada and east of the Mississippi. The war had been expensive, so Britain demanded taxes from its American colonies on goods such as tea and sugar. The colonists refused to pay. At the so-called Boston Tea Party on December 16, 1773, they even threw British tea into Boston Harbor to show their defiance. Tensions grew between the two sides.

In September 1774 in Philadelphia, the colonies pledged to support Boston. That winter, their soldiers prepared for war against Britain's redcoat troops.

Early battles

Fighting broke out in Lexington, Massachusetts, in April 1775. After an initial victory, the redcoats fell back to Boston and were surrounded. At the battle of Bunker Hill, they lost many men to the ill-trained but fierce American patriots before finally defeating them.

The colonies formed a regular army and appointed George Washington to lead it. Not all colonists supported the revolution, and many were still loyal to the British king. The war divided many families, sending brother to fight against brother.

When spring came, Washington's men managed to drive the redcoats out of Boston. But the British, under General Sir William Howe, moved on to New York, where they captured the harbor by September 1776. Washington's exhausted troops retreated to Trenton, New Jersey.

Although the British won the battle of Bunker Hill, the American soldiers fought so bravely that they renewed the fighting spirit of all the colonial troops.
▼

▲ *Washington and his troops spent the harsh winter of 1777 at Valley Forge, getting ready to fight again in spring.*

Meanwhile, the colonies had passed the Declaration of Independence on July 4. The patriots were now fighting for the freedom of the United States of America. On Christmas Eve and in January, Washington's men dealt blows to the British at Trenton and Princeton. Howe's men fought back, taking Philadelphia in September 1777. Washington's cold, hungry men spent the winter training at their camp at Valley Forge, Pennsylvania.

France enters the war

British forces under General John Burgoyne had been marching south from Lake Champlain toward Albany. Through the summer of 1777 they had suffered defeats in Bennington, Vermont, and at Freeman's Farm, New York. Eventually Burgoyne surrendered to General Horatio Gates at Saratoga, in October.

At this point, the king of France, Louis XVI, realized that the Americans might just win, and, instead of giving secret military aid, he began to openly support them. This greatly worried the British. Their troops in Philadelphia, now led by General Sir Henry Clinton, made a ragged withdrawal to New York in June 1778.

War in the South

The British turned their attention to the South. Redcoats under General Charles Cornwallis scored victories over Gates's troops in 1780. But when Cornwallis left to gather troops, General Nathanael Greene, who had replaced Gates, rallied the patriots and pushed the British back to Savannah and Charleston. Cornwallis entered Yorktown, where he was pinned down by American and French troops. In September 1781, a French fleet defeated Royal Navy vessels in Chesapeake Bay.

Victory

On October 9 General Cornwallis surrendered, and the war was over. A peace treaty was signed in Paris, France, on September 3, 1783. The agreement gave complete independence to the 13 colonies, which joined together to form the United States of America.

AMAZING FACTS !

Deborah Samson (1760–1827) was a schoolteacher who joined the fight for independence. She disguised herself as a man and enlisted in the army as "Robert Shurtliff." In one battle she was hit in the thigh by a musket ball, but she dug it out with her own knife so the doctors would not learn her secret. When the truth came out, "Shurtliff" was given an honorable discharge, and Samson became a national heroine.

SEE ALSO: Colonial America; Declaration of Independence; Franklin, Benjamin; French and Indian Wars; Paine, Thomas; Revere, Paul

✳ AMPHIBIANS

Amphibians are vertebrates (animals with a backbone) that are adapted to live both on land and in water. They are found in all parts of the world except Greenland and Antarctica.

There are more than 4,000 kinds of amphibians, divided into three main groups: frogs and toads, salamanders and newts, and caecilians. In the early stages of their life, the groups appear similar, but as adults they look different.

Frogs and toads have four legs and no tails. Their strong, long back legs are used for leaping and swimming. Salamanders and newts have long tails. They have four legs, but these are short and weak and are more suited to walking than jumping. Caecilians look like worms. They have no legs and burrow in the ground.

All amphibians are cold-blooded: They do not make their own body heat, so their body temperature depends on the temperature of their surroundings.

Amphibians have well-developed senses. Frogs and toads depend on their vision to find food. Salamanders have good vision and hearing and rely on both senses to hunt. Caecilians either have very small eyes or no eyes at all. They rely on smell to hunt, using two tentacles, or feelers, near the mouth to pick up food scents. Most amphibians are able to produce sounds, but only frogs and toads use their voices to communicate with each other. They send warnings or mating calls.

Young amphibians eat either plants or insects and other animals, or a mixture of plant and animal food. Adults eat mostly insects. Many types of frog and salamander have a long, sticky tongue that they can flick out to catch flies or other prey. Amphibians are themselves hunted by many diffferent kinds of mammals, birds, and snakes. Some use camouflage and can escape their enemies by standing still, to blend in with their surroundings. Some salamanders have tails that can break off so that the salamander escapes and leaves its hunter holding the tail. The skin of many amphibians has glands that let off poison. This irritates the mouth of an attacker so that it lets go.

Life cycle

Most amphibians live in water for the early part of their life and on land for the adult part. The young are known as larvae and hatch from eggs. The larva of a frog or toad is called a tadpole. The larvae look

An axolotl is a rare type of salamander that is able to breed without developing adult features.
◄

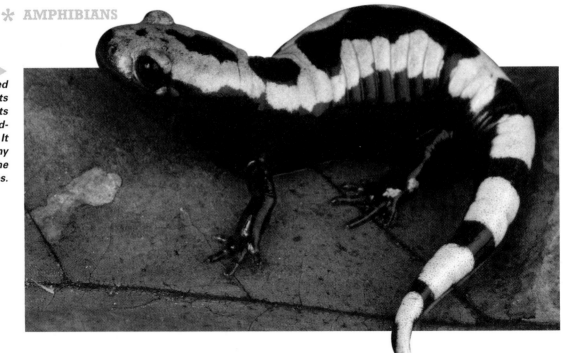

▶
The marbled salamander gets its name from its striking black-and-white markings. It is found in many parts of the United States.

AMAZING FACTS !

The Japanese giant salamander grows to over 5 ft. (1.6 m) in length. One species of caecilian reaches lengths of over 4 ft. (1.2 m).

Some tree frogs from the Amazon rain forest produce highly poisonous substances. The natives of the rain forest used the poison on their darts to make hunting more efficient.

like fish and have a tail to propel them along. They breathe through gills, which are organs on the sides of their head that take oxygen from the water and pass it into the larvae's blood. Gradually the larvae go through a series of changes that turn them into adults. This process is called

metamorphosis.   For many amphibians, this involves growing legs, losing their tails, and developing lungs to replace their gills. Some kinds of salamander do not develop lungs, but are able to absorb oxygen through their skin.

Environment

Frogs and toads are the most common amphibians. They live mostly in wet or damp places such as ponds, marshes, or rain forests. Some toads are able to live in dry areas, including deserts. Salamanders and newts generally live in lakes and streams and under damp logs on forest floors. Axolotls are a rare kind of salamander found only in Mexico. They seldom develop into adults, but are able to breed. They remain in water and breathe through three sets of gills. Caecilians are found only in the tropics and subtropics. They usually live underground, but some live in water as adults.

SEE ALSO: Animals; Frogs and Toads

✳ ANCIENT CIVILIZATIONS

Beginning about 8000 B.C., people created societies based on farming. These societies gradually became more organized, and out of them grew what we call civilization.

The term *ancient civilization* is used by historians to describe those civilizations that developed before A.D. 500. The world's oldest civilization developed about 6,500 years ago, when people in Mesopotamia (modern Iraq) formed a highly organized society, with cities, laws, and a shared culture and religion.

The Sumerians and Babylonians

The southern plain of Mesopotamia between the Tigris and Euphrates rivers was named Sumer. Its earliest people were called Sumerians. Another people called Semites also settled along the rivers. From 4500 B.C. onward, both peoples began to build cities.

Each city had its own ruler, who tried to obtain more land. Around 1890 B.C., Babylon, one of the Semite cities, conquered and ruled the entire plain, which became known as Babylonia.

The Sumerians learned how to make bronze for weapons, tools, and ornaments. They invented the potter's wheel and the world's first wheeled carts, drawn by oxen. They also invented a form of writing called cuneiform, which means "wedge-shaped."

People living in cities need laws. The most famous collection was issued by Hammerabi, king of Babylon, in about 1750 B.C. There were different laws for free people and for slaves. Most ancient civilizations allowed slavery, and prisoners of war were often kept as slaves rather than killed.

Ancient Egypt

About 3200 B.C., a king named Menes (or Narmer) brought the land along the Nile River in Egypt under his rule and founded a civilization that lasted over 3,000 years. Egypt was one of the richest and most civilized lands in the world.

Indus civilization

In 1922 scholars unearthed the ruins of cities built about 4,000 years ago in the Indus Valley of India. Mohenjo-Daro and Harappa each had between 20,000 and 50,000 inhabitants and a system of sewers that would not be equaled until modern times. A disaster of some kind struck in about 2000 B.C. Invaders might have conquered the cities, or maybe the climate changed and people moved away.

Assyrian and Persian civilizations

A thousand years after Hammerabi, Babylon was no longer a great power. In 710 B.C. the Assyrians, who lived in the hills to the north, conquered the city. The Assyrian army had swift battle chariots and strong, iron weapons. Their king,

The ruins of the Indus Valley city of Mohenjo-Daro in Pakistan as they are today.
▼

An artist's impression of how the royal palace at Knossos in Crete might have looked. It covered 5 acres (2 ha) and had 1,200 rooms.

conquered by an Iranian people called the Persians. The Persian Empire became the largest the world had seen. As well as Iran, it included modern Turkey, Egypt, Israel, Jordan, Lebanon, Syria, Iraq, Afghanistan, and part of Pakistan.

Cretan civilization

Crete is an island in the Mediterranean Sea. About 5,000 years ago, the Cretans traded with Egypt, Syria, Italy, and lands even farther away. Although it is not clear exactly what happened, the island's greatest city, Knossos, suffered a disaster about 1400 B.C. People continued to live there for another 300 years, but its great days were over.

Ashurbanipal, who ruled from 669 to 626 B.C., conquered an empire that included Egypt and Babylonia.

A few years after Ashurbanipal's death, Babylonia revolted, and in 612 B.C. the Babylonians destroyed Nineveh, the Assyrian capital. In 539 B.C. Babylon was

Greek civilization

About 800 B.C., Greeks began to form city-states, or *polis*. From about 500 B.C., one of the most important city-states was in Athens, the modern capital of Greece. Athenians created beautiful buildings,

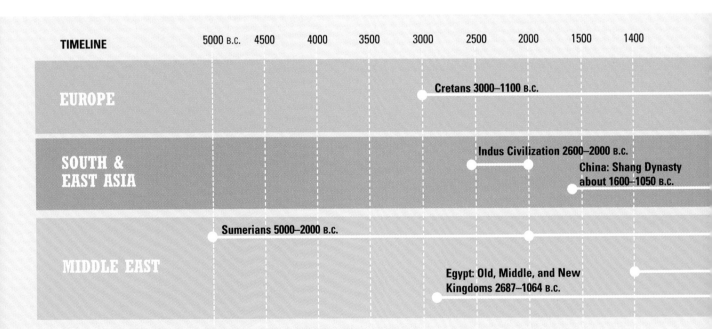

TIMELINE	5000 B.C.	4500	4000	3500	3000	2500	2000	1500	1400
EUROPE					Cretans 3000–1100 B.C.				
SOUTH & EAST ASIA						Indus Civilization 2600–2000 B.C.		China: Shang Dynasty about 1600–1050 B.C.	
MIDDLE EAST	Sumerians 5000–2000 B.C.					Egypt: Old, Middle, and New Kingdoms 2687–1064 B.C.			

This carved stone column shows Hammerabi, king of Babylon (standing), receiving a set of laws from Shamash, the god of justice (sitting).

years, he ruled an empire that extended from Greece east to the Indus River. Alexander the Great, as he was known, established cities throughout his realm that became centers of Greek culture.

Roman Empire
While Alexander was empire-building in the East, Rome was fighting to control Italy in the West. For hundreds of years, Rome then ruled a great empire, which came to include Egypt and Greece. The Romans built a vast network of roads and bridges. They brought peace and prosperity to the peoples they ruled.

China
China, cut off from the rest of the world by mountains and deserts, was ruled by great families called dynasties. In 221 B.C. Huang Ti became the land's first emperor. The civilization that developed was the most advanced of its time. The Chinese invented items such as paper and gunpowder centuries before the West.

wrote literature, and made advances in government, law, politics, science, math, and philosophy (the meaning of life).

In 336 B.C. a 20-year-old, Alexander, became king of Macedonia (now part of northern Greece). He attacked and defeated the Persian Empire. Within 10

SEE ALSO:
Alexander the Great;
China; Egypt, Ancient;
Greece, Ancient;
Roman Empire

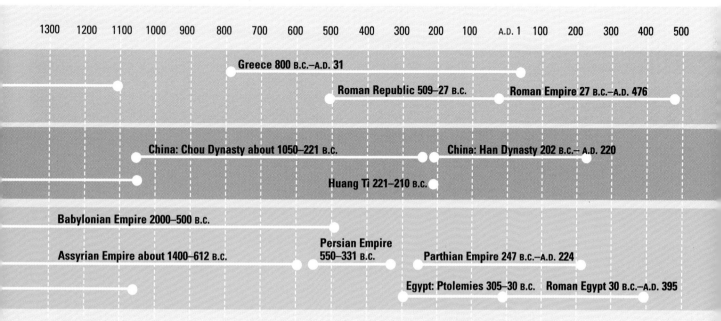

| 1300 | 1200 | 1100 | 1000 | 900 | 800 | 700 | 600 | 500 | 400 | 300 | 200 | 100 | A.D. 1 | 100 | 200 | 300 | 400 | 500 |

Greece 800 B.C.–A.D. 31

Roman Republic 509–27 B.C.   Roman Empire 27 B.C.–A.D. 476

China: Chou Dynasty about 1050–221 B.C.   China: Han Dynasty 202 B.C.– A.D. 220

Huang Ti 221–210 B.C.

Babylonian Empire 2000–500 B.C.

Persian Empire 550–331 B.C.

Assyrian Empire about 1400–612 B.C.   Parthian Empire 247 B.C.–A.D. 224

Egypt: Ptolemies 305–30 B.C.   Roman Egypt 30 B.C.–A.D. 395

✳ ANDERSEN, HANS CHRISTIAN (1805–75)

Andersen was a writer of magical stories, and in many ways his own life was like a fairy tale. He escaped poor beginnings to become Denmark's most famous author.

▲
Hans Christian Andersen understood children, and they loved to sit at his feet while he told his magical tales.

SEE ALSO:
Children's Authors

Hans left his hometown of Odense when he was only 14 to seek his fortune as an actor at the Royal Theater in the capital city of Copenhagen. However, he was tall and awkward, and he could not sing or dance. At the theater they told him to get an education and gave him some money. At 17, Hans was older than the other students, and the schoolmaster made fun of him. Finally he was taken away to be taught privately.

After his schooling, Hans spent many years traveling. He wrote poems, books, and plays, with some success. It was not until he was 30 that he wrote any fairy tales. Hans put many pieces of his own life into his stories. His gawky appearance was the basis for *The Ugly Duckling*, which points out that the qualities that make you feel lonely or different are sometimes the very qualities that can make you special.

Hans's first small book of fairy tales became popular almost immediately. His fame grew rapidly. After years of hardship and loneliness, he came to be honored throughout the world. Yet he never lost the ability to see everything with the clear, innocent eyes of a child.

✳ ANGELOU, MAYA (1928–)

Maya Angelou's writings paint a vivid picture of the life of a black woman in 20th-century America.

SEE ALSO:
African Americans;
Civil Rights;
Literature

Maya Angelou was born Marguerite Johnson in 1928 in St. Louis, Missouri. Her parents' marriage broke up, and she and her brother were raised in rural Arkansas by their grandmother. Maya, as she was nicknamed, had a difficult childhood, but she was extremely intelligent and loved writing and music.

In 1940 Maya moved to San Francisco with her mother. She won a scholarship in drama and dance. In the 1950s, she changed her name to Maya Angelou while performing in cabaret. She moved to New York in the late 1950s and became interested in politics and civil rights. She spent part of the 1960s teaching and writing in Africa.

In 1970 Angelou published *I Know Why the Caged Bird Sings*, the story of her early years. It became very successful. Further accounts of her life have appeared, and today she is one of America's most celebrated writers. Angelou is also famous as a poet. Volumes of her verse include *Just Give Me a Cool Drink of Water 'fore I Diiie* (1971). In 1993 she wrote a poem for the inauguration of President Bill Clinton.

▲
Maya Angelou's books on her varied and sometimes difficult life have become best-sellers.

✳ ANIMALS

The term *animal* is used to describe a vast number of different species that live on Earth, from worms to human beings.

◄ *The cheetah is a carnivorous predator whose spotted fur acts as camouflage, enabling it to blend into its surroundings and creep up on its prey.*

The animal kingdom is a large group of living things, or organisms, that share certain features. Generally, animals have body parts, such as limbs; they are able to move about; they cannot make their own food (unlike plants) and so have to take it from their surroundings; they are able to sense their environment; and they are able to reproduce.

The two main animal groups are vertebrates and invertebrates. All the members of the first group have backbones (vertebrae). The best-known vertebrates are mammals, birds, reptiles, amphibians, and fish. Invertebrates do not have backbones. The most familiar invertebrates are arthropods, such as insects, crabs, spiders, and millipedes; sponges; mollusks, such as snails, slugs, and octopuses; coelenterates, such as jellyfish and coral; and worms.

Variety of animal life

Groups of animals may share some characteristics, yet every kind of animal has its own lifestyle and is suited to living in a particular type of environment, or habitat. Over millions of years, the behavior and body structure of each animal species have adapted to a particular way of life in order for the species to survive. For example, meat-

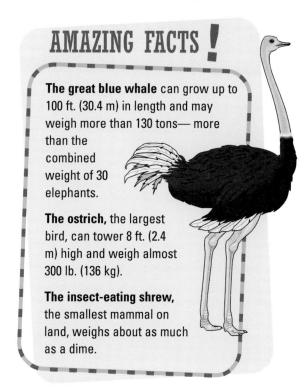

AMAZING FACTS !

The great blue whale can grow up to 100 ft. (30.4 m) in length and may weigh more than 130 tons— more than the combined weight of 30 elephants.

The ostrich, the largest bird, can tower 8 ft. (2.4 m) high and weigh almost 300 lb. (136 kg).

The insect-eating shrew, the smallest mammal on land, weighs about as much as a dime.

eating animals—known as carnivores—have developed long, sharp teeth for tearing and chewing flesh.

Animals move around in different ways. A streamlined shape and fins enable fish to move through water. Mammals usually have legs that allow them to stand and walk on land. Amphibians and reptiles have legs that extend outward from the sides of the body, which they use to leap or crawl. Most birds and many insects have wings that enable them to travel through the air using powered flight.

Survival behavior

In order to survive, animals need to find food, defend themselves from attack, communicate with other members of their species, and reproduce.

Predators are carnivores that hunt other animals. Scavengers, such as vultures, do not hunt for themselves, but eat the remains of animals killed by predators. Most mammals are herbivores; that is, they eat only plants. Animals that eat both plant and animal products are known as omnivores and include human beings.

The male peacock displays its amazing multi-colored tail feathers in an effort to attract mates (female peahens).

SEE ALSO: Amphibians; Birds; Corals and Coral Reefs; Crabs; Ecology; Evolution; Extinction; Fish; Insects; Mammals; Millipedes and Centipedes; Reproductive System; Reptiles; Snails and Other Mollusks; Spiders and Scorpions; Worms

Many animals are herbivores, which means that they eat only plants. The giant panda's diet consists almost entirely of bamboo shoots.

Some animals, such as wolves, hunt in groups; others hunt alone. Some have highly developed senses, especially sight and smell, which they use to find food.

When a predator appears, an animal will often remain motionless in order to make itself undetectable. Some animals use camouflage—the way their shape or color blends in with their surroundings—to conceal themselves. Other animals rely on bright colors or patterns that serve as warning signals to enemies; or scales, shells, and spines that act as armor.

Each animal species shares a language of sound and behaviors that is recognized by all its members. Animal calls are used to warn, to defend, to claim territory, or to find a mate. Scent is also used for identification and in mating.

Simple animals, such as sponges, need only one parent to reproduce, but most need a male and a female parent. Many fish and insects do not protect their eggs or babies. They produce vast numbers of eggs so that at least some survive. Most birds and mammals have few young. They often look after their offspring until they are able to care for themselves.

✳ ANTARCTICA

On many maps, Antarctica looks quite small. This is misleading: The southern continent is larger than either Australia or Europe.

Antarctica, the continent that surrounds the South Pole, is the coldest, windiest, most remote place on Earth. It is 5.5 million sq. miles (14.2 million sq. km) in area, and its rocky surface is blanketed with a vast ice sheet up to about 3 miles (5 km) thick. This ice sheet holds 70 percent of the world's fresh water, although Antarctica gets no rain, and in some places very little snow. The thickness of the ice gives Antarctica the greatest average elevation (height above sea level) of any continent. Without the ice, much of Antarctica would actually be under seawater.

ANTARCTICA

ANTARCTIC OCEAN
Queen Maud Land
Weddell Sea
Antarctic Peninsula
Enderby Land
Ronne Ice Shelf
American Highland
Ellsworth Land
Transantarctic Mountains
South Pole ×
Marie Byrd Land
Ross Ice Shelf
Wilkes Land
Ross Sea
Adélie Coast
ANTARCTIC OCEAN

Between late fall and early spring, the sun does not rise on the South Pole. Antarctica loses huge amounts of heat during the darkest months. Even when the sun does return in spring, much of its energy is reflected directly back into space by the snow-white terrain. Fierce winds, pulled downhill by the force of gravity, make the continent a very difficult place to live. The winter temperature inland averages about –94°F (–70°C). The weather on the coast is milder.

In the ocean around Antarctica, the wind never stops blowing. The air is so cold that the water freezes over. At the coasts lie enormous ice shelves—some as large as the state of Texas. Slow-moving "rivers" of ice, called glaciers, creep from the continent's center to the ice shelves. At the edge, pieces of ice break off to become icebergs. These are a danger to shipping, but they gradually melt as they float northward.

In winter a belt of ice up to 1,000 miles (1,600 km) wide surrounds the continent. Although much of it melts during the summer, the sea ice still extends between 100 and 500 miles (160–800 km) from the continent.

Plants and animals
The Antarctic mainland is almost empty of life. Only a few insects, mosses, and grasses survive along the warmer coasts.

➡

AMAZING FACTS !

In 1983 scientists at the Russian Vostok Station recorded the world's lowest temperature: −128.6°F (−89.2°C).

Inland, lichens and simple organisms called algae live in the cracks in rocks. In contrast, the ocean teems with life. About 27 types of seabird breed in the region. They include penguins, which are sleek swimmers that breed on the ice and hunt in the sea. Seals and whales are common. Swarms of tiny, shrimplike creatures called krill are an important source of food for fish, birds, and whales.

Millions of years ago, Antarctica lay farther north. It once had a tropical climate, supporting forests that were home to reptiles and marsupials (small, pouched mammals). Later, the landmass drifted south, causing most of the wildlife to die from the cold.

The Ross Ice Shelf is more than 1,000 ft. (300 m) thick and moves forward into the sea about half a mile (1 km) a year.

No people are native to Antarctica; until 1820 no one was certain that the continent existed. In the early 1900s,

▲

Penguins are flightless birds. Although they are clumsy on land, where they come to breed, they are fast swimmers.

many explorers tried to be the first to reach the South Pole. The race was eventually won by Roald Amundsen of Norway, on December 14, 1911.

International continent
The Antarctic Treaty, signed in 1959, protects Antarctica's environment. It ensures that scientists from all nations share their knowledge of the continent. Today there are about 40 scientific research stations from different countries in Antarctica. Some countries want to mine and drill the continent for its vast reserves of mineral resources, but 24 countries have agreed not to do so until 2041 at the earliest.

Scientists drill deep into Antarctica's ice to sample layers of snow that fell thousands of years ago. This informs them about patterns of atmospheric pollution. They also monitor the ice cover to see whether climate change is having any effect. If the ice melts, many of the world's low-lying coastlines will be flooded.

SEE ALSO: Arctic; Byrd, Richard E.; Climate; Continents; Exploration and Explorers; Glaciers; Pollution

✳ ANTHONY, SUSAN B. (1820–1906)

Susan B. Anthony was a pioneer in the movement for women's rights. Her work in the United States helped spread the campaign to other parts of the world.

Susan Brownwell Anthony led the campaign to give women the same political rights as men. However, the 19th Amendment, which finally granted women the right to vote, was not introduced until 1920, 14 years after Anthony's death.

Anthony was born in 1820, in Adams, Massachusetts, to a family of Quakers. She became involved in two important reform movements of the time—antislavery and temperance (stopping people from drinking alcohol). In 1850 she met Elizabeth Cady Stanton, a leader in the women's rights movement. They

persuaded the New York state legislature to pass a law allowing women to keep the money they earned. Until then, women's income had become the property of their husbands. In 1872 Anthony began to campaign for women to be given the same voting rights as black men had been given in 1870. Her work continued until she retired in 1900.

SEE ALSO: Women's Rights

▲
Women received the vote in 1920 as a result of Susan B. Anthony's campaign for women's rights.

✳ APES, MONKEYS, AND PRIMATES

Apes and monkeys, along with human beings, belong to a group of animals called primates. The main difference between apes and monkeys is that monkeys have tails and apes do not.

Primates are among the most intelligent of mammals. Their well-developed brains are particularly good at seeing and controlling movement. Almost all primates have fingers, and sometimes toes, that can grasp objects. They use these to climb trees, to clasp food, and, in the case of humans, to hold tools.

Most primates live in the tropics and subtropics of Africa, Asia, and the Americas. Human beings are the only primates to have spread through most of the world.

Primates have fewer offspring than other mammals. The young stay with their

◄
The gorilla is the largest primate. A male can weigh about 600 lb. (272 kg). There are probably fewer than 10,000 mountain gorillas left in the wild.

AMAZING FACTS !

The smallest primate is the pygmy mouse lemur, found in Madagascar. It weighs about 1 oz. (30 g).

The siamang gibbon has arms that span more than 5 ft. (1.5 m), more than twice the length of its body.

mother longer, to learn behavior from her and the other members of the group. Their diet is based mainly on plants. Although some monkeys eat insects, human beings are the primates most likely to eat meat.

There are 233 species of primate, and they form two main groups: prosimians and anthropoids. Prosimians include aye-ayes, galagos, lemurs, lorises, pottos, and

Squirrel monkeys live in communities of a few dozen members, divided into smaller groups. Pregnant females form their own group, as do adult males.

tarsiers. They are nocturnal—active at night—and usually have very large eyes. They tend to be smaller than other primates, are not so intelligent, and often live in small groups.

Anthropoids include human beings, monkeys, and our closest relatives, the apes. Anthropoids have color vision and

can see in three dimensions. This helps them to move about safely in trees. They are diurnal—active during daylight.

Apes

Anthropoids are divided into several further groups. There are two families of apes: great apes and lesser apes. Great apes include chimpanzees, gorillas, orangutans, and bonobos. The lesser apes include the gibbons.

Chimpanzees are the most intelligent apes. Some have learned how to use simple tools to get food. Scientists have even trained them to use sign language to communicate with humans.

Monkeys

Monkeys also divide into two groups, making up 133 different species in all. New World monkeys, from Central and South America, include marmosets, tamarins, douroucoulis, and woolly, howler, spider, and squirrel monkeys. Old World monkeys inhabit Africa, Asia, and a very small part of Europe (Gibraltar). They include macaques, langurs, baboons, guenons, and colobus monkeys.

Most Old World monkeys live on the ground for much of the time. New World monkeys are graceful climbers that seldom leave the trees. Some have a so-called prehensile tail that serves as another hand while they are swinging from branch to branch.

Most apes and monkeys are social animals: That is, they live in groups. Among the apes, only orangutans live alone. Chimpanzees live in groups of between 15 and 80 individuals. Among the monkeys, baboons and macaques form the largest communities. A group of plains baboons may number 300 animals, although it is usually fewer than 100. Some species live in smaller, family units.

Environment

One species of primate—humans—poses the biggest danger to other primates. Habitats, especially the tropical rain forests, are vanishing because of human activities, such as clearing land for agriculture and cutting down trees for timber. Both the golden lion tamarin, which is one of the smallest primates, and the mountain gorilla, one of the largest primates, are threatened with extinction. Conservationist groups try to establish forest sanctuaries (safe places) where primates can be protected and their habitat preserved. But numbers of primates continue to decline, and it is quite likely that in just a few years, some of our closest relatives will exist only in zoos, if at all.

SEE ALSO: Animals; Conservation; Endangered Species; Mammals; Rain Forests

Chimpanzees have been taught how to use simple tools and sign language.

✳ ARCHAEOLOGY

Archaeologists investigate the past: They search the sites of ancient cities and houses for clues about the people who used to live there.

The word *archaeology* comes from two Greek words—*archaios* (ancient) and *logos* (study or talk). So *archaeology* means "the study of the past." Archaeologists base their study on the objects that people leave behind. Foundations of buildings, tools, weapons, and even the remains of meals that people ate all give archaeologists information about how ancient people lived. They can learn about their trade, how they found their food, whether they worshiped gods, and so on.

Uncovering the past

Over thousands of years, artifacts (things made by people in the past) become buried under layers of building rubble and earth that pile up over ancient towns and other settlements. Archaeologists study history and legends to find a likely place to dig. Sometimes it may be on a remote hillside that local people believe was the site of an ancient city. At other times it may be in the middle of a modern city, where builders are excavating a site for a new building. Wherever they start to dig, archaeologists keep a careful record of everything they find.

Archaeologists have various ways of dating artifacts. Sometimes they assess an object's age by the depth at which it was found beneath the surface. For more

▶ *Archaeologists excavating Anasazi ruins near Sand Canyon Pueblo, Cortez, Colorado.*

👀
SEE ALSO:
Ancient
Civilizations;
History;
Myths and
Legends;
Tutankhamun

accurate dating, they use a method known as carbon dating. All living things receive a set amount of radioactive carbon (carbon-14, or C-14) from the outer atmosphere. When a plant or animal dies, C-14 begins to leave it at a set rate. Scientists are able to measure the amount of radioactive carbon left in material that was once alive, such as wood or bone. They can then figure out when the artifact was made.

✳ ARCHITECTURE

Architecture is the art of designing buildings. Architects look at the needs of people at home, in offices and factories, and in public spaces.

The development of architecture has been a long process. Builders of the past had to learn from experience which materials were reliable and how best to hold those materials together.

First buildings

The earliest people lived in caves. They discovered how mud could be formed into bricks or used to hold rocks together, and they started to build homes to protect themselves from danger and the weather. They found that round or oval buildings were the easiest to construct, and added roofs of leaves and grass supported by wooden poles.

The first Egyptian pyramid, which dates back over 5,000 years, is the earliest record of an architect-designed building. It was a tomb for Zoser, the pharaoh, or king, and was built by the architect Imhotep. Tombs and temples in ancient Egypt were vast and usually highly decorated or carved with inscriptions.

The towns of early Greek civilizations were often built on hills and surrounded by strong walls to protect them from enemy armies. The Greeks introduced elegant columns and carved friezes to create temples with pleasing proportions. They discovered how to put stone blocks together with metal bars for strength, and developed trusses—wooden beams arranged in a triangle that could support large roofs, similar to rafters today.

The Roman civilization built even larger cities than the Greeks. Buildings for homes and workplaces were grouped around public buildings such as temples and arenas. The Romans found a way of building arches to make doorways with a

Westover Plantation in Virginia was built around 1730 in the Palladian style.

semicircle of specially shaped stones arching over the upright pillars. Among the Romans' most impressive structures were tiered aqueducts (bridges carrying channels of water). Some of them still stand today.

The Middle Ages
After the fall of the Western Roman Empire in the fifth century A.D., building skills declined. Until the 11th century, the main material used in western Europe was wood. In eastern Europe, the Byzantine style of architecture focused on religious buildings, richly decorated, and often topped by huge domes. In India and East Asia, the most impressive buildings were Buddhist shrines.

GREAT ARCHITECTS
Some of the world's best-known buildings—especially the very oldest ones—have no named architect. The following are among the most famous architects. The "see also" box (next page) indicates entries on others.

Imhotep (about 2650 B.C.)
Ancient Egyptian who built the pyramid of Zoser, Saqqara (above).

Brunelleschi, Filippo (1377–1446)
Italian who designed the great domed cathedral in Florence, Italy.

Palladio, Andrea (1508–80)
Influential Italian stylist who built villas and palaces in Italy.

Wren, Sir Christopher (1632–1723)
English architect who designed St. Paul's Cathedral, London.

Sullivan, Louis Henry (1856–1924)
American architect famous for designing skyscrapers, including the Wainwright Building in St. Louis, MO.

Gropius, Walter Adolf (1883–1969)
American architect who specialized in buildings using steel, plate glass, and reinforced concrete.

Mies van der Rohe, Ludwig (1886–1969)
American architect who designed the Lake Shore Drive Apartments, Chicago, and other glass-clad skyscrapers.

Le Corbusier (Charles-Édouard Jeanneret) (1887–1965)
Swiss architect who devised French mass housing projects.

Fuller, (Richard) Buckminster (1895–1983)
American inventor and engineer who pioneered geodesic domes.

Aalto, Alvar (Hugo Alvar Henrik) (1898–1976)
Finnish architect of Baker Hall, MIT, Boston, MA, and many European public buildings with interiors with wooden siding.

Gehry, Frank (Owen) (1929–)
American architect of the Guggenheim Gallery, Bilbao, Spain.

Rogers, Richard (1933–)
English codesigner of the Georges Pompidou Center, Paris, France.

Piano, Renzo (1937–)
Italian codesigner of the Georges Pompidou Center.

In the 11th century, there was a huge increase in the number of buildings constructed in western Europe. Important buildings such as castles were made from stone. Magnificent churches and cathedrals were built to glorify God, and to start with, their style was based on the Roman principles of curved arches and solid shapes. However, by around 1150, architects had developed the Gothic style, with high ceilings, elegant pointed arches, steeply sloping roofs, and towering spires.

Palladian style

One of the most important architects of the 16th century was Andrea Palladio of Vicenza, Italy, who built villas (palaces and country homes) for wealthy people in and around Florence and Rome. He influenced many later architects in both Europe and America. Meanwhile, in Japan the emphasis was on simplicity and natural materials. Homes were built of wood and

made to withstand earthquakes. Earthquake-proofing did not feature in designs by Western architects until the 20th century.

Modern architecture

In the 1800s, cast iron, steel, reinforced concrete, and large sheets of glass became available for use in buildings. These new materials greatly influenced the architecture of the 20th century. Buildings became taller and better looking, and were sometimes used for more than one purpose. Many architects today are concerned about conserving energy, and other environmental issues.

SEE ALSO: Egypt, Ancient; Greece, Ancient; Lin, Maya; Pei, I. M.; Roman Empire; Skyscrapers; Wright, Frank Lloyd

✳ ARCTIC

In the Arctic, the sun does not rise in winter and shines all night during the short summer. The icy Arctic Ocean surrounds the North Pole.

▲ **Arctic ice covers the Beaufort Sea off Tigvariak Island, Alaska.**

Ice covers the northern waters of the Arctic Ocean all year round. In summer some of the ice melts, and ships can navigate parts of the ocean.

Most of the Arctic land forms a vast, treeless plain called the tundra. Snow covers the ground for 10 months of the year. In summer the sun briefly warms the thin topsoil, allowing plants to flower. There are rocky islands in addition to the tundra. Greenland, the largest of them, is

mostly covered in ice. Many birds and thick-furred mammals live in the Arctic. The waters of the region are rich in fish, seals, whales, and porpoises.

People

Humans have lived in the Arctic for thousands of years. The Inuit live in Alaska, Canada, Greenland, and Siberia. Native Americans live in some areas of the North American Arctic. The Lapps live in northern parts of Finland, Norway, and Sweden, and in Russia. Arctic Siberia's native peoples include the Chukchi, Koyaki, and Yakuts. Most Arctic peoples follow traditional occupations, such as

ARCTIC

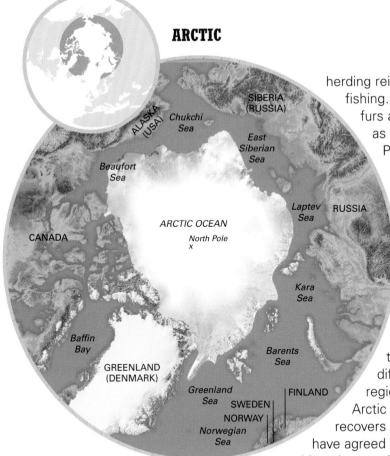

ARCTIC OCEAN
North Pole
x

ALASKA (USA)
Chukchi Sea
SIBERIA (RUSSIA)
East Siberian Sea
Beaufort Sea
Laptev Sea
RUSSIA
CANADA
Kara Sea
Baffin Bay
Barents Sea
GREENLAND (DENMARK)
Greenland Sea
FINLAND
SWEDEN
NORWAY
Norwegian Sea

herding reindeer, hunting, and fishing. Resources include animal furs and fish. Minerals such as coal and gold are mined. Petroleum is extracted from Arctic regions of Alaska and Canada.

Exploration

The first travelers to the Arctic were Norsemen from Scandinavia. Later explorers tried unsuccessfully to sail around the north of the other continents. With today's technology, it is not difficult to explore the region, but the ecology of the Arctic is easily damaged and recovers very slowly. Many nations have agreed on measures to protect this unique region.

SEE ALSO:
Antarctic;
Exploration
and
Explorers;
Greenland

* ARGENTINA

Argentina is a large country in South America. It is bordered by the Atlantic Ocean, Bolivia, Brazil, Chile, Paraguay, and Uruguay.

Argentina is the second-largest country in South America, next in size to Brazil. It is a land of contrasts. There are vast prairies stocked with cattle, steamy swamps, icy islands lashed by storms, and towering mountains. A great farming nation, Argentina also has many cities, busy ports, and factories.

Land and climate

Argentina is divided into five main land zones. The Andes Mountains form most of Argentina's western border with Chile. In the north, high peaks rise from the Puna, a high plateau. The southern Andes are lower. The Gran Chaco, in the far north, is a great lowland covered by areas of thick rain forest and swamp. Its rivers often overflow in the wet season, causing floods. The Gran Chaco is the hottest part of the country.

Mesopotamia, to the east of the Gran Chaco, is a fertile plain lying between the Paraná and Uruguay rivers. Rainfall is heavy here. The pampas are the center of Argentina's agriculture. Here, too, are the big cities and industrial plants.

Patagonia is a region of dry, windswept plateaus. It is the coldest part of the country. Sheep graze its thin soil. The area includes the southernmost part of South

Argentina's national flag

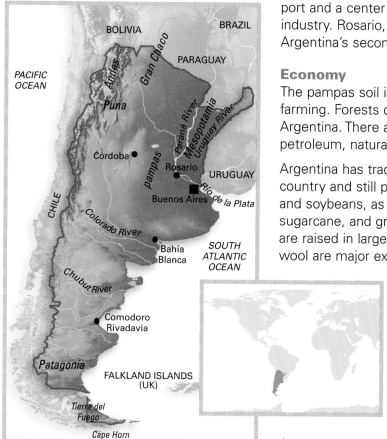

port and a center of commerce and industry. Rosario, on the Paraná River, is Argentina's second-largest city.

Economy

The pampas soil is fertile and ideal for farming. Forests cover about one-fifth of Argentina. There are deposits of petroleum, natural gas, coal, and iron ore.

Argentina has traditionally been a farming country and still produces wheat, corn, and soybeans, as well as cotton, sugarcane, and grapes. Cattle and sheep are raised in large numbers; beef and wool are major exports. Today the country also has many industrial plants making leather products, iron, chemicals, and autos.

History

Argentina won independence from Spain in 1816. Over the next century, wealthy landowners farmed more and more of the pampas,

America, Tierra del Fuego. Here penguins live on islands off Cape Horn. Argentina claims several islands in the Atlantic Ocean, including the Islas Malvinas (Falkland Islands).

People

Argentina has a small native population, but most Argentines are descended from Europeans. Some are mestizos—a mixture of European and Indian. The Spanish started arriving in the 1500s. Between the mid-1800s and the early 1900s, a rush of settlers came from all over western Europe.

Today more than 85 percent of the population live in cities and towns. Buenos Aires, the capital, lies on the Río de la Plata (River Plate). It is Argentina's chief

KEY FACTS

OFFICIAL NAME:
República Argentina

AREA:
1,068,297 sq. mi. (2,766,889 sq. km)

POPULATION:
37,032,000

CAPITAL & LARGEST CITY:
Buenos Aires

MAJOR RELIGION:
Roman Catholicism

MAJOR LANGUAGE:
Spanish

CURRENCY:
Peso

raising wheat and beef cattle on great ranches. New settlers came from Europe, but life was hard for poor people.

The army seized power in 1943. Working people liked Colonel Juan Perón, and he was elected president in 1946. But he was a harsh ruler. Perón was thrown out in 1955. Since then there have been many changes of government.

▶ *Although most Argentine cattle farming takes place on the pampas, there are also ranches in Patagonia, where this picture was taken. Cowhands in Argentina are called gauchos.*

SEE ALSO: South America

✳ ARMSTRONG, LOUIS (1900–71)

Louis Daniel Armstrong was a legendary American jazz musician, singer, and popular entertainer. His hometown, New Orleans, Louisiana, was also the birthplace of jazz music.

As a young boy, Armstrong loved to follow the brass bands that marched down the streets of New Orleans. First he learned to play the cornet and then the trumpet. In 1922 Joe "King" Oliver asked Armstrong to join his jazz band as a trumpeter. They made many records.

Armstrong later formed his own bands: the Hot Five and the Hot Seven. To show off his skills, he took a solo turn at playing each tune on his trumpet. Soon jazz musicians everywhere were playing solos. From the 1930s onward, Armstrong sang, performed in variety shows, and starred in Hollywood movies. He was an inventive singer and used his voice like a musical instrument, often singing nonsense sounds instead of real words. This is called scat singing.

Armstrong was called "Satchmo" because his mouth looked as wide as an open satchel bag. He was hugely popular and won a whole new audience for jazz.

SEE ALSO: Music

▶ *Louis Armstrong was one of the founders of jazz.*

✳ ART AND ARTISTS

Making works of art is one of the oldest human activities. Throughout history there have been different styles, or art movements. And the word *art* has many meanings.

Types of art

When we think of art, we perhaps think of the great works of painting and sculpture created by master artists. Painting and sculpture are known as the fine arts or the major arts, and are created primarily to be looked at. But these are only a small part of the art made around the world.

Decorative arts

The term *decorative arts* is used to mean a kind of art that is useful as well as beautiful. Decorative objects such as cups, rugs, or furniture have a practical use aside from their beauty. Someone who makes decorative art objects is often called an artisan. Artisans use many different materials, such as straw, beads, feathers, glass, and paper, and they shape metals, precious stones, wood, and ivory.

In Western society there was originally little difference between fine and decorative arts. In Europe until about the 15th century, sculpture

This Chinese bronze vessel depicting a monster dates from about the 13th century B.C. ▶

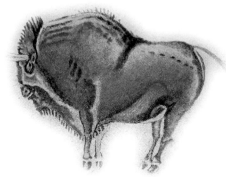

▲ *This bison was found with other cave paintings in Altamira, Spain. These works of art date from between 16,000 and 9,000 B.C.*

was always a part of architecture, and paintings were used to decorate church altars. Gradually a gap developed between decorative and fine art. However, in Asia there was no distinction between the two kinds of art. Much of what we call decorative art was the art most highly prized by Asians. For example, in China some of the finest bronzes ever made, decorated with carvings based on dragons, snakes, and birds, were vessels for wine and food. In Japan, lacquer (highly polished varnish) objects and figures were greatly valued.

Folk art

The term *folk art* is used to describe art produced by people using traditional techniques passed down to them through the generations. It especially applies to art produced by people living in rural areas. Some folk art is simple craftwork created for everyday use. More elaborate works are usually made for an important purpose such as a religious ceremony. Throughout history each culture has produced its own characteristic folk art.

Mass production

The Industrial Revolution, the period of economic growth that began in the mid-1700s, marked the start of mass production. For the first time, millions of people could afford to buy decorative arts. By the 1900s, factories were mass-producing many craft objects such as textiles and furniture—items that had once been made by hand.

After World War II (1939–45), technical advances, such as improved color printing in books, made fine art more accessible to a wider audience. Meanwhile, courses at schools and colleges helped more people appreciate art. But not everyone agrees about what art is. Most people think that a work of art should appeal to both the mind and the senses: It should make the viewer think about the subject depicted as well as feel some emotion. There are fresh ideas in art all the time, and the history of fine art is reflected in a series of movements that have developed in different cultures, remaining popular until a new style has emerged.

History of fine art

The earliest paintings were made on the walls of caves by Stone Age peoples about 20,000 years ago. The paintings depicted the animals they hunted for food, such as bison, reindeer, and ibex.

Egyptian art

In the ancient Egyptian civilization, which arose about 5,000 years ago, artists created images and statues to celebrate their rulers, who were believed to be gods. Kings were buried in huge tombs called pyramids, inside which were rooms decorated with carvings and paintings of their deeds. The figures in Egyptian art were not painted to look lifelike. Later civilizations, such as those of the Cretans and the Greeks, created statues that

looked more human, or more specifically, like representations of perfect humans. Roman art was more realistic and expressive. When Germanic people overran the Roman Empire in the fifth century A.D. and converted to Christianity, they turned to religious art.

Medieval Christian art

For nearly a thousand years, most European art was related to the church. Medieval paintings and sculptures showed saints, martyrs, and scenes from the Bible. It was only in the 1400s that artists became concerned with individual human beings, and they tried to make their works realistic. For the first time, too, artists were recognized as being different from craftspeople. These changes took place in a period known as the Renaissance, which means "rebirth." Artists and scholars

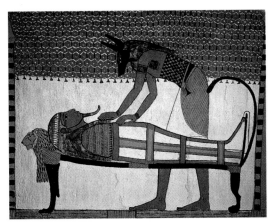

This wall painting from the tomb of an Egyptian official dates from the 14th century B.C.

believed they were returning to the art produced in the past.

In the centuries after the Renaissance, artists continued to try to capture what was most important and truthful about people and the world around them. They included the Italian painter Michelangelo and the Dutchman Rembrandt. Many artists tried to create "rules" about how to make a good picture and what sort of scene it should portray. ➡

American art

The earliest artists in America were native people who had lived there for thousands of years before European settlement. They made beautiful pottery, jewelry, and carvings. Early American painting and sculpture was influenced by European— especially English—art after the settlers arrived in the early 1600s. But in portrait painting, for example, Americans created more realistic likenesses. During the 1800s, landscape painters worked on romantic views of the wilderness. By the end of the century, there was a growing interest in realism.

Impressionism

A major change in the creation of art came with Impressionism, a style developed by a group of French artists in the mid-to-late 1800s. Impressionists were more concerned with the fresh, free way they applied their paint in dabs or strokes of color to the canvas than with the subjects of their pictures. The French artist Auguste Rodin transformed the art of sculpture by creating surfaces that seemed alive.

At the beginning of the 20th century, Georges Braque (1882–1963) and Pablo Picasso (1881–1973) developed Cubism, a style of painting influenced by African art. They represented subjects as a series of simplified, angular forms. More artists began painting abstract works. Abstract art did not try to show anything that was real. Instead, Wassily Kandinsky and others liked to work with color and shape. In the mid-1920s, a new movement called Surrealism became popular in Europe. The Surrealists, such as Salvador Dali, based their images on dreams and fantasy.

Modern art in the United States

At the start of World War II, many artists fled Europe for New York. The city became the center of modern art, and a style called Abstract Expressionism developed. Paintings in this style usually appear disorderly, but the way paint is applied to the canvas reveals the artist's feelings. By about 1960, a new kind of style, known as Pop Art, had emerged. Pop Artists aimed to make art fun and use it to mirror society. Their subjects were drawn from

This autumn river landscape is the work of French Impressionist Claude Monet (1840–1926). ▶

▶ *Claude Monet in his famous garden at Giverny, France.*

American popular culture. Other artists favored Minimal Art, a kind of abstract art based on how shapes look in different lights and colors.

A more recent development is Conceptual Art, or "idea art." Its followers believe that the idea of a work of art is more important than the end product. The result is a breaking down of boundaries between the arts. Artists convey ideas through music, performance, photography, and video, as well as painting, drawing, and sculpture.

Salvador Dali (1904–89) was a Spanish Surrealist painter and experimental filmmaker.

GREAT ARTISTS

This is a short list of some of the world's most famous artists. The "see also" box indicates entries on other important ones.

Praxiteles (4th century B.C.)
Athenian sculptor considered to be the greatest of his time.

Giotto (Giotto di Bondone) (about 1267–1337)
Italian painter who began to develop realistic ways of painting.

Raphael (Raffaello Sanzio) (1483–1520)
Italian painter famous for his set of wall paintings in the Vatican, Rome.

Titian (Tiziano Vecelli) (about 1488–1576)
Italian painter from Venice famous for his use of color and depiction of human character.

Goya (Francisco José de Goya y Lucientes) (1746–1828)
Spanish painter whose imaginative work depicted subjects as varied as court life and scenes of war.

Hokusai (Hokusai Katsushika) (1760–1849)
Japanese landscape artist and printmaker.

Turner, J.M.W. (Joseph Mallord William) (1775–1851)
English painter whose work experimented with capturing the effects of light.

Whistler, James Abbott McNeill (1834–1903)
American painter whose landscapes and portraits evoked moods rather than accurately reflected color.

Cézanne, Paul (1839–1906)
French painter whose methods greatly influenced modern art.

Rodin, Auguste (1840–1917)
French sculptor famous for his portrayal of the human body.

Monet, Claude (1840–1926)
French landscape painter and one of the founders of Impressionism.

Sargent, John Singer (1856–1925)
American painter famous for his portraits of fashionable society.

Kandinsky, Wassily (1866–1944)
Russian painter and pioneer of abstract art.

Klee, Paul (1879–1940)
Swiss painter whose colorful works portrayed a world of poetry and music.

Rothko, Mark (1903–70)
American Abstract Expressionist who painted rectangular masses of color with fuzzy edges that seemed to float across one another.

Dali, Salvador (Filipe Jacinto) (1904–89)
Spanish Surrealist who painted dreamlike images using a highly realistic technique.

Pollock, (Paul) Jackson (1912–56)
American Abstract Expressionist who splashed and dripped paint onto canvas.

Warhol, Andy (1928–87)
American Pop Artist famous for his paintings based on subjects featured in newspapers and advertisements, such as cans of soup.

SEE ALSO:
Cassatt, Mary; da Vinci, Leonardo; Folk Arts; Homer, Winslow; Kahlo, Frida; Michelangelo; O'Keeffe, Georgia; Picasso, Pablo; Rembrandt van Rijn; Renaissance; van Gogh, Vincent

✳ ASIA
Asia is the largest and most heavily populated continent. Once colonized by Europeans, its peoples now govern themselves.

Land and climate

Asia occupies nearly one-third of Earth's total land surface and is home to about 60 percent of its people. It has the world's highest peak—Mount Everest—and its lowest point—the shoreline of the Dead Sea, 1,300 ft. (400 m) below sea level.

Asia forms the larger, eastern portion of an enormous landmass known as Eurasia. Many islands, including those making up the nations of Japan, Indonesia, and the Philippines, border the continent and form part of it. Politically Russia forms part of Europe, but much of its territory is in Asia.

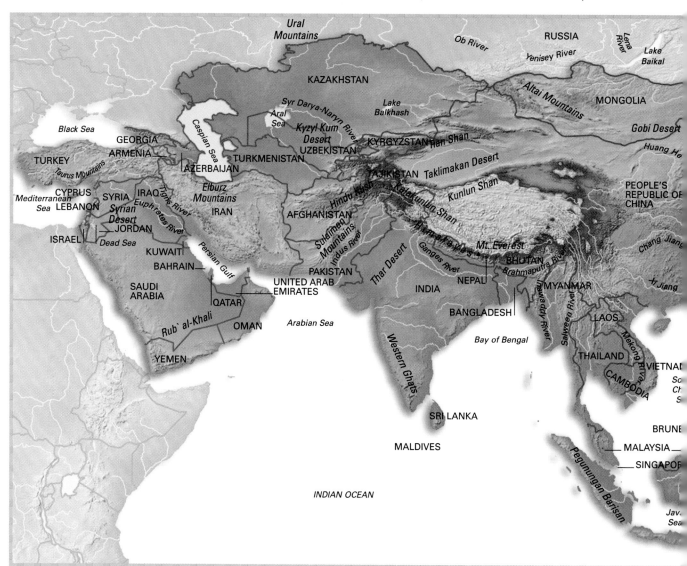

In the heart of Asia is the great mountain chain of the Himalayas, which include Everest. The Himalayas are part of an even larger mountain system that stretches from Turkey to China. Asia has some of the world's most forbidding deserts, including the Gobi of Mongolia and China and the Rub` al-Khali (Empty Quarter) of Saudi Arabia. Vast treeless plains, or steppes, cover much of Central Asia. Farther north is a broad belt of pine forest known as taiga.

Much of Asia is cold and dry in the winter and warm and dry in the summer. The mountain ranges that cross Asia act as a huge wall. They keep the cold winds of the Arctic from blowing to the south and the hot winds of the south from blowing north. Winters in Siberia are among the coldest on Earth, while temperatures around the Persian Gulf can reach 120°F (49°C). Parts of Southwest Asia receive as little as 4 in. (100 mm) of rain a year, whereas northeast India is one of the wettest regions on Earth.

Plants and animals
Much of Asia has poor soils, particularly in the interior, which is too high, dry, or cold to farm. The most fertile places, where crops can readily be grown, are along the river valleys and in some coastal areas. Southeast Asia's tropical rain forests include valuable hardwoods such as teak and mahogany.

Polar and brown bears, Arctic foxes, reindeer, and elk live in North Asia. The orangutan lives in the tropical forests of Sumatra and Borneo. India has many large mammals, including the Bengal tiger, the Indian rhinoceros, and the Asian elephant.

People
Asia is home to many different peoples, who speak a great variety of languages. Most of the population lives in three regions—South Asia (the Indian subcontinent), Southeast Asia, and East Asia (China, Japan, and Korea).

About two-thirds of Asia's people earn their living from the land. Major crops include rice, wheat, corn, rubber, tea,

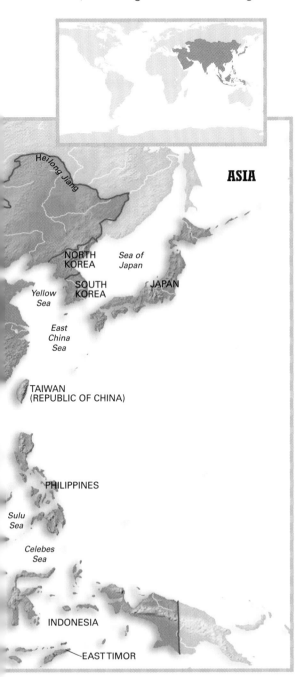

ASIA

Heilong Jiang

NORTH KOREA

Sea of Japan

SOUTH KOREA

JAPAN

Yellow Sea

East China Sea

TAIWAN (REPUBLIC OF CHINA)

PHILIPPINES

Sulu Sea

Celebes Sea

INDONESIA

EAST TIMOR

KEY FACTS

AREA:
about 17,297,000 sq. mi. (44,780,000 sq. km)

POPULATION:
3,682,550,000

COUNTRIES:
48

LARGEST COUNTRY:
China

SMALLEST COUNTRY:
Singapore

RELIGIONS:
Islam, Hinduism, Buddhism, Taoism, Shinto, animism, Sikhism, Confucianism, Judaism, Christianity

LANGUAGES:
Many, including Urdu, Hindi, Tamil, Persian, Chinese, Japanese, Korean, Hebrew, Turkish

sugarcane, cotton, soybeans, and silk. Nomadic (wandering) herders in Central and Southwest Asia depend on livestock.

Asia has some of the world's largest cities, including Tokyo (Japan), Seoul (South Korea), Shanghai (China), and Mumbai (Bombay, India).

Natural resources

Asia is rich in mineral resources. The Persian Gulf area is the world's single-largest source of petroleum. Japan is the most industrialized nation in Asia. China and India are a distant second and third.

History

The earliest human settlements in Asia date from around 3500 B.C. in three great river valleys: the Tigris–Euphrates in Southwest Asia, the Indus in South Asia, and the Huang He (Yellow River) in East Asia. These civilizations developed the world's first writing and legal codes.

The Gobi desert is in east–central Asia. In summer the climate is hot, but in winter it is bitterly cold.
▼

Major Physical Features

DESERTS
- Arabian 500,000 sq. mi. (1,295,000 sq. km)
- Gobi 400,000 sq. mi. (1,036,000 sq. km)
- Turkestan 220,000 sq. mi. (569,800 sq. km)
- Taklimakan 125,000 sq. mi. (323,750 sq. km)
- Thar 100,000 sq. mi. (259,000 sq. km)

MOUNTAIN RANGES & HIGHEST POINTS
- Himalayas: Mt. Everest 29,078 ft. (8,863 m); total of 30 peaks above 24,000 ft. (7,315 m)
- Kalakunlun Shan (Karakoram) 4 peaks above 26,000 ft. (7,925 m)
- Kunlun Shan 25,338 ft. (7,723 m)
- Tian Shan 24,406 ft. (7,439 m)
- Hindu Kush 24 peaks above 23,000 ft. (7,010 m)
- Elburz 18,510 ft. (5,642 m)
- Altai 14,783 ft. (4,506 m)
- Pegunungan Barisan 12,484 ft. (3,805 m)
- Sulaiman 11,295 ft. (3,443 m)
- Ural Mountains 6,217 ft. (1,895 m)

RIVERS
- Chang Jiang (Yangtze) 3,915 mi. (6,299 km)
- Yenisey-Angara 3,442 mi. (5,538 km)
- Huang He (Yellow River) 3,395 mi. (5,463 km)
- Ob 3,230 mi. (5,197 km)
- Lena 2,734 mi. (4,399 km)
- Mekong 2,702 mi. (4,348 km)
- Heilong Jiang (Amur) 2,700 mi. (4,344 km)
- Syr Darya-Naryn 1,876 mi. (3,018 km)
- Brahmaputra 1,800 mi. (2,896 km)
- Indus 1,790 mi. (2,880 km)
- Salween 1,750 mi. (2,816 km)
- Euphrates 1,740 mi. (2,800 km)
- Xi Jiang (Si-Kiang) 1,650 mi. (2,655 km)
- Ganges 1,553 mi. (2,499 km)
- Irrawaddy 1,300 mi. (2,092 km)
- Tigris 1,150 mi. (1,850 km)

LAKES
- Caspian Sea 143,550 sq. mi. (371,800 sq. km)
- Lake Baikal 11,780 sq. mi. (30,500 sq. km)
- Aral Sea 11,600 sq. mi. (30,000 sq. km)

The first great Asian empire, the Mauryan, was established in the fourth century B.C. and created unity in India. Under its greatest ruler, Asoka, Buddhism and great monumental art flourished.

In China the Han dynasty, or ruling family (202 B.C.–A.D. 220), established an empire and extended its influence in Central and Southeast Asia. The Han adopted Confucianism, a system of ethical teachings founded by the philosopher Confucius. During this period, Christianity appeared in Southwest Asia, and Buddhism began to spread to East Asia.

In the seventh century A.D., Muslims (followers of Islam) took over most of North Africa, Southwest Asia, and northern India. In East Asia, China flourished under the Tang and Sung dynasties from about 600 to 1200.

In the 13th century, Genghis Khan, a Mongol warrior, gained control of much of Asia from China to Russia.

Many Europeans came to Asia in the 1500s and carved out empires. In the 20th century, the desire for self-rule became a powerful force in Asia. From World War II (1939–45) onward, all countries gained their independence.

SEE ALSO: Ancient Civilizations; Buddhism; Central Asia; China; Continents; Genghis Khan; Indian Subcontinent; Indonesia; Iran; Iraq; Islam; Israel; Japan; Korea; Malaysia; Middle East; Palestine; Philippines; Religions; Russia and the Baltic States; Southeast Asia; Turkey and the Caucasus

The tiger is one of many rare and beautiful species that are found in the wild only in Asia.

✳ ASIAN AMERICANS

About 4 percent of the U.S. population are Asian Americans—people with origins in East Asia, Southeast Asia, or the Indian subcontinent.

Asians began to immigrate to the United States in the mid-1800s, when Chinese people were attracted to the "Gold Mountain" on the American West Coast. Other Chinese workers came to Hawaii to work on plantations. Young farm workers from southern China came to San Francisco to work in mines and to help build the new railroads. By 1882 there were more than 100,000 Chinese workers in the United States, but then the government passed laws to stop the flow of immigrants.

Improving civil rights
For the next 80 years, only a few Asians were allowed to immigrate. They were mainly students and businessmen and some refugees who wanted to flee the Communist regime of China in the mid-1900s. Those who came had few rights: They were not allowed to vote or take U.S. citizenship. All that changed after the Civil Rights Act of 1964. Chinese Americans who were already in the United States campaigned for social

equality, and thousands of Chinese came from their homelands to be reunited with their families.

Since the early 1970s, most Asian immigrants have been well-educated people who have studied science and technology. They have made an important contribution to U.S. expertise in these areas. People who had moved from China to other parts of Asia also made their way to America in search of work and a safe place to live. Chinese are now the largest group of Asian Americans.

Japanese immigrants
From 1600 to 1868, people were not allowed to enter or leave Japan without permission. In 1868 the Japanese emperor was overthrown, and the nation began a development program that made it the strongest power in Asia. The first Japanese immigrants came to Hawaii and California. By 1920, 300,000 of them lived in the United States. In 1941, when Japan entered World War II (1939–45), Japanese Americans were moved to relocation camps because they were regarded as enemies. After the war, it was a long time before Japanese people were accepted, but by 2000 more than one million Japanese lived in the United States, mainly on the West Coast.

Other groups
Smaller groups of immigrants have come from other countries in East or Southeast Asia. Koreans came in search of work before World War II, and refugees came during and after the Korean War (1950–53). Koreans are now one of the fastest-

A Chinese worker pans for gold with other miners in California around 1855. Asian immigrants joined the flood of fortune-seekers from all parts of the world who hoped to become rich in the United States.

growing ethnic groups in the United States. Indochina (Laos, Cambodia, and Vietnam) is another area where war and politics have driven first refugees and then workers to the United States in search of safer lives and better incomes.

Asian Indians from India, Pakistan, Bangladesh, and Sri Lanka traditionally emigrated to Europe (particularly the United Kingdom). More recently, however, some emigrants from those countries have begun to move to Canada and the United States, where they have settled in many of the major cities.

Filipino migration

Another major group of Asian Americans are Filipinos (people from the Philippines), who came in search of better jobs. Many of them started out working as domestics in U.S. cities.

Generally Asian Americans are well-educated. In 2000, 44 percent of Asians and Pacific Islanders age 25 and over living in the United States had a bachelor's degree or a higher university degree, and 86 percent of them had a high school diploma.

DID YOU KNOW?

The main countries of origin of Asian Americans are as follows:

Cambodia, China, India, Japan, Korea, Malaysia, Pakistan, Philippines, Thailand, Vietnam

Asia includes most of Turkey and a large part of Russia. When we talk about people of Asian origin, however, the term does not generally refer to people from countries to the west of Pakistan and north of China and Mongolia.

SEE ALSO:
Asia; China; Immigration; Indian Subcontinent; Japan; Korea; Korean War; Malaysia; Philippines; Southeast Asia; World War II

A delighted Asian American student holds up her diploma at a graduation ceremony at the University of Indiana.

✳ASTEROIDS 👀➡ ✳COMETS, METEORS, AND ASTEROIDS

✴ ASTRONAUTS

Men and women who travel in space are called astronauts, a modern word that comes from ancient Greek and means "sailors of the stars."

The United States began its manned space travel program in the late 1950s. For some years its space agency, the National Aeronautics and Space Administration (NASA), lagged behind the Soviet Union. But in 1969 the United States won the race to put a man on the moon.

Soviet pioneers

The first person in space was Soviet cosmonaut Yuri Gagarin, who made a single orbit of Earth in April 1961. (The word *cosmonaut* is the Russian equivalent of *astronaut*; it means "sailor of the universe.")

The first NASA manned space-flight program was Project Mercury. Its objectives were to orbit Earth, investigate a human's ability to function in space, and recover both crew and spacecraft safely. The seven astronauts hired for Project Mercury were all Air Force test pilots with at least 1,500 hours of flight time who had flown 50 miles (80 km) above Earth. Because of the small size of the Mercury capsule, the astronauts could not be over 5 ft. 11 in. (180 cm) tall.

Toward the moon

The second U.S. manned space program, begun in 1962, was named Gemini because its capsules had two-man crews (*gemini* is Latin for "twins"). Gemini capsules were larger than the Mercury craft, so the nine men chosen could be up to 6 ft. (183 cm) tall. The maximum age for astronauts was reduced from 40 to 35 years old. Civilian test pilots could qualify.

The third series of missions was the Apollo program (1963–72), which aimed to land humans on the moon and bring them safely back to Earth. Of the 14 men originally selected, six were not test pilots but scientists.

The age of the space shuttle

In 1978 NASA named 35 new candidates for positions as astronauts aboard the space shuttle. Six were women—the first U.S. female astronauts. Since then candidates have been recruited each year, and astronauts from other nations also take part in shuttle flights.

The first Soviet cosmonauts were also experienced jet pilots, but some later missions were carried out by men without

Astronauts prepare to board Apollo 11 for the first manned moon landing in July 1969.

FAMOUS ASTRONAUTS

Gagarin, Yuri (1934–68)
On April 12, 1961, the Soviet Union became the first nation to put a human into space when Gagarin orbited the Earth in *Vostok 1*.

Glenn, John (above) (1921–)
In February 1962 Glenn became the first American to orbit Earth.

Tereshkova, Valentina (1937–)
This Soviet cosmonaut was the first woman in space. She orbited Earth in June 1963.

Leonov, Alexei (1934–)
In March 1965 cosmonaut Leonov became the first person to leave a spacecraft on a "spacewalk," or extravehicular activity (EVA).

Armstrong, Neil (left) (1930–), and **Aldrin, Edwin "Buzz"** (1930–)
On July 20, 1969, these U.S. astronauts became the first humans to step on the moon. **Michael Collins** (1930–) was the third crew member.

Young, John (1930–), and **Crippen, Robert** (1937–)
These U.S. astronauts were the first to fly in the space shuttle, in April 1981.

Ride, Sally (1951–)
Orbiting Earth in the shuttle in June 1983, Ride was the first American woman in space.

a military or piloting background. The Russians led the way for women in space—in 1963 Valentina Tereshkova became the first female in space.

Astronauts are trained for space-flight conditions, such as weightlessness, and on-board emergencies. There are full-scale spacecraft models at NASA's Lyndon B. Johnson Space Center in Houston, Texas, and elsewhere.

An astronaut takes a walk in space outside the International Space Station in July 2001.

Astronauts in weightless conditions aboard the space shuttle Endeavour in 1992.

SEE ALSO: Spacecraft; Space Exploration

✳ ASTRONOMY

Astronomy is the study of everything in the universe beyond Earth. It is one of the oldest sciences. About 10,000 years ago, people used astronomy to decide when to plant and harvest crops.

Our first real knowledge of ancient astronomy dates from about 2,500 years ago, when Greek astronomers carefully recorded what they had learned. They believed that Earth was at the center of the universe and that the stars and other planets circled Earth.

Beginning of modern astronomy

The Polish astronomer Nicolaus Copernicus (1473–1543) was the first person to suggest correctly that Earth revolved around the sun, not the other way around.

An early astronomer observing the stars through a telescope, an instrument first used and possibly invented by Galileo Galilei.
◄

The Italian scientist Galileo Galilei (1564–1642) was the first to use a telescope to study the sky. Like Copernicus, he believed that the planets orbited, or circled, the sun, but he could not explain why. The English scientist Isaac Newton (1642–1727) discovered that all objects possess a force called gravity that attracts other objects. A large object such as the sun produces enough gravity to hold the planets in orbit around it. Moons orbit planets for the same reason.

Ancient and modern constellations

People in ancient times first noticed that groups of stars seemed to form patterns that did not change, even though the stars themselves moved across the sky. These groups of stars are called constellations, which means "clusters of stars." People named many constellations after gods and spirits, who were believed to live in the sky. One group of 12 constellations became known as the zodiac, meaning "circle of animals." People began to use the movements of the sun, moon, and planets within these constellations to predict the future. This practice is called astrology. It is still popular today.

Ancient peoples of the Northern Hemisphere identified 36 constellations in addition to the ones in the zodiac. In the 1500s, Europeans sailed to the Southern Hemisphere, where they saw thousands of stars unknown to northerners. Later astronomers grouped these stars, as well as many fainter ones in the northern sky, into new constellations. In 1931 astronomers recognized a total of 88 ancient and modern constellations.

Moving galaxies

In the early 1900s, astronomers realized that some distant, glowing clouds they could see in the night sky were in fact huge groups of stars, or galaxies. There are billions of galaxies in the universe, and each contains billions of stars. Most galaxies are clustered together in groups.

By the 1920s, as telescopes became more powerful, astronomers noticed that galaxies outside the cluster that contains Earth's Milky Way galaxy were moving away from one another. This means that the universe is expanding. By the 1960s, many astronomers believed that this

expansion began about 10 to 15 billion years ago with a huge explosion, which they called the Big Bang.

Black holes

Astronomers still do not know what lies at the center of galaxies. Some think they may contain a black hole. Black holes form when a large star dies. As the star cools and becomes smaller, its gravity becomes stronger and causes it to collapse under its own weight. Any matter or energy attracted inward by this force is unable to escape. Black holes are invisible. We know that they exist because gas from neighboring stars throws out x-rays that can be detected from Earth as the gas is about to be sucked into the hole.

An artist's impression of a black hole at the center of a swirling whirlpool of hot gas.

▼

SEE ALSO: Big Bang Theory; Comets, Meteors, and Asteroids; Earth; Galaxies; Galilei, Galileo; Gravity; Jupiter; Mars; Mercury; Moon; Neptune; Newton, Isaac; Planets; Pluto; Rockets; Satellites; Saturn; Solar System; Space Exploration; Stars; Stonehenge; Sun; Telescopes; Universe; Uranus; Venus

Sagittarius is one of the 12 constellations of the group known as the zodiac.

▼

✳ ATLANTIC OCEAN

Covering about one-fifth of Earth's surface, the Atlantic Ocean is the planet's second-largest body of water. Only the Pacific Ocean is larger.

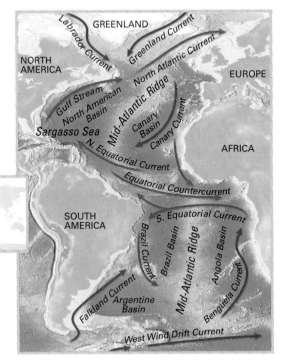

clockwise direction, and in the South Atlantic counterclockwise. The Gulf Stream of the North Atlantic carries warm water north along the eastern coast of the United States and then turns northeast, bringing warm weather to western Europe. In the South Atlantic the warm Brazil Current travels south from the equator along the eastern coast of Brazil.

History

To early peoples, the world did not exist beyond the Atlantic Ocean. In 1492 Christopher Columbus started a new era of exploration, when he sailed across the Atlantic to the Americas. As traders crisscrossed the ocean and Europeans settled in the Americas, the Atlantic became—and today remains—a vital highway between Europe and America.

Some of the great rivers of the world, including the Amazon and the St. Lawrence, empty into the Atlantic. These rivers pick up many minerals from the land and wash them out to sea, making the Atlantic the saltiest of the oceans.

The 700-ft. (215-m) Cliffs of Moher in County Clare, Ireland, are constantly pounded by the Atlantic.
▼

Warm and cold currents

The Atlantic is divided by the equator into the North Atlantic and the South Atlantic. In the North Atlantic the currents flow in a

KEY FACTS

AREA:
Over 41,000,000 sq. mi. (106,000,000 sq. km), including connected seas

AVERAGE DEPTH:
About 12,800 ft. (3,900 m)

DEEPEST SPOT:
30,249 ft. (9,220 m) in

the Puerto Rico Trench, in the North Atlantic

WIDTH:
From 1,850 mi. (2,980 km), between Brazil and Senegal, to more than 4,000 mi. (6,400 km) between Florida and the Strait of Gibraltar

👀 SEE ALSO: Columbus, Christopher; Exploration and Explorers; Oceans and Seas; Pacific Ocean

✳ ATMOSPHERE

The atmosphere is a thin layer of air that protects Earth from the burning sun and the freezing cold of space. Without it life could not survive.

Earth's atmosphere is a mixture of gases, water vapor, and dust particles. Almost four-fifths of the air is made up of nitrogen. Nearly one-fifth of air is oxygen, which is essential for almost all life. People and animals need oxygen to breathe and to turn food into energy. There are only small amounts of carbon dioxide in the air, but this gas, too, is vital to life on Earth. Green plants use carbon dioxide in the process of making food.

Water vapor enters the atmosphere by evaporating from oceans, lakes, rivers, and the earth's surface. Clouds and fog form from the vapor. The water in clouds can evaporate back into the atmosphere or fall as rain, sleet, or snow.

Layers

Between the ground and the edge of outer space, Earth's atmosphere has five different layers. The lowest layer is called the troposphere and extends up to about 12 miles (19 km) high. It is here that most of Earth's weather forms.

The next layer, up to about 30 miles (50 km) high, is the stratosphere. It contains the ozone layer. Ozone is a gas that absorbs most of the sun's ultraviolet radiation, so that only small amounts reach Earth. That is important because too much ultraviolet radiation can cause skin cancer and cataracts in the eyes. The ozone layer is damaged by the long-term use of chlorofluorocarbons (CFCs), gases that were used until recently in nearly all aerosol sprays, refrigerators, and air-conditioning systems.

Above the stratosphere, up to about 50 miles (80 km) high, is the mesosphere. Temperatures here are very low. Meteors burn up in this layer.

Between 50 and 250 miles (80–400 km) high is the thermosphere. This layer contains an area called the ionosphere, which reflects radio waves back to Earth.

Over 310 miles (500 km) above Earth's surface is the exosphere. It is the outlying layer of the atmosphere. The exosphere contains almost no gases. It continues into outer space until it merges with the atmosphere of the sun.

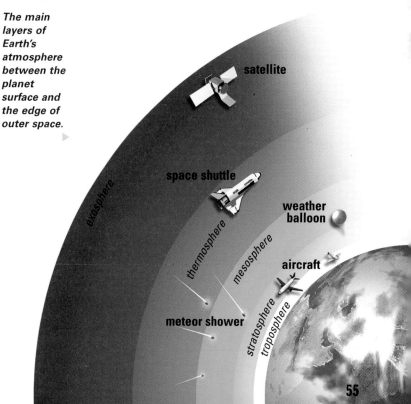

The main layers of Earth's atmosphere between the planet surface and the edge of outer space. ▶

satellite

space shuttle

weather balloon

thermosphere

mesosphere

aircraft

exosphere

stratosphere

troposphere

meteor shower

SEE ALSO: Climate; Earth; Environment; Pollution; Space Exploration; Sun; Weather

✳ ATOMS AND MOLECULES
An atom is the smallest piece of matter that can exist naturally on its own. A molecule is made up of two or more atoms.

STRUCTURE OF AN ATOM

Electrons form a fuzzy cloud that moves around the nucleus.

The nucleus consists of protons and neutrons.

▶ *An atom is made up of tiny particles called protons, neutrons, and electrons.*

👀

SEE ALSO:
Chemistry;
Elements;
Matter

Atoms are the basic building blocks of our world. These tiny particles make up every type of matter in the universe—solid, liquid, and gas. Matter is anything that takes up space (volume) and has mass.

Too small to see
An atom is unimaginably tiny. For example, the period at the end of this sentence has a diameter of about 0.02 in. (0.5 mm). If the period were made up of pure carbon, it would contain about two million carbon atoms placed side by side. If each atom were magnified to be the size of the period, the magnified period would be about 1.2 miles (2 km) across.

Atoms cannot be seen. Scientists figured out that they must exist by observing the behavior of chemicals. Scientists used to think that atoms were the smallest particles of matter. But in the early 1900s, they discovered that atoms contain tiny subatomic particles. At the center of the atom is a nucleus (plural, *nuclei*). The nucleus contains two kinds of subatomic particles—protons and neutrons. Particles called electrons move around the nucleus. The electrons are so small that it is impossible to identify their exact position at any particular moment. Most of them are likely to be in a region around the nucleus called the electron cloud. Each electron, however, stays within a shell, a bit like the layers of an onion.

Elements and compounds
A group of atoms bound together is called a molecule. When atoms of the same type bind together, they form the molecules of a chemical element. When different types of atoms combine, they form the molecules of a compound. A compound is a substance made up of two or more elements in which the elements are always combined in exactly the same proportion. For example, water is a compound made up of the elements hydrogen and oxygen. A single molecule of water contains one atom of oxygen and two atoms of hydrogen.

AMAZING FACTS!

It would take about two trillion fine grains of pollen to make up 0.035 oz. (1 g) of mass, which is about the mass of a paper clip. Yet each one of those tiny pollen particles would contain about 20 billion atoms.

✳ AUSTRALIA AND NEW ZEALAND

Australia is an island country lying between the Pacific and Indian oceans. To the southeast of Australia, in the South Pacific Ocean, is the island country of New Zealand.

AUSTRALIA

Land and climate
Australia has a low-lying landscape, except for a mountain range in the east. Most of the people live in the cities to the east of this range. The hot, dry interior is called the outback. January and February are the hottest months; July is the coolest. Summer temperatures in the outback can exceed 100°F (38°C).

Plants and animals
In dry areas, there are eucalyptus trees with leaves that conserve water. In the northeast, tropical rain forests flourish. Animals include kangaroos, koalas, and emus (large, flightless birds). There are also many snakes, spiders, and jellyfish.

People and economy
Australia's native people, the Aborigines, have lived there for 40,000 years. Their ancestors came on boats from lands in Southeast Asia.

Australia is a major producer and exporter of agricultural products. The country's mineral resources include gold, bauxite (aluminum ore), uranium, and oil. Service industries are the fastest-growing sector.

Australia's national flag

KEY FACTS

OFFICIAL NAME:
Commonwealth of Australia

AREA:
2,967,895 sq. mi. (7,686,848 sq. km)

POPULATION:
18,886,000

CAPITAL:
Canberra

LARGEST CITY:
Sydney

MAJOR RELIGIONS:
Protestantism, Roman Catholicism

MAJOR LANGUAGE:
English

CURRENCY:
Australian dollar

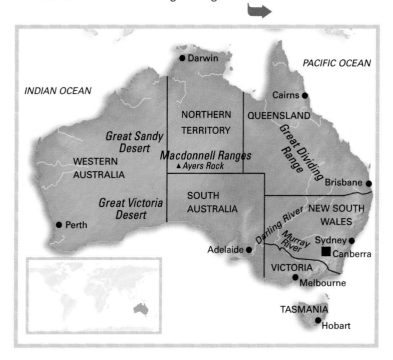

Ayers Rock, called Uluru by the Aborigines, is the largest outcrop of its type in the world.

History

In 1642 the Dutch sailor Abel Tasman visited the island of Tasmania. In 1770 the British explorer James Cook arrived at Botany Bay, near what is now Sydney. It was there that the first British settlers landed in 1788. More British settlers followed. Australia became a nation in 1901. In more recent years, Asian settlers have added to Australia's population.

NEW ZEALAND

New Zealand's national flag

Land and climate

New Zealand is made up of two large islands—North Island and South Island—and some small outlying islands. Both main islands have mountains; some are active volcanoes. There are geysers and hot springs, and earthquakes are common. The summers are mild, and the winters are cool and rather stormy, though frosts are rare in the lowlands. The weather is extremely changeable.

The Maoris are the native Polynesian people of New Zealand. Today they are outnumbered by people of British descent. ▼

Plants and animals

Natural vegetation, known as native bush, once covered half of New Zealand, but settlers have cleared much of it for crops or conifer plantations. Along the southwest coast are dense rain forests, and ferns are plentiful. The country is rich in bird life. Flightless birds survived there because they had no natural enemies. The best-known example is the kiwi, which has short legs and small, stumpy wings. New Zealand has no native land mammals except bats.

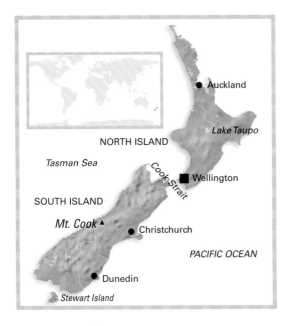

People and economy

New Zealand's first inhabitants, the Maoris, came from Polynesia in the 1300s. British settlers arrived from the 18th century onward. The country became independent from Britian in 1907. Most people live on the North Island. The country's economy depends heavily on its sheep and cattle, which yield meat, dairy, and wool products.

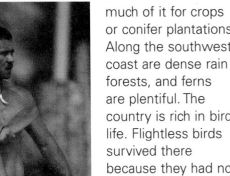

KEY FACTS

AREA: 104,454 sq. mi. (270,534 sq. km)	**MAJOR RELIGIONS:** Protestantism, Roman Catholicism
POPULATION: 3,862,000	**MAJOR LANGUAGE:** English
CAPITAL: Wellington	**CURRENCY:** New Zealand dollar
LARGEST CITY: Auckland	

SEE ALSO: Aborigines; Exploration and Explorers; Marsupials

✳ AUSTRIA
Austria is a small country lying in the heart of Europe. It has a rich history and was once the center of a vast European empire.

Land and climate
Austria is dominated by mountains: The Alps, the highest mountains in Europe, extend across western Austria. The Danube River forms a wide valley running across eastern Austria. Climate varies between the country's regions. The mountains have heavy snowfall in winter.

People
Most Austrians speak German, but in some areas they feel more closely linked to neighboring states, such as Slovenia and Slovakia.

Economy
The Austrian economy is based mainly on industry. Most factories are in the Danube valley. The leading manufactured goods include machinery, textiles, and chemicals. Austria is also popular with tourists.

History
In 1278 the Hapsburg family took control of Austria. They built an empire that spread across Europe from Spain north

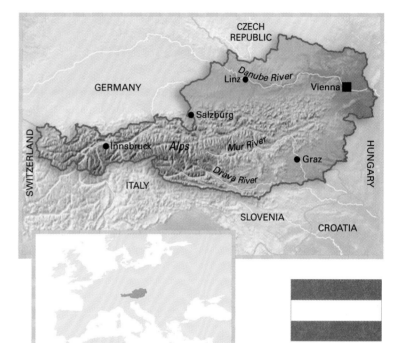

Austria's national flag

to the Netherlands and beyond Hungary to the east. The empire (known as the Holy Roman Empire) was eventually destroyed in 1806 by the French general Napoleon Bonaparte. The Hapsburgs ruled until the end of World War I (1914–18), when emperor Charles I was forced to step down. Austria became a republic.

In 1938 Austria was swallowed up by Nazi Germany. When World War II ended in 1945, Austria was divided among the Allies. It became independent in 1955.

KEY FACTS

OFFICIAL NAME: Republik Österreich

AREA: 32,374 sq. mi. (83,849 sq. km)

POPULATION: 8,211,000

CAPITAL & LARGEST CITY: Vienna

MAJOR RELIGION: Roman Catholicism

MAJOR LANGUAGE: German

CURRENCY: Euro

SEE ALSO: Central Europe; Napoleon; World War I; World War II

*AUTOMOBILES ➣ see *CARS

*AZTECS

The Aztecs were an Indian people based in Central America. Their empire was conquered by the Spanish in the early 16th century.

▲
This turquoise serpent once decorated an Aztec high priest's clothing. It was probably one of many treasures given to Cortés by Montezuma.

The Aztec Empire was based on a city called Tenochtitlán. The city was built on islands in a lake in the valley where Mexico City now stands. The city was founded by a people called the Mexica in 1325. In 1430 the battling local tribes made an alliance that formed the basis of the Aztec Empire. It stretched from Mexico as far as what is now Guatemala.

Aztec cities were ruled by kings who tried to gain control over other cities. Any city controlled by a neighboring king had to pay taxes in the form of gold, food, and other goods. The Aztecs tried to please their many gods by making human sacrifices. The victims were taken to temples on top of huge stepped pyramids, where a priest cut their chests open and tore their hearts out.

Food and trade
The Aztecs grew corn, beans, squash, and other crops in gardens on islands in the lake. They built the islands by piling up rich soil from the lake bottom. Merchants from the lowlands brought other food to the city's markets, including cacao beans, which are the source of chocolate.

Fall of the empire
Hernán Cortés, a Spanish conquistador, came to Tenochtitlán in 1519. The emperor, Montezuma II, welcomed Cortés. He thought the Spaniard was the returning priest-king Quetzalcóatl. But Cortés killed Montezuma and joined forces with other Aztec cities to destroy Tenochtitlán in 1521, ending Aztec rule. Today more than a million Nahua people, descended from the Aztecs, live in central Mexico.

MEXICO
Tenochtitlán
Gulf of Mexico
Bay of Campeche
Yucatán Peninsula
● ● Teotihuacán
● Mexico City
BELIZE
PACIFIC OCEAN
GUATEMALA

▲
This map shows the extent of the Aztec Empire around 1500.

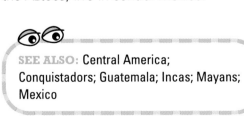

SEE ALSO: Central America; Conquistadors; Guatemala; Incas; Mayans; Mexico

BACH, JOHANN SEBASTIAN (1685–1750)

Johann Sebastian Bach was the greatest member of a family of more than 50 musicians who lived in central Germany between 1500 and the 1800s.

Bach was born in 1685 in Eisenach. He became an orphan at age 10 and went to live with his older brother, a church organist. Bach went to school in Lüneburg, where he sang in the choir and studied with the organist George Böhm. In 1703 Bach became church organist at Arnstadt. He began to write music. He married his cousin in 1707 and moved to Weimar, where he spent 10 years working for the duke of Weimar.

Bach then entered the service of Prince Leopold of Anhalt in Cöthen. In the next six years he composed many of his best-known instrumental works, including the Brandenburg concertos. His wife died in 1720, and he married again. He had 20 children; several of his sons became well-known composers. In 1723 Bach became director of music at St. Thomas's Church and School in Leipzig. He kept this job until his death in 1750.

Bach's work was published only after his death.

SEE ALSO:
Music

BALBOA, VASCO NÚÑEZ DE (1475–1519)

The explorer Vasco Núñez de Balboa was the first European to see the Pacific Ocean from America.

Balboa was born in Spain in 1475. In about 1500, he settled on the island of Hispaniola (now Haiti and the Dominican Republic). He fell into debt and escaped on a ship to San Sebastián in Colombia. When the ship arrived, the town was in ruins. Balboa took charge and led the people to Panama, where they started a colony called Darien. Balboa became its governor. Local Indians told Balboa that a great sea lay to the south and he decided to find it. He set out with Spanish troops and Indians across the mountains of Panama. On September 25, 1513, Balboa climbed the final peak alone and saw the Pacific Ocean. He named it the South Sea. Balboa was executed for treason by the new governor of Darien.

SEE ALSO: Central America; Conquistadors; Exploration and Explorers; Pacific Ocean; Panama

Balboa carried his raised sword into the Pacific Ocean to claim it for the King of Spain.

BALKANS see GREECE AND THE BALKANS

✳ BALLOONS AND AIRSHIPS

Balloons are aircraft made of a large bag filled with hot air or gas, with a basket for passengers. Airships are large balloons with engines.

Ballooning is a popular sport. It is best in open country, far from tall buildings, traffic, and high-tension wires. Balloonists travel where the wind takes them.

One of the best-known airships in the United States is the Goodyear blimp, seen here over Three Rivers Stadium in Pittsburgh, Pennsylvania.

History of balloons

The first big balloons were built in 1783 by the French brothers Joseph and Jacques Montgolfier. On November 21 two more Frenchmen sailed over Paris in a balloon—the first humans ever to "fly." In 1785 Jean Pierre Blanchard, a Frenchman, and John Jeffries, an American, crossed the English Channel in a gas balloon. Balloons were used in wars, including the Civil War (1861–65), to spy on enemy troops or to carry messages. In the 20th-century world wars, unmanned balloons were launched to get in the way of enemy bombers.

Modern balloons can go very high and stay up for a long time. They are used to explore the upper atmosphere and to look into space through on-board telescopes. Ballooning is also a popular sport. There are long-distance races, accuracy tests, and chases. In 1999 Bertrand Piccard and Brian Jones made the first nonstop balloon flight around the world. It took them just 19 days.

A modern balloon is an enormous bag made of nylon or plastic. The bag is filled with hot air or gas that is lighter than the air outside. This causes the balloon to rise. The pilot and passengers ride below in a basket, or gondola. They must go where the wind takes them.

An airship is a cigar-shaped, gas-filled balloon. They often have a stiff "skeleton" (metal framework) to hold its shape. This type is called a rigid airship. It floats like a balloon but is powered by engines with propellers that make it possible to steer in any direction.

History of airships

In 1852 Henri Giffard flew the first powered airship over Paris, steering it with a steam-powered propeller. In 1900 the first rigid airship was flown by a German company belonging to Ferdinand von Zeppelin. Inside these Zeppelins, as rigid airships are often called, was a metal framework that held hydrogen-filled bags. Zeppelins had gasoline engines to power their propellers. More than 100 of these rigid airships were built, but they were not the ideal aircraft. The future of aviation was with airplanes.

DID YOU **KNOW?**

Airships first proved useful during World War I (1914–18). Britain and Germany both used airships for gathering information behind enemy lines and on bombing raids. After the war, airships began carrying commercial passengers. Transatlantic flight was possible for the first time. Between 1928 and 1937 the *Graf Zeppelin* airship completed 144 flights across the North Atlantic.

The *Hindenburg* was the largest Zeppelin ever built. It was fitted with luxurious furniture and a kitchen equipped to prepare grand meals for up to 50 passengers. It made its first flight in April 1936. During the course of the year it made ten transatlantic crossings between Germany and the United States.

However, the *Hindenburg* was filled with huge amounts of hydrogen, a highly flammable gas. One evening in early May 1937, at the end of its first flight of the year to America, the airship was docking in Lakehurst, New Jersey, when it suddenly burst into flames. Within 30 seconds the *Hindenburg* lay in a smoking ruin on the ground. It was carrying 97 people; 35 died. Despite months of investigation no final conclusion was reached as to what had caused the explosion, but the disaster meant the end of the airship industry.

SEE ALSO:
Aircraft;
Atmosphere;
Warfare

✳**BALTIC STATES** ✳**RUSSIA AND THE BALTIC STATES**

✳ BANKING

Banks are trustworthy institutions that look after money and valuables and lend or change money. Their clients range from individuals to giant corporations and governments.

If you have money that you do not want to spend, you may deposit it at a bank. Your deposit will be recorded in a checking or savings account. The account is an agreement between you and the bank. It has a unique code that ensures your deposits are credited to you alone. If you need money, you may ask a bank to make a loan (lend you money).

When you deposit savings, you earn interest. This is a fee paid to you for the use of your money. Interest is calculated as a percentage of the amount you deposit. Money deposited in a bank as savings is loaned to borrowers at a higher interest rate than is paid to savers. The interest the bank receives is used to pay interest to depositors and to pay for the bank's operating costs.

History
The practice of lending or looking after money dates back thousands of years. The earliest bankers had strongboxes

▲
A money changer lending money to a nobleman in the 15th century.

in which money could be left for safekeeping. People also borrowed money in exchange for a fee.

Modern banking began in Italy during the late 1500s. In England during the 1600s, the first bankers were jewelry makers who looked after people's valuables in safe vaults. They issued paper receipts, or notes, in exchange. Eventually people began to use the paper notes as money.

▲

The First National Bank in Cumberland, Maryland, in about 1910.

The American banking system started in 1781, when the first state banks were established. The system quickly grew out of control and several banks failed. After 1863 the national banking system was modernized, and in 1913 Congress set up the Federal Reserve System to control the nation's money supply.

Types of banks

Most American banks are commercial banks, chartered (given a license to operate) by national or state government. They offer loans, take deposits, and manage checking accounts. Other banks specialize in, for example, investments (lending money to business enterprises for a share in the profits) or long-term loans for home-buyers.

The World Bank was set up to help finance reconstruction work after World War II (1939–45). Since that time it has assisted underdeveloped countries by offering them long-term loans.

👀 SEE ALSO: Economics; Money; Stock Markets; World War II

✳ BASEBALL

Baseball has been called America's national pastime. Today about 2,500,000 players in some 30 countries play in baseball leagues.

New York Yankees outfielder and slugger Joe DiMaggio follows through after a swing during a mid-1940s game.

▼

Baseball was first played about 150 years ago. The rules as they are played today have changed very little over the last century. The game is played on a field marked out with a diamond consisting of the home plate and three other bases, with a position marked for the pitcher (who throws the ball) in the center. There are two lines, running from home base through first and third bases, that define where the batter can hit the ball. The area between the lines is called fair territory; the area outside them is foul territory.

There are two teams of nine players that take turns batting or fielding. The batting team is called the offensive team; the fielding team is the defensive team.

Members of the offensive team take turns batting the ball out into the field and trying to score a run by running around the bases and back to home plate. The defensive team's fielders try to catch the ball (to get the batter out) and then, if there is another runner still heading for a base, throw it to that

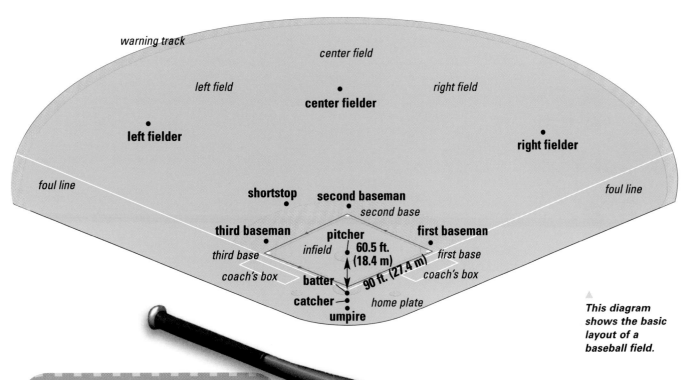

warning track

center field

left field

right field

center fielder

left fielder

right fielder

foul line

shortstop

second baseman

second base

foul line

third baseman

pitcher

first baseman

infield

60.5 ft.
(18.4 m)

third base

first base

90 ft. (27.4 m)

coach's box

batter

coach's box

catcher

home plate

umpire

This diagram shows the basic layout of a baseball field.

DID YOU KNOW?

An official baseball has a cork center surrounded by layers of rubber and tightly wound yarn. The outer cover, made of bleached white cowhide, is stitched on with thick red thread. The ball weighs between 5 and 5¼ oz. (142–49 g) and is 9 to 9¼ in. (23–24 cm) in circumference. Until recently all bats had to be made of wood (usually ash but sometimes hackberry or hickory). Today aluminum bats are permitted at every level of competition except the minor and major pro leagues, where wood is still required. A bat must be no more than 2¾ in. (7 cm) in diameter at the thickest part and no more than 42 in. (107 cm) long.

baseman. The fielders can also get the runners out by tagging them with the ball between bases. Runners can stop at any base if it is not safe to run on.

Three strikes and you're out

When the pitcher thows the ball toward the batter, the ball must pass over home plate within an area called the strike zone. The top of the strike zone is a point midway between the top of the batter's shoulders and the top of the pants. The bottom of the strike zone is level with the top of the knees. If the pitch goes through the strike zone, and the batter does not swing, a strike is called on the batter. A strike is also called if the batter swings at the ball and misses, or if the batter hits the ball into foul territory. The batter is out when three strikes have been made.

The visiting team bats first. The teams change sides when three batters are out. When three home players are out, the first inning is over. A normal game has nine full innings, but the game ends and the home team wins if it is ahead after the first half of the ninth inning (or takes the lead in the second half of the ninth inning).

Teams and leagues

Baseball is played at many different levels. Teams are grouped together in leagues, including professional major and minor, and college and school leagues. Little League Baseball is a nonprofit organization that runs baseball and softball leagues for people between ages 8 and 18, with teams of up to 15 players.

There are 30 teams in major league baseball: 28 based in U.S. cities and two in Canadian cities. The teams are divided into two leagues: 14 in the American League and 16 in the National League. Each league has an Eastern, a Central, and a Western Division. The major league season lasts from April until October. Every team plays a total of 162 games during the regular season. The teams that have won the most games in a season play in playoff games to determine which teams will compete in the World Series.

Baseball has traditionally been played by men, but more women are taking up the game, especially in the United States and Japan.

SEE ALSO: Sports

✳ BASKETBALL

Basketball is one of the most popular indoor sports in the world. The game was invented in 1891 by Dr. James A. Naismith. Today it is played and watched in more than 15 countries.

Basketball is a fast, exciting game that demands skilled ball play and good teamwork. It originated when Dr. Naismith, a physical education teacher in Springfield, Massachusetts, needed to keep his students occupied during the winter months. He attached a basket to the balcony at each end of the gym and established some basic rules. Since then the rules have developed, and official dimensions have been established, although court sizes may differ according to the age of the players and the size of the gym in which the game is played. Basketball can also be played on outdoor courts.

The object of the game is to get the ball into the appropriate basket (a hoop at each end of the court). Each team defends the basket at its own end of the court (the backcourt) and tries to shoot the ball into the basket at

The most important skill in basketball is shooting for the basket. A player can choose any of several different kinds of shot, but all require good balance, concentration, and lots of practice.

teammate. Players may not hold, push, slap, or trip an opponent. Such violations are called personal fouls, for which free throws are given from the free-throw line. If a player commits five personal fouls (six in professional competitions), he or she is disqualified from the game and replaced by a substitute.

If the ball goes off the court, or out-of-bounds, the team that was not the last to touch it throws the ball into play again. There are time limits set on how long a player can hold the ball, how long an offensive player can stay inside the free-throw lane, and how long a team can be in possession of the ball.

A field goal is a basket made from the court during normal play and scores two points. Three points are counted for a field goal shot from beyond the three-point line.

the other end (the frontcourt). The team in possession of the ball, and trying to score, is said to be on offense. The team without the ball, and trying to prevent the other team from scoring, is said to be on defense. Players can advance the ball up and down the court only by passing (throwing) it or dribbling (bouncing) it.

Players and play

There are five players on each team: a center, two forwards, and two guards. Positions are not fixed, but the center is usually the tallest player and takes a position close to the opponents' basket; the forwards are stationed to the sides of the center, along the end lines, or farther out on the wings; and the guards (usually smaller and quicker than the center and forwards) play a defensive role. Teams also have several substitute players.

The game begins with a "jump ball" at the center of the court. The referee tosses the ball in the air between two opposing players (usually the centers). Each one jumps up and tries to tap the ball to a

Michael Jordan, formerly of the Chicago Bulls, goes for the hoop.

A goal from a free throw counts one point. The team that scores most points wins the game.

High school basketball games are played in four 8-minute quarters. Younger teams play four 6-minute quarters. College games are divided into four 10-minute quarters, professional games into four 12-minute quarters. In the second half of the game, the teams "trade" ends, and each shoots for the basket it defended in the first half. Teams can call a time-out (a short halt) at any time, when substitutes may come on to give the other players a rest.

Diagram of a basketball court. The dimensions may vary slightly.

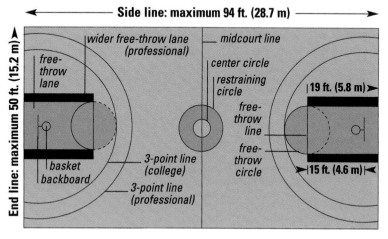

Conferences

The National Basketball Association (NBA) now has 29 teams (28 in U.S. cities and one in Canada) divided into the Eastern and Western Conferences. Each team normally plays 82 games in a season. At the end of the regular season, the top 16 teams compete in a series of playoffs to determine the NBA champion.

SEE ALSO: Sports

✳ BATS

Bats are the only mammals that fly through the air with wings. They are found in almost every part of the world except the polar regions.

AMAZING FACTS!

The smallest species of bat (and of mammal) is Kitti's hog-nosed bat. It weighs $1/10$ oz. (1.5 g) and has a 6-in. (15-cm) wingspan.
The largest species of bat is the flying fox, which weighs 3 lb. (1.5 kg) and has a 6-ft. (2-m) wingspan.
Vampire bats (left) from South and Central America feed on the blood of cattle and other mammals.

Most bats live in large groups called colonies. Many eat insects, but others eat fruit or nectar, and a few eat fish or meat, while vampire bats feed on blood. Nearly all bats are nocturnal (active at night).

Finding their way

A bat's wing is not like a bird's wing. A bird's wing is formed chiefly of feathers, but a bat's wing is a double layer of skin stretched over the thin bones of its "arm" and "fingers," and linked to its legs. Because they fly at night, bats have to use a kind of radar to find their way around. Each bat sends out ultrasonic sounds (sounds that are too high for people to hear). When the sound waves hit an

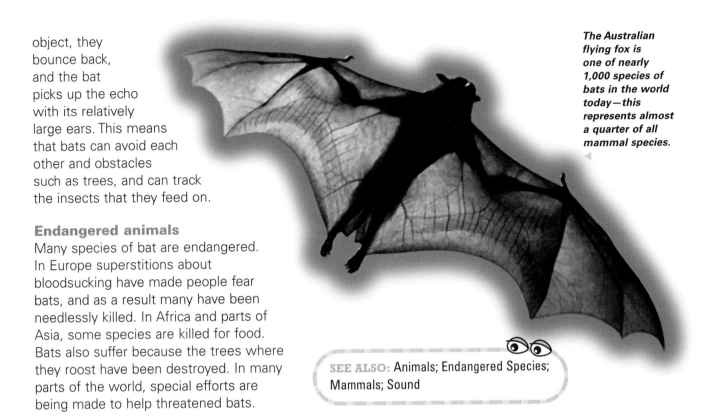

object, they
bounce back,
and the bat
picks up the echo
with its relatively
large ears. This means
that bats can avoid each
other and obstacles
such as trees, and can track
the insects that they feed on.

The Australian flying fox is one of nearly 1,000 species of bats in the world today—this represents almost a quarter of all mammal species.

Endangered animals
Many species of bat are endangered.
In Europe superstitions about
bloodsucking have made people fear
bats, and as a result many have been
needlessly killed. In Africa and parts of
Asia, some species are killed for food.
Bats also suffer because the trees where
they roost have been destroyed. In many
parts of the world, special efforts are
being made to help threatened bats.

SEE ALSO: Animals; Endangered Species;
Mammals; Sound

✱ BEARS
Most bears live in forests in mountain regions. They feed mainly on the meat of other mammals, but also eat plants and sometimes fish.

Bears, including the American black bear
and the grizzly bear (a type of brown
bear), have powerful legs and long, sharp
claws that they use for climbing trees.
Their thick fur protects them against cold
winters in their mountain homes.

Bears spend much of the day feeding:
They need lots of leaves, nuts, and berries
to fuel their huge bodies. Some bears are
good at fishing. They catch salmon as the
fish swim up streams toward their
breeding grounds. Bears also chase small
mammals, such as young deer.

Bears are aggressive animals. Male bears
fight each other over females. She-bears
are at their most dangerous when they

Although bears are rather awkward when they move on land, they are extremely agile when climbing trees.

are rearing their young: If they think their cubs are threatened, they may attack other bears and even people.

Other bears

Polar bears live in the northern Arctic around the North Pole. They have almost white fur that camouflages them against the ice and snow. They feed mainly on seals and young walrus, which they catch either by stalking at the ocean's edge or by waiting beside ice holes. They also eat fish and, in the summer, grass and herbs. Polar bears are strong swimmers.

Other bears include the Himalayan black bear, which has a mane of thick fur; the insect-eating sloth bear of India and Sri Lanka; and the small, shorthaired Malayan sun bear. Most bears live in the Northern Hemisphere. The one exception is the spectacled bear, found in South America.

SEE ALSO:
Animals;
Arctic;
Hibernation;
Mammals

AMAZING FACTS!

Kodiak bears are the world's largest carnivores (meat-eaters). They live on Kodiak Island, AK, and on the neighboring mainland. Males are up to 9 ft. (2.8 m) long and weigh up to 1,700 lb. (780 kg).

Bears generally live alone, except during the breeding season.

In winter bears fall into a deep sleep that is like hibernation, but their body temperature does not drop, and they still have their normal bodily functions.

Polar bears have thick fur on the soles of their feet to help them grip ice.

✳ BEETHOVEN, LUDWIG VAN (1770–1827)

Beethoven was one of the greatest composers of classical music. His achievement is even more amazing because he was deaf for much of his life.

Ludwig van Beethoven was born in 1770 in Bonn, Germany. His father was an alcoholic and wanted his son to earn money by performing. He often dragged young Ludwig out of bed to practice the piano. By the age of 13, Ludwig was already working as an organist. After his mother died, when he was 18, Beethoven had to take charge of the family. He played for many princes in and around Vienna, Austria.

Then, about 1799, Beethoven discovered that he was going deaf. After this he developed a new musical style that reflected his violent emotions. At about this time Beethoven composed the Fifth

Ludwig van Beethoven in his late thirties.
▼

Symphony, one of the most popular and influential of all his works. By 1820 he was so deaf that he could communicate only in writing. But this was his most creative period, during which he wrote his greatest works: the last five piano sonatas, the Mass in D (*Missa solemnis*), the Ninth Symphony, and the last five string quartets.

In 1826 his nephew Karl tried to commit suicide. This badly affected Beethoven's health. He died on March 26, 1827.

SEE ALSO: Music

✳BELGIUM ⟶see⟶ ✳ NETHERLANDS, BELGIUM, AND LUXEMBOURG

✳ BELL, ALEXANDER GRAHAM (1847–1922)

Alexander Graham Bell is credited with being the inventor of the telephone. From an early age, he was interested in speech and hearing.

Bell was born in Edinburgh, Scotland. He inherited an interest in speech and sound from his grandfather and father. By the age of 16, Bell was teaching music and speech.

While studying how the human voice works, Bell came upon the work of Hermann von Helmholtz, a German scientist who had used electric vibrations to make vowel sounds. Bell began to study electricity so that he could repeat Helmholtz's experiments.

Bell went to Boston, Massachusetts, and continued his experiments. He wondered if an electric current could be made to vary, just as the air varies with sound waves. Then any sound, including human speech, could be carried by electricity. This was the idea behind the telephone.

On March 10, 1876, Bell transmitted the first spoken telephone message by wire from one electrical instrument to another worked by his assistant in the next room. By the end of 1877, he had formed the Bell Telephone Company.

Bell's famous first telephone message—"Mr. Watson, come here. I want you"—was spoken to his assistant when Bell spilled some acid.

SEE ALSO:
Electricity;
Sound;
Telephones;
Tongue and
Speech

✳ BIBLE

The Bible is a collection of books that forms the basis of the beliefs and laws of two religions, Judaism and Christianity.

The Christian Bible is divided into two parts: the Old Testament (39 books, originally in Hebrew, about events before the birth of Jesus Christ) and the New Testament (27 books, originally in Greek, about Jesus). Jews use the Hebrew Bible, which is almost the same as the Old Testament. The Torah (the first five books) sets out the laws of Judaism.

The books of the Bible are the work of many different writers. They include religious laws, stories to illustrate how people should lead their lives, and songs of praise called psalms. There are also history books. Some stories, such as those of Adam and Eve, Noah and the flood, and Abraham, the founder of Judaism, are also found in the Koran, the sacred writings of Islam. The books of the Hebrew Bible were handed down by word of mouth for hundreds of years, but the books of the New Testament were written soon after the events they describe.

Pope John Paul II raises a copy of the Bible during Mass in Israel.

Translations

The Christian Bible was soon translated into Latin, which was the most widely known language at the time. In the 1500s, Christians in western Europe were divided into Roman Catholics and Protestants by a dispute called the Reformation. A German translation of the Bible by Martin Luther (a Protestant) set the pattern for many later versions in other languages. The best-known English Bible is the King James Version, which was published in 1611 and is still used today. The first American English version of the

This manuscript of the Bible dates from the 1200s.

Bible appeared in 1901. The Bible has also been translated into modern languages.

SEE ALSO: Buddhism; Christianity; Islam; Judaism; Koran; Reformation; Religions; Torah

* BICYCLES AND MOTORCYCLES

All bicycles and motorcycles have two wheels. Bicycles are propelled by their riders; motorcycles have engines.

In 1818 a German inventor, Karl von Drais, was the first person to build a bicycle. It was made of wood and named a running machine (*Laufmaschine*) because the rider had to stride along to make the cycle move. It was followed in the 1870s by the Ordinary, or penny-farthing (named for the largest and smallest British coins of the time). This cycle had a tiny rear wheel and a huge front wheel, with pedals attached to the hub. Finally, in 1885 John Kemp Starley came up with the Rover Safety, a bicycle with a chain that linked the pedals to the rear wheel. Starley's design has been modified and improved to produce the bicycles we know today.

There are modern bicycles for many different purposes: touring bikes, mountain or trail bikes, and racing bikes. The most advanced racing bikes have lightweight, carbon-fiber frames and

A typical modern bicycle. The rider's gloves, helmet, and sunglasses are for protection.

wheel spokes that are enclosed to reduce drag from the air. Very narrow, high-pressure tires reduce friction as the cyclist races along; even the helmet and clothes the cyclist wears are designed to reduce wind resistance. The recumbent bike is a new idea: The rider lies back in a seat, with his or her feet on pedals in front that drive a chain attached to the rear wheels.

Motorcycles

The first motorcycle to appear in public had a gasoline engine attached to a wooden-framed bicycle. It was built in 1885 by the German Gottlieb Daimler. Today's motorcycles are often as powerful as cars. Usually riders control the throttle and the front-wheel brake through controls on the handlebars. A foot pedal controls the rear-wheel brake.

SEE ALSO: da Vinci, Leonardo

AMAZING FACTS!

In the 1490s artist and inventor Leonardo da Vinci drew a bicycle with a chain to drive the wheels. **Daimler's 1885 motorbike** (below) had outrigger wheels on either side that could be raised and lowered to stabilize the bike. **The yearly Tour de France** bicycle race lasts up to 25 days; riders cover about 2,500 miles (4,000 km).

✳ BIG BANG THEORY

The Big Bang is a theory that explains how the universe began. The theory is backed up by scientific data about light and radiation traveling through the universe.

For much of human history, scientists believed that either Earth or the sun was at the center of the universe. By the 1800s, telescopes allowed astronomers to observe faint patches of light in the sky.

Hubble's discovery

In the late 1920s, the American astronomer Edwin Hubble suggested that these lights were other galaxies. He used an instrument called a spectroscope and discovered that some of the galaxies were moving away from Earth at great speeds. The galaxies create patterns of light in the spectroscope: If the patterns are near the red end of the spectrum, they are moving away from Earth. This is known as Red Shift.

Astronomers realized not only that the universe is much larger than previously

View from the Hubble Space Telescope.

Hubble's views of the universe reveal galaxies back to the beginning of time.

thought, but also that it is expanding. If we look back through time, at one stage the galaxies must have all been in the same place. This leads to the question, how did the universe begin?

By the 1960s, many scientists thought that the universe may have begun with a tremendous explosion, which they called the Big Bang. They searched for evidence that such an explosion had taken place.

According to the Big Bang theory, at the beginning of time (10–15 billion years ago) the early universe would have been very dense, small, and hot—so hot, in fact, that matter could not have existed, although radiation (energy) could. The universe would have appeared as a bright "fog" of radiation reaching in all directions. As the universe expanded, it cooled until the

radiation fog began to clear, and the energy turned into matter: First hydrogen atoms formed, and then helium. According to the theory, radiation from the Big Bang should be detectable throughout the universe today, not as visible light but as microwave radiation. In 1965 two American scientists, Arno Penzias and Robert Wilson, discovered this type of radiation coming from all directions in the sky. Known as cosmic background radiation, it may be the remnant of the Big Bang and the farthest back into time astronomers have observed.

SEE ALSO: Astronomy; Galaxies; Matter; Telescopes; Universe

* BILL OF RIGHTS
The Bill of Rights added 10 amendments to the Constitution to set out the basic rights of citizens. Its aim is to keep the government from abusing power.

The right to trial by jury is one of the many basic human freedoms protected by the Bill of Rights.

Several states approved the Constitution on the understanding that the priority of the new government would be to adopt a bill of rights that guaranteed individuals certain basic privileges. The Bill of Rights officially became part of the Constitution on December 15, 1791.

The bill's 10 amendments
The First Amendment guarantees freedoms of religion, speech, and the press, as well as the right to assemble and to petition the government. The Fourth, Fifth, Sixth, and Eighth amendments also deal with the rights of individuals. They are designed to protect people against government's abuse of power, especially in criminal proceedings. The Fourth Amendment protects

individuals from unreasonable searches and seizures (either of themselves or of their property) by law-enforcement officials. The Fifth Amendment keeps someone from being tried twice for the same crime. It states that people cannot be forced to give evidence against themselves, and those accused of a crime must be properly notified of the charges and given a fair hearing. The Sixth Amendment secures the right of an accused person to have a lawyer and to a public trial by jury. The Eighth Amendment bans "cruel and unusual punishments" of convicted criminals.

Three other amendments address specific concerns. The Second Amendment notes the need for a "well regulated militia" (a body of citizen soldiers who serve during times of emergency or war) and declares that the people's right "to keep and bear arms shall not be infringed." The Third

During the Revolution citizens called minutemen agreed to go on military duty "at a minute's warning."

Amendment prevents the government from making citizens shelter soldiers in their homes. The Seventh Amendment ensures trial by jury in civil suits.

The Ninth Amendment states that the people have rights that are not specified in the Constitution or the Bill of Rights. The 10th Amendment declares that the states or people retain the powers not delegated to the United States by the Constitution.

SEE ALSO: American Revolution; Congress; Constitution, United States; Supreme Court; United States Government

* BIOLOGY

Biology is the scientific study of organisms, or living things—the way they work, their structure, and their interrelationships.

It is easy to say that biology is the scientific study of living things, but how do we know what is living and what is not? To answer this question, biologists have figured out a set of characteristics that are shared by all organisms.

All living things are made of cells. Most cells are so small that they can be seen only under a microscope. Some organisms, such as bacteria, consist of just one cell. Others might have billions.

All organisms need energy to live. Animals get energy from food. Green plants and some small organisms get energy from the sun through photosynthesis.

Organisms grow as they get older. They become larger and change shape. Organisms create new individuals of the same type to replace those that die. This is called reproduction.

Evolution

Organisms can sense and respond to changes in their world. In order to survive, an organism must adapt to such changes. As winter sets in, for example, the fur of an arctic fox turns white and thick to keep it warm and make it less visible against the snow. The organisms that adapt best to changes in the environment are most likely to survive and reproduce.

FAMOUS BIOLOGISTS

The following are among the most influential biologists in history. The "see also" box indicates entries on other important ones.

Hippocrates (about 460–377 B.C.) Greek physician who introduced scientific methods to medicine.

Harvey, William (top left) (1578–1657) English physician who described the circulation of blood in the body.

Van Leeuwenhoek, Antonie (left) (1632–1723) Dutch naturalist who made many discoveries with a microscope.

Carolus Linnaeus (von Linné, Carl) (1707–78) Swedish botanist who classified the living world, giving each plant and animal a scientific name.

Schleiden, Matthias (Jakob) (1804–81), and **Schwann, Theodor (Ambrose Hubert)** (1810–82) German scientists who developed cell theory.

Mendel, Gregor (Johann) (1822–84) Austrian monk and botanist who developed the theory of heredity and genetics.

Biologists at work

Biology is divided into many fields. People who study plants are called botanists. Those who study animals are zoologists. Some zoologists concentrate on specific types of animals. Ornithologists study birds, and marine biologists study animals that live in the oceans and seas. Some biologists study particular parts of organisms. Biochemists study chemical reactions in organisms; geneticists study genes, which determine the qualities organisms inherit from their parents. Ecologists study how living organisms relate to each other in their environment.

SEE ALSO: Animals; Biomes; Botany; Carson, Rachel; Cells; Darwin, Charles; Ecology; Evolution; Genetics; Human Body; Photosynthesis; Plants; Scientific Instruments; Scientists; Zoology

✳ BIOMES

Biome is the scientific term for a community of specific types of plants and animals that covers a large area of the earth's surface.

A type of biome is usually the result of the type of climate in a region. The major land biomes are grasslands (called prairies in North America, savannas in Africa, steppes in Asia, pampas in South America), deserts, chaparrals, deciduous forests, coniferous forests, tundra, and tropical rain forests. Aquatic biomes exist in rivers, lakes, and oceans.

Most kinds of biomes can be found on every continent except Antarctica. Each place has unique plant and animal species, yet the plants and animals of a particular biome tend to be similar regardless of where they are. For example, cacti are common in the southwestern deserts of the United States. In African deserts, there are similar prickly plants called euphorbs. Both have adapted similarly to living in the hot, dry desert biome.

In many parts of the world, biomes have been altered by people. For example, in the grasslands of the Sahel, in western Africa, domestic animals have overgrazed the land so that the thin layer of topsoil has blown away. This process is called desertification. People in Central and South America and Southeast Asia have been destroying the tropical rain forests. This may affect the world's climate.

Grasslands

Grasslands are a biome in which the average annual rainfall is 10 to 40 in. (254 to 1,016 mm). Animals include large herds of grazing animals, such as zebras and gazelles, and predators, such as lions, leopards, and hyenas.

Deserts

A desert is a biome in which there is less than 10 in. (254 mm) of rain annually. The days are very hot, and the nights are cold. Succulents, plants that store water in their leaves or stems, grow there. Many animals stay underground during the day and come out at night.

Chaparrals

Chaparrals are dense growths of shrubs and trees. They are found on the coasts of the Mediterranean Sea, in southern California, central Chile, the southern tip of Africa, and southern Australia. Some

areas average as little as 10 in. (254 mm) of rain a year. Moist air from the oceans prevents conditions from being as severe as those in the desert. The main plants are tough evergreen shrubs with small, leathery leaves. Most of the animals that live there are adapted to a dry climate.

Deciduous forests

The forests of eastern North America, Central Europe, eastern China, and the southeast coast of Australia are made up of deciduous trees, or trees that grow and shed their leaves in a seasonal pattern. Deciduous forests tend to have rich soil. Rain falls all year, averaging about 40 in. (1,016 mm). Many plants and animals flourish, including ferns, fungi, and deer.

Coniferous forests

Temperate coniferous forest is found in moist, coastal environments, including the northwest Pacific coast of North America

Human activity is a major threat to biomes. Here a part of the Amazon rain forest in Brazil is burned down to create space for an enlarged cattle ranch.
▼

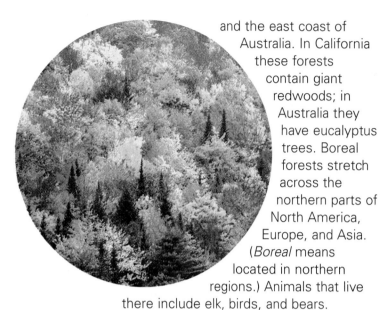

and the east coast of Australia. In California these forests contain giant redwoods; in Australia they have eucalyptus trees. Boreal forests stretch across the northern parts of North America, Europe, and Asia. (*Boreal* means located in northern regions.) Animals that live there include elk, birds, and bears.

The beautiful fall colors of a deciduous forest in Maine.

Tundra

North of the boreal forest lies the treeless tundra. Beneath it is a layer of frozen ground called permafrost, which may be over 1,000 ft. (305 m) thick. The soil on top of the permafrost thaws for only eight weeks in summer, when the tundra teems with life. After summer, many mammals go to the forests, and the birds fly south.

Tropical rain forests

In these biomes around the equator, annual rainfall averages between 80 and 200 in. (2,000–5,000 mm), and falls year-round. Temperatures hover just below 80°F (27°C) day and night. This biome has the greatest variety of life, ranging from parrots to monkeys and jaguars.

SEE ALSO: Climate; Conservation; Deserts; Ecology; Forests; Grasslands; Oceans and Seas; Rain Forests; Wetlands

* BIRDS

Birds are found in every area of the world—there are more than 9,000 species. Although most birds can fly, a few have evolved into flightless creatures.

*The fossilized remains of an **Archaeopteryx**, thought to be the earliest species of bird.*

Most scientists now believe that birds evolved from small two-legged dinosaurs called theropods.The earliest known bird is *Archaeopteryx*, which lived about 150 million years ago. It was about the size of a bluebird and had feathers and wings. It could probably fly, but not very well.

Feathers and flight

A bird's feathers perform several different jobs: They smooth and streamline its body, enabling it to move easily through the air or water; they also protect the bird's skin and help it maintain its body temperature even in temperatures below zero.

There are three basic types of flight: flapping, gliding, and soaring. Most birds use flapping flight—that is, after they take off, they continue to fly by moving their wings up and down. When gliding, birds keep their wings extended and coast downward. During soaring flight, birds use the energy of rising columns of warm air, called thermals, to fly without having to flap their wings.

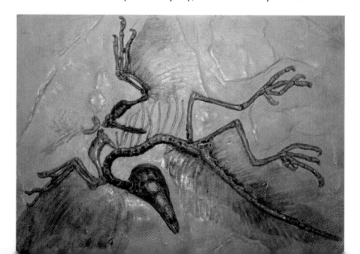

Like all birds of prey, the red-tailed hawk has a powerful hooked bill and sharp talons for seizing its victims and tearing them to pieces.

AMAZING FACTS!

The Cuban bee hummingbird is the smallest living bird. It weighs about 1/20 oz. (1.6 g) and is about 2 in. (5 cm) long. It moves its wings 70 times a second when flying or hovering in front of flowers.

The ostrich lays a gigantic egg that can weigh up to 4 lb. (1 kg). The tiny Cuban bee hummingbird's egg is only 1/4 in. (5 mm) long and weighs 1/100 oz. (0.25 g). More than 5,000 hummingbird eggs would fit inside an ostrich egg.

The nest built by the male dusky scrub fowl of Australia is a gigantic mound of rotting leaves, sticks, and grass that can sometimes measure 36 ft. (11 m) across and over 16 ft. (5 m) high.

The feather cloak of the Hawaiian King Kamehameha I took at least a hundred years to make and used about 450,000 feathers from more than 80,000 birds.

Skeleton and muscles

The body systems of birds are all adapted to flight. Over time the skeleton of the bird has developed into an airy and lightweight yet strong frame. Birds have a large breastbone, or sternum, that protects their internal organs and supports the muscles that power flight. The largest muscles are the pectoral (breast) muscles. They join the sternum to the long bone of the wing. When they contract during flight, the bird's wings are pulled down. Other, smaller muscles contract during flight to pull the wings up.

Feeding

Birds feed on a wide variety of food, from fruit and seeds to dead animals. Their beaks are adapted to suit their diet. For example, an eagle has a powerful hooked bill to tear its prey to bits. Because birds have no teeth, their digestive system must grind up food to obtain its energy.

Nearly all birds have a stomach made up of two parts. The first part secretes strong digestive juices. The second part, called the gizzard, has muscular walls that grind food. Birds often swallow small stones and grit to aid the grinding.

Birds have a higher body temperature, a faster heart rate, and a greater need for oxygen than mammals, so they have to eat a lot of food to fuel their bodies. When flying, birds require 10 to 20 times more oxygen than they need when they are at rest. To get the extra oxygen, birds increase their rate of breathing. ➡

The great horned owl has large eyes that enable it to see well in the dark and detect movement at great distances. ▼

Senses

In general, birds have the best vision of all animals. Their hearing is also well developed, especially in night birds such as owls. Only a few birds have a good sense of smell. The kiwi is nearly blind and relies on smell to find its food.

Communicating

Ducks are birds that live on and near water.
▼

Bird songs sound beautiful, but birds do not sing to make music. They sing to attract mates and to tell other birds to stay off their territory (an area they consider theirs). Birds usually have between 5 and 14 songs, but some species have more.

Reproduction

All birds lay eggs and care for them in some way. Some lay eggs on bare cliff ledges; others build nests to hold the eggs. Many birds die during their first year of life. The greatest threats are bad weather and predators.

The migration cycle

Billions of birds travel to warmer southern countries in the winter, when food supplies are scarce: These birds are called migrants. They return north to breed because there are fewer predators there.

SEE ALSO: Animals; Conservation; Dinosaurs; Endangered Species; Fossils; Migration

* BLIZZARDS

A blizzard is a very strong wind carrying snow. It can bury roads under snowdrifts, cut off whole towns from the outside world, and kill people from the cold.

The National Weather Service describes a blizzard as a storm lasting at least three hours, with winds stronger than 35 mph (56 kph), and so much snow in the air that it is possible to see for a distance of only a quarter-mile (400 m) or less. Some blizzards contain freshly falling snow. Others simply pick up fallen snow and whip it up in the air.

During a blizzard, the air temperature near ground level is usually about 20°F (–7°C). In a severe blizzard, it can sometimes drop below 10°F (–12°C).

What causes blizzards?

High winds can occur when a warm, low-pressure air mass meets a cold, high-pressure air mass. When one of the air masses contains a lot of moisture, a rainstorm or snowstorm can result. An especially violent storm may lead to a blizzard. Sometimes blizzards strike when a jet stream (high-altitude air current) carries cold air over a long distance and suddenly dips down into a warm air mass.

In North America, blizzards are often caused when warm, moist air from the oceans collides with icy blasts of air from Canada. The Great Plains region, from the Great Lakes south to Texas, usually suffers the worst blizzards, since there are few obstacles to slow the wind.

Some of the worst-ever North American blizzards struck in 1888. In January howling winds blew snow across the Dakota Territory, Montana, Minnesota, Nebraska, Kansas, and Texas. More than 230 people died. Blizzards struck again in mid-March, burying the East Coast in deep snowdrifts. In recent years there have been severe blizzards in February 1978, March 1993, and January 1996.

Why are blizzards dangerous?
Blizzards can affect all forms of transport, and "whiteout" conditions—when there is a drier, more powdery snow—seriously reduce visibility. Roads become slippery or are blocked. Houses may suffer frozen water pipes and loss of electric power.

The cold can kill people caught out in the open. Its effect is made worse by the wind-chill factor: how cold people and animals actually feel. An air temperature of 0°F (–18°C) plus a wind of 15 mph (24 kph) makes your body feel as cold as –19°F (–28°C). This is deadly: Frostbite (frozen flesh, often hands, feet, nose, or ears) can set in within a half hour. Children and the elderly are especially at risk of hypothermia. This occurs when body temperature drops dangerously low. The person may lose consciousness and die.

SEE ALSO:
Climate;
Weather

The very young and the very old are most at risk in blizzards.

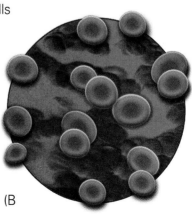

✳ BLOOD
Blood is like a river of life flowing through your body. It carries food to the cells, takes waste away from them, and helps defend you against disease.

Blood flows around the body through tubes called blood vessels. The vessels that carry blood away from the heart to the rest of the body are arteries. Veins carry blood back to the heart. More than half the blood in the human body is plasma, a liquid that can carry dissolved chemicals around the body. There are three types of solid carried in the plasma: red cells, white cells, and platelets.

There are more red blood cells in the body than any other kind of cell. They pick up oxygen from the air that is breathed into the lungs and carry it to the cells that need oxygen to work. White blood cells fight against microbes such as viruses and bacteria that cause disease. They create antibodies—proteins that can make the microbes harmless. The platelets form a substance to make blood clot. This stops you from bleeding to death if you are cut.

Blood groups
Everyone has similar red blood cells, but on the outside of the cells are molecules called antigens. If you have a transfusion of blood from someone with different antigens, your blood may make the cells in the new blood clump together and block your arteries and veins. There are four basic groups: group A (with A antigens), group B (B

Human red blood cells magnified 450 times under a microscope.

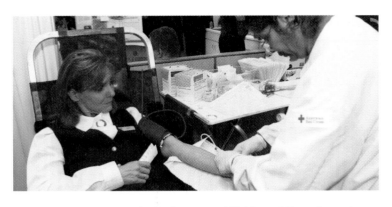

A woman gives blood to help others who have lost their own. Doctors must ensure that donors and recipients have matching blood.

antigens), group AB (A and B antigens), and group O (neither A nor B antigens). Another set of antigens divides people into two types, Rhesus positive (Rh+) and Rhesus negative (Rh–).

SEE ALSO: Cells; Heart and Circulatory System; Human Body

AMAZING FACTS!

An average adult makes 200,000,000,000 blood cells every day in the bone marrow (a soft area in the middle of the bones).

If you took all the red blood cells from an average person and stacked them on top of each other, they would reach 31,000 miles (50,000 km) into the sky.

Insects (below) and spiders do not have a heart to circulate blood. Instead, they have a liquid that works like blood, carrying oxygen and food around their bodies.

---

*BOATS see * SHIPS AND BOATS

---

* BOLÍVAR, SIMÓN (1783–1830)

For nearly 300 years, most of South America was under Spanish rule. Simón Bolívar freed Venezuela, Ecuador, Bolivia, and Colombia from Spain.

Simón Bolívar is still known to the people of South America as El Libertador — the liberator.

Bolívar was born into a noble family at Caracas, Venezuela, on July 24, 1783. When he was 16, he was sent to Spain and then spent seven years studying in Europe. Inspired by the revolutions in America and France, he vowed that he would free his country from Spanish rule. In 1811 he and a group of patriots seized Caracas and declared Venezuela's independence. But they were crushed by Spanish troops, and Bolívar fled. He spent years in exile, gathering supporters. Finally, in 1819 Bolívar's army defeated the Spanish army in Colombia. Two years later,

Bolívar liberated Venezuela and in 1822 freed Ecuador. Venezuela, Colombia, and Ecuador were united into the republic of Gran Colombia, with Bolívar as its president. Bolívar helped liberate Peru, and in 1825 Upper Peru was renamed Bolivia in his honor. Gran Colombia later fell apart, and Bolívar died on December 17, 1830.

SEE ALSO: Bolivia; Colombia; Ecuador; Peru; South America; Spain; Venezuela

✷ BOLIVIA

Bolivia lies in the heart of South America, between the towering Andes Mountains and the rain forests of the Amazon River Basin.

◄ *Aymará musicians playing reed pipes and drums to celebrate a traditional pre-Christian Bolivian farmer's festival.*

Land and climate

Bolivia is one of only two countries in South America that has no coastline. The other is Paraguay. Bolivia's chief city, La Paz, is the world's highest capital, at 12,000 ft. (3,600 m) above sea level.

The Andes separate Bolivia from the west coast of South America. The mountains are at their widest here and are divided into two ranges called cordilleras. The Western Cordillera forms the border with Chile. Between the Western and Eastern cordilleras is a high plateau called the Altiplano. It is where most of the population lives, particularly around Lake Titicaca, which is the highest navigable lake in the world at 12,500 ft. (3,810 m). Deep valleys in the Eastern Cordillera drain down to the Amazon Basin and Brazil, while in the southeast, plains extend into Paraguay and Argentina.

Because of Bolivia's altitude there are great differences between day and night temperatures. However, there is little difference in temperature between summer and winter. The dry season lasts from May to November. Between December and February, there are heavy rains on the Altiplano and tropical storms on the lowlands.

People

More than half of Bolivia's people are Aymará and Quechua Indians. The Aymará are descended from a civilization that first emerged around Lake Titicaca over 1,000 years ago. The Quechua are descended from the Inca civilization of 700 years ago. About 15 percent of the people are of Spanish descent. Spain tried to convert the Indians to Christianity, but they continue to hold traditional festivals.

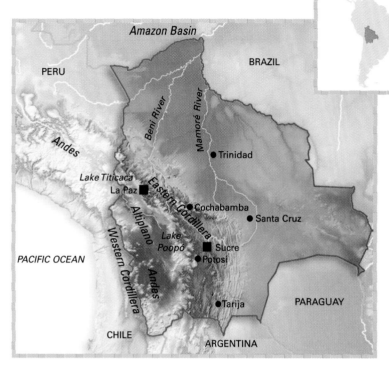

Important agricultural products include soybeans, coffee, cotton, sugarcane, corn, and rice.

History

The Aymará civilization was at its height between A.D. 600 and 900. In the 15th century, it was conquered by the Incas of Peru, who came to mine the mountains for silver and tin. The metals attracted Spanish invaders in the 1500s. Inspired by a leader named Simón Bolívar, the Indians fought Spanish rule and declared independence in 1825. Since then Bolivia has had an unsettled history, with many different governments.

SEE ALSO: Bolívar, Simón; Conquistadors; Incas; South America

Bolivia's national flag

Economy

Bolivia has a strong farming tradition. Most of the farms are on the Altiplano. Llamas and alpacas, long-necked animals related to camels, are native to the region. They are used to pull carts and carry loads. Their fur and meat are also valuable.

KEY FACTS

OFFICIAL NAME:
República de Bolivia

AREA:
424,165 sq. mi.
(1,098,587 sq. km)

POPULATION:
8,329,000

CAPITALS:
La Paz
(government); Sucre
(constitutional)

LARGEST CITY:
La Paz

MAJOR RELIGION:
Roman Catholicism

MAJOR LANGUAGES:
Spanish, Quechua, Aymará

CURRENCY:
Bolivian peso

Aymará Indians established a civilization on the shores of Lake Titicaca over 1,000 years ago. These dwellings, called adobe, are made from bricks or baked mud.

✳ BOONE, DANIEL (1734–1820)

Daniel Boone was one of America's greatest pioneers and frontier heroes. He blazed trails and led the first white settlers into Kentucky.

Daniel Boone was born on November 2, 1734, at Oley, a frontier settlement in Pennsylvania. At an early age, he learned how to avoid being caught by Native Americans while hunting in the woods.

In 1751 Boone moved to North Carolina. He fought for the British in the French and Indian War (1756–63), and then raised a family. In 1769 he crossed the Appalachian Mountains to explore Kentucky. In 1775 he cleared the Wilderness Road through the Cumberland Gap, a natural pass in the mountains. He built Boonesborough, a fort on the Kentucky River, and brought settlers to the region. In 1778 Boone lived for several months among the Shawnee

people. The Native Americans planned raids on the settlers, but Boone used his skills as a leader and a scout to prevent bloodshed.

Boone later held several public offices. He had no legal claim to the lands he had explored because he had not followed the correct legal procedures. In 1799 he moved westward to Missouri. He died on September 26, 1820.

SEE ALSO: French and Indian Wars; Native Americans

Boone leading settlers through the Cumberland Gap to Kentucky.

✳ BOTANY

Botany is the branch of biology that studies plants, including their classification, structure, physical composition, and ecology.

Plants are essential to all life on Earth. Only plants can capture the energy of the sun and use it—in a process called photosynthesis—to make food. Animals cannot do this and so depend on plants for food, as well as for the oxygen that plants create during photosynthesis. Botanists have identified about 300,000 different varieties of plant.

Branches of botany
There are many specialists within botany. Some botanists study plants in relation to the environment, investigating how soil and water affect their growth and development. Others study the history of

plants on Earth. This might involve investigating fossils and other evidence of species that became extinct thousands of years ago. This branch of botany is called paleobotany.

Some botanists concentrate on particular varieties of plant. The study of fungi is called mycology; the study of ferns is called pteridology. Bacteriology, the study of bacteria, is a branch of botany that is important in medicine, because bacteria cause many diseases. Other botanists study different kinds of crops or investigate extracting materials such as rubber or drugs from plants.

Widely known as Linnaeus, the Swedish botanist and naturalist Carl von Linné created the modern system of plant classification.

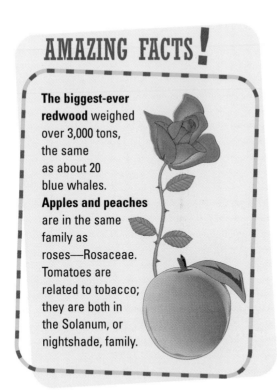

AMAZING FACTS !

The biggest-ever redwood weighed over 3,000 tons, the same as about 20 blue whales.
Apples and peaches are in the same family as roses—Rosaceae. Tomatoes are related to tobacco; they are both in the Solanum, or nightshade, family.

Plant classification

Every known variety of plant, from the smallest moss to the largest redwood tree, has a unique botanical name. This follows the system originally devised by the Swedish naturalist Linnaeus (1707–78) in his book *Species Plantarum*, which was published in 1753. Under Linnaeus's method, the white pine belongs to the genus, or group, *Pinus*, and its species, or kind, is *strobus*. So, wherever you are in the world, the scientific name for the white pine is always the same: *Pinus strobus*. This method of naming botanical species is called plant taxonomy.

SEE ALSO: Biology; Diseases; Ecology; Flowers; Fossils; Fungus; Photosynthesis; Plants; Trees

✳ BRAIN AND NERVOUS SYSTEM

The brain controls the nerves, the spinal cord, and the sense organs (such as eyes and ears): Together, these body parts are known as the nervous system.

The brain is divided into different parts. The cerebellum controls body movement. The biggest part of the brain, the cerebrum, controls thinking, learning, memory, and imagination. The brain stem connects these parts to the spinal cord and contains the medulla, which keeps the blood flowing and the lungs breathing.

An average adult brain weighs about 3.1 lb. (1.4 kg). It consists of two kinds of cell: neurons (nerve cells) and glia (glial cells). Neurons send information through the body; some neurons are the longest cells in the body. Glia do not send out information; their job is to clean, feed, protect, and support the neurons.

There are three main types of neuron: Sensory neurons respond to light, temperature, sound, smell, taste, and touch; motor neurons control muscles and movement; and interneurons relay information between the other two. Most nerves are invisible to the naked eye, but some can be up to 3 ft. (1 m) long.

Nervous system

The nervous system is divided into the central nervous system and the peripheral nervous system. The spinal cord and the brain form the central nervous system. The spinal cord consists of nerves that run through the neck and back. These nerves are protected by the spinal column. The brain and spinal cord process incoming messages and send out messages to the organs and body parts on the periphery, or outside, of the body. The messages are carried by the branching network of nerves that make up the peripheral nervous system. The process by which neurons carry the messages involves both chemistry and electricity.

AREAS OF THE BRAIN

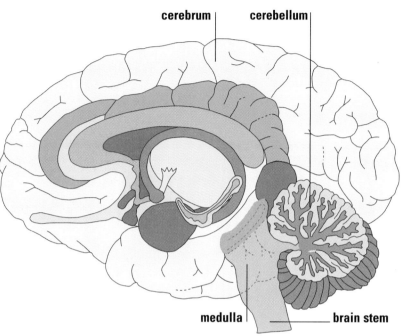

Diagram showing the main areas of the human brain. The largest part is the cerebrum.

This magnetic resonance image (MRI) shows clearly the link between the brain and the spine. The body shape has been altered by an artist.

The spinal cord responds to some messages without involving the brain. If you touch something hot, for example, your hand recoils automatically without thinking. This is called a reflex action.

There are two main types of peripheral nerves: Sensory nerves carry messages to the central nervous system; motor nerves carry messages from the central nervous system to all parts of the body.

The autonomous nervous system is part of the peripheral nervous system. It controls vital organs such as the heart, stomach, and lungs. These nerves operate automatically—or without you having to think about them.

Brain disorders
The brain is so important to the body that any damage to it can have effects on the rest of the organism. The brain can be

damaged by accident, such as a blow to the head, or by illnesses, such as epilepsy, which causes major electrical discharges within the brain. Some brain diseases are caused by neurons in certain parts of the brain breaking down.

Some people also suffer from mental illnesses, such as depression, which affect their moods and thought patterns. Mental illness is not fully understood, but it can often be controlled through drugs.

SEE ALSO:
Cells;
Human
Body

Other animals
In most larger animals, brains and nervous systems operate in a way similar to those of humans. Single-celled organisms do not have nervous systems, and other simple animals, such as jellyfish, have a collection of nerve cells—a nerve net—but no brain.

AMAZING FACTS!

The human brain accounts for just 2 percent of the body's weight, but uses up to 20 percent of the body's oxygen supply.
Scientists estimate that the human brain contains more than 100 billion neurons (nerve cells).

✳ BRASS 🔍see ✳ MUSICAL INSTRUMENTS

✳ BRAZIL
Brazil is the largest country in South America. It occupies almost half the continent's area and is home to more than half its population.

Typically colorful and riotous carnival celebrations in Rio de Janeiro mark the start of Lent.

Land and climate
Brazil has a mixture of hilly and low-lying areas. It is divided into five regions: the northeast, the east, the south, the central west, and the Amazon Basin. Each region contains several states.

The Amazon Basin is a vast area of rain forest, jungle, and swamp formed by the Amazon River and its tributaries. The world's largest tropical rain forest, the region is home to many rare animals.

Most of Brazil has a tropical climate—the air is moist and sticky. In parts of the Amazon Basin, temperatures stay near 95°F (35°C) all the time. Ocean breezes

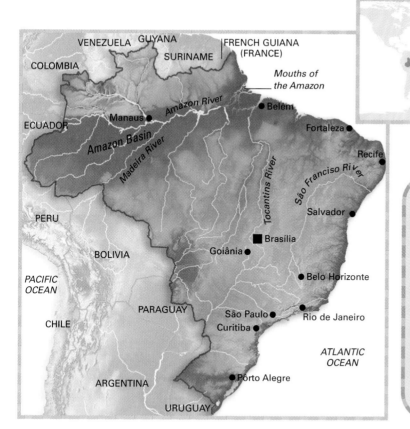

VENEZUELA GUYANA
SURINAME
FRENCH GUIANA
(FRANCE)
COLOMBIA
Mouths of the Amazon
ECUADOR
Manaus
Amazon River
Belém
Amazon Basin
Fortaleza
Madeira River
Recife
PERU
São Francisco River
Tocantins River
Salvador
Brasília
BOLIVIA
Goiânia
Belo Horizonte
PACIFIC OCEAN
PARAGUAY
São Paulo
Rio de Janeiro
Curitiba
CHILE
ATLANTIC OCEAN
ARGENTINA
Pôrto Alegre
URUGUAY

Brazil's national flag

KEY FACTS

OFFICIAL NAME:
República Federativa
do Brazil

AREA:
3,286,478 sq. mi.
(8,511,965 sq. km)

POPULATION:
170,115,000

CAPITAL:
Brasília

LARGEST CITY:
São Paulo

MAJOR RELIGIONS:
Roman Catholicism,
Evangelical
Protestantism

MAJOR LANGUAGE:
Portuguese

CURRENCY:
Real

bring cooler weather to the Atlantic coast, and south-central Brazil has mild winters. In the far south, snow occasionally falls.

People

Most Brazilians are mestizos (people of mixed European, African, and Indian ancestry). Others have come from Japan, the Middle East, and Europe, especially Portugal. A few Indians still live in remote areas of the tropical rain forest.

Brazil has a rich cultural heritage. Its contemporary music and dance are popular all over the world. The nation's favorite sport is soccer: The Brazilian national team has won the World Cup more often than any other country.

Economy

Brazil is an important producer of coffee, cacao (the source of cocoa and chocolate), sugar, fruits, and tobacco. Farmers raise great herds of cattle, horses, and hogs.

The great statue of Christ the Redeemer overlooking Rio de Janeiro.

89

Brazil is also a leading industrial nation. Many of its factories, which turn out textiles, cars, chemicals, and other products, run on hydroelectric or nuclear power. Minerals, gemstones, ores, and wood products are important exports. Tourism and other services, such as education and business, are also important to the national economy.

São Paulo is the chief industrial city of Latin America and the largest city in Brazil. It is the center of the nation's textile industry. The city of Curitiba rivals São Paulo as a center of coffee production. The large carnival (street party) in the beautiful city of Rio de Janeiro attracts many tourists each year. Belo Horizonte, Brazil's third-largest city, is a major commercial and industrial area. Belém is the main port for Amazon River shipping.

SEE ALSO:
Circuses and Carnivals; Portugal; South America

History

Brazil's earliest inhabitants were Indians. More than 100 native tribal groups inhabited the land. They did not plant crops, but hunted animals and gathered fruits and berries.

Portuguese explorers came in search of gold in 1500. Portugal then ruled Brazil for more than 300 years. Settlers brought slaves from Africa to work on plantations. Brazil became independent from Portugal in 1822, but was ruled by a Portuguese emperor. In 1888 slavery was abolished. Brazil became a republic in 1889.

Throughout the 20th century, Brazil faced problems such as rebellions and falling coffee prices. The government is hard-pressed to build enough schools and hospitals for the soaring population. The rain forest is being destroyed by settlers.

✳ BRIDGES

Bridges are structures that carry pedestrians, cars, and trains across rivers, valleys, and canyons, or between islands.

There are more than 500,000 bridges in the United States today. Most of them are designed to carry automobile or railroad traffic, but some are intended for pedestrians only. Most bridges are so short that they do not have names, and most travelers do not even notice going over them. There are some bridges, however, that are famous for their length, for their outstanding design, and for their beauty. Others are known as examples of great engineering.

The Golden Gate suspension bridge in San Francisco, California.

Types of bridges

Bridges must be strong enough to support their load. They need to be stable enough to withstand natural forces such as temperature changes, wind, and earthquakes. They must also stand up to corrosion due to moisture, air pollution, and road salt. When deciding which kind of bridge to build, engineers consider how far the bridge must span, how deep in water or earth they must go to find solid support, and how much traffic the bridge

must carry. These considerations help them choose the type of bridge and the right materials.

The first bridge was probably a fallen tree across a stream—a basic beam bridge. Beam bridges have a wooden, concrete, or metal deck (for a road or railroad to run on), supported at both ends. They can be strengthened with trusses—triangular supports made of metal or wood.

The ancient Romans discovered that they could span greater distances by building arched bridges. By the early 1800s, engineers had perfected this technique. The bridge across Sydney Harbor, Australia, built in 1932, is an arched structure made of concrete and steel.

Cantilever bridges work on a principle similar to arch bridges: Two cantilevers (like projecting shelf supports) are built out toward each other from opposite sides. Each cantilever rests on a pier (solid support) and is anchored to the bank behind the pier. The cantilevers are joined in the middle by a truss.

Suspension bridges

All of the world's longest and best-known bridges are suspension structures. The oldest known bridges of this type were made from ropes that were slung across a gap and tied at both ends. A wooden pathway hung on shorter ropes from the two main ropes.

Modern suspension bridges have brick or concrete towers, with the main cables running above them, so that the bridges can span wide rivers, straits, and estuaries. The first modern suspension bridges were introduced by the German-American engineer John A. Roebling. He is famous for constructing the Brooklyn Bridge in New York City. The bridge was completed in 1883.

For smaller spans, cable-stay bridges are used. They are similar to suspension bridges, but the supporting cables run from the deck to the top of the tower and back down to the deck on the other side. Several towers may span wide gaps.

Some bridges have to open to allow large ships to pass beneath. The two sides may lift up to create an opening, the bridge may swing around on a pivot, or the central section may lift out of the way.

Famous bridges

London Bridge across the Thames River, England, is one of the most famous structures in history. The original bridge

A covered bridge spans the Housatonic River in Litchfield County, Connecticut.
▼

was a series of stone arches. It was completed in 1209 and took over 30 years to build. Until the 1700s it was the only bridge across the Thames in London. The bridge was a focus for London life and even had houses built on it. It was rebuilt in the 1830s and again in the 1970s. Stones from the second bridge were shipped to Lake Havasu City, Arizona, where the bridge was reconstructed over an arm of the Colorado River.

Venice, Italy, has about 400 bridges crossing its many canals. One of the most famous is the Bridge of Sighs, built around 1600. It is believed that prisoners sentenced to death could be heard sighing as they crossed the bridge on their way to execution.

👀

SEE ALSO:
Roman Empire

AMAZING FACTS!

The main span of the Akashi Kaikyo suspension bridge, near Kobe, Japan, is 6,529 ft. (1,990 m) long.
The 23-mile (37-km) Kojima-Sakaide road and rail link between Honshu and Shikoku islands, Japan, is made up of three suspension bridges and two cable-stay bridges, plus truss bridges and viaducts.
The world's longest road bridge is the 24-mile (38-km) Pontchartrain Causeway across Lake Pontchartrain, LA.

❋ BUDDHISM

Buddhism is one of the oldest religions. It is based on the teachings of a man who said he had found the cause of unhappiness and its cure.

A modern Buddhist monk sounding a bell at a monastery in Bangkok, Thailand.

Buddha is believed to have been a Hindu prince named Siddhartha Gautama, who lived 2,500 years ago. His father tried to keep Siddhartha from knowing what an unhappy place the world really was, but he discovered sickness and death on trips outside the palace. For the first time, he realized that unhappiness is a part of life. He gave up all wealth and pleasures, sure that this would help him understand life.

After six years of failure, Siddhartha sat beneath a tree and vowed not to move until he understood the whole meaning of life. Insight came to him in one day, but he remained in a state of bliss under the tree for another 49 days. He then became known as a buddha (meaning "enlightened one"). He taught for the next 45 years, until his death in about 483 B.C.

Teachings and beliefs
There are no gods in Buddhism. Unlike many other religions, Buddhism is not based on belief in a supreme creator. Instead, Buddhists respect and worship the Buddha and his teachings.

The most important Buddhist teachings are the Four Noble Truths, which are: All is suffering; the origin of suffering is ignorance and desire; suffering comes to an end in nirvana; there is a way, or path, to reach nirvana and buddhahood.

Buddhists believe that nirvana is a state of inner peace and understanding. Misery and suffering are caused because we desire things, people, or life itself. But it is possible to find inner peace (nirvana) by following Buddhism, eliminating ignorance, and losing our desires.

Buddhists believe that people die and are reborn again. This is called reincarnation. Those who lead a good life are reborn into a better life, while bad people suffer more the next time around. Those who lose all desire will eventually reach nirvana.

The Buddhist life
The qualities needed to lead a good life include morality, compassion, and respect for others. Some Buddhists follow stricter rules than others. Some enter monasteries to escape the world's desires; many visit holy sites and public shrines to make offerings of food or flowers. In a Buddhist's life, much time is spent sitting quietly and peacefully. Today Buddhism is a major religion in Asia, but there are many Buddhists in other countries, including the United States. The best-known form of Buddhism in the West is Zen, which began in China and is now practiced mainly in Japan.

SEE ALSO: Asia; Hinduism; Religions

✳ BUTTERFLIES AND MOTHS
There are about 112,000 different species of moths and butterflies in the world. In the United States and Canada alone, there are probably about 11,000 species.

Butterflies and moths are flying insects that often look very much alike. In general, butterflies are usually brighter in color than moths. They are active by day, while most moths are night creatures and are attracted by light. A moth has a thicker, more hairy body.

Both butterflies and moths have two pairs of wings, but while a resting moth usually folds its forewings back upon its hind wings, a butterfly at rest leaves its wings full and erect.

A butterfly, like a moth, has two antennae, or feelers, on its head. A butterfly's antennae have slightly enlarged tips, like clubs, while a moth's antennae do not. In some moth species, the antennae have featherlike plumes.

▷ An adult butterfly develops from an egg that becomes a caterpillar.

Life cycle
Butterflies and moths pass through four stages of development in their life cycles. The first stage is the egg. Adult females lay eggs on a plant their young will eat.

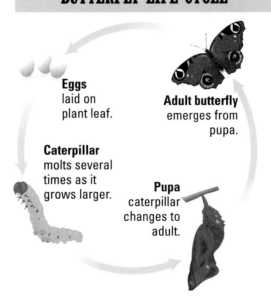

BUTTERFLY LIFE CYCLE

Eggs laid on plant leaf.

Adult butterfly emerges from pupa.

Caterpillar molts several times as it grows larger.

Pupa caterpillar changes to adult.

Many flowering plants rely on butterflies to pollinate them so that they can reproduce.

Each egg hatches into a wormlike larva, or caterpillar. A caterpillar feeds constantly and may eat once or twice its own weight in leaves each day. After several days of feeding, the caterpillar outgrows its skin. It molts, splitting the skin and crawling out. A caterpillar may shed its skin four or five times in all.

In the third stage, the caterpillar enters a resting state and is called a pupa. Some burrow behind bark or into the ground to pupate. Others rest in a silken cocoon, which they make by spinning thread from the mouth. (Silk cloth is made from the threads in the cocoon of the silkworm moth.) During the pupa stage, which may last from two weeks to a whole winter, the caterpillar's body changes completely.

The butterfly or moth crawls out of the cocoon in a new, adult form. Blood flows into its wings, and in a few hours it can fly off to live out its fourth, or adult, stage.

Wings
The wings of many adult butterflies and some moths come in many beautiful shapes and colors. Some species of butterfly have large spots like eyes on their wings. These markings fool predators into believing that the butterfly is a larger, stronger creature, such as an owl. Yellow and black or red and black markings are warning colors that tell the butterfly's enemies that it is poisonous. Bright colors also help butterflies of the same species to recognize one another for mating. Some wings have dull colors that blend in with their surroundings and help the butterfly or moth to hide from enemies.

The wings are covered in rows of tiny scales, as fine as dust. The scales account for the scientific name for butterflies and moths: They are called Lepidoptera, which means "scaly winged."

Senses and feeding
Moths and butterflies can see, smell, and taste very well. Their most important sensing tools are their antennae, which they use for smelling and touching. Some species of butterfly are also able to smell through "noses" on their feet.

Butterflies have two large compound eyes. They are very sensitive to ultraviolet light from the sun. Flowers have special markings that show up in this light. The markings guide a butterfly to the center of a flower to find nectar—its chief food. A butterfly's mouth is formed from a long, hollow tube called a proboscis. It allows the butterfly to suck up nectar like liquid through a straw.

AMAZING FACTS!

The female Queen Alexandra Birdwing of New Guinea is the world's largest butterfly, with a wingspan of up to 12½ in. (32 cm).

Hawkmoths can fly at speeds of up to 30 mph (48 kph). Hummingbird hawkmoths can fly backward as well as forward.

Butterflies need flowers for food, but flowers depend on butterflies, too. As a butterfly feeds on nectar, its body brushes against pollen grains from the flower. When the butterfly visits another flower, the pollen on its body rubs off and fertilizes the second flower. This process is called pollination.

Migration

Many butterflies, and some moths, migrate during certain seasons of the year. The monarch is the best known of the migrating butterflies. Monarchs spend winter along the Gulf of Mexico and other southern areas. Through spring and summer, they go north to Canada and the United States. Each generation of caterpillars feasts on new milkweed plants. With the cooler fall weather, monarchs fly back south in great swarms.

Silk moths spin a cocoon to protect their eggs.

SEE ALSO:
Flowers;
Insects;
Migration;
Pollination

✳ BYRD, RICHARD E. (1888–1957)

Rear Admiral Richard E. Byrd was America's greatest Antarctic explorer. A daring aviator, he was the first man to fly over the South Pole.

Byrd was born on October 25, 1888, in Winchester, Virginia. In 1912 he graduated from the United States Naval Academy.

On May 9, 1926, Byrd and his copilot, Floyd Bennett, took off from Spitzbergen in the Arctic Ocean to head for the North Pole. According to them, they found it, circled for a while, then returned to Spitzbergen about 16 hours later. For their achievement, they won the Medal

Richard E. Byrd holding a sundial compass during a trip to the Antarctic.

of Honor. The men would have been the first people ever to have flown over the North Pole, but there are now doubts about the men's claim.

In 1928 Byrd led his first expedition to Antarctica. From his base, Little America, airplanes explored the continent. On November 28–29, 1929, Byrd and three crewmen, including his pilot Bernt Balchen, made the first flight over the South Pole. Byrd's second Antarctic expedition (1933–35) was for scientific purposes. He lived alone for five months in a tiny cabin under the snow while gathering weather information. Byrd led two more expeditions in the 1940s. He died on March 11, 1957.

SEE ALSO:
Antarctica;
Arctic;
Exploration
and
Explorers

✳ BYZANTINE EMPIRE

The Byzantine Empire grew out of the Roman Empire after A.D. 330, when Emperor Constantine moved his government from Rome to Byzantium.

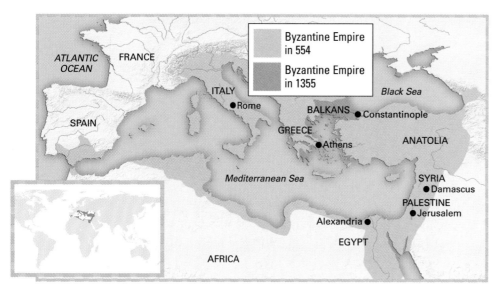

Map showing the extent of the Byzantine Empire, which grew through sea trade across the Mediterranean.

A thousand years ago, Constantinople was the largest and probably the richest city in the world. Its wealth came from trade. The city stood at a crossroads. All ships carrying goods between the Mediterranean Sea and the Black Sea had to pass Constantinople. The main road from Europe to the Middle East also ran through the city. The emperors taxed all goods that passed in and out of the capital.

Byzantium was an ancient Greek city that became known as Constantinople, for the emperor. After Constantine died in A.D. 337, later emperors found it hard to rule the vast Roman Empire.

Constantinople

In 395 the empire was split—the east was ruled from Constantinople and the west from Rome. Rome later lost most of the Western Empire (Italy, Spain, France, Britain, and northwest Africa). The eastern part survived and became known as the Byzantine Empire. Its official language was Greek. The empire was under constant attack, but it lasted for centuries due to its strong armies.

Byzantine culture was influenced by the writings of ancient Greeks such as Plato and Aristotle. It is because of this that ancient learning was kept alive, for Greek was not studied elsewhere at the time.

Although the Byzantine Empire was Christian, it resented the authority of the pope in Rome. But the pope thought that the eastern emperors had too much power. The eastern and western churches divided in 1054. Churches of Byzantine origin today include the Greek Orthodox Church and the Russian Orthodox Church.

In 1204 Crusaders conquered Constantinople. The empire ended in 1453, when the Turks captured the city.

Dating from about A.D. 1000, this Byzantine mosaic depicts the Virgin Mary holding the infant Jesus.

SEE ALSO:
Christianity;
Crusades;
Greece,
Ancient;
Roman
Empire

C

✳ CABOT, JOHN (ABOUT 1451–98)

John Cabot was probably the first European since the Vikings to set foot on the North American continent, in 1497.

He was born Giovanni Caboto in Genoa, Italy. He became a merchant and grew frustrated by the long overland journey needed to transport goods from the East. Caboto believed that the earth was round and that it would be easier to reach Asia by sailing west across the Atlantic Ocean.

He asked the monarchs of Spain and Portugal to finance a voyage to reach China (then called Cathay) by sea. They refused, but King Henry VII of England agreed. In May 1497 Caboto set sail. On June 24 he reached what was probably the east coast of modern Canada. This landing was the basis for the British claim to North America. Because of his English links, he is known by the English form of his name, John Cabot.

Cabot returned to England believing that he had found the northeast coast of Asia. He went on a second voyage the following year, when it is thought he died in a storm.

> **SEE ALSO:** Canada; Exploration and Explorers

This painting shows the departure of John Cabot and his son Sebastian from Bristol, England.

✳ CACTUS

A cactus (plural, *cacti*) is a plant that has adapted to very dry conditions. Cacti originated in North and South America.

Cacti grow mainly in hot, dry areas in South and Central America and the Southwestern United States. Some species grow as far north as Canada. People have now introduced cacti to many other parts of the world.

Cactus roots spread out close to the surface of the ground, absorbing scarce rainwater quickly before it dries up, or evaporates. The water is stored in the stem of the cactus. The outside surface of the cactus is thick and waxy, which keeps the water from escaping.

In other plants, water is lost through the holes, or pores, in the leaves, but cacti have very few pores, helping keep water in. The cactus often has spines to protect it from animals seeking food or water. ➡

Cacti have spines on their surface to keep off animals that would use them as a source of food and water.

Kinds of cacti

There are around 1,500 species of cacti. The best known are the prickly pears, which have a sweet, juicy fruit and often large, colorful flowers. The biggest cactus is the saguaro, which can grow to 40 ft. (12 m) tall and live for more than 200 years. Woodpeckers and desert owls often live in holes in the saguaro.

Close relatives of the saguaro include the organ-pipe cactus, which looks like a church organ, and the night-blooming cereus, or wax candle, cactus. This cactus normally resembles a bundle of sticks, but white blooms appear on it for one night each year.

Desert water source

Barrel cacti can reach a height of 12 ft. (3.6 m) and can be over 3 ft. (1 m) in diameter. They store water in their trunks. People lost in the desert have survived by cutting the top off the plant, pounding the pulp, and drinking the liquid that escapes.

The small hedgehog and pincushion cacti are frequently grown as decorative plants in gardens and homes.

AMAZING FACTS!

A species of barrel cactus called the bisnaga can grow to 9 ft. (2.7 m) in height and have a diameter of 3 ft. (1 m). Bisnagas this large are probably more than 1,000 years old.

SEE ALSO: Biomes; Deserts; Plants

✳ CAESAR, JULIUS (ABOUT 100–44 B.C.)

Julius Caesar was a politician, soldier, writer, and leader of the Roman republic. His name, Caesar, became the title of the Roman emperors.

Gaius Julius Caesar was born into a noble family and began his political career in 78 B.C. In 59 B.C. he formed an alliance with Pompey, a famous general, and Crassus, a rich nobleman. This three-man pact was called the First Triumvirate.

Caesar was elected as a consul, became governor of three provinces, and successfully fought the Gauls in France and the Britons in England. Pompey, his previous ally, later became jealous of him, and a civil war broke out between them. Caesar eventually won this conflict at the battle of Pharsalus in 48 B.C.

Caesar returned to Rome in 45 B.C. and was named dictator. The following year he was appointed dictator for life by the Senate. Other important Romans, such as Brutus and Cassius, thought this was too much power for one man, and they plotted against Caesar. He was stabbed to death on March 15, 44 B.C.

Julius Caesar ruled ancient Rome from 49 B.C. until his murder five years later.

SEE ALSO: Cleopatra; Roman Empire

✳ CALENDARS

A calendar is a system that keeps track of days, months, and years. Today the word is also used for a schedule of events or meetings.

In early history, people measured the passing of time by the seasons and the changes in the sun and moon's position. More than 10,000 years ago, the ancient Egyptians had a calendar similar to the modern, Western one. It had 12 months, and each month had 30 days, making a year of 360 days. However, the earth takes nearly 365¼ days to orbit the sun, so the calendar lost a few days every year.

Other civilizations, such as the Babylonian and the Chinese, also used a system of years containing between 360 and 365 days divided into 12 months. The Jews probably got the idea of a seven-day week from the Babylonians. The Roman calendar—which forms the basis of most modern systems of time measurement—was in turn based on the Jewish system.

Julian and Gregorian calendars

Beginning in the second century B.C., the Romans gave their calendar a 12-month system. But their year had only 355 days, putting the calendar out of sequence with the sun. In 46 B.C. Julius Caesar introduced a 365-day system, with an extra day every four years (leap year). It became known as the Julian calendar.

The Julian calendar was still not a perfect match with the seasons. In A.D. 1582 Pope Gregory XIII adopted a new calendar that brought the year back into line with the seasons. This was the Gregorian, or New Style, calendar. North America and Britain adopted this calendar in 1752, but Greece switched only in 1923.

From the 500s onward the Christian church numbered years from the date of the birth of Jesus Christ. Years after this date are labeled A.D. *Anno Domini* is Latin for "in the year of our Lord." Those before it are called B.C. (before Christ).

Today the Gregorian is the most widely used calendar, but there are others. The Chinese calendar puts its years in groups of 12, each named after an animal. The Hebrew calendar of the Jewish religion begins 3,760 years before A.D. 1, and the Islamic calendar begins 622 years after it, with the flight of Muhammad from Mecca to Medina.

A French calendar from about 1450 showing the month of November.

DID YOU KNOW?

Most of the names in English for the days of the week come from the ancient Germanic and Norse tribes of northern Europe.

Sunday	Sunnadag, "Day of the sun"
Monday	Monandag, "Day of the moon"
Tuesday	Tiu, the god of war
Wednesday	Odin, or Wotan, ruler of the gods
Thursday	Thor, god of thunder
Friday	Frigga, wife of Odin
Saturday	Saturn, Roman god of agriculture

SEE ALSO:
Ancient Civilizations;
Aztecs;
Caesar, Julius; Egypt, Ancient;
Holidays and Festivals;
Islam;
Judaism;
Time

*CANADA

Canada, in northern North America, is the second-largest country in the world, after Russia. Much of its land area is unsuitable for human habitation.

Canada's national flag

Land and climate

Canada has coastlines on three oceans—the Atlantic, the Pacific, and the Arctic. Its border with the United States crosses four of the five Great Lakes and Niagara Falls. The land includes the Interior Plains, or prairies, part of the Great Plains, and the northern part of the Rocky Mountains. In the far north, winter temperatures can fall below 0°F (−18°C) and snowfall can reach 118 in. (300 cm).

Plants and animals

Canada's most important plants are trees. There are about 150 native species, including maple, Douglas fir, and aspen. The earliest industry in Canada was the animal fur and skin trade. Bison were hunted so much that they are now protected on reserves. Native animals include grizzly bears and coyotes.

An aerial view of Long Beach in the Pacific Rim National Park, British Columbia.

People and economy

The largest group of Canadians is of British ancestry (about 28 percent of the population). The next largest group is French-speaking people (about 23 percent). Eighty-five percent of the population lives within 180 miles (300 km) of the U.S. border. More than one-quarter of the people live in Vancouver, Montreal, or Toronto, Canada's biggest cities.

Service industries, including tourism, make up the largest part of the economy. Other industries include manufacturing, agriculture, and fishing. There are rich mineral resources throughout the country.

History

The earliest inhabitants of Canada were Inuits, who arrived from Asia about 25,000 years ago. Leif Eriksson, a Viking explorer, probably landed in Newfoundland in about 1000 B.C., but there was not a proper European settlement until 500 years later. In 1497 Giovanni Caboto (John Cabot) reached Newfoundland. In 1534 Jacques Cartier claimed the Gulf of St. Lawrence for France and named the area Kanata.

By the end of the 1500s, French and English settlers were competing for the

KEY FACTS

OFFICIAL NAME:
Dominion of Canada

AREA:
3,851,809 sq. mi.
(9,976,185 sq. km)

POPULATION:
31,081,900
(2001 census)

CAPITAL:
Ottawa

LARGEST CITY:
Toronto

MAJOR RELIGIONS:
Roman Catholicism, Protestantism

MAJOR LANGUAGES:
English, French

CURRENCY:
Canadian dollar

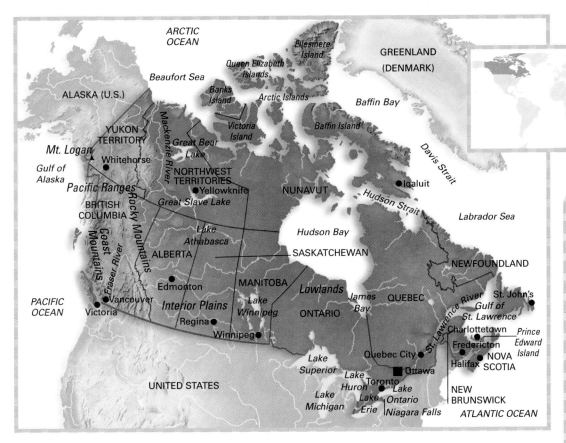

ARCTIC OCEAN
Ellesmere Island
GREENLAND (DENMARK)
Beaufort Sea
Queen Elizabeth Islands
ALASKA (U.S.)
Banks Island
Arctic Islands
Baffin Bay
YUKON TERRITORY
Victoria Island
Baffin Island
Mackenzie River
Great Bear Lake
Davis Strait
Mt. Logan
Whitehorse
Gulf of Alaska
NORTHWEST TERRITORIES
Yellowknife
NUNAVUT
Iqaluit
Pacific Ranges
Great Slave Lake
Labrador Sea
BRITISH COLUMBIA
Rocky Mountains
Lake Athabasca
Hudson Strait
Hudson Bay
Coast Mountains
Fraser River
ALBERTA
SASKATCHEWAN
NEWFOUNDLAND
PACIFIC OCEAN
Edmonton
MANITOBA
Lowlands
James Bay
QUEBEC
St. John's
Vancouver
Interior Plains
Lake Winnipeg
ONTARIO
Gulf of St. Lawrence
Victoria
Regina
Charlottetown
Prince Edward Island
Winnipeg
Fredericton
NOVA SCOTIA
Lake Superior
Quebec City
Halifax
UNITED STATES
Lake Huron
Ottawa
Toronto
Lake Michigan
Lake Erie
Lake Ontario
Niagara Falls
NEW BRUNSWICK
ATLANTIC OCEAN

SEE ALSO:
American Revolution;
Cabot, John;
Champlain, Samuel de;
Exploration and Explorers;
French and Indian Wars;
North America, Geography;
Vikings

fur trade. Humphrey Gilbert claimed Newfoundland for England in 1583, and Samuel de Champlain founded Quebec, a French settlement, in 1608. By 1689 the French and English were in open conflict, and by 1760 Canada was British.

French people in a British state

There was still a large minority of French-speaking settlers in Canada, and the Quebec Act of 1774 gave them legal and religious rights. American settlers were angry that their land was subject to French law. The act became one of the causes of the American Revolution. The Act of Union in 1840 united the territories of Upper and Lower Canada (now Ontario and Quebec). In 1867 the British North America Act created the Canadian Confederation, comprising Ontario, Quebec, New Brunswick, and Nova Scotia.

In the 1880s, a métis (part-French, part-Native American) called Louis Riel led the Northwest Rebellion of prairie settlers. Riel was executed in 1885, but he became a figurehead for French-speakers who were unhappy at the increasing power of the Canadian state.

After 1945 Canadian French-speakers campaigned to make Quebec independent from Canada. The separatist Parti Québécois took control of the province in 1976, but gave up calls for full independence in 1995. In 1982 the Constitution Act gave Canada the right to amend its own constitution without permission from Britain.

Europeans trading with native Canadians during the 1700s.

101

✳ CANALS

Canals are artificial channels, or ditches, filled with water. They were built originally to drain swamps or irrigate dry land.

SEE ALSO:
China; Egypt;
Egypt,
Ancient;
Lakes;
Oceans and
Seas;
Panama;
Rivers

Early in history people found another important use for canals—transportation. A canal can join two cities. It can give inland areas access to the sea. Rivers, lakes, and seas can be linked by canals to provide shorter or safer water routes.

How canals work

Canals can be built all on one level, or they can go from one level to another by means of locks. Locks are sections of a canal with watertight gates at each end. A ship going from a lower to a higher level in a canal sails into a lock through its open lower gates. The gates are shut behind it. Water is then allowed to flow into the lock until the level of water inside it is as high as the water in the upper level of the canal. Finally the upper gates are opened, and the ship goes on its way.

If a ship is going down to a lower level, the process is simply reversed, and water is let out through small openings in the gates. If the gates themselves were opened to let water in or out, a torrent would rush in or out with terrific force, damaging the ship or washing away the canal banks.

History of canals

Nearly 4,000 years ago, the ancient Egyptians built one of the earliest known canals for transportation. It connected the Nile River with the Red Sea. The world's greatest canal system is the Grand Canal of China, which was completed in around A.D. 620. Including its side branches, it stretches more than 1,678 miles (2,700 km).

One of the most famous artificial waterways of modern times is the Suez Canal, built in Egypt between 1859 and 1869 to link the Mediterranean and the Red seas. It enabled ships to go from Europe to Asia without having to sail around Africa.

The Panama Canal, completed in 1914, links the Atlantic and Pacific oceans, eliminating the long trip around the southern tip of South America.

A container ship passes through the 100-mile (160-km) Suez Canal in Egypt.

✳ CAPITALISM

Capitalism is an economic system in which most of the industries and businesses in a country are privately owned by individuals, rather than by the government.

The word *capitalism* comes from the money, or capital, of private individuals. Capitalists are people who use their own wealth (or other people's money) to make more wealth. Though capitalists simply want to make money, this does not mean that they can charge very high prices or sell bad goods. If they do, they may lose business to others with lower prices or better goods. Competition forces capitalists to sell the best goods at the lowest possible price.

Competition is an important feature of capitalism. The profits made by individual capitalists help the economy of a whole country. As capitalists make profits, they can expand their businesses and put more people to work.

Early capitalism
Before the 1700s, the ruling classes of most countries had tight control over production and trade in order to protect their economic and military strength. But with the Industrial Revolution, which began in the mid-1700s, came a new middle class of wealthy merchants and factory owners with large amounts of capital. Many people believed that capitalism would work best if governments allowed business to run itself. But as industry grew unchecked, factory owners often abused their power. They forced workers to labor long hours in dangerous conditions for low pay.

Reformers cried out against these conditions. One of the most outspoken was the German thinker Karl Marx

(1818–83), a founder of communism. In 1867 he published *Das Kapital*, claiming that capitalism must die of its own cruelty and greed. Labor unions (groups that protect workers' rights) had begun to develop. Most unionists believed that bad working conditions could be improved without killing the capitalist system. Laws also brought changes to capitalism. By the late 1800s, some companies were so powerful that they had almost no competition. (One all-powerful company acting alone is known as a monopoly. A group of such companies is called a trust.) The Sherman Antitrust Act (1890) outlawed monopolies in the United States.

Capitalism today
Many nations today combine capitalism with government control of the economy. For example, a government may own vital industries such as the railroads, while allowing private ownership of other industries. Most people in democratic countries support free enterprise. But they also want government to stop capitalism from running out of control.

This French cartoon from 1908—showing a rich capitalist trampling on ordinary people—represents capitalism out of control.

SEE ALSO:
Communism; Economics; Labor; Trade

✳ CARIBBEAN ISLANDS

The Caribbean Islands largely consist of the Greater Antilles and the Lesser Antilles. The Antilles are the main island group of the West Indies.

The islands stretch for more than 2,000 miles (3,220 km) and form the boundary between the Caribbean Sea and the Atlantic Ocean. The Greater Antilles include the four largest islands—Cuba, Hispaniola (shared by Haiti and the Dominican Republic), Jamaica, and Puerto Rico. The Lesser Antilles include Barbados, the Leeward Islands, and the Windward Islands. The Virgin Islands and the northern islands of the Netherlands Antilles are usually classified as parts of the Lesser Antilles. To the north the Bahamas and the Turks and Caicos Islands are outside the Caribbean area.

Land and climate

The islands are part of two partly submerged mountain chains that reach their highest point in Hispaniola. The mountains have been worn away on many of the Lesser Antilles, but some of the other islands still have active volcanoes.

The region has a moderate climate, cooled by the breezes of the trade winds. Temperatures range from about 70 to 85°F (21–29°C). Hurricanes often develop in the late summer or early fall.

▲

Downtown Kingston, the capital of Jamaica and the home of reggae music.

People and economy

The original Carib Indian inhabitants of the islands died out soon after European settlement. Today most Caribbean peoples are descended from Africans brought to the region to work as plantation slaves.

For centuries the chief products of the Caribbean were sugar, coffee, and spices.

KEY FACTS

GREATER ANTILLES:
Cuba, Hispaniola (Haiti and the Dominican Republic), Jamaica, Puerto Rico (U.S.)

LESSER ANTILLES:
Anguilla (Br.), Antigua and Barbuda, Aruba (Neth.), Barbados, Bonaire (Neth.), Curaçao (Neth.), Dominica, Grenada, Guadeloupe (Fr.), Martinique (Fr.), Montserrat (Br.), Saba (Neth.), St. Eustatius (Neth.), St. Kitts and Nevis, St. Lucia, St. Martin (Fr.–Neth.), St. Vincent and the Grenadines, Trinidad and Tobago, British Virgin Islands, U.S. Virgin Islands (St. Croix, St. John, St. Thomas)

OTHER ISLANDS:
Cayman Islands (Br.), Margarita (Venez.), Tortuga (Venez.)

STATUS:
All Caribbean islands are independent except where noted:
Br. = Britain
Fr. = France
Neth. = Netherlands
U.S. = United States
Venez. = Venezuela

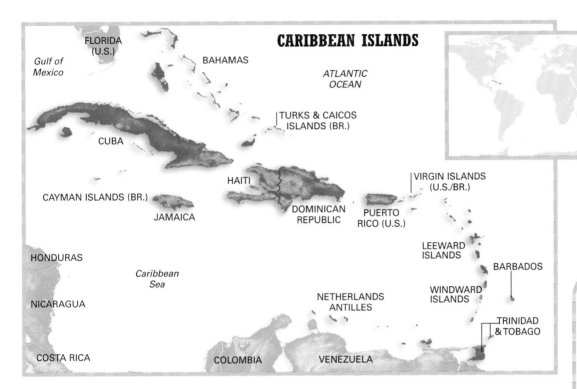

CARIBBEAN ISLANDS

FLORIDA (U.S.)

Gulf of Mexico

BAHAMAS

ATLANTIC OCEAN

TURKS & CAICOS ISLANDS (BR.)

CUBA

CAYMAN ISLANDS (BR.)

HAITI

JAMAICA

DOMINICAN REPUBLIC

PUERTO RICO (U.S.)

VIRGIN ISLANDS (U.S./BR.)

HONDURAS

Caribbean Sea

LEEWARD ISLANDS

BARBADOS

NICARAGUA

NETHERLANDS ANTILLES

WINDWARD ISLANDS

TRINIDAD & TOBAGO

COSTA RICA

COLOMBIA

VENEZUELA

SEE ALSO:
Columbus, Christopher; Cuba; Jamaica; Spanish–American War

However, industry is now Puerto Rico's main source of income. Cuba has one of the world's largest deposits of nickel, and Jamaica produces bauxite (aluminum ore). Tourism is important for all the islands.

History

Christopher Columbus reached the Caribbean in 1492. The Spanish then colonized the Greater Antilles. For the next 300 years, Spain vied with other European nations for power in the region. The British finally gained dominance. Haiti was the first Caribbean state to gain independence, in the late 1700s. The Dominican Republic followed in the mid-1800s. As a result of the Spanish–American War (1898), Cuba won its independence, and Puerto Rico became a territory of the United States. In 1917 the United States bought St. Croix, St. John, and St. Thomas (the U.S. Virgin Islands) from Denmark. Cuba became a republic in 1902. Most British-owned islands became independent between 1960 and 1980.

St. John, one of the three main U.S. Virgin Islands, which lie about 40 miles (64 km) east of Puerto Rico.
▼

* CARS
Cars are self-propelled vehicles that travel on land without rails. They are a form of automobile, a term that also covers trucks and buses.

Henry Ford and his son, Edsel, in the 1905 Model F Ford outside their home in Detroit, Michigan.

The first self-powered road vehicle was built by a Frenchman, Nicolas Cugnot, in 1769. It was a three-wheeled steam engine designed to pull cannons. It was never fully tested because it crashed during a trial run.

Later efforts by the Englishman Richard Trevithick and the American Oliver Evans had little success. It was not until the late 1800s that the car as we now know it began to take shape.

The German engineers Gottlieb Daimler and Karl Benz both created working, engine-driven automobiles in 1886. In the 1890s, French engineer Emile Levassor built a car with spring suspension and clutch-and-gear transmission. The next big idea was the brainchild of the Americans Ransom E. Olds and Henry M. Leland, who found it profitable to build all their vehicles from standardized parts.

Although cars provide many benefits to society, they have several disadvantages, including congestion and pollution.

The greatest advances in car manufacture, however, were made by Henry Ford, who developed the assembly line that made mass production possible. In the Ford plant, cars under construction were moved down the line on a conveyor belt, and each worker had a few simple tasks to perform, over and over, many times a day.

Cars for the masses
Before the assembly line, it took 728 minutes to build a car. On the assembly line, it took 93 minutes. Between 1908 and 1925, the cost of a Model T car fell from $850 to $290. Cars were now affordable by ordinary people. In the next few decades, developments such as hydraulic brakes, safety glass, and car radios made driving safer and more fun.

By the 1960s, the massive increase in car use was causing pollution problems. In the 1970s, there were gasoline shortages, and manufacturers made cars smaller and more efficient. More recently, battery-powered cars have been developed to protect Earth's resources, but they are still not generally used.

How a car works
Most cars are powered by internal-combustion engines. They are started by an electrical system that makes a spark, and they are powered by liquid fuel—

INSIDE A CAR

The average
modern car
contains about
14,000 different
parts. These are
some of the
most important.

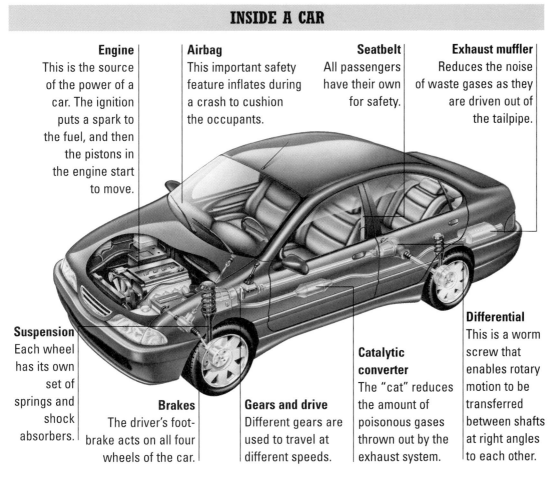

Engine
This is the source of the power of a car. The ignition puts a spark to the fuel, and then the pistons in the engine start to move.

Airbag
This important safety feature inflates during a crash to cushion the occupants.

Seatbelt
All passengers have their own for safety.

Exhaust muffler
Reduces the noise of waste gases as they are driven out of the tailpipe.

Suspension
Each wheel has its own set of springs and shock absorbers.

Brakes
The driver's foot-brake acts on all four wheels of the car.

Gears and drive
Different gears are used to travel at different speeds.

Catalytic converter
The "cat" reduces the amount of poisonous gases thrown out by the exhaust system.

Differential
This is a worm screw that enables rotary motion to be transferred between shafts at right angles to each other.

either gasoline or diesel. When mixed with air and burned, the fuel generates expanding gases. The gases form energy that is used to turn a shaft that then turns the car's wheels. The transmission, or

gearbox, of a car uses gears to match the engine's speed to the desired road speed. The device that controls the transmission is called the clutch. Transmissions may be automatic or manual.

Oil protects the various engine parts from rubbing against each other, and a cooling system prevents overheating. The exhaust removes waste gases. The suspension is a set of springs and shock absorbers that soften unevenness in the road and help the car take corners smoothly.

Today most cars have safety features such as airbags. Yet many people are killed and injured on the road each year. The car provides many benefits, but it must be used with care.

AMAZING FACTS!

In the United States there are about two people per car; in China there are more than 1,300 people per car.
In a year American motorists travel about 2 trillion miles (3.2 trillion km).
The longest car ever built is a 26-wheel limousine, 100 ft. (30.5 m) long.

SEE ALSO:
Engines;
Fossil Fuels;
Pollution

✳ CARSON, RACHEL (1907–64)

American marine biologist Rachel Carson is widely regarded as the founder of the modern environmental movement.

Rachel Carson at work in a government research laboratory.

Rachel Louise Carson was born in Springdale, Pennsylvania. Her interest in nature began in early childhood. She graduated from Pennsylvania College for Women in 1929 and received a master's degree from Johns Hopkins University in 1932. Starting in 1936 she worked for the Fish and Wildlife Service. Carson began to write books about marine life. *The Sea Around Us* (1951) won the National Book Award for nonfiction. Her most famous book was *Silent Spring* (1962), in which she warned that the chemical sprays used by farmers were poisoning the environment. The spring was silent, she explained, because pesticides had killed the birds and other living things. The book was criticized by industrial firms, but further research supported many of Carson's findings and led to restrictions on pesticide use.

Carson died in 1964. The Rachel Carson National Wildlife Refuge in Maine was named for her in 1970.

SEE ALSO: Ecology; Environment; Pollution

✳ CARTOONS AND ANIMATION

A cartoon was originally a rough drawing done to prepare for a painting. Today the word refers to a drawing, or a series of drawings, with a message.

This 1798 cartoon by James Gillray makes fun of the struggle between Britain and France for military supremacy in Europe.

Cartoons can tell a simple joke or a long story. They can be funny and zany or serious and political. They can appear on a printed page or on a TV or movie screen as animation (moving pictures).

Cartoons as we know them began in the 1700s, when printed books and pictures became cheaply available. Artists such as the Englishman James Gillray (1756–1815) and the Frenchman Honoré Daumier (1808–79) used their skills to attack politicians. Cartoons became common in European papers and magazines. The first famous American cartoonist was Thomas Nast (1840–1902), who attacked political corruption in *Harper's Weekly* magazine.

In the 1900s, one-panel cartoons—cartoons with a single picture—were very popular in magazines such as *The Saturday Evening Post*, but gradually comic strips took their place. The only magazine in the United States that still has large numbers of one-panel cartoons is *The New Yorker*, which has published great cartoonists such as James Thurber and Charles Addams. One-panel cartoons are still popular in other countries.

AMAZING FACTS !

The first cartoon with a soundtrack was *Steamboat Willie*, made in 1928. It starred Mickey Mouse.

Mickey Mouse was the first nonhuman to win an Academy Award® (or Oscar®).

Walt Disney has won more Academy Awards® than anybody else, with 26 Oscars® over 37 years.

The Simpsons is the longest-running animated series on television.

Animation

Cartoons that are filmed to give the illusion of movement are called animation. There are three main kinds of animation: flat pictures, three-dimensional models, and computer-generated animation.

Primitive animation existed well before the movies. Devices called magic lanterns contained simple drawings that appeared to move when the machine was rotated. The idea behind two-dimensional animation is the same. Each drawing is photographed individually. There are very slight differences between the drawings, so that when the frames are run together at speed, the figures appear to be moving. Some animation is drawn directly onto paper, which is then photographed, but most cartoons of this type are now created on transparent sheets called cels. Most of the famous movies of the Walt Disney studios, such as *Snow White*, *The Jungle Book*, and *Beauty and the Beast*, were made this way. It is also the most usual technique for TV cartoons such as

The dinosaurs in Jurassic Park were created by combining full-size and small-scale models with computer-generated images.
▼

Walt Disney
(1901–66) drawing
a sketch of
his first great
cartoon character,
Mickey Mouse.

The Flintstones, The Simpsons, and Rugrats. Some movies combine animated pictures and live action—examples include Mary Poppins and Who Killed Roger Rabbit?

Three-dimensional model animation is done in a similar way. Models are moved a tiny fraction at a time, and each move is photographed. An early example of this technique was the 1933 movie King Kong. More recently, filmmakers have used clay models. In Nick Park's Chicken Run, for example, simple actions such as a character scratching his head involved hundreds of tiny movements and took many hours to shoot.

The first big success of computer animation was Jurassic Park, an action movie released in 1993 and directed by Steven Spielberg. Computer-generated dinosaurs were used to menace the humans. Later movies, such as Toy Story and Monsters, Inc., were made entirely with this technology. Computer animation is also used to create video games.

SEE ALSO: Films

✱ CASSATT, MARY (1844–1926)

Mary Cassatt was the foremost American woman painter of the 1800s. She was associated with a group of French painters called the Impressionists.

Mrs. Duffee
Seated on a
Striped Sofa
Reading, painted
by Cassatt in 1876.

Mary Stevenson Cassatt was born in Allegheny City, Pennsylvania. She was the daughter of a businessman. After studying art in Philadelphia and Italy, she settled in Paris, France, in 1873. Her paintings soon attracted praise.

Cassatt quickly became friendly with most of the major French artists of the day and was particularly close to Edgar Degas. She was largely responsible for bringing their work to the attention of art lovers in the United States. On her advice, her wealthy American friends and relations bought paintings by Degas, Claude Monet, and other Impressionists.

Cassatt was mainly a painter of figures. Her favorite subjects were mothers and children. From the 1890s, she became increasingly influenced by Japanese art.

Cassatt remained in France for the rest of her life. She continued painting until 1917, when she went blind. In 1996 her painting In the Box sold in New York City for $3.67 million, the highest price ever paid for a work by a female artist.

SEE ALSO: Art and Artists

✳ CASTLES

A castle is a building or group of buildings with fortifications to protect it from outside attack. It may be a garrison for soldiers or a home for nobles.

Many castles were built in Europe between the 900s and the 1400s. During this period, known as the Middle Ages, kings often granted land to wealthy nobles. In return, nobles swore loyalty to the monarchs and promised to supply them with armed fighting men called knights. The noblemen built castles from which their knights could control and defend the surrounding countryside.

Construction

Castle design changed greatly over the centuries. Early castles were built of earth and timber, but beginning about 1000 onward, most were made almost entirely of stone. A large stone castle was very expensive to build. Materials often had to be transported over long distances. Construction could take 20 years and employ more than 2,000 workers.

Many castles had a tall stone structure called a keep at the center. Thick-walled and fireproof, it was one of the safest places in the castle. Around the keep ran high stone walls and a deep trench filled with water, called a moat. The castle was protected by a raisable gate called a portcullis and a drawbridge that could be raised or lowered over the moat.

Attacks on a castle

A castle could be attacked in several ways. The attackers could attempt to climb over the walls, try to knock them down with special machines such as battering rams, or tunnel under the walls, causing them to collapse. Because castles were difficult to defeat by direct assault, attackers would often settle down for a siege. They tried to prevent supplies from reaching the castle and so starve the occupants into surrender. A siege could take months or even years.

Soldiers defend a castle from attack during the Middle Ages. ▼

Castles today

By the 1500s, castles were less effective because of the invention of gunpowder. Cannons could smash down the stoutest walls. People made their castles more comfortable or moved into houses. Few castles today are used as homes. Some have been turned into museums, but most have fallen into ruin.

Harlech Castle, Wales, in the United Kingdom, has two thick walls, circular towers, and a strong, secure central gatehouse. ▼

👀

SEE ALSO: Architecture; Knights and Chivalry; Middle Ages; Warfare

✳ CATS AND BIG CATS

There are about 36 different species in the cat family. They are all carnivores—animals that feed on the meat of other creatures.

Scientists divide cats into four groups. The largest group has 28 species, including domestic cats, wildcats, pumas, and lynxes. Another group consists of the big cats, including lions, tigers, jaguars, leopards, and snow leopards. The other two groups contain one species each—the cheetah and the clouded leopard.

Distribution

Cats are native to all the continents except Australia and Antarctica. They are adaptable creatures that live in a wide variety of habitats, from open plains to jungles and snowy mountain peaks. The cougar, or puma, is the most widely distributed wildcat. It can be found from northern Canada almost to the southern tip of South America. At the opposite extreme, the little Iriomote cat inhabits only the island of Iriomote in southern Japan. This rare and secretive creature was discovered in 1967.

The ancient Egyptians worshiped cats. This bronze sculpture of a cat-god dates from about 500 B.C.
▶

The ancient Egyptians were the first people to tame, or domesticate, wildcats that lived in the desert close to human settlements. These animals looked similar to modern domestic cats. By 1500 B.C. the Egyptians kept cats as pets and even worshiped them as gods. At about the same time, people had also begun to domesticate cats in India and China.

Characteristics of cats

Cats vary widely in size, but they share many characteristics. They are muscular, with rounded heads and short muzzles, or snouts. Their forward-looking eyes are set well apart. That gives them a wide field of vision, which helps as they scan the landscape for prey. In the rear of each eye is a layer of cells that reflects light, enabling cats to see clearly at night.

Cats have very good hearing and a keen sense of smell. Their teeth are adapted for seizing prey and tearing flesh. They have pads on their feet, and they walk silently on their toes—that helps them creep up on their prey.

Cats' clawed toes help them grip the ground, scramble up trees, and cling to prey. All cats but the cheetah can retract their claws into bony coverings, called sheaths, when they are not in use.

Except for lions, cats are solitary animals. For most of their lives they live alone, coming together only when it is time to mate. After mating, most male cats immediately go off on their own.

Female cats stay with their young and care for them until they are able to fend for themselves. However, lions live in family groups called prides. A typical pride has about 15 members, consisting of a male leader, one or two other adult males, several females, and their young. Most of the hunting is done by the lionesses—males do very little.

traditional medicines. Big cats are killed because they attack livestock and sometimes people.

As more land is developed for human use, there is less space available for cats and their prey. Nature reserves help protect cats, and there are now laws against hunting endangered species. However, some furs are still sold illegally.

SEE ALSO: Animals; Egypt, Ancient; Endangered Species; Extinction; Mammals

DID YOU KNOW?

The sand cat of North Africa and western Asia can live in the desert without ever drinking water. It remains in its burrow or in the shade of a shrub during the heat of the day. At night it hunts for small rodents, lizards, and insects. They supply all the fluid the sand cat needs to survive in the desert.

Reproduction

All cats are born blind and helpless. Like other mammals, newborn cats feed on milk produced by their mother. They grow very rapidly. A lion cub weighing several pounds at birth can double its weight in two weeks. In 10 weeks it can weigh almost 20 lb. (9 kg).

Soon the mother cat begins to teach her young to hunt. Often she will catch prey but not kill it. Instead she carries it to the cubs and then releases it for them to chase. After long weeks of practice, they learn how to make a kill.

Young lions learn to hunt by watching their elders creep up on game and attack it. When they are about six months of age, they begin learning to stalk prey. By the time they are a year old, they have learned to kill their own prey with the help of the adults. It may be a few months more before they can handle the task alone.

The future of cats

The populations of many species of cat have decreased so much that some are now threatened with extinction. Vast numbers are killed for their beautiful coats and their body parts, which are used in

The snow leopard is native to Central Asia. It is also known as an ounce.

✳CAUCASUS see ➧ ✳ TURKEY AND THE CAUCASUS

✴ CAVES

Caves are geological features that are formed when water containing acid flows through or beats against limestone rocks and hollows them out.

Over millions of years, water has created many spectacular caves in previously solid rock. The rocks inside the caves can take a wide range of amazing shapes and sizes. The most famous are icicles of stone called stalactites, which grow downward from ceilings, and candles of stone called stalagmites, which grow up from the floor.

Sea caves are formed by the pounding of waves on rocky cliffs. When hot, melted rock, or lava, from a volcano cools, it forms a hard crust, but the fiery interior flows on. The hollow, hardened tubes left behind are lava caves. They are usually only a yard or so underground. Moving sheets of ice called glaciers also sometimes form caves.

Life in caves

Some animals use caves for temporary shelter but do not live there all the time. During the winter, bears, snakes, and many insects sleep in caves. Other animals spend more of their lives deep in caves. Some, such as rats and bats, go outside to find food. But some insects, fish, and salamanders spend their whole lives in black caves.

Most caves are found by accident. But speleologists, the scientists who study caves, can sometimes locate them by following the paths of streams when they disappear underground. There are about 17,000 known caves in the United States.

SEE ALSO: Amphibians; Bats; Bears; Geology; Glaciers; Volcanoes

▷ *Stalactites and stalagmites in Carlsbad Caverns, New Mexico.*

AMAZING FACTS !

The longest known cave stretches for over 330 miles (531 km) in the Mammoth system, KY.

One of the world's deepest caves is on the border between France and Spain. It is 3,280 ft. (1,000 m) deep.

✳ CELLS

Cells are the basic units of life. Some tiny forms of life consist of only one cell. The human body is made of billions and billions of cells.

Most cells are so small that they can be seen only with a microscope. In fact, the existence of cells became known only after the microscope was invented in the late 16th century. They were first noticed in plant tissues. This is not surprising, because most plant cells are larger than animal cells. In the 1660s, Robert Hooke of England first used the word *cell* when he was examining thin slices of cork with an early microscope.

Cell size
An average animal cell is about one-thousandth of an inch long. The smallest cells are probably bacteria. They can hardly be seen even with a microscope. Nerve cells are probably the largest cells. Some of them are over 3 ft. (1 m) long.

Cells convert food substances such as sugar into energy that is used to do various kinds of work. There are a great many different types of cells. Each kind usually specializes in one particular activity. For example, in animals some cells expand and contract; they are muscle cells. Cells that are sensitive to light form the retina (layer at the back of the eye) in humans and animals.

Cell structure
All cells are made up of three main parts: the cell membrane (the outer layer), the cytoplasm (the main body of the cell), and the nucleus (the core of the cell). Cytoplasm contains many complicated structures. This is where new cell material—more living matter—is produced and old material is broken down and expelled.

With a few exceptions, a single cell does not live very long. Most kinds of cell can divide into two new cells exactly like the original. This process is called cell division. As long as divisions continue, aging and death are postponed. As cells multiply in this way, the body they are part of continues to grow.

Anything that stops cell multiplication stops growth. Even in a grown human, cells are always dying and need to be replaced. In time, cell replacement becomes slower, and the body ages.

Enlarged, colored images of the three types of human blood cell—a platelet (blue), a white cell, and a red cell.

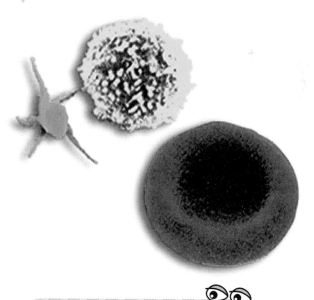

SEE ALSO: Blood; Eyes and Vision; Genetics; Heart and Circulatory System; Human Body; Microscopes; Plants

✳ CENTRAL AFRICA

The countries of Central Africa include Burundi, Cameroon, Central African Republic, Chad, Equatorial Guinea, Gabon, and Rwanda.

Land and climate

Central Africa's other countries are the Republic of Congo (Congo-Brazzaville), the Democratic Republic of Congo, and the islands of São Tomé and Príncipe.

The dominant feature of the region is the Congo River. Its vast basin straddles the equator, and the climate in lowland areas is hot and humid, with high seasonal rainfall. Its floodplains are home to forests, swamps, and grasslands.

Local farmers sell their produce at a market in Maroua, northern Cameroon. Agriculture plays an important role in the Central African economy.

People and history

For longer than recorded history, the forests of Central Africa have been home to peoples such as the Mbuti. Adults do not usually grow over 5 ft. (1.5 m). Europeans called them pygmies. Other peoples of the region include the Tutsi and Hutu in Rwanda and Burundi. Most native Central Africans speak one of the Bantu languages. The majority live in the country, often in small villages ruled by a chief.

Central Africa traded copper, salt, and textiles with other parts of Africa. In the 15th century, the Arabs brought the Islamic religion and took away slaves. In the 1880s, European powers divided up Central Africa. The colonies all gained their independence between 1960 and 1975.

SEE ALSO: Africa; Islam; Slavery

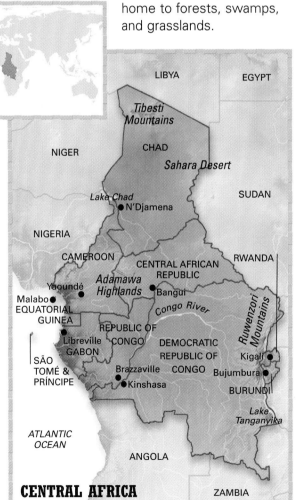

CENTRAL AFRICA

LIBYA
EGYPT
Tibesti Mountains
NIGER
CHAD
Sahara Desert
Lake Chad
N'Djamena
SUDAN
NIGERIA
CAMEROON
CENTRAL AFRICAN REPUBLIC
RWANDA
Yaoundé
Adamawa Highlands
Bangui
Malabo
EQUATORIAL GUINEA
Congo River
Ruwenzori Mountains
REPUBLIC OF CONGO
Libreville
GABON
DEMOCRATIC REPUBLIC OF CONGO
Kigali
SÃO TOMÉ & PRÍNCIPE
Brazzaville
Kinshasa
Bujumbura
BURUNDI
Lake Tanganyika
ATLANTIC OCEAN
ANGOLA
ZAMBIA

☀ CENTRAL AMERICA

Central America is an isthmus (a narrow bridge of land) that connects North and South America. It has coasts on the Pacific Ocean and the Caribbean Sea.

The term *Central America* generally refers to Guatemala, Honduras, El Salvador, Nicaragua, Costa Rica, and Panama—countries that share a common history. Geographically, Belize is included, although it has a very different history.

Land and climate

Most of Central America is either hilly or mountainous. There are many volcanoes, some of which are still active. Earthquakes are common. There are two main breaks in the mountains—one in Nicaragua and one in Panama. These two countries are mostly low-lying and have areas of dense jungle. Northern Guatemala and much of Belize are also jungle lowland. Most people in Guatemala, Honduras, Costa Rica, and El Salvador live in the highlands.

The Central American climate is tropical, and temperatures are generally high. The highland regions experience wet and dry seasons, but the low-lying regions have heavy rainfall throughout the year.

Plants and animals

Eastern lowland Central America is covered by rain forest. Southwestern Costa Rica has a rare habitat called cloud forest, which is dripping wet throughout the year. Native mammals include jaguars, ocelots, peccaries, and spider monkeys. North American animals such as pumas have migrated to the region. There are many reptiles, birds, and insects, although the wildlife is threatened by the growing human population.

People

Guatemala is a largely Indian nation. Its citizens are descendants of the Mayans, whose empire flourished in the region before the Europeans arrived. Honduras, El Salvador, and Nicaragua also have a strong Indian heritage, although the people today are mainly mestizo—of mixed Indian and European (chiefly Spanish) ancestry. The population of Costa Rica is mostly Spanish in origin. Many people in Belize are descended from black African slaves brought there from the West Indies. Panama has a mixture of all these groups.

▲
Central America was once home to the Mayan people, who were talented artists and sculptors. This figure is an incense burner.

◄
Volcán Poás is an active volcano in Costa Rica. It stands in a national park full of forest wildlife.

Economy

Central America is mainly an agricultural region. The chief export crops are coffee, bananas, and cotton. Sugarcane and rice flourish along the coast. Hemp (used in making rope) and chicle (used in chewing gum) are important products of the jungle regions. Forested areas provide valuable hardwoods such as mahogany.

The region has limited resources and one of the highest population growth rates in the world. Industry cannot provide enough jobs for the landless, and falling export prices make it harder for governments to meet the needs of their peoples.

The populations of most Central American countries have long been divided into wealthy landowners and poor campesinos (peasants). Land ownership is both the chief form of wealth and the main source of political power. The majority of the population depend on the big landowners for their living. Some campesinos can find work only in busy seasons of the year. Others labor on the big estates in return for the right to grow food for their families on a small patch of ground.

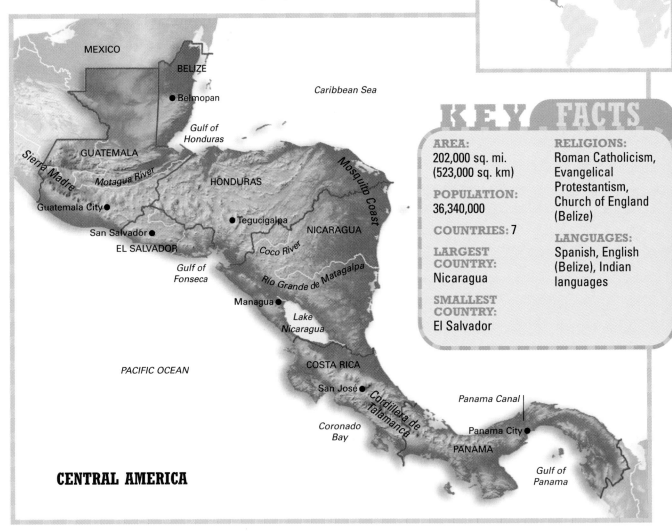

KEY FACTS

AREA:
202,000 sq. mi.
(523,000 sq. km)

POPULATION:
36,340,000

COUNTRIES: 7

LARGEST COUNTRY:
Nicaragua

SMALLEST COUNTRY:
El Salvador

RELIGIONS:
Roman Catholicism, Evangelical Protestantism, Church of England (Belize)

LANGUAGES:
Spanish, English (Belize), Indian languages

CENTRAL AMERICA

Map labels: MEXICO, BELIZE, Belmopan, Caribbean Sea, Gulf of Honduras, Sierra Madre, GUATEMALA, Motagua River, HONDURAS, Mosquito Coast, Guatemala City, Tegucigalpa, San Salvador, NICARAGUA, EL SALVADOR, Coco River, Gulf of Fonseca, Rio Grande de Matagalpa, Managua, Lake Nicaragua, PACIFIC OCEAN, COSTA RICA, San José, Cordillera de Talamanca, Panama Canal, Coronado Bay, Panama City, PANAMA, Gulf of Panama

The white-throated capuchin is a small monkey that lives in the forests of Central America.

between liberal and conservative groups. The disputes often led to civil wars and sometimes to military invasions of neighboring countries. By the early 1900s, some leaders had become dictators who stayed in office for long periods of time. They often used threats and violence to remain in power against the wishes of the people. Armies also grew powerful and usually supported the interests of the wealthy landowners.

Since World War II (1939–45), there have been revolutions across Central America led by people seeking social and economic change. New civilian governments were elected in Costa Rica in 1948; Guatemala, Honduras, and El Salvador in the 1980s; and Nicaragua in 1990.

Cars and pedestrians crowd a busy street in downtown San Salvador, the capital city of El Salvador.

History

Maya-speaking peoples have lived in the northern part of Central America for about 3,000 years. Mayan civilization reached its height from about A.D. 325 to 975.

Christopher Columbus sailed along the coast of Central America in 1502. The Spanish explorer Vasco Núñez de Balboa arrived in 1513. The Spanish conquered the region and controlled it for 300 years. In 1821 Guatemala, El Salvador, Honduras, Nicaragua, and Costa Rica became independent from Spain. Panama gained independence from Colombia in 1903. Belize was a British colony until 1981.

During the 1800s, much of Central America was torn by political struggles

SEE ALSO: Balboa, Vasco Núñez de; Columbus, Christopher; Guatemala; Mayans; North America, Geography; Panama; South America

✳ CENTRAL ASIA
The five republics of Central Asia—Kazakhstan, Kyrgyzstan, Tajikistan, Turkmenistan, and Uzbekistan—were parts of the former Soviet Union.

About two-thirds of Central Asia are desert. Kazakhstan is mostly steppe grassland, which is too dry for agriculture. The Aral Sea was once the world's fourth-largest body of inland water, but drainage has drastically reduced its size.

Most of the population lives along riverbanks or in the foothills of the south and southeast. Nearly all Central Asian languages are related to Turkish. Central Asia is mainly Muslim. Cotton is the largest crop. Most industry is in and

around the capital cities. Resources include natural gas in Turkmenistan and Uzbekistan and oil in Kazakhstan.

By 3500 B.C. the people of the steppes were the first in the world to ride horses. This gave them the military strength to conquer parts of China, India, and Europe. Russia controlled much of Central Asia in the 1500s. After the Russian Revolution of 1917, the area was split into five republics under Soviet control. In 1991 the republics declared independence.

A shepherd tends his flock on the upland plains of Kazakhstan.

SEE ALSO:
Asia; Russia and the Baltic States

120

✳ CENTRAL EUROPE

The countries of Central Europe are Austria, Germany, Switzerland, and tiny Liechtenstein.

Land, people, and economy

The far north of Central Europe is low, flat, and cold, with vast conifer forests. Farther south the land is very mountainous. The region is densely populated. Most people speak German, but Switzerland has three other official languages: French, Italian, and Romansch—an old, rarely spoken language derived from Latin. Most people in the region are Roman Catholics or Protestants. Industry is important in Central Europe. Germany is a leading industrial nation in the world and Europe's main automobile manufacturer. Tourism is strong in Austria, Switzerland, and Liechtenstein.

History

Germanic tribes have lived in Central Europe since the time of Christ. In A.D. 800 Charlemagne, the leader of the Frankish tribe, became emperor of a vast territory in Central and western Europe known as the Holy Roman Empire. This empire collapsed in 1806, and power passed to Germany and Austria-Hungary. These Central Powers, along with Turkey, were defeated in World War I (1914–18).

Under its leader Adolf Hitler, Germany fought again in World War II (1939–45). In 1938 Germany took control of Austria. Germany was split into the Communist-controlled German Democratic Republic

CENTRAL EUROPE

(East Germany) and the Federal Republic of Germany (West Germany) in 1949. The country was not reunited until 1990.

Switzerland has been a democracy for over 700 years. It has not fought in a war for nearly 200 years. The tiny state of Liechtenstein is ruled by a monarchy, but Switzerland represents it abroad.

The Limmat River flows through Zurich. The city is the center of Switzerland's banking and manufacturing.
▼

👀

SEE ALSO: Ancient Civilizations; Austria; Charlemagne; Communism; Eastern Europe; Europe; Germany; Middle Ages; Roman Empire; World War I; World War II

✳ CHAMPLAIN, SAMUEL DE (ABOUT 1567–1635)

Samuel de Champlain was the founder of Quebec and one of Canada's most famous explorers. His books tell vivid stories of life in the New World.

As an explorer and mapmaker, Champlain earned the title "Father of New France."

Champlain was born in Brouage, France. After an expedition to the West Indies, 1599–1601, he was appointed royal geographer to King Henry IV of France.

Champlain first visited Canada in 1603, sailing up the St. Lawrence River as far as present-day Montreal. He later mapped the Atlantic coast as far south as Cape Cod. In 1608 Champlain was sent to establish a fur-trading post at Quebec. He traveled westward across Lake Nipissing, Lake Huron, and Lake Ontario into New York, making the first known record of explorations of these regions.

In 1612 the fur companies appointed Champlain governor of Quebec. England and France went to war in 1628, and Champlain was forced to surrender his fort in 1629. He returned in 1633 and found Quebec in ruins. Champlain rebuilt the colony and started a settlement at Trois-Rivières on the St. Lawrence River.

SEE ALSO: Canada; Exploration and Explorers; North America, Geography

✳ CHARLEMAGNE (ABOUT 742–814)

Charlemagne was an important king in the Middle Ages. He ruled the Franks, a Germanic tribe, in what is now France, and built a great empire.

Charlemagne united much of Christian Europe into one state.

In 768 Charlemagne inherited half of his father's kingdom, which had grown to include much of western Europe. In 771, when his brother died, he became sole ruler of the Franks. He spent most of his reign expanding his lands and converting his subjects to Christianity. By 800 his kingdom covered most of modern France, Belgium, the Netherlands, Switzerland, Austria, western Germany, northern Italy, and parts of Spain and eastern Europe.

Charlemagne encouraged farming, trade, and religion, and developed a code of laws. He was particularly interested in education and created a palace school at Aachen (in modern Germany). In 800 Pope Leo III placed a crown on Charlemagne's head, declaring him emperor of the Romans, successor of the great Caesars of ancient Rome.

Charlemagne left his kingdom to his son, Louis I. After Louis's death, the empire was divided among his three sons. The modern nations of western Europe came from these kingdoms.

SEE ALSO: Central Europe; France; Middle Ages; Roman Empire

✳ CHAUCER, GEOFFREY (ABOUT 1340–1400)

Geoffrey Chaucer was medieval England's greatest writer. He put much humor and feeling into the tales he wrote about the lives of ordinary people.

Geoffrey Chaucer was the son of a London wine merchant. In 1356 he became a page in the household of Prince Lionel, a son of Edward III. A military expedition took him to France, where he was taken prisoner. He returned to England in 1360 and later married one of the queen's attendants.

Chaucer composed his first long poem, *The Book of the Duchess* (1369), on the death of a prince's wife. It was written in the poetic style then popular in France. About 1386 he began the *Canterbury Tales*. It is in the form of a very long poem and is about a group of Christian pilgrims traveling to a shrine at Canterbury. Each pilgrim is a colorful, unique character who tells a story during the journey.

Chaucer took ideas from many other works, but he wrote in an entirely original way—with earthy humor and deep insight. His verse is in a style of English no longer used today, with unfamiliar words. For many readers, this adds to the character of the language.

Chaucer was one of the first great European writers to use humor in his work.

SEE ALSO: Literature; Middle Ages

✳ CHAVEZ, CESAR (1927–93)

Cesar Chavez fought for the rights of Mexican-American farm laborers. He founded the union that became the United Farm Workers.

Cesar Estrada Chavez was born in Yuma, Arizona. He spent his childhood as a migrant farmworker and then served in the United States Navy. From 1952 he began working with immigrants in California, encouraging them to register as voters, and helping with immigration problems. At the time, many immigrants worked on farms in bad conditions and for low wages.

In 1962 Chavez began to organize the National Farm Workers Association. By 1965, 1,200 families had joined. Chavez used nonviolent tactics, such as fasting, to draw attention to his campaign. His inspiration was the Indian leader Mohandas Gandhi.

Chavez arranged strikes and boycotts of farm produce. These efforts persuaded growers to sign contracts with union members. The union later became known as the United Farm Workers, and joined AFL–CIO, the main union movement in the United States.

After his death, Chavez was awarded the Presidential Medal of Freedom, the highest civilian honor in the United States.

Labor leader Cesar Chavez in 1989. He was awarded the Medal of Freedom posthumously, in 1994.

SEE ALSO: Gandhi, Mohandas; Hispanic Americans; Labor

✳ CHEMISTRY

Chemistry is the science that deals with the structure and properties of substances and the changes that these substances undergo.

Atomic theory is one of the most fundamental parts of the science of chemistry. It states that all substances are made up of tiny particles far too small to be seen with even the strongest microscopes. These tiny particles are called atoms. Everything—glass, brick, iron, water, the stars, and your own body—is made up of atoms.

There are many kinds of atoms. So far scientists know of at least 114 different types. Most of them are quite rare. Only about a dozen kinds of atoms are common on Earth.

Then how can there be so many different things on Earth? The answer is that atoms are like the letters of the alphabet—all English words are built out of only 26 letters. Even just a few kinds of atoms can combine into many different arrangements. Each arrangement makes up a different substance.

Chemical and physical changes
Understanding how substances can change is essential to understanding chemistry. Not all changes are chemical changes, however.

For example, you can break up a bar of iron into tiny pieces. Each piece is still iron because the arrangement of atoms has not been changed. This is a physical change. You can magnetize a piece of iron, or let an electric current pass through it. These, too, are physical changes.

Chemical changes—sometimes also called chemical reactions—are different. If you heat a mixture of powdered iron and sulfur, for example, a blackish material forms in which you can no longer see separate bits of grayish iron or yellow sulfur. The new material has a new set of properties unlike those of either iron or sulfur. It is a substance called ferrous sulfide. When the iron and sulfur were heated, each sulfur atom combined with an iron atom, forming molecules of ferrous sulfide. A new arrangement of atoms was formed, and it made up a new substance with new properties.

Chemical changes go on all around us. Whenever coal or oil burns, that is a chemical change. The rusting of iron is a chemical change. When food is cooked, it goes through many chemical changes.

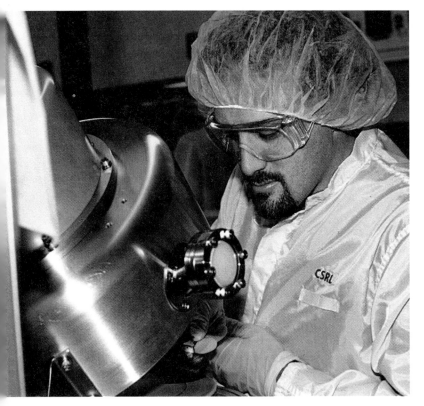

A researcher using a device that can detect and analyze tiny amounts of chemicals. ▼

Making heat, for example on a stove or in an oven, is a chemical change, or a reaction between fuel and air. Using the heat to cook food makes further chemical changes.

Chemical changes also go on inside the body at all times. These are the many kinds of changes that interest a chemist.

Branches of chemistry
Chemistry overlaps many other sciences. For example, some chemists might want to know how fast reactions go and what can be done to change their speed. They might want to know how a salt solution can carry an electric current. Questions like these are answered by using methods similar to those used by scientists called physicists. This branch of chemistry is called physical chemistry.

Chemists also study the many chemical processes that take place inside living organisms. They might want to know how foods are broken down and digested in the body, or how to change the chemical abilities of tiny bacteria, for example. Their field of study is called biochemistry.

The study of compounds containing carbon is called organic chemistry

because carbon comes from living or once-living organisms. The study of other compounds is called inorganic chemistry. Analytical chemistry identifies and studies the different chemical substances that make up mixtures.

Specialized branches of chemistry include astrochemistry—the study of the origin and interaction of chemicals in space. Geochemistry deals with the chemical properties of the earth. It is related to geology and is used in areas such as mineral-ore processing. Nuclear chemistry is concerned with nuclear power and the safe disposal of nuclear wastes. Environmental chemistry focuses on the effect of chemicals on the natural world.

Chemistry is put to use in the search for new energy sources, in efforts to fight disease, to improve agricultural yields, and to increase the world's food supply. Chemistry, in fact, touches many parts of our lives and has been put to use since human history began.

SEE ALSO:
Atoms and
Molecules;
Biology;
Cells;
Elements;
Geology;
Matter;
Nuclear
Power;
Physics;
Scientists

* CHIEF JOSEPH (1840–1904)

Joseph, born In-mut-too-yah-lat-lat ("Thunder Rolling in the Heights"), was chief of the Nez Percé people and a brilliant military leader.

Chief Joseph, aged about 50. He became chief when he was 31, after the death of the previous chief, his father.

Joseph was born in the Wallowa Valley in what is now Oregon. In 1863 the government ordered the Nez Percé to move from their traditional lands to a reservation in Idaho. For 13 years, the Nez Percé ignored the order, but the situation became worse when gold was discovered in the area. In 1877 the government sent agents to enforce the removal.

Joseph had become chief of the Nez Percé in 1871, when his father died. He decided to escape with his people into Canada. For more than three months he led them on a 1,000-mile (1,600-km) journey across the Rockies. On the way,

despite being outnumbered ten to one, he fought and won more than a dozen battles against some of the Army's best officers. About 30 miles (50 km) from the Canadian border, troops commanded by General Nelson A. Miles attacked the Nez Percé. Chief Joseph surrendered on October 5, and Miles promised that his people could return to their native lands.

Miles's promise was broken, however. Despite Joseph's efforts, the Nez Percé were sent to a reservation in Oklahoma. Joseph died in Washington in 1904.

SEE ALSO: Native Americans

* CHILDREN'S AUTHORS

Today many books are written especially for young readers. Children have also taken over a few adult books as their own.

Books were expensive items before the printing press was invented in the 1400s. Few people could read, and tales, nursery rhymes, and songs were passed on by recitation or song. Even after printed books became available, it was years before books were produced especially for children. One of the first was a picture book called *The Visible World in Pictures*, published in English in 1659. Printers also produced little booklets called chapbooks that sold for a penny each. Most were for

Children's literature has often featured magical figures such as this witch in Rapunzel.

adults, but some had stories that appealed to children. Books for children at this time often had a strong moral or religious tone.

The first fairy tales
In 1697 a collection of eight stories was published in France. It included "Cinderella," "The Sleeping Beauty," and "Little Red Riding Hood." In 1729 it was published in English with the title *Tales of Mother Goose*. A London publisher, John Newbery (1713–67), saw that there was a market for books aimed at children. In 1744 he published *A Little Pretty Pocket-Book*, a tiny book full of fables and poems.

FAMOUS CHILDREN'S AUTHORS

These are just a few of the most famous children's authors. The "see also" box indicates some other important ones.

Grimm, Jacob (1785–1863), and **Grimm, Wilhelm** (1786–1859)
German scholars who put together a collection of folk stories widely translated as *Grimm's Fairy Tales*.

Alcott, Louisa May (1832–88)
American novelist whose *Little Women* (1868–69) related the everyday lives of four teenage sisters.

Carroll, Lewis (Charles Lutwidge Dodgson) (1832–98)
Clergyman and tutor at Oxford University, England, who wrote *Alice's Adventures in Wonderland* (1865), a masterpiece of "nonsense" literature.

Stevenson, Robert Louis (1850–94)
Scottish author of adventure stories, including *Treasure Island* (1883) and *Kidnapped* (1886).

Barrie, J. M. (James Matthew) (1860–1937)
Scottish novelist and playwright. His play *Peter Pan*, about a boy who would not grow up, was first performed in 1904.

Potter, Beatrix (1866–1943)
English author who wrote and illustrated books with animals as characters, such as the tales of Peter Rabbit and Jemima Puddle-duck.

Milne, A. A. (Alan Alexander) (1882–1956)
English author of *Winnie-the-Pooh* (1926) and *The House at Pooh Corner* (1928).

Lewis, C. S. (Cyril Staples) (1898–1963)
English literature tutor at Oxford University, England. His tales of Narnia are full of Christian references.

Dahl, Roald (1916–90)
English author of humorous books, including *Charlie and the Chocolate Factory* (1964) and *The Witches* (1983).

Blume, Judy (1938–)
American author best known for books that deal with issues facing young people.

Rowling, J. K. (Joanne Kathleen) (1965–)
English author (right) whose Harry Potter novels, about a boy's adventures at a school for wizards, are popular with both adults and children.

It was so successful that he published more books, including the *History of Little Goody Two-Shoes* (1765). It was probably the first book written for children, with illustrations drawn especially for it. Since 1922 the John Newbery Medal has been awarded annually by the American Library Association (ALA) to the author of the most distinguished American children's book of the year.

In the 1800s, more books written for children appeared. *Grimm's Fairy Tales* were folktales collected by the Grimm brothers in Germany. From Denmark came Hans Christian Andersen's *Fairy Tales and Stories*. In England Edward Lear's *Book of Nonsense* (1846) was a collection of amusing short poems illustrated with cartoons by the author. *Alice's Adventures in Wonderland* by Lewis Carroll was published in 1865.

Color picture books
Until the 1860s, all illustrations in children's books were black-and-white. Then the English printer Edmund Evans brought out nursery rhyme picture books with color illustrations by Walter Crane. Another artist who worked on children's books was Randolph Caldecott (1846–86). Since 1938 the Caldecott Medal has been awarded annually by the ALA to the artist of the most distinguished American picture book for children. ➡

The Mad Hatter's tea party in Alice's Adventures in Wonderland by Lewis Carroll.

New realism

By the late 1800s, the dividing line had become less clear between books written especially for children, adult books with children as their leading characters, and books meant for adults that became popular with children. Important novels of this time were Harriet Beecher Stowe's *Uncle Tom's Cabin* (1852), Louisa May Alcott's *Little Women* (1868–69), and Mark Twain's *Adventures of Tom Sawyer* (1876).

The number of books for children greatly increased in the 1900s. Stories for older children began to deal with harsher subjects, such as children abandoned by their parents, divorce, old age, and death.

Fantasy continued to be a popular trend in children's books. In many fantasy tales, animals behave like humans, as in *Charlotte's Web*. Written in 1952 by E. B. White, this is perhaps the most popular American children's book. In other fantasies, strange things happen to the child hero or heroine. In the Harry Potter books by J. K. Rowling, Harry escapes his grim home to enter a school for wizards.

SEE ALSO: Andersen, Hans Christian; Myths and Legends; Seuss, Dr.; Twain, Mark; White, E. B.; Wilder, Laura Ingalls

✳ CHILE

Chile lies along the southwestern coast of South America, separated from Argentina by the Andes, one of the world's highest mountain chains.

Land and climate

Chile stretches more than 2,600 miles (4,180 km) from north to south but averages only 100 miles (160 km) in width. It is generally cold and rainy in the south and hot and dry in the north.

In parts of the Atacama Desert, no rainfall has ever been recorded. This area attracts settlers because of its mineral deposits.

The Central Valley lies between the Andes and a range of coastal mountains. The soil is fertile, and the climate is mild. Over two-thirds of the population live in this region, mainly in the cities of Santiago and Valparaíso. Most of Chile's industry is also located here, as are most of the big farms.

Chile claims parts of Antarctica but this is not recognized internationally. The official boundary stops at Cape Horn. Chile and Argentina share the island of Tierra del Fuego (Land of Fire). Chile owns other islands off its west coast, including the Juan Fernández Islands and Easter Island, which is known for the great stone heads that people there carved long ago.

People

The Chilean people are mainly of mixed Indian, Spanish, and other European descent. The remaining true Indians number only about 500,000. About 85 percent of the population live in cities and urban areas. A huge gap still separates the

KEY FACTS

OFFICIAL NAME:
República de Chile

AREA:
292,257 sq. mi.
(756,945 sq. km)

POPULATION:
15,211,000

**CAPITAL &
LARGEST CITY:**
Santiago

**MAJOR
RELIGION:**
Roman Catholicism

**MAJOR
LANGUAGE:**
Spanish

CURRENCY:
Peso

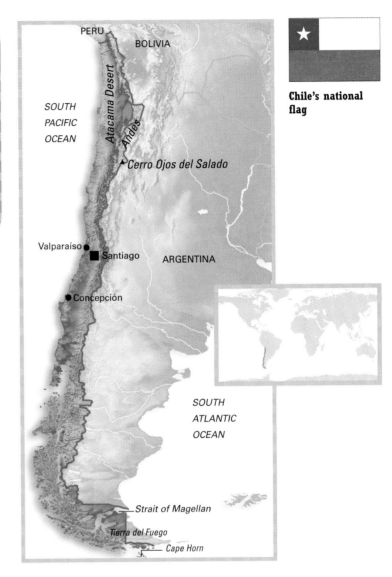

Chile's national flag

few rich people from the many poor. Wealthy Chileans own the factories, banks, and large farms and ranches.

In the cities, there is a growing middle class of doctors, teachers, clerks, and soldiers. Poor Chileans live in rural shacks or city slums. They try to earn a living as farmhands, miners, factory workers, and laborers. However, one in four of all Chileans has no job.

Economy

Farming employs about 20 percent of the Chilean workforce. Fruits, wines, and vegetables are among Chile's leading agricultural exports. Chile is the world's largest producer of copper. Other important metals are molybdenum, iron ore, gold, and silver. Iodine and boron are valuable by-products of nitrate mining. Processed foods, wood and wood products (including paper), textiles, and

◄ *Archaeologists puzzle over the massive stone statues on Easter Island, which is owned by Chile. But nobody knows the origin of the stones.*

transportation equipment and machinery are some of the chief manufactured products. Commercial fishing is also a major industry.

History

Indians lived in Chile for thousands of years before the Spanish arrived in the 16th century. The first Spaniards came to Chile from Peru, looking for riches. The Indians struggled against Spanish conquest for two centuries, although after 100 years, fighting and disease had reduced their number by two-thirds. ➡

Independence

When the French invaded Spain in 1808, they removed the Spanish king. Chileans founded their own government in 1810. After several battles with the Spanish, Chile became independent in 1818.

Chileans then fought one another for control. Periods of stability alternated with war. In 1925 Chile adopted a new constitution with a strong presidency.

In 1973 the Chilean military, led by General Pinochet, overthrew President Allende. The Pinochet regime restored economic stability but committed many human rights abuses. In 1988 Pinochet

A view of Constitution Plaza, the main square in the center of Santiago, Chile's capital city. ▶

was rejected as president, paving the way for a democratic election.

SEE ALSO: Incas; South America

* CHINA

The People's Republic of China is home to one-fifth of the world's population and is the world's third-largest country in area.

Land and climate

China's geography is varied. The north, where the Huang He (Yellow River) flows, is cold and dry. The south, which includes Guangzhou (Canton) and Hong Kong, is much warmer. The two areas are divided by the Chang Jiang (Yangtze), the third-longest river in the world.

Chinese pilots in 1969 holding up Mao Zedong's "Little Red Book" of his thoughts. ▼

History

From ancient times, Chinese rulers have passed power to brothers or sons, forming dynasties, or ruling families. China's name comes from the Ch'in (Qin) dynasty, founded in 221 B.C.

For many centuries, China was far ahead of Europe in terms of prosperity, technical and scientific knowledge, art, and culture. The Chinese invented many things, such as gunpowder, paper, and printing, long before they were known in the West.

In the 13th century, the Venetian explorer Marco Polo visited the court of the Emperor Kublai Khan. The Portuguese reached China by sea in the 1500s. But it was not until the 19th century that China traded widely with Europe.

The last emperor was forced out in 1912, and China became a republic. The first president was Sun Yat-sen, who led a party named the Kuomintang. In 1949, after a civil war, the Communists, led by Mao Zedong, took control. The Kuomintang leader, Chiang Kai-shek, fled to Taiwan. In 1950 China invaded and occupied Tibet. However, many people still do not recognize Chinese authority there.

China's national flag

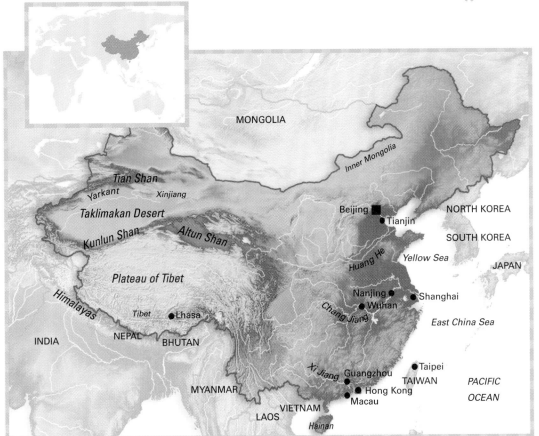

MONGOLIA

Inner Mongolia

Tian Shan

Yarkant   Xinjiang

Taklimakan Desert

Kunlun Shan   Altun Shan

Plateau of Tibet

Himalayas

Tibet ●Lhasa

INDIA   NEPAL   BHUTAN

MYANMAR

VIETNAM

LAOS

Hainan

Xi Jiang Guangzhou TAIWAN PACIFIC
●Hong Kong   OCEAN
Macau

Beijing■ ●Tianjin   NORTH KOREA
                      SOUTH KOREA

Huang He   Yellow Sea   JAPAN

Nanjing● ●Shanghai
●Wuhan
Chang Jiang   East China Sea

Taipei

In the 1960s, Mao Zedong launched the Cultural Revolution. Young people were made to join the Red Guards and encouraged to publicly criticize those teachers and parents who were not committed to the Communist Party.

For many years, the United States did not recognize the People's Republic of China. Then in 1972 President Richard M. Nixon became the first president to visit the country. The United States officially recognized China in 1979.

After Mao Zedong's death in 1976, the government began to introduce capitalism to China. However, that did not mean the people were free to do what they liked. When students demonstrated for political reforms in Beijing's Tiananmen Square in 1989, the government sent in soldiers and

Part of the Great Wall of China, which was built in ancient times to keep out invaders from the north. ▼

KEY FACTS

OFFICIAL NAME: People's Republic of China

AREA: 3,696,527 sq. mi. (9,573,998 sq. km)

POPULATION: 1,284,958,000

CAPITAL: Beijing

LARGEST CITY: Shanghai

MAJOR RELIGIONS: Buddhism, folk religions

MAJOR LANGUAGE: Chinese (Mandarin dialect official)

CURRENCY: Yuan

to itself as the Republic of China. Hong Kong and Macau are both in southern China. Macau was ruled by Portugal from 1557, and Hong Kong became a British colony in 1842. Both were returned to China in the 1990s.

Economy
China has a long tradition of farming. It produces one-third of the world's rice and 40 percent of the world's pigs. The government is aiming to modernize its economy and to expand industry.

A decorated dragon boat on the water in Beijing, China's capital city.

tanks to crush the demonstrations. Hundreds of people were killed.

Taiwan, Hong Kong, and Macau
The People's Republic still sees Taiwan as part of China. However, Taiwan has its own government and economy and refers

SEE ALSO: Ancient Civilizations; Asia; Communism; Marco Polo

✳ CHOPIN, FRÉDÉRIC (1810–49)
Chopin was one of the greatest composers for the piano. The short solo works for which he is best known are like beautifully crafted musical poems.

Chopin began learning the piano when he was only six years old.

Frédéric François Chopin was born near Warsaw, Poland, on March 1, 1810. His mother was Polish, and his father was a Frenchman and a teacher.

As an infant, Chopin heard his mother and sister play the piano. Soon his amazing talent began to show. He played a difficult piano concerto in public when he was only eight years old, and at 15 he published his first composition.

In 1829 Chopin began a concert tour around Europe. His playing won such high praise in Paris that he decided to settle there for life. He never returned to Poland.

In Paris, Chopin played at concerts and taught piano. But above all, he composed. Soon he was recognized as the greatest piano composer of his time. His expressive and melodic music is considered part of the Romantic Age. His best works are compositions for the piano, which include waltzes and Polish dance styles such as polonaises and mazurkas.

While still a young man, Chopin developed tuberculosis. The disease finally took his life on October 17, 1849, at age 39.

SEE ALSO: Music

✳ CHRISTIANITY

Christianity is the world's largest religion, with approximately two billion followers. It is practiced in virtually every country on Earth.

The word *Christianity* comes from the Greek *Christos,* meaning the "chosen one," a translation of the Hebrew *Moshiach,* or "messiah." Christianity is based on the life and teachings of Jesus Christ (about 4 B.C.–A.D. 30), a Jewish preacher who is believed to have lived in Palestine, a province of the Roman Empire, about 2,000 years ago.

According to the Bible, the holy book of Christianity, Jesus preached to the common people that religion was not just something practiced by the priests, but was a moral code that should govern all their thoughts and actions. The Romans were afraid that Jesus was stirring up rebellion. They had him arrested, tried, and crucified (put to death on a cross).

After the crucifixion, Jesus's followers began to spread his message throughout the empire. Despite persecution in the early years, Christianity grew. By 394 it had become the official religion of the Roman Empire.

Splits in the church
In 1054 the Christian church divided into eastern and western branches. This was the result of conflicting beliefs and political rivalries. The eastern branch became the Orthodox Church. The western branch became the Roman Catholic Church, headed by the pope. By the 1500s, the Roman Catholic Church was very powerful and rich. In northern Europe, churchmen began a movement for reform, known as the Reformation. By 1650 Europe was divided between Catholics and Protestants.

Americas
The first European settlements in the Americas were Catholic. With the Reformation, the New World became a site of conflict between Protestant England and Catholic Spain and France. There were also clashes between different Protestant sects. After the creation of the United States, the Constitution guaranteed freedom of religion.

Christians believe in one God who is represented as a trinity, or single deity with three parts: the Father, the Son, and the Holy Spirit. Most Christians believe that Jesus Christ, the Son, was the human form of God, who came to Earth to save people from sin.

A stained-glass window from the 14th century showing Christ on the cross, with his mother, Mary, and St. John.

DID YOU KNOW?

Early Christians used the fish as a secret symbol to identify themselves. Fish symbols were also used to indicate the secret meeting places of the Christians.

SEE ALSO:
Bible;
Middle Ages;
Reformation;
Religions;
Roman Empire

✳**CIRCULATORY SYSTEM** 👀➡ ✳ **HEART AND CIRCULATORY SYSTEM**

✻ CIRCUSES AND CARNIVALS

The origins of the circus date back thousands of years. The carnival had its origin hundreds of years ago in the feasting and merrymaking before Lent.

Circus

Pottery found in ancient ruins depicts acrobats, jugglers, and trained bears. In ancient Rome, an arena called the Circus Maximus was the scene of chariot races and other feats of skill and daring. However, the modern circus developed in England. In 1768 a riding instructor named Philip Astley found that he could ride standing up if his horse cantered in a circle of a certain size at a constant speed while both he and the horse were leaning slightly inward. This led to the circus ring. One day Astley interrupted his feats with some clowning. The audience laughed at the sight of a bumbling rider trying to climb on a horse—and falling off.

On August 27, 1785, Thomas Pool put on the first American circus in Philadelphia, Pennsylvania. One of the best-known names in American circus history is that of P. T. Barnum (1810–91). In 1871 he organized a traveling circus called the "Greatest Show on Earth." Ten years later, Barnum teamed up with James A. Bailey to create the Barnum & Bailey Circus.

A poster from 1895 advertising the Barnum & Bailey Circus.

Carnival

The word *carnival* comes from the Latin expression *carne vale!* ("flesh, farewell!"). Carnivals are still held each year in Europe and the Americas to mark the start of Lent, a time when some Christians give up meat or treats such as candy. Among the most famous carnivals are those of Munich, Germany, and Rio de Janeiro, Brazil. Carnivals often include parades of colorful floats, street dancing, fireworks, and fancy-dress balls.

The carnival season begins officially on Twelfth Night (January 6). But most of the celebrating occurs on Fat Tuesday, just before the beginning of Lent.

Traveling carnivals

Carnivals that move from town to town originated in the United States in the late 1890s. Traveling carnivals always play outdoors, and their season runs from early spring to late fall. The "front end" of the show lot is lined with refreshment stands, with everything from cotton candy to hot dogs, and games of skill and chance, with prizes for the winners. At the "back end" of the lot are the rides, such as the merry-go-round, and often a huge fun house.

DID YOU KNOW?

The French call the last carnival before Lent "Mardi Gras," or "Fat Tuesday," from the custom of using up cooking fats on the day before Lent. The most famous U.S. Mardi Gras is held in New Orleans, LA.

SEE ALSO: Holidays and Festivals

✳ CITIES
Cities are the largest communities in which people live and work. People live in cities because they find something there that they want or need.

Cities originally developed on sites where people could obtain regular supplies of food from the surrounding area. Some were on hills, which made them easy to defend. Some were near a source of water. Others grew up where trade routes crossed or around shrines built to gods. The earliest cities were formed in Mesopotamia (modern Iraq) in about 4500 B.C. The greatest city of ancient times was Rome, the capital of present-day Italy, which ruled much of Europe from 50 B.C. to A.D. 476.

Cities today
Cities usually house the offices of major business and government organizations, as well as universities, museums, and places of worship. Because cities are so crowded, land is expensive, and people often live in apartment buildings. Transport can also be a problem, with traffic jams, pollution, and noise. Despite this, many people choose to live in cities.

▲
A nighttime view of Seoul, South Korea, which has grown from a population of one million in 1945 to over 10 million.

LARGEST U.S. CITIES		THE WORLD'S LARGEST CITIES	
	Population		*Population*
1. New York City, NY	21,199,865	**1.** Tokyo, Japan	26,500,000
2. Los Angeles, CA	16,373,645	**2.** São Paolo, Brazil	18,300,000
3. Chicago, IL	9,157,540	**3.** Mexico City, Mexico	18,300,000
4. San Francisco, CA	7,039,362	**4.** New York City, U.S.	16,800,000
5. Philadelphia, PA	6,188,463	**5.** Mumbai (Bombay), India	16,500,000
6. Boston, MA	5,819,100	**6.** Los Angeles, U.S.	13,300,000
7. Detroit, MI	5,456,428	**7.** Kolkata (Calcutta), India	13,300,000
8. Dallas, TX	5,221,801	**8.** Dhaka, Bangladesh	13,200,000
9. Washington, D.C.	4,923,153	**9.** Delhi, India	13,000,000
10. Houston, TX	4,669,571	**10.** Shanghai, China	12,800,000

Figures for metropolitan areas (city center and surrounding built-up area) from the U.S. Census for 2000. The U.S. defines these areas in a different way than the United Nations.

Figures for agglomerations (the city and its suburbs) from the United Nations in 2001. These calculations give smaller populations for New York and Los Angeles than the U.S. Census.

SEE ALSO:
Ancient Civilizations;
Roman Empire;
Towns and Villages

✳ CITIZENSHIP

A citizen is an official member of a political body, such as a country. Citizenship includes a wide range of rights and responsibilities.

Living in a country does not necessarily make someone a citizen of that country. For most people, citizenship is determined by the country where they are born or by the nationality of their parents. Citizens of one country who live in a foreign country are known as aliens. Their rights and duties are determined by political treaties and by the laws of the country in which they stay.

Being a citizen

The idea of citizenship is very old. In the city-state of Athens, in ancient Greece, citizenship was granted to males of certain classes. It meant that a man could vote, take part in government, and serve in the military. Women, slaves, and most foreigners did not have such rights. Over the years, the idea of citizenship developed. Today citizenship gives protection under the law and often grants rights such as schooling and welfare. Citizens are also able to vote and to run for political office. In exchange, adult citizens usually have to pay taxes, be available for jury service, and in some cases perform military service.

Democracy

This is the model of citizenship under a democratic system. Democracy is another idea first proposed in ancient Greece. It means rule by the people, rather than by an individual or a small group. It is based on the belief that all should have the same

Immigrants to the United States at a naturalization ceremony held in Seattle, Washington, in 1994.

rights and freedoms and that people should be free to govern themselves. In the modern world, democracy takes many forms. However, it usually means that all adult citizens can vote to choose their representatives in government. They can also run for election themselves. Another important feature of democracy is freedom of speech. This means that citizens are free to express an opinion without fear of punishment. Other privileges of democracy include religious and political freedom.

Many people do not live in democratic states. They cannot change their governments by peaceful means. Often they are not allowed to speak out against the government. Nondemocratic governments may use police and military force to punish those who oppose them.

Elections

In a democratic society, citizens have a say in who will be in government. The process that allows people to make their choice is called an election, and the act of choosing is called voting. Usually the person or group with the most votes takes office. In the United States, the most important elections are for the presidency, held every four years.

In most countries, citizens running for office join a political party, a group that shares views about how society should work. Some political parties campaign for lower taxes. Others campaign for the rights of ethnic or religious groups. In the United States, the two main parties are the Republicans and the Democrats.

U.S. citizenship

The first official written explanation of American citizenship was included in the

Americans put their votes in a ballot box as they vote for a president in 2000.

14th Amendment to the Constitution (1868). Section 1 of this amendment declares that "All persons born or naturalized in the United States, and subject to the jurisdiction thereof, are citizens of the United States and of the State wherein they reside." This wording places national citizenship before state citizenship. In other words, Americans are first citizens of the United States and then citizens of the state in which they live.

Naturalization is the legal way in which people change their citizenship. Usually any person who has entered the United States as a legal immigrant may become a naturalized citizen. They must be over 18 years old and have lived in the United States for five years and for at least six months in the state where they apply. Applicants must pass an examination and take an oath of allegiance. Naturalized citizens have all of the rights granted to natural-born citizens, except that they may not become president or vice president.

SEE ALSO: Constitution, United States; Greece, Ancient; United States Government

❋ CIVIL RIGHTS

Everyone wants freedom, equality, and justice. The term *civil rights* refers to guarantees by law of fair and equal treatment for all people.

Other terms, such as *civil liberties* and *human rights,* are often used to mean the same thing. Civil rights include freedom of speech, religion, and assembly (meeting together for a common purpose); the right to take part in the political process (to vote); and the right to fair and equal treatment under the law.

In the United States, the civil rights movement refers to the campaign for civil rights fought by African Americans in the 1950s and 1960s.

Threats to civil rights
Governments often try to restrict people's civil rights. In a dictatorship (that is, rule by one party, the army, or a single leader), the rights of the people are often reduced. It may be that they are not allowed to vote freely. Even in democracies the government may attempt to hold onto its power by silencing its critics. It may try to censor or control radio and television, newspapers, books, and movies.

Because people's civil rights have been threatened throughout history, most countries recognize that laws are required to protect them. Many nations have drawn up legal documents listing the rights guaranteed to their citizens. The first such document in the West was the Magna Carta (1215), which forced the king of England to grant certain rights to his barons. Many centuries later, in 1689, the English Parliament, or legislative body, passed a law that included a bill of rights. The law made Parliament, which represented the people, more powerful than the king and ensured that the people would have certain basic liberties.

The Bill of Rights
When the first U.S. Congress met in 1789, it proposed a bill of rights similar to the English one. The Bill of Rights became law in 1791. However, it did not guarantee equal treatment for all. For example, until slavery was abolished in 1865, African Americans had no legal rights whatsoever.

Although later amendments to the Constitution abolished slavery, made ex-slaves citizens, and gave African-American men the right to vote, prejudice against blacks meant that the new laws often were ignored. Many states, particularly in the South, passed laws that segregated (separated) blacks from whites in public life. For more than half a century, these laws effectively gave whites legal permission to treat blacks as second-class citizens. In 1954 the Supreme Court ruled that racial segregation in public schools was unconstitutional.

King John signing the Magna Carta in 1215. The charter gave certain rights and liberties to the English barons.

Rosa Parks in 1956 sitting in the front of a bus. Blacks were supposed to sit at the back and give up their seats to white people. When Rosa Parks refused to do this in 1955, she sparked the modern civil rights movement.

In 1955 a black seamstress in Alabama named Rosa Parks refused to give her seat on a bus to a white man. Parks was arrested. Blacks in Alabama launched a boycott of the bus system and chose a young minister, Dr. Martin Luther King Jr., to lead their protest.

Civil rights movement

Many African Americans began to press for desegregation and civil rights. King and thousands of others were repeatedly jailed for protesting racial segregation. On August 28, 1963, more than 200,000 people of all races gathered at the Lincoln Memorial in Washington, D.C., to urge the government to take action against racial discrimination and segregation. King made a stirring speech that appealed for justice.

On July 2, 1964, President Lyndon B. Johnson signed into law the Civil Rights Act. The bill protected every citizen's right to use public facilities, to seek work, and to vote. However, many law-enforcement officers, particularly in the South, failed to protect the rights of blacks at the polls. This prompted another demonstration, in 1965, in which 30,000 blacks and whites, led by Dr. King, marched from Selma to Montgomery, Alabama. This resulted in the Voting Rights Act of 1965, which did away with literacy tests or payment as a requirement for voting.

DID YOU KNOW?

On August 28, 1963, Martin Luther King Jr. made a famous speech that is known as *"I have a dream"* because that was one of its key phrases. Here are two excerpts from the speech:

"I have a dream that my four little children will one day live in a nation where they will not be judged by the color of their skin but by the content of their character."

"When we let freedom ring, when we let it ring from every village and every hamlet, from every state and every city, we will be able to speed up that day when all of God's children, black men and white men, Jews and Gentiles, Protestants and Catholics, will be able to join hands and sing in the words of the old Negro spiritual, 'Free at last! Free at last! Thank God Almighty, we are free at last!'"

SEE ALSO:
African Americans; Bill of Rights; Citizenship; Constitution, United States; Human Rights; King, Martin Luther, Jr.; Parks, Rosa; Slavery; World Government

✳ CIVIL WAR

The American Civil War was a four-year war (1861–65) between the federal government of the United States and 11 rebel Southern states.

There were many reasons for the outbreak of war. Tensions had been rising between Northern and Southern states for many years, mainly because of the differences between their economies.

In the South, farmers grew tobacco and cotton on large plantations, using slaves to work the land. Trade in black slaves from Africa began in the early 17th century. For years the whole country practiced slavery, but it mostly disappeared in the North. In the South, however, as demand for cotton and tobacco increased, planters needed more slaves. A way of life developed based on whites being able to buy and sell blacks. Blacks had few or no rights.

Union troops in the trenches at Petersburg, Virginia, during General Grant's nine-month siege of the city in 1864.

As the United States grew in the early 1800s, slave owners wanted to be able to take slaves to new territories, such as California. But many people in the North firmly opposed any expansion by slave owners. By the 1850s, some Northerners were calling for the abolition of slavery, while some Southern states were threatening to leave (secede from) the Union to protect their right to keep slaves.

Secession

In 1860 the Republican Party picked Abraham Lincoln as its candidate for president. Because Lincoln opposed the spread of slavery, Southerners saw him as an enemy. When he won the election, South Carolina left the Union. Mississippi, Florida, Alabama, Georgia, and Louisiana followed. They established a new nation, the Confederate States of America, with Jefferson Davis as president.

Virginia, Arkansas, Tennessee, Texas, and North Carolina later joined the original Confederate states. In the border states of Kentucky and Missouri, Unionists and Secessionists fought for control.

War began on April 12, 1861, when the Confederates fired on the Union's Fort Sumter in Charleston, South Carolina.

Both sides began to organize their armies. In July 1861 the first major battle of the war was fought at Bull Run, Virginia. It ended in a huge defeat of the Northern forces, but it settled nothing.

Although both sides had initial victories, the Confederates gained the upper hand under their brilliant general, Robert E. Lee. At the battle of Gettysburg, Pennsylvania, in July 1863, more than 28,000 Confederates and 23,000 Union soldiers were killed, wounded, or missing.

AMAZING FACTS!

Never before had there been so much slaughter and suffering in a war. More American soldiers—both Union and Confederate—died in the Civil War than died in the two 20th-century world wars combined.

In 1864 President Lincoln made General Ulysses S. Grant commander in chief of the Union armies. A few months later Grant headed for Richmond, Virginia, while General William T. Sherman marched South to Atlanta, Georgia, which he captured and burned in September. He then began his famous March to the Sea, cutting across Georgia to Savannah, which he captured on December 21.

Slavery abolished

In January 1865 Congress passed the 13th Amendment to the Constitution, forever prohibiting slavery in the United States. Lee surrendered on April 9. On April 14 an actor named John Wilkes Booth assassinated Lincoln. The North's victory resulted in the abolition of slavery, the granting of citizenship to the freed slaves, and the preservation of the Union. However, many Southern cities, towns, and plantations were destroyed, and the Southern economy collapsed.

General Robert E. Lee in the Appomattox Court House, Virginia, signing the surrender that ended the Civil War on April 9, 1865.

SEE ALSO: Abolition Movement; African Americans; Civil Rights; Confederacy; Constitution, United States; Emancipation Proclamation; Slavery

✳ CLEOPATRA (60–30 B.C.)

Cleopatra VII, queen of Egypt, was the last of the Macedonian family that ruled Egypt from 323 B.C. After she died, Egypt came under Roman rule.

A statue of Queen Cleopatra, who captivated two powerful Romans.

When her father died in 51 B.C., Cleopatra became joint ruler with her brother Ptolemy XIII, but he drove her out of Egypt three years later. With the assistance of the Roman general Julius Caesar, she returned to Egypt in 47 B.C. and ruled with another brother, Ptolemy XIV. He was later killed, and Cleopatra's son Caesarion (whose father was, she claimed, Julius Caesar) became the new co-ruler.

After Caesar's death, Cleopatra supported another Roman general, Mark Antony, in his attempt to become ruler of Rome. They married and had three children. Antony's campaign ended when he lost the battle of Actium in 31 B.C. Antony and Cleopatra both committed suicide, and Egypt fell under Roman domination. According to legend, Cleopatra used an asp—a poisonous snake—to kill herself.

Cleopatra was not beautiful, but her intelligence and self-confidence made her attractive to powerful men. Her story has inspired authors and film directors, from William Shakespeare's play *Antony and Cleopatra* to the 1963 movie *Cleopatra*.

SEE ALSO: Caesar, Julius; Egypt, Ancient; Roman Empire; Shakespeare, William

✳ CLIMATE

Climate is the overall state of weather in a place over a long period of time. Weather, on the other hand, is caused by changes in the atmosphere.

This satellite image of Earth shows land and sea temperatures, as well as cloud formations.

It might be cold and rainy where you are now. However, if it is usually warm and sunny, then the climate is said to be warm and sunny despite today's weather.

Scientists learn about the climate of a place by studying its weather and the types of plant that grow there. The two most important weather conditions that describe a place's climate are temperature and precipitation (the moisture that falls to the ground as rain or snow).

Why are climates different?
The differences in climate from place to place are caused by various factors, but the main one is distance from the equator. This distance is measured in degrees of latitude. Near the equator (0° latitude), the sun is never far from being directly overhead at noon. Regions close to the equator remain warm all year round. Near the poles, at 90° latitude, the sun is never very high in the sky and there are cold climates. In the middle latitudes, the sun is high in the sky in summer and low in winter, so places like Portland, Maine (about 45° north latitude), have warm summers and cold winters.

▲
Greenpeace is one of the many environmental groups that are concerned about climate change. Their 1999 Arctic expedition proved that the ice pack is melting fast, and that wildlife, such as this walrus, is suffering as a result.

Other factors that control climate include altitude (height above the ground) and closeness to water. Temperatures usually fall as altitude increases because the air is less dense and does not hold as much heat. Water temperature changes more slowly than land temperature, so coastal areas tend to have milder winters and cooler summers than places inland. Winds also affect the climate because they carry heat and moisture.

Climate change

Climates have changed throughout Earth's history. Climate change may be due to changes in the amount of energy from the sun or the amount of dust in the atmosphere. In recent years, scientists have discovered that temperatures are gradually rising around the world. This trend is known as global warming. It is important to learn more about how climate changes because it affects our environment and way of life.

▲
A scientist in Idaho measures the depth of snow. It is vital to work how much water will be available for farming and other uses.

> **SEE ALSO:** Atmosphere; Environment; Fossil Fuels; Navigation; Pollution; Weather

✳ CLOCKS AND WATCHES

Clocks and watches are counting mechanisms that measure the passage of time. They make regular movements at equal intervals.

Modern clocks and watches are driven in one of three ways—mechanically by systems of springs and cogwheels, by electricity, or by atomic power.

The earliest clocks

Ancient Babylonians and Egyptians used sundials, or shadow clocks, to divide daylight into short, equal periods. The Egyptians used clepsydra, or water clocks, that were equally effective by day and night. The Greeks built astrolabes, instruments that told time by measuring the altitude of stars. In Greece and Rome, portable sundials were worn as jewelry.

Mechanical clocks date from the late Middle Ages. They all have an internal source of energy—today a falling weight, a wound spring, or an electric current—that is regulated so that the clock runs accurately. The weight, spring, or current turns a wheel and a system of gears that move the clock's hands.

The accuracy of clocks improved in the 1600s, after the Dutch scientist Christiaan Huygens

▶
This clock tower in Padua, Italy, was created in 1344 by Jacopo Dondi.

143

(1629–95) introduced the pendulum into weight-driven clocks. The oscillation, or swinging, of the pendulum ensures that the gear wheels move regularly. In the 1700s, wear-resistant jewels were built into clocks to reduce friction in the gears.

Wristwatches

Wristwatches became popular in the 1920s. The earliest examples were self-winding. Battery-powered watches were introduced in the 1950s.

Modern electronic watches are powered by quartz crystals, which vibrate at their natural frequency. Digital quartz watches display time in numbers, using LEDs (light-emitting diodes) or LCDs (liquid-crystal displays).

Electric clocks are powered by motors synchronized with the alternating current (AC) power line. The rotational speed of the motor is reduced by gears.

SEE ALSO:
Calendars;
Navigation;
Time

Atomic clocks

The most accurate clocks today are atomic. They measure time by the oscillations of chemical elements. Such clocks may be accurate to within one second over thousands or even millions of years. They are used to correct errors in nonatomic clocks.

AMAZING FACTS!

Atomic clocks measure time by counting the regular, natural vibrations of atoms, typically those of the elements cesium, hydrogen, or nubidium. In 1967 the standard second was established as the time it takes a cesium atom to vibrate 9,192,631,770 (more than nine billion) times.

✳ CLOTHING

Clothes are both useful and ornamental. Humans need them to protect their bodies and like them because they can be made fashionable and stylish.

The more advanced a society becomes, the more attention people pay to dress. From ancient times, people have enjoyed adorning their bodies with clothing, makeup, and jewelry. Dress began to signify people's place in society—their status or occupation. People also dressed in special ways for important events such as weddings, parties, or funerals.

Clothing around the world

Climate usually influenced the type of clothing that developed in different parts of the world. People living in cold climates generally wore tight-fitting clothes made of heavy, warm materials. In warmer climates, people wore loose, lightweight garments that provided protection from the sun and allowed cool air to circulate around their bodies.

Other factors that caused differences in clothing were the types of fibers available and differing ideas of beauty. Clothing for special occasions was often governed by custom or tradition. Many people still wear national or traditional costumes, such as the Scottish kilt, to celebrate festivals and landmark events. Other national costumes are still used for everyday wear—for example, the Indian sari.

A model wears a Ralph Lauren design on the catwalk during the New York Fashion Week, 2002.

Changes in fashion

In Oriental and Islamic cultures, early clothing traditions were later codified (established as rules to be followed). Respect for tradition discouraged changes in styles of dress.

People in the West admired change and experimentation in clothing styles. The styles of a particular period in history tell us a great deal about the people who wore them—such as their religious and political beliefs, their feelings about themselves and the world around them, and the extent to which their technology had developed.

Many everyday items of clothing worn in the West today were unknown in ancient times. It was not until the Middle Ages, for example, that men began to wear *braies*—two separate, loose-fitting woolen leggings held together at the waist by a drawstring and at the lower leg by linen bands. They developed into a "pair of pants," or trousers. Trousers gradually became acceptable clothing for women in the 20th century.

A French military officer in the dress uniform of the 1690s.

The clothing industry

Until the 19th century, most clothing was made by hand for an individual. Fashionable clothes were elaborate and expensive. Fashion was for the royal and the rich. By the 1820s, however, there was an increasing demand for affordable, ready-to-wear clothes.

The invention of the sewing machine revolutionized garment production. One of the earliest machines was made by Elias Howe in 1846, but it was clumsy and slow. The invention of the foot-treadle machine by Isaac M. Singer a few years later freed both hands of the operator for sewing. A foot pedal turned the wheel, moving the needle up and down.

As mass production increased, dressmakers and tailors noticed that certain sizes came up over and over again. It became possible to work out a system of standard patterns. It was still many years, however, until manufacturers could make ready-to-wear clothes that fit well. ➥

New fabrics

For centuries all fabrics came from natural fibers: silk from the silkworm, linen and cotton from plants, and wool from sheep. In the late 1800s, artificial fibers were developed. They were cheaper to produce and less likely to wrinkle. In the 1980s, people began to return to natural fibers.

A modern mass-production clothing factory in Tamil Nadu, India.

Design and manufacture

Fashion design did not become an industry until the mid-1800s, with the founding of the House of Worth in Paris, France. Today Paris is still a world center of fashion, as are New York, London (England), Milan (Italy), Tokyo (Japan), and several other major cities.

If a fashionable design is chosen to be mass-produced, cardboard or plywood patterns are made for each section of the sample garment. Different sizes are obtained by changing the dimensions of the original pattern. Each garment may be worked on by several people. Garments are packed and shipped to stores.

SEE ALSO: Fabrics and Cloth; Manufacturing; Middle Ages

✳COAL ᴮᵉᵉ ✳ FOSSIL FUELS

✳ COLOMBIA

Colombia is in the northwestern part of South America. It is the fourth-largest country on the continent and has the second-largest population.

Colombia's national flag

Land and climate

Colombia has coasts on the Pacific Ocean and the Caribbean Sea. Three great ranges of the Andes Mountains divide Colombia into regions: the highlands, the eastern plains, and the coastal lowlands. Most of the major cities and farmland are in the highlands. Most people live on the coastal plain along the Caribbean coast.

The Pacific coastal lowlands are one of the wettest areas in the world. Temperatures depend on altitude (height). The Caribbean coastal plain has an average temperature of 82°F (28°C), but temperatures in the Andes are lower.

The main river is the Magdalena, which runs for 1,000 miles (1,600 km) between the central and eastern Andes and flows into the Caribbean.

People

About 58 percent of Colombia's people are mestizos, that is, of mixed European and native Indian ancestry. Another 20 percent are of European ancestry, and 14 percent are mulatto—of mixed European and African ancestry. There are also smaller groups of mixed African and Indian Colombians. Pure-blooded Indians account for only 1 percent of the population.

The official language is Spanish. Roman Catholicism is the religion of 90 percent of the Colombian people.

Famous Colombians of recent years include the novelist Gabriel García Márquez and many soccer players, such as Carlos Valderrama and Rene Higuita.

Economy

Service industries such as banking and retail make up 55 percent of Colombia's economy. Manufacturing accounts for 26 percent, and 19 percent comes from agriculture.

Coffee is the most important crop, followed by bananas, sugar, flowers, and tobacco. In the 1990s, oil production became a major part of the country's economy. Colombia is also the world's biggest producer of emeralds. Cultivation of coca and the illegal cocaine trade are estimated to bring in $300 million a year.

The mountains in Colombia make transportation difficult. Much long-distance travel is by river or air. Tourism has been badly affected by recent violence.

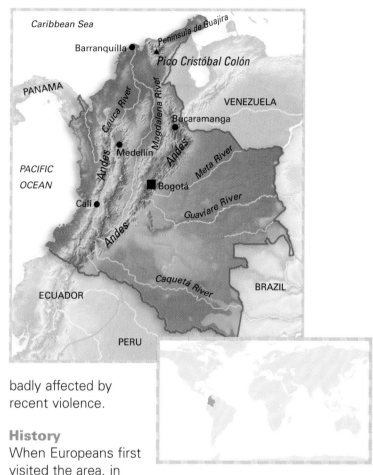

History

When Europeans first visited the area, in 1499, Indian tribes lived there. Colombia was named for the explorer Christopher Columbus. In 1549 the Spanish conquerors created the colony of New Granada, which included what we now

Laborers weeding the corn crop on an estate in the valley of the Magdalena River.

know as Ecuador, Panama, and Venezuela. In 1810 an independent government was set up, and in 1819 Venezuelan Simón Bolívar became president of the Republic of Gran (Greater) Colombia. In 1830 Venezuela and Ecuador became two separate countries.

From 1899 to 1902, a civil war, known as the War of a Thousand Days, took place. In 1903 the United States attempted to lease (rent) part of Panama from Colombia to build a canal. When Colombia refused, the Panamanians rebelled and announced their independence.

There was more unrest after 1948, when Jorge Eliér Gaitán, an important political leader, was assassinated. The following

SEE ALSO:
Bolívar, Simón; Columbus, Christopher; Ecuador; Panama; South America; Venezuela

KEY FACTS

OFFICIAL NAME: República de Colombia

AREA: 439,735 sq. mi. (1,138,914 sq. km)

POPULATION: 42,321,000

CAPITAL & LARGEST CITY: Bogotá

MAJOR RELIGION: Roman Catholicism

MAJOR LANGUAGE: Spanish

CURRENCY: Peso

nine years were known as *La Violencia* (the violence). Antigovernment rebels and drug-trade gangs have been the cause of more recent violence.

✳ COLONIAL AMERICA

During the colonial period (1607–1776), a number of European countries established settlements in America. The dominant colonies were English.

This map shows the boundaries of the 13 English colonies in about 1732. Their western borders were still open.

Before 1600 most inhabitants of North America were Native Americans. Soon after, however, European settlers began to move to America. They moved because they hoped for a better life—the chance to own land and become more prosperous. Some came because they wanted to worship God in their own way. Many European countries at that time expected people to attend the official state church and pay taxes to support it. Those who refused could be sent to prison.

The first colonies
The Spanish were the first settlers. From 1565 onward, they established settlements in modern Mexico, the American Southwest, and Florida. They mined gold and silver and built America's first Christian churches.

The English set up their first permanent colony at Jamestown, Virginia, in 1607. However, a year later only one-third of the settlers were still alive. Some had been killed by Native Americans. Most died from cold, hunger, and disease. The colony later recovered and prospered.

The Pilgrims

The second permanent English colony was Plymouth. It was settled by a group known as the Pilgrims. They sailed from England on a ship called the *Mayflower* in September 1620. Aboard were just over 100 passengers. About one-third were Puritan Separatists who had broken away from the Church of England and were seeking religious freedom in America. In return for land, they would earn money for the venture's merchant backers in London. The *Mayflower* first landed at the tip of Cape Cod, Massachusetts, 10 weeks after leaving England. The Pilgrims explored the coast, and in December they chose Plymouth as the site of their colony.

As the English settled along the eastern seaboard, other European powers also rushed to establish colonies. Sweden established New Sweden on the Delaware River in 1638, but the colony was taken over by the Dutch in 1655.

New Amsterdam, as the Dutch named their fort on Manhattan, was the main settlement of a colony called New Netherland. The colony passed into English hands in 1664, and New Amsterdam was renamed New York.

The French claimed New France in present-day Canada and later the vast territory west of the Mississippi River, which they called Louisiana. The French were less interested in settlement than in the fur trade and converting the native peoples to Christianity.

Life in the English colonies

By 1669 there were 13 English colonies along the East Coast from New Hampshire in the north to Georgia in the south. Life differed from colony to colony.

New England in the 1600s was a land of tidy fields and villages. The church was the center of religious, social, and political life. New England had more schools than any other region of colonial America. The first college in the colonies, Harvard, in Cambridge, Massachusetts, was set up in 1636.

In the Middle Colonies—including New York, New Jersey, and Pennsylvania—lived people from different nations who spoke different languages and worshiped in different ways. They traded many products, such as grain and barrels of

Early settlers building a walled settlement at Jamestown, Virginia, in 1607. At first many of the English settlers died, but by 1619 the settlement was flourishing. Less than 150 years later, the English flag was flying over 13 colonies. The colonies declared their independence in 1776.

salted beef and pork. Trade helped them become prosperous. Large towns emerged, such as Philadelphia.

In the colonies south of Chesapeake Bay, many people lived on plantations that grew tobacco and rice. Both crops required a lot of labor. Planters used slaves to do the work. There were few schools and churches, and families lived a long way apart. The southern colonists produced many things wanted in England, such as tobacco. When prices were high, southerners could make good money.

Family life
Most people worked, played, learned, and worshiped at home. Men made all the decisions concerning their families and

worked to support them. Women worked in the home and raised the children. A large family was essential because children were needed to share the work. Half the people of colonial America were under 16 years old.

The Frontier
The colonial population grew. By the 1760s, colonists were moving west. By 1775 settlers had crossed the Appalachian Mountains and were beginning to move into Kentucky and Tennessee.

SEE ALSO: American Revolution; Slavery; United States of America

The Governor's mansion in Williamsburg, Virginia, is kept as it was in colonial days.

*COLORS
Everyone knows what color is, but how can it be explained in words? Imagine trying to explain color to someone who has been blind from birth.

Although we are surrounded by different colors, such as these bright city lights, we cannot always describe the colors we see.

To understand color, it is necessary to understand light. Light is a series of waves. The waves have various lengths. Objects absorb some wavelengths and reflect others. It is the reflected wavelength that gives an object its color. So, grass is green because it reflects green light waves but absorbs other light waves. Objects need light to give them color. At night grass might look dark-gray, not green. That is because the light is not reflecting from it.

White light can be made up of three basic colors—red, green, and blue—called primaries. All other colors are mixtures of the primaries. White objects reflect all lengths of light waves.

Mixing different colors of paint is not the same as mixing light. When paint primaries—yellow, red, and blue—are mixed, they make black.

The animal world

Color is all around us—think of advertising billboards, color television and movies, brightly colored T-shirts and sneakers. Color is not just for decoration, however. Animals use it for display, such as the bright feathers that a peacock uses to attract mates. They can also use it for protection—Arctic animals are often white, so their enemies cannot see them in the snow. A chameleon is a type of lizard that can change its color so that it blends in with different surroundings.

How humans use color

Humans use color as well. Think how confusing a basketball game would be if all the players were wearing yellow clothes. Transportation would be very dangerous—we need to see the difference between red and green lights, and between white lines and black roads. We might find it difficult to explain what color is or to describe different colors, but they are an essential part of our world.

A visitor to the San Francisco Exploratorium explores the "Wall of Light" exhibit. All the colors that we see are made up of three primary colors— red, green, and blue.

SEE ALSO:
Animals;
Light;
Newton, Isaac;
Physics

✳ COLUMBUS, CHRISTOPHER (1451–1506)

Christopher Columbus sailed westward across the Atlantic Ocean in 1492 with the hope of finding a sea route to Asia. Instead he discovered the New World of the Americas.

Christopher Columbus (Cristoforo Colombo in Italian) was born in Genoa, Italy, in 1451. Genoa was a busy seaport, and Christopher worked as a sailor and fisherman. He was soon joining merchants on trading trips along the coast of the Mediterranean Sea. Between voyages he studied mapmaking and geography.

By 1476 he was in Portugal, then the greatest seafaring center in Europe. He became interested in the writings of travelers such as Marco Polo, who had voyaged to Cathay (China) in 1275 and described a land with many jewels, silks, and spices.

Searching for a route to Asia

In Columbus's time, the spice trade route between Europe and Asia was very slow. Merchants transported goods partly by sea and partly overland. Columbus believed that an easier and direct route to Asia would be westward across the Atlantic Ocean. His studies of old writings made him believe that the earth was much smaller than it really is. The Spanish rulers Ferdinand and Isabella eventually agreed to finance a voyage, and Columbus set off with a crew of about 90 men in three ships—the *Niña*, the *Pinta*, and the *Santa Maria*—on August 3, 1492.

After 70 days, they reached the islands now called the Bahamas. Columbus thought that he was in the East Indies and called the inhabitants "Indians." He had discovered what Europeans would soon call the New World of the Americas. (Of course, it was not a New World to the millions of Native Americans already living there.) Columbus spent the next 10 weeks exploring the islands of the Caribbean. He returned to Spain believing he had reached Asia. In the next 12 years, he made three more expeditions to the area.

Columbus never found the gold and jewels he had expected. Reports of

chaotic conditions in the Spanish colonies reached Ferdinand and Isabella. In 1500 Columbus was removed as governor of the Indies and sent back to Spain in chains. Although he was released and made a final voyage along the coast of Central America, he never regained his former prestige. He died in 1506.

Today historians have recognized Columbus's navigational skills. Not only did he find the best route across the ocean to the Americas, but he also found the best eastern route back to Europe—routes that are still used hundreds of years later.

▶
Christopher Columbus was one of the greatest navigators in history.

👀
SEE ALSO:
Caribbean Islands;
Central America;
Exploration and Explorers;
Marco Polo

✳ COMETS, METEORS, AND ASTEROIDS
Comets, meteors, and asteroids are all pieces of matter left over from billions of years ago when the solar system was first formed.

Comets
A comet is a mass of ice, rocks, and dust. Comets are usually found in the outer regions of the solar system. Sometimes, however, a comet is pulled closer to the sun. As the comet gets hotter, the outer layers turn to gas and form a long "tail."

Some comets can be seen from Earth, but only when they are near the sun. Halley's comet comes into view every 76 years; the last time it was visible from Earth was 1986. A new comet, Hale-Bopp, was discovered on July 23, 1995. It is a lot brighter and larger than Halley's comet.

Asteroids
An asteroid is a small planet made of rock and metal. Most asteroids in the solar system orbit, or circle, the sun between Mars and Jupiter. This area is known as the asteroid belt. In 1996 the NEAR (Near Earth Asteroid Rendezvous) probe was launched. It orbited an asteroid named

Comet Hale-Bopp, a very bright comet, was discovered by Alan Hale in New Mexico and Thomas Bopp in Arizona at the same time.

▶

433 Eros and took pictures of the surface. Scientists believe that asteroids were formed by the same processes that helped form the solar system.

Meteors and meteorites
Sometimes tiny pieces of comets or asteroids reach Earth's atmosphere and burn up, leaving a bright trail. They are called meteors, or shooting stars.

Meteorites are meteors that strike Earth. They are usually very small and do little damage. However, some meteorites have left large dents, or craters, in the earth's surface. One crater, in the Yucatan Peninsula, Mexico, is 110 miles (180 km) across. Based on the size of this crater, many scientists believe that about 65 million years ago, a meteorite caused the extinction of the dinosaurs.

Before space travel to the moon, meteorites were the only material from outside Earth that scientists could examine. They can learn a lot about the formation of the planets by studying the substances contained in meteorites.

A meteorite crater in Arizona. It is about 50,000 years old and about 656 ft. (200 m) deep.

SEE ALSO:
Dinosaurs;
Extinction;
Planets;
Solar
System;
Space
Exploration

* COMMUNICATION
Communication means sending and receiving information. The word *communicate* comes from the Latin *communicare*, which means "to share."

Communication requires a sender; a recipient, that is, someone to receive it; a message, or the idea you want to communicate; and a medium, that is, the method of carrying the message. Originally people sent and received messages by sound or by gesture. This direct communication took place only at one time and over a short distance. When people began writing their ideas in words and pictures, this meant that knowledge was no longer limited to what a person could see directly or be told by others.

Today modern communication systems carry messages over long distances.

Telephones convey spoken messages, and computer systems give data to people. Printing, television, radio, and the Internet, often called the mass media, are all tools for communicating with many people.

SEE ALSO: Alphabet; Computers; Internet; Languages; Media; Myths and Legends; Newspapers and Magazines; Photography; Printing; Radio; Sound Recording; Space Exploration; Telecommunications; Telephones; Television; Video Recording; Writing

COMMUNICATION TIMELINE

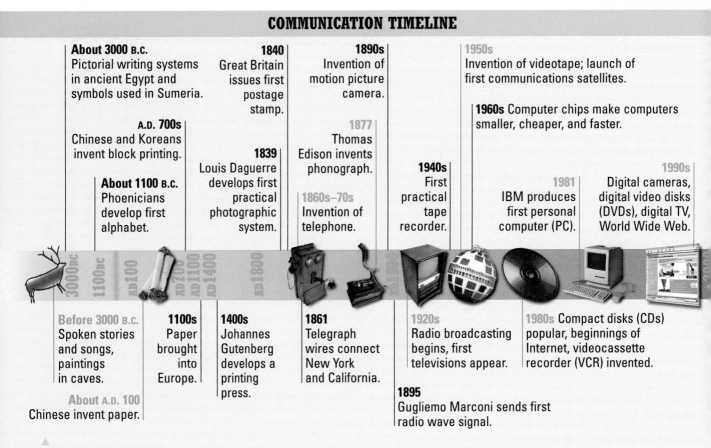

About 3000 B.C. Pictorial writing systems in ancient Egypt and symbols used in Sumeria.

A.D. 700s Chinese and Koreans invent block printing.

About 1100 B.C. Phoenicians develop first alphabet.

1840 Great Britain issues first postage stamp.

1839 Louis Daguerre develops first practical photographic system.

1890s Invention of motion picture camera.

1877 Thomas Edison invents phonograph.

1860s–70s Invention of telephone.

1940s First practical tape recorder.

1950s Invention of videotape; launch of first communications satellites.

1960s Computer chips make computers smaller, cheaper, and faster.

1981 IBM produces first personal computer (PC).

1990s Digital cameras, digital video disks (DVDs), digital TV, World Wide Web.

Before 3000 B.C. Spoken stories and songs, paintings in caves.

About A.D. 100 Chinese invent paper.

1100s Paper brought into Europe.

1400s Johannes Gutenberg develops a printing press.

1861 Telegraph wires connect New York and California.

1895 Gugliemo Marconi sends first radio wave signal.

1920s Radio broadcasting begins, first televisions appear.

1980s Compact disks (CDs) popular, beginnings of Internet, videocassette recorder (VCR) invented.

This timeline shows some of the key inventions in the history of communication.

✳ COMMUNISM

Communism, which began as a collection of ideas, grew into a political movement that shaped much of the world's history during the 20th century.

The word *communism* was first used to refer to any society in which property would be owned "communally" (by everyone) rather than by individuals. This idea is very old—the Greek thinker Plato referred to it in the 300s B.C.

Modern theories of communism, however, began much later, after the Industrial Revolution. In the mid-1700s, industry developed rapidly in Western Europe. Factory laborers worked hard for low pay, while factory owners grew rich. Many

people thought this system unfair. They believed that the hardships of workers would end if property were owned by all the people, rather than privately owned. They called their ideal system socialism or communism. The German thinker Karl Marx (1818–83) believed that one day the workers in industrial societies would take over the farms and factories, and then establish a new, fair communist society. People who followed his revolutionary ideas were known as Marxists.

Lenin and the Soviet Union

It was a Marxist, Vladimir Ilyich Lenin (1870–1924), and his political party, the Bolsheviks, who swept to power in Russia in the 1917 revolutions. Lenin established the Union of Soviet Socialist Republics (USSR) throughout Russia. His party became known as the Communist Party.

Lenin believed that the Communist Party should exercise total, one-party control. The party seized all the farms and factories, and controlled all trade, but the people were not ready for a Marxist revolution. After Lenin died, Joseph Stalin (1879–1953) struggled to keep power. He had thousands of citizens killed or imprisoned.

Soviet collapse

Many other countries fell under Communist rule in the 1940s. The Soviet Communist system failed in the USSR and Eastern Europe in the late 1980s, and Communist regimes were replaced by elected governments. By 1991 the Soviet empire had collapsed. Today Communist rule survives only in the People's Republic of China, Cuba, and North Korea.

The Russian revolutionary Vladimar Ilyich Lenin in a political poster. Lenin ruled the USSR from 1917 until his death in 1924.

DID YOU KNOW?

Most Communist flags and emblems were red, representing the blood shed by workers in their struggle. Against the red background of the Soviet flag, a crossed hammer and sickle stood for the unity of the industrial workers and the peasants. A five-pointed star symbolized the unity of the five continents then recognized—Africa, America, Asia, Australia, and Europe.

SEE ALSO: Capitalism; Eastern Europe; Economics; Industrial Revolution

✳ COMPUTERS

Computers come in many shapes and sizes, and serve many purposes. They help society function, often without people being aware of them.

Computers control stoplights and factory operations. They monitor banking transactions. They scan bar codes at checkouts. They link schools, businesses, governments, and people around the world. There are computer chips in cars, radios, televisions, and home appliances.

A computer is a system of electronic components that work together to store, retrieve, and process data. The parts that sit on the desk (the hard drive and monitor) or that you hold in your hand are known as hardware. Software is the instructions that tell hardware what to do. Computers can be programmed to perform different jobs, and that makes them different from simple calculators.

Hardware

There are three parts to computer hardware: processing units, input and output devices, and memory and storage. The central processing unit (CPU) makes

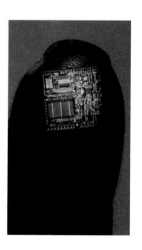

A tiny computer chip—a world of information at your fingertips.

INSIDE A PERSONAL COMPUTER

A typical modern desktop computer.

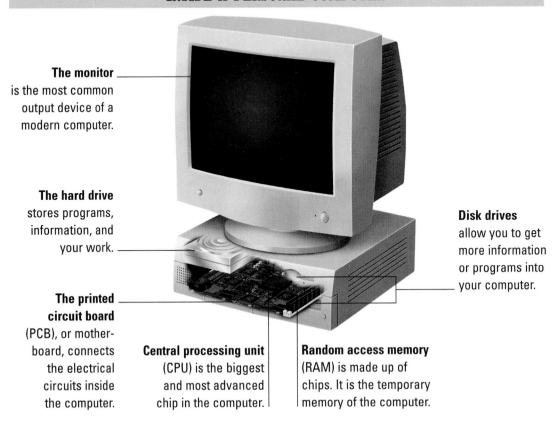

The monitor is the most common output device of a modern computer.

The hard drive stores programs, information, and your work.

Disk drives allow you to get more information or programs into your computer.

The printed circuit board (PCB), or motherboard, connects the electrical circuits inside the computer.

Central processing unit (CPU) is the biggest and most advanced chip in the computer.

Random access memory (RAM) is made up of chips. It is the temporary memory of the computer.

its calculations using digital data, a variety of information expressed in binary form (series of 1s and 0s). The CPU must be given information to process—the input. Input devices include a keyboard and a mouse. The results are called output. Output can be displayed on screen, printed on paper, saved onto disk, or sent to another computer over a network.

For storing and finding data, a computer has memory and disks. Memory is usually temporary and is located inside the computer on small electronic components called chips. Disks are slower, but can hold larger amounts of data and store information for a much longer time.

For the computer hardware to do useful work, it needs software—instructions that tell the computer what to do and how to do it. A specific set of instructions is called

a program. One program, the operating system, has instructions for running all the hardware components and for managing the actions of other programs.

Programming languages
The language of computers is machine language—a series of 1s and 0s that are converted into "on" and "off" electrical pulses. The electrical pulses tell the computer what to do. Programmers find machine language hard to understand, so they use other languages that contain words and symbols. A special program translates the programmers' instructions into machine language.

Beginning in the 1960s, computers miles apart could be connected to networks. Millions of computers are now connected in a worldwide network—the Internet.

History of computers

Since ancient times, people have used machines to count and calculate. But it was not until the early 1800s that the English mathematician Charles Babbage built what many people consider to be the first true computer. Early computers were mechanical. When people discovered electricity, computers became much faster. Further inventions during the 1900s led to the first personal computers (PCs) in the early 1980s. Computers have many advantages, but also present problems, such as people called hackers accessing information illegally, or creating viruses that destroy data and damage programs.

Computer games

Advances in computer technology have made computer games highly popular. By the early 1990s, PC games were widespread. Many of the games test a player's ability to react quickly and with skill to the action on the screen.

SEE ALSO: Communication; Electronics; Internet; Robots; Telecommunications

A high school student uses a special program to improve her writing skills.

✳ CONFEDERACY

The Confederacy was an alliance of Southern states that withdrew from the United States and declared their own nation. The split sparked the Civil War.

South Carolina was the first state to withdraw (secede) from the Union on December 20, 1860. It withdrew after the election of President Abraham Lincoln, who wanted to stop the spread of slavery. Southern farmers needed slaves to work on the cotton and tobacco plantations.

Georgia, Florida, Alabama, Louisiana, and Mississippi quickly followed South Carolina's lead. Delegates from the states met in Montgomery, Alabama, the Confederacy's first capital, on February 4, 1861. They drafted a constitution creating a new republic called the Confederate States of America, with Jefferson Davis as president and Alexander H. Stephens as vice president. The capital was later moved to Richmond, Virginia. Texas, Virginia, Tennessee, Arkansas, and North Carolina then joined the Confederacy. Missouri, Kentucky, and Maryland did not secede, but supplied troops to both sides during the Civil War.

Civil War

The American Civil War began on April 12, 1861, when Confederate troops fired on Fort Sumter in Charleston, South Carolina. The Confederacy was at a disadvantage in many ways. It had a smaller population

Jefferson Davis (1808–89) was president of the Confederate States of America.

In the 1800s, a white landowner oversees black cotton pickers at work in Texas.

than the North, fewer factories, inferior railroads, and very little currency. The South thought that the sale of cotton to Europe would bring in money, that their farms would provide enough food for the army, and that the ability of their soldiers would win victory even though the North had more men and better arms.

But the South was wrong. Europe found other cotton suppliers. Much of the farmland fell to Union armies. The South could not match the North's ability to produce military equipment. The Confederacy survived for four years, mainly due to the courage of its soldiers and the skill of its generals, such as Robert E. Lee. After some early Confederate victories, the tide turned in 1863. On April 9, 1865, Lee surrendered.

Military defeat meant the end of the Confederacy. The Southern economy was in ruins. Farms, towns, and cities had been destroyed. It would be many years before the South began to recover.

SEE ALSO: Abolition Movement; Civil War; Emancipation Proclamation; Slavery

✳ CONGRESS

The Congress of the United States consists of the House of Representatives and the Senate. Together they make the laws of the federal government.

A two-chamber system
In 1787 the states of the new United States sent delegates to the Constitutional Convention. This was a meeting to decide how the government of the nation would operate. They decided that the legislative branch—the section that creates laws—would consist of two chambers, or houses. This arrangement is called a bicameral system.

A major reason why Congress has two houses is that the bicameral system resolved a serious conflict. The heavily populated states wanted representation in Congress to be based on population. The less heavily populated states believed that representation in this way would mean

that their voices would not be heard, and so they insisted on equal representation. The convention overcame this obstacle by agreeing on the Great Compromise. This allowed for the House of Representatives (usually known simply as the House) to be elected on the basis of population, but it also provided for equal representation for each state in the Senate.

The Senate
Each state has two senators, no matter what the size of its population. Senators were originally appointed by the legislatures of their states. Under the 17th Amendment to the Constitution, ratified in 1913, they are now elected by popular

vote. Senators must be at least 30 years of age, and have been U.S. citizens for at least nine years. They serve for a term of six years. Senate elections take place every two years, with one-third of the senators retiring or running for re-election. The vice president of the United States presides over the Senate.

The House of Representatives

Most states are divided into areas called congressional districts. There are 435 districts in total, and each one elects a member to the House of Representatives. California, the state with the largest population and therefore most districts, elects 52 representatives to the House. States with smaller populations (Alaska, Delaware, Montana, North Dakota, South Dakota, Vermont, and Wyoming) elect just one representative each.

House representatives must be at least 25 years old and have been U.S. citizens for at least seven years. They serve for a term of two years. The House is presided over by the Speaker of the House, who is nominated by the majority political party.

How the houses work together

A bill—a proposal for a new federal law—must have the approval of both houses of Congress.

However, the Senate has special responsibility for foreign affairs. Under the Constitution, two-thirds of Senators must agree to any treaty

COMPARING THE SENATE AND THE HOUSE OF REPRESENTATIVES

	Senate	House
Members	100	435
Term of office	6 years	2 years
Minimum age	30 years	25 years
Presiding officer	U.S. vice president	Speaker

with a foreign power. The House has a special role in laws relating to tax and finance. Revenue-raising measures can be introduced only in the House. All other bills may be introduced in either chamber.

Much of the work involved in considering bills goes on at committee stage. There are 22 committees in the House and 16 in the Senate. Each committee has a special area of interest, such as agriculture or education. The majority of bills are rejected in committee.

If a bill survives the committee stage, it passes to the floor of the House or the Senate. Here all representatives or senators can discuss it and may attempt to bring amendments—changes to the wording or content. If it passes this stage, it is sent to the other chamber, where the process begins all over again. Because a bill rarely passes both chambers in the same form, a conference committee is

The Capitol Building in Washington, D.C., is one of the nation's most famous and treasured landmarks. Congress meets here to make federal laws.
▼

The House of Representatives is a legislative body with 435 elected members.

president for signature. He is permitted to veto the bill—to refuse to authorize it. However, if two-thirds of the House and Senate support the bill, they can overrule the president's veto.

At first this system might seem complex, but it is part of the system of "checks and balances" provided in the Constitution. No branch of government can have so much power that it can act entirely alone.

Congress can also propose amendments to the Constitution and declare war on another country. The House has the power to impeach, or bring charges against, federal officials for misconduct.

selected to work out differences. Any agreement reached must again be approved by both the Senate and the House. The final step in the passage of a bill comes when it is placed before the

SEE ALSO: Constitution, United States; Presidency, The; Supreme Court; United States Government; Vice Presidency, The

* CONQUISTADORS
Conquistador is the Spanish word for "conqueror." It is used to describe the Spanish leaders who took over parts of America in the 1500s.

Aztecs welcome the conquistador Hernán Cortés to their lands.

The most famous conquistadors are Hernán Cortés, who conquered Aztec Mexico, and Francisco Pizarro, who conquered Inca Peru. The conquistadors

were only seeking personal wealth and adventure, but in the process they created a vast empire for Spain in the Americas.

Cortés and the Aztecs
In 1504, eager to gain fame and fortune, Hernán Cortés (1485–1547) sailed from Spain to the West Indies, where he became a planter on the island of Hispaniola. In 1519 he set off for Mexico with 11 ships, 600 men, and 16 horses.

At that time Mexico was ruled by the Aztec emperor Montezuma (or Moctezuma) II. His empire stretched from the Pacific Ocean to the Gulf of Mexico and south to the modern border of which were new to them. The soldiers brought new diseases, such as smallpox, which killed thousands of Aztecs.

Pizarro and the Incas

Francisco Pizarro (about 1475–1541) sailed from Spain to America in 1502. In 1513 he joined Spanish explorer Vasco Núñez de Balboa. They were the first Europeans to cross the narrow strip of land in Central America known as Panama and reach the Pacific Ocean.

In Panama, Pizarro heard of Peru, the heart of the Inca Empire. He set off for Peru in 1531 and kidnapped Atahuallpa, the Inca ruler. After a ransom was paid, Pizarro had Atahuallpa killed. With news of his death, the Inca armies retreated, and Pizarro took Cuzco, the Inca capital, in 1533. In 1535 he founded Lima, now the capital of Peru.

SEE ALSO:
Aztecs;
Balboa,
Vasco
Núñez de;
Exploration
and
Explorers;
Incas;
Mexico;
Peru; Spain

AMAZING FACTS !

Atahuallpa, the last Inca emperor, offered to fill a room with gold as a ransom for his release by Pizarro. The Incas brought gold and silver objects from every corner of the empire. Pizarro and his men melted them all down. The final amount came to 24 tons of gold and silver—the richest ransom ever paid.

Guatemala. Yet within two years, Cortés had overthrown the Aztec Empire. There were many reasons for his victory. The Aztecs thought the Spaniards were gods. They feared the Spanish guns and horses,

✳ CONSERVATION

Conservation is the protection of Earth's natural resources—air, water, soil, forests, grasslands, wildlife, and minerals—from harm or destruction.

People rely on natural resources for food, water, housing, clothing, and energy. We need to manage these resources carefully so that they may last for future generations. The use of resources is an increasingly important issue as the human population continues to grow.

There are two main types of natural resource: renewable and nonrenewable. Soil, water, plants, and animals are renewable because they can usually replace themselves at the same rate at which they are used.

Fossil fuels (coal, oil, and natural gas) are nonrenewable. They take thousands of years to form and are destroyed by use. They provide most of the energy used by

people for heating, transport, and manufacturing. Minerals also have limited supplies, but most can be reused or recycled. Conservation of nonrenewable resources focuses on using them efficiently so that supplies last as long as possible, and locating new sources of and substitutes for these resources.

History of conservation

Early humans were too few in number to do any major damage to the environment. The Industrial Revolution, which began in the mid-1700s, led to new technologies and—with improvements in medicine, food production, and water supplies— population growth. By the end of the 1800s, many people were concerned

The Grand Canyon in Yellowstone Park, Wyoming, the world's first national park.

the Sierra Club. Other groups include the National Audubon Society and the Wilderness Society.

Conservation in action
We can all contribute to protecting the environment. To conserve energy, for example, we can insulate our homes. We can walk, ride bicycles, or take trains rather than drive. We can also help by recycling paper, glass, metal, and plastic. Governments have an important role to play by passing laws to conserve natural resources and protect the environment.

about the waste of resources and destruction of the environment. Hunting had wiped out several species of animal in the United States. In 1872 the Yellowstone area in Wyoming became the world's first national park, a protected area.

Today many organizations work to save threatened areas, protect natural resources, and create effective systems of conservation. One of the largest and most active organizations in the United States is

SEE ALSO: Atmosphere; Carson, Rachel; Climate; Ecology; Endangered Species; Energy; Environment; Extinction; Fossil Fuels; Natural Resources; Pollution

✳ CONSTITUTION, UNITED STATES
The U.S. Constitution is the world's oldest written constitution still in use. It is a system of basic laws and principles on which our government is based.

One of the important principles on which the Constitution is based is the division of power among the three branches of the federal government. The legislative branch (represented by Congress) has the power to create laws; the executive branch (represented by the president and his advisers) has the power to enforce laws; and the judicial branch (represented by the Supreme Court and other courts) has the power to review and reverse laws.

History
When the United States gained its independence from Great Britain in 1783, most Americans felt a greater loyalty to

their individual states than to their new country. They did not want to create a strong national government far away from their homes, over which they would have little or no control.

These feelings caused leaders to organize the new American government according to a document known as the Articles of Confederation. Its main purpose was to enable the states to cooperate if they were attacked by a foreign enemy. However, the states still had a great deal of independence, and the new Congress did not have the power to make the states obey it. As time passed, however, people began to realize that they needed a stronger national government for all the states to achieve common goals.

The Constitutional Convention

Delegates from 12 of the 13 states (all except Rhode Island) gathered in Philadelphia, Pennsylvania, to work out the best form of government. The Constitutional Convention opened on May 25, 1787. It was attended by scholars, war leaders, and politicians, including Alexander Hamilton, Benjamin Franklin, and George Washington. James Madison earned the nickname "Father of the Constitution" because it was mainly his ideas and energy that kept the convention moving toward its goal.

A struggle soon developed between delegates from the large and small states. The states with most people supported a plan to give states with large populations a larger share of decision-making power. Less populous states, however, supported a plan by which every state, regardless of its size, would have the same representation within the government.

The convention came to a standstill until delegates from Connecticut came up with a clever solution. One of the two houses of the new Congress (the House of Representatives) would be elected according to the states' populations. The other house, the Senate, would give an equal voice of two members to each state, no matter what its size. The delegates agreed on most of the remaining issues.

Signing the Constitution

On September 17, 1787, the Constitution was signed by 39 of the original 55 delegates. However, according to the Constitution, nine of the 13 states had to adopt, or ratify, the document before it could become effective.

Delaware was the first state to approve the Constitution. But some of the larger states, including Massachusetts, New York, and Virginia, remained undecided. The Founders knew that the new government would have no chance of succeeding without the support of these states. So they mounted a campaign in defense of the Constitution.

Some people, known as antifederalists, believed the Constitution would make the national government too powerful. They thought that each state should have more power. Their idea was for the Constitution to contain a bill of rights, which would guarantee citizens certain privileges that the government could never take away.

The Constitution of the United States of America provides the framework for the federal (national) government and lays down the division of responsibilities between the federal and the state governments.

The 1787 Constitutional Convention in Independence Hall, Philadelphia, Pennsylvania.

states depended on reaching an understanding that the bill of rights would be the new government's first priority. On June 21, 1788, New Hampshire became the ninth state to ratify the document. New York and Virginia followed soon after, ensuring that the government had the support it needed. In 1791 the 10 amendments, the Bill of Rights, were added to the Constitution. They defined and protected the rights of the American people. Sixteen further amendments followed, each reflecting the changing needs of American society.

The Bill of Rights

John Hancock, a leader of the Revolution, then proposed that a bill of rights be added as a group of amendments, or changes, to the original Constitution. Ratification in Massachusetts and in almost all of the other uncommitted

SEE ALSO: American Revolution; Bill of Rights; Congress; Franklin, Benjamin; United States Government; United States of America

✳ CONTINENTS

A continent is a large landmass on the surface of the earth. It may contain many more than one country, and usually includes islands that lie off its coasts.

It is generally accepted that there are seven continents. In order of size (largest first), they are Asia, Africa, North America, South America, Antarctica, Europe, and Australia.

In some cases, Europe and Asia are said to be a single continent, Eurasia. When Europe and Asia are treated as separate continents, the boundary between them is agreed to run along the eastern edge of the Ural Mountains. From there it extends around the northern coast of the Caspian Sea to the Caucasus Mountains, and on to the northern coast of the Black Sea.

Asia, Europe, and Africa form what is known as the Old World. North America and South America make up the New World. Two continents—Australia and Antarctica—are islands. All together, the seven continents cover 29 percent of the earth's surface area. Oceans and other bodies of water cover the rest.

Distribution and movement

With the exception of Antarctica, all the continents are broader in the north than in the south. About two-thirds of the world's land surface lies in the Northern Hemisphere—that part of the earth north of the equator.

The continents did not always lie in their current positions. Over millions of years, the different landmasses have been pushed together and pulled apart by the shifting of Earth's crust. More than 200 million years ago, the continents formed a single landmass called Pangaea. Gradually Pangaea separated into northern and southern halves known as Laurasia and Gondwanaland. These masses eventually drifted apart to form the continents we know today.

This view of Earth shows the continents of North and South America as seen from space.

second-most populous continent. Europe ranks third in population, despite being the second-smallest continent. Antarctica has no inhabitants other than a few scientists.

Population

Asia, the largest continent in area, also has the most people. Africa, the second-largest continent in area, is also the

SEE ALSO: Africa; Antarctica; Asia; Australia and New Zealand; Earth; Europe; Geography; Geology; Maps; Mountains and Valleys; North America, Geography; Oceans and Seas; Plate Tectonics; South America

✴ CORALS AND CORAL REEFS

Corals are cnidarians, or coelenterates—animals related to jellyfish and sea anemones. In tropical oceans, they form large colonies, called reefs.

Corals

A live coral is called a polyp. Its body is made up of a double-layered, baglike structure called a sac, with an opening (the mouth) surrounded by a ring of tentacles. The mouth leads to a pouch (the gut). The inner layer of the coral polyp produces a substance that forms a hard cup-shaped skeleton into which the polyp can withdraw its tentacles for protection.

Corals do not have internal organs, such as brains or lungs. They rely on the movement of water to bring oxygen to the tissues in their gut and remove waste. Their tentacles have tiny, spearlike

structures that catch tiny organisms for food. They may also release a mild poison, which protects the coral from attack.

Corals reproduce in two ways. Sexual reproduction takes place when eggs and sperm form inside the polyp and are released into the water, where they meet. They form a larva that may swim for weeks before it eventually settles on the ocean floor and grows into a new polyp.

Asexual reproduction, or budding, occurs when a polyp divides in two, or when new polyps "bud" from the tissue around the original polyp. These polyps continue to bud and grow into coral colonies. Colonies

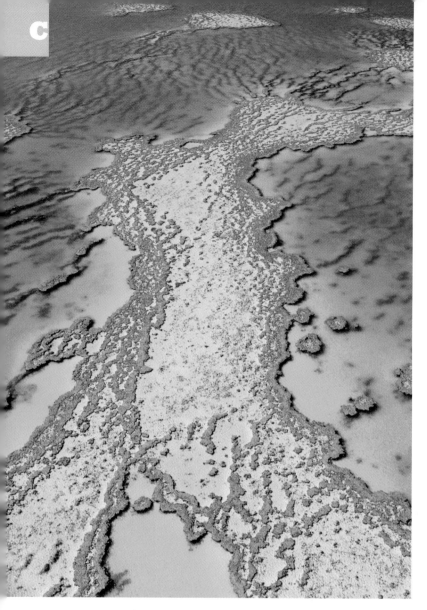

huge, bumpy rocks in shallow waters. However, they are living structures, always growing. When a coral dies, it leaves its hard limestone skeleton behind to form a tiny part of the reef. The reefs provide habitats for many other sea species, and protect shorelines from incoming waves.

Reefs form in shallow, mainly warm water. They are usually found in the Indo-Pacific region, from the east coast of Africa to Hawaii; and in the western Atlantic region, from Bermuda to Brazil.

Coral reefs are popular places for fishing and leisure activities. However, human activity has caused great damage to the reefs. Overfishing and pollution can kill a reef. Rising ocean temperatures, possibly caused by global warming, are also a problem: When the water is too warm, coral polyps lose their color and are unable to reproduce. More than 25 percent of the world's coral reefs have already died.

The Great Barrier Reef, off the northeast coast of Australia, is the world's longest coral formation. It stretches over 1,250 miles (over 2,000 km) and consists of a series of reefs and coral islands.

grow both outward as new polyps bud and upward as the base of the polyp pulls itself up and the polyp makes a new skeletal layer above the old one.

Coral Reefs
In warm tropical seas, tiny, single-celled plants called zooxanthellae live inside the cells of corals. They use energy from the sun to convert carbon dioxide and water into oxygen and carbohydrates. This process is called photosynthesis. It gives the corals energy to increase growth and skeleton production. When this occurs, large structures called coral reefs are created. At first glance, these look like

SEE ALSO: Animals; Ecology; Endangered Species; Environment; Fish; Jellyfish; Oceans and Seas; Photosynthesis; Seashores

✳ COWS

Farmers today keep about 1.3 billion cows throughout the world. Milk and meat are just two of the many useful products cows provide.

Cows are valuable domestic livestock. As well as providing dairy and beef products, they also supply materials for goods such as leather, soap, oil, fuel, and medicines.

Cows are often referred to as ruminants because of the way they digest their food. When a cow chews and swallows, the food is partly digested in a part of the stomach called the rumen. The part-digested food, or cud, is brought back up into the mouth and chewed again before being finally swallowed. This way of feeding allows cows to digest tough plants, so cows can be raised even in parts of the world with poor farmland.

Cows and cattle

Cows belong to the Bovidae, a large family of mammals that also includes sheep, goats, and antelopes. Humans first domesticated (tamed and bred) cows about 6,000 years ago. The ancestor of most cow breeds was the aurochs, a species of wild cattle that roamed Europe and Asia. Today the aurochs is extinct. Surviving wild cattle include buffalo, water buffalo, and bison.

Adult females are called cows, while young females are heifers. All males are known as bulls, unless they have been operated on so that they cannot breed. Then they are called steers. A newborn is called a calf. A group of cows is called a herd.

Dairy cows

Dairy farming is big business, producing butter, cheese, and yogurt as well as milk. By far the most popular cow breed in the

In the United States, a typical cow-calf producer owns between 35 and 40 cows, although some producers own up to 40,000 cows.

United States is the Holstein. A dairy cow produces milk only when she has had a calf. She is then milked twice a day at the farm. In the United States, the average dairy cow gives 16,000 lb. (7,260 kg) of milk each year.

Beef cows

The most common beef cow breeds in the United States include the Brahman, Angus, Hereford, and Simmental. Beef cows may be bred on one farm, raised on another, and "finished" (fattened up) on a special grain diet on a third farm. Not all beef, however, comes from mature, grain-fed beef cattle. Dairy cows and breeding cows are also used for meat when they are no longer productive. Their meat, called cow beef, is generally used for ground beef or sausages. Veal is beef that comes chiefly from milk-fed dairy calves.

Some cow breeds produce both milk and meat. These include the Milking Shorthorn, South Devon, and Red Poll.

DID YOU KNOW?

In India, the nation which has the most cattle in the world, the cow is seen as sacred by the Hindus who live there. Hindus do not kill cattle or eat their meat. Instead the cattle in India are raised for draft (pulling heavy loads) and milk rather than for beef.

SEE ALSO:
Agriculture;
Animals;
Mammals

✳ CRABS

Crabs are fast-moving crustaceans—animals whose bodies are covered with hard shells. Most of the 4,500 kinds of crab live in or near the ocean.

A crab has three main body parts, covered by a large shell, called a carapace. The head section has two moveable stalks that support the eyes. The middle section is called the thorax. The abdomen is at the rear, usually folded under the thorax.

Crabs are decapods—they have 10 limbs, attached to the thorax. Four pairs are legs. Crabs walk sideways, rather than forward. The two front limbs are chela, or claws. They use these to capture prey, and in self-defense. They also have appendages on the head, including antennae, used for feeling and smelling, and mouth parts.

The shell

The crab's shell, or exoskeleton, supports and protects its soft body parts. The shell is made of a hard material called chitin. A crab sheds several shells as it grows. The only exception is the hermit crab. To protect itself, the hermit crab pushes its long, soft abdomen into a shell that once belonged to a marine snail. When it grows too big for a shell, it looks for a larger one. The size of crabs varies greatly. Pea crabs are less than ¼ in. (6 mm) in diameter. Giant spider crabs can have leg spans of up to 12 ft. (3.7 m).

The life of a crab

Crabs hatch from jelly-covered eggs, usually laid in the ocean. Developing crabs pass through four stages before becoming adults. The first two stages take place inside the egg. Most crabs hatch as a zoea, a swimming larva, with two pairs of swimming limbs. The exception is freshwater crabs, which hatch with all their limbs.

Crabs are not picky eaters. Small fish and shellfish are their preferred food, but they also eat seaweed and algae, scraping the food off rocks with their claws. Some species, such as the fiddler crab, are scavengers, eating the remains of dead animals and plants.

Crabs are a favorite food of many seabirds and some fish. They are also a popular food for humans in many countries. Blue crabs and Dungeness crabs are among the most common crabs eaten by people.

SEE ALSO:
Animals;
Oceans and
Seas;
Seashores

Crustaceans, such as this Sally Lightfoot crab, are animals without a backbone. They have bodies made up of segments.

DID YOU KNOW?

Many spider crabs hide from predators by covering themselves with pieces of seaweed and sponges. They have hairlike hooks on their bodies and legs, and give off sticky secretions to keep the fragments attached.

✳ CRAZY HORSE (ABOUT 1849–77)

Tashunca-Uitco, or Crazy Horse, was a chief of the Oglala Sioux who firmly resisted white occupation of the northern Plains.

A memorial to the Sioux chief Crazy Horse. Started in 1948, it is still being carved.

In 1854 Sioux chief Crazy Horse was present at the Grattan massacre, the first clash between U.S. troops and the Sioux, which took place near Fort Laramie, Wyoming. All the soldiers were killed. In the 1870s, Crazy Horse fought to keep white gold miners out of the Black Hills, a region his people held sacred. In 1873 he took part in two skirmishes with Lieutenant Colonel George Custer's troops on the Yellowstone River.

Followers of Crazy Horse formed the Sioux Confederation, which later defeated Custer and the Seventh Cavalry at the Battle of the Little Bighorn in 1876. In the battle, Crazy Horse served as a field leader. He surrendered to the U.S. Army in May 1877, but was fatally stabbed by a guard while trying to resist imprisonment in September.

As a memorial his portrait is being carved from the solid rock of Thunderhead Mountain in South Dakota. When completed, the statue will be 563 ft. (171.6 m) tall, making it the world's largest mountain carving.

SEE ALSO: Native Americans

✳ CRIME AND LAW ENFORCEMENT

Laws are created to protect people and property. A crime is an act that is forbidden by law. The police and courts enforce the law.

In the United States, crimes are classified according to their seriousness. Major crimes are called felonies: They include murder, theft, and assault. Less serious crimes—such as vandalism and public drunkenness—are misdemeanors.

Reasons for crime

People commit crimes for different reasons. Some people's personalities may make them more likely to take drugs or be violent. Poor living conditions may also contribute to crime. Criminals may see theft as a quick way to make money. People sometimes commit crimes for political reasons. When this involves violence, it is called terrorism.

Police on a drug raid arrest a suspected dealer. The police arrest and charge suspects, but it is the task of the courts to examine the evidence and decide whether they are guilty or innocent.

The criminal justice system

The police are responsible for enforcing the law and preventing crime. When a crime is committed, they try to solve it and arrest a suspect. They may call on scientists and psychologists to help.

The police cannot decide whether a person is guilty. After a person is arrested and charged, he or she goes to court. The charged person is known as a defendant and has an attorney. The state provides a prosecuting attorney to argue that the defendant is guilty. The court is led by a judge, but it is often a jury of ordinary people who make the final decision.

If the person is found to be not guilty, he or she goes free, but if the person is found guilty, the court must decide on a punishment. This ranges from a fine for a minor offense to a prison sentence, or the death penalty, for more serious crimes.

DID YOU KNOW?

Fingerprints are the impressions of the ridges of the fingertips. They are used as a means of identification. No two people in the world, not even identical twins, have the same fingerprints. Only ink and paper are required to take fingerprints, making it both simple and inexpensive. The Federal Bureau of Investigation (FBI) has nearly 170,000,000 prints on file.

SEE ALSO: Law; Prisons; Supreme Court

✴CROCODILES see ✴ALLIGATORS AND CROCODILES

✴ CRUSADES

The Crusades were wars undertaken by Christians to defeat people they believed were enemies of their religion, and to protect Christianity's holy sites.

The best-known crusades were launched between 1096 and 1291 to conquer Palestine (modern Israel, Lebanon, and Syria). This area, known as the Holy Land, was sacred to Christians because Jesus Christ lived and died there. The area had been ruled by Muslims (followers of Islam) for over 300 years. Muslims allowed Christians to visit as pilgrims the holy places where Jesus had been.

By the 11th century, it was more difficult for pilgrims to visit the Holy Land. Pope Urban II (pope 1088–99) asked Christians to drive the Muslims out of Palestine. Many people responded. Some went for religious reasons, others to win glory, land, and money, and some for adventure.

The First Crusade

The First Crusade, begun in 1096, was a success. Although the Crusaders were outnumbered by the Muslims, they won. In 1099 the Crusaders took Jerusalem, a city holy to Christians and Muslims. They killed many of the people there and stole their valuables. The Crusaders divided the lands into states for themselves, one of

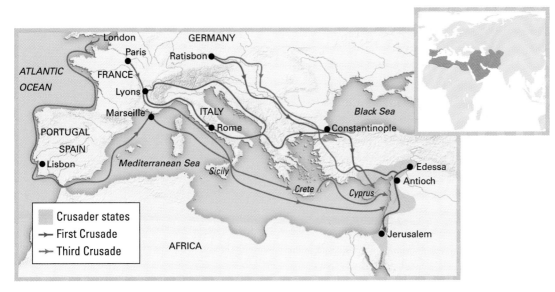

The small map shows the Islamic Empire in 750. The large map map shows the routes taken on the First Crusade (1096–99) and the Third Crusade (1189–92).

SEE ALSO:
Byzantine Empire;
Christianity;
Islam;
Knights and Chivalry;
Middle Ages

the most important being Jerusalem. The Crusaders ruled only a narrow strip of land, mostly along the Mediterranean coast. Muslim rulers won back the territory, and in 1187 a powerful Muslim leader, Saladin, recaptured Jerusalem. The West continued to send Crusaders to the East. The Fourth Crusade (1202–04) never reached the Holy Land. Instead it conquered and partially destroyed the Christian city of Constantinople. This played a major role in driving apart the Christians of Western Europe and the Orthodox Christians of the East. In 1291 Muslims conquered the last of the Crusader states.

✳ CUBA

Cuba is the largest and most populous country in the Caribbean Sea. It lies only 90 miles (145 km) from the southern tip of Florida.

Land and climate
Cuba consists of one large island and more than 1,600 little islands. About 40 percent of the country is mountainous. The climate is semitropical.

People and economy
Most of the original Native American people of Cuba died within 100 years of Spanish conquest during the early 1500s. Today most Cubans are of Spanish and African ancestry. Major products are sugar, coffee, fruit, and cigars. Since the collapse of the Soviet Union in the 1990s, Cuba's economy has suffered. Tourism has become an important source of income.

History
Cuba was claimed for Spain in 1492 by Christopher Columbus and remained a Spanish colony until 1898. The United States became involved in Cuba's war against Spain. It then occupied Cuba from 1899 to 1901 and from 1906 to 1909, and continued to be a powerful economic influence there after independence.

In 1958 revolutionaries led by Fidel Castro overthrew President Fulgencio Batista. Under Castro, Cuba became a Communist country. Because Castro received support from the Soviet Union, the United States cut off relations with Cuba in 1961. Cuban exiles, trained in the United States, landed

KEY FACTS

OFFICIAL NAME:
República de Cuba

AREA:
44,218 sq. mi. (114,524 sq. km)

POPULATION:
11,201,000

CAPITAL & LARGEST CITY:
Havana

MAJOR RELIGION:
Roman Catholicism

MAJOR LANGUAGE:
Spanish

CURRENCY:
Cuban peso

Cuba's national flag

SEE ALSO:
Caribbean
Islands;
Columbus,
Christopher;
Communism;
Spanish–
American
War

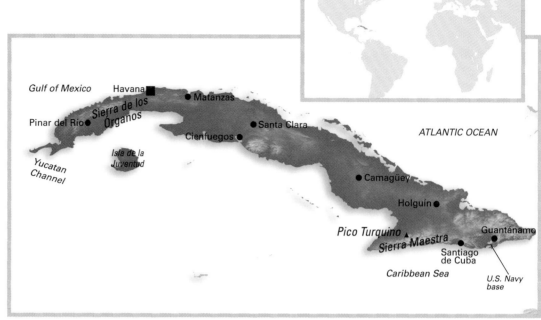

Gulf of Mexico — Havana — Matanzas — Pinar del Rio — Sierra de los Organos — Cienfuegos — Santa Clara — ATLANTIC OCEAN — Yucatan Channel — Isla de la Juventud — Camagüey — Holguín — Pico Turquino — Sierra Maestra — Guantánamo — Santiago de Cuba — Caribbean Sea — U.S. Navy base

at the Bay of Pigs but failed to overthrow Castro. In 1962 the United States found Soviet missiles in Cuba, which led to a confrontation between the Americans and the Soviets. The missiles were eventually removed. The United States still maintains trade restrictions against Cuba, although it has a naval base there.

* CURIE, MARIE (1867–1934) AND PIERRE (1859–1906)
Marja Sklodowska was born in Poland. In 1891 she went to college in Paris, France, and changed her name to Marie. In 1895 she married Pierre Curie.

Marie and Pierre Curie in their laboratory in 1898. They worked together to discover radium.

The couple worked together studying the invisible radiation given off by the element uranium. They discovered that the atoms of some elements are constantly breaking down. This gives off radiation that can pass through other materials. These elements are described as radioactive.

In 1903 the Curies and another scientist, Antoine Henri Becquerel, won the Nobel Prize in physics. Pierre Curie died in a street accident in 1906. Marie continued her research and won a second Nobel Prize—this time in chemistry—in 1911 for discovering the elements radium and polonium. She was the first person to receive two Nobel awards in science. When she died, in 1934, it was found that she had been poisoned by exposure to radioactivity.

In 1935 the Curies' daughter Irène and her husband, Frédéric Joliot-Curie, were awarded the Nobel Prize in chemistry.

SEE ALSO: Atoms and Molecules;
Chemistry; Elements; Nobel Prize; Scientists

✳ DAMS

A dam is a barrier that controls a flow of water. Dams may be built to store water, to prevent flooding, or to generate electricity.

The earliest dams were built in Egypt and Israel as long ago as 2500 B.C. They were usually made of rocks, earth, and wood. Today most dams are made of concrete and reinforced with steel.

The most common kind of dam are embankment dams. They are made of earth or rock and earth. The highest dams in the world, the Rogun and the Nurek in Tajikistan, are examples of this type. Timber dams are easy to build but do not last over time. They are sometimes built as temporary structures while a permanent dam is being built.

Major dams

There have been a number of important dam projects in the United States during the last 100 years.

The Tennessee Valley Authority (TVA) project, a series of dams begun in 1933, controlled the flow of the Tennessee River. It saved many areas from flood damage and provided low-cost energy to the region. The water is used to power turbines to create electricity—this is called hydroelectric power. However, many residents had to move from their homes, as farmland was flooded by reservoirs. Other important dams include the Grand Coulee in the Columbia River Basin and the Hoover Dam on the border of Arizona and Nevada. They were also built in the 1930s and provide electricity to vast areas of the United States.

The Hoover Dam is one of the world's largest dams. The dam wall is a massive 1,244-ft. (379-m) concrete arch that stretches between the deep canyon walls of the Colorado River.

By 2009 the world's largest dam will be the Three Gorges Dam on the Chang Jiang (Yangtze) River in China. It will supply one-tenth of China's electricity needs, but 1.3 million people have been forced to move because of it. The dam may also cause environmental problems.

▲
The Hoover Dam controls the Colorado River and provides hydroelectricity.

SEE ALSO: Electricity; Energy; Floods; Natural Resources; Water

✳ DANCE

A dance is a series of rhythmical steps and body movements, usually in time to music. Dance has been performed throughout human history.

Religious dance

Some of the earliest dances recorded in history were performed in ancient Greece in the fifth century B.C., as part of religious ceremonies. Many peoples in Africa, Australia, and other areas had similar religious dances. They performed them to ask their gods for a good harvest, victory in war, and other blessings. Many Native American peoples still perform these dances. For example, Pueblo Indians dance for rain.

Dancing for pleasure

Dancing for fun became popular in Europe in the 1300s. Country folk began to hold social dances in their villages. The nobles (people of high birth or rank) thought these dances were too wild, so they changed them to suit life in castles and royal courts. Ballroom dances, such as the minuet and the quadrille, had their origins in folk dance. When the waltz was introduced in Europe in the mid-1800s, it was considered shocking because couples had not danced with their arms around each other before. Many European dances, such as the polka from eastern Europe, came to North America with immigrants.

Dance often develops as music changes. In the 1900s, jazz music led to energetic dances such as the jitterbug and the lindy hop. In the 1960s, the twist became the first popular dance in which partners did not touch each other. In the 1970s, disco dancing to records became popular. Break-dancing to hip-hop music arrived in the 1980s. At the same time, line dancing to country music made use of older American dance steps.

Dancing as performance

During the 1500s, dance became part of dramatic entertainments, called masques, that were held at royal courts. In 1661 King Louis XIV of France founded the Royal Academy of Dance in Paris. This was the beginning of what is now known as ballet, a style of expressive dancing based on precise steps with graceful gestures and movements.

In the 1900s, choreographers—people who devise dance movements—and dancers began to break away from the strict, formal rules of European ballet. Popular forms of dance influenced professional performers. Dancers such as Fred Astaire, Ginger Rogers, and Gene Kelly brought tap and jazz dancing to the Hollywood screen. Broadway musicals, too, often became noted for their dance. Today's pop stars, such as Janet Jackson, can be superb dancers as well as singers and musicians.

Ginger Rogers and Fred Astaire in the 1938 movie Carefree. Tap dancing was popular in Hollywood films of the period. ▶

SEE ALSO:
Films;
Greece,
Ancient;
Music

✱ DARWIN, CHARLES (1809–82)

Charles Darwin's theory of evolution—how plants and animals developed from earlier forms of life—forever changed the way people see the world.

Charles Robert Darwin was born into a wealthy and well-known English family. From an early age, he showed an interest in nature. After leaving college in 1831, he became the naturalist on the ship H.M.S. *Beagle* for a five-year voyage to South America and the Pacific.

Darwin observed the geology and the animal and plant life wherever the ship visited. His studies of animals on the Galápagos Islands were very important. When he returned to England, in 1836, he began to develop the theory of natural selection. This is the idea that species develop because animals and plants best suited to their environment are the ones most likely to reproduce and survive.

In 1858 Darwin read an essay by the English scientist Alfred Russel Wallace. It came to the same conclusions that Darwin had reached. Darwin quickly published his ideas in a book called *On the Origin of Species by the Means of Natural Selection*. It sold out in a single day.

Many people attacked Darwin's theory of evolution because it seemed to go against established scientific ideas. It also went against the Bible's version of the creation of life on Earth. Darwin later argued that humans and apes are descended from a single species. His ideas were eventually accepted by most scientists, and he received Britain's highest scientific award for his work.

Charles Darwin's work changed our concept of nature and man's place within it.

SEE ALSO:
Biology;
Evolution;
Scientists

✱ DA VINCI, LEONARDO (1452–1519)

The most versatile talent of his age, Leonardo da Vinci was a painter, sculptor, architect, military engineer, inventor, musician, and scientist.

Leonardo was born in Vinci, Italy, which is why he is called Leonardo da ("from") Vinci. In 1469 he became apprenticed to the artist Andrea del Verrocchio in Florence. In 1482 Leonardo went to work for the duke of Milan. He supervised court entertainments, built military equipment, installed central heating in the duke's palace, and painted *The Last Supper*.

Leonardo filled notebooks with ideas for inventions. By studying his drawings of machines, 20th-century engineers have been able to build working models of them. Leonardo used mirror (backward) writing to protect his ideas.

Leonardo had many different interests. He studied the human body, dissecting (cutting up) dead bodies to see what they looked like inside. He also studied the structure of plants, making many discoveries about their growth.

In 1503 Leonardo returned to Florence, where he painted his most famous picture, the *Mona Lisa*. He died in France on May 2, 1519.

SEE ALSO: Art and Artists; Inventors and Inventions

This is thought to be a self-portrait of Leonardo da Vinci, sketched in about 1512.

✳ DECLARATION OF INDEPENDENCE

After the Constitution, the Declaration of Independence is the most famous and important legal document of the United States of America.

The Declaration of Independence was formally adopted on July 4, 1776, by representatives of the 13 original colonies. It announced that the United States was a nation separate from its old British rulers. The location of the meeting, the Pennsylvania State House in Philadelphia, became known as Independence Hall. Printed copies of the Declaration were distributed up and down the coast from New Hampshire and Massachusetts to South Carolina and Georgia. Americans still celebrate their country's birthday every year on July 4.

The Declaration
The Declaration was written mainly by Thomas Jefferson (1743–1826). The first part outlines the basic rights of all American citizens. The second part describes some of the wrongs that the British committed against Americans' rights. It states that all men are born equal. This does not mean that they are born equal in wealth, talent, or health. It means that they are equal in rights whether they are rich or poor. Everyone has the right to live, to be free, and to be happy.

The Declaration also states that governments exist only to protect the lives, liberties, and happiness of the people. If the people have a government that they do not like, they have the right to change it. This is one of the most important practices in a democracy.

The Declaration states that every person has the right to be treated as a human being—with dignity and with justice. In many times and places, people have not been treated that way. Americans themselves have not always met these high standards. However, President Abraham Lincoln (1809–65) said that the Declaration tells Americans what they ought to do, and they must try to live up to it.

On July 8, 1776, the Liberty Bell called citizens to hear the first public reading of the Declaration of Independence.

👀
SEE ALSO:
American Revolution;
Civil Rights;
Constitution, United States;
United States of America

✳ **DEMOCRACY** 👉 see ✳ **CITIZENSHIP**

✳ DESERTS

A desert is an area where there is very little water. Deserts are not necessarily hot, dry, and sandy— they may be cool or even covered with ice.

Most dry deserts receive less than 8 in. (200 mm) of rainfall in a year. There may be months or even years between storms. Most of the rain that does fall evaporates in the dry air before it soaks into the ground.

Dry desert plants must be able to store water in their roots or stems. Cacti are the best plants of this type. Animals must also be able to live with little water. Reptiles, such as snakes, obtain water from food. Mammals, such as gazelles and kangaroos, often travel long distances to isolated water holes. A place in the desert with enough water for plant growth is called an oasis. The water comes from underground layers of rock.

In tropical dry deserts the summers are extremely hot, while winters might be cool, sometimes with frost. Examples of this type of desert include the Sahara in northern Africa and the Atacama in northern Chile.

Dry deserts in the middle latitudes, such as the Gobi in Central Asia, are warm in the summer but bitterly cold in the winter. The ground is often frozen and cannot absorb water.

Cold deserts

Cold deserts form in areas where there are constantly low temperatures. They have little plant life and few inhabitants. Most of the high plateaus of the world are cold deserts. Ice deserts occur in the Antarctic and Arctic.

Reclaiming deserts

People have tried hard to make deserts habitable. Some peoples, such as the nomadic, or wandering, Bedouin of the Sahara, have lifestyles adapted to desert life. Water pipelines and irrigation have made it possible to build cities in deserts, such as Las Vegas in the Nevada desert.

Deserts often contain great mineral wealth. People live there to extract gold, diamonds, natural gas, and oil. New deserts may be formed by human activity, especially by using too much water or by overgrazing grassland. This process is called desertification.

SEE ALSO:
Antarctica;
Arctic;
Biomes;
Cactus

THE WORLD'S LARGEST DRY DESERTS

Sahara, Africa	3,500,000 sq. mi. (9,065,000 sq. km)
Australian	600,000 sq. mi. (1,554,000 sq. km)
Arabian, Middle East	500,000 sq. mi. (1,295,000 sq. km)
Gobi, Asia	400,000 sq. mi. (1,036,000 sq. km)
Kalahari, Africa	225,000 sq. mi. (582,750 sq. km)
Turkestan, Asia	220,000 sq. mi. (569,800 sq. km)
Taklimakan, China	125,000 sq. mi. (323,750 sq. km)
Sonoran, North America	120,000 sq. mi. (310,800 sq. km)
Namib, Africa	102,000 sq. mi. (264,000 sq. km)
Thar, Asia	100,000 sq. mi. (259,000 sq. km)
Somali, Africa	100,000 sq. mi. (259,000 sq. km)

◄ *A chameleon walks across dunes in the Namib Desert.*

✻ DICKENS, CHARLES (1812–70)
Charles Dickens is one of the greatest English writers. His most famous novels include *Great Expectations* and *Oliver Twist*.

Charles Dickens was a favorite author of Queen Victoria.

Charles John Huffam Dickens came from a poor and humble background. He spent his childhood working in a factory because his bankrupt father could not afford to send him to school. This deeply affected the young Charles.

As a young man, Dickens worked on a newspaper, where he soon discovered his gift for writing novels. Many of his works were published in weekly installments. His first book, *The Pickwick Papers*, was published between 1836 and 1837.

Dickens's novels are full of laughter and tears and are famous for their larger-than-life characters. Although he became successful, Dickens never forgot his poor roots. He was a campaigning novelist who wrote passionately about what was wrong with English society during the Victorian period: poverty, corruption, abuse of children, dirt, and disease. When his books exposed these injustices, politicians tried to make conditions better. Dickens never stopped working. He continued to give public readings from his works even when he became ill. He died at age 58.

SEE ALSO: Literature

✻ DICKINSON, EMILY (1830–86)
Although few of Emily Dickinson's poems were published during her lifetime, today she is recognized as one of America's best poets.

Emily Elizabeth Dickinson was born in Amherst, Massachusetts. Her father was strict, and it was said that he did not want his three children to read any book other than the Bible. At school, however, Emily enjoyed reading many authors.

After studying science for a year at a Bible school, Emily returned home, where she spent more and more time alone. She became a very private and, according to townspeople, a rather odd woman. She had begun to write poetry, but she kept it secret from almost everyone. In all, Dickinson wrote nearly 2,000 poems, although only seven were published before her death. Her work is now much loved and admired. Her poems are written mainly in short, unrhymed verses and often deal with unusual subject matter.

SEE ALSO: Literature

This drawing of Emily Dickinson was reproduced in an edition of her collected poems in 1925.

✻**DIGESTIVE SYSTEM** 👀➡ ✻**STOMACH AND DIGESTIVE SYSTEM**

DINOSAURS

Dinosaurs are reptiles that first appeared on Earth about 230 million years ago. They became extinct (died out) about 65 million years ago.

No human has ever seen a living dinosaur. We have only known about them since the 1800s, when paleontologists— scientists who study fossils—pieced together remains such as bones, footprints in rock, and eggs to discover what dinosaurs looked like. In 1841 Richard Owen, an English scientist, created the name *dinosaur* (from the Greek for "fearfully great lizard").

Sometimes paleontologists made mistakes when trying to identify dinosaurs. That is because it is very rare to find a complete skeleton. They have therefore had to make guesses about the parts that are missing. But they now generally agree that dinosaurs can be divided into two main groups, Saurischia and Ornithischia.

Saurischia

Saurischia means "lizardlike hip." Dinosaurs of this type had hipbones similar to those of modern crocodiles. They are subdivided into two further groups. Theropoda, or "beast feet," were carnivores (meat-eaters) that walked upright on their back legs. They had huge feet, usually with three or more toes. Their front limbs were very small.

The first Theropoda appeared in the Triassic period about 225 million years ago. They included *Coelophysis*, which was about 9 ft. (2.7 m) long. In the next geological period, the Jurassic, which began about 200 million years ago, lived *Allosaurus*, which was 30 ft. (9 m) long. It had sharp teeth and curving claws to slash its prey to shreds.

The most famous dinosaur lived during the Cretaceous period (about 144 million to 65 million years ago): *Tyrannosaurus* ("tyrant lizard") was about 50 ft. (15 m) long and weighed about 7 tons.

The other Saurischia were the Sauropoda, or "lizard feet." They were usually herbivores (plant-eaters), and they walked on all four legs. The earliest sauropod was *Plateosaurus*. Later the massive *Apatosaurus* (also called *Brontosaurus*,

This backbone was dug up in Big Bend National Park, Texas, in 1999. Scientists believe that it is from an Alamosaurus.

248–213 million years ago
The Triassic period, during which the first dinosaurs appeared on Earth.

213–144 million years ago
The Jurassic period, during which stegosaurs became widespread.

Stegosaurus

248-213 MILLION YEARS AGO

TRIASSIC *Coelophysis*

213-144 MILLION YEARS AGO

JURASSIC

▲
This timeline shows the main events during the evolution and decline of the dinosaurs.

meaning "thunder lizard"), with its huge legs, slender head, and long neck and tail, emerged. These dinosaurs weighed more than 30 tons.

Ornithischia
The other major group of dinosaurs is the Ornithischia ("birdlike hip"). Despite their name, Ornithischia were land-dwelling creatures. They were plant-eaters.

The Ornithischia group is subdivided into two smaller groups, Ornithopoda and Stegosauria. Ornithopoda ("bird feet") resemble modern birds, but many were much bigger than any bird we have ever seen. *Iguanodon*, for example, measured about 30 ft. (9 m) in length and weighed more than 4 tons. Many later Ornithopoda,

such as the hadrosaurs, had strange bumps or crests on their heads. Scientists believe they might have been used to smell or make sounds.

Stegosauria were dinosaurs with plates, armor, or horns. They first appeared during the Jurassic period. *Stegosaurus* ("plated lizard") had a small head and a brain the size of a walnut, although its body was up to 30 ft. (9 m) in length. It had one or two rows of bony plates along its backbone. *Triceratops* was a stegosaur that resembled modern rhinoceroses.

Among the other animals that lived during the age of the dinosaurs and later became extinct were pterosaurs, which flew, and ichthyosaurs, which lived in the oceans.

The end of the dinosaurs
No one knows for certain why the dinosaurs died out. Earth's climate may have changed, killing off the plants and animals that made up the dinosaurs' diet. The shape of the land and the seas shifted, and that may have destroyed the dinosaurs' habitats.

Another theory is that Earth was struck by a meteorite (a large lump of rock from space). It caused a massive cloud of dust that blocked out the sunlight and killed the plants that the dinosaurs ate. Some

DID YOU KNOW?

Most scientists believe that dinosaurs were covered by leathery skin, like modern reptiles. But a fossil of a young dinosaur of the type called dromaeosaur, found in China in 2001, has made some scientists think again. Around the body were imprints that seemed to show down and feathers. So, the scientists are asking, were the mighty dinosaurs something like big birds?

144–65 million years ago
The Cretaceous period, at the end of which dinosaurs became extinct.

Triceratops

Apatosaurus

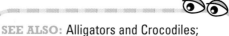
CRETACEOUS

Tyrannosaurus rex

people now think a star exploded and showered Earth with deadly radiation. The problem with these theories is that they do not clearly explain why many other species did not die out. The ancestors of modern animals—including humans—survived whatever killed off the dinosaurs. Scientists can make guesses, but they may never know for certain.

SEE ALSO: Alligators and Crocodiles; Archaeology; Comets, Meteors, and Asteroids; Extinction; Fossils; Reptiles; Rhinoceroses

✳ DISEASES

A disease is any illness or sickness that affects the normal functioning of an animal or plant. Every disease has its own set of effects, or symptoms.

The symptoms of a disease can be visible or invisible. Visible symptoms include spots or rashes. Invisible symptoms might be pain or tiredness. Doctors examine the patient and carry out tests to find the cause of disease. Diseases that develop quickly but are short-lived are known as acute. Chronic diseases last a long time.

Infectious diseases

Many diseases are caused when the body is invaded by unhealthy organisms called microbes. Bacteria and viruses are the main groups of microbes that can cause infectious diseases. They can enter the body in various ways—for example, from insect bites. They can be passed from one

A mosquito bite can transmit the disease malaria to humans.

person to another by sneezing or by sharing eating and drinking utensils.

Bacteria damage the body by creating poisons called toxins. Bacterial infections include tuberculosis and typhoid fever. Viruses invade cells and then reproduce within them. Viral diseases include influenza and measles.

Fighting disease
A healthy human body usually protects itself through its immune system. White blood cells destroy invading microbes. But sometimes the immune system goes wrong. This may be because it has already been weakened by another infection. Alternatively, the disease may be inherited. Acquired immune deficiency syndrome (AIDS) is a disease that weakens the immune system so that it is unable to fight off other diseases.

Congenital and hereditary diseases
Congenital diseases are those caused during or before birth. If a pregnant woman contracts rubella (German measles), her child may be born deaf.

The genes we get from our parents may cause hereditary diseases. These include hemophilia, when the blood cannot clot.

Neoplastic diseases
Neoplastic diseases occur when cells begin to divide too quickly. The result is a tumor, which may lead to cancer. Cancer may be hereditary, or it may be triggered by other causes, such as smoking.

SEE ALSO: Blood; Genetics; Health; Human Body; Medicine

✻ DOGS, WOLVES, AND OTHER WILD DOGS
Dogs are members of the Canidae family of mammals. There are about 35 different species, including coyotes, foxes, jackals, and wolves.

Most members of the dog family, or canids, are good runners, with muscular, deep-chested bodies and slender legs. They have four toes on each paw, plus a thumblike toe on each forepaw and sometimes on the rear feet as well. They walk on their toes, which

Bloodhounds are used as tracker dogs because of their strong sense of smell.

are well padded. Dogs have 42 teeth—some for gripping and tearing flesh, some for cutting, and others for grinding food.

Dogs have superb hearing and fairly good eyesight, but their keenest sense is smell. They are able to detect a scent weeks after its source is gone. Dogs use their voices regularly. Domestic dogs bark to raise an alarm, to show aggression or fear, or as a cry for help. Growling usually means "Stay away." Dogs may also howl, whimper, or whine to show their feelings.

Wild canids
Some wild canids look very like domestic dogs. Others are quite unusual and hardly resemble dogs at all. However, they all

share a common ancestor, *Tomarctus*. Around 15 million years ago *Tomarctus* roamed the earth's forests.

The largest wild canid is the gray wolf. It was once common, but human settlers, fearful of wolves, killed so many of them that today they are found only in remote parts of northern North America and on rugged mountains in Europe and Asia. Wolves live in family groups called packs. The pack works together to hunt prey. With their deep chests and long legs, wolves can trot for hours without tiring.

Coyotes and jackals are wild canids that look like small, rangy wolves. They may form packs or pairs, though some coyotes live alone. Coyotes are found from Alaska to Central America. Jackals live in Africa and south-central Asia. The African wild dog and the Asian dhole are similar animals. They also hunt in packs.

Foxes are small canids that live mostly alone or in pairs. There are more than 20 fox species around the world, from the snowy Arctic to the hottest deserts. The red fox is often seen in towns, eating garbage that has been left lying around by humans.

Other wild canids include the rare bush dog of the Amazon jungles, the Australian dingo, and the maned wolf of the South American grasslands.

Dogs and people
Our pet dogs are descended from wolves. They were domesticated, or tamed and raised by people, more than 12,000 years ago. Today dogs depend on people for food, shelter, and safety. They give a great deal in return. Some are trained to guard property. Others herd farm animals, work with hunters, sniff out bombs or drugs at airports, or search for survivors at disaster scenes. Specially trained dogs assist people who cannot see or hear, or who use a wheelchair.

Breeds of domestic dog
It is because of these special tasks that there are so many different breeds of dog. New kinds of dogs were bred to perform specific tasks. The American Kennel Club classifies purebred dogs in seven groups: working, sporting, hound, terrier, herding, toy, and nonsporting.

The working breeds are dogs that are most often used by the police or on guard duty. This group includes Doberman pinschers, German shepherds, and Rottweilers. Dogs that pull sleds, such as the Siberian husky, are also working dogs.

The sporting breeds are widely used as hunting dogs. German shorthaired pointers and English setters are among the dogs trained to locate game birds for hunters. Some breeds have been trained to fetch animals and birds after they have been shot down.

A North American gray wolf rests on a rock.
▼

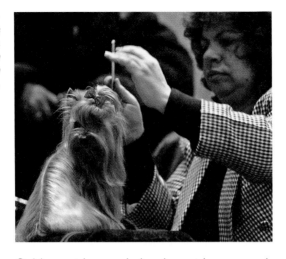

▶ *A woman combs a Yorkshire terrier, a toy breed, at a dog show in Moscow, Russia.*

SEE ALSO:
Animals;
Mammals

Golden retrievers, Labrador retrievers, and Chesapeake Bay retrievers recover birds from water and bring them to the hunters. Dachshunds were originally bred in Germany to chase badgers. Hunters on horseback often follow a pack of

foxhounds as they trail a fox. Bloodhounds have a remarkable sense of smell. Police sometimes use them to hunt for people.

Terriers were bred and trained to hunt rodents. Breeds such as the Manchester terrier and the Cairn terrier could catch mice and rats and shake them to death.

Herding breeds chase and direct farm animals. They round up stray sheep and cattle, move herds from one field to another, and guard livestock from danger. Herding breeds include the collie and the Shetland sheepdog.

Most tiny dogs are called toy breeds. This group includes the Chihuahua, the toy poodle, and the Shih Tzu. These breeds have been kept as house pets for hundreds, sometimes thousands, of years and are especially popular as show dogs.

✳DOLPHINS 👀see ✳WHALES AND DOLPHINS

✳ DOUGLASS, FREDERICK (1817–95)

Frederick Douglass was one of the most dynamic leaders of the abolition movement, which worked to get rid of slavery.

▲ *Douglass was the first black to hold a high government position.*

Frederick Douglass was born Frederick Augustus Washington Bailey in Maryland. He was the son of a white father and a slave mother. He learned to read and write while working as a house slave. In 1838 he escaped to the North and changed his name.

In 1841 Douglass addressed a meeting of the Massachusetts Anti-Slavery Society. He spoke so well that some people doubted he could ever have been a slave. In response, he wrote an autobiography entitled *Narrative of the Life of Frederick Douglass*.

In 1845 Douglass went on a lecture tour of England, earning the money to buy his freedom. In 1847 he founded *North Star*, an antislavery newspaper. During the Civil War (1861–65) he organized regiments of black soldiers. After the war, he became a leader of the Republican Party. From 1889 to 1891, he was U.S. minister to Haiti.

SEE ALSO: Abolition Movement; African Americans; Civil Rights; Civil War; Emancipation Proclamation; Slavery

✳ EARS AND HEARING

Hearing is the sense that receives sound. Ears receive sound waves and change them into signals that the brain translates into the sensation of sound.

Sound is described by volume—how loud it is—and by frequency—how high or low it is. Volume is measured in decibels. A normal conversation is about 65 decibels. Frequency is measured in hertz. Most people can hear frequencies between about 16 and 20,000 hertz.

People hear sounds when they pick up vibrations called sound waves. The waves enter the ear and strike the eardrum, causing a vibration that moves tiny bones inside the skull. This sends a message along the auditory nerves to the brain.

The brain does not just register the volume and frequency of sounds. It also makes sense of them. A loud rock band

and a pneumatic drill might sound similar, but the human brain can tell them apart.

Many animals need more sensitive hearing than humans so they can hear their prey. Dolphins and bats make ultrasonic sounds that are too high-pitched to be heard by the human ear.

When a person cannot hear the normal range of volume or frequency, he or she has a hearing impairment. If someone cannot hear sounds below 90 decibels, the condition is identified as deafness.

SEE ALSO:
Bats; Brain and Nervous System; Human Body; Sound; Whales and Dolphins

AMAZING FACTS !

The Beatles' album *Sergeant Pepper's Lonely Hearts Club Band* (1967) ends with a sound so high-pitched that humans cannot hear it—but dogs can.

A blue whale can make low-frequency noises with a volume of 188 decibels. By comparison, a jumbo jet on takeoff only makes a sound of 120 decibels.

INSIDE THE EAR

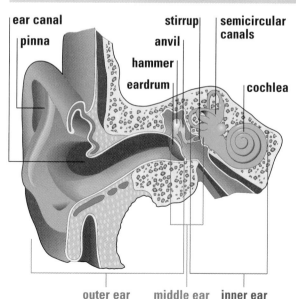

ear canal
pinna
hammer
eardrum
stirrup
anvil
semicircular canals
cochlea
outer ear   middle ear   inner ear

The outer ear is made up of the pinna, which is the part that you can see, and the ear canal. The middle ear contains three tiny bones that connect the inner and the outer ear. The inner ear has sensory receptors for hearing, and it controls balance.

✱ EARTH

The planet Earth is a vast mass of rock surrounded by layers of air, circling the sun. About 71 percent of Earth's surface is covered by water.

Scientists believe Earth was formed about 4.6 billion years ago, probably from tiny pieces of dust and gases produced when the sun was created. For the first billion years there was little or no life on the planet. Its atmosphere was probably made of carbon dioxide and steam.

No one knows when life began. The earliest traces suggest that it first appeared in the oceans about 3.8 billion years ago. These early life-forms were simple organisms with only one cell each. Very slowly life developed into more complex organisms. Between 600 and 240 million years ago, life began to develop on land. The first humans appeared about six million years ago.

Earth in space
All the light, heat, and energy on Earth comes from the sun. Earth orbits (revolves around) the sun at a distance of about 93 million miles (150 million km). On a complete orbit, it travels about 590 million miles (950 million km). Each orbit lasts about 365 days—one year. The moon, about 240,000 miles (386,200 km) away, is the planet's only natural satellite. The moon completes an orbit of Earth once every 29 days—a lunar month.

Earth itself is spinning, and each complete rotation lasts about 24 hours—one day. The most northerly point on Earth is the North Pole, and the most southerly spot is the South Pole. Imagine a line connecting the North and South poles

◄
This photograph of Earth was taken from the moon in 1994 by the space mission Clementine.

through the center of Earth. This imaginary line is the axis on which the planet spins.

Earth's structure
Earth is basically spherical, or ball-shaped, but is slightly flattened at the poles. Its diameter is about 7,923 miles (12,751 km) at its widest point, called the equator, where its circumference (the distance all the way around the surface) is 24,902 miles (40,067 km).

Beneath the surface, Earth is made up of three layers. The topmost layer is called the crust. Its thickness varies from about 22 miles (35 km) on land to only 3 miles (4.8 km) beneath the oceans. The crust is made mainly of granite and basalt rocks.

Below the crust is the mantle, which accounts for about four-fifths of the planet's volume. The core—the center of Earth—is made mostly of iron, which is molten because it is under enormous heat and pressure.

Probably because of the iron at its center, Earth is a magnet. It has two magnetic poles, one at the north of the planet, the other at the south. These magnetic poles are close to, but not exactly at, the geographic North and South poles.

Ever-changing Earth
The map of Earth has not always looked the way it does today. Over 150 million years ago, Africa and Europe were joined to North and South America, and the Atlantic Ocean did not exist. Australia and Antarctica formed a single continent, and India was a large island.

Earth 200 million years ago. Laurasia and Gondwanaland split to form the continents we know today.

Since then, however, vast sections, or plates, of the planet's crust and upper mantle have gradually shifted position, splitting the land apart to form the map we know today. This process is called continental drift.

Today the planet consists of several large plates and a number of smaller ones. Sometimes plates rub against each other, and the rocks they are made of are driven up to form massive mountain ranges. The longest mountain ranges are about 30,000 miles (50,000 km) long, but they are largely invisible because they lie submerged beneath the Atlantic, Indian, and Pacific oceans.

The surface of Earth is still constantly changing, but the process is usually so slow that we cannot see it happening. Many changes are caused by air, water, and wind, which wear away rocks and mountains over millions of years. This process is called erosion.

Other changes are caused by geological forces that originate deep inside the planet. They can be much more sudden and violent than erosion. Strains between Earth's plates can produce shock waves that result in earthquakes.

Molten rock-forming material (lava) from the mantle can escape onto the surface through gaps in the crust called volcanoes. Almost all earthquakes and volcanic activity take place where the edges of certain plates meet.

Geologists examine a lava stream near an active volcano in Hawaii.

KEY FACTS

POSITION IN THE SOLAR SYSTEM:
Third planet from the sun

AVERAGE DISTANCE FROM THE SUN:
93,000,000 mi. (150,000,000 km)

SOLAR ORBIT:
365.25 Earth days

DIAMETER:
7,923 mi. (12,751 km)

MASS:
6.6 sextillion tons

ATMOSPHERE:
Mainly nitrogen (79 percent) and oxygen (20 percent). Also small amounts of other gases (argon, carbon dioxide, helium, hydrogen, krypton, neon, and xenon) and dust

AXIAL ROTATION:
23 hours 56 minutes

SEE ALSO: Atmosphere; Calendars; Continents; Earthquakes; Geology; Mountains and Valleys; Oceans and Seas; Planets; Plate Tectonics; Solar System; Volcanoes; Weather

* EARTHQUAKES

An earthquake is a sudden release of natural energy onto the surface of the earth, generated by the movement of rocks deep underground.

This great crack in the pavement was caused by an earthquake that hit Taiwan in 1999.

The shaking movements sent out by earthquakes are called seismic waves. Scientists who study these movements are called seismologists. These experts used to believe that all earthquakes were caused by slippages, called faulting, in rocks in the lowest reaches of the earth's outermost layer, or crust. But they now think that faulting is only a secondary cause of earthquakes, and that most shock waves originate in the mantle, the layer below the crust. Here masses of steam are produced. As the steam moves slowly upward, it heats rocks in its path, eventually dislodging them and producing added effects that may eventually be felt on the surface.

Measuring earthquakes

Thousands of earthquakes happen every year, but most are so small that they can be detected only by the most sensitive scientific equipment. One or two are huge: They may cause vast destruction and alter the appearance of the earth.

During an earthquake, the point at which the greatest amount of seismic movement takes place is called the focus. The point on the earth's surface directly above the focus is called the epicenter. The effects of the earthquake are usually strongest near the epicenter. The magnitude, or

AMAZING FACTS!

An earthquake in Shanxi, China, in 1556 is thought to have killed at least 830,000 people and measured 8.0 to 8.3 on the Richter scale.
A cat survived for 80 days lying beneath a collapsed building after being buried by an earthquake in Taiwan in 1999.

total amount of energy, released by an earthquake is usually measured on the Richter scale. The strongest earthquakes measure about 8.6 on this scale.

Making predictions

People can neither prevent earthquakes nor predict when they will happen. However, they are more likely to happen in certain areas, such as along the San Andreas Fault in California and in parts of Japan. Houses and other structures in these areas are built to survive shocks. Earthquakes generally happen along the boundaries of the tectonic plates in the earth's crust.

Earthquakes beneath the ocean floor can produce huge waves called tsunamis that move rapidly across the ocean. They can cause great damage if they reach land.

SEE ALSO: Earth; Geology; Plate Tectonics

✳ EAST AFRICA

The countries of East Africa are Djibouti, Eritrea, Ethiopia, Kenya, Somalia, Tanzania, and Uganda. Some experts include the island nations of Comoros, Madagascar, Mauritius, and the Seychelles.

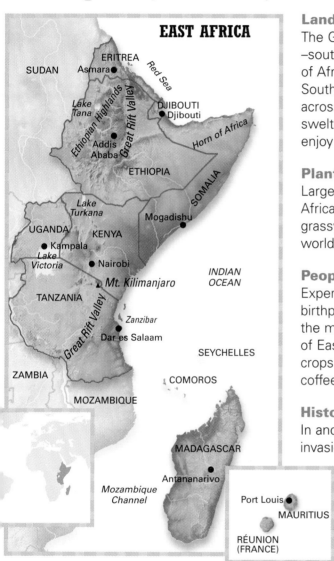

EAST AFRICA

Land and climate
The Great Rift Valley carves a wide north–south line through East Africa. The Horn of Africa lies to the northeast of the Rift. South of the Horn, much of the region lies across the equator. While lowland areas swelter in tropical heat, the highland parts enjoy a more pleasant climate.

Plants and animals
Large areas of savanna and forest in East Africa are protected as national parks. The grassy plains are home to some of the world's richest wildlife.

People and economy
Experts believe that East Africa was the birthplace of modern humans. Swahili is the most common language. The majority of East Africans farm the land. Popular crops grown for export include bananas, coffee, sugarcane, tea, and tobacco.

History
In ancient times, tribal chiefs ruled. Arab invasions from the seventh century onward brought Islam to East Africa. Europeans arrived in the 19th century; many seized land for colonies. Only Ethiopia stayed independent. East Africa's countries gained independence in the 1960s and 1970s. Since then there has been much conflict in Eritrea, Ethiopia, Somalia, and Uganda.

◄

Between the ages of about 14 and 30, the Masai men of Kenya are called morans *(junior warriors). During this time they train to become senior warriors.*

SEE ALSO:
Africa;
Kenya

✴ EASTERN EUROPE

The countries of Eastern Europe are Belarus, Czech Republic, Hungary, Moldova, Poland, Russia, Slovakia, and Ukraine.

Land and climate

Russia lies partly in Europe and partly in Asia. The Ural Mountain range marks the division between the continents. The western half of Russia is considered to be part of Eastern Europe.

The region forms part of the Central European Plain—the most densely settled area of the continent, with many large rivers. The Volga, Europe's longest river, flows through Russia. The region also has some of the greatest climate extremes in the continent. The lowest winter temperatures occur in the tundra of northern Russia; the southern part of Russia receives very little rain.

People and economy

Most people in Eastern Europe speak a language from the Slavic group. Roman Catholicism is the main religion in Poland, the Czech Republic, and Slovakia. In Russia, Ukraine, and Belarus most people belong to the Eastern Orthodox Church.

Eastern Europe, especially Poland, Russia, and Ukraine, is rich in coal. Russia also has large deposits of oil. Manufacturing mainly takes place in Poland, the Czech Republic, Ukraine, and the Urals area of Russia.

History

Slavic tribes have lived in Eastern Europe since the time of Christ. The Slavs first lived between the Volga and Oder rivers. By the end of the first millennium, the West Slavs, ancestors of modern Czechs, Poles, and Slovaks, had settled in north-

EASTERN EUROPE

LATVIA
LITHUANIA
Baltic Sea
RUSSIA
Moscow●
● Minsk
BELARUS
RUSSIA
Vistula River
● Warsaw
GERMANY
POLAND
● Prague
CZECH
REPUBLIC
● Kiev
UKRAINE
Dniester River
Dnieper River
SLOVAKIA
● Bratislava
AUSTRIA
● Budapest
● Chisinau
HUNGARY
MOLDOVA
Sea of Azov
SLOVENIA
ROMANIA
CROATIA
SERBIA &
MONTENEGRO
Black Sea

central Europe. The East Slavs—the future Russians, Ukrainians, and Belorussians—had advanced to the east. Hungarians trace their history to the Magyars, a people with a unique language and culture. In the 1500s, the Ottoman Turks, who were building a vast empire across Asia and Eastern Europe, invaded Hungary. They held it until the end of the 1600s, when it joined the Austrian empire.

In the 11th and 12th centuries, Germanic peoples had moved into Slavic territory. By the end of the 18th century, Poland was divided up among Prussia (a German state), Austria, and Russia. Russia had been expanding westward since the 16th century. This land was lost after World War I (1914–18), and Poland was re-created.

In the years following World War II (1939–45), Europe was divided politically. Russia became part of a Communist superstate, the Soviet Union, which put Communist governments in power across Eastern Europe. Much of Western Europe allied itself with the United States. This period was called the Cold War because the United States and the Soviet Union threatened to go to war, but never did.

From 1989 to 1991, the Eastern European Communist states replaced their governments with democratically elected ones. In 1991 the Soviet Union broke apart into the republics from which it had been formed. Czechoslovakia split into the Czech Republic and Slovakia in 1993.

The historic capital city of Prague in the Czech Republic. As well as being the commercial and financial center of the country, its rich culture and history attracts many tourists.

The Biebrza National Park in eastern Poland is the largest area of marshes and peat lands in this part of Europe.

SEE ALSO: Byzantine Empire; Central Europe; Communism; Europe; Hungary; Poland; Russia and the Baltic States; World War I; World War II

✳ECHINODERMS see ✳STARFISH AND OTHER ECHINODERMS

✳ ECOLOGY

Ecology is the study of the complex and ever-changing relationship between living things—organisms—and their environment.

▲
Ecologists have discovered that the number of lodgepole pine seedlings in Yellowstone National Park, Wyoming, has increased tenfold since the 1988 forest fires.

Habitats and ecosystems

All plants and animals are suited to a particular habitat—the place and natural conditions in which they live; for example, a forest floor. The plants and animals of a particular habitat form groups called communities. A small community might be all the organisms living in a rotting log. The number of species within a community is called species diversity. Variety of species is called biodiversity. An ecosystem is a community of living things plus the nonliving things they need to survive. In particular, it is the way in which all the organisms interact with their environment and with each other. When it is considered as an ecosystem, a forest is more than a group of trees; it is a complex of soil, air, water, minerals, bacteria, animals, and birds.

Energy and food webs

Ecologists try to understand how the relationships between organisms and their surroundings change and why. They study the flow of nutrients and energy between living and nonliving things. For example, in a forest ecosystem, a tree uses energy from the sun to produce new growth. Its roots draw nutrients from the soil. When the leaves fall off, they rot on the ground, returning nutrients to the soil. Ecologists also study the relationships between living things in a community. One way to do this is to study which organisms eat other living things. These links are described in food chains. Within an ecosystem such as a pond, members of different food chains feed on each other to form a set of interconnecting chains called a food web.

Ecosystems change constantly. Some changes are caused by natural events such as fires or floods. An ecosystem that is functioning well may even benefit from natural change. However, human activities, such as clearing a forest, can cause dramatic change that leads to the loss of biodiversity. Ecology shows that any changes humans make in the environment affect all the organisms in it.

SEE ALSO: Biomes; Environment; Food Chains; Forests; Pollution; Soil

✷ ECONOMICS

Economics is the study of the way money, goods, and services are made and used in a society. The part of a society's activity that produces wealth through goods and services is called the economy.

In a market economy, people have a wide variety of products to choose from.
▼

People need food and shelter to survive. Many people also want luxuries—things that they do not need. As well as these items, people also use services, such as education. Economists define a society by how it makes these goods and services, and how it consumes or uses them.

Economists study how economic systems work. They try to forecast how economic conditions will change. With governments and businesses, they try to keep prices stable, reduce unemployment, and keep a balance between collecting government taxes and ensuring that people have enough money for goods and services.

Types of economy

In some nonindustrial parts of the world, people operate in small family or tribal groups. They produce what they need to survive. There is little or no trade with outside groups. This is called a traditional economy. In some more developed areas, governments tell people what to produce. They set prices and control trade. This is a command economy. China is an example of this system.

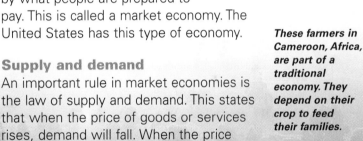

In other societies, the government takes little role in the economy. People can mostly buy or sell what they want. Prices are determined by what people are prepared to pay. This is called a market economy. The United States has this type of economy.

These farmers in Cameroon, Africa, are part of a traditional economy. They depend on their crop to feed their families.

Supply and demand

An important rule in market economies is the law of supply and demand. This states that when the price of goods or services rises, demand will fall. When the price falls, demand will rise. At the same time, if the price rises, the supply will rise; if the price falls, supply will also fall. Supply and demand work together to help set prices.

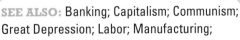

SEE ALSO: Banking; Capitalism; Communism; Great Depression; Labor; Manufacturing; Money; Stock Markets; Trade

✳ ECUADOR

Ecuador is on the Pacific coast of South America. The equator crosses the country north of the capital, Quito. *Ecuador* is the Spanish word for "equator."

Ecuador's national flag

Land and climate

The coastal lowlands (*costa*) include tropical forests and rich agricultural land. In the center of the country are the Andean highlands (*sierra*). The *Oriente* (eastern region) includes tropical forests and important oil deposits. Ecuador owns the Galápagos Islands, about 600 miles (965 km) off the coast. They are famous for their wildlife.

The higher peaks of the Andes Mountains stay snow-covered all year. Rainfall is heaviest in the *Oriente*, with 100 in. (2,500 mm) or more of rain a year.

People and economy

About 80 percent of Ecuador's population are Indians or mestizos. Mestizos are people of mixed Indian and European (mainly Spanish) ancestry. The rest are of Spanish, black, or mixed black ancestry. The blacks are descendants of slaves who were brought from Africa during the period of Spanish rule.

Just over half the population lives in rural areas, mostly either in the sierra or in the costa regions.

KEY FACTS

OFFICIAL NAME: República del Ecuador	**MAJOR RELIGION:** Roman Catholicism
AREA: 103,930 sq. mi. (269,180 sq. km)	**MAJOR LANGUAGES:** Spanish, Quechua, other Indian languages
POPULATION: 12,646,000	
CAPITAL: Quito	**CURRENCY:** U.S. dollar
LARGEST CITY: Guayaquil	

Petroleum is Ecuador's biggest industry. One-third of the workforce is employed in agriculture. Bananas, coffee, cacao, and sugarcane are the main crops. Shrimp, tuna, and balsa wood are major exports. In 1999 the Ecuadorean economy collapsed, and the government adopted U.S. currency to encourage stability.

History

In the late 1400s, the area that is now Ecuador became part of the Inca Empire. Spain defeated the Incas in the 1530s, founding a new city at Quito in 1534. In the 1800s, Ecuadoreans rose up against Spanish rule, winning their freedom in 1822. Ecuador became an independent republic in 1830. For much of the 20th century, it suffered from political unrest.

SEE ALSO: Incas; South America

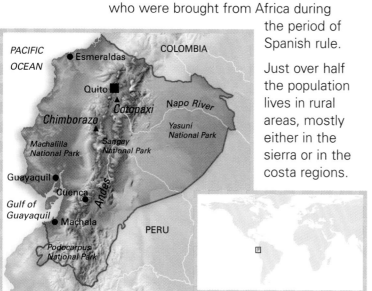

PACIFIC OCEAN — COLOMBIA — Esmeraldas — Quito — Cotopaxi — Napo River — Chimborazo — Yasuní National Park — Machalilla National Park — Sangay National Park — Andes — Guayaquil — Cuenca — Gulf of Guayaquil — Machala — PERU — Podocarpus National Park

✳ EDISON, THOMAS ALVA (1847–1931)

Thomas Edison was one of the most important inventors ever, making discoveries in electric light, sound recording, telegraphy, and telephones.

Thomas Edison pictured with his phonograph. It was the first machine that reproduced sound from a recording.

Thomas Alva Edison was born in Milan, Ohio, on February 11, 1847. Although he was clever, he did not do well at school, so he was taught at home. When he was 12, he got a job selling newspapers on the Grand Trunk Railroad and later became a telegrapher. That made him want to improve the way telegraphs worked.

In 1876 Edison set up an "invention factory" at Menlo Park, New Jersey. There he built the first phonograph, an early version of the record player. He was also the first person to build a workable electric light system. He set up a movie studio, and his company produced the first movie that told a story, *The Great Train Robbery*, in 1903.

It was eight minutes long. Next he developed the first storage battery that could be used over and over again.

Edison received 1,093 patents in the United States—more than anyone before or since. A patent gives an inventor the exclusive right to make, use, and sell a new invention for a period of time.

SEE ALSO: Communication; Electricity; Films; Inventors and Inventions; Sound Recording; Telecommunications

✳ EDUCATION

Education is the gaining of knowledge and skills. People start learning almost as soon as they are born, and the process carries on throughout life.

Most ancient cultures made education available for boys only. Girls did not go to school for many centuries.

In ancient Greece, education was intended to prepare young men for playing a part in society. They were taught reading, writing, math, singing, and sports. The greatest teacher was Socrates (about 470–399 B.C.). His followers, who included Plato and Aristotle, set up schools that instructed the young in philosophy (the art of thinking).

The Romans took many ideas about education from the Greeks and spread them throughout their empire. When the

Western Roman Empire collapsed in the fifth century, education in Europe declined. For many years, even kings were unable to read. Only boys intending to be priests got a good education.

Renaissance and the modern era

The great expansion in learning that began in the 1300s was called the Renaissance. After 1455 the development of the printing press made books cheaper and more widely

A stone relief carving showing a schoolmaster in ancient Rome instructing a pupil.

available. The Reformation, the period in the 1500s when many people broke away from the Roman Catholic Church, also had an effect on education. The Bible was translated from Latin into local languages, so people could read it for themselves. However, churches and religious bodies still controlled most schools.

In the 1700s, thinkers like Jean-Jacques Rousseau (1712–78) argued that education should give more freedom to children and use less discipline. Governments began to pay for education, and girls got better access to learning. From the 1900s, most Western countries began providing state-funded education to all children, usually for about 10 years from age five.

Education in the United States

In colonial America, children learned to read and write by memorizing religious passages. By the end of the 1800s, state-funded schools were providing basic education in all states. Many schools remained racially segregated until 1954.

Today states still have control over the public schools within their borders. Each state is divided into school districts, run by school boards. Most districts organize their schools on a "ladder" system. Children begin with preschool and elementary schools, moving to middle or junior high schools, and then to high schools. After high school, many students go on to colleges and universities.

SEE ALSO:
Ancient
Civilizations;
Colonial
America;
Greece,
Ancient;
Reformation;
Renaissance;
Roman
Empire

* EGYPT

Egypt is a republic in northeastern Africa. The remains of ancient Egyptian civilization make it a popular area for tourists and archaeologists.

Egypt's national flag

Land and climate

Two waterways dominate Egypt: the Nile River, which flows north 930 miles (1,500 km) to the Mediterranean Sea; and the Suez Canal, which links the Mediterranean with the Red Sea.

Deserts to the east and west squeeze 95 percent of Egypt's population into the narrow Nile Valley and delta, which make up only about 5 percent of the country's land area. The Sinai Peninsula includes Jabal Katrina, Egypt's highest point, at 8,625 ft. (2,629 m).

Summer temperatures in the south can reach 110°F (43°C) during the day. The Mediterranean coast is cooler, but still warm and dry all year. Rainfall is limited.

People

Although Egypt is on the African continent, most of its people are Arabs.

The majority are Muslim, although 7 percent belong to the Coptic Christian faith. Arabic is the official language.

Economy

The Nile Valley is a fertile agricultural area, and farming employs nearly 30 percent of the workforce. Cotton, vegetables, and rice are important crops.

Industry and mining, especially of petroleum products, are increasingly important. Revenue from tourism provides foreign currency, but this has suffered in recent years because of political unrest, including terrorist attacks.

History

In A.D. 640 Arab Muslims invaded Egypt. The earliest Arab settlement was at Al-Fustat, south of modern Cairo. In 1517 the Ottoman Turks took control. Ottoman

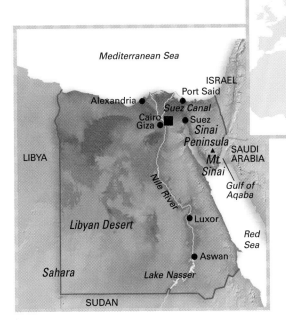

Mediterranean Sea

ISRAEL
Port Said
Alexandria
Suez Canal
Cairo · Suez
Giza
Sinai
Peninsula
Mt. SAUDI
Sinai ARABIA
LIBYA
Gulf of
Aqaba
Nile River
Luxor
Libyan Desert
Red
Sea
Aswan
Sahara Lake Nasser
SUDAN

Britain occupied Egypt in 1882. Egypt did not regain independence until 1922. In 1952 a military coup overthrew the Egyptian king. Gamal Abdel Nasser became president in 1954. He took control of the Suez Canal, and British and French troops invaded.

Egypt and Israel went to war in 1967 and 1973. In 1979 Nasser's successor, Anwar el-Sadat, signed a peace treaty with Israel. Other Arab states, and many Egyptians, objected, and Sadat was assassinated in 1981. In 1982 Israel completed its withdrawal from the Sinai Peninsula, which it had been occupying since 1967.

governor Mehemet Ali, who ruled Egypt between 1805 and 1848, founded a dynasty that gained independence. He began a program of reform. When the Suez Canal opened in 1869, Britain and France increased their interest in Egypt.

SEE ALSO: Canals; Egypt, Ancient; Middle East

* EGYPT, ANCIENT

The civilization of Egypt was one of the most important of ancient times. It was based in the valley of the Nile River.

In about 3200 B.C., a ruler named Menes, or Narmer, united the cities of northern and southern Egypt on the Nile River, founding one of the first great empires of the ancient world. Menes was the first king, or pharaoh, of the first dynasty (ruling family). Thirty-one dynasties ruled

The Great Sphinx at Giza, which was carved in about 2500 B.C. It has the body of a lion and the head of a man—the face is a portrait of King Khafre of Egypt's Old Kingdom.

This map shows the area influenced by Egyptian culture. All the great cities of ancient Egypt were near the banks of the Nile River, where the land was fertile enough to grow crops. ▶

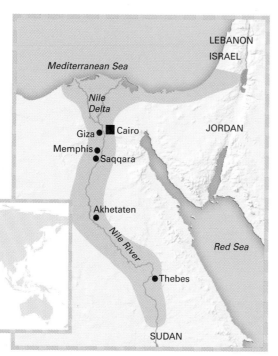

Egypt until Alexander the Great conquered it in 332 B.C. The dynasties are grouped into periods of stability (called the Old, Middle, and New Kingdom) and periods of unrest when several people claimed the throne. One of Alexander's generals ruled Egypt as Ptolemy I. The last of his descendants was Cleopatra VII. After her death, Egypt became a Roman province.

The ancient Egyptians worshiped many gods. The most important was Re, the sun god. Egyptians believed that the pharaohs were his descendants. Because Egyptians believed in life after death, the bodies of important people were mummified, or preserved. Dead pharaohs were placed in pyramids. The most famous pyramids are at Giza, on the west bank of the Nile River.

SEE ALSO: Alexander the Great; Alphabet; Ancient Civilizations; Archaeology; Cleopatra; Egypt; Religions; Roman Empire; Rosetta Stone; Wonders of the World; Writing

* EINSTEIN, ALBERT (1879–1955)
Albert Einstein was one of the most important scientists in history. He developed ideas that changed people's view of the universe.

Einstein was born in Ulm, Germany. He grew up in Munich, where his father ran a small factory. At college he studied math and physics and later worked in an office in Switzerland, checking applications for patents (official documents protecting new inventions). In his free time, he worked on his theory of relativity—the idea that light, gravity, and time are all related. In 1905 he published his work. At first few people understood his ideas, but those ideas began to alter the way people thought.

In 1914 Einstein went to work at Berlin University and continued to publish his theories. After World War I (1914–18), he became recognized internationally. In 1921 Einstein was awarded the Nobel Prize in physics. In 1933, when the Nazis took power in Germany, Einstein accepted a position at Princeton University. Although he hated war, he persuaded President Roosevelt to promote the development of the atomic bomb. Einstein died on April 18, 1955. His ideas influenced many areas, including science and philosophy.

▲
Albert Einstein in 1920, the year before he received the Nobel Prize in physics.

SEE ALSO: Algebra; Nobel Prize; Physics

✳ ELECTRICITY

Electricity provides lighting, heat for cooking, cooling for refrigeration, and power for many things such as computers, televisions, trains, and subways.

People observed electricity long before they knew how to use it. The ancient Greek scientist Thales (about 625–547 B.C.) rubbed amber (fossilized tree resin) with a woolen cloth. Afterward the amber attracted small, light materials, such as lint. The Greek word for amber is *elektron*, and this gives us the word *electricity*.

Scientists now know that all matter is made of tiny atoms. The nucleus—the center of the atom—contains one or more protons, particles with a positive charge, and neutrons, particles with no charge. Electrons, particles with a negative charge, circle the nucleus. An atom usually has the same number of protons and electrons. That makes it electrically neutral—neither positive nor negative. In some kinds of atoms, electrons farthest from the nucleus are loosely held and can easily be set free.

If two substances are rubbed together, the loose electrons are pulled off the atoms in one of the materials and stick to the atoms in the other. Materials that lose electrons are positively charged, and materials that gain electrons are negatively charged. Opposite charges attract each other; like charges repel. The charge attracting the lint is called static electricity.

More discoveries

The Italian Alessandro Volta (1745–1827) found that he could generate electricity from a chemical reaction between metals and salt water. His discovery was called the voltaic pile. Later the English scientist Humphrey Davy (1778–1829) joined voltaic piles together to produce an even stronger current—a battery. The English scientist Michael Faraday (1791–1867) found that a moving magnet inside a coil of wire generates an electrical charge. This is the basis for electrical generators and motors. Electricity really became useful only in about 1830. But since then it has greatly changed the way people live.

▲ *A bolt of lightning is an electrical current caused by a buildup of static electricity.*

◄ *A girl touches a special device called a Van de Graaff generator. The generator creates a negative charge of static electricity. As her hairs become charged through the dome, they repel each other and stand on end.*

SEE ALSO: Atoms and Molecules; Electronics; Inventors and Inventions; Magnetism; Matter

✻ ELECTRONICS
Electronics is a technology that uses electricity to communicate and process information. It is central to many pieces of modern equipment.

Electronics is the basis of a wide range of products we use, from televisions and computers to robotics and high-tech cars. It manipulates, or varies, electrical current. The current flows around a closed path called a circuit.

Electrical signals

Electrical currents that carry information are called electrical signals. There are two basic types. An analog signal is a wavelike current that can vary in volume or strength, called amplitude. A digital signal uses a series of standard pulses that represent numbers. Both types of signal can be varied by devices named semiconductors. They include transistors, diodes, and integrated circuits (ICs). All semiconductor devices can control the flow of electrical current and so operate computers, radio and television receivers, and many other electronic systems.

Electrical current

Electrical current flows at different rates depending on the material. Most metals allow current to flow through them easily. They are called conductors. Copper is an example of a conductor. Materials such as glass allow almost no current to flow through them. They are called insulators. Materials called resistors limit the amount of current that flows through them.

Semiconductors

A semiconductor is halfway between a metal and an insulator. Its ability to conduct current can be adjusted by changing the electrical pressure, or voltage, that is applied to the material by a source of electricity, such as a battery. The most common semiconductor used in transistors and integrated circuits is silicon (an element found in sand).

When semiconductors are linked with resistors and capacitors (devices that store electrical charge) into an electronic circuit, they can perform a wide variety of jobs. Transistors increase, or amplify, an electrical signal; resistors slow it; and capacitors store it.

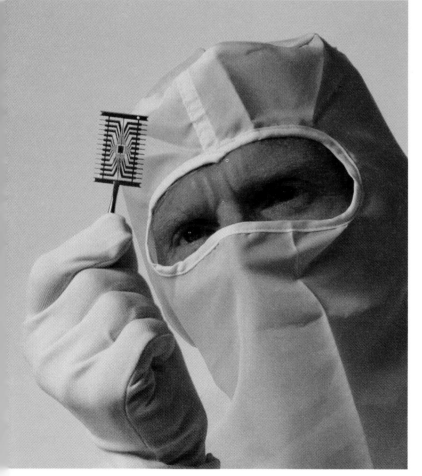

A technician holds up a computer chip. Computer chips in radios, home appliances, televisions, and cars help people use these and many other products daily.

Diodes move electricity in one direction only. This quality means that they are used to turn voices, images, and computer data into signals that can be sent by radio or wire. Diodes on the receiving end change the signals back into their original form. Diodes have many other uses in electronics. Some can give off light when an electrical current passes through them, as in the display of a digital clock. Others can detect light and turn it into electricity.

Integrated circuits

An integrated circuit, also called a microchip, is a semiconductor wafer containing thousands of tiny resistors, capacitors, and transistors. ICs are assembled onto circuit boards for use in many different products.

Integrated circuits are classified as either linear ICs or digital ICs. One common type of linear IC is the operational amplifier, which is used in audio devices such as tape recorders or compact disc players. Most integrated circuits are digital ICs. These are used in computers, robot controllers, and communications networks. Two common types of digital

ICs are the microprocessor chip, or microprocessor, and the memory chip. A microprocessor acts like the "brain" of a personal computer. It contains all the circuits a computer needs to perform calculations. A memory chip stores data as a huge series of tiny electrical charges. Some memory chips are able to store data that would add up to 60,000 printed pages of text.

The future

The most important developments in electronics have been the production of devices that are much smaller, faster, and cheaper. In the future, these devices will be able to do more complicated things, such as perform many different calculations at the same time. Electronics has made possible the modern age of computers and telecommunications. And it seems certain to have a big effect on our lives in the future.

Workers in Vietnam assemble circuit boards for televisions and stereos. Each worker wears a special wristband that discharges static electricity. That prevents static from damaging the electronic components.

DID YOU KNOW?

Many electronic devices are so small that they are called microelectronic devices. *Micro* means "one-millionth" and refers to objects about a millionth of a meter in size. And electronic devices are getting even smaller. This new technology is called nanotechnology. *Nano* means "one-billionth" and refers to objects a thousand times smaller than microelectronic devices. Nanotechnology may lead to computers with incredibly tiny circuits that are many times faster than current ones.

SEE ALSO: Atoms and Molecules; Computers; Electricity; Elements; Metals; Telecommunications

✳ ELEMENTS

Chemical elements are the basic substances out of which everything in the universe is made. Iron, aluminum, and sulfur are common elements.

A chemical element is a piece of matter that cannot be broken down into anything simpler by chemical or physical means (excluding nuclear reactions). Every atom of an element is identical and unlike that of any other element. Each element has its own chemical symbol. Usually the symbol is the first letter of the element's name or the first letter and one other. For instance, the chemical symbol for carbon is C, and the symbol for aluminum is Al. Sometimes the symbol is taken from the Latin name. For instance, the Latin word for iron is *ferrum*, and the chemical symbol for iron is Fe.

A high school student in a chemistry laboratory. Behind him is a poster showing the periodic table, which lists all the chemical elements.

Atomic number

The most important property that separates one element from another is the internal structure of its atoms. Each atom contains three types of particles: protons, which carry a positive electrical charge; negatively charged particles called electrons; and neutrons, which have no charge at all.

The defining characteristic of any element is the number of protons it contains. For example, carbon atoms have six protons, hydrogen atoms have one each, and oxygen atoms have eight protons. Normally, an atom has an equal number of electrons and protons.

From the way the electrons are arranged, scientists can predict—even if they have

ISOTOPES OF HYDROGEN

 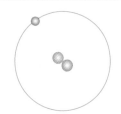 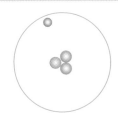

ordinary hydrogen   deuterium   tritium

⊙ **electron**   ⊙ **proton**   ⊙ **neutron**

The three different forms, or isotopes, of hydrogen have their own names. Deuterium and tritium are heavier than ordinary hydrogen.

not seen for themselves—how an atom will react chemically. They can tell properties such as stability (the ease with which an element changes when exposed to other elements). They can also predict boiling point (the temperature at which an element turns from liquid to gas).

Atomic mass

Chemical elements also differ from each other in weight, or atomic mass. Atoms are too small to weigh on scales, so their atomic mass is expressed in relation to the supposed mass of a carbon atom. It is taken to be 12 atomic mass units, or amus. Although all atoms of the same element have the same number of protons and electrons, the number of neutrons they contain may vary. These different forms of the same element are called isotopes.

Although every atom of every element is identical, some elements can take more than one physical form; the different forms are called allotropes. Carbon, for example, may take the form of diamond, the

hardest natural substance, or graphite, the soft so-called "lead" in pencils.

The periodic table

In 1869 the Russian chemist Dmitri I. Mendeleev published a periodic table of the elements. He ordered them by their atomic mass and chemical properties. Mendeleev also showed several gaps in the 60-odd elements known at that time and boldly predicted the properties of three elements that were as yet undiscovered. Gallium, germanium, and scandium were discovered within the next 15 years, and their properties closely matched Mendeleev's descriptions.

Seventy-five of the first 103 chemical elements in the periodic table are metals. Metals are characterized by their conductivity, luster (sheen), and ductility (capacity to be drawn into threads). Seventeen elements are nonmetals—for example, carbon and sulfur. Between the metals and the nonmetals are elements called semimetals or metalloids, such as silicon. The periodic table is still the most important chemistry reference there is. An element's position in the table gives many clues about its properties.

A crystal of sulfur. Sulfur has the atomic number 16. It is a yellow nonmetallic element that occurs naturally.

SEE ALSO:
Atoms and Molecules; Chemistry; Matter

✴ ELEPHANTS

Elephants are the largest land animals in the world. There are two species: African elephants are usually bigger and heavier than Indian elephants.

Elephants are mammals. They have several distinctive features aside from their large size. Their long trunk is used for breathing, smelling, touching, feeding, drinking, lifting heavy objects, and trumpeting. No other animal has a nose with so many uses.

Elephants are equally remarkable for their tusks. They are extremely long teeth that continue to grow during the elephant's life. They are made of bony material called ivory. Elephants have always been hunted for their tusks. The ivory is carved into sculptures and ornaments.

Adult elephants have little hair on their thick, wrinkled skin, but their tails are tipped with wiry hair, and their eyelashes can be over 5 in. (12 cm) long. Elephants need a great deal of food. A big male may eat up to 500 lb. (225 kg) of plant material, such as leaves, bark, fruit, and grasses, a day, and drink between 20 and 40 gallons (75–150 l) of water.

Elephant herds

Most elephants live in herds of 10 to 50 animals, most of whom are related. The leader is usually an old cow (female). Most adult bulls (males) live apart from the herd, but visit it often. The female carries her unborn young for 20 to 22 months before birth, the longest period for any mammal.

Elephants and people

Elephants have been used to serve the needs of people for at least 5,000 years. Their size and strength have been used to lift heavy objects, carry heavy loads, and even lead armies into battle. Killing elephants for their tusks is now illegal, but elephant hunting continues to take place.

A family of African elephants. The tusk of an adult can measure 11 ft. (3.4 m) long.
▼

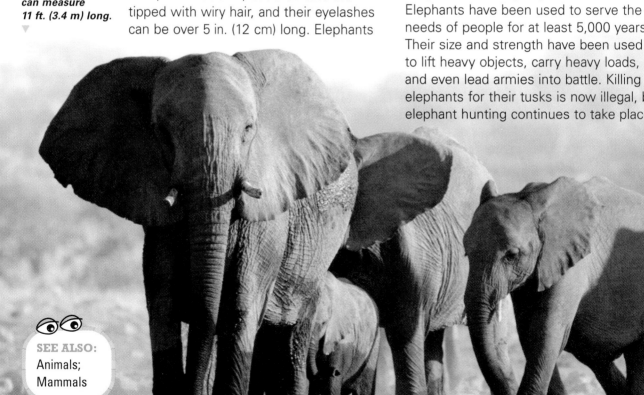

SEE ALSO:
Animals;
Mammals

✳ ELLINGTON, DUKE (1899–1974)

Edward Kennedy Ellington, known as "Duke," was one of the most important orchestra leaders and composers in the history of jazz music.

Ellington played over 20,000 performances.

Ellington began studying piano at age seven, and at age 17 he began to play professionally. He formed an orchestra in New York City in 1923 and soon became nationally famous. For four years, he and his orchestra were stars at the Cotton Club, Harlem's best-known nightspot.

Ellington wrote over 1,000 jazz and nonjazz works. With the help of his highly talented band members, Ellington grouped instruments together in unexpected and effective new ways. His most popular numbers are songs like "Mood Indigo," "Sophisticated Lady," and "Satin Doll." The works that best demonstrate his genius as a composer and arranger are pieces such as "Ko-ko" and "Concerto for Cootie."

Important members of his orchestra included drummer Sonny Greer, saxophonists Ben Webster and Johnny Hodges, trumpeter Cootie Williams, and composer and arranger Billy Strayhorn.

SEE ALSO: Music

✳ ELLIS ISLAND

During the 60 years it operated, over 12 million people passed through Ellis Island's immigration center on their way to the United States of America.

The island

Ellis Island lies about 1 mile (1.6 km) southwest of the tip of Manhattan Island, New York. It is about 27 acres (11 ha) in area. The island was originally called Oyster Island by the early Dutch colonists. It was later known as Gibbet Island, due to its use as a site for hanging pirates. (A gibbet was a frame where criminals were hanged.) In the 1770s, a merchant named Samuel Ellis bought the island and gave it his name. The state of New York bought Ellis Island in 1807, then sold it to the U.S. government.

The immigration center

Immigration to the United States slowed during the Civil War (1861–65), but began to increase after 1870. Starting in the 1880s, millions of people from eastern and southern Europe endured long, cramped voyages across the Atlantic in the hope of a new life. Many were Jews escaping religious persecution (cruel and unfair treatment) in their own countries.

For most of the 1800s, the United States government used Ellis Island as a fort and an arsenal. In 1892 it became a center to process immigrants. At its peak, in the early 1900s, one million

A customs official at Ellis Island attaches labels to the coats of a German immigrant family.

people passed through Ellis Island in a year. Every immigrant had to undergo a medical, psychological, and legal exam. Successful applicants traveled by ferryboat to New York City. Many settled there. Others went on to Boston, Chicago, and other cities across the United States. Only 2 percent of the arriving immigrants were excluded from entry.

The government introduced restrictions on immigration in the 1920s. During World War II (1939–45), the island was used as a detention center for enemy aliens (foreigners). Ellis Island was officially closed in 1954. In 1990 the main building reopened as a museum devoted to the history of immigration.

Ellis Island was a gloomy, unattractive place in many ways, but it is important for what it represents—the opportunity for immigrants from all over the world to make a new life in America.

SEE ALSO: Immigration; United States of America

✳ EL NIÑO

Every two to seven years, world weather patterns are disrupted, often with disastrous results. The cause is a natural phenomenon called El Niño.

El Niño is a warming of water in the Pacific Ocean off the northwest coast of South America. The phenomenon usually starts around Christmastime. It takes its name from the Spanish for "little boy," which refers to the infant Jesus.

During an El Niño year, the westward trade winds over the Pacific near the equator weaken. This weakening allows warm water from the western Pacific to move eastward along the coasts of Ecuador and Peru. It evaporates, resulting in heavy rains over South America, in the east Pacific. Meanwhile, in the west Pacific, Indonesia experiences drought.

The warm water can also prevent a natural process called upwelling. This normally occurs when cold water rises, carrying nutrients from the ocean depths to the surface. Without this process, fish and other marine life can starve.

Scientists do not fully understand why El Niño happens, or why it happens in some years and not in others, but they have discovered that El Niño has been occurring for at least 15,000 years. The El Niño event of 1997–98 ranked as the second-strongest in the last century. It was responsible for more than a year's worth of extreme weather, which caused over 2,000 deaths and billions of dollars in damages worldwide.

La Niña

Another phenomenon is called La Niña— the Spanish for "little girl." It often follows an El Niño year, but is less frequent. It occurs when the southeast trade winds strengthen and unusually warm water is piled up in the west Pacific. This leads to excessive rainfall in the west and dry conditions in the east Pacific, where water temperatures near the equator are unusually cold.

In a La Niña year, winters are cooler than normal in the northern United States, and warmer in the south. In an El Niño year, this is reversed.

The El Niño storms of 1998 caused serious damage to communities in northern California.

SEE ALSO: Climate; Floods; Oceans and Seas; Pacific Ocean; Weather

✳ EMANCIPATION PROCLAMATION

On September 22, 1862, President Abraham Lincoln issued a proclamation freeing slaves. It changed the course of American history.

Lincoln warned that unless the states of the Confederacy returned to the Union by January 1, 1863, he would declare their slaves to be "forever free." This famous document is known as the Emancipation Proclamation because it emancipated, or freed, the slaves.

The Confederate states in the South of the country seceded, or withdrew, from the Union because they knew that Lincoln would prevent the spread of slavery when he became president. This led to Civil War (1861–65) between the North and the South because Lincoln was determined to restore the Union.

In 1862 Lincoln decided that putting an end to slavery would help the North win the war. Many people tried to persuade him to withdraw the proclamation, but the final version was issued on January 1,

1863. The Emancipation Proclamation itself did not end slavery, but it led directly to the adoption of the 13th Amendment to the Constitution in 1865, which made slavery illegal in the United States. Although Lincoln did not live to see his proclamation become law, he is still remembered as the Great Emancipator, the man who freed the slaves.

A portrait of Abraham Lincoln with the text of the Emancipation Proclamation.

SEE ALSO: African Americans; Civil War; Confederacy; Constitution, United States; Slavery

✳ ENDANGERED SPECIES
An endangered species is any species of animal, plant, or living thing that will die out, or become extinct, unless action is taken to prevent its decline.

Endangered species are in immediate danger of extinction. Species that are likely to become endangered in the near future are called threatened. Species that are not in immediate danger, but have small populations and so could move quickly toward extinction, are called vulnerable or candidate species.

Scientists estimate that 20,000 species of plant are in danger of extinction across the world. In the last 400 years, more than 500 types of animals and plants have disappeared from the North American continent. At least 1,000 more are endangered or threatened.

Some of the world's endangered animal species are well known, such as tigers and African elephants. Many more, however, are small and unfamiliar to most people. The Moapa dace, a small fish, lives only in about 2 miles (3.2 km) of a river in Nevada. The Madison Cave

isopod, a tiny crustacean, is found only in one Virginia cave. Both species are endangered. No matter how small or unfamiliar it is, each species of living thing has its own role in keeping the world of nature in balance. When a species becomes extinct, this has an effect on other species. They might rely on it for food, or as protection from predators. The extinction of one species can threaten others with the same fate.

The human effect
At one time, living things were primarily endangered by natural events, such as the extremely cold climate of the Ice

The black rhino is hunted for its horn, which is used in traditional medicine.

Age or the geological changes caused by earthquakes or volcanoes. Now the greatest problems facing plants and animals are human activities that harm the environment on which plants and animals depend. One of the biggest dangers is the destruction of habitats. For example, the tropical rain forests are home to over half the species of animals and plants living on Earth. Every hour, several thousand acres of tropical forest are cleared for human use. In the process, many species are being wiped out.

Pollution can also harm habitats. For example, acid rain caused by pollution in the United States falls on Canada and endangers fish living in its northern lakes.

Other human activities that cause problems include illegal hunting, or poaching, capturing wild animals for the pet trade, and the introduction of a new species into a habitat. For example, foxes, cats, and dogs introduced to Australia are responsible for the extinction of nine mammals and for endangering more than a dozen other species.

Some countries claim that policies to protect endangered species are bad for their people. Norway and Japan oppose international controls on the hunting of whales. Many people in these countries

rely on whaling for their jobs. In some developing countries, people survive by poaching endangered animals, to eat or to sell.

But humans often suffer when species become endangered. Overfishing of cod and other species in the North Atlantic means that stocks are in danger of dying out. If this happens, fishermen will lose their jobs, and whole communities will break up. Pollution can endanger animals and plants, but it can also enter human bodies when people eat those species.

Protecting endangered species

Conservation organizations, such as the World Wide Fund for Nature and Friends of the Earth, are working to conserve species and habitats. International agreements and national laws have been established to protect endangered species. Examples include the end of the trade in ivory, which comes from elephants' tusks.

If the numbers of a species drop to a dangerous level, many zoos and parks run breeding programs. With such programs, it is hoped that offspring can be raised in captivity and then later be returned to the wild. But if humans continue to build and develop on natural habitats, often destroying them in the process, many endangered species will exist only in artificial environments.

A five-day-old jaguar cub, an animal in danger of extinction, being fed at a zoo.

SEE ALSO: Conservation; Ecology; Environment; Extinction; Pollution

✳ ENDOCRINE SYSTEM

The endocrine system of the human body produces chemicals called hormones. Hormones "tell" parts of the body to carry out specific actions.

Hormones are usually produced by organs called glands. Endocrine glands release hormones directly into the blood. The bloodstream carries the hormones to where they will do their work. There are several glands in the endocrine system, each doing different jobs. The pea-size pituitary gland is at the base of the brain. It controls the growth of the body. The hypothalamus is the part of the brain that contains major control centers for the nervous system. It produces hormones that start or stop the production of hormones by other glands. The thyroid gland in the neck produces hormones that regulate the rate at which body cells burn food for energy. The adrenal glands are on top of the kidneys. The outer layer of the adrenal glands produces hormones that help regulate sugars, proteins, minerals, and body fluids. The inner layer produces a hormone called adrenalin that helps the body react to emergencies. The pancreas—a long, thin organ behind the stomach—produces the hormone insulin, which helps to control the level of sugar in the blood. Lack of insulin leads to a serious disease called diabetes. The male and female sex organs also produce sex hormones that help the body to develop.

The human endocrine system consists of glands and other hormone-producing cells. Glands are organs that produce specific chemicals. ▶

👀

SEE ALSO:
Blood; Brain and Nervous System; Human Body; Reproductive System

ENDOCRINE SYSTEM

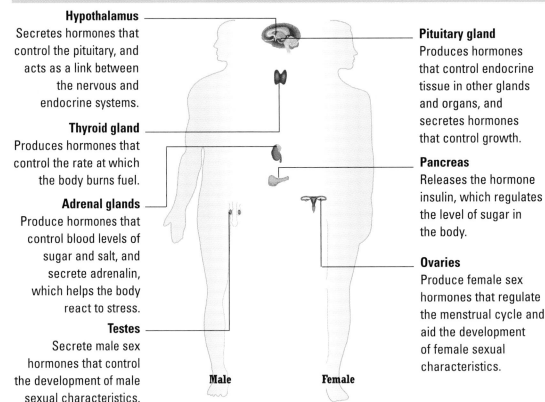

Hypothalamus
Secretes hormones that control the pituitary, and acts as a link between the nervous and endocrine systems.

Thyroid gland
Produces hormones that control the rate at which the body burns fuel.

Adrenal glands
Produce hormones that control blood levels of sugar and salt, and secrete adrenalin, which helps the body react to stress.

Testes
Secrete male sex hormones that control the development of male sexual characteristics.

Pituitary gland
Produces hormones that control endocrine tissue in other glands and organs, and secretes hormones that control growth.

Pancreas
Releases the hormone insulin, which regulates the level of sugar in the body.

Ovaries
Produce female sex hormones that regulate the menstrual cycle and aid the development of female sexual characteristics.

Male   **Female**

☀ ENERGY

Energy is everywhere in many different forms, from sunlight to motion. Energy can be converted from one form to another, but it can never be destroyed.

Scientists define energy as the ability to do work. In physics, work is done when a force applied to an object moves it in the direction of the force. If a woman hammers a nail into wood, she exerts a force to drive the nail into the wood. If she stands without moving, holding a heavy weight, she is not doing any work because the position of the weight remains unchanged. The weight has not been moved any distance by force.

Different forms of energy

Work can be done in various ways. Each way represents a different kind of energy. The two most basic kinds of energy are potential energy and kinetic energy. When the hammer is raised but not moving, it has potential energy—it is capable of doing work. When the head hits the nail, it has kinetic energy. The word *kinetic* comes from a Greek word meaning "motion." Together, kinetic energy and potential energy are known as mechanical energy. Kinetic energy is also closely related to heat energy. An object is hot because its atoms (the tiny particles that make up all matter) are always in motion.

Most of the time that energy is used to do work, part of it is wasted as heat. Most of the energy of the hammer, for example,

goes to heating up the nail and the head of the hammer. Only a small part of the energy actually moves the nail.

Sources of energy

Ancient peoples used only the energy their bodies obtained from food. When they learned to use fire, they changed the chemical energy of wood into heat and light. The chemical energy in wood comes from the energy of the sun. Plants absorb energy from the sun and change it into chemical energy through a process called photosynthesis. The energy in coal, oil, and natural gas also comes from the sun.

Other sources of energy include nuclear energy, which releases the energy in the nucleus of an atom. Fears about the safety of nuclear power plants have prompted scientists to turn to natural forms of energy such as the sun, wind, and water. However, at the moment it is difficult to produce large amounts of electricity from natural energy.

When wood is burned, its chemical energy is turned into heat energy and light energy.

SEE ALSO: Atoms and Molecules; Chemistry; Electricity; Engines; Fossil Fuels; Heat; Matter; Nuclear Power; Photosynthesis

Wind turbines gather kinetic energy from the wind and convert it to electricity.

✳ ENGINES

Engines are machines that turn some form of energy into mechanical energy, which is then used to do work. Engines are defined by the kind of energy they convert.

Windmills and water mills were some of the earliest engines. They harness the energy of wind and moving water, and are still used to pump water and make electricity. Most other engines turn heat energy into movement. Heat engines almost always burn a chemical fuel, such as wood, coal, oil, or gasoline, to produce the heat. Heat engines include steam, gasoline, diesel, jet, and rocket engines.

Steam engines

The first true engines ran on steam, which is produced when water is boiled. Steam occupies much more space than the water from which it is made. So when steam is produced in an enclosed space, it pushes parts of the steam engine to create movement.

Fuel to heat the water is burned outside the engine. For this reason, steam engines are called external-combustion engines. *External* means "outside," and *combustion* means "burning." The water is heated in a boiler, and the steam is then piped into the engine.

In 1712 Thomas Newcomen, an English blacksmith, built the first successful piston-operated steam engine. A piston is like a stopper that slides back and forth inside a cylinder (a tube closed at one end). A rod on one end of the piston connects to a wheel. Steam enters the cylinder and pushes the piston, which turns the wheel. Newcomen's engine was used to pump water out of flooded coal mines. In later years, steam engines were built to pull trains.

Today the steam turbine has replaced the piston engine. A turbine is a set of metal blades attached to a central rotor. It looks like a pinwheel, or a fan, and it fits inside a tube. A fluid or gas rushing through the turbine pushes the blades, making the rotor spin to provide power for the work. Steam turbines power electric generators and large ships.

Internal-combustion engines

An internal-combustion engine is a heat engine that burns fuel and air inside the engine itself. Most internal-combustion engines are gasoline or diesel engines. Gas engines have many uses, from simple lawn mowers to powerful racing cars. Diesel engines power most heavy trucks, buses, and locomotives.

Jet engines

During the 1930s, engineers worked on jet engine designs. The first jet plane, a German Heinkel, flew in 1939, but the jet plane was not widely used until after 1945. It is now in widespread use in military and other aircraft.

Some manufacturers are working on the design of cleaner engines that are able to run on hydrogen or electricity instead of fuel.

SEE ALSO: Aircraft; Cars; Energy; Force and Motion; Fossil Fuels; Machines; Rockets; Ships and Boats; Trains and Railroads

ENGINE TYPES

STEAM ENGINE

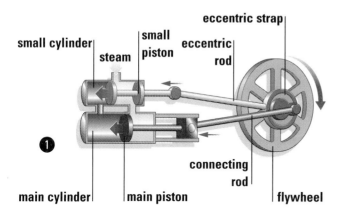

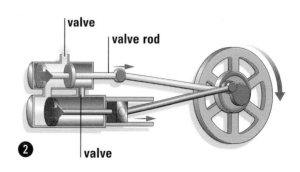

(1) Steam presses on the main piston, pushing it toward the end of the cylinder. That pulls the connecting rod toward the engine, making the wheel turn. As the flywheel turns, so does the eccentric strap, pushing the eccentric rod left.

(2) The valve rod links the eccentric rod to the smaller piston, which is pushed to the end of the cylinder. That makes steam in the main cylinder switch to the left-hand side. The larger piston moves to the right, restarting the whole process.

◄
Steam is produced when water is boiled. This happens outside the engine. When steam is piped in, it pushes parts of the engine so that they move.

FOUR-STROKE INTERNAL-COMBUSTION ENGINE

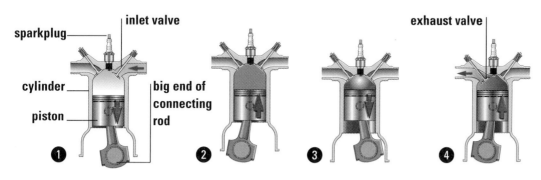

Fuel is burned inside the cylinder in the internal-combustion engine. The piston is connected by a crankshaft and connecting rod to a wheel that drives the machine. The sparkplug lights the fuel. When the piston moves down, it sucks fuel and air into the cylinder through the inlet valve (1). The piston moves up, compressing the fuel and air (2). The fuel and air expand as they burn and push the piston down (3). The piston moves up, pushing burned gases out of an exhaust valve (4).

◄
The internal-combustion engine has many advantages over the steam engine. Its design led to the invention of the automobile.

✳ENGLAND 🔍see🔍 ✳UNITED KINGDOM

✳ ENVIRONMENT

The environment is the name for the surroundings in which animals and plants live, and which tend to influence their development and behavior.

All living things, or organisms, interact with and influence their surroundings. Organisms form a network of interconnected environmental systems called biomes. A rain forest is a biome, as is a desert. The branch of science that studies the way organisms relate to their environment is called ecology.

Natural events such as droughts, floods, or fires may cause some damage to the environment, but they are temporary disturbances. Over the course of time, the environment will come back into balance.

Humans, however, have had a greater effect on the environment than any other species. Not everything they have done has been good for it.

Greenhouse effect

A big problem for the environment today is how Earth's climate is changing. Earth's atmosphere is full of different gases. The gas carbon dioxide is produced by natural events such as forest fires and volcanoes. Together with another gas, methane (produced by decaying organic matter), and water vapor, carbon dioxide builds up in the air. These gases act like the glass in a very large greenhouse, trapping the sun's heat. This natural greenhouse effect keeps the earth warm enough to support all the plants and animals that live there.

Global warming

Since the early 1980s, experts have noticed that temperatures are gradually getting higher around the world. This is called global warming.

Many scientists believe that global warming may be caused by the burning of fossil fuels in homes, factories, and cars. These fuels (coal, oil, and gasoline) release carbon dioxide and other greenhouse gases into the atmosphere when they are burned. As a result, Earth's natural greenhouse effect has become unbalanced.

Farmers in Sumatra need land for houses and crops, but by using it they have destroyed the forests.
▼

DID YOU KNOW?

The population of the United States has grown by 13 percent in the last 10 years—and 83 percent in the last 50 years. The Census predicts that the population could increase from today's 284 million to 400 million by 2050. That means another 116 million people who will need water, food, energy, and housing. Because Americans use more resources than any other country in the world, U.S. overpopulation has a more damaging effect on the environment than overpopulation in other countries.

Environmental problems

Global warming and the greenhouse effect can cause serious problems in the environment. In Antarctica, for example, the giant ice sheets that cover the frozen continent have been slowly melting. As a result, the extra water makes sea levels rise, which could cause flooding in coastal areas around the world.

There are other environmental problems connected to the changing climate. Global warming causes drought (very long periods without rain) and bad storms. Plant and animal species that have adapted to the climate of the area where they live may die out as the climate changes. People with farms may have to move if there is not enough or too much rain, and their crops and livestock are affected. Tropical diseases harmful to people, such as malaria, may also spread.

People and the environment

Since the 1950s, the world's population has more than doubled, and all people need food, water, and shelter. The increased demand on natural resources can unbalance the environment, causing problems for other species. Many have become extinct (died out completely) or are endangered (in danger of extinction).

It is only recently that people have started to worry about the effect they are having on the environment. They have now begun to think about halting various damaging practices. For example, should people cut down fewer trees to preserve the rain forests, have fewer children to keep population numbers down, stop driving cars, and be prepared to pay more for their electricity?

The dry, cracked earth of this field in Thailand is the result of drought. Environmental problems, such as global warming, are causing climate changes around the world.

There are no easy answers to these questions. If logging is banned, people who live by harvesting timber will have no income. What gives one person the right to tell another not to start a family or to stop driving a car?

Most people agree that environmental problems must be sorted out. But they do not always agree on the solutions.

SEE ALSO: Biomes; Carson, Rachel; Climate; Conservation; Ecology; Endangered Species; Energy; Extinction; Food Chains; Fossil Fuels; Natural Resources; Pollution

✳**EQUATOR** 🔖 ✳**NAVIGATION**

⚹ EUROPE

Europe is the world's second-smallest continent, after Australia, but its long history as a world power makes it important out of all relation to its size.

Land, climate, and people

Europe and Asia occupy the same landmass, but they are considered to be separate continents. The boundary runs north to south from the Ural Mountains to the Caspian Sea. Sea air brings mild, wet weather to western Europe. In Central Europe, winters are cooler and summers hotter. The Mediterranean region is hot and dry in summer. Europe is the most densely populated of the continents, with one-seventh of the world's population.

History

Europe has a long, complex history. Its countries have regularly changed borders. One of the first great civilizations arose 3,000 years ago in Greece. Greece was later conquered by Rome. At its height, the Roman Empire covered most of Europe. From the fifth to the ninth centuries A.D., the Franks, a Germanic tribe, ruled much of Europe. They built up the power of the Roman Catholic Church.

Beginning in the 1300s, there was great artistic and cultural activity in Europe, a period called the Renaissance. Further change took place when the Protestant Church broke with the Roman Catholic Church in northwest Europe. The Industrial Revolution began in Britain in the mid-1700s. Cities across Europe grew as people moved to work in factories. After the American Revolution, Britain lost many of its American territories, but, with other nations, claimed new lands in Africa and Asia. Power struggles between the nations of Europe led to World War I (1914–18). The Russian Revolution in 1917

led to the creation of the Soviet Union. Germany led Europe into World War II (1939–45). After the war, the Soviet Union spread communism across Eastern Europe. The Soviet Union broke up in 1991. In 1957 six European nations formed the European Economic Community to make trade easier. In 1993 it was renamed the European Union (EU). In 2002, 12 EU states adopted a new currency, the euro.

SEE ALSO: American Revolution; Ancient Civilizations; Austria; Central Europe; Communism; Eastern Europe; France; Germany; Greece, Ancient; Greece and the Balkans; Hungary; Iceland; Industrial Revolution; Ireland, Republic of; Italy; Middle Ages; Napoleon; Netherlands, Belgium, and Luxembourg; Poland; Portugal; Reformation; Renaissance; Roman Empire; Russia and the Baltic States; Scandinavia; Spain; United Kingdom; World War I; World War II

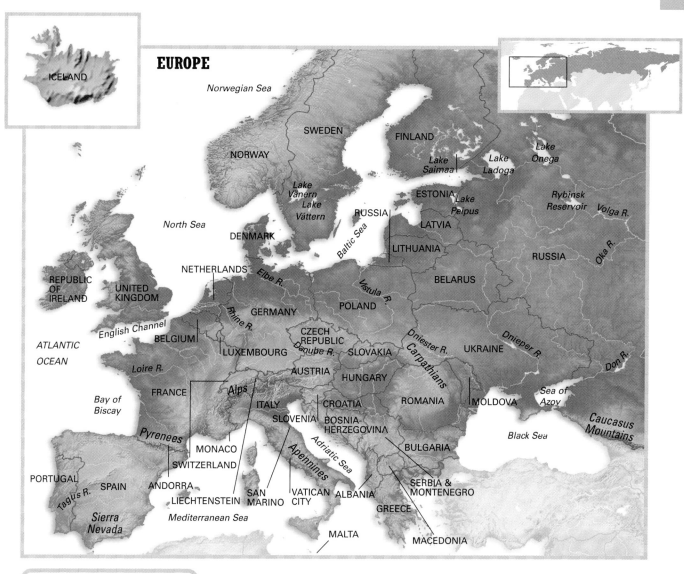

ICELAND

EUROPE

Norwegian Sea

SWEDEN

FINLAND

NORWAY

Lake Onega

Lake Saimaa

Lake Ladoga

Lake Vänern

Lake Vättern

ESTONIA

Lake Peipus

RUSSIA

Rybinsk Reservoir

Volga R.

North Sea

DENMARK

LATVIA

Baltic Sea

LITHUANIA

RUSSIA

Oka R.

NETHERLANDS

Elbe R.

BELARUS

Vistula R.

REPUBLIC OF IRELAND

UNITED KINGDOM

GERMANY

Rhine R.

POLAND

English Channel

BELGIUM

CZECH REPUBLIC

Dniester R.

Dnieper R.

UKRAINE

Don R.

LUXEMBOURG

Danube R.

SLOVAKIA

Carpathians

ATLANTIC OCEAN

Loire R.

AUSTRIA

HUNGARY

FRANCE

Alps

Bay of Biscay

ITALY

SLOVENIA

CROATIA

ROMANIA

MOLDOVA

Sea of Azov

BOSNIA-HERZEGOVINA

Caucasus Mountains

Pyrenees

Adriatic Sea

BULGARIA

Black Sea

MONACO

Apennines

SWITZERLAND

PORTUGAL

SPAIN

ANDORRA

LIECHTENSTEIN

SAN MARINO

VATICAN CITY

ALBANIA

SERBIA & MONTENEGRO

Tagus R.

Sierra Nevada

Mediterranean Sea

GREECE

MALTA

MACEDONIA

Major Physical Features

MOUNTAIN RANGES & HIGHEST POINTS

- Caucasus 18,510 ft. (5,642 m) at Mt. Elbrus

- Alps 15,780 ft. (4,810 m) at Mt. Blanc

- Sierra Nevada 11,411 ft. (3,478 m) at Mulhacén

- Pyrenees 11,169 ft. (3,404 m) at Pico de Aneto

RIVERS

- Volga 2,193 mi. (3,529 km)
- Danube 1,770 mi. (2,848 km)
- Dnieper 1,424 mi. (2,291 km)
- Don 1,220 mi. (1,963 km)
- Oka 930 mi. (1,496 km)
- Dniester 840 mi. (1,352 km)
- Rhine 820 mi. (1,319 km)
- Elbe 725 mi. (1,167 km)
- Vistula 668 mi. (1,075 km)
- Loire 634 mi. (1,020 km)
- Tagus 626 mi. (1,007 km)

LAKES

- Ladoga 6,826 sq. mi. (17,679 sq. km)
- Onega 3,753 sq. mi. (9,720 sq. km)
- Vänern 2,156 sq. mi. (5,584 sq. km)
- Rybinsk 1,757 sq. mi. (4,551 sq. km)
- Saimaa 1,690 sq. mi. (4,377 sq. km)
- Peipus 1,373 sq. mi. (3,556 sq. km)
- Vättern 738 sq. mi. (1,911 sq. km)

*EVOLUTION

Evolution is the slow, gradual change or development of the characteristics of animals and plants over many generations.

Some people, especially those who believe the literal truth of the Bible, question whether evolution exists. Most scientists, however, believe that evolution explains how all living things descend from common ancestors in a pattern that resembles a family tree.

Evidence of evolution
Large changes in life-forms happen over thousands or millions of years. Because evolution takes place too slowly to see, scientists look for evidence that it has occurred. Fossils, which are the remains of ancient life, provide the best evidence. Different fossils are found in rocks of

different ages. This shows how life on Earth has changed. Fossils also show that groups of animals or plants have evolved from other groups. For example, fossils indicate that amphibians, such as frogs, evolved from fish that were capable of breathing air and moving on land.

Different modern species often share similar features. This suggests that they inherited them from a common ancestor. For example, the front limbs of lizards, birds, bats, whales, and people all have the same basic structure, even though they are used very differently. So it seems likely that a common ancestor of these animals had this bone arrangement.

How evolution takes place
The theory that explains why organisms, or living things, change over time is called natural selection. It was developed by the English naturalist Charles Darwin (1809–82). The theory is based on three basic facts about animals and plants.

DARWIN'S FINCHES

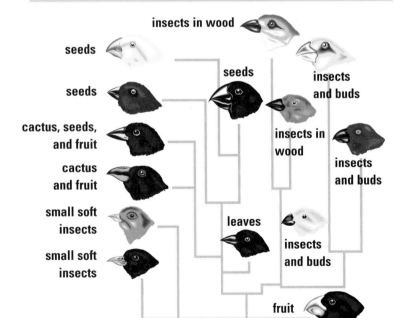

insects in wood

seeds

seeds

seeds

cactus, seeds, and fruit

insects and buds

cactus and fruit

insects in wood

small soft insects

insects and buds

small soft insects

leaves

insects and buds

fruit

From studying finches, Charles Darwin found that different species had different types of beaks depending on what types of food they ate.

The humpback whale is a mammal that breathes air but is specially adapted to life in the sea.

First, individuals within a species vary slightly from one another. They inherit these differences from their parents. Second, plants and animals produce more offspring than are able to survive. This causes competition for limited resources such as food. Third, some individuals are better (or worse) competitors for these resources based on their individual traits. Organisms with traits that are helpful in a certain environment will, on average, survive and reproduce better than those with less favorable traits. The favorable traits will thus be passed on to more offspring and will become more common in the overall population.

Traits are determined by combinations of genes. These are biological instructions that control how every living creature generally appears, how it functions and reproduces, and even partly how it behaves. Sometimes when genes are passed from the parents to the offspring, bits are accidentally changed. These changes are known as mutations. Some produce variations without causing harm, but most are harmful. Evolution could not exist without variations because there would be no possibility of change.

Adaptation

Traits that enable a species to fit better into its environment are called adaptations. They result from natural selection. For example, the giraffe's long neck is an adaptation for eating leaves from treetops. Ancestors of the giraffe did not have long necks. But those animals that had slightly longer necks than others could find more food simply because they could reach it. Longer-necked giraffe ancestors therefore survived to have more offspring than shorter-necked giraffes. The result is the modern giraffe, the world's tallest land animal.

Rates of change

Evolution can happen quickly. In just a few decades many species of insects have evolved to resist insecticides, the poisons farmers use to kill them. This is because insects have many generations in a short space of time. Fossils show that in some organisms small changes occurred over long periods, perhaps millions of years.

Giraffes can feed from leaves that cannot be reached by other animals.

SEE ALSO: Darwin, Charles; Dinosaurs; Fossils; Genetics; Geology

✳ EXPLORATION AND EXPLORERS

Throughout history people have set out into unknown territories. The earliest explorers looked for new lands in which to hunt and settle.

The ancient civilizations around the Mediterranean Sea sent out expeditions in search of new trade. From about 2500 B.C., the Egyptians sent ships to the mysterious land of Punt, thought to be on the east coast of Africa. The Phoenicians, a people from the coast of Lebanon, were great seafarers. In about 500 B.C., Hanno sailed out of the Mediterranean through the Strait of Gibraltar and established colonies on the coast of Africa.

The Vikings of Scandinavia were daring adventurers. From about A.D. 800, they sailed longboats up the rivers of northeast Europe. They settled in Britain and France and colonized Iceland, Greenland, and what later became Russia. In about A.D. 1000, Leif Eriksson sailed from Greenland and reached North America.

In the Middle Ages, the Crusades (wars to free the Holy Land from the Muslims) created interest in eastern lands. A great traveler was Marco Polo (1254–1324), who journeyed with his father and uncle from Venice, Italy, to Beijing in China.

This map shows the routes taken by some of the greatest explorers. ▼

KEY TO ROUTES
Viking expeditions (8th–10th centuries)
Marco Polo (1271–95)
Christopher Columbus (1492–1504)
John Cabot (1497)
Vasco da Gama (1497–99)
Ferdinand Magellan (1519–22)
Samuel de Champlain (1613–15)
Captain James Cook (1768–79)
Lewis and Clark (1804–06)
David Livingstone (1841–73)

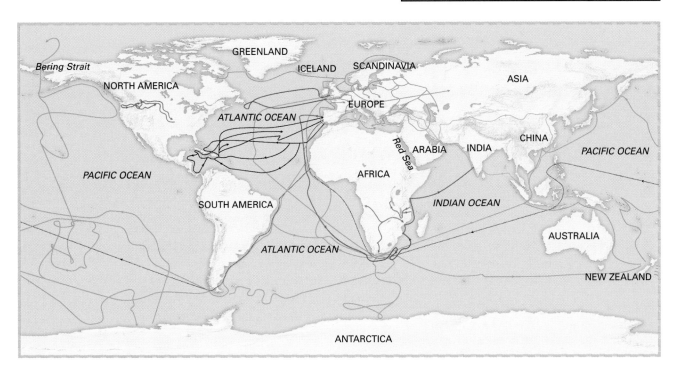

Great age of exploration

In the 1400s, improved navigational techniques meant that sailors could take longer voyages. Europeans looked for sea routes to the East so that they could transport spices more cheaply. Portugal explored the west coast of Africa. In 1488 Bartolomeu Dias (about 1450–1500) sailed around the southern tip of Africa. In 1497 Vasco da Gama (about 1460–1524) took this route, but continued east to India.

Christopher Columbus (1451–1506) sailed from Spain across the Atlantic Ocean in 1492 and reached the Bahamas. In 1519 the Portuguese Ferdinand Magellan (about 1480–1521) was sent by Spain to discover a sea route to Asia by sailing southwest across the Atlantic Ocean. He found what was later named the Magellan Strait at the tip of South America and then sailed across the Pacific Ocean to the Philippines. Magellan was killed, but one of his ships returned to Spain, having sailed all the way around the world.

The Americas

Many Spaniards followed Columbus to the Americas. In 1521 the Aztec Empire of Mexico was conquered by Hernán Cortés (1485–1547). In 1500 Pedro Álvares Cabral (about 1468–1520) discovered Brazil for Portugal. Spaniard Francisco Pizarro (about 1475–1541) conquered the Inca Empire of Peru between 1531 and 1533.

In 1497 the Italian John Cabot (about 1451–98) was sent by England to explore eastern Canada. In the early 1500s, the French explored the lands along the St. Lawrence River, later the center of the colony of New France. Frenchman Samuel de Champlain founded Quebec in 1608.

In 1804–06 Meriwether Lewis (1774–1809) and William Clark (1770–1838) were the first European Americans to explore the Missouri River and find a route to the Pacific coast.

The Pacific and Australasia

The Englishman Captain James Cook (1728–79) made three trips to the Pacific Ocean, exploring the coasts of New Zealand and eastern Australia. He also discovered the Hawaiian Islands and sighted Antarctica. Cook claimed the east coast of Australia for England in 1770.

Africa and Asia

Europeans did not explore much of Africa until the 1800s. Among the most famous explorers were the Scotsmen Mungo Park (1771–1806) and Dr. David Livingstone (1813–73). Park charted the course of the Niger River, and Livingstone discovered the Zambezi River. The interiors of Arabia, Central Asia, and China were not explored by the Europeans until the 1700s.

The Polar regions

Soon after Europeans first went to North America, they explored the Arctic. The Northeast Passage—the seaway along the top of north Norway and Siberia to the Bering Strait—was navigated in 1878–79. The first crossing of the Northwest Passage was completed in 1906. The American Robert Peary (1856–1920) reached the North Pole in 1909. In 1911 Norwegian Roald Amundsen (1872–1928) was the first to set foot on the South Pole.

SEE ALSO: Antarctica; Arctic; Balboa, Vasco Núñez de; Byrd, Richard E.; Cabot, John; Champlain, Samuel de; Columbus, Christopher; Conquistadors; Crusades; Egypt, Ancient; Hudson, Henry; Lewis, Meriwether; Marco Polo; Navigation; Peary, Robert E.; Space Exploration; Vikings

✳ EXTINCTION

A species of plant or animal becomes extinct when its last living member dies. In recent times, human activity has been a major cause of extinction.

Why species become extinct

All species evolve, or change to survive in their environment. These changes take place over many thousands of years. Sometimes the environment changes so much that a species cannot survive. Climate can also change, or a food supply can run out.

However, there have been five times during Earth's history when at least three-quarters of all species alive have become extinct within a few million years. These episodes of rapid dying off of many species are known as mass extinctions. The dinosaurs are the best-known examples. Nobody knows with certainty why the dinosaurs died out so quickly. Other prehistoric animals, such as the woolly mammoth and the sabre-toothed tiger, have also become extinct. Periods of extreme climate change, like the Ice Age, killed off many animals and plants.

Park rangers in the Central African Republic with illegally hunted ivory. Trade in ivory was banned worldwide in 1989 in an attempt to protect elephants. However, hunting continued, and elephants are still endangered.
▼

Extinction today

One of the greatest mass extinctions in Earth's history is happening at the moment. Scientists estimate that between 18,000 and 55,000 species become extinct each year, mostly because of the activities of humans. Species that are in immediate danger of dying out are known as endangered.

By converting forests to farms and building roads and houses, humans destroy the habitats of many plants and animals. This process, called deforestation, drives out native species. If its habitat disappears completely, a species may become extinct. The orangutan, a great ape that lives in the jungle regions of Southeast Asia, is one species threatened by the destruction of its habitat. The destruction of the Amazon rain forests in South America has caused the extinction of thousands of different animals and plants. Some smaller species are destroyed before humans know they ever existed.

Hunting also causes species to die out. The dodo, a large flightless bird, was hunted to extinction by settlers on the island of Mauritius in the central Indian Ocean by 1681. Some whale species came close to the same fate. Today, animals such as elephants, black rhinoceroses, and some parrots are hunted or captured illegally, and their survival is threatened as a result.

Extinctions may also occur when humans introduce new species to areas where they do not live naturally. For example, cats and rats introduced to islands have

The dodo was a
species of
flightless bird
bigger than a
turkey. It was
hunted to
extinction by the
end of the 1600s.

caused the extinction of many species of ground-nesting birds that had no defense against these predators. In the British Isles, the American gray squirrel threatens the survival of the native red squirrel. Humans have also killed off species that they regarded as threats to their own livestock. This was the fate of the Tasmanian marsupial wolf, which became extinct in the 1930s.

Environmental damage caused by pollution, such as oil spills, can also pose a serious threat to many species. Species that have thrived for many millions of years can be put in danger by a single moment of carelessness. Chemicals released into water supplies can make fish and other species infertile—unable to reproduce. Climate change, which may be caused by industrial production of carbon dioxide and other gases, may also be responsible for extinctions.

The end of extinction?

Some species that are believed to be extinct turn out to be alive. For example, scientists thought that a bony fish called the coelacanth died out 70 million years ago. Then, in 1938, a new specimen was found in the Indian Ocean.

Some people believe that science may one day be able to bring species back from extinction. With gene technology and cloning, scientists might be able to use the preserved bodies of mammoths and other extinct species to bring plants and animals back to life. At present, however, this is just science fiction.

SEE ALSO: Dinosaurs; Endangered Species; Evolution; Pollution

✳ EYES AND VISION

For humans and many other animals, vision—the sense of sight—is the most important of the senses. We see when light forms images in the eyes. The brain then interprets these images.

An adult human eye is about the size of a table-tennis ball. Most of its surface is made of a tough layer called the sclera. At the front of the eye is a clear layer called the cornea.

Inside the sclera is the choroid layer. Part of the choroid forms the colored iris. In the center of the iris is the pupil. Behind the iris is a clear, rubbery lens. At the back of the eye is the retina, which contains light-sensitive cells.

How we see

Light enters the eye through the pupil. Muscles control the size of the pupil— when light is very bright, the pupil automatically becomes smaller. Other muscles control the shape of the lens, which makes focusing possible. Without this, it would only be possible to see objects clearly at a certain distance.

Light passes through the lens and lands on the retina. Here there are two kinds

Light enters the eye through the pupil, passes through the lens, and lands on the retina, where it triggers a message that travels down the optic nerve to the brain.
▶

of light-sensitive cells, the rods and cones. Rods make it easier to see in dim light. Cones allow us to see fine detail. Together they make color vision possible. When light reaches the retina, it triggers a message to a nerve cell. This message passes along a nerve fiber in the optic nerve, toward the brain. The brain then interprets the message as sight.

Eye problems

The most common eye problems occur when the cornea and lens cannot focus properly. Nearsightedness and farsightedness happen when light does not focus on the retina. These problems are corrected with eyeglasses or contact lenses. More serious disorders include cataracts—cloudy areas on the lens—and glaucoma—high pressure in the eyeball.

INSIDE THE EYE

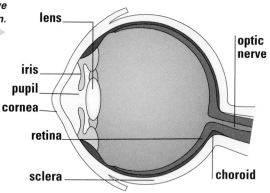

lens
optic nerve
iris
pupil
cornea
retina
sclera
choroid

SEE ALSO: Brain and Nervous System; Human Body

✳ FABRICS AND CLOTH

Fabrics and cloth are materials made from fibers such as cotton and wool. A fabric or cloth that has been woven or knitted is called a textile.

Almost every culture uses fabrics in some form. Examples include denim jeans, knitted shawls, and wool carpets. They can be made by hand or by machine.

History

Archaeologists have discovered that Europeans used plant fibers to make ropes and fishing nets in about 8000 B.C. The Egyptians spun and wove linen in which they wrapped their dead. Before 2000 B.C., the Chinese raised silkworms and made silk from their cocoons. Native people in the Americas used cotton, llama hair, and yucca fibers to make cloth for centuries before the Europeans arrived.

Silks and other rich fabrics became important to traders in Europe and Asia from about A.D. 100. Skilled weavers and printers produced beautiful fabrics, and their work influenced artists in other countries. But most people wore rough clothes made from wool or plant fibers.

The Industrial Revolution began in England in the 1700s with the invention of new machines that made spinning and weaving faster and less expensive. Rayon was one of the first artificial fibers to be developed in the late 1800s as a substitute for silk. Other artificial fibers, such as nylon, acetate, and polyester, followed in the 1900s.

How cloth is made

The raw materials used to make cloth come from animal, plant, or chemical sources. Cotton, linen, and raffia come from the stems, seeds, bark, or leaves of plants. Wool and cashmere are among the fibers that come from the fleece of sheep, goats, and other animals. Most fibers developed in the last 100 years are chemical in origin.

Most cloth is created from fibers that have been spun into yarns—continuous

A woman holds a basket of silkworms feeding on leaves. Silkworms are the fat, white larvae of the white moth, and they spin the delicate fibers of silk.
▼

A woman weaves fabric in Nepal. Although some people still weave and spin by hand, it is more common today for the process to be done by a machine.

strands of fibers—through a process called spinning. The spinner draws out the short fibers and twists them together into lengths. Sometimes two or more materials are spun together. For many centuries, spinning took place on a wheel that was operated by hand or foot. Today it is more likely to be a mechanical process.

Synthetic fibers are plastics, made from raw materials such as coal and alcohol. Chemicals are mixed to produce a gluey liquid that is forced through tiny holes in a metal nozzle called a spinneret. This makes long, thin strands called filaments. The filaments are hardened, stretched, washed, bleached, and dried, then wound onto spools. Synthetic yarn is made from several filaments wound together.

Nonwoven cloth

Once the yarn is made, there are two main ways to prepare a cloth—nonwoven and woven. Nonwoven techniques include felting, knotting, and looping. In felting, fibers are arranged as a mat, and heat, moisture, and friction are applied to press the fibers together. Nomadic (wandering) peoples in Central Asia make tents from wool felt. Felt made from wool or fur is often used to make hats.

Fishermen have used knotting to make their nets for many centuries. A more complex knotting technique is macramé, often used for decorative wall hangings. The most common examples of looping are knitting and crochet.

Weaving

Nonwoven techniques use a single set of yarns. In weaving there are always at least two sets of yarns. The warp yarns are held on a loom, and the weft yarns are interlocked between them, at right angles. Extra yarns can be inserted and pulled up to form loops, called pile. Velvet and corduroy are examples of pile fabrics.

Dyeing and printing

Color can be added to fibers before yarns are spun or to finished fabrics. Until the 1800s, all dyes came from natural sources, such as plants. Most dyes today are synthetic. If part of the cloth is covered during dyeing, the dye will not color that part. One such covering technique is tie-dyeing, where string is knotted around the fabric. The Chinese and Indians used wooden blocks to print designs on fabrics before the first century A.D. Later, large presses, like those used for printing books, were used.

SEE ALSO: Clothing; Industrial Revolution; Manufacturing; Trade

✱FARMING see➡ ✱AGRICULTURE

☀ FILMS

Films—also known as motion pictures, movies, or cinema—are one of the most popular forms of entertainment today. Filmmaking is a mixture of technology, art, and business.

The forerunner of movies was the magic lantern, a popular form of entertainment in the 1800s. It was a box with a series of images inside that spun very quickly in front of a light source. The still images changed so fast that they appeared to be moving. The next development was systems that made photographic images appear to move.

Modern films consist of long reels of flexible plastic. They are divided into frames. Each frame contains an image that is very slightly different from the next. When these reels are run through a projector, we see the images against a white screen. Because they run so quickly, it looks as if the images are moving.

Early film

The first movies were very short and simple. Audiences were happy to look at images of everyday scenes, such as workers leaving a factory, because the illusion of movement was exciting on its own. However, moviemakers were soon making stories on film.

The epic **Gone with the Wind,** *set during the Civil War, is one of the most popular films of all time.*

In the early 1900s, several studios set up in the Hollywood area of California. In 1927, *The Jazz Singer* was the first movie with a built-in soundtrack. Now moviegoers could hear their favorite stars speak and sing. The 1920s also saw the first Academy Award® ceremony. These prizes, also known as Oscars®, go to the best directors, actors, and other contributors to films in a year. The 1930s and 1940s are known as the Golden Age of Hollywood. Actors such as Clark Gable and Joan Crawford provided glamour and escapism during the bleak days of the Great Depression and World War II (1939–45).

In the 1960s, films became more realistic and dealt with difficult social and political issues. More recently, special effects have become very important. Movies like *Jurassic Park* and *Toy Story* set new standards for what can be achieved in film.

Making a film

Almost all films begin with a script— a document that tells the story and lays out what the characters say and do. Sometimes the story is

Now in 70 mm. wide screen and full stereophonic sound!

DAVID O. SELZNICK'S PRODUCTION OF MARGARET MITCHELL'S
"GONE WITH THE WIND"

Winner of Ten Academy Awards

**CLARK GABLE
VIVIEN LEIGH
LESLIE HOWARD
OLIVIA de HAVILLAND**

▲
Charlie Chaplin was one of the first big stars of silent films. His comic genius still makes people laugh today.

Halle Berry shows her delight at winning the Best Actress Academy Award® in 2002. It was the first time that an African American won this category.

based on a book, a TV show, or another work that already exists. Once the script is written, the key people are the producer and the director. The producer finds money to finance the project and keeps overall control. It is the director's job to interpret what is in the script and to help the actors give their best performances.

Actors

To many filmgoers, the actors are the most important part of a film. Some fans go to any film that features their favorite performer. At times producers have to persuade stars to take roles in their films by offering big sums of money. But most actors have to audition for roles—they perform a section from the script in front of the director and the producer. If they seem right for the part, they get the job.

After the actors have performed the script and their work is recorded on film, the work is not over. For a 90-minute movie, there may be many hours of film. The editor and the director work together to choose the best pieces of film and to put them together to make a movie that entertains and makes sense as a story. Other technicians may add sound effects or special visual effects. Nowadays these effects are often created with computers.

The producers will often show a finished version to a test audience to see what they think. Sometimes, depending on the reaction, the film is re-edited. Or a director might return to a movie some years after its release and make further changes, often using new technology that was not available when the film was first made.

DID YOU KNOW?

We think of Hollywood as the home of movies, but the country that produces the most feature films is India. The film industry based in the city of Mumbai (Bombay) is known as Bollywood. In its early days, in the 1930s, it produced as many as 1,000 feature films a year in all of India's major languages. The stories are frequently based on Indian myths. Romance, action, songs, suspense, and dance are all important features of a Bollywood film.

SEE ALSO: Cartoons and Animation; Computers; Dance; Television

✳ FIREFIGHTING

Fires cause thousands of deaths and billions of dollars' worth of damage every year. Without firefighters this destruction would be even greater.

Every day in the line of duty, firefighters risk their lives to save others. Three hundred forty-three firefighters died in the terrorist destruction of the World Trade Center on September 11, 2001.

Firefighters at work

Firefighters must respond to a fire whenever and wherever it occurs. Once on the scene, they work together in a tight-knit team. They must attach the pumps on the fire truck to fire hydrants, connect hoses to the hydrants, and carry the hoses where they are needed. Usually several firefighters have to handle a single hose because the water pressure is too powerful for one person to control. As the fire rages, the firefighters go in and out of the burning building with the hoses, trying to put out the flames. Others aim water at nearby buildings to prevent sparks from setting those buildings on fire as well.

Firefighting has special dangers at night and in cold weather. People in a burning building may have been asleep when the fire broke out, so firefighters have to search for people trapped or those overcome by smoke or poisonous gases. In cold weather, water from the hoses may freeze, making surfaces more slippery than usual.

Backdraft

Another danger firefighters face is a backdraft explosion, a burst of flames that shoots out toward the firefighters. It occurs when a superheated room, filled with gases from the fire, suddenly gets a fresh supply of oxygen. When firefighters make holes through which gases may escape, they can lessen the danger of backdraft.

Firefighters are also trained to respond to other emergencies, such as cutting people free from car wrecks and giving first aid to injured people.

A firefighter tackles a blazing building in Syracuse, New York.

AMAZING FACTS!

The great fire of Chicago, IL, on October 8, 1871, killed 300 people, destroyed 17,450 buildings, and caused $200 million worth of damage.

A fire in Boston, MA, on November 9, 1872, destroyed 775 buildings and caused $75 million worth of damage. Firefighters could not control the blaze because the horses that usually pulled their engines were all sick with an infectious disease.

SEE ALSO: World Trade Center

✳ FISH

Fish live in water. They are vertebrates—that is, animals with a backbone and an internal skeleton. There are over 21,000 different species of fish.

Salmon can leap tall waterfalls in a single bound, soaring 6 ft. (1.8 m) in the air.

The background picture shows double-saddle butterfly fish near a coral reef.

Not all animals that live in water are fish. Some, such as whales, are mammals; others, such as frogs, are amphibians. The characteristics that set fish apart from other animals include breathing oxygen from the water, having fins, and being cold-blooded (dependent on their surroundings for body temperature).

Fish have forms that are contoured, or shaped, to help them swim smoothly through water. All have mucus-coated skins. Most have movable fins, and many have scales. Fish use their respiratory organs, usually gills, to get oxygen from the water.

Most bony fish have an organ called a swim bladder that fills with gas like a balloon. The swim bladder enables fish to float, to hover, and to sink. Many bottom-dwelling fish do not have swim bladders. Sharks and rays also lack one. To keep from sinking to the bottom, they must swim constantly.

The eyes of most fish are placed on either side of the head. In many species, each eye moves independently. This gives fish a wide view of what is in front of, behind, below, and above them. Many fish have a keen sense of hearing. They also depend heavily on their sense of smell to locate prey, detect predators, and communicate.

Life cycle

Fish come together to spawn, or produce young, sometimes in pairs or in schools, which are large, teeming groups. In most fish the female lays its eggs in the water, and they are fertilized there by sperm released into the water by the male. The fertilized eggs then develop and hatch in the water. Young fish, or fry, emerge from the eggs. Some are cared for by the parent fish; however, most fend for themselves. Some fish feed mainly on plants, such as algae and seaweed. Most fish eat other fish, as well as worms, insects, and shellfish.

Early in their lives, about 80 percent of fish live in schools. However, only about 20 percent of adults live in large groups. Fish form schools because there is safety in numbers, mates are readily available, and it is easier for a fish to travel through water in the wake of the fish in front of it.

Where fish are found

Although 97 percent of the world's water is found in the oceans, only 58 percent of all fish are marine, or saltwater, species.

Less than 1 percent of the world's water is fresh, and yet it contains 41 percent of the fish species alive today. The remaining 1 percent of fish can live in either fresh or salt water.

In the oceans, most fish live within the top 600 ft. (183 m) of coastal waters. However, deep-sea fish have been collected from a depth of more than 27,000 ft. (8,200 m). Some fish live only in certain places, such as the Arctic Ocean, while others are found all over the world.

Overharvesting and pollution has greatly reduced the fish

KINDS OF FISH

Ichthyologists, scientists who study fish, have divided fish into two main groups: jawless fish and jawed fish. Jawed fish are further divided into cartilaginous fish and bony fish.

Jawless fish include lampreys and hagfish.

Jawed fish

Cartilaginous fish, or Chondrichthyes, include sharks, skates, and rays. They have skeletons made of cartilage, which is the same material that forms people's outer ears and nose. There are about 800 species.

Bony fish, or Osteichthyes, are by far the largest group of fish. They are divided into four groups of fish species: lungfish, coelacanths, bichirs, and rayfinned fish. Rayfinned fish are the largest group of fish alive today.

AMAZING FACTS !

The dwarf goby of the central Indian Ocean is no bigger than a pencil eraser, reaching only about ⅓ in. (0.8 cm) in length.

The whale shark, found in the warm areas of the Atlantic, Pacific, and Indian oceans, can grow to lengths of 42 ft. (13 m) and weigh 16 tons.

Cod lay as many as 100 million eggs in a season.

populations in nearly three-quarters of the world's fisheries. Regulations are needed to preserve fish populations, but many countries disagree on the course of action to take.

SEE ALSO: Animals; Ecology; Migration; Oceans and Seas; Pollution

✳ FITZGERALD, ELLA (1917–96)

Ella Fitzgerald was one of the greatest jazz and popular music singers of the 1900s. Her style of singing was a huge influence on later performers.

Ella Jane Fitzgerald was born in Newport News, Virginia, and grew up in New York City. She first achieved fame as a singer in the 1930s with Chick Webb's Big Band. Her first big hit was "A-Tisket, A-Tasket" in 1938. She was popular for her clear, flexible voice and her skill at scat singing—singing with nonsense syllables, instead of words. After Webb died in 1939, she led the band for three years.

In the 1950s, she began to record the "Songbook" series of albums. Each one was devoted to the works of a single American songwriter, or songwriting team, such as George Gershwin, Cole Porter, or Irving Berlin. Many of her versions of

these songs set a high standard for future singers to compare themselves against. She later recorded contemporary pop songs written by rock bands, such as the Beatles and Cream. She also performed bossa nova and opera.

Ella won many awards during her career, including 13 Grammys. Despite suffering from diabetes, which affected her sight and general health, she performed until the early 1990s. She died in 1996.

▲ *Ella Fitzgerald was known as the "First Lady of Song."*

SEE ALSO: Gershwin, George; Music

✳ FITZGERALD, F. SCOTT (1896–1940)

The American writer F. Scott Fitzgerald invented the phrase *The Jazz Age* to describe the society of the 1920s that he portrayed in his novels and stories.

Francis Scott Key Fitzgerald was born in St. Paul, Minnesota. He went to Princeton University, but left in 1917 to join the U.S. Army. In 1920 he published his first novel, *This Side of Paradise*. In the same year, he married Zelda Sayre.

In 1925 Fitzgerald published his most famous book, *The Great Gatsby*. It is the story of a wealthy, attractive man who turns out to have made his fortune through crime. Fitzgerald's other works include *The Beautiful and Damned* (1922) and *Tender Is the Night* (1934). His characters are almost always rich and appear to be happy, attractive, and successful. However, they often have dark

secrets and are unhappy beneath the surface. In the author's words, all his stories have "a touch of disaster" in them. This reflects the lives of the Fitzgeralds—Zelda suffered from mental health problems, and Scott was an alcoholic.

In 1937 Fitzgerald became a movie scriptwriter. Hollywood was the setting for his final, unfinished novel, *The Last Tycoon*. He died on December 21, 1940. He was only 44 years old.

▲ *F. Scott Fitzgerald's* The Great Gatsby *is considered to be a classic American novel.*

SEE ALSO: Literature

✳ FLAGS

A flag is a piece of cloth, often attached to a pole or staff. It is decorated with a design and used as an emblem, a symbol, or as a means of signaling.

There are special flags for nations, states and provinces, counties and cities, and for international organizations like the United Nations. Thousands of different military flags are also in use, as well as personal rank flags—including the banners used by kings, queens, and presidents.

The design of each nation's flag has special meaning. Many flags have symbols such as stripes, stars, animals, and crosses. The symbol of an eagle might represent strength or a famous ruler. Even colors usually have meaning. For example, blue might represent the waters surrounding an island nation.

The earliest forerunners of modern flags were made about 5,000 years ago in ancient India, China, and Egypt. Known as standards, they were not cloth, but carved figures secured on the tops of poles. They were used for signaling to and from ships and during battles because they could be seen from a long distance.

In the Roman Empire, troops carried a red or purple flag hung from a crossbar attached to a pole. This kind of flag was called a *vexillum*, from the English word *vexillology*, which means "the study of flags." The Chinese may have been the first to invent cloth flags. By about A.D. 1000, most flags in Europe were cloth, although carved standards were still used.

The U.S. flag

Over the years the U.S. flag, the Stars and Stripes, has been changed 27 times, mostly by the addition of stars to represent new states. The very first American flag, however, had no stars on it at all: It showed the Union Jack, the symbol of Great Britain. After the Declaration of Independence, Americans wanted to show that they were no longer loyal to the mother country but to the "new constellation" of American states. The 13-star flag was designed by Francis Hopkinson, a member of the naval board. Tradition says that the first flag was sewn by Betsy Ross. When the original 13 states increased to 15, two more stars

A Union cavalry flag from the Civil War (1861–65).

TYPES OF FLAGS

STARS & STRIPES

▷ *The U.S. flag through the years, from the late colonial period to the present.*

| 1776 | 1777–95 | 1795–1818 | 1912–59 | Present day |

On the earliest U.S. flag, the 13 stripes represented the original states, and the Union Jack showed that they belonged to Britain. After independence, the British inset was replaced with 13 stars. After Vermont and Kentucky joined the Union, the flag acquired another two stars and two stripes. In 1912 the number of stripes reverted to 13, and each state had its own star.

TYPES OF FLAGS CONTINUED

UNION JACK

The design of the Union Jack is a combination of the flags of the three countries that make up the United Kingdom.

St. George's Cross (England)

St. Andrew's Cross (Scotland)

St. Patrick's Cross (Ireland)

The flag of the United Kingdom, often known as the Union Jack, is an overlay of the flags of St. George (for England), St. Andrew (for Scotland), and St. Patrick (for Ireland). The overlay is quite intricate and is often drawn incorrectly. The flag is twice as wide as it is high.

INTERNATIONAL CODE FLAGS

Used on ships, each flag can represent either a single letter or a message.

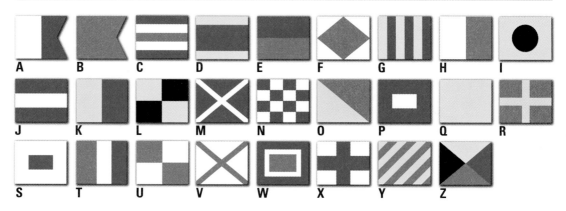

One of the best-known ship's flags is that standing for *P*. It is the Blue Peter, which is flown when a ship is about to sail. Other meanings include *C*: Yes; *H*: Pilot on board; *N*: No; *O*: Man overboard; *Q*: *Request pratique* (permission to use a foreign port); *V*: Require assistance.

were added to the flag, together with two more stripes. In 1818 Congress passed a new law. It said that there should be 13 stripes for each of the original 13 colonies and one star for each state. For many years, the stars were arranged in various ways. In 1912 President Taft established an official pattern.

Signal flags

The crews of ships at sea communicate by using a special group of flags and pennants known as the International Code of Signals. They are colorful and simple in design so that they can be seen from far away. The code consists of a flag for each of the 26 letters of the English alphabet, 10 flags for the numbers zero through nine, a code pennant to indicate that a message is in code, and three repeater pennants that are used to restate the messages on previously hoisted flags. Another group of message flags is plain-colored with specific meanings. The most familiar are the white flag meaning "truce" and the red flag meaning "danger."

SEE ALSO: Communication; Roman Empire

✳ FLEMING, ALEXANDER (1881–1955)

Anyone who has taken penicillin to cure an infection owes a debt to the Scottish scientist Alexander Fleming, who discovered this "wonder drug."

Alexander Fleming was born on a farm near Darvel, Scotland, and left school when he was 13. However, when he was 20, he began studying medicine in London, England. When he finished his studies, he began work as a bacteriologist in the laboratories of St. Mary's Hospital. He worked there for the rest of his life.

In 1928 Fleming was growing bacteria in flat, open dishes. One day he noticed some mold on one of the dishes. He noted that no bacteria were growing near the mold. Further experiments showed that a chemical in the mold had killed the microbes. Fleming named the chemical penicillin. It first became widely used in

World War II (1939–45) to treat wounded servicemen. Without penicillin, many thousands would have died of infections. Two other scientists, Howard Florey and Ernest Chain, were the first to produce penicillin in large quantities. But without Fleming's chance discovery, their work would have been impossible. Fleming received a knighthood in 1944. The following year, he, Florey, and Chain received the Nobel Prize for medicine.

SEE ALSO: Fungus; Medicine; Nobel Prize; Scientists

Sir Alexander Fleming holds a dish containing penicillin, a mold that cures a wide range of illnesses.

✳ FLOODS

Floods occur when the level of a body of water rises too high for its banks and water pours onto the surrounding land. They may cause severe damage.

Floods have many possible causes. Heavy rainstorms can increase the amount of water in a river, making it overflow. If the surrounding land is hard or waterlogged, it cannot absorb the extra water. If farms or buildings are near the river, they may be invaded or submerged by water. There may even be loss of life.

Tropical storms can also cause flooding. Hurricanes and typhoons may bring destructive winds and rain to coastal areas. Underwater earthquakes can cause tsunamis—huge, fast-moving waves that can flood coasts.

Another cause of floods, especially in mountain areas, is melting snow. If snow

In the wake of Hurricane Floyd, the Tar River floods part of Greenville, North Carolina, in 1999.

AMAZING FACTS !

A cyclone hit Bangladesh in 1970, causing widespread floods. Over 500,000 people died. Another cyclone in 1991 killed over 138,000 people. **Flooding in China** along the Yangtze River valley in 1931 caused the deaths of over three million people from disease, drowning, or starvation. **The worst floods in the United States** occurred in 1993, when the waters of the Mississippi and Missouri rivers flooded 16 million acres in nine states, causing dozens of deaths and $10 billion worth of damage.

melts too quickly, and the ground is too frozen to let the water soak in, great torrents may pour down the sides of mountains, flooding the valleys below.

Flood protection

The shape of land near a river can make the area more or less likely to flood. In North America, the major tributaries of the Mississippi River often flood. Elsewhere the basins of the following rivers are particularly at risk: the Huang He (Yellow River) in China, the Indus River in Asia, and the Danube River in Europe.

Floods cannot be fully prevented, but steps can be taken to protect people and property. Drainage systems can be built to keep floodwater off the land. Dams can control the flow of rivers and prevent them from bursting their banks. Levees are high riverbanks that allow rivers to carry more water. Reservoirs are huge artificial lakes that can hold excess water.

SEE ALSO: Dams; Earthquakes; Hurricanes and Typhoons; Rivers

* FLOWERS

There are approximately 240,000 different kinds of flowering plants, or angiosperms. They live on every landmass except Antarctica.

The flowers of the rafflesia, from the jungles of Southeast Asia, measure up to 3 ft. (0.9 m) across and weigh more than 15 lb. (6.8 kg).

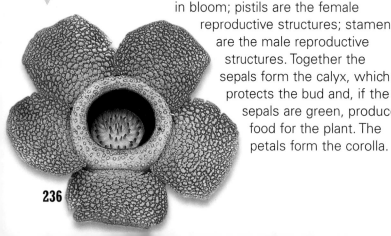

A typical flower has four main parts. The sepals are the leaflike structures that cover the flower bud; petals are the delicate leaves that make up the most noticeable part of the flower when it is in bloom; pistils are the female reproductive structures; stamens are the male reproductive structures. Together the sepals form the calyx, which protects the bud and, if the sepals are green, produces food for the plant. The petals form the corolla.

The reproductive structures are responsible for producing seeds. The pistil is divided into three parts: the ovary, at the base of the pistil, encloses and protects the ovules, which hold the eggs; the stigma is the sticky top of the pistil; the style is the thin tube connecting the stigma and the ovary.

Each stamen is made up of two parts: the slender filament, which sticks up from the base of the flower, and the anther, which sits on top of the filament. Inside the anther are two sacs containing pollen grains. The pollen grains produce sperm.

The life of a flower

All flowers have a similar life cycle. A flower starts as a tightly closed bud. As the petals and other structures inside the bud grow, the bud swells and eventually opens. After the bud bursts, and the sepals begin to fold away, the petals start to unfurl. At this time the reproductive structures and the glands, called nectaries, begin to grow. The nectaries produce the sweet liquid called nectar.

Pollination, the transfer of pollen from the anther to the stigma, takes place once all the structures are fully developed. This process is called self-pollination if the pollen from a stamen lands on the pistil of the same flower. It is known as cross-pollination when the pollen is transferred from the stamens of one flower to the pistil of a flower on another plant of the same kind. This transfer happens when bees, butterflies, moths, or birds become covered with sticky pollen grains as they drink flower nectar. When they land on another flower, their bodies brush the sticky surface of the stigma, transferring the pollen. Some flower species rely on the wind to transfer pollen. Instead of showy flowers or nectar, they make huge amounts of pollen, which wafts away on the wind.

PARTS OF A FLOWER

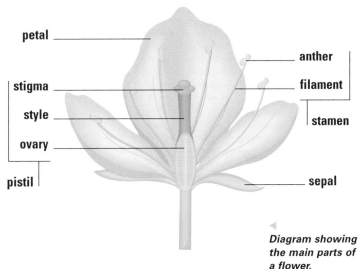

petal · anther · filament · stamen · stigma · style · ovary · pistil · sepal

◀ Diagram showing the main parts of a flower.

By the time the seeds are beginning to form, the flower has died. The flower's ovary may ripen into a fleshy fruit, such as an apple, or a dry, hard fruit, such as a nut. Animals may collect and eat the fruits and unknowingly scatter the seeds. Other fruits may float away on the wind or water. If conditions are favorable for a seed to sprout once it is released from its fruit, it can grow into a mature plant that produces its own flowers.

Some flowers produce flowers and fruits within a single year,

Frailejones are found only in the Andes Mountains in South America.

then die. These species are called annuals. Biennial species take two years to produce their flowers and fruits, after which time they die. Perennial species live for many years. Some flower one or more times a year; others may live for decades before flowering and producing seeds.

Saving our flowers

Many species of flowers are endangered or threatened with extinction. Some flowers, including certain orchids and cacti, have been collected by people who sell them to florists. Others are endangered because their habitats have been destroyed. When flower species are endangered, the animal pollinators, such as butterflies, that depend on the species for food can also become threatened.

SEE ALSO:
Cactus;
Conservation;
Endangered
Species; Fruit;
Insects;
Plants;
Pollination

AMAZING FACTS!

The common duckweed has the smallest flowers of any plant. They measure only $1/16$ to $3/16$ in. (1.6 to 4.8 mm) in length and weigh just a fraction of an ounce.

The world's largest flowering plant is a Chinese wisteria that was planted in 1894 in Sierra Madre, CA. It spreads its branches over nearly an acre and weighs 25 tons. It is estimated that more than 1.5 million flowers decorate its branches during its five-week flowering period.

✳ FOLK ARTS

Folk art is art produced by people using traditional techniques that have been passed down to them through the generations.

The term *folk art* is usually used to describe creative work made in the tradition of the artist's culture or local area. It especially applies to art produced by people living in rural areas. As well as paintings and sculpture, examples of folk art can include clothing, furniture, utensils, toys, and quilts. Some pieces may be simple craftwork intended for everyday use; others may be highly decorated art that has been made for an important purpose such as a religious ceremony.

Folk artists often learn by watching their elders or by becoming apprentices in a craft. Some folk artists learn by teaching themselves. Increased trade and communications have changed the practice of folk art, but they have not made it disappear.

Folk arts around the world

Folk arts differ from country to country, and even from village to village. However, there are also similarities between the works of people living thousands of miles apart. For example, calligraphy—decorative writing—has existed for many years in

▶ *At Santa Clara Pueblo, New Mexico, an artist decorates a piece of pottery.*

Europe, in China and Japan, and in the Islamic world. Calligraphers put their designs in books, on posters, even on walls and on pottery. When people from different cultures meet, they exchange ideas, and the arts of various regions take on new influences and techniques.

Many great artists have taken their influences from various folk art traditions. The Italian painter and sculptor Amedeo Modigliani (1884–1920) based his style on the simplified shapes used in African art. The French artist Henri de Toulouse-Lautrec (1864–1901) took ideas from Japanese printing techniques.

North American folk arts

Native American peoples were creating beautiful things well before the arrival of the first European settlers. Clothing, tent material, tools, even weapons, often carried woven or carved designs. Many of these images had religious meanings. Folk art made by the early settlers reflected their homeland traditions. Dutch and German influences were especially strong.

Artists and craftspeople began to use the raw materials of their new land. Religious groups such as the Shakers (who originally came from England) and the Amish (who originally came from Switzerland and Germany) developed their own styles, which still influence modern home design. Shaker furniture from the 1800s can be very valuable today.

Folk art was especially successful in the more remote, rural areas of the United States until about 1900. After that, advances in industry and communications meant that people were able to buy everyday goods that they would have made previously. Textiles could be mass-produced on large looms in factories, and furniture could be made with power tools.

An Amish woman sits at her sewing machine, surrounded by quilts she has made.

However, many of the traditions of American folk art still exist. People continue to make quilts and carve toys using traditional methods. They are interested in the old ways of doing things, and the process helps them to understand the lives of their ancestors.

True folk art continues today, as new immigrants bring the traditions of lands such as Mexico, Nigeria, and Vietnam to North America. These traditions may remain distinct within their communities or neighborhoods, or they may mix with other art forms to make new traditions. What is certainly true is that folk arts will never die out completely.

SEE ALSO: Art and Artists; Colonial America; Fabrics and Cloth; Native Americans

✳ FOOD

If animals are to survive and thrive, they need a regular supply of food. But for humans, food can be far more than simple fuel.

Food in history

Early humans spent much of their time searching for food and ate whatever they could find. They picked plants and berries and ate insects and shellfish. Later, as people learned to make tools, they fished and hunted for their food.

A woman carries food and decorations on her head as part of a village festival in Bali.

Humans gradually began to grow crops and to keep animals for meat, milk, and eggs. At first each family or tribe grew enough to feed their own group. As agriculture improved, people grew more food than they needed. They traded the surplus to get other things they wanted. Markets and fairs were set up at which people exchanged food and other goods.

Food in society

Most animals eat food just to survive. For humans, eating delicious food is one of life's greatest pleasures. What we choose to eat may be influenced by our ethnic identity, religious beliefs, social status, or where we live. And every person has individual habits and food preferences. But although people eat in various ways, the practice of sharing a meal with family and friends is common across the globe. Even if the food is very simple, the act of eating together provides a chance to relax and talk, and can improve the quality of life.

Sometimes food is part of a celebration. In North America, people often eat turkey at Thanksgiving, as the Pilgrims are said to have done. In other cultures, special foods mark weddings, birthdays, or religious or national occasions.

Food can help to maintain links to people's cultures. For example, some Jewish people throughout the world follow rules about what they can and cannot eat.

Immigrants bring the foods and recipes of their native lands to their new countries. In many big cities, there are restaurants and shops that provide food from Italy,

China, India, Japan, Latin America, and many other regions. These give people comforting memories of the lands they have left behind and provide new eating experiences for the native populations.

Food supply

The amount of energy that a food supplies is measured in units called calories. The average adult needs about 2,800 calories per day to maintain health. The world's food supply provides enough calories to maintain this level. However, 800 million people do not consume enough calories. At the same time, many people in the developed world consume far too many calories. Combined with an inactive lifestyle, this can lead to obesity (excessive fatness), heart disease, diabetes, and other problems.

The world's population has expanded rapidly over the last 100 years. It currently stands at about six billion, and is expected to rise to nine billion by 2050. Improved techniques in farming and irrigation have helped food producers keep up with this increase. Scientific advances, such as genetic manipulation, have created new strains of crops that give increased yields and resist disease.

However, this is not enough to guarantee food supplies in the poorer parts of the

world. Mismanagement, corruption, and natural disasters such as floods and droughts affect food production in many countries. Also, many farmers in Africa, Asia, and South America produce food for European and North American buyers. This does not encourage the best use of resources. Western supermarkets often demand food that will stay fresh and look attractive for long periods. This is not always the most nutritious food.

People in the West receive a large proportion of their calories from animal sources—meat, dairy, and eggs—which is not an efficient use of farmland. As an average across the whole world, people get only 16 percent of their calories from animal foods. If we want to reach a stage where every person has enough to eat, Westerners will have to cut down on the amount of animal foods they eat.

▲
Throughout the world, families enjoy mealtimes together as a chance to relax and talk.

SEE ALSO: Agriculture; Health; Stomach and Digestive System

✳ FOOD CHAINS

A food chain is made up of a series of living creatures, or organisms, each one using the next one in the chain as part of its food supply.

Energy from food is transferred from one organism to the next. The first organisms in the chain are primary producers. They use a process called photosynthesis to obtain energy from the sun. The primary producers on land are green plants. Tiny organisms known as plankton are the primary producers in water. Primary consumers eat primary producers. On land, primary consumers are plant-eating animals—herbivores— such as cows. Secondary consumers— carnivores—feed on primary consumers. Bacteria and fungi are both primary and secondary consumers. They feed on dead plants and animals, converting them into nutrients that can be reused by other organisms in the food chain. They are called decomposers.

The osprey—a meat-eating bird of prey—is a secondary consumer.

Food webs and communities

A community is made up of all the different species that live and interact with one another in a certain area. Food chains interact to form food webs when members of different chains feed on one another. Energy is transferred though the community in the form of food, although it decreases at each stage of the chain. The primary consumer receives

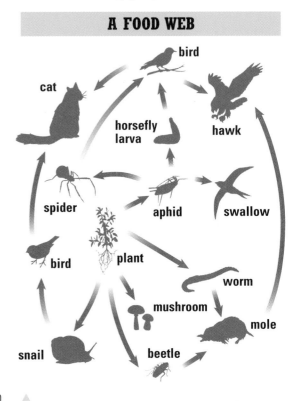

A FOOD WEB

bird

cat

horsefly larva

hawk

spider

aphid

swallow

bird

plant

worm

mushroom

mole

snail

beetle

A simplified food web: It is formed from several food chains in which each organism eats others and is in turn eaten. The arrows show the direction of nutrient flow.

10 percent of the energy produced by the primary producer. The secondary consumer gets 10 percent of the primary consumer's energy (only 1 percent of the original energy). That is why primary producers are such an important part of a community. Without them there would be no food energy.

SEE ALSO: Animals; Ecology; Energy; Environment; Fungus; Photosynthesis; Plants

✳ FOOTBALL

Football is one of the most popular sports in the United States. The game is played on a large field between two teams of 11 players each.

The first game resembling modern football was played in 1874. Football was based on soccer and rugby. (In many countries, the term *football* refers to soccer.) For many years, it was an amateur game, mainly played in colleges. Canadian football is very similar to the U.S. game.

The American Professional Football Association was formed in 1920. It became the National Football League (NFL) two years later. The first Super Bowl, then played between the champions of the NFL and the American Football League, was held in 1967. The Super Bowl is now played between the champions of the two NFL conferences—the American Football Conference and the National Football Conference.

The field

A football field is 120 yards (110 m) long and 53⅓ yards (49 m) wide. The main playing area is 100 yards long, with a goal line at each end. It is divided every 5 yards by a yard line extending from side line to side line. The 10 yards behind each goal line are the end zones. At the back of each end zone is a goal with a crossbar 10 ft. (3 m) above the ground.

How football is played

The object of the game is to score more points than the opponent by advancing a ball past the opposing team's goal line. During a game, possession of the ball switches between teams. Each team has players making up the offense, who play when their team has the ball, and others who make up the defense and play when the opponents have the ball. The offense tries to move the ball toward the opponents' goal line. The defense tries to tackle (knock down) the ball-carrier. Other offensive players try to block defensive players and stop them from tackling.

Before a game begins, the captains toss a coin. The winner of the toss chooses to kick off or receive the ball, or else selects which goal to defend. For kickoff at the beginning of the game, the ball is placed on the 30-yard line (35-yard line in college and high school) of the kicking team. The kicker runs forward and kicks it. ➡

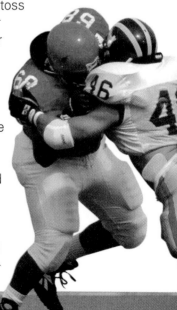

A Boston University running back bursts through a hole in University of Delaware's defense. Boston University's offensive linemen are blocking any tackles. ▼

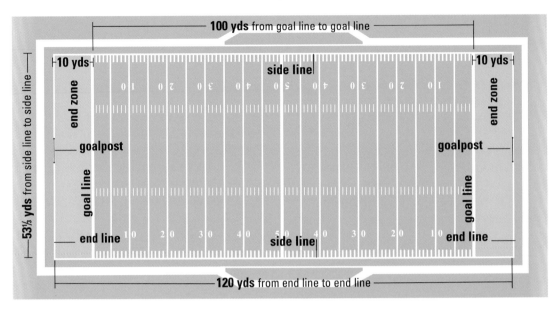

The football field is covered with natural grass or artificial turf. Each end zone has a goal line, and the side lines mark the edge of the field.

A football is oval in shape and has laces on one side, which makes it possible for players to get a good grip on the ball.

Any member of the opposing team may catch the ball and run toward the kicking team's goal. When he is tackled or goes out of bounds, the ball is ruled down, or dead. Play starts again where the ball was ruled down. The offensive and defensive teams face each other. One of the offensive linemen, the center, snaps the ball between his legs to the quarterback. To keep the ball, the offensive team must gain at least 10 yards in four plays, or downs. If the team fails to gain 10 yards after three plays, it may decide to punt, or kick, the ball deep into the opposing team's territory.

A team can advance the ball by carrying it or throwing it forward to a teammate. The defense can try to take the ball away from the offense (create a "turnover") at any time. Defensive players can block a punt or catch a punted ball as it lands in the field of play and run with it. If an offensive player fumbles or drops the ball, a defensive player can take it. Defensive players can also intercept a pass.

A professional or a college game lasts 60 minutes. A high school game lasts 48 minutes. The game is divided into four quarters of 15 or 12 minutes, with a halftime intermission between the second and third quarters. The teams change goals at the end of each quarter.

Scoring

A touchdown is worth six points. A team scores a touchdown by running or passing the ball across the opponents' goal line. Long runs and passes are some of the most exciting plays in football. After a touchdown a team can score extra points by kicking the ball over the crossbar for one point or by running or passing it into the end zone for two points. A field goal, when the ball is kicked over the crossbar from the ground, is worth three points. A safety occurs when a defensive player tackles a ball-carrier behind his own goal line. It is worth two points.

SEE ALSO: Sports

☀ FORCE AND MOTION

A force is an influence that changes the motion of an object or distorts its shape. The study of forces and motion forms a branch of physics called dynamics.

Forces act on all objects, from the protons and neutrons in the center of every atom to the largest stars in the universe. We make constant use of force and motion: throwing a ball, walking down the sidewalk, and riding a bicycle all need a force to produce the desired motion.

Galileo's breakthrough

While ancient Greek and Roman scientists knew forces existed, they did not realize how forces influenced the motion of objects. The first great breakthrough came in the late 1500s. Italian scientist Galileo Galilei (1564–1642) was attending a cathedral service in Pisa, Italy, when he noticed a lamp swaying back and forth on the ceiling. Galileo noted that each complete cycle of the lamp took about the same time, but the lamp swung through less distance in each successive cycle. He realized that some kind of draining force was reducing the distance through which the lamp swung in each cycle. Take away this force, and the lamp would swing through the same distance forever. Galileo also realized the difference between speed and velocity. He showed that speed is the rate of movement, while velocity is speed in a particular direction.

Velocity and acceleration

The velocity of an object changes if a force is applied to it. A change in velocity is known as acceleration. Positive acceleration is increasing velocity. Negative acceleration, or deceleration, is decreasing velocity. Acceleration also occurs when an object moves in a circular motion—for example, the motion of Earth around the sun. Circular acceleration constantly changes the direction of the object, but the speed of the object does not necessarily have to increase.

Newton's laws of motion

Galileo's ideas about forces and motion laid the foundations for the three laws of motion formulated by English scientist Isaac Newton (1642–1727). His first law states that an object moving at a steady speed in a fixed direction will continue to do so unless a force changes its speed or direction of motion. In other words, an object will only accelerate or decelerate if a force is applied. Newton's second law states that the acceleration depends on the size of the force and the mass of the object. The third law states that whenever a force acts on an object, there must be an equal reaction in the opposite direction. ➡

Scientists call all changes in velocity acceleration. However, non-scientists say that a car is accelerating when it increases its speed and decelerating when it slows down.
▼

RESULTANT FORCES

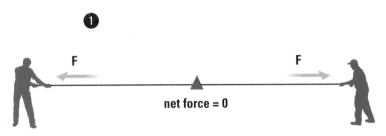

❶

net force = 0

(1) Two people pull against each other on a rope with equal force F. The net force is zero since the two forces act in opposite directions.

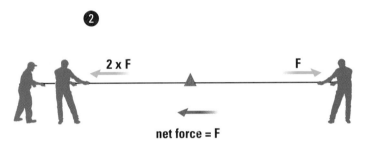

❷

2 x F

F

net force = F

(2) Two people now pull against one person, all with equal force F. The net force is F and will act in the direction of the two-person team.

In honor of Newton's work, all forces are measured in units called newtons (N). One newton (1 N) is the force required to accelerate one kilogram (1 kg) of mass at a rate of one meter per second per second ($1 m/s^2$).

Different forces

There are many different forces. When you ride a bicycle, for example, your foot applies a mechanical force on the pedal to move it. In the case of Galileo's lamp, a mechanical force called air resistance, or drag, slowed down the lamp. Mechanical forces occur when objects touch each other. Other forces act on objects without touching them. For example, gravity is a force that pulls objects toward the center of Earth. Electromagnetism is a force that

AMAZING FACTS !

As well as developing his laws of motion, Newton also discovered that the force of gravity causes objects to accelerate toward the ground at a rate of 32 ft./s^2 (9.8 m/s^2). If a person fell out of an airplane from a height of 32,000 ft. (9,754 m) above Earth, it would take them 45 seconds to hit the ground, assuming there was no air resistance. Of course, on Earth there is always air resistance.

holds molecules together. Forces called weak and strong nuclear forces act within the nucleus of an atom. All these forces act over a distance and arise from a field of force. Physicists call these four forces—gravity, electromagnetism, the strong and the weak nuclear force—the fundamental forces of the universe.

Interacting forces

Often more than one force acts on an object at any one time. All the forces combine to produce a net, or resultant, force. If the combined forces move an object, they are called unbalanced forces.

If the combined forces do not move the object, they are called balanced forces. An object is said to be in equilibrium if all the forces combine to produce no net force.

SEE ALSO: Atoms and Molecules; Energy; Galilei, Galileo; Gravity; Matter; Newton, Isaac; Physics

FORESTS

Forests cover more than 30 percent of the earth's land surface. The world's largest forest regions are in Asia and South America.

Forests are found all over the world. However, trees must have a frost-free growing season of at least three months. They also need a lot of water during this time. The North and South poles, the tops of some mountains, deserts, and some prairies are therefore bare of forests.

Types of forests

There are two basic types of trees in forests: hardwoods and softwoods. The majority of trees are hardwoods—broad-leaved trees such as oaks, maples, and hickories. Softwoods, such as pine, firs, and spruce, have needle-shaped leaves and bear seeds in cones, which means they are often called conifers.

Hardwood forests include rain forests, which grow in steamy tropical and subtropical regions. Other hardwood forests grow in temperate regions such as the United States, northern Europe, and eastern China. Softwood forests grow

The variety and lushness of the hardwood trees at McKittrick Canyon, in Guadalupe National Park, are rare for this part of Texas. They are due mainly to the presence of natural springs and streams.

in areas with long winters and moderate to high rainfall. The forests of northern Europe and Asia are called taiga or boreal forests. Subalpine forests grow at high altitudes. Cloud forests grow on tropical mountains with heavy rainfall.

Importance of forests

Forest soils are giant sponges. They soak up rain, so that it seeps slowly into the ground. When trees are cut, the soil is exposed and washes or blows away. Then rain runs off quickly, causing floods.

Trees increase the supply of oxygen and absorb carbon dioxide, helping keep the atmosphere in balance, so that life on Earth can continue. Forests provide food and shelter for a large population of birds and other animals. Millions of people enjoy forests as places for recreation. Forests are also important commercial resources, providing timber for fuel, building houses, and papermaking.

About a quarter of the world's forests have been cleared, either to build on or to harvest the wood commercially. Diseases, insects, and fires take an annual toll of trees almost equal to the volume cut by people. Since trees are an important natural resource, it is important to make every effort to protect them.

SEE ALSO: Biomes; Conservation; Environment; Floods; Rain Forests; Trees

Some of the world's tallest trees grow in Redwood National Park, California. Redwoods can reach a height of over 300 ft. (91 m) and live to be 2,000 years old. In the 1900s, the survival of this forest was in doubt, but today it is protected.

✳ FOSSIL FUELS

Fuels are materials that are burned to produce heat, light, and power. The most common fuels—oil, coal, and natural gas—are called fossil fuels.

Formation of fossil fuels

Fossil fuels were formed as ancient plants and microscopic animals died and their remains settled in layers on the ground or at the bottom of swamps.

Over time, heat and pressure caused the dead plants and animals to change form. All fossil fuels were formed by this basic process, but the various types of fuel were formed from different plants and animals under a variety of conditions, in different places, and at different times.

The energy in fossil fuels originally came from the sun. In a process known as photosynthesis, plants trap energy from the sun to turn water and carbon dioxide into food. When a fossil fuel is burned, it releases the energy stored in plants that lived millions of years ago.

Workers drilling for petroleum, or crude oil. Oil supplies more energy today than any other type of fuel.

Oil/Petroleum

Petroleum—from the Latin words for "rock" and "oil"—has numerous purposes. It is also known as crude oil. Deposits of petroleum lie deep under solid rock. Huge drills are used to find these deposits and bring the oil to the surface. The process that converts petroleum into useful products is called refining.

Refined petroleum heats buildings and powers generators to produce electricity. It can be made into gasoline, which powers cars and other motor vehicles. Other major fuels derived from petroleum are diesel and jet fuels. Petroleum is the basic material for plastics, synthetic fibers, asphalt (a substance used to pave roads and runways), and many other products.

Petroleum is one of the most important substances in world economics. The production of oil in various Arab nations affects the whole political process in the Middle East. Countries have gone to war to safeguard oil stocks and pipelines.

Coal

Coal comes from the remains of ferns and mosses that grew in swampy forests millions of years ago. Heat and pressure gradually transformed the dead plant material into layers, or seams, of hard, black rock. Deep, or underground, mining has been used for centuries to extract coal, often in dangerous conditions. Today miners are most likely to use machines to do the actual cutting.

Coal contains a high percentage of the element carbon. This makes it burn slowly with a clean flame, so it is good for

A coal miner stands alongside a drilling machine. Coal was first mined by chopping away at the coal wall, or face, with pickaxes. Today machines are often used to dig the coal more efficiently.

heating houses. Today, however, one of its most important uses is to generate electricity. Coal is also a vital ingredient in steel refining and in the production of some fertilizers and other chemicals.

Natural gas

Sometimes fossil material deep within the earth takes the form of a gas. Natural gas is usually found with petroleum. It is a mixture of gases consisting mostly of methane gas. When natural gas is drawn out of the ground, it is usually dissolved in liquids. It is later separated from these liquids and then transported in pipelines to consumers. It is a common home heating fuel, but is also used in cooking and in generating electricity.

Renewable and nonrenewable resources

Because fossil fuels come from the breakdown of natural materials, they are always being produced. However, this process takes millions of years. The human race uses these materials much faster than they are created. That is why these fuels are classified as nonrenewable resources. If we rely on nonrenewable fossil fuels, sooner or later we will run out. So it is important to investigate other, renewable resources such as solar, wind, and water power. Nuclear energy is also an efficient use of resources, but there are questions over its safety. There is further concern over the effects that the burning of fossil fuels may have on the environment. For example, the burning of gasoline in vehicles causes air pollution. And burning coal, in particular, may also contribute to global warming.

SEE ALSO:
Conservation;
Energy;
Environment;
Fossils; Natural
Resources;
Nuclear Power;
Photosynthesis;
Pollution

A natural gas plant where the liquid fuel is extracted from deep within the earth. Gas supplies about 30 percent of the energy used in the United States and Canada.

✳ FOSSILS

Fossils are the remains or evidence of life in ancient times. There are many kinds of fossil because plants and animals were preserved in different ways.

Only a small part of the earth's early life has been fossilized, or preserved as fossils. Usually they are organisms with a skeleton or a shell; the soft parts of animals or plants are seldom preserved.

Kinds of fossil

Sometimes, in very hot, dry areas, a piece of bone or a tooth of an ancient animal is preserved. In moist areas, bone material or woody material is gradually replaced with minerals, creating a fossil.

If an animal had a shell, it may fill with sand after its death. The shell disappears, but the sand inside turns to stone, creating a mold of the inner shape of the shell. The same thing can happen when the body of an animal decays, leaving a hollow mold that slowly fills with minerals, forming a cast of the animal's shape.

The footprint of an ancient animal or the outline of a leaf can be preserved under layers of sand, which harden into rock. Tree sap, tar, and ice can also preserve organisms. Insects became trapped in the sticky sap of trees. The resin hardened into amber, and the insect inside became a fossil. Many types of animals accidentally fell into tarpits. Their flesh decayed, but their bones and teeth were preserved.

Entire woolly mammoths, giant elephants that lived over 10,000 years ago, have been found in frozen soil or in the ice of glaciers. Their bodies did not decay or turn into fossils, but were frozen in ice. If they thaw out, their flesh begins to decay.

The fossil record

Scientists who study fossils are called paleontologists. By studying fossils, they can find out about life long ago and the environment that existed then. In some places, such as the Grand Canyon, Arizona, it is possible to see the layers of rock that have built up over millions of years to form the earth's surface. Each layer contains different types of fossils. The sequence of layers is called the fossil record. By studying it, paleontologists can track how life forms evolved, or changed, through time.

This fossil fish was found in Germany. It dates from between 163 and 144 million years ago.
▼

👀

SEE ALSO: Dinosaurs; Earth; Evolution; Extinction; Geology

✳ FRANCE

France is the largest country in western Europe. It has borders with Spain, Andorra, Italy, Monaco, Switzerland, Germany, Luxembourg, and Belgium.

Land and climate
France has a varied landscape. Mountains called the French Alps run north from the Mediterranean and include Mont Blanc. At 15,780 ft. (4,810 m), Mont Blanc is the highest peak in western Europe. Other ranges include the Jura and Vosges mountains and the Pyrenees. The Massif Central covers one-sixth of France. It is mostly plateaus (high flatland).

The south is warm and dry, while the Atlantic and northern coasts are cooler. High mountains are snow-capped all year.

People and economy
The French are descended from many ethnic groups. Celts settled in Brittany and Norse people settled in Normandy. Alsace, Flanders, and Corsica were settled by people of German, Dutch, and Italian ancestry, respectively. Recently, immigrants from France's former colonies, mainly those in North Africa, have arrived.

Before World War II (1939–45), France had a mainly agricultural economy. Today industrial production is more important, especially cars, aircraft, and armaments. The country's cheeses and wines are world-famous, and tourism is one of the largest industries.

History
By 50 B.C., the Roman general Julius Caesar had defeated the Gauls of France—a Celtic people who had lived there for many centuries. Rome ruled the area for the next 400 years.

After the Romans left, Germanic tribes invaded Gaul. In 481 Clovis founded the first great Frankish kingdom, from which France takes its name. Clovis was France's first Christian ruler. The greatest Frankish king was Charlemagne, who ruled from 768. His empire included Germany and much of Europe.

In the following centuries, there was much conflict with England. In the 1300s, a series of wars began, now known as the Hundred Years' War. At first England occupied large areas of France. But in the early 1400s, a young farm girl called Joan of Arc led the French army to victory against the English, who were eventually driven out of France.

In the 1500s, there was bitter conflict between Catholics and Protestants, or Huguenots. Henri IV, a Huguenot, became king in 1589, but he converted to Catholicism. In the early 1600s, two high-ranking church officials (cardinals), Richelieu and Mazarin, controlled France. When Mazarin died in 1661, King Louis XIV (1638–1715) announced

The dukes of Bourbon and Orléans are captured by the English. The battle of Agincourt in 1415 was one of many battles fought between the English and French during the Hundred Years' War.

The Eiffel Tower, Paris, is a 984-ft. (300-m) iron structure. It was finished in 1889 to commemorate the 100th anniversary of the French Revolution.

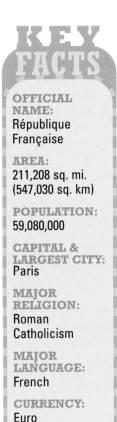

OFFICIAL NAME:
République Française

AREA:
211,208 sq. mi.
(547,030 sq. km)

POPULATION:
59,080,000

CAPITAL & LARGEST CITY:
Paris

MAJOR RELIGION:
Roman Catholicism

MAJOR LANGUAGE:
French

CURRENCY:
Euro

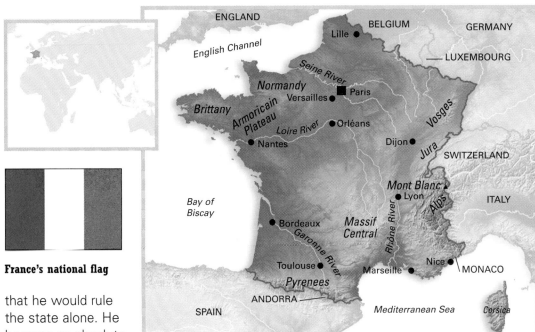

France's national flag

that he would rule the state alone. He became an absolute monarch with total control over his people. He built a grand palace at Versailles to show off his power.

France's economy declined after Louis XIV's death. France also lost overseas territories, such as Canada, to Britain between 1756 and 1763. The country was close to bankruptcy, and King Louis XVI lost the confidence of the people.

On July 14, 1789, a mob stormed the Bastille, a fortress in Paris that was viewed as a symbol of the monarchy. The event marked the start of the French Revolution. July 14 is still celebrated as France's national holiday. Thousands of people died on the guillotine. Finally, in 1793 King Louis XVI and Queen Marie-Antoinette were executed.

France was soon at war with most of Europe. Napoleon Bonaparte, who made himself emperor in 1804, became master of almost all of Europe. However, in 1815 he was defeated by an alliance of European powers and sent into exile.

The French then alternated between a republican government and a return to monarchical government. In 1852 Napoleon's nephew became Emperor Napoleon III. Many people hoped he would recapture the glory of his uncle's rule. However, Napoleon was defeated by the German state of Prussia in 1870. France became a republic again.

Germany occupied much of northeastern France during World War I (1914–18) and the whole country during World War II (1939–45). Many French people fought against the occupation. The Allies liberated France in 1945. In recent years, France has become a leading member of the European Union (EU), an economic and political grouping of European countries.

SEE ALSO: Caesar, Julius; Central Europe; Charlemagne; Europe; Napoleon; Roman Empire; World War I; World War II

✳ FRANKLIN, BENJAMIN (1706–90)

Benjamin Franklin was a diplomat, scientist, inventor, and writer. His ideas make him one of the most influential Americans of all time.

Benjamin Franklin was born in Boston, Massachusetts. He left school early to train as a printer. By the age of 42, he was able to retire and pursue other interests.

The first of Franklin's many inventions was a stove. He never patented (registered to make a profit) his inventions, because he believed that new ideas should be used to benefit everyone. Franklin's particular interest was electricity. He is famous for his dangerous experiment in 1752, where he used a kite as a lightning conductor during a thunderstorm.

In 1754 Franklin attended a conference in Albany, New York, to discuss defense against Native American attacks. His plan to unite the colonies later formed the basis for the first constitution of the United States. He helped to draft the Declaration of Independence in 1776. He was also mainly responsible for the Treaty of Paris, which officially ended the American Revolution in 1783.

Franklin was president (governor) of Pennsylvania in his 80s. He also argued for the abolition of slavery. He died on April 17, 1790.

> **SEE ALSO:** American Revolution; Constitution, United States; Declaration of Independence; Electricity; Inventors and Inventions

▲ *Franklin came up with new ideas and produced inventions that still influence our lives today.*

✳ FRENCH AND INDIAN WARS

Between 1689 and 1763, France and Great Britain fought four wars in North America. They are known as the French and Indian wars.

The French first came to Canada in 1534. The English began settling in North America in 1607. By 1750 there were about 90,000 French and about 1.5 million British in the colonies. Conflict became inevitable as the two nations competed for land and the fur trade. Native Americans were involved in the French and Indian wars only as supporters of the French and the British forces.

The first three wars
The first war between Great Britain and France in North America was fought between 1689 and 1697. Neither country

◄ *General James Wolfe, the British leader, dies on the battlefield on the Plains of Abraham near Quebec, Canada, in 1759.*

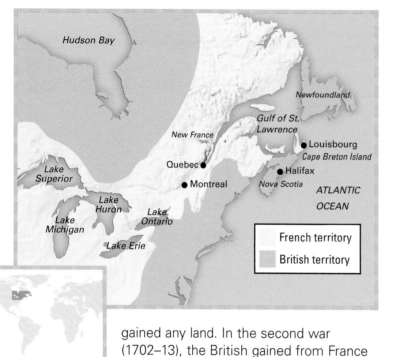

This map shows French and British lands in 1756.
◀

A third war spread from Europe to North America in 1744. The British took the French fortress of Louisbourg but returned it in the peace treaty of 1748 in exchange for land in other parts of the world.

The French and Indian War

The fourth war is the one usually called the French and Indian War. It was officially declared in 1756. The French won early victories, but in 1758 the British captured several fortresses. They won a decisive victory at Quebec on September 13, 1759. However, war between France and Great Britain continued in Europe until 1763.

gained any land. In the second war (1702–13), the British gained from France the Hudson Bay area, Newfoundland, and Acadia, which they renamed Nova Scotia.

SEE ALSO: Canada; Louisiana Purchase; United States of America

❋ FROGS AND TOADS

Frogs and toads form a group of amphibians with tailless bodies, bulging eyes, and well-developed hind legs that are used for leaping or hopping.

Frogs and toads all have short, round bodies with large, flat heads and four legs. Frogs usually have longer hind legs, enabling them to jump long distances. Toads are more likely to waddle.

There are more than 3,700 species of frogs and toads—the majority are frogs. They are found in all areas of the world except Antarctica. However, they are most common in the tropics. They live in a range of

A red-eyed tree frog from the rain forests of Costa Rica hides on a leaf and waits to catch insects for food.
▼

habitats, usually wet places such as ponds, marshes, and rain forests. Toads tend to have thicker skin than frogs, which makes them better able to live in dry parts of the world.

Like other amphibians, frogs and toads do not make their own body heat. Their body temperature depends on the temperature of their environment. To survive, they have to avoid temperature extremes. In freezing temperatures, they stay warm under piles of leaves or burrow into the muddy bottoms of ponds or streams.

As adults, frogs and toads eat mainly insects. They usually have a long, sticky

F

AMAZING FACTS!

The poison arrow frogs of Central and South America are the most toxic animals in the world.

The golden poison arrow frog, found in western Colombia, contains enough poison to kill 100 adult humans.

Some species of aquatic frog do not have a tongue. Instead, they have taste buds on their front limbs.

Sharp-nosed frogs from South Africa are only about 2½ in. (6.4 cm) long, but can jump more than 16 ft. (4.9 m).

tongue that can whip out, catch prey, and quickly flick it back into their mouth.

Frogs and toads vary greatly in size, although most are about 6 in. (15 cm) in length. The largest is the Goliath frog of West Africa, which can be as long as 1 ft. (30 cm). The Cuban frog is under ½ in. (1.3 cm) in length.

Most frogs and toads defend themselves with camouflage. This means that the colors, patterns, and textures of their skin blend in with their environment, so that their enemies and prey cannot easily see them. Some species, such as the European green toad, can change color for added protection. Most frogs and toads also produce poison. An animal that tries to eat a frog or toad may spit it out because the poison burns the inside of its mouth.

Life cycle

Most frogs and toads mate in water. The male signals with a distinctive call that he is ready to mate. Each species makes a different noise: the bullfrog's call sounds

like "jug-o-rum," while the Mexican burrowing toad makes a noise more like "whoa." The males of some species have pouches in their throats called vocal sacs. These amplify (make louder) their mating calls. Frogs and toads usually mate in large groups, so these calls can be very loud.

When a male and female pair up, they cling together. The male, which is usually smaller, hangs onto the female's back. The female releases eggs, called spawn, into the water, and the male releases sperm

Toads usually have a thicker, drier skin than frogs.

An adult frog develops from a tadpole that hatched from an egg.

FROG LIFE CYCLE

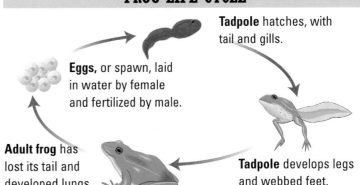

Tadpole hatches, with tail and gills.

Eggs, or spawn, laid in water by female and fertilized by male.

Adult frog has lost its tail and developed lungs.

Tadpole develops legs and webbed feet.

onto them. The cane toad releases the most eggs—up to 35,000 at one mating. The tiny Cuban frog releases only one egg at a time.

Most of the spawn will be eaten by predators. An egg that survives produces a young tadpole—a legless, fishlike creature with a long tail. A tadpole develops into an adult in stages, as its legs grow and its tail shrinks away. Its gills gradually disappear and lungs develop, so that it can breathe on land. This process is called metamorphosis.

Frogs, toads, and humans

Like many other animals, frogs and toads have suffered from human activity in recent years. Their habitats are destroyed by water pollution or land development. Many thousands are squashed by

automobiles as they cross roads to reach their breeding places. In a few areas, people have built tunnels under roads to enable frogs and toads to travel to the other side in safety.

Frogs and toads are valuable to humans. They eat large numbers of insects and are very good at controlling insect pests that carry disease and destroy crops. The marine toad has been introduced to tropical areas to control insects that damage sugarcane. Scientists are also studying how to make new drugs from the poisons produced by frogs and toads.

SEE ALSO: Amphibians

✳ FROST, ROBERT (1874–1963)

Robert Frost was one of America's most popular poets. He spent much of his life in New England, and his poetry reflects the land and people of that area.

Robert Lee Frost was born in San Francisco, California. His father died in 1885, and his mother moved Robert and his sister to live with their grandparents in Lawrence, Massachusetts.

Robert became interested in poetry during his years at high school. He went to college for less than a year before leaving to try several jobs, including teaching and farming. His first real poem, "My Butterfly," was published in the journal *The Independent* in 1894.

In 1895 Robert married his high school sweetheart Elinor. The couple had six children, but two died young. In 1912 the family moved to England. By the time they returned to the United States in 1915,

▲ *Robert Frost's poetry was admired for its use of informal language to describe everyday events and ordinary people.*

Robert had published two collections of poems, *A Boy's Will* and *North of Boston*.

Robert was invited to read and lecture in schools and colleges. His style, based on everyday language, made him the most celebrated poet in America. In 1924 he received the first of four Pulitzer prizes. He continued to gather awards into old age.

President John Kennedy honored Robert by asking him to read a poem, "The Gift Outright," at his inauguration ceremony in 1960. Robert Frost died in 1963.

SEE ALSO: Literature

✳ FRUIT

The name *fruit* is usually given to any fleshy part of a plant that has developed from a flower and has seeds, such as apples and strawberries.

Some produce that are usually considered to be vegetables, such as tomatoes and cucumbers, are actually fruits. But most people do not think of them as fruit because they are not eaten as dessert.

In most parts of the world, fruits grow wild. Early people gathered fruits long before they grew crops for food. When they began to cultivate crops, they planted the seeds from the best fruits. In time the fruit from cultivated plants became better than the wild fruits.

Spread of fruit

As people began to travel, they took fruit seeds with them. In this way many fruits spread from the places where they first

Cranberries grow in boggy areas of North America. They are picked with hand rakes or special machines. Native Americans ate these berries, and European settlers used them in cooking.

grew to other parts of the world where the climate was also suitable. Oranges, for example, are native to Southeast Asia and have been grown in China for centuries. They reached Europe in the ninth century. Christopher Columbus is thought to have brought citrus fruits to America in 1493.

Cultivation of fruit

Today fruits native to many different areas of the world are grown wherever the climate is suitable. Apples, peaches, pears, plums, and grapes are grown in all lands having temperate (mild) climates.

Most fruit is picked by hand. Once fruit is harvested, it may be shipped to be sold fresh, put into cold storage, or processed. In the processing plant, it may be canned, frozen, dried, or squeezed for juice.

DID YOU KNOW?

Before 1850, very few Americans had tasted a banana, although Alexander the Great had reported finding bananas growing in India in 327 B.C. Scientists believe the roots of banana plants were carried to the east coast of Africa by a people who moved there in ancient times. From there the banana plant was carried across the African continent to the west coast by early Arab traders. When Portuguese explorers visited West Africa in 1482, they found bananas growing there and took them to the Canary Islands. In 1516 a Spanish missionary brought the banana to the Caribbean island of Hispaniola. In the late 1800s, ships began to bring bananas to American ports.

SEE ALSO: Agriculture; Alexander the Great; Columbus, Christopher; Plants

*FUNGUS

A fungus is an organism that does not have chlorophyll, the green substance that many plants use to make food.

There are more than 50,000 known species of fungus or fungi (plural). Molds, mushrooms, and yeast are some of the most familiar types of fungi.

People eat mushrooms and use yeast to make bread and beer. Some fungi form the basis for antibiotics and other drugs. Other fungi, however, cause disease in food crops, plants, and animals.

The structure of fungi

Fungi are unicellular (made of one cell) or multicellular (made of many cells). Unicellular fungi can be as small as $\frac{1}{5,000}$ inch (5 micrometers), while a multicellular fungi can spread for miles.

Multicellular fungi, such as molds and mushrooms, are made from many long, threadlike cells called hyphae (single, *hypha*). Hyphae grow and branch into a tangled mass called a mycelium. The mycelium helps the fungus perform two important functions—absorbing nutrients

Fly agaric are highly poisonous fungi.
▼

and reproducing. The reproductive mycelium forms special structures that produce the reproductive cells, or spores. The spores are scattered by air currents, water, and living things.

How fungi obtain food

Fungi are not like other plants. Green plants contain a pigment called chlorophyll that allows them to get food and energy from sunlight. Fungi feed on living things, decaying plants and animals, and organic matter—material that once came from plants or animals. Fungi help maintain the balance of nature because they recycle nutrients. They return digested nutrients to the soil, providing an enriched environment for new plant growth. Fungi also release carbon dioxide, which can be used by plants, into the atmosphere.

SEE ALSO: Diseases; Ecology; Food Chains; Photosynthesis

✳GALAXIES

A galaxy is an enormous group of stars. All the stars that we can see from Earth without a telescope are part of a single galaxy called the Milky Way.

There are billions of galaxies in the universe. They can be elliptical, irregular, or spiral in shape. The most common shape is an ellipsis—roughly like an egg. They usually contain only stars, with little or no dust or clouds of gas.

Galaxies with irregular shapes can be between 9,000 and 32,000 light-years in diameter. (A light-year is the distance light travels in one year: about 6 trillion miles, or 9.6 trillion kilometers.)

The least common shape is the spiral. These galaxies are like pinwheels wound around a nucleus or a bar of stars, gas, and dust at the center. The Milky Way is an example of a spiral galaxy.

The Milky Way
Scientists believe that the Milky Way galaxy is about 10 billion years old. The nucleus, at the center, is a tremendous source of energy and exerts a powerful gravitational pull on the rest of the galaxy, which rotates around it at great speed. Earth's solar system orbits around it at a speed of about 155 miles (250 km) a second. Even at this rate, it takes about 250 million years to complete one orbit.

The central bulge revolves around the nucleus. The bulge is about 3,000 light-years across. Extending from it is the galactic disk, containing the spiral's arms. Earth is on the inner edge of an arm of the Milky Way called Cygnus. Around the disk is the outermost part of the Milky Way, a huge halo of dim stars.

Studying the galaxies
For many years, people did not know that the Milky Way contained stars. The Italian scientist Galileo (1564–1642) was the first person to study it with a telescope. In the 1920s, the American astronomer Edwin Hubble worked out that there are many other galaxies and that the universe was much larger than anyone had realized.

SEE ALSO:
Astronomy;
Big Bang
Theory;
Galilei,
Galileo;
Gravity; Solar
System; Stars

Only the brightest stars in this spiral galaxy can be seen individually.
▼

* GALILEI, GALILEO (1564–1642)

Galileo Galilei was one of the world's most important scientists. His discoveries were often based on simple observations.

Galileo's lively scientific writings appealed to ordinary readers.

Galileo Galilei was born in Pisa, Italy. He went to college to study medicine, but he was more interested in science. At that time, the writings of Aristotle, the great scientist of ancient Greece, were accepted as absolute truth. Aristotle had stated that heavy objects fall faster than light ones. By rolling balls of different weights down a slope and timing them, Galileo discovered that all objects fall at the same rate when there is no air resistance. This proved Aristotle wrong and made Galileo unpopular.

Galileo made his first telescope in 1609. He made an important discovery the following year when he observed that the planet Jupiter had moons that revolved around it. This supported Copernicus's discovery 60 years earlier that Earth and the other planets circled the sun. Since Aristotle's time, people had believed that all planets revolved around Earth. The Catholic Church supported Aristotle's beliefs and imprisoned Galileo. He spent his final years confined to his villa in Florence, but he continued to write and teach. By the time he died in 1642, he had laid the groundwork for modern physics.

SEE ALSO: Astronomy; Force and Motion; Gravity; Physics; Scientists; Telescopes

*GANDHI, MOHANDAS (1869–1948)

Gandhi was the most important leader in the history of modern India. He is often known as Mahatma, meaning "great soul."

Mohandas Karamchand Gandhi was born in Porbandar, India, on October 2, 1869, into a large Hindu family. When he was 18, he went to London, England, to study law.

In 1893 Gandhi went to work as a lawyer in South Africa. Indians in that country were treated harshly, and Gandhi led a campaign of nonviolent resistance against the government called civil disobedience. He spent time in jail in South Africa, but won some reforms.

Return to India
In 1915 Gandhi returned to India, which was then part of the British Empire. He joined the Indian National Congress, a political party working for the independence of the country.

Gandhi's protests were always nonviolent and used a method called passive resistance. He led boycotts—refusing to buy British goods—and fasts—refusing to eat. The British had put a tax on salt, which led to much hardship for poor people, who could not afford to buy it. Gandhi led a march to the sea, where his followers made salt from seawater, which was against the law. The march forced the British to allow people to gather salt for their own use.

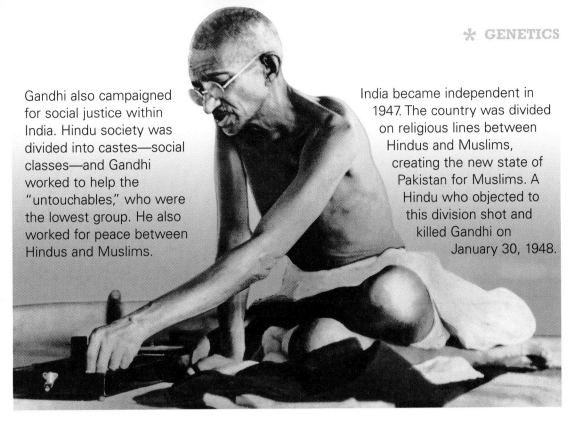

Gandhi also campaigned for social justice within India. Hindu society was divided into castes—social classes—and Gandhi worked to help the "untouchables," who were the lowest group. He also worked for peace between Hindus and Muslims.

India became independent in 1947. The country was divided on religious lines between Hindus and Muslims, creating the new state of Pakistan for Muslims. A Hindu who objected to this division shot and killed Gandhi on January 30, 1948.

Gandhi lived very simply and wore only plain, homemade clothes.

SEE ALSO:
Hinduism;
Indian
Subcontinent;
Islam; King,
Martin Luther,
Jr.; South
Africa

✳**GAS** 〖see〗▸ ✳**MATTER**

✳**GASOLINE** 〖see〗▸ ✳**FOSSIL FUELS**

✳**GEMS** 〖see〗▸ ✳**MINERALS AND GEMS**

✳ GENETICS

A branch of biology, genetics is the study of heredity, reproduction, evolution, and the development of all forms of life.

Genes are biological instructions that control how every living creature appears, functions, reproduces, and even partly how it behaves. They are found inside the cells of the body and are inherited, or passed down, from one generation to the next. You may inherit dimples from your mother or the ability to roll your tongue from your father. These features, or traits, are determined by combinations of genes that are different for every person. While each individual is unique, most genes are common to everyone. In fact humans share many of the same genes with other animal species—from the simple fruit fly to our close cousin the chimpanzee.

Although genetics has been studied since the mid-1800s, the greatest advances in the field were made at the end of the 1900s. Modern breakthroughs have enabled doctors to diagnose and treat previously incurable diseases, police to investigate crimes, and agricultural scientists to design better crops. ➡

In 1997 Dolly the sheep (below, right) was the first animal to be cloned using cells from an adult sheep. This process raises a difficult moral question: Is it right for humans to create life in this way?

The complete collection of genes for each organism is called its genome. Each species has its own unique genome.

Heredity and variation

Genes are the basic units of heredity—the inheritance of traits from one generation to the next. Genes determine physical features, including your sex, height, and hair and eye colors.

When variations in genes are harmful, they result in what are called genetic disorders. These diseases are inherited by offspring from their parents. They are caused by mutations—alterations to the normal genetic makeup.

The genetic code

Genes are "written" in a language called the genetic code, which is contained in deoxyribonucleic acid, or DNA. Every molecule of this chemical is shaped like a twisting ladder, often called a double helix. One DNA molecule can contain thousands of genes and forms a long, threadlike part of a cell called a chromosome. In humans and other animals, chromosomes are found in every cell in the body except red blood cells. Chromosomes come in pairs that are similar in size and shape. Half of the chromosomes come from the individual's mother, the other half from the father. Different species have different numbers of chromosomes in their cells. The fruit fly has only four pairs. Humans have 23 pairs, or a total of 46 chromosomes.

SEE ALSO: Agriculture; Cells; Diseases; Endangered Species; Evolution; Human Body; Medicine; Reproductive System

* GENGHIS KHAN (ABOUT 1167–1227)

Genghis Khan was a military conqueror who created the greatest land empire in history. It stretched across Asia and parts of Europe.

Genghis Khan was born in Siberia in about 1167. He was named Temüjin. His family belonged to a wandering Mongol tribe. After his marriage, he joined the army of Wang Khan and won many victories against rival tribes. By 1204 Temüjin ruled all the Mongol tribes.

In 1206 a great council of Mongol nobles renamed Temüjin Genghis Khan, which means "universal ruler." Genghis Khan drew up the Great Yasa, a code of laws, which required loyalty, discipline, and unity among all Mongols.

In 1207 Genghis Khan began a series of invasions. He himself led an elite group of 10,000 warriors. His cavalrymen were very loyal and always prepared for battle. By 1215 they had captured Peking (now Beijing, in China). Genghis Khan then turned his armies west. By 1220–21, they had reached the Caspian Sea.

Genghis Khan died in Mongolia in 1227, either from a wound or a fall from a horse. He left behind an enormous empire that included all of Central Asia, most of China, and parts of the Middle East and Russia.

This detail from a Persian manuscript from the 14th century shows Genghis Khan proclaiming himself emperor.

SEE ALSO: Asia; Warfare

✳ GEOGRAPHY

Geography is the study of Earth's various physical features—the land itself, climate, and soils—and humans' relationship to them.

Physical geography

Physical geography is mostly concerned with the physical environment of regions (areas with similar features). The study of the development of landforms, such as mountains, is called geomorphology. Biogeography is the study of how environmental factors, such as soil and temperature, affect living things.

Climate is the overall state of weather in a region. The study of climate is called climatology. Climate has the greatest influence on plant and animal life, and in turn on the people who depend on them.

Human geography

Human geography is concerned with people and how they live. A people's culture includes their language, literature, art, customs, laws, religion, clothing, food, and housing. When cultural geographers study a group of people, they investigate things such as how the people obtain food or how they trade with each other.

The study of how groups of people are distributed is called population geography, or demography. Economic geographers study why certain economic activities, such as the trading of goods between countries, take place where they do.

Political geographers study how laws and government actions affect landscapes. Urban geographers study how cities and landscapes affect one another. Historical geographers study the changes in landscapes and settlements over time.

History of geography

The first real geographer was Thales, a Greek who lived over 2,600 years ago. Thales kept maps of where he traveled, and collected information from other travelers. From about A.D. 400, much of the knowledge of the Greeks was forgotten. But the Arabs of North Africa and Arabia continued making maps. In the 1400s, explorers sailed uncharted oceans, and geographical knowledge grew again. By the late 1700s, all the continents had been sighted. For the first time, people knew about the world's lands and peoples.

Early geographers gathered information mainly by exploring. Today they can collect data without ever surveying a region on the ground. Since the 1960s, math and technology have made geography much more scientific. Statistics (the study of mathematical trends), computers, and satellites help geographers measure and analyze information more accurately.

SEE ALSO:
Biomes;
Climate;
Earth;
Economics;
Exploration and Explorers;
Geology;
Internet;
Maps;
Mathematics;
Population and Censuses;
Technology

Despite the physical geography of Ecuador's Chota Valley—a dry area located high in the Andes Mountains—agriculture is successful there, thanks to good irrigation.

G

✳ GEOLOGY

Geology is the scientific study of the origin, history, composition, and structure of Earth since the planet formed 4.6 billion years ago.

The word *geology* comes from the Greek words for "earth science." There are numerous branches of geology. They include mineralogy (study of minerals), geomorphology (study of the processes that produce landforms), petrology (study of rocks), paleontology (study of fossils), stratigraphy (study of the rock layers, or strata), and astrogeology (study of the evolution of planets and their satellites). There are also economic geologists, mining geologists, and petroleum geologists. All these branches connect with each other and with other fields, such as physics and chemistry.

Scientists divide geological time into periods based on the kinds of animals and plants that existed during those times. The names of the periods are mostly taken from the areas where their rocks were studied. Few traces of life have survived from the Precambrian era.

History of geology

Ancient peoples believed that Earth had been created by magic or by gods. Around 2,500 years ago, ancient Greek scholars began to focus their explanations of the earth and its geological features on observations of nature. This was the start of modern geology.

A geologist takes a sample of rock on a field trip to Antarctica.

GEOLOGICAL TIMELINE

Precambrian era

Earth formed. Single-celled organisms developed. Soft-bodied plants and animals evolved. Earth's atmosphere gained oxygen.

single-cell algae

4,600 –590 Million Years Ago

Paleozoic era

Cambrian period
Life was restricted to the seas. The first vertebrate, a small fish, appeared.

trilobite

590–248 Million Years Ago

Ordovician period
Seas spread across much of North America. Shellfish were plentiful.

ammonite

Silurian period
Animals and plants moved onto the land.

Devonian period
The Age of Fish. Large fern trees and other plants developed on land. The first amphibians appeared.

icthyosaur

Pennsylvanian/ Mississippian (Carboniferous) period
The Coal Ages. Plant growth in swampy lands laid the basis of coal deposits. The first reptiles and giant insects developed.

Permian period
Cone-bearing trees appeared. Climates changed, and glaciers covered many areas. The Appalachian Mountains formed.

In the 1500s, Georgius Agricola, a German doctor, wrote the first modern textbook on rocks, minerals, fossils, and metals. In 1795 Scottish geologist James Hutton proposed that Earth was constantly changing as a result of erosion and mountain-building forces. The first geological map showing the strata of different ages was drawn in 1815 by the English engineer William Smith. Geologists plotted a chart that showed the changes in rock strata and fossils over time. In the 1900s, they proved that Earth's landforms had originally been one large continent named Pangaea. Later Pangaea broke up into smaller continents that drifted very slowly apart. This movement is called continental drift.

Geologists also showed that comets or asteroids occasionally collided with Earth, perhaps causing mass extinctions of animals and plants.

Today many geologists look for natural resources that have not yet been found, such as oil, minerals, and even fresh water. They also study volcanoes, flood plains, and earthquake faults in an effort to reduce the dangers that these natural hazards pose to people living nearby.

Arches National Park, Utah. This natural feature was formed by wind erosion of surrounding layers of softer rock.

SEE ALSO: Climate; Comets, Meteors, and Asteroids; Continents; Dinosaurs; Earth; Earthquakes; Fossil Fuels; Fossils; Minerals and Gems; Plate Tectonics; Volcanoes

Mesozoic era

Triassic period
The first dinosaurs and first small mammals appeared.

Jurassic period
An inland sea formed in North America. More dinosaurs developed, and the first birds appeared.

brachiosaur

Archaeopteryx

Cretaceous period
Dinosaurs reached their peak and died out. Fruit trees and flowering plants developed. North America's inland sea drained, and the Rocky Mountains formed.

Cenozoic era

Tertiary period
Small mammals developed. Climates varied. Primitive horses, monkeys, and other new mammals appeared. Grains and grasses developed. Apes developed in Africa and Asia. The Alps and Himalayas had formed by the end of this period. Ocean and land life resembled that of modern times. Primitive humans appeared.

Quaternary period
Glaciers covered Earth. Woolly rhinos and mammoths appeared and died out. Modern humans developed. They learned to grow plants, raise animals, and use metals.

woolly mammoth

man

✳ GEOMETRY

A branch of mathematics, geometry is the study of space, shape, and measurement. The word comes from the Greek meaning "to measure the earth."

The ancient Babylonians and Chinese were able to calculate the areas and volumes of some shapes. But modern geometry really began in about 300 B.C. The ancient Greek mathematician Euclid set down mathematical statements that needed no proof and called them axioms. He reasoned that other statements based on axioms must also be true and called them theorems. This system is still the way new mathematics is created today.

SEE ALSO:
Egypt, Ancient;
Greece, Ancient;
Mathematics

TRIANGLES AND CIRCLES

Pythagoras's Theorem

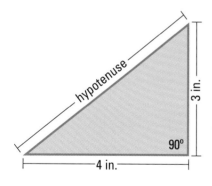

The ancient Greek mathematician Pythagoras (about 580–500 B.C.) worked out an important theorem about right triangles. He stated that the square of the hypotenuse is equal to the sum of the square of the other two sides. For example, if one side measures 3 in., its square is 3 x 3 = 9 in. If another measures 4 in., its square is 4 x 4 = 16 in. So the square of the hypotenuse is 9 + 16 = 25, and 25 = 5 x 5, so the length of the hypotenuse is 5 in.

Circles

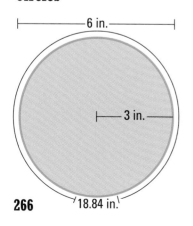

To calculate the circumference of a circle, multiply the diameter of the circle by a special number called pi. The symbol for pi is π, and its value is about 3.14. If the diameter of the circle is 6 in., for example, multiply 6 x 3.14 to get a circumference of 18.84 in. To calculate the area of a circle, multiply the radius by itself (square it), and multiply that number by pi. So the area is 3 x 3 x 3.14 = 28.26 sq. in.

GEOMETRIC TERMS

Angle: a wedge shape formed when two lines meet. Angles are measured in degrees.
Circle: a figure surrounded by a line (circumference) on which all points are the same distance from the center.
Diameter: a straight line from one side of the circumference of a circle to the other through the center.
Hypotenuse: the longest side of a right-angled triangle.
Parallel: two or more lines that are a constant distance apart and never meet.
Polygon: a two-dimensional shape made of straight lines.
Quadrilateral: a polygon with four sides.
Radius: a straight line from the center of a circle to the circumference.
Right triangle: a triangle with one angle of 90 degrees.
Square: a quadrilateral with all sides the same length and all angles 90 degrees.
Squared: a number multiplied by itself is said to be squared.
Triangle: a polygon with three sides.

Egypt's pyramids were designed according to strict geometric principles. Each has a square base and four sloping triangular sides.
▼

☀GERMANY

Germany is positioned in the heart of Europe and has few natural barriers to mark its borders. Its area makes it the sixth-largest country in Europe.

Land and climate

Germany is divided into three geographical regions: the northern lowlands, the central uplands, and the southern mountains. In the northern lowlands, forests alternate with meadows and marshy lakes. In the central uplands there are deep river valleys and forested hills. The Black Forest and the Bavarian Alps are in the south.

The Rhine River, with a total length of about 820 miles (1,319 km), is the chief river of Germany and the most important commercial waterway in western Europe.

Most of Germany has a fairly mild climate. Inland regions in the south and east normally have hotter summers and colder winters. There is more rain in summer.

Economy

Nearly 45 percent of workers in Germany are employed in industry. The coal mines of the Ruhr region provide fuel for factories. Germany is one of the world's chief steel producers and is Europe's leading car manufacturer. It is also famous for its cameras, lenses, and precision instruments. After the United States, it is the leading producer of plastics.

People and history

Germanic peoples arrived in northern and Central Europe at least 2,000 years ago. Among the largest tribes were the Franks and the Saxons. By A.D. 800, the ruler of the Franks, Charlemagne, had conquered many European lands to create a vast kingdom that would later become known as the Holy Roman Empire. By the 14th century, the Holy Roman emperor had lost control to rulers of individual states.

In 1701 Frederick I took the title of king of Prussia (one of the German states). Prussia developed a strong army and an efficient government. Under Frederick II (ruled 1740–86), it became a major power.

In 1871 Otto von Bismarck (1815–98), chancellor to the Prussian king, united Germany by force. The country became a strong commercial and naval power. Britain, France, and Russia united against Germany and Austria-Hungary. World War I (1914–18) broke out between the European powers, later joined by the United States. When Germany lost, it was stripped of some of its land and had to pay $33 billion to the United States, Britain, France, and Russia.

Germany's national flag

Modern German automobile manufacturers have factories worldwide. This is the Mercedes-Benz assembly plant in Sacramento, California.

Two soldiers stand on either side of the remains of the Berlin Wall. The wall, built by the East Germans in 1961 to divide the German capital, was destroyed in 1989.

KEY FACTS

OFFICIAL NAME:
Bundesrepublik Deutschland

AREA:
137,803 sq. mi. (356,910 sq. km)

POPULATION:
82,220,000

CAPITAL & LARGEST CITY:
Berlin

MAJOR RELIGIONS:
Protestantism, Roman Catholicism

MAJOR LANGUAGE:
German

CURRENCY:
Euro

SEE ALSO:
Central Europe; Communism; Europe; Great Depression; Holocaust; World War I; World War II

Hitler's rise

The worldwide depression, which started in the United States in 1929, hit Germany especially hard. By 1933 more than six million people were out of work. The National Socialists, or Nazis, a political party led by Adolf Hitler, gained more and more votes. Hitler became chancellor in 1933. By 1934 he had established himself as *führer*, or supreme leader, and turned Germany into a police state. Jews lost their rights, and many fled the country.

In 1938 Germany annexed, or occupied, Austria. In 1939 Hitler invaded Poland, and World War II (1939–45) broke out. German victories brought most of Europe under his control. In 1941 Hitler invaded the Soviet Union. This marked the beginning of a change in Hitler's fortunes. In 1945 Germany was forced to surrender, and Hitler committed suicide.

East and West divided

The country was immediately divided into four zones of occupation. In 1949 West Germany was formed from the British, French, and U.S. zones, and East Germany from the Soviet zone.

For about 45 years, the German people lived in a divided land. West Germany had a democratic form of government. East Germany was a Communist state. In October 1990 the two Germanys were finally reunited. One of the greatest challenges that faced the new government was to bring the economic level of East Germans up to Western standards.

A great castle in Bavaria in the south of Germany, built between 1869 and 1886.

✳ GERSHWIN, GEORGE (1898–1937)
George Gershwin was one of America's best-loved composers of popular music. He is famous for his Broadway musicals.

George Gershwin was born in Brooklyn, New York. At the age of 14, he published his first popular song. He played the piano so well that he left school for Broadway—New York City's theater district—where he got a job demonstrating songs for a music publisher.

His first hit was the song "Swanee," in 1919. Gershwin often worked with his older brother Ira, who wrote the words, or lyrics, to his music. Their first big success was the musical comedy *Lady, Be Good!* in 1924. In 1931 they wrote *Of Thee I Sing*, which won the first Pulitzer Prize for a musical.

In 1924 Gershwin was asked to write for a jazz orchestra. In less than three weeks, he had composed one of his most famous works, *Rhapsody in Blue*. In 1935 George and Ira produced *Porgy and Bess*, a folk opera about blacks in America's South. The next year, the Gershwins went to Hollywood, California, to write film musicals. George died of a brain tumor there on July 11, 1937.

George Gershwin, an American composer who mixed jazz rhythms and harmonies with traditional orchestral music.

SEE ALSO: Music

✳ GHANA
Ghana is a nation in West Africa. Formerly the British colony of the Gold Coast, it became independent and changed its name in 1957.

Land and climate
Ghana's coast consists of sandy beaches and mangrove swamps. Dense tropical forest once covered the south of the country, but there has been much deforestation. Grassland, or savanna, covers the north and the center. The climate is hot and often dry. There is little rain in the north from October to May.

People and economy
There are more than a dozen ethnic groups in Ghana, speaking more than 50 dialects. The main groups in the center and south include the Ashanti and Fanti. The Dagomba and Mamprusi live in the north. The majority of Ghanaians are

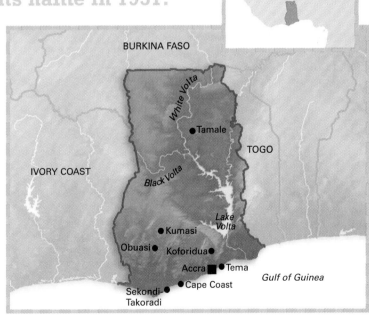

Ghana's national flag

KEY FACTS

OFFICIAL NAME:
Republic of Ghana

AREA:
92,099 sq. mi.
(238,537 sq. km)

POPULATION:
20,212,000

CAPITAL & LARGEST CITY:
Accra

MAJOR RELIGIONS:
Christianity, traditional African religions, Islam

MAJOR LANGUAGES:
English (official), Hausa, various other African languages

CURRENCY:
New cedi

farmers. Cacao, which makes chocolate, is the main cash crop, but farmers are gradually changing to other crops.

History
The Portuguese were the first Europeans to arrive on the coast, in 1471. They named the region the Gold Coast, because the precious metal was so plentiful. It later became a major source of slaves for the New World.

In 1844 Britain signed a treaty with the Fanti people, putting their land under British protection. Britain bought Danish and Dutch coastal colonies before founding the Gold Coast colony in 1874. Britain fought two wars with the Ashanti after Ashanti expansion into the colony.

The colony won its independence in 1957 and was renamed Ghana. It became a republic in 1960, with Kwame Nkrumah as the first president. Power shifted back and forth between civilian and military rulers for some years until a new multiparty constitution came into force in 1992.

SEE ALSO: Africa; West Africa

*GLACIERS
A glacier is an enormous mass of ice so thick that it moves under the pressure of its own weight and the force of gravity.

Glaciers can develop wherever the amount of snow falling in winter is greater than the amount that melts in summer. As snow builds up over many years, the lowest layers are compressed by the weight of the layers above. They slowly change, first to a dense material called firn, and finally to ice.

Eventually the ice becomes so thick and heavy that it begins to move downhill under the force of gravity. It can do this because, under pressure, ice is not a rigid solid like steel. It can flow or creep—but very slowly. When the mass of ice is thick enough to flow, it is called a glacier.

New ice constantly forms at the glacier's origin, or accumulation basin. But the leading edge (or snout) of the glacier slowly moves into warmer regions, where it may begin to melt. Alternatively it may reach the sea and calve (break off), forming icebergs.

Glacial erosion
As a glacier slowly moves across land, it picks up rocks and dirt and carries these materials along. A glacier can break rock and reshape the land through the huge pressure of its ice, the effects of freezing and thawing, and the grinding action of the debris it carries.

The Chatteboi Glacier in the foothills of the Himalayas in northwest Pakistan.

AMAZING FACTS❗

The Jacobshavn Glacier, in Greenland, is the fastest known glacier—it moves up to 4 miles (about 6 km) a year and forms many icebergs as it calves (breaks off) and falls into the sea.

Ice sheets

A glacier that covers a high mountain plateau is called an ice cap. When an ice cap grows to cover vast areas of land, it is called an ice sheet. There are two continental ice sheets: The one in the Northern Hemisphere covers more than 80 percent of Greenland; the one in the Southern Hemisphere covers about 97 percent of Antarctica.

SEE ALSO:
Antarctica;
Gravity;
Greenland;
Mountains
and Valleys;
Rivers

✳GLASS

Glass is a hard, brittle, transparent or translucent solid. It is used for making many things, including windows, windshields, and ornaments.

Dating from the sixth century A.D., this Roman multicolored glass jar is decorated with images of a man standing with raised arms, a tree, and a date palm.

Glass is formed when silica, a variety of quartz often found in sand, is heated with soda ash or potash to temperatures of 2,600°F (1,427°C). This process may happen naturally or artificially. Other ingredients can be added to give glass special qualities and color.

History

Nobody knows when the first glass was made. The oldest surviving glass artifacts are Egyptian beads dating from about 2500 B.C. For centuries glass objects were made in molds or around sand-clay cores. It was a difficult process, and glass jewelry and utensils were very expensive.

Some time before the first century A.D., glassmakers discovered that by blowing air through a pipe into molten glass, they could make cups and bottles more easily, quickly, and cheaply.

After the fall of the Western Roman Empire in the fifth century, many glassmaking techniques were lost. By the 11th century, they had been rediscovered, and European craftsmen made beautiful colored windows for churches, called stained glass. Glassmakers still did not know how to make large panes, so few homes had glass windows. During this period,

AMAZING FACTS!

Pyroceram, a heat-resistant ceramic glass, can withstand the temperatures generated on the exterior of a spacecraft as it reenters Earth's atmosphere.

Panes of glass can be made so tough that they are bulletproof.

Fiberglass, spun from glass fibers, is fireproof. It may be mixed with plastic to form a strong, lightweight material used to make cars, boats, golf clubs, and fishing rods.

glassmaking flourished in Islamic countries such as Egypt, Iran, and Syria. It was not until the 15th century that glassmakers in Venice, Italy, began to lead the world in glass manufacturing.

Since the early 1900s, glass has become an everyday commodity. It can now be melted, rolled, blown, and molded by automatic processes. Thermostats keep furnaces and lehrs—cooling ovens—at constant temperatures.

SEE ALSO: Art and Artists; Egypt, Ancient; Manufacturing; Middle East; Roman Empire

* GRASSLANDS

Grasslands are one of the world's richest biomes (communities of specific plants and animals). They are also known as pampas, prairies, savannas, or steppes.

Grasslands account for about 25 percent of Earth's land surface. They occur on every continent except Antarctica. They are usually found in the middle of continents in what is known as a rain shadow—the side of a mountain range on which rain is less likely to fall.

Grasslands typically have a wet season and a dry season, hot summers, cold winters, drying winds, and prolonged droughts. They receive 10 to 40 in. (254–1,016 mm) of rainfall a year.

Temperate grasslands are found in central North America and also in Argentina,

Russia, and China. In Argentina the grasslands are known as pampas; in Russia they are called steppes.

Fire is very important to the ecology of grasslands. It burns and clears trees, shrubs, and herbs, but it does not damage grasses, because their main growing parts are below ground. Burned vegetation adds nutrients to the soil, helping grasses grow.

America's breadbasket

Grassland soil is widely used for farming. In the United States, the vast grasslands in the middle of the country are often

Bison grazing on grasslands. These biomes support the largest herds of animals in the world.

called "America's breadbasket." North America has three different types of grasslands, or prairies—the tall-grass, mixed-grass, and short-grass prairies. The tall-grass prairies of the eastern Midwest are the wettest, and their soil is thick and rich in organic matter. Their grasses can grow as high as 5 ft. (1.5 m).

The mixed-grass prairies in the middle of the Midwest receive about 15 to 25 in. (380–635 mm) of rainfall, or precipitation, per year, and the grasses grow 2 to 3 ft. (0.6–1.0 m) high. The short-grass prairies, in the western Midwest, receive only about 10 in. (254 mm) of rain a year. Their soil is thinner than that of the other two types, and their grasses grow to about 2 ft. (0.6 m) in height.

Although trees are rare on grasslands, a few species have adapted to life in this biome. For instance, the box elder, the silver maple, and the redbud can all be found on grasslands in the United States.

Savannas
Savannas are hot all year round. In South America, they occupy an area of land 10 times the size of Colorado. Savannas and grasslands cover 65 percent of Africa.

SEE ALSO: Africa; Agriculture; Argentina; Biomes; China; Ecology; North America, Geography; Plants; Russia and the Baltic States; South America; Trees

✳GRAVITY
Gravity is a natural force. Every time you drop a ball from your hand or throw it upward or straight ahead, it is pulled back to Earth by gravity.

Physical events that occur repeatedly, reliably, and invariably are said to conform to a natural law. The force of gravity is one such law—any object on Earth that is dropped or thrown will behave in much the same way, according to the same principle, every time.

Isaac Newton
The first person to figure out the law of gravity was the English scientist Isaac Newton (1642–1727). Newton was puzzled about the motion of the moon. He wondered why the moon did not just fly off into space; what force kept it in its

The laws of gravity apply on Earth, which has a great mass that draws objects to it. Outer space lies beyond the planet's gravitational pull, so objects and astronauts there are weightless.

LAW OF GRAVITY

tube without air (a vacuum)   **air-filled tube**

> *In a vacuum, any two objects dropped together will reach the ground at the same time. In normal conditions (far right), air slows objects down: The larger surface area of the feather will make it fall more slowly than the marble.*

orbit, or curved path, around Earth? According to legend, Newton's ideas were influenced by seeing an apple falling from a tree. This showed him that Earth is pulling all objects toward itself. The force that pulled the apple to the ground must be the same as the one that keeps the moon in orbit around Earth. Newton showed that every object must have gravity, and that every object, or body, pulls on every other body. This is known as the theory of universal gravitation.

SEE ALSO: Earth; Force and Motion; Galilei, Galileo; Matter; Newton, Isaac; Solar System; Space Exploration

---

✻GREAT BRITAIN 🔜 ✻UNITED KINGDOM

✻ GREAT DEPRESSION

An economic depression is a time when the economy is doing badly. Unemployment is high, incomes and profits fall, and many businesses fail.

The economic downturn that started in the United States in 1929 was called the Great Depression because it was the longest and worst of its kind in history. Its ill effects were felt worldwide.

The 1920s in the United States were a period of great prosperity. In 1928 Herbert Hoover was elected to the presidency. On the surface, the economic boom seemed to be continuing. However, not all Americans had shared in the prosperity of the decade. Farmers, coal miners, and some industrial workers had suffered hard times. The stock market had reached great heights. But there were warning signals that stocks were overpriced and that too

many people were buying them with borrowed money, gambling that stock prices would rise even higher.

Wall Street Crash
On October 29, 1929, the stock market collapsed. The economy quickly spiraled downward. Unemployment rose steadily, until a quarter of the labor force was out of work. Workers who were able to keep their jobs often found their salaries cut drastically. Many businesses went bankrupt, and almost half of all banks failed as investors, fearful of losing their money, hurriedly withdrew their deposits. The only help available to the needy was a

The stock market on October 29, 1929, known as "Black Tuesday." After several days of panic, the market finally crashed.

In 1930 President Hoover raised taxes on imported goods, called tariffs. Other countries did the same, and international trade suffered, making the Depression worse. The Depression was not all Hoover's fault, but he became unpopular. Near city dumps and along railroad tracks, the homeless huddled in shacks made of corrugated iron and old boxes. These areas became known as "Hoovervilles."

The Great Depression continued after Franklin D. Roosevelt was elected president in 1932 and introduced his revolutionary New Deal. It ended at the start of World War II in 1939, when American factories were flooded with orders for arms and ammunition.

SEE ALSO:
Economics;
Stock
Markets;
United
States of
America;
World War II

form of home relief, which provided small sums of money for food. The economy suffered a further blow in August 1930, when a drought struck the Plains states. A million farmers lost their year's crop.

GREECE, ANCIENT

The civilization of ancient Greece centered around the Aegean Sea, the region that today includes Greece and the western part of Turkey.

Ancient Greece was not a single country ruled by one person. Instead there were a number of independent communities with a common language and culture.

City-states
About 800 B.C., Greeks began to form city-states, or *polis*. Each governed itself. Some had only a few thousand inhabitants, but some, such as Athens, had as many as 250,000. City-states were set up as far from Greece as France and Spain. There were several different forms of government in the city-states. Some were tyrannies, ruled by one person who had absolute power. Some were oligarchies—ruled by a small group of rich

The ancient Greek world reached to Sicily and Anatolia, far beyond the borders of mainland Greece.

275

Greek dramatists wrote plays 2,000 years ago that are still performed. These two models of actors are wearing comic masks that were made from clay in about 50 B.C.

people. Others were democracies, from the Greek word *demos,* meaning "people." They were not democracies in the modern sense. Women and slaves could not take part in political debate.

Religion, philosophy, and literature

Greek thinkers laid the foundations of modern science and philosophy over 2,000 years ago. One of the most important developments in Greek thought was philosophy. Great thinkers and teachers such as Socrates, Plato, and Aristotle considered questions about the purpose of life and morality. Their works still influence modern philosophers.

Greek literature—poetry, plays, and histories—is also still studied. The most famous poems are the *Iliad* and the *Odyssey,* written by Homer; the most famous playwrights are Aristophanes, Sophocles, and Euripides.

One thing that united the Greeks was their religion. They believed in many gods, whose personalities were very human. The gods were believed to inhabit Mount Olympus, and there were ceremonies and sacrifices in their honor. The Olympic Games, dedicated to Zeus, the king of the gods, were held every four years.

Athens and Sparta

From about 500 B.C., the two most influential city-states were Athens and Sparta. Athens was the important center for philosophy and literature. Public life

Sculptors and builders in ancient Greece created beautiful statues and temples. The Parthenon, Athens, was built to house a statue of the goddess Athena.

▼

focused on the *agora*, or marketplace, which lay below the Acropolis, the hill where the main temples stood. Most political debate took place at the *agora*.

Athens was an important military power and had a particularly strong navy. The strongest army in ancient Greece was that of Sparta. Spartan boys entered military school there at the age of six and did not return to their families until they were 30.

The Spartans became concerned about the growing power of Athens, and war broke out between the two states in 431 B.C. The Spartans cut off shipments of food to Athens, and the Athenians were starved into defeat in 404 B.C.

The decline of Greece

The last great Greek leader was Alexander of Macedon, also known as Alexander the Great. His conquests stretched as far from Greece as India. Greek culture then dominated large parts of Europe, Asia, and Africa. It continued to be important even after political control passed to the Roman Empire. The last of the Greek states to fall to Rome was Egypt, in 30 B.C.

SEE ALSO: Alexander the Great; Ancient Civilizations; Citizenship; Literature; Myths and Legends; Olympic Games; Philosophers; Roman Empire; Theater

✻ GREECE AND THE BALKANS

The Balkan Peninsula, with Greece at its southernmost tip, extends into the western end of the Mediterranean Sea.

The Balkans include Albania, Bulgaria, Greece, and Romania, plus the countries that once made up Yugoslavia: Croatia, Macedonia, Bosnia-Herzegovina, Slovenia, and the new confederation (partnership) of Serbia and Montenegro.

Land and climate

The region is mountainous: Along the coasts of Croatia, Serbia and Montenegro, and Albania, an extension of the European Alps forms an impressive barrier that drops down to the Adriatic Sea. The climate is continental, with cold winters, hot summers, and year-round rainfall.

People

In ancient times, the Balkans were dominated by the Greeks, the Romans, and then the Byzantine Empire. Control passed to the Turkish Ottoman Empire in

the 16th century and then to the Austro-Hungarian Empire in the 18th century.

Communism

By the end of the 18th century, the Balkan peoples wanted independence. They gained it separately and at different times. In 1912 Serbia, Bulgaria, Greece, and Montenegro defeated Turkey in the First Balkan War. Serbia wanted to be free from the Austro-Hungarian Empire. In 1914 Bosnian Serbs assassinated the Austrian Archduke Franz Ferdinand and his wife in Sarajevo and started World War I.

In 1919 a peace treaty created a new kingdom that became Yugoslavia in 1929. After World War II (1939–45), the Balkan countries became Communist states, with

Dubrovnik, in Croatia, is a port on the Adriatic coast. Much of the city dates back to the 13th century.

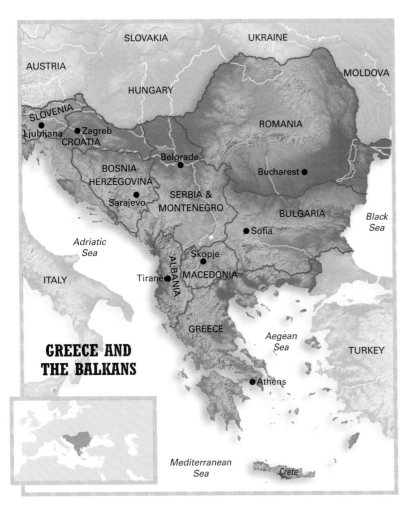

GREECE AND
THE BALKANS

AREA:
200,000 sq. mi.
(518,000 sq. km)

POPULATION:
50,000,000

COUNTRIES: 9

LARGEST COUNTRY:
Romania

SMALLEST COUNTRY:
Slovenia

RELIGIONS: Islam,
Eastern Orthodoxy,
Roman Catholicism

LANGUAGES:
Serbo-Croatian,
Slovenian, Albanian,
Bulgarian, Greek,
Romanian

the exception of Greece. Some countries came under the control of tyrants, and gradually the Balkan states abandoned Communism. Yugoslavia split up in the 1990s, when different ethnic groups fought for control.

SEE ALSO: Byzantine Empire; Central Europe; Communism; Europe; Greece, Ancient; Roman Empire; Turkey and the Caucasus; World War I; World War II

✱ GREENLAND
Greenland, or Kalaallit Nunaat, is the world's largest island. Geographically it is part of North America, but politically it is part of Denmark.

**Greenland's
national flag**

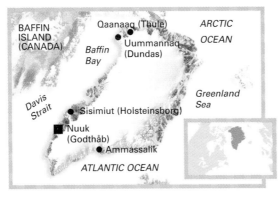

Land and climate
Most of Greenland's area is covered by a massive ice cap. The ice-free land is primarily along the coast, which is rimmed by mountains. Five-sixths of the island lies inside the Arctic Circle. Summers are short and cool, with average temperatures of about 50°F (10°C) in the south and 41°F (5°C) in the north. In winter temperatures fall to 18°F (–8°C) in the south and –5°F (–20°C) in the north.

Plants and animals

The few patches of soil support grasses and heather. Mosses and lichens grow on barren rock. Trees grow only in a few places in the southwest. Animals include arctic foxes, wolves, polar bears, and caribou. The sea is home to seals, whales, cod, and crabs.

People and economy

Most native Greenlanders are a mixture of Inuit and Dane. All Greenlanders are bilingual in Inuktitut (the official name of the Greenlandic language) and Danish.

Greenland's main industries are fishing and fish processing, which employ about one-quarter of the workforce. There are deposits of oil, lead, diamonds, and other substances, but extraction is difficult because of the climate and lack of transportation.

History

Greenland was settled in a series of Inuit migrations between about 4000 B.C. and 1000 B.C. In A.D. 982 an Icelander named Eric the Red was exiled to the island. He named it Greenland to attract settlers. Over the centuries, the climate grew colder, and the farms disappeared. In 1721 a Scandinavian missionary, Hans Egede, established a new settlement, and it became a Danish colony. Between 1776 and 1950, Denmark was Greenland's only trading partner. In 1953 the island fully became part of Denmark. In 1979 Greenlanders took control of their own affairs. Foreign policy is still the responsibility of Denmark.

SEE ALSO: Arctic; Iceland; North America, Geography; Scandinavia

✳ GUATEMALA

Guatemala was the center of the ancient Mayan civilization for many centuries. It is the most populous country in Central America.

Land and climate

Guatemala has a varied landscape. The highlands contain a range of volcanic mountains, running from the border with El Salvador in the south to Mexico in the west. The Pacific coastal plain is a humid region in the south.

The climate is tropical, with a rainy season from May to mid-October. The lowlands have temperatures between 77° and 86°F (25–30°C). Temperatures are lower in the higher areas, which include the main centers of population.

People and economy

About 43 percent of Guatemalans are *indígenas*—native people descended from

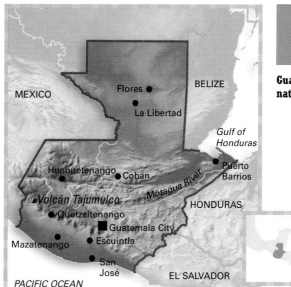

Guatemala's national flag

KEY FACTS

OFFICIAL NAME:
República de Guatemala

AREA:
42,042 sq. mi.
(108,889 sq. km)

POPULATION:
11,385,000

CAPITAL & LARGEST CITY:
Guatemala City

MAJOR RELIGIONS:
Roman Catholicism, Evangelical Protestantism

MAJOR LANGUAGES:
Spanish (official), various Mayan languages

CURRENCY:
Guatemalan quetzal, U.S. dollar

SEE ALSO:
Central America;
Mayans

the Mayans. The other major group is made up of *ladinos*, who are either of mixed Spanish and Mayans descent, or are *indígenas* who have abandoned the culture of their ancestors.

Guatemala is the most industrialized nation in Central America. Just under half of the population is involved in agriculture, and coffee is the most important crop.

History

The Spanish invaded Guatemala in 1524 and defeated the warring Mayans. In 1840 the country became independent. Until the 1940s, most Guatemalan governments acted in the interests of the military and commerce. Conditions for peasants and native people were very poor. A period of democracy followed a revolution in 1944. However, in 1954 a military coup overthrew the president. Violent conflict began between the military and rebel forces in 1960. Civilian rule was restored in 1986. In 1996 the government and guerrillas agreed to stop fighting, but more than 100,000 people had been killed.

* GUTHRIE, WOODY (1912–67)

Woody Guthrie was a leading folk singer and composer in the United States. His songs often addressed social issues and problems.

Woodrow Wilson Guthrie was born in Okemah, Oklahoma, on July 14, 1912. He had little formal schooling and soon became a wandering singer. The Great Depression of the 1930s made a deep impression on him, and he wrote songs about social injustice and disadvantaged people. In the 1940s, he performed alongside Pete Seeger in a group called the Almanac Singers. They performed in migrant labor camps and at union meetings.

Guthrie wrote more than 1,000 songs. The best known include "This Land Is Your Land" and "Union Maid." He suffered from an inherited disease called

The folk singer Woody Guthrie in 1943.

Huntington's chorea and died in New York City on October 3, 1967.

Guthrie's music was not commercially successful for most of his lifetime. He was also unpopular because of his liberal politics. However, his work was a huge influence on many folk and rock performers of the 1960s and later, especially Bob Dylan and Guthrie's own son Arlo. His brave example in addressing social problems in his songs is followed by alternative and hip-hop artists today.

SEE ALSO: Great Depression; Music

*HABITATS see *ECOLOGY

*HAMILTON, ALEXANDER (1755–1804)

Alexander Hamilton was one of America's greatest statesmen. He was the first secretary of the Treasury, a role in which he set up a federal bank.

Alexander Hamilton was born in the West Indies. In 1772 he attended King's College (later Columbia University) in New York. At the start of the American Revolution in 1775, he joined the Continental Army. He became General George Washington's aide-de-camp (military assistant).

President Washington appointed Hamilton secretary of the Treasury in 1789. Hamilton retired in 1795, but remained a trusted adviser of the president.

In the presidential election of 1800, Aaron Burr and Thomas Jefferson received the same number of votes. The election was decided by the House of Representatives. Jefferson was elected president, and Burr became vice president.

Hamilton had led the fight to block Burr's election. The hatred between the two men lasted for years. It eventually led to a fight, called a duel, on July 11, 1804. Hamilton was mortally wounded and died the next day. He is commemorated on the 10-dollar bill.

An oil painting of Alexander Hamilton by the artist John Trumbull.

SEE ALSO: American Revolution; Banking

*HEALTH

Health can mean simply the absence of disease, or it can be a feeling of fitness and well-being. The most important part of health is keeping the body well.

Nutrition

One of the most important ways that people can look after their health is by having a varied diet. Nutrition is the science that deals with how the body uses food. Food supplies the body with vital nutrients. Carbohydrates, fats, and proteins are nutrients that provide energy. Carbohydrates are found in sugars and grains. Fats are found in meat, fish, dairy foods, eggs, and nuts. Eating too many fats can cause obesity and heart disease. Proteins, which are also vital to building and repairing body tissue, are found in

Fruit contains vitamins and minerals that are essential for physical well-being. It is also a source of fiber, which helps prevent health problems.

meat, fish, eggs, dairy foods, and beans. Vegetarians do not eat food from animal sources (meat, poultry, fish, sometimes dairy products and eggs), so they need to make sure that they get enough protein from nuts, seeds, and beans. Vitamins and minerals are other important nutrients. Vitamins help cells function normally. They are found in a variety of fruits, vegetables, nuts, and seeds. Calcium, a mineral found in dairy foods and green vegetables, is important for bone growth. Fiber, which is found in whole wheat foods, vegetables, and cereals, is important for digestion.

Water is essential to life, so it is important to drink enough of it. Many people drink less water than they should.

Exercise

Exercise tones the muscles, helps keep bones strong, and reduces weight. Moderate activity every day benefits the heart and lungs and helps the body process food more efficiently.

Sleep

Getting enough sleep allows the body to recover from the work of the day and to build up energy. Elementary and high school students need about 8 to 10 hours of sleep each night. Dreaming may be important for learning and memory.

Regular exercise helps the body stay healthy. Wearing protective equipment to prevent injuries is important.

Avoiding hazards

Tobacco is the main cause of lung cancer and contributes to other cancers. It also contributes to heart disease and a lung disease called emphysema. Alcohol can also be harmful. Heavy drinking can seriously damage the brain, liver, and heart. It also plays a large role in accidents—half of all fatal highway crashes are related to drinking. Other drugs, such as cocaine, marijuana, and tranquillizers, can all damage physical and mental health.

Accidents and injuries can be avoided by using a seat belt when traveling by car and by wearing the right protective equipment, such as a helmet or knee pads, when biking or playing certain sports.

Preventing disease

Many infectious diseases can be prevented by immunization with vaccines. Most people in the United States have been immunized against diptheria, whooping cough, polio, and tetanus. People living or traveling in other parts of the world may need vaccines for diseases like typhoid and yellow fever.

Hand washing and general cleanliness help prevent the spread of colds, flu, and food poisoning. Brushing one's teeth helps prevent cavities and gum disease.

Mental health

Health is not just a question of the body functioning well. Some people can be very

✳ HEAT

People use the words *hot*
that have high or low tem
however, heat is not the s

Heat is a form of energy that exists inside
matter. Matter is anything that takes up
space and has mass. The more matter
there is, the more heat energy there is,
whether the temperature is high or low.
There is more heat energy in a large
iceberg than in a cup of hot coffee.

Heat is measured in calories. One calorie
of heat will raise the temperature of 1
gram (0.03 ounces) by 1°C (34°F). Another
measurement is the British thermal unit
(BTU). A BTU will raise the temperature of
1 lb. (454 g) of water by 1°F (–17°C).

Temperature

Molecules, the tiny particles that make
up matter, are always moving and giving
off energy. Temperature measures the
average kinetic energy, or energy of
motion, of a molecule. There is more
average energy in the molecules of hot
matter than there is in cold matter.

Temperature is measured on a number
of scales. Scientists use the Celsius,
or centigrade, scale, in which water
freezes at 0°C and boils at 100°C. It
was developed in 1742 by the Swedish
astronomer Anders Celsius.

AMAZING FACTS!

The sun is the source of most of
Earth's energy. The center of the
sun is approximately 27,000,000°F
(15,000,000°C). Many other stars
are even hotter.

well physically, but might feel sad, angry,
or confused. If these feelings last a long
time, the person might have a mental
health problem. There are many mental
illnesses. Depression is the most
common. These illnesses need to be
treated by experts, such as psychiatrists.
Mental and physical health are often
linked. For example, stress can worsen
conditions such as high blood pressure
and ulcers.

Some aspects of a healthful environment
are outside the control of the individual,
although our actions and choices influence
them. Air that is safe to breathe, water
that is free from disease, and food that is
not dangerous to eat all depend to a large
part on government and state regulation.

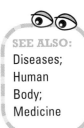

SEE ALSO:
Diseases;
Human
Body;
Medicine

✳HEARING 👉 ✳EARS AND HEARING

✳ HEART AND CIRCULATORY SYSTEM

The circulatory system is the network that carries
blood around the human body. The heart is the most
important organ in this system.

Blood is the remarkable fluid that keeps
us alive. It contains millions of cells that,
among other things, transport oxygen and
help fight infection. Red blood cells carry
oxygen to all parts of the body and
remove waste carbon dioxide. White
blood cells combat infection, clear away
worn-out cells, and attack cells that
become malignant (cancer-causing).

Blood vessels

The human circulatory system consists
of three different kinds of blood vessels—
arteries, capillaries, and veins. Arteries
carry blood away from the heart. As
arteries branch out, carrying blood to
every part of the body, they split into

tiny blood vessels called capillaries. As the
blood returns to the heart, the capillaries
link up to form veins. Veins contain
valves—flaps that keep the blood from
flowing backward. Without valves, blood
would be pulled back by gravity into the
lower part of the body.

The heart

The heart is a pump made of muscle.
It has four chambers: the right and left
atrium and the right and left ventricle.
There are flaps, called valves, between
the chambers and also at the outlets to
the arteries that carry blood away from the
heart. These valves snap shut to stop the
blood from flowing backward. ➡

Blood that has gathered oxygen from the lungs is pumped by the heart around the body through the arteries (colored red). Used blood carrying carbon dioxide returns to the lungs through the veins (colored blue).

Superior vena ca
Large vein that collec
used blood from th
head and arm

Inferior vena ca
Large vein that tak
used blood back to th
heart and lung

Renal ve
Collects used bloc
from the kidney

THE HEART

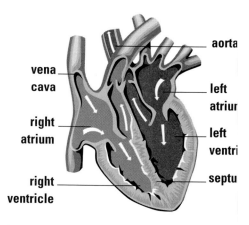

vena cava

aorta

right atrium

left atriur

right ventricle

left ventri

septu

▲
The heart is the driving force of the circulatory system. A thick wall, called the septum, divides the heart into halves, named left and right in accordance with the heart's owner rather than the observer. Valves, which open and close, divide each half into upper and lower parts.

Blood flows into the
veins all over the bod
right ventricle, then o
where it picks up a fr
and unloads its carbo

AMAZING

Your body contains
miles (100,000 km)
Some are so tiny t
seen with the nake

✳ HELICOPTERS
Helicopters are aircraft with large rotating blades that can fly in any direction—forward, backward, to the side, straight up—as well as hover in one place.

In the late 1400s, the Italian artist and inventor Leonardo da Vinci designed a flying machine called a *helixpteron*, from the Greek words for "spiral" and "wing." It had a large screw on top, which was meant to pull the machine up in the air. No one knows whether he built the machine.

In 1903 the Wright brothers made the first successful airplane flight. Twenty years later, a Spanish engineer named Juan de la Cierva built the autogiro. It had wings and a propeller, like an airplane, but it also had rotor blades on top. French, German, and American engineers developed the first practical helicopters in the late 1930s. In 1939 the Russian-American Igor Sikorsky perfected the single-rotor design that is still in use.

How helicopters work
The blades of a helicopter are powered by an engine. As they cut through the air, the shape of the blades makes the air pressure below greater than the pressure above. This causes lift. The same principle allows airplanes to fly. Airplanes, however, need to move forward to produce lift. A

A Coast Guard Jayhawk HH-60J helicopter patrols over New York City. It can stay airborne for about six hours.
▼

helicopter can stay still, while its blades move through the air and produce enough lift for flight. This allows helicopters to move in any direction or hover on one spot. The amount of lift changes when the pilot alters the pitch, or angle, of the blades. When the angle is larger, the lift is greater. The pilot has two main controls: one to change the pitch of all the blades at once, and one to alter the pitch on one side or at the front or back. They make the helicopter go up and down or sideways, forward, or backward. A small rotor on the tail stops it from swinging around from the movement of the large rotors.

Unlike airplanes, helicopters do not need long runways for takeoff and landing. Because they can hover, they are useful for rescues at sea or on mountains. Rescuers use a line to lift people or lower supplies.

SEE ALSO: Aircraft; da Vinci, Leonardo; Engines; Wright, Orville and Wilbur

DID YOU KNOW?

In the late 1700s, two French scientists demonstrated a working model that used the same principles that helicopter designers now take for granted. It consisted of a stick with feathers stuck into a cork at each end. When they spun the stick, it "flew" for a few seconds. The model was based on an ancient Chinese toy.

well physically, but might feel sad, angry, or confused. If these feelings last a long time, the person might have a mental health problem. There are many mental illnesses. Depression is the most common. These illnesses need to be treated by experts, such as psychiatrists. Mental and physical health are often linked. For example, stress can worsen conditions such as high blood pressure and ulcers.

Some aspects of a healthful environment are outside the control of the individual, although our actions and choices influence them. Air that is safe to breathe, water that is free from disease, and food that is not dangerous to eat all depend to a large part on government and state regulation.

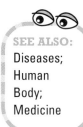

SEE ALSO:
Diseases;
Human
Body;
Medicine

✳HEARING 👉 ✳EARS AND HEARING

✳ HEART AND CIRCULATORY SYSTEM

The circulatory system is the network that carries blood around the human body. The heart is the most important organ in this system.

Blood is the remarkable fluid that keeps us alive. It contains millions of cells that, among other things, transport oxygen and help fight infection. Red blood cells carry oxygen to all parts of the body and remove waste carbon dioxide. White blood cells combat infection, clear away worn-out cells, and attack cells that become malignant (cancer-causing).

Blood vessels
The human circulatory system consists of three different kinds of blood vessels— arteries, capillaries, and veins. Arteries carry blood away from the heart. As arteries branch out, carrying blood to every part of the body, they split into tiny blood vessels called capillaries. As the blood returns to the heart, the capillaries link up to form veins. Veins contain valves—flaps that keep the blood from flowing backward. Without valves, blood would be pulled back by gravity into the lower part of the body.

The heart
The heart is a pump made of muscle. It has four chambers: the right and left atrium and the right and left ventricle. There are flaps, called valves, between the chambers and also at the outlets to the arteries that carry blood away from the heart. These valves snap shut to stop the blood from flowing backward. ➡

CIRCULATORY SYSTEM

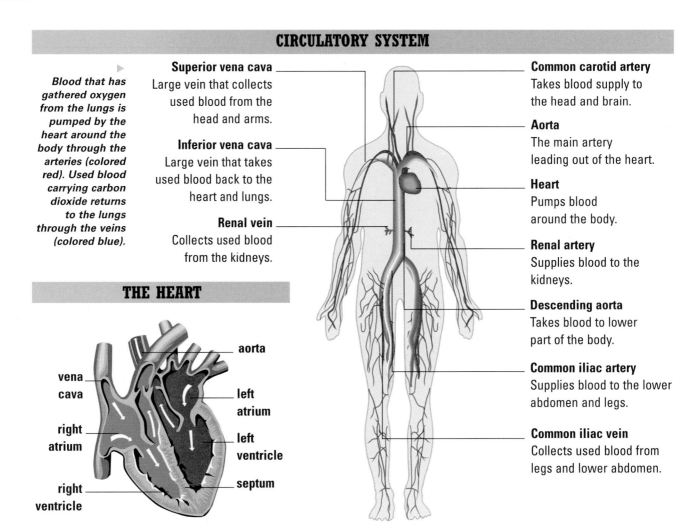

Blood that has gathered oxygen from the lungs is pumped by the heart around the body through the arteries (colored red). Used blood carrying carbon dioxide returns to the lungs through the veins (colored blue).

Superior vena cava
Large vein that collects used blood from the head and arms.

Inferior vena cava
Large vein that takes used blood back to the heart and lungs.

Renal vein
Collects used blood from the kidneys.

Common carotid artery
Takes blood supply to the head and brain.

Aorta
The main artery leading out of the heart.

Heart
Pumps blood around the body.

Renal artery
Supplies blood to the kidneys.

Descending aorta
Takes blood to lower part of the body.

Common iliac artery
Supplies blood to the lower abdomen and legs.

Common iliac vein
Collects used blood from legs and lower abdomen.

THE HEART

aorta

vena cava

right atrium

right ventricle

left atrium

left ventricle

septum

The heart is the driving force of the circulatory system. A thick wall, called the septum, divides the heart into halves, named left and right in accordance with the heart's owner rather than the observer. Valves, which open and close, divide each half into upper and lower parts.

Blood flows into the right atrium from veins all over the body. It streams into the right ventricle, then out toward the lungs, where it picks up a fresh supply of oxygen and unloads its carbon dioxide. The oxygen-rich blood then moves to the left atrium, down to the left ventricle, and through the aorta to the rest of the body. The heart fills and empties in a rhythmic cycle called the heartbeat. The heartbeat rate is controlled by special cells in the heart. An adult usually has a rate of about 70 beats a minute, but exercise, fear, or sleep can speed up or slow down the rate.

AMAZING FACTS!

Your body contains more than 62,000 miles (100,000 km) of blood vessels. Some are so tiny that they cannot be seen with the naked eye.

SEE ALSO: Blood; Cells; Human Body; Lungs and Respiratory System; Muscular System

* HEAT

People use the words *hot* and *cold* to describe things that have high or low temperatures. To a scientist, however, heat is not the same as temperature.

Heat is a form of energy that exists inside matter. Matter is anything that takes up space and has mass. The more matter there is, the more heat energy there is, whether the temperature is high or low. There is more heat energy in a large iceberg than in a cup of hot coffee.

Heat is measured in calories. One calorie of heat will raise the temperature of 1 gram (0.03 ounces) by 1°C (34°F). Another measurement is the British thermal unit (BTU). A BTU will raise the temperature of 1 lb. (454 g) of water by 1°F (–17°C).

Temperature

Molecules, the tiny particles that make up matter, are always moving and giving off energy. Temperature measures the average kinetic energy, or energy of motion, of a molecule. There is more average energy in the molecules of hot matter than there is in cold matter.

Temperature is measured on a number of scales. Scientists use the Celsius, or centigrade, scale, in which water freezes at 0°C and boils at 100°C. It was developed in 1742 by the Swedish astronomer Anders Celsius.

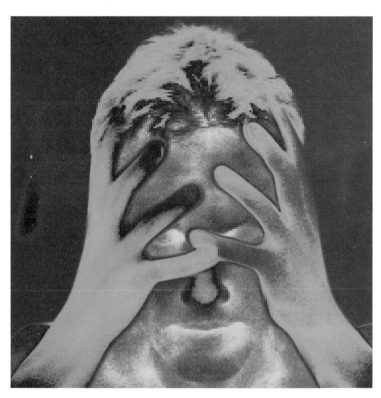

In the Fahrenheit scale, named for the German physicist Gabriel Fahrenheit, water freezes at 32°F and boils at 212°F. On the Kelvin scale, named for the British scientist Lord Kelvin, water freezes at 273.16K (kelvins). Absolute zero, the temperature at which no more heat energy can be removed from matter, is known as 0K.

Thermodynamics is the study of heat and its relation to other forms of energy. The three laws of thermodynamics state that: Energy cannot be created or destroyed; heat naturally flows from a warmer body to a cooler body; and it is impossible to reduce temperature to absolute zero.

Thermograms record differences in temperature. This image shows a man holding his head. Red shows the warmest temperature.

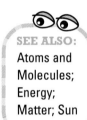

SEE ALSO:
Atoms and Molecules; Energy; Matter; Sun

AMAZING FACTS !

The sun is the source of most of Earth's energy. The center of the sun is approximately 27,000,000°F (15,000,000°C). Many other stars are even hotter.

✳ HELICOPTERS

Helicopters are aircraft with large rotating blades that can fly in any direction—forward, backward, to the side, straight up—as well as hover in one place.

In the late 1400s, the Italian artist and inventor Leonardo da Vinci designed a flying machine called a *helixpteron*, from the Greek words for "spiral" and "wing." It had a large screw on top, which was meant to pull the machine up in the air. No one knows whether he built the machine.

In 1903 the Wright brothers made the first successful airplane flight. Twenty years later, a Spanish engineer named Juan de la Cierva built the autogiro. It had wings and a propeller, like an airplane, but it also had rotor blades on top. French, German, and American engineers developed the first practical helicopters in the late 1930s. In 1939 the Russian-American Igor Sikorsky perfected the single-rotor design that is still in use.

How helicopters work

The blades of a helicopter are powered by an engine. As they cut through the air, the shape of the blades makes the air pressure below greater than the pressure above. This causes lift. The same principle allows airplanes to fly. Airplanes, however, need to move forward to produce lift. A

A Coast Guard Jayhawk HH-60J helicopter patrols over New York City. It can stay airborne for about six hours.

▼

> ## DID YOU KNOW?
>
> In the late 1700s, two French scientists demonstrated a working model that used the same principles that helicopter designers now take for granted. It consisted of a stick with feathers stuck into a cork at each end. When they spun the stick, it "flew" for a few seconds. The model was based on an ancient Chinese toy.

helicopter can stay still, while its blades move through the air and produce enough lift for flight. This allows helicopters to move in any direction or hover on one spot. The amount of lift changes when the pilot alters the pitch, or angle, of the blades. When the angle is larger, the lift is greater. The pilot has two main controls: one to change the pitch of all the blades at once, and one to alter the pitch on one side or at the front or back. They make the helicopter go up and down or sideways, forward, or backward. A small rotor on the tail stops it from swinging around from the movement of the large rotors.

Unlike airplanes, helicopters do not need long runways for takeoff and landing. Because they can hover, they are useful for rescues at sea or on mountains. Rescuers use a line to lift people or lower supplies.

SEE ALSO: Aircraft; da Vinci, Leonardo; Engines; Wright, Orville and Wilbur

✳ HEMINGWAY, ERNEST (1899–1961)

The American author Ernest Hemingway wrote with a distinctive style that strongly influenced later generations of writers.

Ernest Hemingway was born in Oak Park, Illinois. He wrote for his high school newspaper and literary magazine, then worked as a reporter for the *Kansas City Star*. There he developed his trademark writing style of short, simple sentences, made up mainly of nouns and verbs. He tried to avoid comment and descriptions of emotion; instead he described actions. His dialogue sounded natural and was brief and to the point.

During World War I (1914–18), Hemingway joined the Red Cross. His experiences formed the basis for the novel *A Farewell to Arms* (1929). His other major novels were *The Sun Also Rises* (1926), *For Whom the Bell Tolls* (1940), and *The Old Man and the Sea* (1952). For this last work, Hemingway won the Pulitzer Prize. In 1954 he was awarded the Nobel Prize in literature for his novels and short stories.

Hemingway married four times. He had a great passion for hunting and fishing. At different times, he lived in Paris, France; Key West, Florida; Havana, Cuba; and Ketchum, Idaho. By 1960 he was in poor health and suffering from depression. In 1961 he took his own life.

All his life, Ernest Hemingway was a keen angler and hunter.

SEE ALSO: Literature; Nobel Prize

✳ HIBERNATION

Animals that hibernate remain inactive during the winter. That enables them to survive when the climate is harsh and food is scarce.

Many animals live in environments with long, cold winters. Some migrate to warmer places or grow thicker coats. Others become inactive, reducing their metabolism—the body processes that use energy—and surviving on stored body fat or food. This state is called hibernation. Bats, hedgehogs, and many rodents, such as squirrels, chipmunks, and hamsters, all hibernate. The only hibernating bird is the common poorwill.

Shutting down

When an animal hibernates, it goes into a state called torpor. Its heart rate drops to just a few beats per minute. Its body heat also falls gradually, so it is only just above air temperature. Its rate of breathing falls. A small animal will reach torpor faster and more easily than a large one. In this state, an animal might seem to be asleep or even dead. It is still alive; but because its body is not using much energy, it does not need to find food to avoid starvation. Some

A hazel dormouse hibernates in its nest. Hibernation is similar to, but different from, sleep.

animals come out of hibernation several times over the winter. They eat stored food, then return to torpor.

After the period of hibernation, usually when the weather is warmer, the animal slowly comes out of torpor. Some species have special fat that gradually returns their body temperature to normal. Others produce heat by shivering their muscles. When the animal's body functions return to normal, it has to look for food again.

SEE ALSO:
Amphibians;
Animals;
Bears;
Migration;
Rodents

Other forms of inactivity

A few species, such as some frogs and fish, enter a sleeplike state during summer to avoid extreme heat. Inactivity of this type is called estivation. Estivating animals burrow into mud and suspend all activity until summer is over.

Some mammals and birds go through brief periods of inactivity—sometimes only a few hours—during the winter. They include skunks, lemurs, nighthawks, and hummingbirds.

Some animals appear to hibernate but do not really do so. A female bear sleeps through much of the winter, living on her own fat. But she is easily woken and warms up quickly.

Ectotherms—cold-blooded animals—sometimes go through a process called dormancy, which closely resembles hibernation. The main difference is that ectotherms cannot warm themselves up and so have to rely on increases in the temperature of the surrounding air to rouse them from dormancy.

✳ HINDUISM

Hinduism is a major world religion, with about 900 million followers. It began in India thousands of years ago.

Hinduism is unlike Christianity, Islam, and Judaism in two important ways. First, it recognizes several holy books, not just one. The oldest and holiest of the Hindu books, far older than the Bible, are the four Vedas. (*Veda* means "knowledge" or "wisdom.") Others include two long story-poems, the *Ramayana* and *Mahabharata*. Second, many Hindus worship more than one god. Some of the best-known gods include Vishnu, Shiva, and the elephant-headed Ganesha. Popular goddesses include Durga, Kali, and Lakshmi. All Hindus

◄

A Hindu woman bathes in the sacred waters of the Ganges River in Varanasi, India.

believe that there is one unifying spirit, called Brahman, that runs through everything in the world. The gods represent different sides of Brahman.

Reincarnation

In Hinduism, just as in Buddhism, Jainism, and Sikhism (other religions from India), followers believe in reincarnation, or being born again. When a person dies, he or she is born again into a new body. The cycle of death and rebirth continues until the person's soul (inner being) understands life so clearly that he or she is finally set free from this world.

For the Hindu, this means that life must be lived as purely as possible, in the hope of a better rebirth. So Hindus try to follow set rules of behavior. They must honor their family, fast (go for periods without food), and meditate (spend time in quiet thought). Hindus worship at shrines in their homes and in temples, making offerings to favorite gods or goddesses. Some important annual Hindu festivals include Navratri and Holi. Hindus also celebrate Divali, or the festival of lights.

Caste system
One of the more complicated aspects of Hinduism is its caste system. This is the ancient belief that everyone belongs to a level, or caste, in society. The highest, purest caste is that of priests and scholars, called Brahmans. Outside the four main castes are people called

untouchables, who traditionally did work that others saw as unclean. In 1947 laws were passed in India to make discrimination against untouchables illegal. However, the caste system remains an important part of family and social life.

A statue of the Hindu god Ganesha in Java, Indonesia.

SEE ALSO: Indian Subcontinent; Religions

✳ HIPPOPOTAMUSES
The hippopotamus, or hippo, is a huge, brown mammal with a large head and four legs. Hippos live in the wild only in Africa.

The word *hippopotamus* means "river horse." The animal is called this because it spends a lot of time in the water. The hippo also has wide nostrils and small ears like a horse. In fact it is more closely related to the pig.

Big beasts
A large hippo can be 5 ft. (1.5 m) tall and as much as 12 ft. (3.6 m) long. It can weigh more than 3½ tons. Apart from the whale, the hippopotamus has the largest mouth of all mammals. It has six tusks (long, pointed teeth) in its mouth, two in the upper jaw, and four in the lower jaw. Hippos will usually hide in the water rather than attack other animals, but they can be dangerous if startled.

Life in the water
Hippopotamuses spend their days resting in pools, rivers, or lakes. They like to float

with only their eyes, nostrils, and ears showing above the surface of the water. They often dive and walk along the bottom of lakes and rivers, where they feed on water plants. They are able to close their nostrils and ears to keep out water, and can stay submerged for as long as nine minutes. Hippos eat mostly at night, when they walk as far as several miles inland to eat grass.

Baby hippopotamuses are often born in the water. They can swim almost immediately and can feed from their mother under water. The baby sometimes rides on its mother's back.

More than a million years ago, different types of hippos lived in Africa, India, and Europe. Now they are found in wild herds

When a hippo dives, it shuts its ears and nostrils to keep out water.

Hippos spend their days in water. They often live in herds of between 20 and 40 members.

only in tropical Central Africa. Because hippos sometimes eat farmers' crops, many of them have been killed or driven away from farms. Today they live mainly around rivers and lakes in parks set aside for wild animals.

SEE ALSO: Animals; Mammals

* HISPANIC AMERICANS

Hispanic Americans, also known as Latinos, are U.S. residents who were born in or whose ancestors came from Spanish-speaking lands.

Spanish settlers arrive at St. Augustine, Florida.

Almost two-thirds of Hispanic Americans come from Mexico. Many others are from Puerto Rico, Cuba, the Dominican Republic, and Central or South America. They are united by their most common religion, Roman Catholicism, and by the Spanish language, which most still speak. Hispanic Americans are reminders that Spain, a Roman Catholic country in western Europe, once ruled vast areas of the Americas.

History

When the Spanish founded St. Augustine in Florida in 1565, they became the first group of Europeans to settle in what is now the United States. Spanish traders, miners, and priests later settled the Southwest. They forced out some Native Americans and mixed with others. They also brought slaves from Africa to work for them. That explains why some modern Hispanic Americans still practice Native

American and African customs. The Spanish also colonized all of South America except Brazil. They quit their colonies in the 19th century.

Migration

For over 150 years, people from former Spanish colonies have been migrating north to the United States in search of work and a better life. They settled in Spanish-speaking neighborhoods, called barrios, in large cities like Los Angeles.

For the first generations of Hispanic American immigrants, life was a struggle. Restaurants refused to serve them, and their children were often bullied at school for speaking or writing Spanish. Hispanic American workers were paid less than half the amount earned by non-Hispanics. But through hard campaigning, Hispanic Americans and other ethnic groups have gradually won rights, such as education in Spanish (or another native tongue), and fairer pay.

Culture

Today there are about 37 million Hispanic Americans. Their vibrant culture, from food and festivals to art, music, and literature,

is now woven into the fabric of everyday life in the United States. So, too, is their language. Many of the words that Americans use regularly are of Spanish origin; examples include *tornado* and *mosquito*. Some familiar place names are derived from Spanish, including Florida (Spanish for "floral") and Colorado ("red"). It was early Spanish settlers who taught other Americans how to tame wild horses and how best to raise cattle. From the Spanish came the cowboy culture, along with such words as *lasso*, *stampede*, *bronco*, and *rodeo*.

Today in nearly every U.S. town there are restaurants serving Hispanic American cuisine. Nachos, tacos, chili, and fajitas have become almost as American as apple pie. In music, Hispanic Americans have brought their sounds to American jazz, pop, and folk, from traditional

Carnival (the start of Lent) is celebrated on the streets of Little Havana in Miami, Florida.

291

Mexican ballads and Texan/Mexican accordion and guitar melodies to the salsa beat of the Caribbean.

Hispanic American painters have enriched U.S. culture with their art, especially the murals (wall paintings) of Los Angeles. The writings of authors such as Sandra Cisneros, Nicholasa Mohr, and Judith Ortiz Cofer describe what life is like for Hispanic Americans in the United States. A number of Hispanics have become celebrities. They include Salma Hayek and Jennifer Lopez.

Holidays and festivals

Special religious holidays include *El Día de los Reyes*, or Three Kings' Day, on January 6, and *Semana Santa*, the Holy Week of Easter. On *El Día de los Muertos*, the Day of the Dead, which is celebrated in the fall, families take gifts to the graves of their relatives. Local saints and feast days are recognized with pilgrimages (visits to holy sites). A girl's *quinceañera*, or 15th birthday celebration, is a special occasion that marks her passage to womanhood. Other important holidays include *Cinco de Mayo* (May 5), which remembers the defeat of French invaders by the Mexican Army in 1862.

SEE ALSO: Central America; Holidays and Festivals; Immigration; Mexico; Music; South America; Spain; Spanish–American War; United States of America

✳ HISTORY
History is the branch of knowledge that records and explains past events. Historical writings are often set out in the order in which things happened.

BLACK DEATH TO SEPTEMBER 11, 2001—A HISTORICAL TIMELINE

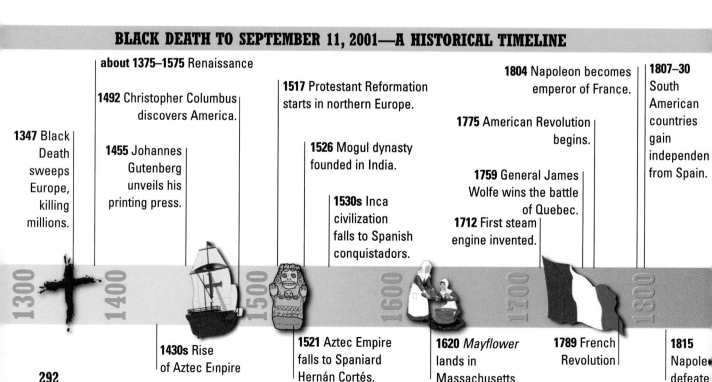

about 1375–1575 Renaissance

1492 Christopher Columbus discovers America.

1517 Protestant Reformation starts in northern Europe.

1804 Napoleon becomes emperor of France.

1807–30 South American countries gain independen from Spain.

1347 Black Death sweeps Europe, killing millions.

1455 Johannes Gutenberg unveils his printing press.

1526 Mogul dynasty founded in India.

1775 American Revolution begins.

1530s Inca civilization falls to Spanish conquistadors.

1759 General James Wolfe wins the battle of Quebec.

1712 First steam engine invented.

1300   1400   1500   1600   1700   1800

1430s Rise of Aztec Empire

1521 Aztec Empire falls to Spaniard Hernán Cortés.

1620 *Mayflower* lands in Massachusetts.

1789 French Revolution

1815 Napole defeate

Many people believe that understanding what has already happened might help humanity avoid making the same mistakes in the present or future. The philosopher George Santayana (1863–1952) once wrote that "Those who cannot remember the past are condemned to repeat it."

In the past, people learned history as if it were a simple record of events. They learned the names of powerful people and their great achievements. Children learned long lists of dates, so that they knew when wars happened, or when governments made important laws.

The modern approach

Historians still believe that such records of events are the foundation of history. However, in recent decades they have also begun to explore different types of history. Instead of studying the few privileged and powerful people in a society, they believe it is just as important to learn about the lives of the many millions of ordinary people. What did they eat? What gods did they worship? And in what way?

History is more than documents. This painting from an ancient Greek vase helps scholars learn about life at the time it was made, about 400 B.C.

As well as studying the lives of a wider range of people, modern historians also use a wider range of evidence. They used to concentrate on written accounts. Now they draw on subjects such as biology, economics, geology, psychology, and sociology. They also refer to folklore, myths, and everyday documents, such as household accounts.

Some historians study a tiny part of history in great detail—they try to discover facts about life in a single village at a particular time, for example. Others study the rise and fall of whole civilizations. ➡

1914–18 World War I

1917 Russian Revolution; formation of Communist Soviet Union

1945–90 Cold War

1905 Einstein's theory of relativity

1948 Founding of State of Israel

1920–33 Prohibition in United States

1859 Darwin publishes *On the Origin of Species.*

1950–53 Korean War

1945 Atomic bombs dropped on Japan.

mid 1950s–75 Vietnam War

1991 End of Soviet Union

1929 Wall Street Crash; start of Great Depression

1871 Germany united as a single state.

1933 Hitler comes to power in Germany.

1969 First man on the moon

1994 End of apartheid in South Africa

1886 Benz and Daimler invent automobile.

1903 First powered flight by Wright brothers

1939–45 World War II

1953 Structure of DNA discovered.

2001 World Trade Center destroyed and Pentagon damaged in terrorist attacks.

Some historians study politics; others study ideas or genealogy (the history of families). Some specialize in the history of wars and warfare. There are also historians who study history before the existence of records, which is called prehistory.

A complex subject

Although history seems simple, it is often very complicated. Any event can have many interpretations. For Americans, for example, Christopher Columbus's arrival in the "New World" in 1492 helped lead to the creation of the United States. But for Native Americans, Columbus's arrival was a disaster. It brought enslavement by the Europeans and disease that killed millions of people. Which view is correct? There are many other examples that show that history is not a single story but many intertwined stories.

The history of history

The Western tradition of history has its origins in the Hebrew Bible and ancient Greek writings. These works have influenced the study of history in Europe, America, and the Islamic world.

The non-Western tradition began in ancient China but spread to Japan, Korea, and elsewhere. Since the time of the Chou dynasty (about 1000 B.C.), Chinese historians have traditionally taken evidence from a wide range of sources, rather like Western historians today.

SEE ALSO: Ancient Civilizations; Archaeology; Myths and Legends; Philosophers; Renaissance; United States of America; Writing

* HOCKEY

Ice hockey is a fast game played on ice. Field hockey is played on grass or turf. Both games involve two teams competing to score goals.

Ice hockey

Ice hockey is played on an oval covered in ice with a goal at each end. Each team tries to shoot the puck (a small rubber disk) into the opposite goal net, and prevent their opponents from scoring.

Only six players from each team are on the ice at any one time—goalie, two defensemen, center, left wing, and right wing. They are joined by a referee and linesmen. Everyone wears protective clothing. Each player has a hockey stick, which usually has a curved blade. At any time substitutes can replace teammates.

The game has three 20-minute periods. To start a period, or to restart play after interruptions, the referee drops the puck

between the two centers. This is called a face-off. Each center tries to gain possession of the puck and build an attack toward the other team's goal. In front of each goalpost is a semicircle known as the crease. If an attacking player is in the crease when a goal is scored, the goal does not count. There are rules to govern play, as well as penalties for foul play.

History

British soldiers probably played the first hockey games in 1855 on the frozen surface of Lake Ontario. Around 1875, students at McGill University in Montreal wrote the first rules of the game. The National Hockey Association was founded in 1910, but was replaced in 1917 by the

National Hockey League (NHL). There are 30 U.S. and Canadian teams in the league. Each year the Stanley Cup is awarded to the best professional team.

The International Ice Hockey Federation in Switzerland controls international play and stages the world championship each year. Men's ice hockey became an official Olympic Winter Games sport in 1920, and women have competed since 1998.

Famous teams and players

Top pro teams include the Montreal Canadiens, the New York Islanders, and the Edmonton Oilers. Outstanding NHL players have included Ray Bourque, Gordie Howe, Bobby Hull, Guy Lafleur, Mario Lemieux, Howie Morenz, Bobby Orr, Maurice Richard, and Wayne Gretzky.

Field hockey

Field hockey is played on a grass field divided into two halves with a goal cage at each end. The striking, or shooting, circle

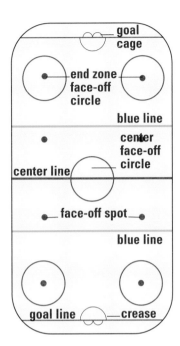
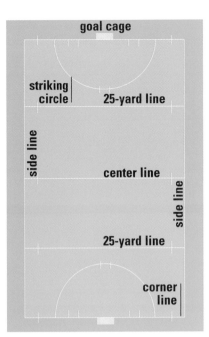

Standard layouts of an ice hockey rink (above, left) and a hockey field (above, right). Field hockey is played on grass or synthetic turf.

Wayne Gretzky sets up a shot in an All-Star game. Mark Howe is about to check.

is a half-circle drawn around each goal mouth. It marks the area within which an attacker's stick must touch the ball in order to score a goal.

There are 11 players on each team. Players move the ball down the field with their sticks in an attempt to shoot it past the goalkeeper into the goal. Each goal scores one point. Games are divided into two periods of 30 or 35 minutes. The team with the most points at the end wins the game. Penalties are given for rough or foul play.

History

Field hockey is the oldest known ball and stick game.

American Kelli James and South Korean Cho Eun-Jung battle for the ball in a 1996 Olympic women's field hockey match.

Similar games date back over 4,000 years, and variations were played in different parts of the world. The English invented the modern sport during the 1800s. The game was introduced to the United States in 1901, and it quickly grew in popularity. The International Hockey Federation (FIH) was founded in 1924.

In the United States, field hockey is played by girls and women at high school and college levels, while both men and women compete in clubs and leagues throughout the country. The Olympics included men's field hockey on the official program for the first time in 1908, with women's field hockey joining in 1980.

SEE ALSO: Olympic Games; Sports

* HOLIDAYS AND FESTIVALS

Holidays and festivals are special days that bring people together—to celebrate triumphs, to pray, to remember heroes or loved ones, or just to have fun.

The jack-o'-lantern made from a pumpkin is a traditional Halloween decoration. The name Halloween comes from "All Hallows' Eve," the night before All Saints', or All Hallows', Day on November 1.

The word *holiday* comes from "holy day"—a day to offer prayers or celebrate a religious event. For Christians, Christmas and Easter are the high points of the year. They mark the birth and the resurrection of Jesus Christ. Rosh Hashanah, Yom Kippur, and Passover are major Jewish holidays. During Ramadan, a month of purification and reflection, Muslims fast each day from sunrise to sunset. Some Muslims also celebrate Mouloud, a nine-day period marking the birth of Muhammad, the founder of Islam.

The passing year

The start of a new year is celebrated throughout the world as a time for entertaining, visiting, and giving gifts. The dates may vary according to the calendar used. New Year's Day is celebrated on January 1 in countries where Christianity is the main religion. The Jewish new year starts in September or October, and the Chinese new year is in January or February. Hindus celebrate the start of a new "year" every three months.

There are holidays that celebrate the coming of spring and the gathering of the harvest. They include Thanksgiving Day, which dates back to 1621, when the first

British settlers celebrated their harvest with the Native Americans who taught them survival skills.

Honoring people
Every country has holidays that honor its founders and heroes. They include former monarchs and presidents, leaders of revolution, and great thinkers. In South America, for example, on July 24 the Venezuelan Simón Bolívar (1783–1830) is honored in all the countries he helped free from Spanish rule—Colombia, Peru, Bolivia, Ecuador, and Venezuela. Bolívar is known as *El Libertador* (the liberator).

Patriotic holidays
Nations mark special dates in their history with celebrations. Independence Day, July 4, marks the birth of the United States in 1776. In Canada, July 1 celebrates the day in 1867 when the provinces of Canada, Nova Scotia, and New Brunswick were united as the Dominion of Canada.

Fun festivals
In countries where there are many Roman Catholics, the street parties and parades of carnival are popular. There are famous carnivals in New Orleans, Louisiana; Rio de Janeiro, Brazil; and Nice, France. ➡

DID YOU KNOW?

Americans are not the only people to give thanks for a good harvest. In the Pongal festival in southeast India, people thank the gods and the cattle that helped plow the fields. Cattle, held sacred in India, are adorned with flowers. July's Crop-Over celebration in Barbados goes back to the 1800s, when slaves yelled "Crop Over!" at the end of the annual sugarcane harvest. And in the West African nation of Nigeria, the Igbo people celebrate Iriji, the New Yam festival. The fun includes wrestling, dancing, and a feast of freshly picked yams.

Thousands of Muslims gather in the Grand Mosque, Mecca, to mark the anniversary of the night when the Koran was revealed to the prophet Muhammad in A.D. 610.

297

Dragon dancers celebrate Chinese new year in Hong Kong. There are 12 animals in the Chinese zodiac. The year 2000 was the year of the dragon.

On October 31, many people celebrate Halloween by wearing costumes, carving jack-o'-lanterns, and partying. Children travel from door to door yelling "Trick or treat!" and collecting candy. Such customs date back to ancient Europe. People believed that witches, demons, and spirits of the dead roamed the earth on the eve of November 1. Priests lit bonfires to drive away the spirits and offered them food to prevent their return.

SEE ALSO: Buddhism; Calendars; Christianity; Circuses and Carnivals; Hinduism; Islam; Judaism; Religions

* HOLOCAUST

Between 1933 and 1945, six million European Jews were systematically killed by Germany's ruling Nazi Party. This mass murder is called the Holocaust.

▲
A Jewish citizen of Warsaw, Poland, in 1940. He is wearing the Star of David, the symbol of Judaism.

In the early 1930s, about nine million Jews lived throughout Europe. The Jews had been persecuted since Roman times for many reasons such as religion, culture, and tradition.

Adolf Hitler's Nazi Party came to power at a time of economic crisis in Germany. Defeat in World War I (1914–18) and worldwide depression had brought poverty and mass unemployment. Hitler blamed these problems on the Jews. Other groups he labeled as being as "unworthy of life" as the Jews included Roma (gypsies), communists, intellectuals, Jehovah's Witnesses, homosexuals, and the disabled. Many from these groups were also murdered during the Holocaust. Hitler believed that all these people stood in the way of building a German empire of only pure-blooded whites, or Aryans.

Under a Nazi law of 1935, German Jews lost their citizenship. They had to wear a yellow Star of David on their clothing as identification and were barred from many jobs and from mixing with non-Jews. They were forbidden to enter non-Jewish shops. In one 24-hour period in November 1938, nearly every synagogue in Germany was destroyed. Thousands of Jews were arrested and sent to concentration camps.

World War II
On September 1, 1939, Hitler's army invaded Poland. By the middle of 1940, most of Europe was under Nazi control. The Nazis crowded the Jews into tiny sections of cities, called ghettoes, where they were given almost no food, water, or heat. Many died of cold, sickness, or hunger. Beginning in 1942, the Nazis moved the Jews to concentration camps

such as Auschwitz and Dachau. Many of them were gassed to death soon after they arrived. This was the Nazis' so-called "Final Solution" to the "Jewish problem."

Allied soldiers were unprepared for the horrors they saw when they liberated the camps in 1945. After the war, Nazi leaders were punished for their crimes.

SEE ALSO: Communism; Europe; Germany; Great Depression; Human Rights; Judaism; World War I; World War II

✴ HOMER, WINSLOW (1836–1910)
Winslow Homer was one of the most important American painters of the late 1800s. He is best known for his pictures of rural life and of the sea.

Winslow Homer was born in Boston, Massachusetts. He had little formal artistic training, but by the age of 21 he was working as an illustrator. At 23 he moved to New York City to work for the magazine *Harper's Weekly*. His first major job for the magazine was to sketch the presidential inauguration of Abraham Lincoln. *Harper's* sent Homer to Virginia during the Civil War (1861–65) to draw battle scenes. However, he found that his talent lay in sketching everyday life in the camps. He decided to give up illustrating to concentrate on his oil painting.

After the war, Homer painted pictures of rural life, summer resorts, and childhood themes. In 1873 he began working in watercolor. He created a realistic style with skillful use of light and shadow.

During 1881 and 1882, Homer lived in a small fishing village in northeastern England. The sea became his favorite subject matter. He returned to the United States and settled in Prout's Neck, a lonely point on the coast of Maine. His finest paintings, such as *The Fog Warning* (1885), explored the theme of humanity versus nature. He also painted in the Bahamas, Cuba, Florida, and the Adirondack Mountains in New York State. He lived alone in Prout's Neck until his death in 1910.

Winslow Homer in about 1905. His dramatic paintings of the sea give a sense of the powerlessness of humans against the forces of nature.

SEE ALSO: Art and Artists; Civil War

✳ HORSES

More than any other species of animal, horses changed the history of civilization. They remain important to humans for work, pleasure, and sports.

Horses are four-legged mammals. They have long tails, and a mane of hair between their pointed ears. Their long legs end in hard hooves that act as shock absorbers when they gallop over firm ground. Their flaring nostrils allow them to take in large amounts of oxygen during exercise. They are herbivores—plant-eaters—with large, grinding teeth to break down tough grasses.

The horse in history

For thousands of years, humans hunted horses for food. About 4,500 years ago, people learned that horses were useful for carrying loads and for riding, and they began to tame them. Different civilizations developed different breeds of horses. Arabs bred the strong, swift Arabian horse for riding and warfare. European peasants bred strong little ponies to haul carts.

On horseback or in horse-drawn carriages, people could travel much faster overland than they could on foot. In the 13th century, the Mongol cavalry (soldiers who fight on horseback) of Genghis Khan conquered a vast empire in Central Asia and westward into Russia and beyond.

In 1519 the Spanish brought horses to Mexico. This was the first time these animals had been on the American mainland for many thousands of years. Horses were vital to the early colonists of the continent for travel, farming, and cattle ranching. The horse remained the main method of overland transport in most of the world until the expansion of the railroads in the second half of the 1800s.

The horse family

Other domesticated members of the horse family are the donkey and the mule. A mule is the offspring of a female horse and a male donkey and is always sterile—unable to reproduce. Wild members of the family include the zebra and various species of wild ass found in Africa and Asia.

Horses spend much of their time grazing in fields.

SEE ALSO:
Animals;
Genghis
Khan;
Mammals;
West, The
American

✳ HOSPITALS

Hospitals are places where sick or injured people receive medical care. They are also centers for educational and research programs.

Although a hospital is a building or a number of buildings, the most important part of it is the people who help make patients better. They include doctors and nurses as well as laboratory technicians, cleaners, cooks, and maintenance and office workers. Each one has a special job that contributes to the care of the patients and the organization of the hospital.

Hospital departments

There are many different kinds of hospitals. Some treat only people with one kind of disease. Others treat only one age group, such as children. Most hospitals are short-term, general hospitals. They are split into departments that provide different kinds of care. Sick children under 16 are admitted to the pediatrics department. This department often has play facilities and space for parents to stay overnight with their children. Some pediatric departments have schoolrooms and teachers, so that the children who are patients at the hospital do not miss out on their education.

In North America, most births take place in obstetrics departments. They are usually on a separate floor to keep the mothers and babies free from infection.

Operations are performed in the surgical department. Patients are given drugs, called anesthetics, that make them lose consciousness before and during surgery. Afterward they go to a recovery room until the effects of the anesthetic wear off.

The busiest department is usually the emergency department, which is where people go when they suffer an injury or

▲ *A 15th-century illustration showing patients in a ward at the Hôtel Dieu in Paris. Medical treatment at the time was extremely limited, and lack of space meant that patients had to share beds.*

illness that must be treated urgently. Emergency patients need to be seen as quickly as possible. This is why the emergency department is usually on the first floor of the hospital. Radiology (X-ray) departments and laboratories are usually near the emergency department.

Very sick patients go to the intensive care unit (ICU) or coronary care unit (CCU). Here department staff constantly check their blood pressure, pulse, breathing, and other body functions.

People who do not need to stay in the hospital overnight are treated as outpatients. Staff may need to perform tests on them or give them treatment. Inpatients stay for the night or for a longer period.

History of hospitals

In early history, places of worship cared for the sick. The first separate medical institutions appeared in Rome, Italy, in

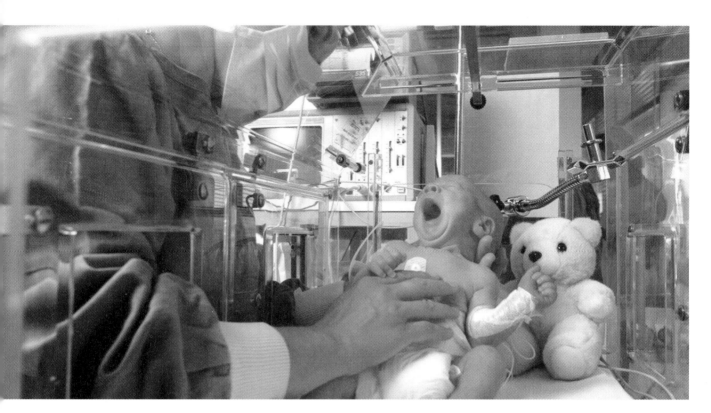

When a baby is born early, he or she is often put in an incubator, which acts like a greenhouse, regulating the surrounding temperature and the amount of oxygen in the air.

SEE ALSO:
Diseases;
Franklin,
Benjamin;
Medicine;
Surgery;
X-rays

the first century A.D. The word *hospital* comes from the Latin word *hospitium*, meaning a place to receive guests.

The first North American hospitals were built in the 1700s. Their main purpose was to confine patients with infectious diseases. Later, hospitals were built to provide care and treatment for the poor. Wealthy people were still treated in their homes. The first not-for-profit, or voluntary, hospital in North America was the Pennsylvania Hospital in Philadelphia, founded in 1751 by Benjamin Franklin and Dr. Thomas Bond.

Hospitals became much safer and more effective in the 1800s due to the discovery of antiseptics, which help prevent infection, and anesthetics, which kill pain. In the first half of the 1900s, the discovery of sulfa drugs and antibiotics also helped medical staff to treat disease and operate more safely.

In recent years, developments such as transplant surgery and laser treatment have greatly increased the range of services that a hospital can offer. Illnesses and injuries that once killed people can now be treated fairly easily by skilled staff.

AMAZING FACTS

The oldest hospital in the Western world is the Hôtel Dieu, in Paris, France. It was established around A.D. 600 by Saint Landry, the Bishop of Paris.

The United States has about 6,800 hospitals. These range in size from small rural buildings with fewer than 25 beds to large urban complexes with 3,000 beds.

✳ HOUSING

Housing **is a term for all the different types of homes that people have created. A home is, at its most basic, a place where people find shelter.**

Early humans lived in caves or made shelters from branches and leaves. When people began to grow crops and raise animals, they also built huts made of mud, with roofs of dried grass.

In about 8000 B.C., people in Asia and the Middle East began to live in permanent settlements. They made homes with long-lasting materials such as sun-dried mud bricks. Some buildings had two stories.

Stone buildings

In ancient Greece, a typical house was a single-story dwelling with stone or brick walls. In ancient Rome, wealthy people lived in large stone houses built around courtyards. People who could not afford to live in a private house rented apartments.

In Europe during the centuries following the fall of the Western Roman Empire in the fifth century A.D., wealthier people built stone castles with thick walls for safety. In the 1300s, rich people began to decorate their homes with wall hangings and furniture, but poor people continued to live in thatched huts or timber houses.

When explorers and colonists arrived in the New World in the 1600s, they brought their methods of home building with them from Europe. It is possible to tell which areas of North America were first occupied by which people—from England, France, the Netherlands, or Spain—by the styles of the oldest dwellings. Settlers in the southern American colonies built houses that were suited to the warm, humid climate. Settlers in the East and West built log cabins.

In the self-help program in Indianola, Mississippi, people learn basic house-building skills by building their own homes.

Growth of cities

Beginning in the 1700s, the Industrial Revolution meant that cities in Europe and North America began to get crowded as people came to work in factories. People lived in rows of poorly built tenements, hemmed in on three sides by neighboring buildings.

The first American apartment buildings, in New York City, were based on those in Paris, France. Middle-class families began to move to the edges of cities, where homes were more affordable. The development of railroads and, later, cars meant that people could live in the suburbs and work in the city centers.

In the 1800s and 1900s, plumbing and power supplies became standard in new houses. But many poorer people still lived in dangerous, unhealthy, and unpleasant conditions, even in wealthy countries.

Housing today

Today concrete is the most common material for housing in the developed world. Although technology means that the environment within the home can be controlled by air conditioning and central heating, houses still vary according to the local climate and the materials available.

Village elders gather near the mud walls around beehive-shape houses in Syria.

In most big cities around the world, space is limited and land is expensive. People often live in apartments, which may be built for that purpose or converted from large houses. Houses tend to be built in rows—they have their own front doors but share walls. In the suburbs and rural areas, homes are often built farther apart.

Some homes are mobile. In the United States, some people live in homes that can be pulled by trucks or cars. In northern Europe, some people live in houseboats on rivers and canals. In other parts of the world, such as Mongolia, people live in tents and follow their herds of livestock.

For many people, the most important factor in choosing a home is money. Many people rent their homes—they pay money to the owner of the property to live there. People who want to buy their homes often take out a mortgage. A company makes a loan that the homeowner pays back over a period of years.

Housing problems

In many parts of the world, there are millions of people who are homeless, or who live in poor-quality housing in slums and shantytowns. Even in the United States, the richest nation in the world, there are people who live on the streets or in homes that put them at risk of fire or sickness. The Department of Housing and Urban Development (HUD) is in charge of housing matters. There are many private and charitable groups that help the homeless and poorer people.

SEE ALSO: Architecture; Castles; Cities; Colonial America; Industrial Revolution; Roman Empire; Towns and Villages

✱ HUDSON, HENRY (UNKNOWN–1611)

The English navigator Henry Hudson was an important explorer of North America who increased Europeans' knowledge of the world.

In 1607 Henry Hudson sailed in a small ship called the *Hopewell* from England to the icy waters around Greenland and Spitsbergen. His aim was to find a route to Asia via the North Pole. Hudson sailed closer to the North Pole than any explorer before him, but had to turn back. The next year he tried again, but without success.

In 1609 the Dutch East India Company trading organization paid Hudson to make another attempt to find a northern passage to Asia. On this occasion his ship, *Half Moon*, reached what is now New York State and sailed up the river that is now named the Hudson. The crew of the *Half Moon* encountered native peoples and claimed the area for Holland.

The following year, in the English ship *Discovery*, Hudson went past Greenland to the bay now named for him. Winter arrived, and the ship got stuck in the ice in James Bay. In the spring Hudson wanted to carry on westward, but his men wanted to return to England. On June 23, 1611, they forced Hudson, his son John, and a few other loyal men into a little boat and set them adrift without food or water. They were never heard from again.

SEE ALSO: Exploration and Explorers

Hudson has a bay, a river, and a strait in North America named for him.

✱ HUMAN BODY

People often compare the human body to a machine, but it can do far more than the most complicated machine ever built.

The human body is made of elements—chemicals that cannot be broken down into simpler substances. The most common elements are carbon, hydrogen, nitrogen, and oxygen. Many of the body's elements join together as compounds. The main compounds in the body are water, proteins, nucleic acids, carbohydrates, and lipids, or fats. Carbohydrates provide the energy for the body's activities. Lipids store fuel and build new cells. Some proteins also build cells, while others take part in chemical reactions. Nucleic acids carry genetic instructions from one generation to the next.

The basic unit of all living things is the cell. Most cells join with other cells to make tissue. There are four main types of tissue: epithelial tissue, which covers the body's surface; connective tissue, which helps join parts of the body; muscle tissue, which makes movement possible; and nervous tissue, which carries nerve signals.

Different kinds of tissue are combined in the body's organs—body parts that perform a specific job. The brain, heart, liver, and lungs are major organs. The skin is an organ that protects the body from air, water, dirt, and germs.

(continued on page 307)

BODY SYSTEMS

SKELETAL SYSTEM

The skeleton provides strength and support for the body and protects soft organs. Bones and muscles allow body parts to move.

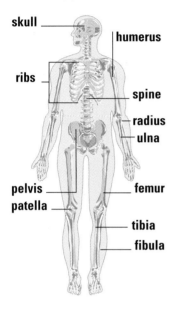

skull
humerus
ribs
spine
radius
ulna
pelvis
patella
femur
tibia
fibula

CIRCULATORY SYSTEM

The heart pumps blood containing oxygen through arteries. Used blood containing carbon dioxide returns through veins.

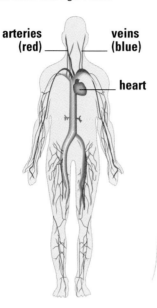

arteries (red)
veins (blue)
heart

RESPIRATORY SYSTEM

The respiratory system provides cells with oxygen so they can produce energy and takes away waste carbon dioxide.

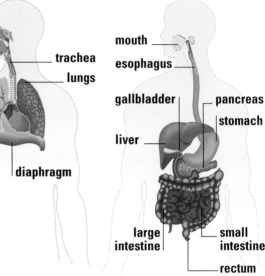

nose
mouth
trachea
lungs
diaphragm

DIGESTIVE SYSTEM

The digestive system breaks down food and converts it into chemicals that the body uses for nourishment; waste is expelled.

mouth
esophagus
gallbladder
pancreas
stomach
liver
large intestine
small intestine
rectum

URINARY SYSTEM

In order to function properly, the body must get rid of its waste. Most of the liquid waste is removed by the urinary system as urine.

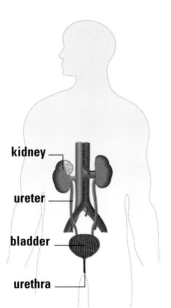

kidney
ureter
bladder
urethra

REPRODUCTIVE SYSTEM

A male reproductive cell, called a sperm, joins with a female reproductive cell, called an ovum, to produce a new human being.

fallopian tube
ovary
uterus
vagina

Female

testicle
penis

Male

ENDOCRINE SYSTEM

The endocrine system produces powerful chemical messengers called hormones. They keep the body working normally.

hypothalamus
pituitary gland
thyroid gland
adrenal glands
pancreas
sex glands

Male   **Female**

MUSCULAR SYSTEM

The body has more than 600 muscles. Muscles move the bones. A simple movement like taking a step requires 200 muscles.

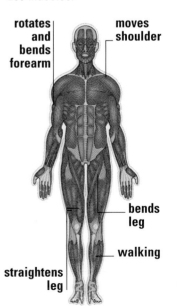

rotates and bends forearm
moves shoulder
bends leg
walking
straightens leg

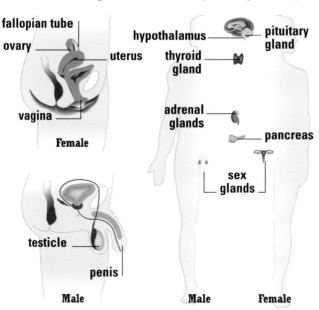

The skeletal system supports the body and protects delicate organs. Some organs work together as systems (see page 306). The various systems perform so well because the body has ways to communicate. For example, the nervous system consists of the brain, nerves, and spinal cord. The endocrine system produces chemicals that work with the nerves to control many body functions.

Blood; Brain and Nervous System; Cells; Diseases; Ears and Hearing; Elements; Endocrine System; Eyes and Vision; Genetics; Health; Hearing; Heart and Circulatory System; Lungs and Respiratory System; Medicine; Muscular System; Reproductive System; Skeletal System; Surgery; Taste and Smell; Teeth; Tongue and Speech; Touch

THE SENSES

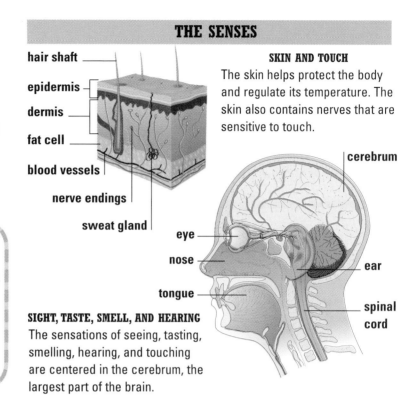

hair shaft
epidermis
dermis
fat cell
blood vessels
nerve endings
sweat gland

SKIN AND TOUCH
The skin helps protect the body and regulate its temperature. The skin also contains nerves that are sensitive to touch.

cerebrum

eye
nose
tongue

ear

spinal cord

SIGHT, TASTE, SMELL, AND HEARING
The sensations of seeing, tasting, smelling, hearing, and touching are centered in the cerebrum, the largest part of the brain.

✴ HUMAN RIGHTS

Human rights are basic freedoms that all people possess. These rights are often abused by repressive governments and in times of war and social unrest.

Human rights include civil and political rights, such as freedom of speech and the right to vote, and economic and social rights, such as the right to work or obtain an education. The idea that all people have rights—regardless of age, nationality, sex, race, religion, or economic status—is relatively new.

Throughout most of history, rights were viewed as privileges granted to people by their rulers. The notion that people are born with natural rights developed only in the 1600s. It formed the basis for the English Bill of Rights and for early state constitutions in America. It was also at the center of the American Declaration

of Independence, which says that "all Men are ... endowed by their Creator with certain unalienable rights" and that "among these are Life, Liberty, and the Pursuit of Happiness."

The idea of individual rights is central to democratic systems of government. A series of terrible events in the first half of the 20th century gave rise to the view that people worldwide should be entitled to the same basic rights, no matter what form of government they live under. These events included political executions in the Soviet Union in the

▲
Daw Aung San Suu Kyi campaigns for human rights in Myanmar.

1930s and the murder of millions of Jews in Nazi concentration camps during World War II (1939–45). Among the charges brought against those responsible for wartime atrocities were "crimes against humanity," a new category of offenses committed against civilians.

Human rights organizations

When the United Nations was founded in the 1940s, one of its main goals was to protect human rights. A committee drew up an international bill of rights, called the Universal Declaration of Human Rights. This sets standards for human rights, but the United Nations has no way to enforce them. Interests such as national security and trade sometimes cause countries to overlook abuses of human rights by governments of other countries.

In 1961 a British attorney named Peter Benenson recognized that governments are not always the best groups to defend human rights. He founded Amnesty International, an organization that now has more than one million members around the world. Amnesty International organizes protests on behalf of victims of torture, political imprisonment, and other violations of rights. It also issues reports on the abuses of rights that continue worldwide.

SEE ALSO: Bill of Rights; Citizenship; Civil Rights; Constitution, United States; Declaration of Independence; Holocaust; Nobel Prize; United Nations; Women's Rights; World War II

* HUNGARY

Hungary is a small nation in east central Europe. The native Hungarians, or Magyars, have a different language and culture from any of their neighbors.

Hungary's national flag

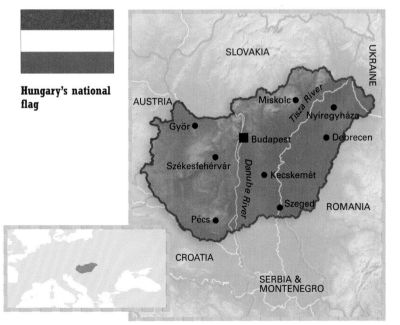

Land and climate

Hungary is divided into two lowland regions, the Great and Little Plains. The Danube River crosses the entire country. The climate is humid and warmer than most of Hungary's neighboring countries.

People and economy

Almost all Hungarian people are Magyars. Other, smaller ethnic groups include Roma (gypsies). Hungary lost two-thirds of its land after World War I (1914–18). As a result, there are large Hungarian minorities in neighboring countries. The Nazis killed most Hungarian Jews during World War II (1939–45). Hungarian is closer to some northern European languages than to those of neighbor states.

KEY FACTS

OFFICIAL NAME:
Republic of Hungary

AREA:
359,919 sq. mi.
(932,190 sq. km)

POPULATION:
10,036,000

**CAPITAL &
LARGEST CITY:**
Budapest

**MAJOR
RELIGIONS:**
Roman Catholicism,
Protestantism

**MAJOR
LANGUAGE:**
Magyar (Hungarian)

CURRENCY:
Forint

Manufacturing employs one-quarter of the population. Agriculture also plays a vital role in the economy.

History

In A.D. 896 a warlike people called the Magyars settled in the Danube basin, the heart of present-day Hungary. They soon dominated the neighboring region. Hungary united with Croatia in 1091 and became the strongest state in east central Europe. The Mongols invaded in 1241, and in 1526 the Turks defeated the Hungarian army at the battle of Mohács. Austria drove out the Turks in the 17th century and took control of the country. An agreement in 1867 gave Hungary its own parliament, but the Austrian emperor ruled as monarch of both countries.

Hungary fought on the side of Germany during both world wars. A Communist government took power in 1948. In 1956 a popular uprising promised reforms, but it was crushed by Soviet troops. János Kádár then led Hungary until 1988. In 1989 most Eastern European countries broke away from Soviet control. Hungary was among them, and free elections were held in 1990, the first in 45 years.

SEE ALSO:
Austria;
Communism;
Eastern
Europe;
Europe;
World War II

✳ HURRICANES AND TYPHOONS

Hurricanes—known as typhoons in Asia—are violent storms, with fast, rain-bearing winds. They occur in many parts of the world and are very destructive.

Hurricanes begin over tropical seas, usually in late summer and early fall along the eastern coast of North America and in the Caribbean. They can happen at any time of year in the Pacific Ocean.

Hurricanes need two "fuels" to start them and keep them going: moist air and heat. As the surface of the ocean heats up, water evaporates into the air. The air above the ocean then becomes moist.

In certain conditions, the warm, moist air begins to form a column. Surrounding air starts to rush toward the column, forming

▶
A man sits near a flooded street in northern Honduras, after Hurricane Mitch in 1998.

a spiral around it. The whole system of air—the column of rising air surrounded by spiraling air—is called a cyclone. As the column of air gets warmer, the winds pick up speed. If they reach more than 74 mph (119 kph), the storm is called a hurricane. Hurricanes often extend up to 500 miles (800 km) in width. Some last a few hours; some as long as two weeks. The average life of a hurricane is six days.

Damage

Hurricanes cause massive damage. At sea, the winds build up waves to a height of 40 ft. (12 m). Hurricane winds of over 100 mph (160 kph) are common. In 1998 Hurricane Mitch killed an estimated 10,000 people and caused over $5 billion worth of damage in Central America.

The greatest hurricane damage on land is from floods. Heavy rains cause rivers to swell and overflow. Strong winds produce another kind of flooding. The wind piles up the surface water of the ocean into high waves and drives them toward the shore, where they may flood the land.

> **DID YOU KNOW?**
>
> In 1950 meteorologists, who study weather, began naming hurricanes. For many years, the names were all female; now they use male names as well. The first storm of the season is given a name starting with *A*. The names continue through the alphabet until the season is over. New names are used every year to avoid confusion.

SEE ALSO:
Floods;
Tornadoes;
Weather

* HURSTON, ZORA NEALE (1891–1960)
Zora Neale Hurston wrote about the lives and folklore of African Americans in the rural South.

A photograph of Zora Neale Hurston taken in Florida in 1935.

Zora Neale Hurston was born in 1891 in Notasulga, Alabama, although during her life she claimed the date to have been 1903, and the place Eatonville, Florida. She left home to join a traveling theater company. She returned to her studies in New York and became part of the "Harlem Renaissance" literary scene, mixing with writers such as Langston Hughes.

Hurston began taking classes in anthropology (the study of human cultures). She was especially interested in folklore, and after graduation she traveled all over the South to do research. She published her findings in *Mules and Men* (1935). Her most famous book is the novel *Their Eyes Were Watching God* (1937), which tells the story of a young African American woman in Eatonville. In 1942 she published her autobiography, *Dust Tracks on a Road*.

After the late 1940s, some people thought Hurston's ideas were too conservative, and her writing fell from fashion. She struggled to make a living as a teacher and domestic servant. When she died in 1960, her work was mostly forgotten. But recent efforts by authors such as Alice Walker have restored Hurston's position as an important African American writer.

SEE ALSO: African Americans; Literature

☀ ICELAND

Iceland is an island nation in the North Atlantic Ocean. Despite its name, much of Iceland is green and relatively warm.

Iceland's national flag

Land and climate

During the Ice Age, all of Iceland was covered by a sheet of glacial ice that eroded away the rock to form Iceland's many fjords and mountain ridges. The glaciers gradually retreated as the climate grew warmer, but 12 percent of Iceland is still hidden by glaciers. The largest of them, Vatnajökull, covers an area nearly three times the size of the state of Rhode Island. The island was formed by volcanic activity. Volcanic energy still provides natural hot water and fuels hot springs called geysers. The average temperature in December is around 32°F (0°C); in June it is 52°F (11°C).

People and economy

The Icelandic people are descendants of Scandinavian Vikings who settled the island in the 800s, and of Celtic people from Ireland. The Icelandic language is similar to Old Norse, and has changed little over the centuries.

Iceland's economy is based on fish and fish processing.

History

Iceland was named by the Norwegian Floki Vilgerdarson, around the year A.D. 860. The first permanent settler was Ingólfur Arnarson, who set up a farm in what is now the capital city of Reykjavik in 874. Other settlers followed from Norway, and they established the world's first democratic parliament, the Althing. Civil war broke out in the 1100s, and the Icelanders accepted Norwegian rule in 1262. Denmark took over Norway in 1380 and ruled Iceland for more than 500 years. Iceland became independent in 1918. In 1944 it became a republic.

OFFICIAL NAME:
Republic of Iceland

AREA:
39,769 sq. mi.
(103,000 sq. km)

POPULATION:
281,000

CAPITAL & LARGEST CITY:
Reykjavík

MAJOR RELIGION:
Evangelical Lutheranism

MAJOR LANGUAGE:
Icelandic

CURRENCY:
Króna

SEE ALSO:
Europe;
Glaciers;
Scandinavia

Map

Denmark Strait
Greenland Sea
Ísafjördhur
Akureyri
Hofsjökull
Langjökull
Vatnajökull
Akranes
Reykjavík
Keflavík
Mýrdalsjökull
ATLANTIC OCEAN
Vestmannaeyjar

✱ IMMIGRATION

Immigration is the voluntary movement of people from one country to another, usually with the aim of permanent settlement in the new country.

This painting shows the Mayflower, the ship that brought the Pilgrims—very early immigrants to America—from Plymouth, England, to the New World in 1620.

Emigration refers to the movement of people out of a country. When people depart from their homelands for new homes elsewhere in the world, they are called emigrants.

Once they arrive in their new countries, they are called immigrants. People who flee their countries because of threats to their safety are usually called refugees, because they seek refuge in other lands.

The United States has been described as a nation of immigrants. In the little more than 200 years of its existence, it has taken in more than 55 million people, from nearly every corner of the world.

Immigration to the New World

Christopher Columbus's "discovery" of the New World in 1492 led to further exploration and the first European settlements in North America. The first colonists in what would become the United States arrived in the 1600s. Some were adventurers seeking a quick fortune. Others came to be free to worship as they pleased. Most, however, were attracted by the plentiful land and hoped to find better economic opportunities than they could expect at home.

The original English settlers were followed by more British and Germans and smaller numbers of French Huguenots (Protestants), Dutch, Scandinavians, and Swiss. A tiny community of Jews settled in the Dutch settlement of New Amsterdam, later renamed New York.

In the years from 1845 to 1855, nearly 1.5 million Irish immigrants arrived in the United States, fleeing poverty and hunger. During this same period, more than one million Germans came to America to escape the upheaval that followed the unsuccessful 1848 revolutions in Europe.

New wave of immigrants

Up until the 1880s, most immigrants came from western or northern Europe. Beginning in about 1890, however, a second great wave of immigration began. The new immigrants included Italians, Slavs, Greeks, and Eastern European Jews. From 1901 to 1910, nearly

8.8 million people arrived. Many of these new immigrants entered the country at New York City. Between 1892 and 1954, more than 12 million immigrants were received and processed at a government immigration facility on Ellis Island.

Asian immigration

The growth of California as a result of the discovery of gold in 1848, and the need for laborers to build the transcontinental railroad, brought the first immigrants from China to the United States. Japanese immigrants began arriving in the late 1800s and early 1900s. Most of the Japanese, as well as many Chinese, came as contract workers to farms on the West Coast or to plantations in Hawaii. Filipinos and other Asians also arrived in the United States during these years.

Many of these immigrants were received and processed at a government facility on Angel Island in San Francisco Bay. Opened in 1910, it was designed to control the flow of Asian immigrants.

Limiting immigration

Many immigrants were welcomed by the growing young nation. However, others were viewed with suspicion and hostility.

The first laws restricting immigration of a particular ethnic group were aimed at Chinese people. At first they were welcomed as a source of cheap labor, but then other workers began to see their lower wages as a threat to their own livelihood. The second group to be excluded was the Japanese.

In 1921 Congress passed the Quota Act, which limited yearly immigration from any country to a specific total. Exceptions were later made for refugees, but the quota system remained the basis of U.S. immigration law until 1965. Congress then began to give priority to refugees

and people who had special skills or close relatives in the United States. In 1978 Congress decided on an annual number of 290,000 immigrants. (In 1990 this figure was raised to 675,000.) Spouses and children of U.S. citizens were not counted as part of the total.

Illegal immigration

Because immigration has been limited, many people have sought to enter the country illegally. The border between the United States and Mexico, in particular, is so easy to cross that it has proved impossible to halt the flow of Mexicans seeking to come to the United States.

Recent immigrants

The newest immigrants to the United States are mainly Asian and Latin American. Many of the Asian immigrants have come as refugees from Vietnam, Cambodia, and Laos following war and unrest in those regions during the 20th century. Others have come from India, China, the Philippines, and South Korea.

Most of the Latin American immigrants have come from Mexico and from countries in the Caribbean, particularly the Dominican Republic, Jamaica, and Haiti. These newcomers are changing the ethnic makeup of the United States.

▲
Border patrol agents round up people trying to enter the United States illegally across the Mexican border at the Rio Grande.

SEE ALSO:
African Americans;
Asian Americans;
Citizenship;
Colonial America;
Ellis Island;
Hispanic Americans

* INCAS

The Incas were an American Indian people who built a vast and powerful empire in the Andes Mountains of Peru in the 1400s.

This map shows the extent of the Inca Empire at its height in the early 16th century.

SEE ALSO:
Aztecs;
Conquistadors;
Mayans; Peru;
South America

According to legend, the god-man Manco Capac was sent to Earth by his father, the sun. Manco Capac founded the city of Cuzco in Peru, and his descendants became Inca emperors. Eventually the Inca Empire stretched from present-day Ecuador south to central Chile.

Spanish conquerors broke up the Inca Empire in the 1500s. When Francisco Pizarro arrived in 1532, Inca land spanned a distance of 2,500 miles (4,000 km). The huge empire was linked by an impressive network of roads and bridges. The Incas were also famous for their architecture. They cut individual stones to fit together exactly. Many Inca buildings still stand.

How the Incas lived
The Incas lived in villages that were grouped into provinces. All men served as soldiers at some time in their lives. Common foods were corn, potatoes, beans, peppers, and guinea pigs. Religion was based on worship of the sun and other gods. People

The Inca city of Machu Picchu, in the Cordillera Blanca Mountains of Peru, was discovered in 1911.

also worshiped their ancestors. The emperor was seen as all-powerful because he was descended from the sun. Our knowledge of the Incas comes from explorers and missionaries and from written accounts kept by two Incas.

The end of the empire
In 1525 the empire was split by a civil war between the brothers Huáscar and Atahuallpa. Atahuallpa had Huáscar executed. Pizarro took advantage of the confusion and captured Atahuallpa. He agreed to free Atahuallpa for a huge ransom, but instead he had Atahuallpa killed. This was not the end of the Incas. Two leaders, both called Tupac Amaru, led unsuccessful revolts against the Spanish in the 1500s and the 1700s. The Inca language, Quechua, is still spoken by half the Peruvian people.

*INDIANS see→ *NATIVE AMERICANS

✳ INDIAN SUBCONTINENT

The Indian subcontinent is made up of India, Sri Lanka, Pakistan, Nepal, Bhutan, and Bangladesh. The Maldives is also sometimes included.

Land and climate

The Indian subcontinent has three main land divisions—the Himalaya Mountains of the north; the lowland plains of the Indus, Ganges, and Brahmaputra rivers; and the Deccan plateau of southern India.

Pakistan contains much of the Indus River. Bangladesh is a low-lying land dominated by the delta (mouth) of the Ganges and Brahmaputra rivers. Nepal and Bhutan lie along the southern slopes of the Himalaya Mountains. Sri Lanka lies off India's southern tip. The Maldives, a small island nation in the Indian Ocean, is sometimes considered to be part of the subcontinent. Forests cover one-fifth of India and much of Bangladesh and Sri Lanka.

Temperatures vary widely from north to south. Intense summer heat brings the monsoon wind, and with it comes heavy rainfall. The monsoon winds move across the subcontinent to the Indian Ocean. Low-lying Bangladesh suffers from tropical storms and flooding, which destroy crops and take many lives. The highlands of Bhutan and Nepal are bitterly cold in winter, with heavy snows.

Plants and animals

The varied plant life of the Indian subcontinent includes bamboo, jasmine, henna, and hemp. Sri Lanka has some of the world's rarest and most beautiful plants, including orchids, hibiscus, and poinsettia. The subcontinent has a wide variety of wild and domesticated animals. Large mammals include the Bengal tiger, the Indian rhinoceros, and the Indian elephant. There are monkeys, crocodiles, and snakes, such as the Indian cobra and python. The water buffalo, used to plow rice fields, is the most important domesticated animal.

People

The subcontinent is home to many different peoples and languages. In India, over four-fifths of the population follow the Hindu religion. The rest of the population are mainly Muslims, followers of Islam. The people of Bangladesh and Pakistan are mostly Muslim. In Sri Lanka the Sinhalese people are Buddhist; the Tamil people are Hindu. The people of Nepal are mainly Hindu. In Bhutan the majority follow Buddhism, and the remainder are Hindu.

Economy

Across the Indian subcontinent, nearly three-quarters of the people make their living from the land. Rice, wheat, sugarcane, cotton, tea, rubber, coffee, coconuts, and spices are important crops and are still largely grown by hand throughout the region.

Industry is expanding rapidly, especially in textiles, food products, and modern machinery. Tourism is an important part of

The Taj Mahal, India, was built in the 1600s by an emperor as a tomb for his wife.

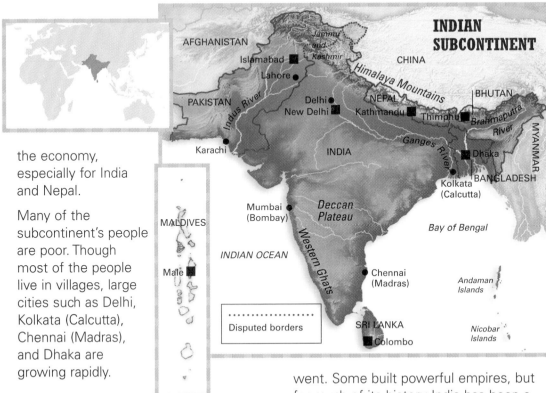

INDIAN SUBCONTINENT

AFGHANISTAN

Jammu and Kashmir

Islamabad

CHINA

Lahore

Himalaya Mountains

PAKISTAN

Indus River

Delhi
New Delhi

NEPAL

BHUTAN

Kathmandu

Thimphu

Brahmaputra River

Karachi

INDIA

Ganges River

Dhaka

MYANMAR

BANGLADESH

Kolkata
(Calcutta)

Mumbai
(Bombay)

Deccan
Plateau

MALDIVES

Western Ghats

Bay of Bengal

INDIAN OCEAN

Male

Chennai
(Madras)

Andaman
Islands

Disputed borders

SRI LANKA

Colombo

Nicobar
Islands

the economy, especially for India and Nepal.

Many of the subcontinent's people are poor. Though most of the people live in villages, large cities such as Delhi, Kolkata (Calcutta), Chennai (Madras), and Dhaka are growing rapidly.

History

One of the world's earliest civilizations developed in the valley of the Indus River more than 4,500 years ago. The area was in northwestern India, but is now part of Pakistan. The remains of two large cities have been found there.

As the centuries passed, invaders settled in the north and west of India, and generations of Indian rulers came and

went. Some built powerful empires, but for much of its history India has been a collection of small kingdoms and states.

In the 1600s, there was a strong Muslim influence under the Mogul emperors. By the 1700s, Portuguese, Dutch, French, and British traders had settled on India's west coast, and in 1877 India became part of

Plantation workers pick tea in Sri Lanka. Tea is also an important crop in Bangladesh and India.

A typical busy street in Dhaka, Bangladesh. Dhaka is the capital and largest city in the country. The city has many historic buildings. As well as being a cultural center, Dhaka is the country's main industrial area.

the British Empire. The Indians rebelled against British rule—first with weapons and then with politics. Indians finally won independence under the leadership of Mohandas Gandhi. In 1947 the British withdrew from India. At the same time, they created the state of Pakistan as a new home for India's Muslims. Ever since, India and Pakistan have fought for ownership of Kashmir, a valley on their border. In 1972 India helped turn the eastern part of Pakistan into what is now Bangladesh. Bangladesh means "Land of the Bengalis." Most of the people in Bangladesh are Bengalis who are related to the Bengalis in neighboring India.

Sri Lanka has also been torn apart by civil war between the minority Tamils, who are Hindu, and the majority Sinhalese, who are mainly Buddhist. The Tamils want their own homeland in northeastern Sri Lanka.

KEY FACTS

AREA:
1,722,145 sq. mi.
(4,460,355 sq. km)

POPULATION:
1,344,467,000

COUNTRIES:
7 (including
Maldives)

**LARGEST
COUNTRY:**
India

**SMALLEST
COUNTRY:**
Maldives

RELIGIONS:
Hinduism,
Buddhism, Islam,
Christianity,
Sikhism, Jainism

LANGUAGES:
Many, including
Hindi, Urdu, Bengali,
Sinhala, Tamil,
Dzongkha, Nepali,
English

SEE ALSO: Ancient Civilizations; Buddhism; Floods; Gandhi, Mohandas; Hinduism; Islam

✱ INDONESIA

Indonesia is a nation made up of thousands of islands that form a long, curving line between the mainland of Southeast Asia and Australia.

Indonesia's national flag

Land and climate

Indonesia's 13,700 islands stretch for about 3,500 miles (5,640 km) from Sumatra in the west to Irian Jaya, the western part of the island of New Guinea. Between Sulawesi and New Guinea are the Moluccas, or Spice Islands—famous for their cloves, nutmeg, and other spices.

The equator runs through Indonesia. The climate is hot and humid, with high seasonal rainfall. Thick rain forests blanket some islands, though many have been cut for lumber or burned to clear land.

People

More than half of Indonesia's huge population lives on Java. Nearly half of all Indonesians work on small farms. About 90 percent follow the religion of Islam, though most people on the island of Bali are Hindus.

KEY FACTS

OFFICIAL NAME:
Republic of Indonesia

AREA:
735,309 sq. mi. (1,904,450 sq. km)

POPULATION:
212,107,000

CAPITAL & LARGEST CITY:
Jakarta

MAJOR RELIGIONS:
Islam, Christianity, Hinduism, Buddhism

MAJOR LANGUAGE:
Bahasa Indonesia

CURRENCY:
Rupiah

History

Some of the earliest human beings lived in Indonesia. Indian traders and priests from Asia came to Sumatra and Java around A.D.100. They brought Buddhism and Hinduism. Islam reached the area in 1100. From the 1500s, European traders came to the islands. By the 1800s, the Dutch controlled Indonesia. In 1945 Indonesia claimed its independence. A bitter war followed; the Dutch did not hand over power until 1949. In recent times, Indonesia has been troubled by revolts against the government and by economic problems.

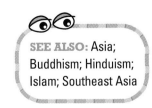

SEE ALSO: Asia; Buddhism; Hinduism; Islam; Southeast Asia

✳ INDUSTRIAL REVOLUTION

The invention of many new machines in the 1700s changed the way that goods were produced and affected how people lived and worked.

The Industrial Revolution began in England in the 1760s. Until that time, all kinds of goods, from clothing to furniture, were made by hand by skilled craft workers. The first leap forward came in about 1764, when James Hargreaves invented the spinning jenny. This was a machine that spun eight threads of yarn at once, doing the work of eight people.

New power

In about 1769, Richard Arkwright had the idea of harnessing the new spinning jenny to a waterwheel to draw power from the energy of a river's flow. He built textile plants, called mills, beside rivers. The mills brought machines and workers together under one roof; they were the first manufacturing plants.

Coal was in high demand in order to make iron, but the coal mines kept flooding. In 1712 Thomas Newcomen designed a steam engine that pumped water out of the mines. In 1769 James Watt patented a more efficient engine that proved to be a far better source of energy than waterwheels in the textile mills.

Rush to the cities

Factories no longer had to be built close to streams or rivers. They began to appear in cities, where the labor supply was more plentiful. Untrained farm laborers soon flocked to urban areas to work. Because the new textile machines were so easy to operate, factory owners could employ the cheapest possible labor, including young children. The laborers worked long hours for very little money and lived in crowded, dirty housing.

American developments

The Industrial Revolution arrived later in the United States. In 1789 an English textile worker named Samuel Slater arrived in New York and set up textile plants. In 1793 the American Eli Whitney invented the cotton gin, a machine that could rapidly comb cotton fibers and prepare them for the textile mills. People began to plant cotton all across the South.

The Industrial Revolution affected many other kinds of manufacturing. Ironworks and steel mills were built to make tools, machines, engines, and railroad tracks. England, where it all began, became one of the world's most powerful nations.

The Coalbrookdale foundry, England, was started in 1709. It pioneered the technique of melting iron with coke, a modified type of coal.

SEE ALSO: Engines; Fabrics and Cloth; Inventors and Inventions; Manufacturing; Trade

✳ INSECTS

Insects are the largest group of animals in the world. There are about one million known species, and more are discovered every year.

Insects have been on Earth for over 350 million years. There are more species of insect than all other species of living creatures put together. The scientific study of insects is called entomology.

Adult insects always have six legs, three on each side of the body. An insect's body is made up of three parts—a head, a thorax, and an abdomen. The thorax is the middle part of the body, and the abdomen is the lowest part.

The praying mantis is a carnivorous (meat-eating) insect that catches and chews its prey.

All insects have a pair of antennae (singular, *antenna*), or feelers, at the front of the head. They usually have one or two pairs of wings. The wings and the legs are attached to the thorax. Most insects have a tough outer shell. The shell is waterproof and also prevents the insect from drying out in extreme heat.

Metamorphosis

A few insects give birth to live young, but most lay eggs. Some insects lay one egg at a time. Others, like termites, can lay more than 10,000 eggs in a day. Most insects go through several forms as they become adults. This is called metamorphosis, from the Greek meaning "change in shape." Ants, bees, beetles, butterflies, moths, and wasps all undergo this process. There are four stages in the process: an egg is laid; the egg hatches into a wormlike larva; the larva eats till grown, then begins a resting stage as a pupa; the adult insect emerges when its body is fully developed.

Some insects, including cicadas, crickets, and dragonflies, do not go through a full metamorphosis. When the young hatch from the eggs, they look like smaller versions of the adults, but with no wings. As they grow, they shed their skin when it becomes too tight and grow a new one—this process is known as molting. Those that are going to fly develop wings.

Senses

Insects feel, smell, and taste with their antennae. Some use their antennae to hear. Antennae are also used to test for humidity or temperature. Using their antennae, insects can smell food and identify the right plants on which to lay their eggs.

Insects taste with tiny hairs on the antennae and mouth. Many insects can also taste with their feet. Hairs on the antennae, outer shell, and feet enable insects to feel. Some insects, such as flies, can feel with their wings.

Most insects have an eye on each side of the head. This helps them see in all directions. Plant-eating insects can see some colors. Most insects also have extra eyes, called ocelli, that are probably for sensing light and dark.

Insects have "ears" on different parts of their bodies. A grasshopper's ears are on its abdomen. Other insects have ears near the tips of the antennae. Insects with the best hearing are those that make sounds, such as cicadas.

The eyes of a fly have thousands of lenses that enable it to detect the slightest movement.

Eating

Insects eat different things in different ways. Some insects eat other insects. The ladybug beetle feeds on aphids (insects that suck the juice from plants). The praying mantis is sometimes a cannibal—after mating, the female eats the male. Dragonflies feed mainly on mosquitoes and gnats. Mosquitoes suck blood from other animals and can pass on diseases, such as malaria. Bees and most butterflies and moths take nectar and pollen from plants. The eating habits of some insects cause problems for humans. Termites can destroy wooden buildings with their powerful jaws. Locusts and Colorado beetles destroy crops.

Movement

When an insect walks, it moves three legs forward at the same time. They are the front and hind legs on one side and the middle leg on the other. This way the insect is always resting on at least three of its legs. Most insect legs end in a pair of claws and a sticky pad to grip surfaces.

Flying insects have very thin wings that look like cellophane. Many insects can move their wings at great speed. A housefly's wings beat about 345 times a second. Hawkmoths and dragonflies can fly at over 30 mph (48 kph).

AMAZING FACTS !

Some beetles can lift 300 times their own weight.

Adult mayflies live for only a few hours. However, some queen termites can live for up to 50 years.

Ants live together in organized communities, or colonies. Some ants live in colonies that contain thousands or even millions of members.

SEE ALSO: Animals; Butterflies and Moths

✳ INTERNET

The Internet is the biggest and most important computer network in the world. In 2002 it was used by an estimated 561 million people.

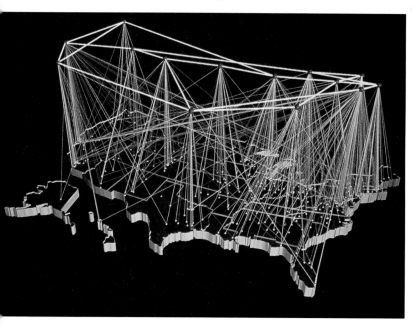

▲
A diagram showing the flow of information traffic over one computer network in the United States during one month. Each main center serves numerous regional users.

The first computers worked in isolation. It was not until the 1960s that they were linked into networks. At first this was on a small scale, from room to room. In the 1960s, the Advanced Research Projects Agency (ARPA), a branch of the U.S. military, developed a system that would eventually be able to connect many networks thousands of miles apart.

At first ARPA wanted a system that would let computers exchange information even if some of them had been damaged by enemy attack. In 1969 their experimental network—ARPANET—linked the University of California at both Los Angeles and Santa Barbara, Stanford Research Institute, and the University of Utah in Salt Lake City. Over the years, other computers in the United States and abroad began to connect to this system, and what is now known as the Internet grew and grew.

For the next 20 years, use of the Internet was restricted almost exclusively to scientists and other professionals. By the 1990s, the cost of computers had greatly dropped, and they were affordable by more people than ever before. As a result, in the last decade of the 20th century the number of people accessing the Internet worldwide probably doubled every 10 months. By 2000 the Internet had reached almost every country in the world, although some countries passed laws to ban it.

What is the Internet?

The Internet is made of thousands of computer networks connected by special computers called routers. Computers can be linked to the Internet by telephone lines, fiber-optic cables, and satellite links. Software called transmission control protocol or Internet protocol (TCP/IP) lets recipients read messages from senders.

E-mail

Ever since the mid-1970s, most of the traffic on the Internet has been communication between individuals by electronic messages (e-mail).

Personal computer
At your home or school.

Internet Service Provider (ISP)
You log on to the Internet using this service.

A typical e-mail address consists of the user's name—for example, jsmith—followed by the "at" symbol (@) and the domain name of the user's computer or local network. The five basic domains are government (abbreviated gov), military (mil), educational (edu), commercial (com), and nonprofit organizations (org). Every country apart from the United States has its own identification letter or letters—for example, "uk" for United Kingdom. This makes up the last part of the address—for example, jsmith@pro-net.co.uk. There is no period at the end of an e-mail address.

World Wide Web

In 1989 the Englishman Tim Berners-Lee invented the World Wide Web. The Web enables any computer with the appropriate software to understand information with instructions written in hypertext markup language (HTML). Each document on the Web has its own unique address, called a uniform resource locator (URL). Today people can access online pictures, sounds, music, and movies, as well as text. Web documents often include links to other documents on the Web. Internet users can browse or surf the Web to get information on almost any subject, and there are many sites on which they can buy goods or enter chatrooms.

Search engines

A problem with the Internet and the World Wide Web has been the huge quantity of information available. Tools called search engines make the information more manageable. People use search engines by typing in key words about their chosen subject; a list of sites that may help them then appears on screen.

No one owns the Internet, and anyone can put up a website. Some sites are controlled, but most are not. This means that in addition to the wealth of valuable information that can be found on the net, there are also sites that are misleading, out of date, incorrect, or even harmful and criminal.

SEE ALSO:
Communication;
Computers;
Media;
Technology

Satellite link
Information can be sent across the world without using telephone wires.

Personal computer
People all over the world can be looking at the same website as you.

Backbone computer
It deals with a lot of websites and information.

Website server
All the pictures, text, and sound files for the website you are looking at are stored here.

Telephone cables
Most of the Internet is joined through telephone wires.

The Internet connects users worldwide.

✳ INVENTORS AND INVENTIONS

An invention is a new and unique technical or scientific solution to a specific problem. Without inventions there would be no progress.

▲ The invention of wheeled vehicles revolutionized transportation— people no longer had to drag or carry loads. This panel, showing a Sumerian horse-drawn cart, dates from about 2500 B.C.

An invention is different from a discovery. Finding a new metal is a discovery; making a new machine is an invention.

Until the invention of paper and printing, knowledge of new technology spread very slowly, and things were often invented or reinvented in different places and at different times. Often historians have no way of knowing who invented a particular thing or when it was invented. Although today we think of inventors as specific individuals, in the past new inventions often came about when many individuals made small improvements to things.

Earliest inventions

Some of the earliest inventions were wooden or stone tools for cutting down trees and killing animals to eat. Later metal tools were invented. The wheel was invented in about 3500–3000 B.C., and people or animals no longer had to carry loads. At about the same time, writing was invented, which meant that people could keep permanent records.

Another great advance was made when people learned to use the energy of natural forces, such as wind and running water. The waterwheel, invented about 2,000 years ago, was the first source of energy that did not rely on muscle power.

Printing using woodblocks was invented by the Chinese around A.D. 700. The

▶ This painting shows a steam engine pumping water from a coal mine in England during the 1700s.

FAMOUS INVENTORS

These are just a few of the people who have become known for their inventions. The "see also" box indicates entries on some others.

Archimedes (about 287–212 B.C.)
Ancient Greek mathematician who invented many things, including a device called the Archimedes' screw, for raising water.

Harrison, John (1693–1776)
English clockmaker who perfected the marine chronometer, a clock so accurate that sailors could calculate their position correctly.

Watt, James (1736–1819)
Scottish instrument maker whose steam engine (patented 1769) was used throughout the mills and factories of the Industrial Revolution.

Daguerre, Louis (Louis-Jacques-Mandé) (1789–1851)
French painter who perfected permanent photographs on silver-coated copper plates—daguerreotypes—in 1839.

Faraday, Michael (1791–1867)
English scientist who discovered that electricity was present in a wire moving close to a magnet, leading to the invention of the electric generator.

Morse, Samuel (Finley Breese) (1791–1872)
American inventor of the electric telegraph, used to send long-distance messages, and an alphabet system of dots and dashes called the Morse code.

and sell the invention or to profit from it by allowing another person or company to sell or use it.

Scientific inventions

The 17th and 18th centuries saw many scientific inventions. The telescope enabled people to study the stars and planets, while the microscope was important for the study of biology. The invention of the steam engine made large quantities of power available. Some of the major discoveries of the early 19th century had to do with electricity. In 1800 an Italian scientist, Alessandro Volta, invented the electric battery, from which an electric current could be obtained. The battery was followed by the electric generator and the lightbulb.

Increased technical knowledge brought many new inventions: the electric telegraph in 1837, the telephone in 1876, and the wireless telegraph (forerunner of the radio) in 1895. The invention of the internal-combustion engine led to automobiles and airplanes. From 1957 communications satellites began to relay telephone calls and television signals worldwide.

Michael Faraday was a chemist and a physicist. He conducted pioneering experiments in electricity and magnetism.

invention of movable type—a more flexible system using metal blocks—in Germany in the 15th century meant that books and knowledge became more widely available.

To safeguard an invention or discovery, many inventors file a patent. A patent is the rights given by a government to an inventor. They include the right to make

SEE ALSO: Aircraft; Ancient Civilizations; Astronomy; Bell, Alexander Graham; Bicycles and Motorcycles; Cars; Communication; Computers; Edison, Thomas Alva; Electricity; Electronics; Engines; Galilei, Galileo; Industrial Revolution; Machines; Magnetism; Microscopes; Photography; Printing; Radio; Robots; Scientific Instruments; Sound Recording; Technology; Telecommunications; Telephones; Telescopes; Television; Video Recording; Wright, Orville and Wilbur; X-rays

*IRAN

Iran, once known as Persia, is a country in southwest Asia. It was long ruled by shahs, or kings, but since 1979 it has been an Islamic republic.

Iran's national flag

Land and climate

Most of Iran is a vast plateau, with mountain ranges on three sides. The east central plateau is desert. The country borders the Persian Gulf, the Arabian Sea, and the Caspian Sea. It has very few rivers, and most of the lakes contain salt water. The climate is generally dry.

People

Most Iranians are descendants of Aryan people who moved to the area from Central Asia before 1000 B.C. The official language is Persian, or Farsi. It is written in Arabic script, but is related to European languages. There are also communities of Arabs, Kurds, Turks, and other ethnic groups. The majority of Iranians are Muslims, who follow Islam.

Economy

Iran has traditionally been an agricultural country, but today its economy depends on the production of petroleum and natural gas. Oil and petrochemicals make up more than 85 percent of Iran's exports.

History

Early rulers of what is now Iran included Cyrus II and Darius I, who created a great Persian empire under the Achaemenid dynasty. The dynasty fell to Alexander the Great in 330 B.C.

In A.D. 642 Arab warriors invaded Persia, bringing the new Muslim faith. For the next 800 years, the region was controlled by foreign powers. From 1501 Shah Ismail Safavid and his successors created a unified nation that resisted attacks from invaders. The Safavid dynasty ruled until

1736. Between 1796 and 1925, the Turkish Qajar dynasty ruled Persia. The last Qajar shah was overthrown in a military revolt, and Reza Khan became shah. He changed the country's name to Iran. His son, Mohammed Reza, became shah in 1941. He faced opposition from religious leaders and was driven out of Iran in 1979. Iran became an Islamic republic, with Ayatollah Khomeini as head of state. In 1980 Iraq invaded Iran, laying claim to a river that forms part of their shared border. This resulted in a war that lasted eight years. The moderate Mohammad Khatami has been president since 1997, but a power struggle remains between reformers and conservatives.

SEE ALSO: Alexander the Great; Asia; Iraq; Islam; Middle East

KEY FACTS

OFFICIAL NAME:
Islamic Republic of Iran

AREA:
633,945 sq. mi. (1,641,918 sq. km)

POPULATION:
67,702,000

CAPITAL & LARGEST CITY:
Tehran

MAJOR RELIGION:
Islam

MAJOR LANGUAGE:
Persian (Farsi)

CURRENCY:
Rial

✳ IRAQ

Iraq is a country in southwest Asia, on the site of some of the world's earliest civilizations. In recent years, it has been hostile to Western powers.

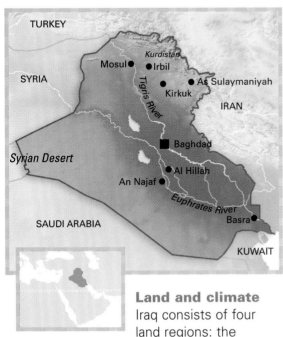

Land and climate

Iraq consists of four land regions: the upper and lower Tigris–Euphrates valleys; the northeastern mountains; and the western uplands. The Tigris and Euphrates rivers provide most of the water, as there is little rain. In summer average temperatures can reach 95°F (35°C).

People and economy

Almost 80 percent of Iraqis are Arabs. This population is split between the two great branches of Islam. Followers of Shi'i Islam make up the majority of Iraqi Muslims. However, the Sunni Muslims of northern Iraq hold political power. The Kurds are the largest minority group. They have long sought their own independent state.

The development of Iraq's oil reserves in the 20th century transformed its economy. But economic sanctions imposed after the Gulf War in 1991 have reduced oil exports.

History

The land now known as Iraq was the site of great empires ruled by the Sumerians, Babylonians, and Assyrians. Between 750 and 1258, Baghdad was an important center of Islamic learning and culture. The area was later ruled by the Mongols and then by the Ottoman Turks. From 1918, after the end of World War I, Britain controlled the region. In 1932 Iraq became independent, and Faisal I was crowned monarch.

In 1958 after a military coup, Iraq became a republic. In 1968 the Baath Party seized power. Saddam Hussein became its leader in 1979. In 1980 Iraq invaded Iran in a border dispute. An eight-year war ensued. In 1990 Iraq invaded its neighbor, Kuwait. The United Nations (UN) imposed sanctions, and when Saddam refused to remove his troops, a U.S.-led force drove the Iraqis out in 1991.

Many people believe that Iraq still holds weapons of mass destruction, against the terms of the Gulf War peace treaty. Iraq allowed UN weapons inspectors into the country at the end of 2002. By early 2003 no chemical weapons had been found. However, the United States, convinced of their existence, led coalition forces into war against Iraq. Saddam Hussein's regime fell three weeks later.

SEE ALSO: Ancient Civilizations; Asia; Iran; Islam; Middle East; Persian Gulf War; United Nations

Iraq's national flag

KEY FACTS

OFFICIAL NAME:
Republic of Iraq

AREA:
169,235 sq. mi.
(438,318 sq. km)

POPULATION:
23,115,000

CAPITAL & LARGEST CITY:
Baghdad

MAJOR RELIGION:
Islam

MAJOR LANGUAGES:
Arabic, Kurdish

CURRENCY:
Iraqi dinar

* IRELAND, REPUBLIC OF

The Republic of Ireland forms the southern part of an island in the North Atlantic Ocean. The northern part—Northern Ireland—is part of the United Kingdom.

Ireland's national flag

SEE ALSO:
Europe;
United Kingdom

Land and climate

The center of Ireland is a plain covered with farm fields and peat bogs. A ring of hills and low mountains surrounds this area. There are many lakes and rivers. Ireland's climate is greatly affected by the surrounding seas. Winters are mild, summers are cool, and, even in the driest months, it often rains.

People and economy

Most Irish people are descended from the ancient Celts, who came from what is now France. Almost everyone speaks English, and Irish Gaelic is spoken in some areas. Irish authors, most of whom write in English, have won fame as novelists, poets, and dramatists. Irish music is popular around the world. The Irish are also sports lovers who enjoy Gaelic football and horse racing.

In the past, Ireland's economy was based on agriculture, but today service industries—especially those related to tourism—bring in more than half of the country's annual income. Irish companies make and export a wide range of goods, including cloth, whiskey, beer, and crystal.

The large amount of rainfall in Ireland makes the countryside very green and has given rise to the nickname "The Emerald Isle."

History

In the fifth century A.D., Saint Patrick introduced Christianity to Ireland. As a result, many monasteries were built, Irish monks introduced Christianity to Europe, and Ireland became a center of learning.

The English first invaded in 1171. From the late 17th century, Protestant English and Scottish settlers governed a Roman Catholic majority. That led to long-running conflict. After a war of independence (1919–21), the island was split into the Irish Free State (now the Republic of Ireland) and Northern Ireland, which is still part of the United Kingdom.

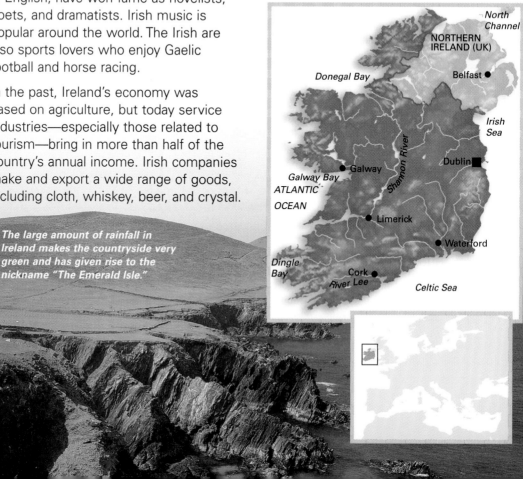

✳ ISLAM

Islam is one of the world's major religions. More than one billion people, called Muslims, follow the teachings of Islam. Muslims believe in Allah.

The Muslim religion is founded on statements, or revelations, that Muslims believe came from Allah through prophets. Those prophets include Abraham, Moses, and Jesus. The most important of all the prophets, however, was Muhammad (about A.D. 570–632).

The prophet Muhammad

Muhammad was born in Mecca, in modern Saudi Arabia. Muslims believe that the archangel Gabriel appeared to him and passed on the teachings of Allah. Muhammad began to preach and attracted many followers. Opponents forced him to flee from Mecca in 622. He went to the city of Medina. His flight is called the *hegira* (migration). It is the starting point of the Islamic calendar. By the time Muhammad died, Islam had become the main religion in Arabia. It soon spread, and today one-fifth of the world's population are Muslims.

Islamic beliefs

The word *Islam* means "submission." Muslims submit to the will of Allah, an all-powerful, loving God. The teachings and laws of Islam are contained in a holy book called the Koran. Other teachings are in the *Hadith*, a collection of stories about the life and sayings of Muhammad.

Islamic law, or *shari'a*, forbids killing, stealing, lying, eating pork, and drinking alcohol. The Muslim also has five key duties, called the five pillars of Islam. *Shahadah* is the profession of faith. Every Muslim must believe that there is one God and that Muhammad is his prophet and messenger. *Salat* is prayer. Muslims must pray five times a day. At noon on Friday, they attend the mosque, the main place of worship. *Zakat* is charity. Muslims must give part of their income to the poor. *Sawm* is fasting. No adult Muslim, apart from pregnant women and the sick, may eat during daylight in the sacred month of Ramadan. The fifth pillar of Islam is *Hajj*, or pilgrimage. All Muslims who can afford to do so must travel to the holy city of Mecca at least once during their life.

A mosque in Washington, D.C. The mosque is the place where Muslims gather for prayer. It also acts as a community center.

SEE ALSO: Calendars; Koran; Religions

329

✳ ISLANDS
An island is a landmass smaller than a continent and completely surrounded by water. Islands vary enormously in size and origin.

Geographers divide islands into two main groups—continental and oceanic. Continental islands were once connected to the mainland. Changes in the earth's crust or sea level caused sections of land to become separated from the main part of a continent. Great Britain is an example of a continental island—it was once part of the mainland of Europe.

Most of the world's islands are oceanic—they were never joined to a continent. Oceanic islands can be volcanic or coral. Volcanic islands are created when lava—liquid rock—erupts beneath the surface of the ocean. The lava cools and becomes solid, and builds up until it rises above sea level. The Hawaiian islands and Iceland are volcanic islands. Coral islands—like those in the South Pacific—are accumulations of tiny sea animals called polyps.

There are other kinds of islands. A tidal island is part of the mainland. When the tide is high, it is cut off and cannot be reached on foot. Barrier islands are made from soil deposited in offshore waters.

Isolation
An island is surrounded by water, so it can be difficult to reach. That means that some islands have unique plant and animal life found nowhere else. When settlers bring new plants and animals with them, they

A coral reef around Vava'u, one of the islands that form the Pacific nation of Tonga.
▼

Keas are the world's only mountain parrot and live only on the South Island of New Zealand. Because thousands were killed in the past, they are now protected.
▼

are in danger of destroying the island's native plants and creatures.

Isolation also makes islands easier to defend. In World War II (1939–45), Germany captured much of continental Europe. But it could not invade the island of Great Britain. Some islands, such as Alcatraz, in California, have been used as prisons because they are hard to escape from. Some small islands are so remote that they have problems with communication. They may not receive food supplies or mail for months because airplanes and boats cannot land there.

SOME IMPORTANT ISLANDS AND ISLAND GROUPS

Aleutian Islands (U.S.)
A group of about 150 volcanic islands that extends about 1,200 miles (1,900 km) southwest from the Alaska Peninsula.

Alexander Archipelago (U.S.)
A chain of more than 1,000 islands off the southeastern coast of Alaska, made up of the summits of submerged mountain ranges.

Borneo
The world's third-largest island, located in the western section of the Pacific Ocean, includes parts of Malaysia and Indonesia and the whole of Brunei.

Canary Islands (Spain)
A group of seven major islands in the North Atlantic Ocean off the northwestern coast of Africa.

Cape Breton Island (Canada)
The island was a separate British colony until 1820, when it was united with Nova Scotia.

Faroe (or Faeroe) Islands (Denmark)
A group of 18 volcanic islands in the North Atlantic Ocean.

Greenland, or Kalaallit Nunaat (Denmark)
The world's largest island is in the North Atlantic Ocean.

Iceland
An island nation in the North Atlantic Ocean.

New Guinea
The second-largest island in the world, in the Pacific Ocean, it is divided between Irian Jaya (Papua), part of Indonesia, in the west, and the nation of Papua New Guinea in the east.

Sicily (Italy)
The largest island in the Mediterranean Sea, it lies just off the southwestern tip of Italy.

SEE ALSO: Australia and New Zealand; Caribbean Islands; Corals and Coral Reefs; Cuba; Endangered Species; Greenland; Iceland; Indonesia; Ireland, Republic of; Jamaica; Japan; Oceans and Seas; Pacific Islands; Philippines; United Kingdom; Volcanoes

✳ ISRAEL

Israel is a small nation on the eastern shore of the Mediterranean Sea in the region known as the Middle East. The modern state was formed in 1948.

Israel's national flag

Land

The center of Israel is a range of hills running north to south. To the east is the valley of the Jordan River. To the west is a coastal plain of varying width. To the south is the Negev Desert.

People and history

About 80 percent of Israel's citizens are Jewish. Many are immigrants from the United States, Eastern Europe, and other areas. The remainder are mostly Arabs. The earliest records of the Jewish people in the area now called Israel date from about 2000 B.C. Over the years, the region, formally called Palestine, was ruled by many other powers. From 1920 to 1948, Palestine was controlled by Britain. During World War II (1939–45), the Nazi Party of Germany killed six million Jews. Many survivors wanted to join the Jews living in Palestine, and Britain supported the idea of a Jewish homeland. On May 14, 1948, David Ben-Gurion (1886–1973) declared the independence of the State of Israel. Within hours neighboring Arab countries, refusing to accept the existence of Israel, attacked the new state. Thousands of Arab Muslims left their homes and land, and traveled to the Gaza Strip and the West Bank. There is still conflict in the region today.

After a war in 1967, Israel occupied the Gaza Strip, the West Bank, and the Golan Heights. The main issue facing Israel today is whether the Palestinians, who make up the majority of the population in the Gaza Strip and the West Bank, should be allowed to form their own state.

SEE ALSO: Asia; Holocaust; Islam; Judaism; Middle East; Palestine; World War II

KEY FACTS

OFFICIAL NAME:
Medinat Yisrael (Hebrew); Dawlat Israel (Arabic)

AREA:
7,876 sq. mi. (20,400 sq. km)

POPULATION:
6,217,000

CAPITAL:
Jerusalem

LARGEST CITY:
Tel Aviv–Jaffa

MAJOR RELIGIONS:
Judaism, Islam, Christianity, Druze

MAJOR LANGUAGES:
Hebrew, Arabic (both official), English

CURRENCY:
Shekel

LEBANON
SYRIA
Mediterranean Sea
GOLAN HEIGHTS
Haifa
Tiberias
Nazareth
Jordan River
WEST BANK
Tel Aviv–Jaffa
Jerusalem
Bethlehem
Dead Sea
GAZA STRIP
Beersheba
JORDAN
Negev
EGYPT
Gulf of Aqaba
Elat

Occupied Territories

✶ ITALY

A country in southern Europe, Italy consists mainly of a long, narrow peninsula shaped like a boot, and many islands, including Sardinia and Sicily.

Land and climate

Italy is dominated by mountains. In the north are the Alps. They rise to heights of between 14,800 and nearly 15,800 ft. (4,500–4,800 m). Another mountain chain, the Apennines, runs from the northwest to the tip of the "boot," in the south. San Marino, one of the world's smallest nations, is located on their eastern slopes.

South of the Alps is the valley of the Po River. It is Italy's largest and most fertile plain, and the site of major cities such as Milan, Turin, Genoa, and Bologna. The cities of Rome and Florence lie on the central plains.

The south is dominated by the great port of Naples. Sardinia and most of Sicily, the more heavily populated of the two islands, are mountainous. The south often has severe earthquakes. Sicily has the highest active volcano in Europe—Mount Etna.

Italy has a generally moderate climate, with regional variations. The Po Valley has damp, warm summers, fairly cold winters with occasional snowfall, and considerable rainfall. In the south and on the islands, winters are cool and rainy, and summers are hot and dry. The mountainous regions on the mainland have the severest winters. Rainfall is heaviest in the north and lightest in the south and on the islands.

Plants and animals

Most of Italy's remaining forests are situated in the north. Trees include fir, larch, oak, beech, and chestnut. Poplars are common in Tuscany (the area around Florence), and olive trees thrive on the lower Apennines. Bears, wild goats, deer, and chamois (a kind of antelope) still live in the mountains.

People and economy

Roman Catholicism is the main religion. Vatican City, the world's smallest country, lies within the city of Rome. It is ruled by the pope, who is the bishop of Rome and head of the Roman Catholic Church.

Before World War II (1939–45), more than half of Italy's workers were employed in agriculture. Today only about one-sixth of the labor force works on the land.

In the 1950s, Italy became one of the founding members of the European Community (or Common Market), an economic union of several western European nations. By the 1970s, Italy had become one of the most powerful industrial nations in Europe. Most industries are located in the north, especially in the triangle bounded by the cities of Turin, Milan, and Genoa.

History

Many legends surround the origins of civilization in Italy, particularly the founding of Rome, but little is actually known about early settlement. The Romans established a republic in about 500 B.C. and built an empire that included much of Europe, northern Africa, and western Asia. The western half of the

Italy's national flag

According to legend, the city of Rome was founded by Romulus. He and his twin brother, Remus, were abandoned by their parents and brought up by a she-wolf.
▼

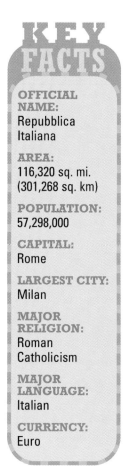

KEY FACTS

OFFICIAL NAME:
Repubblica Italiana

AREA:
116,320 sq. mi.
(301,268 sq. km)

POPULATION:
57,298,000

CAPITAL:
Rome

LARGEST CITY:
Milan

MAJOR RELIGION:
Roman Catholicism

MAJOR LANGUAGE:
Italian

CURRENCY:
Euro

The port of Venice in northeast Italy is built on mud flats and more than 100 islands. Its main thoroughfares are canals.
▷

SEE ALSO:
Byzantine Empire;
Caesar, Julius;
Europe;
Renaissance;
Roman Empire;
World War I;
World War II

The Renaissance, the great rebirth of European culture, began in Italy in the 1300s and lasted to the end of the 1500s.

The areas of land that make up Italy were finally unified between 1859 and 1870. Economic progress was interrupted in 1915, when Italy entered World War I (1914–18). In 1926 Benito Mussolini, leader of the Fascist Party, became dictator (supreme ruler). His alliance with Nazi Germany in World War II (1938–45) left Italy in ruins. Defeat in the war brought an end to fascism and the monarchy. In 1946 Italy became a republic.

Roman Empire collapsed in the fifth century A.D., and power passed to the eastern half of the empire, later known as the Byzantine Empire. The peninsula was broken up into many competing states.

J

✳ JAMAICA

Jamaica is an island nation in the Caribbean Sea, 500 miles (800 km) southeast of the United States.

Land and climate

Jamaica is part of a group of islands known as the Greater Antilles. Much of the country is mountainous, and a limestone plateau covers more than three-quarters of the island. There are many small streams, but few large rivers.

Jamaica has a tropical climate and is sometimes subject to hurricanes. Rainfall is greatest in the Blue Mountains, which can receive up to 150 in. (3,800 mm) of rain in a year.

People

The original inhabitants of Jamaica, the Arawak, died out after European colonization. Today about 90 percent of Jamaicans are descended wholly or partly from the African slaves who worked on sugarcane plantations.

Economy

Jamaica's economy has been weak for many years, with heavy national debts and high unemployment. The trade in illegal drugs has contributed to a growing crime rate. Bauxite accounts for about half of all exports. Tourism is also important for the economy. Reggae music, which began on Jamaica, has raised the country's profile, but little of the money it earns has found its way back to the island.

Jamaica's national flag

History

Christopher Columbus landed in Jamaica in 1494. The Spanish soon settled and brought in African slaves when the native Arawak died from cruelty and disease.

The British took control of the island in the 1600s. They abolished slavery, but many nonwhites still lived in great poverty. Jamaica won a degree of self-government in 1938 and independence in 1962. The country remains in the British Commonwealth and recognizes the British monarch as its head of state.

SEE ALSO: Caribbean Islands; Columbus, Christopher; Slavery

KEY FACTS

AREA:
4,243 sq. mi.
(10,990 sq. km)

POPULATION:
2,583,000

CAPITAL & LARGEST CITY:
Kingston

MAJOR RELIGIONS:
Protestantism, Roman Catholicism

MAJOR LANGUAGE:
English

CURRENCY:
Jamaican dollar

✳ JAPAN

Japan is a nation in the North Pacific Ocean. Its many islands form an arc about 1,500 miles (2,400 km) long off the eastern coast of Asia.

Japan's national flag

Land and climate

The four main islands of Japan are Honshu, Hokkaido, Kyushu, and Shikoku. Honshu has about three-fifths of Japan's land area and is home to four-fifths of its people. Hokkaido, to the north, is rugged and cold. Southerly Kyushu is densely populated. Shikoku, between Kyushu and Honshu, has fewer inhabitants.

Most of Japan is mountainous and heavily forested. There are many volcanoes, and earthquakes are common. Hot, humid summers give way to cool or cold winters, with heavy snow in the north.

People and economy

Japan is one of the world's most densely populated countries. More than 80 percent of the people live in cities. Tokyo, the capital, is the world's largest city. Shinto and Buddhism are the major religions, and most Japanese follow both. Shinto involves the worship of ancestors.

Dancers wear traditional kimono costumes at a cherry blossom festival in Kyoto.

▶ *The white-naped crane is one of Japan's most beautiful and rare native birds.*

Because Japan has little flatland for farming, much of the nation's food is imported. The main locally produced food is rice, which is grown in paddies—or flooded fields—on hillsides.

Since the late 1800s, Japan has grown into an industrial giant known especially for its high-quality cars and electronic goods, such as televisions.

History

The earliest settlers of Japan came from the Asian mainland in about 8000 B.C. By A.D. 400 Japan was a network of small states ruled by powerful clans. Japan was greatly influenced by China and adopted the Chinese writing system and calendar.

The Japanese believed that their emperor was divine. But from about the ninth century he had little real power. Warring clans grew more powerful. Each lord had an army of samurai—skilled warriors who believed that honor was more important than death. By 1185 the Minamoto clan was the most powerful. In 1192 the emperor gave their chief, Yoritomo, the title of shogun, or great general. This began a new style of military government that ruled Japan for the next 700 years.

KEY FACTS

AREA:
145,887 sq. mi.
(377,847 sq. km)

POPULATION:
126,714,000

**CAPITAL &
LARGEST CITY:**
Tokyo

**MAJOR
RELIGIONS:**
Shinto, Buddhism

**MAJOR
LANGUAGE:**
Japanese

CURRENCY:
Yen

During the 1600s, Japan shut itself off from the outside world. No one could leave or enter the country except for a few traders. In 1868 a group of young samurai overthrew the shogun in favor of the Emperor Meiji. They wanted Japan to become the military and commercial equal of Western nations.

Japan increased its trade and developed its industry. It won wars against China in 1894–95 and Russia in 1904–05, and invaded Manchuria in China in the 1930s. During World War II (1939–45), Japan sided with Germany and attacked the U.S. fleet at Pearl Harbor, Hawaii, in 1941. That brought the United States into the war. In August 1945 the United States dropped atomic bombs on the cities of Hiroshima and Nagasaki, and Japan surrendered.

Helped at first by the United States, Japan rebuilt its economy to become one of the world's richest and strongest nations.

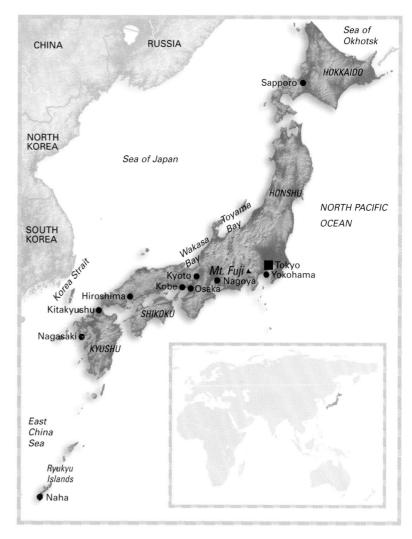

The sacred Mount Fuji, or Fujiyama, is an extinct (inactive) volcano on the island of Honshu. It is 12,388 ft. (3,776 m) high.

SEE ALSO:
Asia;
Buddhism;
Pacific Rim;
Religions;
World War II

JELLYFISH
Jellyfish belong to a group of soft-bodied creatures called cnidarians, or coelenterates. They are some of the most ancient forms of life on Earth.

There are about 200 known species of jellyfish. Most live in coastal waters. They are closely related to corals, sea anemones, and hydras. All cnidarians are invertebrates—they have no backbone.

Body and feeding
A jellyfish has a body shaped like an umbrella or a bell. It is little more than a hollow bag consisting of two layers of cells separated by soft, watery jelly. It has one opening, or mouth. Food is digested by the inside layer of cells.

Tentacles like hanging threads surround the mouth. Some jellyfish have stinging cells in their tentacles. When the jellyfish senses prey nearby, coiled threads with barbed tips spring out of its stinging cells, pierce the victim, and inject it with poison. The tentacles then capture the food and draw it into the mouth.

Movement
Jellyfish are not strong swimmers. Their movements are guided by wherever the ocean currents take them. They change their direction and depth in the water by contracting the muscles around the rim of their body to drive out water and push themselves along.

Jellyfish have basic senses that allow them to tell the difference between light and dark. Some jellyfish migrate between the ocean surface and deep, dark waters every day. Some travel to reproduce in shallow waters during

SEE ALSO:
Animals;
Corals and
Coral Reefs;
Oceans and
Seas;
Seashores

A jellyfish is not a true fish because it does not have a backbone.

AMAZING FACTS!

Some jellyfish, such as the bright blue-and-orange sea blubber, may measure about 12 ft. (3.5 m) in diameter. Their tentacles may extend more than 100 ft. (30 m) beneath them. Other jellyfish are the size of a fingertip.
If a person is badly stung by the box jellyfish, also called the sea wasp, he or she may die from its poison.

the summer and then spend the winter in deeper waters.

Life cycle
An adult jellyfish is called a medusa (plural, *medusae*). The female produces an egg, which is fertilized by sperm from the male. A small larva develops and settles on the ocean floor. It grows into a polyp—a hollow cylinder attached to a rock at one end, with a ring of tentacles surrounding a mouth at the other end. The polyp grows for several months and then "buds" layers that break off and develop into medusae.

✴ JUDAISM
Judaism is the religion of the Jews, a cultural and ethnic group originally from the Middle East that has spread across the world.

The Jews believe that their leader Moses presented his people with a set of laws. Most of these laws are included in the Torah (also called the Pentateuch), the first five books of the Jewish bible. The Jewish bible is the original Hebrew text of what Christians know as the Old Testament.

The Jews entered into a covenant—an agreement—with God. They would keep to his laws, and he would protect them and make their land fertile. The Jews see themselves as the chosen people of God.

Jewish life
The history of the Jews has been marked by long periods of exile and suffering. Jews have settled all over the world, especially in Europe and North America. Over thousands of years, Jews have interpreted their laws and faith in different ways. Some are very orthodox and believe that anything that goes against the Torah is sinful; others are more relaxed and liberal.

The main Jewish place of worship is the synagogue, or shul. The leader of each community is the rabbi, which means "teacher" in Hebrew. The Jewish sabbath runs from sunset on Friday to sunset on Saturday. No work is done during this period. On Friday evening, the whole family gathers for a special meal. On Saturday morning, people attend the synagogue for a service.

The main Jewish festivals are Passover, which celebrates the escape of the Jewish people from Egypt; Rosh Hashanah, the Jewish New Year; and Yom Kippur, or Day of Atonement, when Jews pray for forgiveness for their sins.

When a boy is 13, he becomes a Bar Mitzvah—son of the commandment—and is allowed to read from the Torah in the synagogue. A girl becomes a Bat Mitzvah—daughter of the commandment—at age 12. Orthodox Judaism does not allow women to read from the Torah.

A rabbi serves food during seder, the religious meal shared in the first two evenings of Passover.

SEE ALSO: Bible; Holocaust; Israel; Middle East; Religions; Torah

339

✳ JUPITER

Jupiter is the largest planet in the solar system. It is so vast that more than one thousand Earths could fit inside it.

KEY FACTS

POSITION IN THE SOLAR SYSTEM:
Fifth planet from the sun

AVERAGE DISTANCE FROM THE SUN:
483,000,000 mi.
(778,000,000 km)

SOLAR ORBIT:
11.9 Earth years

DIAMETER:
89,000 mi.
(143,000 km)

MASS:
1,900 quintillion tons

ATMOSPHERE:
Hydrogen, helium

AXIAL ROTATION:
9 hours, 55 minutes

Unlike Earth, Jupiter does not have a solid surface. It is a huge ball of gases, made up of 82 percent hydrogen, 14 percent helium, and 4 percent other elements. It is referred to as a gas giant.

If you were to travel toward the center of this ball, you would find the gases getting hotter and denser, and the pressure increasing. The pressure of the gases, or atmosphere, is so strong at the center that hydrogen becomes a molten metal. Astronomers believe that the planet's deepest layers have a temperature of about 36,000°F (20,000°C).

The circulation of molten metal at the center of the planet creates an electric current, which generates a magnetic field. Jupiter has a magnetic field that is 10 times stronger than the field around Earth.

Moons and clouds

In 1610 the Italian scientist Galileo discovered four moons circling, or orbiting, Jupiter. They were named Ganymede, Io, Callisto, and Europa. Later, astronomers found more moons. Scientists now know of at least 39 moons around the planet.

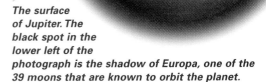

▷ *The surface of Jupiter. The black spot in the lower left of the photograph is the shadow of Europa, one of the 39 moons that are known to orbit the planet.*

The largest, Ganymede, has a diameter of 3,270 miles (5,260 km), slightly larger than the planet Mercury.

Clouds of ammonia and water, some of which are brightly colored with other elements, blow around Jupiter. The most amazing feature of Jupiter's clouds is a huge orange-red area over twice the width of Earth, called the Great Red Spot. It is made up of violently swirling gases rising from deep inside the planet.

In the 1970s, the *Voyager* space probe found that the Great Red Spot has a constant source of energy, rather like an everlasting tornado. *Voyager* also found that Jupiter is surrounded by three rings of rocks. Previously, astronomers believed Saturn to be the only planet with rings.

👀
SEE ALSO: Astronomy; Galilei, Galileo; Planets; Solar System; Space Exploration

▷ *A close-up of Jupiter's Great Red Spot.*

KAHLO, FRIDA (1907–54)

Frida Kahlo was a famous Mexican artist known for her brightly colored self-portraits. Her paintings have gained wide recognition since her death.

Magdalena Carmen Frida Kahlo y Calderón originally wanted to be a doctor, but she was badly hurt in a bus accident in 1925. While she was recovering in bed, she began to paint. She married the Mexican painter Diego Rivera in 1929. Because of their political activities, they were forced to leave Mexico, but they returned in 1933.

Kahlo's style was strongly influenced by Mexican folk art and by the Surrealist styles of European painters. Surrealist painters were very interested in dreams, the strange atmosphere of which they tried to capture in their paintings.

The effects of Kahlo's accident are very important in her work. She was in pain for the rest of her life and could not have children because of her injuries. Her marriage to Rivera was a difficult one, and she clearly expressed her frustrations in her work.

In 1943 Kahlo was appointed professor of painting at La Esmeralda, the Education Ministry's School of Fine Arts. When she died, she left her house in Coyoacán, Mexico City, to the Mexican people. It is now a museum of her life and art.

Frida Kahlo in about 1939. Traditional Mexican clothing and exotic jewelry, set against her dramatic features, became her trademark style.

SEE ALSO:
Art and Artists;
Mexico

*KANGAROOS see *MARSUPIALS

*KENYA

Kenya is a republic in East Africa, on the equator with a coast on the Indian Ocean. Many people visit Kenya, especially to see the amazing wildlife.

Kenya's national flag

Land and climate

The Great Rift Valley crosses Kenya from north to south, with many small, extinct volcanoes along its floor. In the central and southwest regions are fertile highlands and most of the mountains, including Mount Kenya. Lake Victoria, which forms part of the western border, is Africa's largest lake.

Temperatures in the north and along the coast are often around 80°F (27°C). Nairobi, in the highlands, is cooler. Only about one-third of Kenya receives more than 20 in. (500 mm) of rain in a year.

People and economy

SEE ALSO:
Africa; East Africa

Most Kenyans are black Africans. The main peoples are the Kikuyu, whose homeland is the fertile highlands, and the southern Masai, who are nomadic (wandering) cattle herders. There are also small South Asian, Arab, and European communities. About 75 percent of Kenyans work in

KEY FACTS

OFFICIAL NAME:
Republic of Kenya

AREA:
224,960 sq. mi.
(582,646 sq. km)

POPULATION:
30,080,000

CAPITAL & LARGEST CITY:
Nairobi

MAJOR LANGUAGES:
Swahili, other African languages, English

MAJOR RELIGIONS:
Roman Catholicism, Protestantism, traditional African religions, Islam

CURRENCY:
Kenya shilling

agriculture. Coffee, tea, sugarcane, and sisal are important crops. After coffee, tourism is the main source of income.

History

Most scientists believe that East Africa was one of the first homes of prehistoric people. Arab traders began searching for gold on the Kenyan coast about 2,000 years ago. The Portuguese established trading posts between 1498 and 1740, when the Arabs drove them out.

In 1895 Britain established the East African Protectorate and began to build a railroad between Lake Victoria and the coast. Many Europeans settled in the highlands, forcing the Kikuyu off the land. In the 1950s, a Kikuyu movement called the Mau Mau tried to drive out the British. Kenya became independent in 1963. Jomo Kenyatta was president until his death in 1978. Daniel Arap Moi became president the following year and ruled until 2002, when Mwai Kibaki took over. He promised to end political corruption in Kenya.

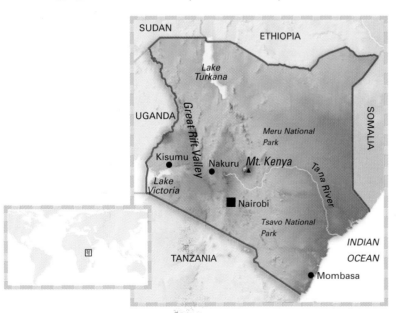

KING, MARTIN LUTHER, JR. (1929–68)

Dr. Martin Luther King Jr. was the most important leader of the movement to obtain rights for African Americans in the 1950s and 1960s.

Martin Luther King Jr. was born in Atlanta, Georgia. His father was the pastor of Ebenezer Baptist Church. King earned degrees at Morehouse College in Atlanta and Crozer Theological Seminary in Pennsylvania. He then went to Boston University, where he earned a doctorate (Ph.D.). In Boston he met Coretta Scott. They married in 1953 and settled in Montgomery, Alabama, where King had been appointed pastor of the Dexter Avenue Baptist Church.

The Reverend Dr. Martin Luther King Jr. was a champion of nonviolent protest in the campaign for civil rights.

First campaigns

At that time buses in Montgomery were segregated—black people had to give up their seats to whites. King led a campaign against the bus company. Black people did not use the buses for 381 days. In 1956 the Supreme Court declared segregation of buses to be against the Constitution.

King was then asked to lead the Southern Christian Leadership Conference (SCLC). The SCLC aimed to win equality for black people without the use of violence.

In 1959 King returned to Atlanta as copastor, with his father, of the Ebenezer Baptist Church. He continued his work with the SCLC. King based his philosophy on the teachings of both Jesus Christ and the Indian leader Mohandas Gandhi, who had helped India win independence from Britain through nonviolent protest.

"I have a dream"

In 1963 King led a march to Washington, D.C., where he made a famous speech to 250,000 people. It is known by one of its key phrases, "I have a dream." In 1964

King won the Nobel Peace Prize for his nonviolent pursuit of justice. The SCLC campaigns helped bring about the Civil Rights Act of 1964 and the Voting Rights Act of 1965.

On April 4, 1968, the day before a scheduled mass march, King was assassinated in Memphis, Tennessee, by a man named James Earl Ray. Martin Luther King Jr. is buried in Atlanta. Since 1986 the third Monday in January has been a national holiday in his honor.

SEE ALSO: African Americans; Civil Rights; Constitution, United States; Gandhi, Mohandas; Nobel Prize

✳ KNIGHTS AND CHIVALRY

Knights were the highest class of warrior in Europe from the 11th to the 14th centuries. They fought on horseback. Their code of behavior was called chivalry.

Between A.D. 850 and 950, western Europe came under attack by warlike peoples, such as the Vikings from Scandinavia and the Magyars from eastern Europe. But from about 950, these invaders were countered by riders wearing armor and riding big, heavy horses. In England they were called knights, from the Anglo-Saxon word *cnight*, meaning "household retainer."

Knights received land from rulers in return for military service. Although the status of knights differed from time to time and from country to country, they became a core part of European society.

Young boys went to live in the home of another knight or noble to be educated. They learned how to ride and fight and how to behave in courtly society. They became squires at about 14 and knights at about 21.

Code of chivalry
The ideals the knight was supposed to uphold were known as chivalry, from the French word *chevalerie*, meaning "cavalry." These ideals were extremely important in medieval society. A knight, for example, should always be generous to the needy and protect the church, women, and all who were unable to defend themselves.

Politeness also became part of the code. Knights curbed their coarse manners in the company of ladies. They believed that a chivalrous knight honored every woman, particularly the one to whom he had given his love. He remained true to her and performed great deeds for her sake.

Preparing to fight
A knight's horse was probably the most valuable thing he owned. His skill as a fighting man depended on a good horse.

Knights take part in a tournament near Calais, France, in 1389.
▷

The armor worn by knights differed from one century to another during the Middle Ages. In the 1100s, a well-armed knight wore a long cloth or leather garment that covered most of his body. Over it he wore chain mail, a network of linked iron rings. It had a hood that fitted over the head and protected the neck. On his head a knight wore a steel helmet, which sometimes had a metal nose protector. In later times the body armor was made of strong metal plates. The helmets had visors that could be lowered to cover the face. The body armor weighed at least 55 lb. (25 kg).

In battle

Knights carried light wooden shields for protection. Their chief weapons were the lance and the sword. The lance, a long pole with a pointed steel head, was for use when the knight was on horseback. The knight pointed his lance straight ahead and rode at full speed against his enemy, trying to run him through or to knock him off his horse. If the knight was forced to dismount, he would go on fighting with his sword, a heavy blade

made of steel. Knights also fought with battle-axes, iron-headed war clubs called maces, and iron balls that swung on chains, called flails.

Tournaments

As a pastime and spectacle, knights took part in tournaments, mock battles fought with flattened lances and blunted swords. Tournaments were often dangerous, and attracted huge crowds of spectators.

SEE ALSO: Castles; Middle Ages; Warfare

By the 1500s, armor gave knights excellent protection, but it was so heavy that it restricted their movement.

DID YOU KNOW?

By 1500 the time of the knight as a warrior was over. Hired foot soldiers with firearms replaced the man on a horse. Knighthood and chivalry did not die out completely. In the United Kingdom, knighthood is still an honor that the king or queen gives to worthy men and women. A male knight is given the title "Sir." His wife is called "Lady." A woman with the rank of knight is called "Dame." Her husband has no title.

✳KOALAS 𝖘𝖊𝖊 ✳MARSUPIALS

✳ KORAN

The Koran (also called the Qur'an) is the sacred book of Islam, the world's second-largest religion. It is one of the most important books in history.

The followers of Islam—Muslims—believe that the Koran contains the actual words, or revelations, of God (Allah) that were delivered to the prophet Muhammad (about A.D. 570–632) by the archangel Gabriel in Arabia. Muhammad recited these words to his followers, and they became the basis of Islam.

Contents

The Koran focuses on the importance of submitting to Allah's will, correct moral behavior, and the coming Day of Judgment. It promises rewards for good and punishment for evil—Paradise and Hell, which are both described in detail.

The Koran also includes many biblical stories, such as those featuring Adam and Eve, Noah and the flood, and Moses. But some of the details of the stories are different from those found in the Bible.

Organization

Unlike the Bible, the Koran is not organized chronologically (in the order in which events happened). It has 114 chapters, called surahs. These are divided into more than 6,000 verses, or ayahs. The chapters are ordered according to length, from the longest to the shortest. Each chapter is designed to stand alone.

Certain themes appear more than once: people's relationship with Allah; politics; and family matters. Although the Koran is seen as the ultimate source of divine instruction, it contains very few laws.

The Koran is written in beautiful, poetic language. Muslims show great respect for their holy book. It must never be laid on the ground or allowed to get dirty. It has been translated into many different languages, but only the original Arabic text is believed to be the true Koran.

▶ *Many Muslims around the world learn Arabic so that they can study the Koran in its original form.*

SEE ALSO:
Bible; Islam; Religions

✶ KOREA

The divided country of Korea lies on a peninsula in East Asia situated between China and Japan.

Korea was liberated from 35 years of Japanese rule in 1945. In 1948 the country was divided into two states—the Republic of Korea (South Korea) and the Democratic People's Republic of Korea (North Korea).

Land and climate

Although Korea has wide, fertile valleys in the south and west that produce rice and other crops, the rest of the countryside is mountainous. Only about one-fifth of the land is suitable for farming.

In the northern inland areas, winter temperatures remain below freezing for five months. Along the coasts in the south, warm ocean currents moderate temperatures so that they rarely fall below freezing. All of Korea has hot summers.

People and economy

Although North Korea is the larger state in area, South Korea has nearly twice as many people. Most of the population is based in lowland areas in the west and south. The main religions are Buddhism, Christianity, and a native Korean religion called Chondokyo, or "religion of the heavenly way." In North Korea, where a Communist government holds power, all forms of religion are strongly discouraged.

The economy of North Korea is controlled by the state. It aims to meet all its own needs for goods and has little foreign trade. By contrast, South Korea produces many goods for export and is the world's 11th-largest trading country.

History

Korea's history dates back thousands of years. China and Japan have been strong influences on Korea throughout its history.

Both North and South Korea were admitted to the United Nations in 1991. Later that year they signed a treaty of reconciliation and nonaggression.

North Korea's national flag

South Korea's national flag

SEE ALSO: Buddhism; China; Communism; Japan; Korean War

KEY FACTS

OFFICIAL NAME:
Democratic People's Republic of Korea (North Korea)

AREA:
46,540 sq. mi. (120,539 sq. km)

POPULATION:
24,039,000

CAPITAL & LARGEST CITY:
Pyongyang

MAJOR RELIGION:
None

MAJOR LANGUAGE:
Korean

CURRENCY:
Won

OFFICIAL NAME:
Republic of Korea (South Korea)

AREA:
38,025 sq. mi. (98,485 sq. km)

POPULATION:
46,844,000

CAPITAL & LARGEST CITY:
Seoul

MAJOR RELIGIONS:
Buddhism, Christianity, Chondokyo

MAJOR LANGUAGE:
Korean

CURRENCY:
Won

✳ KOREAN WAR

The Korean War lasted from 1950 until 1953. It began when the armed forces of the Democratic People's Republic of Korea invaded the Republic of Korea.

United Nations forces patrol through a ruined South Korean village in 1950.

SEE ALSO:
Communism;
Korea;
United
Nations

On June 25, 1950, the military forces of Communist North Korea crossed the 38th parallel, the line dividing Korea into two parts. The attack was aimed at reuniting the country under Communist rule. Two days later, the United Nations approved a resolution, introduced by the United States, asking member nations to provide assistance to South Korea.

United Nations defense

Sixteen countries, under the flag of the United Nations, sent military forces to South Korea's defense. Most troops came from the United States. Many others contributed equipment and supplies. North Korea's main allies were the Soviet Union, which supplied it with arms, and China, which later poured masses of troops into the conflict. Within the first two days of war, the well-equipped and well-trained North Korean forces had pushed aside the outnumbered and poorly trained Republic of Korea army and captured Seoul, the South Korean capital. On September 15, 1950, the United Nations forces launched a combined naval, marine, and army attack on the North Korean-occupied port of Inchon, on South Korea's west coast. It was hazardous and daring, but successful. Seoul was recaptured in late September, and in October North Korean troops retreated back across the 38th parallel.

Peaceful conclusion

By June 1951 a stalemate had developed, with both sides entrenched along the 38th parallel. The war became one of brutal fighting, as each side fought for a small advantage over the other.

The war raged across the Korean peninsula, causing great destruction and loss of life before an armistice (peace agreement) was signed in 1953. Military casualties on both sides exceeded 1.5 million. More than 54,000 Americans had died in action or from injuries and disease. Millions of Koreans had died, and many more were left homeless or refugees.

The Soviet Union proposed negotiations for a ceasefire at the United Nations on June 23, 1951. Talks continued for two years until the armistice was finally signed on July 27, 1953. Militarily, the war ended with a victory for neither side. However, the aggression against South Korea had been repulsed, and the right of states to be free from the threat or use of force had been preserved.

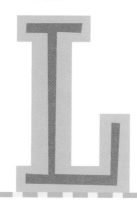

✳ LABOR

Labor is the paid work that people do for others. It also refers to the people who work for another person or an organization.

In the days before industry, most people worked for themselves. They farmed land to produce food for their families or made things and provided services that they could exchange for money. Exceptions included slaves and soldiers.

From the 1700s, the situation changed. Small farms began to disappear, and people worked for rich landowners instead. More people moved to the growing cities. Many of them worked for firms in large factories. Others worked from home, making goods such as matchbooks. They were paid money (wages) according to how many items they made. Conditions were often poor, and wages low. If a worker protested, the employer could fire him or her.

Labor organizations and unions
Beginning in the 1800s, workers began to organize themselves to fight for better working conditions. The groups they formed were sometimes called unions. Governments and employers often opposed these organizations. They broke up meetings and punished organizers.

Different unions wanted different things. Their demands often included higher wages, shorter working days, and safer conditions. Employers argued that this would cost too much. Unions sometimes

organized strikes, when employees refuse to work. Employers would find other people to do the work.

From the late 1800s, working men were able to vote in most European countries. Governments passed laws to protect workers. The laws included safety regulations, rules about the length of time people had to work, and the right to join unions. The powers of unions have varied at different times and in different

▲
The General Strike in Britain in 1926 lasted for nine days. It was an unsuccessful attempt by unions to prevent the wages of coal miners from being lowered.

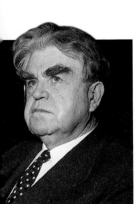

John L. Lewis, called the "roaring lion of labor," was a powerful labor leader in the United States.

SEE ALSO:
Chavez, Cesar;
Economics;
Industrial
Revolution;
Manufacturing

countries. Some unions have links with political organizations, and their industrial action can threaten governments. Examples of this include the British General Strike in 1926 and the actions of the Solidarity union in Poland in the 1980s.

North America

Unions existed in North America beginning in the early 1800s. The labor movement began to grow after the Civil War (1861–65). A very important early labor organization was the Knights of Labor, which had 700,000 members by 1886. After the Haymarket Riots, during a strike in Chicago, unions became unpopular.

The American Federation of Labor (AFL) was a national organization of unions. Most of its members were craftspeople—workers with a particular skill. In 1935 John L. Lewis founded the Committee for Industrial Organization, later the Congress of Industrial Organizations (CIO). The CIO aimed to unite all workers in a particular industry. The AFL and the CIO were rival groups until they merged in 1955.

After the end of World War II, in 1945, the government lifted wage and price controls that benefited workers. This led to many strikes. In response the government passed the Taft–Hartley Act of 1947, which restricted strikes that would endanger the nation's safety or welfare, among other controls. It cut back the power of unions, and membership began to fall.

Labor today

There are still strikes and labor disputes today. But many disagreements between labor and management are settled by discussion or by arbitration—when an independent organization listens to both sides and works out a solution. Unions still protect their members by offering them benefits such as insurance and legal advice. They also campaign for improved working conditions and safety, and on issues such as unequal pay for women and minorities.

In some parts of the world, there are still restrictions on unions and workers' rights. Employers can make people work in dangerous conditions for very little pay. The International Labor Organization (ILO), established in 1919 and now an agency of the United Nations, acts to protect the rights of workers and improve labor conditions across the world.

Members of the Polish labor union Solidarity demonstrate in 1987. The union helped overthrow the government.

LAKES

A lake is an inland body of water in a depression in the surface of the land called a basin. The water in a lake can be fresh or salty.

Lake basins can form in several ways. Some are made by movements of the earth's crust; others are carved out by ice in glaciers or created when river valleys flood. Some lakes form in the craters of extinct volcanoes. Other lakes are artificial, created as reservoirs or behind dams.

How lakes are formed

Lakes are formed when water flows into these depressions. It might enter across the surface, from rivers or streams, or from underground, flowing out of springs or groundwater. When the climate is humid, more water flows into a basin than escapes through evaporation. The level of water in the basin rises, forming a lake. If the climate is dry, water is lost through evaporation, leaving deposits of salty minerals on the bed and sides of the lake.

Many lakes disappear over time. Rivers can form, and they drain water away. Sometimes the basin fills with mud, silt, and vegetation until the lake becomes a swamp. Changes in climate can cause a lake's water to evaporate.

THE WORLD'S LARGEST LAKES

Caspian Sea, Asia	143,550 sq. mi.	(371,800 sq. km)
Superior, North America	31,820 sq. mi.	(82,414 sq. km)
Victoria, Africa	26,868 sq. mi.	(69,588 sq. km)
Huron, North America	23,010 sq. mi.	(59,596 sq. km)
Michigan, North America	22,400 sq. mi.	(58,016 sq. km)
Tanganyika, Africa	12,700 sq. mi.	(32,893 sq. km)
Great Bear, North America	12,275 sq. mi.	(31,792 sq. km)
Baikal, Russia	11,780 sq. mi.	(30,500 sq. km)
Aral Sea, Asia	11,600 sq. mi.	(30,000 sq. km)
Malawi (Nyasa), Africa	11,430 sq. mi.	(29,604 sq. km)

People and lakes

People use lakes for fishing, boating, swimming, and, when they freeze, ice-skating. But people can also damage lakes. Companies and communities use them to dump sewage and other waste. Chemicals can cause weeds and algae to grow too fast. That uses up oxygen in the water and kills off other life in the lake.

Crater Lake, Oregon, stands on the site of a mountain that exploded in a volcanic eruption more than 6,000 years ago.

SEE ALSO:
Dams;
Earth;
Glaciers;
Volcanoes;
Wetlands

✳ LANGUAGES

Language is a set of sounds or symbols that a group of people uses to communicate. Without language much human activity would be impossible.

The word *language* comes from the Latin *lingua*, meaning "tongue." The tongue is the most important organ in human speech. Most languages are spoken first, then written down later. Many animals can communicate with one another, but only humans can communicate complex ideas with speech.

No one knows exactly how our languages developed. Some people think that the first words came from humans attempting to copy sounds from nature, such as running water or animal calls. Over many centuries, different cultures used different sounds to communicate. That is why people from various countries use languages that others cannot understand.

A world of languages
There are nearly 3,000 separate languages in the world today. They range from Chinese, English, and Spanish, which are spoken by billions of people, to tribal languages that are spoken by only a few thousand people. Sometimes it is hard to draw a clear line between a language and a dialect, which is a local variation of a language. Some languages, known as dead languages, go out of existence. The most famous example is Latin, the language of the ancient Romans.

Written language
When all language was spoken, ideas, history, and many other different forms of knowledge were passed from generation to generation because people memorized stories they were told. This is called oral tradition. Beginning in at least 3000 B.C., the ancient Sumerians, who lived in what is now Iraq, developed the earliest known writing, called cuneiform. Each word was a separate, unique picture. The Chinese still use this method of writing.

In about 1100 B.C., the Phoenicians, a Mediterranean people, began to use symbols that stood for sounds rather than words. They arranged these sound symbols to make parts of words. This was the first alphabet. Before this

This clay cylinder from Sumer, dating from about 1800 B.C., is inscribed with cuneiform writing.

In World War II (1939–45), the U.S. Army sent top-secret messages in Navajo, a language that was understood by very few people because it had not been written down.
▷

development, people had to learn a new symbol for each word. Now people needed to learn only a fixed number of symbols to make a written language.

How languages change

If you speak English, you are speaking the same language that George Washington spoke more than 200 years ago. But the way you speak now would sound very strange to the first U.S. president, because languages change over time. People create new words for new things and ideas. Washington would not have known the words *television* or *airplane*.

New words are created and existing ones change their meaning, partly because of need and partly because of fashion. Some people believe that new technological developments, such as e-mail, will make spoken and written English more informal.

Travel affects language. When the Pilgrims came to North America, they spoke the same English as the people of England. Over time British English and American English became different. Americans and Britons have different accents and use different words for the same things. For

example, an elevator is called a lift in Britain. There are similar differences between the Spanish used in Spain and that spoken in South America.

Learning language

Whatever their nationality, most children learn their language from listening to and copying the people around them. The first voice they hear is usually that of their mother, so people's first language is called their mother tongue. Some children are raised in places where more than one language is spoken, and they become bilingual—able to speak two languages. Many people learn languages in addition to their mother tongue.

▲
Chinese children take part in a calligraphy (handwriting) class. Written Chinese contains more than 40,000 characters.

SEE ALSO: Alphabet; Ancient Civilizations; Communication; Ears and Hearing; Tongue and Speech; Writing

☀ LASERS

A laser is an instrument that produces a special kind of light. Laser light can be used to slice through steel or to play your favorite CD.

INSIDE A LASER

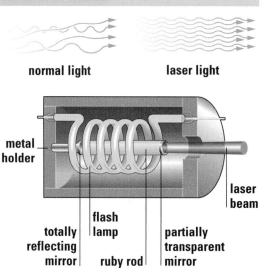

normal light   laser light

metal holder

totally reflecting mirror

flash lamp

ruby rod

partially transparent mirror

laser beam

In a ruby laser the light-emitting medium is an artificial gemstone shaped like a rod with two reflective ends, one coated in a layer of silver, the other partially coated. These ends act as mirrors that control the direction of the laser beam. The energy source is a tube-shaped lamp wrapped around the ruby rod.

Rays of light are swarms of photons (light particles) that travel in waves. The distance between the crest, or top, of one wave and the crest of the next wave is called a wavelength. Different colors of light have different wavelengths.

Ordinary light, such as sunlight, is called "white light," but it is really a mixture of different colors. Rays of white light travel in many different directions and weaken as they go farther from their source.

The word *laser* is formed from the first letters of "light amplification by stimulated emission of radiation." Unlike ordinary light, laser light is only one color. Its rays all have exactly the same wavelength, and they all move together in the same direction without spreading. Because rays

of laser light do not spread, they can be focused by a lens or curved mirror into an intense beam on a very small spot.

Most laser machines have three parts: a light-emitting medium, an energy source to stimulate the medium to emit light, and a device to control the direction of the resulting beam.

A very powerful beam of laser light can heat the spot at which it is aimed to thousands of degrees. That makes lasers useful for welding small components such as battery cases for heart pacemakers.

Lasers are now common in everyday life. Supermarket checkouts use laser scanners to "read" the price of an item from a pattern of lines, called a universal product code (UPC), printed on the package. A compact disk (CD) player bounces laser light off tiny pits in the disk's surface and converts the reflected light into sound. Doctors use beams of laser light to correct vision defects and to remove tumors, skin blemishes, and tattoos.

Lasers can cure vision defects without having to cut the eye.
▼

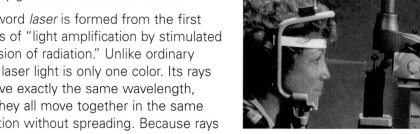

SEE ALSO:
Colors;
Light

☀LATITUDE 🔎see☀ ☀NAVIGATION

☀ LAW

Laws are rules that regulate the actions of citizens and governments. They protect people from harm and try to prevent people from harming others.

Historians believe that people began to make rules for getting along with one another as soon as they began living in groups. The earliest recorded laws date from about 3400 B.C. One of the greatest of the ancient codes of law was that of Hammerabi, king of Babylon (part of modern Iraq) from 1792 to 1750 B.C.

Civil law and common law

In Europe two different systems of law have evolved. In France and some other countries, laws are based on a written code, which judges consult for guidance. This system is called civil law.

In England, by contrast, judges base their decisions on judgments that have already been made in other cases. The English system, known as common law, forms the basis of the law in North America.

In the United States, there are now three levels of law. Federal laws apply to the whole country. State laws operate within a state. Local laws apply to one city or town. All laws must comply with the U.S. Constitution.

Public law and private law

U.S. law can be divided into two broad categories—public law and private law. Public law concerns the legal relationship between the government and citizens. It includes constitutional law, criminal law, regulations of administrative agencies such as the Internal Revenue Service and the Environmental Protection Agency, and the laws governing court procedures. A violation of a person's civil rights, a theft or murder, and cases of illegal pollution are all matters that involve public law.

A judge makes a point to a defendant (right) and her lawyer.

Private law, often also called civil law, regulates the relationships between private individuals and between individuals and businesses. Divorce, business disputes, and house purchases are all covered by private law. In the United States, laws can be made by Congress, by state legislatures, or by local councils.

In some cases, judges reach their verdict alone. In more serious criminal cases, the decision of the court is left to a jury—a team of adults selected from the community. The judge gives them guidance and ensures that the court proceedings are fair.

> **SEE ALSO:** Ancient Civilizations; Congress; Constitution, United States; Crime and Law Enforcement; States and State Governments; Supreme Court; United States Government

* LEWIS, MERIWETHER (1774–1809)

Meriwether Lewis, together with William Clark (1770–1838), led the first overland expedition by European Americans to the Pacific Northwest coast.

Meriwether Lewis was born near Charlottesville, Virginia. As a boy he developed a love of the wilderness and hunting. He served in the militia in Pennsylvania and joined the regular army to fight against Native Americans in the Northwest Territory.

Thomas Jefferson was a friend of Lewis's family. When Jefferson became president, Lewis became his private secretary. For two years, they planned an expedition to find a land route to the Pacific. Lewis selected Lieutenant William Clark, another Virginian who was familiar with the frontier and Native Americans, to share command with him. Congress granted the expedition a fund of $2,500.

Lewis's historic expedition was successful owing to his close work with joint leader William Clark.

The explorers set off up the Missouri River in May 1804. They reached the Pacific Ocean in November 1805. En route they established friendly relations with several Native American peoples. They returned to St. Louis, Missouri, in September 1806.

Jefferson appointed Lewis governor of the Louisiana Territory in 1808. Lewis's service was brief, as he shortly died under mysterious circumstances in Tennessee.

SEE ALSO: Exploration and Explorers; Louisiana Purchase; Native Americans; Sacajawea

---

*LIBERIA see *WEST AFRICA

---

* LIBRARIES

A library is a room or a building with a collection of books, periodicals, and other materials. The first libraries were set up in ancient Egypt and Babylon.

In addition to libraries that are open to the public, many important libraries are attached to schools, colleges, and government organizations. The largest library in the world is the Library of Congress in Washington, D.C.

Most libraries work the same way and have the same rules. Users are expected to be quiet and to take good care of the books, periodicals, and other materials. The most important part of any library— apart from the books and other

resources—is the librarian. He or she is there to help visitors find the books they need and to guide them through the library system and the catalog.

Catalog

The titles of all the books in a library are contained in a catalog. It used to be a system of cards arranged alphabetically in drawers, but many libraries now have computerized catalogs. School libraries and many public libraries use the *Sears*

List of Subject Headings. Big public libraries and most colleges use the Library of Congress subject headings. A standard list of categories enables all librarians to classify books in the same way.

On the shelves

Books are organized under one of two systems: the Dewey decimal system or the Library of Congress system. Both systems use combinations of letters and numbers to help users find the books they want. The classification, or class, numbers are marked on the spine of the book. Under these numbers, the library may add the first few letters of the author's last name. The combination of the class number and the letters is known as the call number. This system makes it possible to pinpoint quickly the whereabouts of any particular book, even in the largest library.

SEE ALSO: Literature; Printing; Writing

LIBRARY CLASSIFICATION SYSTEMS

Dewey decimal classification system

000	General works	600	Technology (applied sciences)
100	Philosophy	700	Arts
200	Religion	800	Literature
300	Social sciences	900	History
400	Language		
500	Pure science		

Library of Congress classification system

A	General works	L	Education
B	Philosophy and religion	M	Music
C	History— auxiliary sciences	N	Fine arts
D	History and topography (except America)	P	Language and literature
E–F	American history	Q	Science
G	Geography and anthropology	R	Medicine
H	Social sciences	S	Agriculture
J	Political sciences	T	Technology
K	Law of the United States	U	Military science
		V	Naval science
		Z	Bibliography and library science

✳ LIGHT

Light is the source of all life on Earth. Without light, plants would not grow, and without plants to provide oxygen, animals would not be able to live.

For many centuries, scientists argued about whether light was made of particles or of waves. Today most scientists agree that both ideas are true. Light is made up of electrical and magnetic forces traveling through space at high speed in waves, and it is also a stream of energy particles known as photons.

Any object that produces light, such as the sun or a flashlight, is called a light source. Other objects do not produce light of their own but reflect the light of other objects

The aurora borealis, or northern lights, is a great curtain of light that appears in the night sky in polar regions.

REFLECTED LIGHT

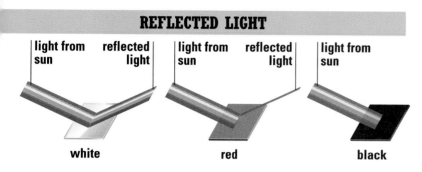

light from sun | reflected light
white

light from sun | reflected light
red

light from sun
black

The surface on the left reflects all seven colors of the spectrum and therefore appears white. The surface in the center absorbs six colors and reflects the seventh, red. The surface on the right absorbs all seven colors and therefore appears black.

that do. For example, the moon is not a source of light. It appears to shine because it is reflecting light from the sun.

The colors of light

The English scientist Isaac Newton discovered that "white" light is made up of several different colors. When sunlight passes through a three-sided pyramid of glass called a prism, it splits into bands of red, orange, yellow, green, blue, indigo, and violet: They are the visible colors of the spectrum. That effect—refraction—happens because light changes direction whenever it moves from one material into another. There are also colors of light we cannot see, called infrared and ultraviolet.

The color of an object depends on the way it reflects and absorbs light. Many objects absorb six colors of the spectrum and reflect the seventh. A red ball appears red because the material of which it is made reflects only that one color.

SEE ALSO: Colors; Eyes and Vision; Heat; Lasers; Newton, Isaac; Physics; Sun

* LIN, MAYA (1959–)

Maya Lin is the architect who designed the Vietnam Veterans Memorial in Washington, D.C., and the Civil Rights Memorial in Montgomery, Alabama.

▲
Architect Maya Lin pictured in Michigan in 2000.

Maya Ying Lin was born in Athens, Ohio. Her parents immigrated to the U.S. from China in 1948. Lin studied architecture and sculpture at Yale University. In her senior year, she won a national competition to design a memorial honoring soldiers who died in the Vietnam War (1957–75). Completed in 1982, the memorial consists of two black granite walls engraved with the names of the 58,000 Americans who died in Vietnam.

In 1988 Lin agreed to design a memorial honoring the civil rights movement. It is made up of a wall inscribed with a quotation from Martin Luther King Jr., a disk bearing the names of 40 people who died in the struggle for civil rights, and a timeline of important events.

Since then Lin has created sculptures and other large-scale works and has designed houses and furniture. She uses recycled, living, or natural material in her work. She lives and works in New York City.

SEE ALSO: Architecture; Art and Artists; Civil Rights; King, Martin Luther, Jr.; Vietnam War

☀ LITERATURE

Literature is written material that has lasting value or interest. It includes imaginative works and factual accounts.

Early literature

The earliest form of literature in ancient times was the long epic story chanted by a musician or poet to an assembled group. The first epic stories to be written down were those of Mesopotamia (now Iraq), where writing began. One of the early epics was *The Epic of Gilgamesh*, a Sumerian poem that dates from about 2000 B.C. The ancient Greeks and Romans wrote works that are still read today, such as the short moral stories called fables written by Aesop.

Beginning in the 1200s, European poets such as Dante, Boccaccio, and Chaucer wrote long works about religion, love, and life. However, most people could not read. When Johannes Gutenberg invented the printing press in the 1400s, books became cheaper and more accessible. Gradually more people learned to read.

Because the stories and cultures of Native Americans were passed down by word of mouth, the first American writers were European colonists and their descendants.

Fiction and nonfiction

Literature is divided into fiction and nonfiction. Fiction is work that the writer invents or imagines. It aims to stir the reader's feelings by describing moods of joy or sadness, by telling exciting stories, and by introducing characters whose emotions can be understood and shared by the reader. Fiction can be in the form of novels, plays, poems, or short stories.

Nonfiction is writing that provides readers with the facts about a certain subject, such as science or history.

Autobiographies, biographies, diaries, and essays are all works of nonfiction. An autobiography is the author's own account of his or her life. A biography is the life of someone other than the author. An essay is a short piece of prose that discusses a subject from a personal point of view.

Drama

A drama is a story meant to be acted out onstage. Serious plays are often called tragedies, especially if they end with the death of the leading character. Comic plays, or comedies, emphasize the ridiculous aspects of human behavior.

The ancient Greeks invented drama, but the great age of dramatic writing was during the reign (1558–1603) of England's Queen Elizabeth I. Playwrights of the time included William Shakespeare, Christopher Marlowe, and Ben Jonson. Like the Greek dramatists, the Elizabethans wrote in

A performance of William Shakespeare's comedy play A Midsummer Night's Dream, written around 1594–96.
▼

359

Don Quixote, the hero of Cervantes's 17th-century novel, was a dreamer who mistook windmills for giants and tried to joust with them. ▶

poetic form. In recent times, most playwrights have written in prose.

Poetry

Poetry differs from prose in having a regular rhythm, sometimes using rhyme. The ancient Greeks wrote epic poems about heroic events. Homer's *Iliad* describes the siege of Troy, and the *Odyssey* tells the adventures of Odysseus on his voyage home from Troy. Lyric poetry is short, songlike, and very personal. The ode, a form of lyric poetry, is dignified in style. Narrative poetry tells a story.

In the early 1800s, poetry was an important literary form. Percy Bysshe Shelley, William Wordsworth, and John Keats are remembered for their lyrics and odes. Samuel Taylor Coleridge's "The Rime of the Ancient Mariner" (1798) is a ghostly tale of magic and mystery. These four poets brought new subjects and a new richness of language into poetry.

American poets such as Henry Wadsworth Longfellow wrote verse about the history of their country. The nation's two greatest poets wrote in the late 1800s. Walt Whitman's work is full of passion for people working together and appreciating nature. Emily Dickinson was much more concerned with the individual's inner thoughts, and often wrote about death.

Novels

A novel is a long story, often with many characters and an involved plot. The earliest known novel comes from Japan. *The Tale of Genji* was written by Lady Murasaki Shikibu in the early 11th century. One of the earliest European novels was *Don Quixote* by the Spaniard Miguel de Cervantes, completed in 1615. *The Power of Sympathy* (1789) by William Hill Brown was the first American novel.

Some of the greatest novelists wrote in the 1800s. They included Charles Dickens, George Eliot, and the Brontë sisters in England; Victor Hugo and Emile Zola in France; and Fyodor Dostoyevsky and Leo Tolstoy in Russia. They all used the novel to study emotions and society.

List of Subject Headings. Big public libraries and most colleges use the Library of Congress subject headings. A standard list of categories enables all librarians to classify books in the same way.

On the shelves

Books are organized under one of two systems: the Dewey decimal system or the Library of Congress system. Both systems use combinations of letters and numbers to help users find the books they want. The classification, or class, numbers are marked on the spine of the book. Under these numbers, the library may add the first few letters of the author's last name. The combination of the class number and the letters is known as the call number. This system makes it possible to pinpoint quickly the whereabouts of any particular book, even in the largest library.

SEE ALSO: Literature; Printing; Writing

LIBRARY CLASSIFICATION SYSTEMS

Dewey decimal classification system

000	General works	600	Technology
100	Philosophy		(applied sciences)
200	Religion	700	Arts
300	Social sciences	800	Literature
400	Language	900	History
500	Pure science		

Library of Congress classification system

A	General works	**L**	Education
B	Philosophy and religion	**M**	Music
C	History— auxiliary sciences	**N**	Fine arts
D	History and topography (except America)	**P**	Language and literature
E–F	American history	**Q**	Science
G	Geography and anthropology	**R**	Medicine
H	Social sciences	**S**	Agriculture
J	Political sciences	**T**	Technology
K	Law of the United States	**U**	Military science
		V	Naval science
		Z	Bibliography and library science

✴ LIGHT

Light is the source of all life on Earth. Without light, plants would not grow, and without plants to provide oxygen, animals would not be able to live.

For many centuries, scientists argued about whether light was made of particles or of waves. Today most scientists agree that both ideas are true. Light is made up of electrical and magnetic forces traveling through space at high speed in waves, and it is also a stream of energy particles known as photons.

Any object that produces light, such as the sun or a flashlight, is called a light source. Other objects do not produce light of their own but reflect the light of other objects

The aurora borealis, or northern lights, is a great curtain of light that appears in the night sky in polar regions.

REFLECTED LIGHT

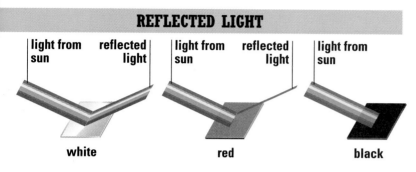

| light from sun | reflected light | light from sun | reflected light | light from sun |

white   **red**   **black**

The surface on the left reflects all seven colors of the spectrum and therefore appears white. The surface in the center absorbs six colors and reflects the seventh, red. The surface on the right absorbs all seven colors and therefore appears black.

that do. For example, the moon is not a source of light. It appears to shine because it is reflecting light from the sun.

The colors of light

The English scientist Isaac Newton discovered that "white" light is made up of several different colors. When sunlight passes through a three-sided pyramid of glass called a prism, it splits into bands of red, orange, yellow, green, blue, indigo, and violet: They are the visible colors of the spectrum. That effect—refraction—happens because light changes direction whenever it moves from one material into another. There are also colors of light we cannot see, called infrared and ultraviolet.

The color of an object depends on the way it reflects and absorbs light. Many objects absorb six colors of the spectrum and reflect the seventh. A red ball appears red because the material of which it is made reflects only that one color.

SEE ALSO: Colors; Eyes and Vision; Heat; Lasers; Newton, Isaac; Physics; Sun

✳ LIN, MAYA (1959–)

Maya Lin is the architect who designed the Vietnam Veterans Memorial in Washington, D.C., and the Civil Rights Memorial in Montgomery, Alabama.

▲ *Architect Maya Lin pictured in Michigan in 2000.*

Maya Ying Lin was born in Athens, Ohio. Her parents immigrated to the U.S. from China in 1948. Lin studied architecture and sculpture at Yale University. In her senior year, she won a national competition to design a memorial honoring soldiers who died in the Vietnam War (1957–75). Completed in 1982, the memorial consists of two black granite walls engraved with the names of the 58,000 Americans who died in Vietnam.

In 1988 Lin agreed to design a memorial honoring the civil rights movement. It is made up of a wall inscribed with a quotation from Martin Luther King Jr., a disk bearing the names of 40 people who died in the struggle for civil rights, and a timeline of important events.

Since then Lin has created sculptures and other large-scale works and has designed houses and furniture. She uses recycled, living, or natural material in her work. She lives and works in New York City.

SEE ALSO: Architecture; Art and Artists; Civil Rights; King, Martin Luther, Jr.; Vietnam War

LITERATURE

Literature is written material that has lasting value or interest. It includes imaginative works and factual accounts.

Early literature

The earliest form of literature in ancient times was the long epic story chanted by a musician or poet to an assembled group. The first epic stories to be written down were those of Mesopotamia (now Iraq), where writing began. One of the early epics was *The Epic of Gilgamesh*, a Sumerian poem that dates from about 2000 B.C. The ancient Greeks and Romans wrote works that are still read today, such as the short moral stories called fables written by Aesop.

Beginning in the 1200s, European poets such as Dante, Boccaccio, and Chaucer wrote long works about religion, love, and life. However, most people could not read. When Johannes Gutenberg invented the printing press in the 1400s, books became cheaper and more accessible. Gradually more people learned to read.

Because the stories and cultures of Native Americans were passed down by word of mouth, the first American writers were European colonists and their descendants.

Fiction and nonfiction

Literature is divided into fiction and nonfiction. Fiction is work that the writer invents or imagines. It aims to stir the reader's feelings by describing moods of joy or sadness, by telling exciting stories, and by introducing characters whose emotions can be understood and shared by the reader. Fiction can be in the form of novels, plays, poems, or short stories.

Nonfiction is writing that provides readers with the facts about a certain subject, such as science or history.

Autobiographies, biographies, diaries, and essays are all works of nonfiction. An autobiography is the author's own account of his or her life. A biography is the life of someone other than the author. An essay is a short piece of prose that discusses a subject from a personal point of view.

Drama

A drama is a story meant to be acted out onstage. Serious plays are often called tragedies, especially if they end with the death of the leading character. Comic plays, or comedies, emphasize the ridiculous aspects of human behavior.

The ancient Greeks invented drama, but the great age of dramatic writing was during the reign (1558–1603) of England's Queen Elizabeth I. Playwrights of the time included William Shakespeare, Christopher Marlowe, and Ben Jonson. Like the Greek dramatists, the Elizabethans wrote in

A performance of William Shakespeare's comedy play A Midsummer Night's Dream, written around 1594–96.
▼

Don Quixote, the hero of Cervantes's 17th-century novel, was a dreamer who mistook windmills for giants and tried to joust with them. ▶

poetic form. In recent times, most playwrights have written in prose.

Poetry

Poetry differs from prose in having a regular rhythm, sometimes using rhyme. The ancient Greeks wrote epic poems about heroic events. Homer's *Iliad* describes the siege of Troy, and the *Odyssey* tells the adventures of Odysseus on his voyage home from Troy. Lyric poetry is short, songlike, and very personal. The ode, a form of lyric poetry, is dignified in style. Narrative poetry tells a story.

In the early 1800s, poetry was an important literary form. Percy Bysshe Shelley, William Wordsworth, and John Keats are remembered for their lyrics and odes. Samuel Taylor Coleridge's "The Rime of the Ancient Mariner" (1798) is a ghostly tale of magic and mystery. These four poets brought new subjects and a new richness of language into poetry.

American poets such as Henry Wadsworth Longfellow wrote verse about the history of their country. The nation's two greatest poets wrote in the late 1800s. Walt Whitman's work is full of passion for people working together and appreciating nature. Emily Dickinson was much more concerned with the individual's inner thoughts, and often wrote about death.

Novels

A novel is a long story, often with many characters and an involved plot. The earliest known novel comes from Japan. *The Tale of Genji* was written by Lady Murasaki Shikibu in the early 11th century. One of the earliest European novels was *Don Quixote* by the Spaniard Miguel de Cervantes, completed in 1615. *The Power of Sympathy* (1789) by William Hill Brown was the first American novel.

Some of the greatest novelists wrote in the 1800s. They included Charles Dickens, George Eliot, and the Brontë sisters in England; Victor Hugo and Emile Zola in France; and Fyodor Dostoyevsky and Leo Tolstoy in Russia. They all used the novel to study emotions and society.

It was also not until the early 1800s that fiction with an especially American flavor was published. Washington Irving wrote stories such as "Rip Van Winkle" and "The Legend of Sleepy Hollow" that are still read today. James Fenimore Cooper's novels, such as *The Last of the Mohicans* (1826), defined the public idea of the American frontier. Great American novels of the period include *The Scarlet Letter* (1850) by Nathaniel Hawthorne, *Moby Dick* (1851) by Herman Melville, and *The Adventures of Huckleberry Finn* (1884) by Mark Twain. American novelists also wrote about the social problems of the growing nation. Harriet Beecher Stowe attacked slavery in *Uncle Tom's Cabin* (1852). Stephen Crane focused on war and poverty. His best-known novel is *The Red Badge of Courage* (1895).

A 19th-century illustration from The Tale of Genji, *the earliest known novel.*

GREAT AMERICAN WRITERS

These are just a few of the many writers who have shaped American literature. The "see also" box (next page) indicates entries on some others.

Irving, Washington (1783–1859)
Short-story writer from New York who was influenced by New England folklore.

Longfellow, Henry Wadsworth (1807–82)
Poet (below) who wrote *The Song of Hiawatha* and "Paul Revere's Ride."

Stowe, Harriet (Elizabeth) Beecher (1811–96)
Author of the antislavery novel *Uncle Tom's Cabin*, which helped bring on the Civil War.

James, Henry (1843–1916)
Novelist who wrote about the relationship between American and European cultures. In 1915 he became a British citizen.

Wharton, Edith (Newbold) (1862–1937)
Novelist who wrote about women in high society in *The House of Mirth* and *The Age of Innocence*, among others.

Cather, Willa (Sibert) (1873–1947)
Novelist whose books, such as *O Pioneers!* and *My Antonia,* often drew on her childhood in Nebraska.

Faulkner, William (Cuthbert) (1897–1962)
Nobel Prize-winning novelist and short-story writer whose works were usually set in Mississippi.

Hughes, (James) Langston (1902–67)
Poet and novelist of the "Harlem Renaissance" literary scene who wrote about the lives of African Americans.

Williams, Tennessee (Thomas Lanier) (1911–83)
Playwright whose works, such as *A Streetcar Named Desire* and *Cat on a Hot Tin Roof,* have become classics of recent American theater.

Salinger, J. D. (Jerome David) (1919–)
Novelist and short-story writer whose most famous work is *The Catcher in the Rye.*

Plath, Sylvia (1932–63)
Poet whose work often dealt with illness and suffering. Her only novel, *The Bell Jar*, was partly autobiographical.

GREAT WRITERS OF THE WORLD

These are just a few of the world's most famous writers. There are many more; the "see also" box indicates entries on some others.

Dante (Alighieri) (1265–1321)
Italian poet who wrote *The Divine Comedy*, the tale of a journey from Hell to Paradise.

Cervantes (Saavedra), Miguel de (1547–1616)
Spanish author of *Don Quixote*, a great study of a deluded, romantic knight and an important early novel.

Milton, John (1608–74)
English poet who wrote the epic *Paradise Lost*, based on the biblical stories of Adam and Eve and Satan.

Goethe, Johann Wolfgang von (1749–1832)
German poet, dramatist, and novelist who wrote *Faust*, the best-known version of a legend about a man who sells his soul to Satan.

Hugo, Victor(-Marie) (1802–85)

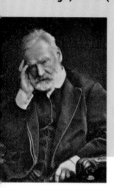

French novelist (left) whose books, such as *Les Misérables*, dealt with social injustice and society's victims.

Brontë, Charlotte (1816–55) (below), **Brontë, Emily (Jane)** (1818–48), and **Brontë, Anne** (1820–49)
English sisters who wrote passionate novels with strong female characters. The best known are Charlotte's *Jane Eyre* and Emily's *Wuthering Heights*.

Eliot, George (Mary Ann Evans) (1819–80)
English novelist who wrote under a man's name. Her most famous work is *Middlemarch*.

Tolstoy, Count Leo (Lev) Nikolayevich (1828–1910)
Russian novelist who wrote *War and Peace* and *Anna Karenina*. A major writer about people's place in history and society.

Woolf, (Adeline) Virginia (1882–1941)
English novelist who developed a style of writing that mimics the flow of thoughts that pass through the mind. Her works include *Mrs. Dalloway* and *To the Lighthouse*.

García Márquez, Gabriel (1928–)
Colombian Nobel Prize-winning novelist who wrote *One Hundred Years of Solitude*, the magical tale of an imaginary South American community.

Modernism

In the 1900s, many novelists focused on the problems of society. John Steinbeck dealt sympathetically with the problems of the poor. Richard Wright, Ralph Ellison, and James Baldwin confronted racism and brought African American literature to a wide readership. But some writers did not deal with society in a straightforward way. James Joyce and Virginia Woolf in Britain and T. S. Eliot and Ezra Pound in the United States were important figures in a movement called Modernism. The language and structure of their writing was new and often difficult for readers. Their work reflected a world where old certainties such as religion and society no longer existed.

Short stories

Short stories are generally between 1,000 and 20,000 words. They usually have only a few characters and focus on a single incident. Among the world's greatest short-story writers have been the Russian Anton Chekhov and the Frenchman Guy de Maupassant. In the United States, the leading short-story writers have included Edgar Allan Poe, O. Henry, Flannery O'Connor, and Katherine Anne Porter.

SEE ALSO: Angelou, Maya; Chaucer, Geoffrey; Children's Authors; Dickens, Charles; Dickinson, Emily; Fitzgerald, F. Scott; Frost, Robert; Hemingway, Ernest; Hurston, Zora Neale; Melville, Herman; Morrison, Toni; Myths and Legends; Nobel Prize; Poe, Edgar Allan; Printing; Shakespeare, William; Steinbeck, John; Theater; Twain, Mark; Whitman, Walt; Writing

✱LONGITUDE see➡ ✱NAVIGATION

LOUISIANA PURCHASE
In a treaty signed on May 2, 1803, the United States bought from France a vast area covering 828,000 sq. miles (2,144,520 sq. km).

The area extended from the Mississippi River in the east to the Rocky Mountains in the west, and from the Gulf of Mexico in the south to the Canadian border in the north.

In the 1500s, this region was explored by Spanish conquistadors. In 1682 a Frenchman—Robert Cavelier, Sieur de La Salle—named it Louisiana in honor of his king, Louis XIV. Early in the 1700s, the French founded settlements along the Mississippi River, the most important being New Orleans.

At the end of the French and Indian wars in North America, France lost its lands east of the Mississippi to Great Britain and gave up Louisiana—New Orleans and French lands west of the Mississippi—to Spain. In 1800, however, Napoleon Bonaparte persuaded the Spanish to sign a secret treaty handing Louisiana back to France.

Crisis over Louisiana
President Thomas Jefferson did not like having a country as strong as France as a neighbor in the west. He feared that if the French controlled New Orleans they would close the Mississippi River to American trade. In March 1803 James Monroe was sent to Paris to negotiate the purchase of New Orleans and an area of land on the Gulf of Mexico. By the time Monroe arrived, Napoleon had already abandoned his plans to build a colonial empire in North America and so had decided to sell Louisiana.

Monroe was startled at being offered so much land, and Napoleon was in a hurry

to finish the business, so the deal was finalized without referring back to Jefferson. The cost was about 80 million francs, or $15 million. Popular enthusiasm swept aside any doubts that Jefferson had when he received the surprising news.

On December 20, 1803, a colorful ceremony was held in New Orleans. The French, Spanish, and Americans watched as the French flag came down and the Stars and Stripes was raised. The following year, Louisiana was divided into the Territory of Orleans, which later became the state of Louisiana, and the District of Louisiana, which was later divided among 14 states.

▲
This map shows (in green) the territory gained by the United States in the Louisiana Purchase of 1803. The current state boundaries are also marked.

SEE ALSO: Conquistadors; French and Indian Wars; Lewis, Meriwether; Napoleon; United States of America

✳ LUNGS AND RESPIRATORY SYSTEM

Respiration is the process of taking in oxygen and removing carbon dioxide from the body by breathing in and out using organs called lungs.

In very simple organisms, respiration occurs when gases pass through cell membranes. More complex animals exchange gas through the skin or, in the case of water-based animals, through the gills. The main respiratory organs of birds, reptiles, and mammals are the lungs.

The human respiratory system

The two lungs take up most of the space inside the chest and are surrounded by the ribs. Air passes from the nose through the pharynx, the larynx (the voice box), then the trachea (the windpipe).

The trachea branches into two tubes. Each tube, or bronchus, enters a lung and branches out many more times. The narrowest of these branches is called a bronchiole, which is about ⅟₂₅ in. (1 mm) wide. Each bronchiole ends in a cluster of tiny sacs called alveoli. Each alveolus is surrounded by tiny blood vessels called capillaries. Oxygen passes from the alveoli to the capillaries and into the circulatory system toward the heart. Waste carbon dioxide moves in the opposite direction, from the capillaries to the alveoli. It leaves the body when the lungs breathe out. If this exchange of gases were to stop for just a few minutes, we would die.

Normal breathing is automatic. The brain coordinates the respiratory system, even during sleep. The lungs do not have any muscles of their own. Breathing depends on movements of a muscle called the diaphragm and the intercostal (between the ribs) muscles.

With each normal breath, an adult takes in about 1 pint (0.5 l) of air. A deep breath can take in six or seven times this amount. During exercise the body requires more oxygen, so the breathing rate speeds up, and breaths become deeper.

RESPIRATORY SYSTEM

The human respiratory system brings in oxygen to give cells energy and takes away waste carbon dioxide. ▶

nose

mouth

larynx

lungs

bronchiole

bronchus

diaphragm

pharynx

trachea

SEE ALSO: Animals; Cells; Heart and Circulatory System; Human Body

✳LUXEMBOURG ⮞see⮞ ✳NETHERLANDS, BELGIUM, AND LUXEMBOURG

* MACHINES

Machines are devices that are used to do work. They can be divided into four broad groups: prime movers, fluid-power, electrical, and mechanical.

Prime movers are machines that convert natural sources of energy, such as running water, wind, oil, and natural gas, into mechanical energy. Common examples include waterwheels, windmills, and internal-combustion engines, such as those that power automobiles.

Examples of fluid-power machines include water pumps and turbines.

Electrical machines are devices such as generators and alternators that power electric motors, loudspeakers, and so on.

Mechanical machines use energy to perform specific work. To do this, they move, or carry out motion. Motion is transmitted mechanically in only three basic ways: by a linkage, by direct contact between surfaces such as gear teeth, or by one or more connectors such as belts, chains, and ropes.

Work

Although in everyday language *work* is a person's job, for scientists it has a special meaning. Work is done when a force moves an object. Physicists define work as force multiplied by the distance over which the force acts. It is measured in foot-pounds. For example, if a task involves lifting a 500-lb. washing machine 6 ft. onto a platform, then 500 x 6 = 3,000 foot-pounds of work will be needed to lift it.

Inclined planes

Machines are devices to reduce effort. A simple way of raising a heavy object is by pushing or pulling it up an inclined plane, or ramp. A ramp is a simple machine.

If the ramp is 10 ft. long, then the effort needed to push the 500-lb. washing machine up it to a height of 6 ft. is only 3,000 : 10 = 300 foot-pounds. The total work is still 3,000 foot-pounds, but the effort has been reduced by the machine. However, this effort figure assumes that the surface of the ramp is smooth and that there is no friction (the resistance encountered when one body moves against another). In reality there is always friction, and the efficiency of any machine is always less than 100 percent.

A torsion-powered catapult. Torsion means "twisting." In ancient and medieval times, these machines hurled large missiles at enemy fortifications. Energy was stored by winding ropes around the catapult with a lever and gear combination. The sudden release of this energy launched large rocks, arrows, or flaming balls.
▼

(continued on page 367) **365**

SOME SIMPLE MACHINES

The diagrams on these pages show the mechanical processes by which some simple machines are made to perform work.

SIMPLE LEVERS

A lever is a rigid bar pivoted around a point called a fulcrum. The lever enables a small force (the effort) to lift a larger force (the load). Among the devices that use the lever principle are scissors, wheelbarrows, and sugar tongs.
▶

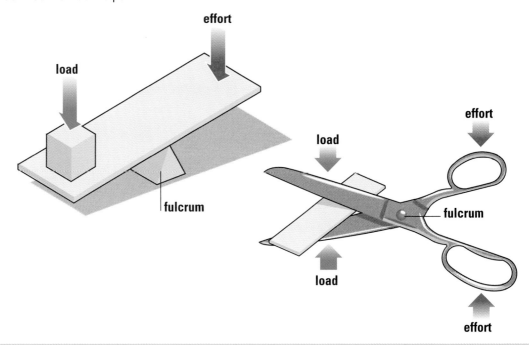

WHEEL AND AXLE

A wheel-and-axle unit is actually a lever, with the axle acting as the fulcrum.
▶

PULLEY

A pulley is similar to a wheel and axle, but has one or more ropes pulling in different directions in order to reduce the effort needed to shift a load.
▶

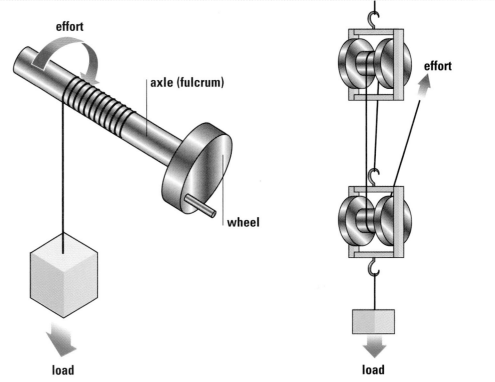

INCLINED PLANE

It is much easier to push a load up an inclined plane, or ramp, than to lift it straight up vertically to the same height.
▶

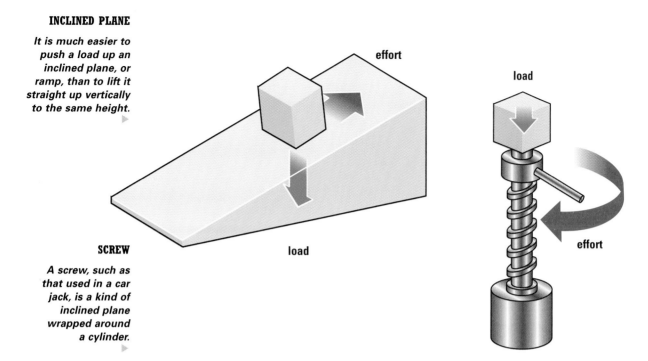

SCREW

A screw, such as that used in a car jack, is a kind of inclined plane wrapped around a cylinder.
▶

Mechanical advantage

Any device such as a ramp that reduces the effort needed to carry out work is called a force multiplier. A broom is another good example of this type of machine—a small movement of the top of the handle is magnified into a larger sweep at the bottom end. The effect of this is to increase not only the distance covered by the sweeping motion, but also the speed at which the sweeping is carried out. Any reduction of effort or increase in speed achieved by a machine is called mechanical advantage.

Levers

Another well-known simple machine is the lever. A lever is a rigid bar that provides the ability to lift when it is turned on a pivot called a fulcrum. An example is the wheelbarrow, in which the wheel acts as the fulcrum. A load of dirt is easier to lift in a wheelbarrow than it would be in a sack. Tools such as pliers and hammers are forms of levers. Our arms are also levers, with our elbows acting as fulcrums.

Other simple machines

In addition to inclined planes and levers, there are other simple machines. These are wedges and screws (both related to inclined planes) and pulleys and wheels and axles (both related to levers).

A wedge consists of a piece of wood or metal that is thick at one end and slopes to a thin edge at the other. It looks like an inclined plane, but works differently. It can hold things together, as in a doorstop, or it can separate or split objects, as in an ax. Knives also use the principle of the wedge to do work by pushing materials apart.

A screw is an inclined plane spiraled around a cylinder, usually of metal. The mechanical advantage of a screw can be seen if you try to remove a cork from a bottle. The cork is harder to take out if you pull the corkscrew straight up than if you twist it.

A pulley is a wheel with a groove around its outer edge that can hold a rope in position. As the rope is pulled, it turns the

HOW GEARS WORK

A gear is a wheel with teeth, or sprockets, cut into its outer edge that fits together (meshes) with a second, similar wheel.

▶ *As the wheels rotate, one wheel moves clockwise and one counterclockwise.*

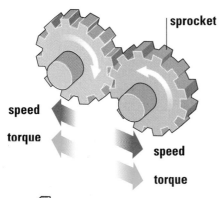

sprocket

speed

torque

speed

torque

▶ *If both wheels need to move in the same direction, a smaller wheel, called an idler, can be placed between them.*

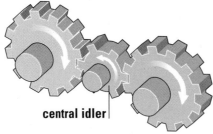

central idler

▶ *If a large wheel drives a small wheel, the speed is doubled, and the power (torque) is halved.*

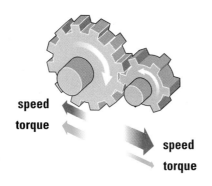

speed

torque

speed

torque

▶ *If a small wheel drives a large wheel, the speed is halved, and the power is doubled.*

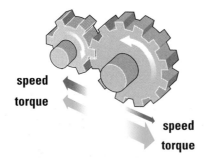

speed

torque

speed

torque

wheel, and the attached load is raised. Pulleys can be fixed in a particular position, for example, to raise a flag up a pole, or they can be movable. Several fixed and movable pulleys can be used together in a lifting device called a block and tackle. By this means a single person may be able to lift a piano.

A wheel and axle is a lever that is able to rotate through 360 degrees. It is similar to a pulley but differs from it in that the wheel is fixed to the axle. A screwdriver is a form of wheel-and-axle machine. So is a bicycle, which functions as a speed multiplier because the pedal sprocket (input) is smaller than the rear wheel (output)—this means that a small turning of the pedal by the cyclist's foot makes a much larger rotation of the wheel that drives the bike along the road.

Gears

The principle of the wheel and axle is used in gears. Gears are two or more wheels with teeth, or sprockets, around the outer rim. When the teeth of two gears interlock, or mesh, and one gear turns, it causes the other gear to turn in the opposite direction. Gears of the same size, with the same number of teeth, turn at the same speed. If one gear is larger than the other, the smaller gear turns faster but the larger one delivers greater turning force, or torque. Gears are used to regulate speed and direction of motion in complex machines, such as cars, bicycles, and clocks, and to increase or decrease the force applied.

👀

SEE ALSO: Electricity; Energy; Engines; Force and Motion; Physics

⭐ MAGNETISM

Magnetism is an invisible force that enables certain objects to pull other things toward them or to push them away.

Every magnet has two ends, or poles: a north pole and south pole. If two magnets are placed close together, the two north poles or two south poles push each other away (repel). A north and a south pole pull toward each other (attract). This push or pull is called a magnetic field.

A magnetic compass works because the earth has a magnetic field, with a north

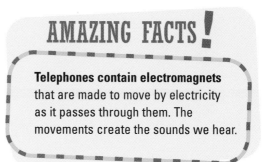

AMAZING FACTS!

Telephones contain electromagnets that are made to move by electricity as it passes through them. The movements create the sounds we hear.

A maglev train is tested at the Railway Technical Research Institute in Japan.

pole and a south pole. The north and south magnetic poles are not in exactly the same places as the geographic north and south poles. Some animals, such as birds, can feel Earth's magnetic field. They use it to find their way when they travel.

Magnetism and electricity

Electricity has positive and negative charges. As with magnetic poles, like charges repel, and opposite charges attract. In the early 1800s, scientists found that when they ran an electric current

through wire, it made a magnet that could be switched on and off. It is called an electromagnet. Electromagnets are used in many devices, including computer disks and video recorders. During the 1950s, scientists developed monorail trains that float above their rails, lifted by the force of electromagnets. They can travel smoothly at very high speeds. Such trains are called maglevs, short for magnetic levitation.

POLE ATTRACTION

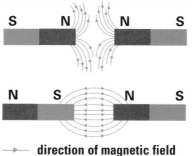

If the like poles of two magnets are placed within range of each other, they will repel (upper diagram). If a south pole is placed within range of a north pole (lower diagram), they will attract each other.

→ direction of magnetic field   N: north pole S: south pole

SEE ALSO: Computers; Earth; Electricity; Electronics; Medicine; Migration; Radio; Sound Recording; Telephones; Television; Trains and Railroads; Video Recording

✳ MALAYSIA

Malaysia is situated on the mainland of Southeast Asia and on one of the islands in the region.

Malaysia's national flag

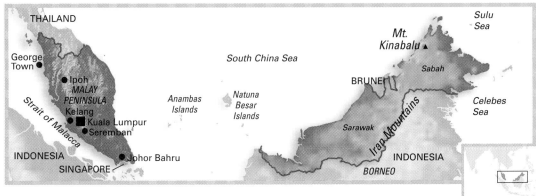

Modern Malaysia was created in two stages. In 1957 what was then Malaya won independence from Britain. The addition of Sabah, Sarawak, and Singapore in 1963 brought Malaysia into being. Singapore formed its own independent nation in 1965.

Land
Malaysia is divided into two distinct regions: Peninsular Malaysia and East Malaysia. In the west, Malaysia occupies part of the Malay Peninsula on the Asian mainland. East Malaysia comprises the states of Sabah and Sarawak on the island of Borneo. Mainland Malaysia is separated from the island by more than 400 mi. (645 km) of the South China Sea.

A mountain chain runs down the middle of the Malay Peninsula. Between the hills and the sea are low-level plains. Most of the peninsula's cities and towns are located on the western coastal plain.

People and economy
Malaysia has a rich and diverse mixture of races and cultures. Native Malays are the largest single group, followed by Chinese. There are also people from India, Pakistan, Sri Lanka, and Bangladesh.

Malaysia leads the world in the production of tin, palm oil, and rubber. It also has large deposits of natural gas, petroleum, bauxite (the main source of aluminum), copper, and iron. Its chief industries are manufacturing, fishing, and mining.

History
The modern history of Malaysia began around 1400, when a Malay ruler founded Malacca, which became the main trading power in Southeast Asia. However, by 1511 Malacca was in Portuguese hands, and by 1824 it was controlled by Britain. During World War II (1939–45), Japan seized Malaya, but Britain reoccupied it in 1945. In 1948 nine Malay states became the Federation of Malaya. Between 1948 and 1960 there was a state of emergency as the government fought Communist rebels. In 1957 two more states joined the federation. Malaysia came into existence in September 1963. Brunei did not join, and Singapore withdrew in 1965.

SEE ALSO: Southeast Asia; World War II

✳ MALCOLM X (1925–65)

Malcolm X was a champion of African American rights. He became famous as a leader of the Nation of Islam, a religious group.

Malcolm Little was born in Omaha, Nebraska. While in prison serving a sentence for burglary (1946–52), he adopted the Islamic religion as practiced by a group that later became the Nation of Islam, or Black Muslims. On his release, he became active in the Nation and changed his name to Malcolm X.

Malcolm X was a skilled speaker and attracted many new members to the Nation. In 1954 he became minister at the Black Muslim temple in Harlem, New York City. He was not afraid to speak out about social and political issues. When President John F. Kennedy was assassinated (killed) in 1963, Malcolm became very unpopular when he said that the act was the result

of hatred in America. He was later suspended from the Nation of Islam.

In 1964 Malcolm X made a pilgrimage to the Islamic holy city of Mecca. He came to believe that whites, like blacks, were victims of a racist society. He formed his own group, the Organization of Afro-American Unity. He was assassinated by three members of the Nation of Islam in Harlem on February 21, 1965.

SEE ALSO: African Americans; Civil Rights; Islam; Slavery

▲
Malcolm X adopted the X in his name because he believed that all African American surnames were slave names.

✳ MAMMALS

Mammals are the only animals that nurse their young with milk. They are also the only animals that have hair.

Characteristics

There are more than 4,000 species of mammals. They all have a diaphragm. This is a muscle that aids breathing by expanding and contracting the chest cavity. The jaws of other vertebrates (animals with backbones) are made up of several bones, but a mammal has only one bone on each side of its lower jaw.

Most mammals have seven neck bones, although the number of bones in their spines varies. Unlike most other animals, mammals are warm-blooded, which means that they are able to maintain a constant body temperature.

Movement

Mammals are found on land, in the trees, in the air, and in the water. Nearly all land mammals use four limbs for walking. Dogs and cats are among the many mammals that walk on the tips of their toes. In horses, deer, and some other mammals, these toes are protected by hard "toenails" called hooves.

Most mammals can swim. Seals, sea lions, and walruses spend most of their lives in the water, and their four limbs are short, flat flippers. Sea cows and whales live their entire lives in the water. Instead of hind limbs they have a broad, flat tail.

Belugas, or white whales, swim off the coast of northern Canada.

Tree-living mammals, such as squirrels and monkeys, have sharp claws to grip tree trunks when they climb. Bats are the only mammals that can fly. Their long, slender forelimbs provide a framework for the thin membranes of skin that form their wings.

Lifestyle

Solitary mammals, such as bears and jaguars, live alone except when breeding. Many mammals, such as monkeys, whales, and deer, live in groups. That helps them find food, look after one another, and escape from predators (hunters).

At certain times of the year, some mammals migrate (travel from one area to another) in search of warmth or food. Other mammals feed heavily and then hibernate (sleep through the winter).

Mammals make babies by sexual reproduction. The male's sperm (sex cell) enters the female's body to fertilize her sex

▷

Cats have sharp teeth and claws to hunt with and also to defend themselves.

cell, the egg. Each fertilized egg, or embryo, grows into a baby. In most mammals, the young grow within the mother, or gestate, for a period before birth. A few mammals, such as the duckbilled platypus in Australia, lay eggs from which the young hatch. Marsupials, such as koalas and opossums, give birth to offspring that are not fully formed. After birth the young feed and grow inside a pouch on the mother's belly.

Food and feeding

Most mammals are herbivores (plant-eaters). Cattle and deer, for example, graze on leaves and shoots; monkeys like fruit. Some mammals, such as lions and weasels, are carnivores (meat-eaters). Mammals that eat both plants and meat are called omnivores. The black bear, for instance, eats berries and buds as well as insects and fish.

Most mammals are prey for carnivores. They can escape in different ways. Most hoofed mammals can run swiftly to avoid being caught and eaten. Porcupines rely on their coat of spines to deter enemies, and armadillos have a coat of scaly armor. Plain-colored, spotty, or striped coats may also help

AMAZING FACTS !

Largest mammal: Blue whale, weight over 130 tons

Smallest mammal: Kitti's hog-nosed bat, length 1.2 in. (3 cm), wingspan 6 in. (15 cm)

Largest land mammal: African elephant, up to 16,500 lb. (7,500 kg)

Tallest mammal: Giraffe (right), 18 ft. (5.5 m) or over

Fastest mammal: Cheetah, 70 mph (113 kph)

Slowest mammal: Sloth, 0.5 mph (0.8 kph)

Longest gestation: Elephant, 20–22 months

Shortest gestation: Opossum, about 12 days

mammals disguise themselves and hide in undergrowth. This form of protection is called camouflage. Whether for defense or attack, mammals have plenty of weapons. Cats attack with sharp teeth and claws, while hoofed mammals slash with hooves, horns, or antlers. Skunks spray a strong-smelling chemical.

The first mammals

Fossilized remains show that the earliest mammals lived at the time of the dinosaurs. They were small creatures that looked like rats or shrews. After the dinosaurs became extinct (died out) about 65 million years ago, the mammal population steadily grew, changed (evolved), and spread all over the world. They began to vary in shape, size, and living habits. Today mammals, especially humans, are the dominant animals on Earth.

SEE ALSO:
Animals; Apes, Monkeys, and Primates; Bats; Bears; Cats and Big Cats; Cows; Dogs, Wolves, and Other Wild Dogs; Elephants; Fossils; Hibernation; Hippopotamuses; Horses; Marsupials; Migration;• Rhinoceroses; Rodents; Whales and Dolphins

✳ MANDELA, NELSON (1918–)

Nelson Mandela was a leader in the struggle against the white minority government's policy of apartheid, or racial segregation, in South Africa.

Nelson Rolihlahla Mandela was born near Umtata, in the Transkei region of South Africa. His father was a chief of the Xhosa people. Mandela studied law and set up practice in Johannesburg in 1952.

Political activism

In 1944 Mandela joined the African National Congress (ANC) and helped form the ANC Youth League. He led the ANC's policy of nonviolent resistance to the government in 1951–52, for which he received his first jail sentence. Mandela was arrested with other ANC leaders and charged with treason in 1956. He was acquitted in 1961. He divorced his first

wife and married Winnie Madikizela in 1958. (They divorced in 1996.)

In 1960 police in Sharpeville shot at unarmed black protesters and the government banned the ANC. Mandela turned to violent action in the fight against apartheid and helped found a military wing of the ANC. He was arrested, tried, and sent to prison for life in 1964. He was kept in Robben Island Prison until 1982 and then moved to a maximum-security prison. His autobiography, *Long Walk to Freedom*, tells the story of these years.

By the late 1980s, South Africa had become isolated within the international

After 27 years of imprisonment, Nelson Mandela emerged to become the first black president of South Africa.

community. The government faced civil unrest at home and trade boycotts and diplomatic pressure from other states. In February 1990 President F. W. de Klerk set Mandela free.

Mandela became the ANC's president in 1991. He shared the Nobel Peace Prize with de Klerk in 1993 for their efforts to end apartheid. Black South Africans voted in elections for the first time in April 1994. The ANC won a majority of seats in the new parliament, and Mandela became the first black president of South Africa. He resigned from the ANC in 1997 and retired from the presidency in 1999. On his 80th birthday, he married Graça Machel.

SEE ALSO: Africa; Nobel Prize; South Africa

✳ MANUFACTURING

Manufacturing is the process of making new products from raw materials, usually on a large scale with the aid of machinery.

Until 250 years ago, most goods were made at home by skilled craftspeople. Many goods were so costly that few people could buy them. The development of modern manufacturing was based on new sources of power and machines.

For centuries the only sources of power were human and animal strength and waterwheels and windmills. That changed in the 1700s. Machines, such as weaving looms, were invented. Later, steam engines provided the power to drive them. Even later, other sources of power were developed, such as electricity. Steel, a strong, workable combination of iron and carbon, replaced brittle iron in the making

of machines and tools. This exciting period of change and growth started in Europe in about 1760 and spread to America. It is known as the Industrial Revolution.

Mass production

During that revolution, industries began using large machines to produce goods. Factories were built to house the machinery. In a system known as mass production, hundreds of factory workers could produce great quantities of an item. Manufactured items cost less to produce than handmade goods, and could be made faster. They were therefore cheaper to buy, and more people than ever before could afford them.

This production line completes thousands of pairs of rubber gloves every day.

Standardization

For successful mass production, parts are standardized—they are all made in the same way and look the same.

This means, for example, that a clock manufacturer will make all the hour hands of a type of clock the same, all the minute hands the same, and so on. As a result, the parts can be put together quickly to make lots of clocks. It is also cheaper for workers to make parts in large quantities than to make a few at a time.

Two Americans came up with the idea of standardization during the early 1800s. Simeon North and Eli Whitney both ran workshops making guns, and each had the idea of using standardized parts.

After all the separate parts were made, a gun was passed from one worker to another, with each worker adding a different part. In time other products, such as clocks, watches, sewing machines, and farm machinery, were produced in the same way.

Assembly lines

Standardization works even better when an assembly line is used. An assembly line is like a long, moving workbench. In 1908 Henry Ford (1863–1947) used an assembly line to build his famous Model T Ford. The bare frame of the car started at one end of the line. As the frame moved along, each worker added a new part. Ford improved the system until the time it took to build a car fell from over 12 hours (before the introduction of the assembly line) to only 1½ hours. Soon cars were being mass-produced in the thousands.

Automation

Automation is a short way of saying "automatic mechanization." It describes the way in which many factory machines are run today. Some machines are now robots. They have "arms" and "hands" that are moved by motors to perform tasks on the assembly line. Bottles, cans, and paper are only a few of the products made by automated machinery. ➥

DID YOU KNOW?

Chemically produced, synthetic (artificial) materials are important in manufacturing. Nylon is a synthetic material first produced in the 1930s by the DuPont Corporation. It is used to make toothbrushes, umbrellas, parachutes, and rope. Other synthetic materials include plastics. They have replaced natural materials because they are easily molded and do not rot.

The original spinning jenny—a machine for spinning wool and cotton yarn—was built in the 1760s by the English inventor James Hargreaves (died 1778).

The industrial world

In 1820 more than two-thirds of Americans worked on the land. As industry grew, people left the farms to work in factories. By 1990 fewer than 3 percent of Americans worked on the land. The number of people working in factories also dropped, mostly because of automation. Today the United States is the world's leading industrial nation—no other country produces a greater quantity of manufactured goods.

SEE ALSO: Cars; Economics; Electricity; Energy; Engines; Fabrics and Cloth; Industrial Revolution; Inventors and Inventions; Machines; Metals; Natural Resources; Plastic; Robots; Technology; Tools; Trade

✳ MAPS

A map is a representation, or a type of picture, of an area. Maps contain useful information and can show city streets, a state or country, or the entire world.

Maps help people find their way from one place to another. They can show information about the land, population, or economic activities. There are also weather, undersea, and star maps. Because the earth is round, a globe gives the most accurate picture of the shapes and sizes of the land and water areas of the earth. Flat maps are easier to handle, however, and they can show small areas in greater detail than a globe. For these reasons, flat maps are more widely used.

History of mapmaking

People have made and used maps throughout history. The oldest surviving maps date back to Babylonian times, over 4,000 years ago. Geographers in ancient Greece were the founders of scientific cartography (mapmaking).

The Romans used maps to help them wage wars, build roads and aqueducts, and administer their conquered provinces. The Polynesians sailed the Pacific guided by maps made of palm fiber and shells. The Chinese also made many maps. The oldest printed Chinese map (1155) was made about 300 years before the first map was printed in Europe.

Between 1470 and 1700, information gathered by explorers led to great advances in cartography. The oldest existing globe (1492) was the work of the

German merchant and navigator Martin Behaim. The first map to use the name *America* was made 15 years later by another German, Martin Waldseemüller. In 1570 the Flemish publisher Abraham Ortelius reproduced many maps of the same size and bound them into the first modern atlas. However, the term *atlas* was not used for a bound volume of maps until the Flemish mapmaker Gerhard Mercator published his *Atlas* in 1595.

In the 1700s, new techniques enabled cartographers to construct much more accurate maps of the world. Today cartographers, assisted by computers, remote sensing devices, and satellite photographs, can make maps of the moon, the planets, and the ocean depths.

Geographic grids

One basic use of maps is to locate specific places or features. To do this, the ancient Greeks invented a geographic grid that is still used today. It is made up of two sets of imaginary lines. One set is a series of circles, called parallels of latitude, that run east and west around the earth. The other set, called meridians of longitude, are north–south lines stretching between the poles. All latitude and longitude grid lines are circles or parts of circles and are shown in degrees (°). Any place on Earth can be located exactly if you know its latitude and its longitude.

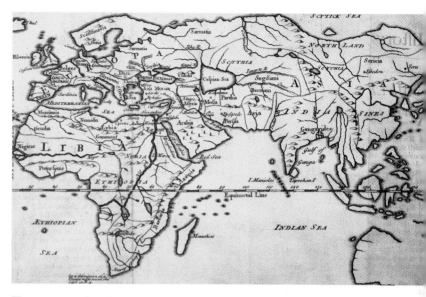

There are other kinds of map grids that help you locate places. Many maps have a series of letters beginning with "A" running across the top and bottom of the map, and a series of numbers beginning with "1" running up or down the right and left edges. To find a place located at A-3 in the map index, look in the box formed where sections A and 3 cross each other.

Direction and distance

Maps tell you direction. On most modern maps, north is at the top of the map. If you face north, east is to the right, west is to the left, and south is behind you.

This 17th-century illustration shows the world as it was known to the Greek historian Herodotus in about 450 B.C. The ancient Greeks created scientific maps, but with less detail than is shown here.

To find a specific place on a map, you need to know its latitude and longitude. The east–west lines are parallels of latitude. The north–south lines are meridians of longitude. New Orleans, for example, is located at 30°N and 90°W.

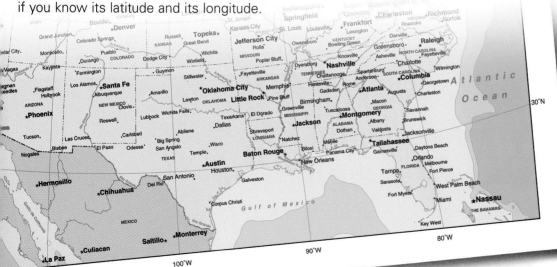

To find the distance between two cities on a map, mark the distance between the two places on the edge of a piece of paper. Place the paper along the graphic scale and read the distance.

Flat maps

"Flattening" a picture of Earth's surface to make a map stretches and distorts the image. Cartographers get around this problem by showing the planet's surface as a series of slices or, more commonly, by stretching or shrinking some areas. That is why Greenland, for example, looks much larger on many maps than it really is in relation to other countries.

Understanding map symbols

Relief, or physical, maps show natural features, such as mountains, oceans, and rivers. Cultural maps include human-made features, such as political boundaries, highways, and towns. Cartographers often use symbols and colors to stand for various features. The outline of an airplane may indicate an airport, for example. Symbols and other information are usually placed in a box called the legend, or key. Maps use different symbols, so always look at the key to see what they mean.

Physical relief features, such as hills and valleys, are hard to depict because they must be shown from above rather than from ground level. To deal with this problem, contour lines mark elevation above sea level. The contour lines link points of the same height.

SEE ALSO: Exploration and Explorers; Geography; Navigation

✳ MARCO POLO (1254–1324)

Marco Polo was a great traveler during the Middle Ages. He was the first European to travel the entire width of Asia, describing the lands and their people.

▲ *Marco Polo described things from his travels in China, such as paper money, that were then unknown in Europe.*

Marco Polo was born in Venice, then an independent city-state in northern Italy. His father and uncle were merchants who journeyed to China. This was the first contact in many centuries between Europe and Asia.

When Marco was 17, he accompanied his father and uncle on their return journey to China and the court of Kublai Khan. He quickly became a favorite of the khan, or emperor, who sent him on special missions to distant parts of the empire.

After 24 years, the Polos returned to Venice. Some time after his return, Marco fought for Venice in a sea battle against Genoa and was taken prisoner. While in prison, he dictated the story of his travels to a fellow prisoner. Today the manuscript is regarded as one of the greatest pieces of travel writing.

At the time, Marco Polo was regarded as a liar. Many Europeans did not believe the wonders he described. In spite of this, his work influenced early mapmakers. It inspired Christopher Columbus to seek a westward sea route to Asia.

SEE ALSO: Columbus, Christopher; Exploration and Explorers; Middle Ages

MARKS

MARS

Mars is the fourth planet from the sun. Its surface features sandy deserts, canyons, volcanoes, and ice caps.

The orbit, or path around the sun, of Mars is more elliptical (oval-shape) than that of most other planets. So the distance from Mars to the sun varies throughout the Martian year. At its closest approach, Mars is 128.4 million miles (206.6 million km) from the sun; at its greatest distance from the sun, it is 154.8 million miles (249.1 million km) away. A year on Mars (the time the planet takes to complete its path around the sun) is almost twice as long as an Earth year.

The red planet

Mars looks distinctly orange or red. This color, associated with anger, led the ancient Romans to name the planet for Mars, their god of war. The color comes from minerals containing forms of iron. The surface of Mars is covered with dark orange or brown boulders and drifts of fine orange sand. The diameter of Mars is a little over half that of Earth. Two small satellites, or moons, named Deimos and Phobos, orbit Mars.

Mars has little atmosphere—there is 600 times more air around Earth than there is around Mars. The air on Mars is usually crisp and clear. Even though almost every day is sunny, it is always cold. Even in the middle of the Martian summer, day temperatures reach no higher than freezing point, 32°F (0°C).

Some scientists believe that Mars once had much more atmosphere, a warmer climate, and flowing water, but that over a

The red color of parts of the surface of Mars is caused by the sands of its many deserts.

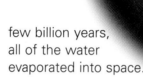

few billion years, all of the water evaporated into space.

Voyages

When the *Mariner 9* spacecraft began its orbit of Mars in 1971, a big dust storm was in progress. The probe's cameras showed nothing but dust and four mysterious spots. As the storm subsided, scientists were surprised to learn that the spots were the tops of four giant volcanoes. The largest of these may have stopped erupting about a billion years ago. In summer 2003 two Mars exploration rovers, *Spirit* and *Opportunity*, were launched. They landed at different locations on the planet in early 2004.

SEE ALSO: Astronomy; Planets; Solar System; Space Exploration

KEY FACTS

POSITION IN THE SOLAR SYSTEM:
Fourth planet from the sun

AVERAGE DISTANCE FROM THE SUN:
142,000,000 mi. (228,000,000 km)

SOLAR ORBIT:
687 Earth days

DIAMETER:
4,200 mi. (6,760 km)

MASS:
642 quintillion tons

ATMOSPHERE:
Carbon dioxide

AXIAL ROTATION:
24 hours, 37 minutes

MARSHES see WETLANDS

✳ MARSUPIALS

A marsupial is any mammal that is born at a relatively undeveloped stage and continues its development in a pouch on the mother's front.

▲
Baby opossums suckling, or being fed, around the entrance to their mother's pouch.

There are more than 240 kinds of marsupials. The best known are kangaroos, koalas, and opossums. Almost all marsupials are found in Australia and on nearby islands. Opossums are the only marsupials that are found in North and South America.

Newborn marsupials

Food is sent to the unborn young of most mammals through a special organ called the placenta. The placentas of most female marsupials are different from those of other mammals, and their young are born at a very early stage.

At birth marsupials are extremely small. Even the newborn of the largest kangaroo is only about the size of a honeybee. The body is hairless. The young marsupial's eyes and ears do not work. The back limbs and tail are tiny stumps, but the front limbs are stronger and end in sharp claws.

Immediately after birth, a newborn marsupial crawls from the birth canal at the base of the mother's tail through the fur to her belly. There it finds a nipple, which it grips with its mouth. The nipple swells within the baby's mouth, so that the baby remains securely attached. In most species, the nipples are located in a pouch, called a marsupium. As the baby gets older, it leaves the pouch for short periods and starts to eat plant foods. When it finally grows too large to climb back into the pouch and nurse, a young marsupial must find all its own food.

Leaving the pouch

The amount of time spent in the pouch varies for different marsupials. When a baby kangaroo—called a joey—is about four months old, it begins to sit up and look out of the pouch. At about eight months, the joey can jump out of the pouch to eat grass or leaves. If anything frightens the joey, it dives back into the safety of the pouch. By the time the joey reaches about 11 months, it is too big to fit in the pouch.

AMAZING FACTS !

The gray kangaroo can reach almost 7 ft. (2 m) in height and weigh up to 200 lb. (91 kg). The kangaroo bounds across the plains of Australia at speeds of over 40 mph (64 kph), covering distances of up to 30 ft. (9 m) in a single hop.

Virginia opossum babies remain in their mothers' pouches for about five weeks. Then they climb onto their mothers' backs. At seven or eight months old, most koalas are too large for the pouch. Like the baby opossum, the young koala rides on its mother's back, holding onto her for safety and comfort.

Kangaroos and koalas

There are more than 50 kinds of kangaroos living in Australia, New Guinea, and other neighboring islands. Along with the pouch of the female kangaroo, probably their best-known characteristic is their hopping way of moving. The kangaroo's strong, muscular tail provides balance when the animal hops and supports it when it stands or moves.

Kangaroos have a varied plant diet. Some eat soft plant matter such as mushrooms, some eat leaves and fruit, and others graze on grasses. Ranchers consider kangaroos a problem because they compete with cattle and sheep for grazing land. Hunting of large kangaroos is permitted in order to keep their populations under control.

The koala, with its large, rounded ears, leathery black nose, and stout body covered with woolly gray-brown fur, looks

A koala clings tightly to the branch of a eucalyptus tree.

like a small bear. A full-grown male koala may weigh up to 30 lb. (14 kg). A female is about 10 lb. (5 kg) lighter in weight.

A female kangaroo with a joey in her pouch.

Koalas spend most of their lives in eucalyptus trees, feeding on the leaves. They sleep for up to 18 hours a day. They are mainly nocturnal, meaning that they are active at night. The koala's diet is among the most specialized of any mammal. Koalas will eat only leaves from about 20 species of eucalyptus trees and may prefer only about five species.

Although some marsupials, such as koalas, are protected by law, they are still endangered. The major threat to marsupials in Australia and the Americas is the destruction of their habitats. As forests are cleared for housing and industrial development, and grasslands are plowed for the planting of crops, their homes and food supplies are destroyed.

SEE ALSO: Animals; Australia and New Zealand; Endangered Species; Mammals

* MATHEMATICS

Mathematics, or math, is the study of numbers and their patterns and relationships. It is also a way of reasoning and analyzing ideas.

▶ *The father of geometry, Euclid, was a Greek who lived and worked in Alexandria (a city in modern Egypt) in the third century B.C.*

Numbers are one of the oldest ideas developed by human beings, older even than writing. The system used all over the world today for writing numbers came orginally from India. In about A.D. 700, Indian mathematicians began using nine symbols for the first nine counting numbers and also created a symbol for zero, or nothing. The Arabs adopted the number system, and in about 1200 it reached Europe. There it replaced the Roman system of writing numbers, which was limited by having no symbol for zero. The new numbers became known as digits, from the Latin for finger, *digitus*.

In the modern system, units (one to nine) are written on the far right of any number. The next digit, written to the left of the unit, is a number of tens, the third digit is a number of hundreds, and so on. Using this system, just 10 symbols—1, 2, 3, 4, 5, 6, 7, 8, 9, and 0—can stand for millions, billions, trillions, and more.

There are different ways of writing or expressing numbers. If 10 is divided by 20, the answer can be written either as a decimal (0.5) or as a fraction (½).

Pure and applied mathematics

Over the thousands of years of its history, mathematics has grown to be a very broad field that includes many branches. However, there are two major divisions of mathematics—pure and applied. Pure mathematics is concerned with problems and questions on a theoretical level, developing theorems (unproved ideas) and formulas. Applied mathematics is concerned with the practical uses of math in the world around us. It uses the principles of pure math to solve problems in such areas as astronomy, business, computer science, economics, navigation, and physics.

Subdivisions of mathematics

The major subdivisions, or branches, of modern mathematics include arithmetic, algebra, geometry, calculus, and probability and statistics.

Arithmetic is the study of numbers and computation. The four basic operations of arithmetic are addition, subtraction, multiplication, and division. Each operation is represented by a sign: + for addition, - for subtraction, x for multiplication, and ÷ for division. Arithmetic is part of everyday life. We use calculators, computers, and cash registers to do computations for us.

Algebra uses symbols, often letters such as **x** and **y**, to represent unknown quantities in a mathematical problem. For example, in the statement **x + 5 = 8**, the letter **x** represents an unknown number. From this information alone, it is possible to work out the numerical value of **x** (3). Statements such as this are known as mathematical equations.

Geometry is the study of space, shape, and measurement. It can be used to figure out the area of a field, the volume of a box, or the size of the moon.

Calculus is the study of change and motion. It is used to work out numerical values that are inconstant and variable, such as the speed of a car, which may be said to be traveling at a steady 50 mph (80 kph), but whose speed is in fact varying, although only slightly, from moment to moment. Calculus is also used to find the areas and volumes of irregularly shaped figures and the lengths of curves. It is a very important tool in modern physics.

Probability and statistics are often considered together. Probability theory is the branch of mathematics concerned with calculating the likelihood of a particular event happening. For example, if you roll a die, there is a one in six chance of rolling a 4. If you keep rolling the die, the chances of a 4 showing at some point increase. But with each roll, the chance of a 4 showing is still one in six because there are six sides to a die, and each number on it has the same chance of

DID YOU KNOW?

The number represented by one followed by 100 zeros—also written as 10^{100}—is called a googol. It was given its name in 1938 by Milton Sirotta, aged nine.

IMPORTANT MATHEMATICIANS

These are a few of the people who made valuable contributions to the science of mathematics. The "see also" box (next page) indicates entries on some others.

Khwarizmi, al- (about 780–850)
Arab who introduced algebra to the West.

Descartes, René (1596–1650)
Frenchman who developed analytic geometry.

Leibniz, Gottfried Wilhelm (1646–1716)
German who invented calculus at the same time as the Englishman Isaac Newton.

Euler, Leonhard (1707–83)
Swiss who wrote more than 900 books on math and introduced several important mathematical symbols, such as pi (π).

Von Neumann, John (1903–57)
Hungarian-born American who developed a computer that enabled the United States to complete the calculations necessary for building and testing its hydrogen bomb.

Turing, Alan Mathison (1912–54)
Englishman who made important contributions to mathematical logic and the development of modern computers.

being rolled. Probability is used in many different situations, from calculating the odds of winning a lottery to determining the chances of inheriting a disease.

Statistics

Statistics applies probability theory to real cases, and provides methods for collecting, analyzing, and displaying information about particular events. The process of using statistics always begins with a question. We might ask "Who is likely to be the next president?" or "What candy bars do teenage girls eat?" or "What is the safest material for building houses?" Researchers find the information, or raw data. They might ask a sample of people for their views. They must make sure that they choose the right people, or their figures will not represent reality. Alternatively, the researchers might take data from newspapers or magazines, from scientific or government records, or from their own observation.

But this is only the start. If researchers ask 2,000 people their preferences for the next president, for example, all they have is 2,000 responses. This is interesting, but it is not much use on its own. A good statistician must make sense of this information. Does one group, such as women, or African Americans, or older people, favor one candidate? Do Texans feel differently from New Yorkers? How strongly do people feel about their choices? What could change their minds? A statistician must analyze the data and present his or her findings in a way that makes the meaning clear.

Graphs

A graph is a visual display of statistical information. With graphs a statistician can present complex information in a way that is easier to understand. There are several kinds of graphs (illustrated below).

Graphs and charts are a way of representing statistical information clearly. These examples show voting trends and results in an election.
▼

A bar graph is used to display and compare the number of people or things in a group. There is a scale on the left-hand side of the graph that shows how many people or things fit into each group. For example, in an election, if 45 percent of voters vote for Ross, the top of Ross's bar is level with the 45-percent mark on the scale.

A circle graph, or pie chart, represents the same data as segments of a circle. One hundred percent is shown as 360 degrees. If 45 percent of voters vote for Ross, 45 percent of the circle—a 162-degree segment—is colored red. Gold has 35 percent, or 126 degrees. Verdi has the remaining 20 percent, or 72 degrees.

Line graphs usually show trends, or how things change over time. For example, in January, Gold had 55 percent of the vote and Ross had 25 percent. In May, Gold's rating has fallen and Ross's has risen. Verdi's rating has stayed about the same.

SEE ALSO: Algebra; Computers; Einstein, Albert; Geometry; Newton, Isaac; Physics

A BAR GRAPH, A PIE CHART, AND A LINE GRAPH

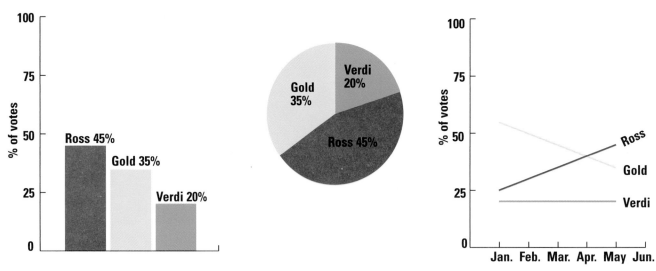

⁎ MATTER

Matter is any substance that has mass and takes up space. This means that almost everything in the universe is matter.

There are three basic forms, or states, of matter: solids, liquids, and gases. A solid resists changes in shape and size. A liquid takes the shape of any container into which it is put. A gas expands indefinitely to fill any container.

All substances change their state when there is a change in temperature. Water is a liquid at room temperature, but it turns into a solid (ice) when it freezes. It turns to steam, which is a vapor or gas, when it is boiled. The temperature at which a solid turns to liquid is called its melting point; the temperature at which a liquid turns into a gas is called its boiling point. When a gas cools and turns into a liquid, it is said to condense; when a liquid turns into a solid, it is said to freeze or solidify. These changes occur at different temperatures for different forms of matter.

Volume and mass

The amount of space that any form of matter takes up is known as its volume. Volume is not linked to weight. An inflated balloon takes up more space than a cell phone, but the phone is heavier.

Mass is not the same as weight. Weight is the force of gravitational attraction between an object and Earth or another astronomical body. Mass does not usually change, but weight changes depending on where an object is. For example, because the moon is less massive than Earth, the force of attraction between the moon and a person on it is less than the force of attraction between Earth and the same person on it. An astronaut weighs less on the moon than on Earth, but has the same mass in both places.

Nuclear changes

All matter is made up of tiny particles called atoms. Atoms are made up of subatomic particles called electrons, protons, and neutrons. Ordinary chemical changes affect the electrons at the surface of the atom. Nuclear changes, which affect the protons and neutrons in the nucleus (plural, *nuclei*), involve much larger quantities of energy. A nucleus can be made to break apart—this process is known as nuclear fission. Nuclei can also be made to join together—this is nuclear fusion. Extreme temperatures are required to achieve nuclear fusion. At such temperatures, matter is in a state called plasma. In this state, atoms break up into free electrons and neutrons. The sun and all other stars are made up of plasma.

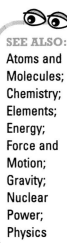

SEE ALSO:
Atoms and Molecules;
Chemistry;
Elements;
Energy;
Force and Motion;
Gravity;
Nuclear Power;
Physics

CHANGES TO MATTER

Matter can be made to change its properties in three main ways.

A metal such as copper can be drawn out into wires or heated until it melts, but it is still copper. These changes are called physical changes. In a physical change, the substance has the same atomic makeup as before, but its form is altered.

copper powder

copper wire

copper bar

When wood is burned, it produces heat and light (fire) and turns into a new form of matter, charcoal. This is a chemical change in which its atomic makeup is altered.

Changes can take place in the atomic nucleus of a form of matter. In a nuclear change, the central core, or nucleus, of an atom is altered. Great amounts of energy are released in the process.

splitting a nucleus

✳ MAYANS

The Mayans are an American Indian people who have lived in southern Mexico and Central America for more than 3,000 years.

The Mayans were based on and around the Yucatán Peninsula.

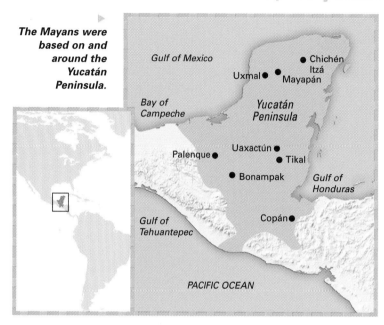

Gulf of Mexico

Chichén Itzá

Uxmal • • Mayapán

Bay of Campeche

Yucatán Peninsula

Palenque • Uaxactún •

• Tikal

• Bonampak

Gulf of Honduras

Gulf of Tehuantepec

Copán •

PACIFIC OCEAN

AMAZING FACTS!

Astronomers using modern observatories and computers have shown that the Mayan astronomical tables were accurate to within one day over the course of 6,000 years.

Earth and Earth to go around the sun. This helped them to work out an accurate calendar, so that they knew when to perform rituals or plant crops.

Food and trade
Most Mayans were farmers who grew corn, beans, squash, tomatoes, and other foods. They wove cotton clothing. There were no wheeled vehicles, so porters carried goods from town to town. The Mayans were great traders and bought goods from as far away as central Mexico.

Writing
The Mayans developed their own system of writing. It was made up of picture symbols called hieroglyphs.

During the ninth century, many Mayan cities were abandoned, and the kings and priests lost their power. Historians think that wars and bad harvests might have caused the decline. The Spanish arrived in the 1520s. They forced the Mayans to work on large plantations. Today there are nearly five million people who continue to speak Mayan languages and carry on the traditions of their ancestors.

The Mayan civilization flourished between the third and ninth centuries A.D., which historians call its classic period. There were 40 Mayan cities, each with its own king who ruled with the help of his nobles. The Mayans were a warlike people, and each king tried to conquer rival kings. The warriors wore armor of quilted cotton and fought with axes, clubs, and spears.

Religion
Priests were in charge of religious ceremonies, which included making offerings of blood and human sacrifices to the gods of the sun, moon, and rain. The victims of these sacrifices were often prisoners of war.

The priests also acted as astronomers. They observed the positions of the sun, moon, and stars and calculated exactly how long the moon took to go around

SEE ALSO:
Astronomy;
Aztecs;
Central
America;
Conquistadors;
Guatemala;
Incas; Mexico;
Writing

* MEDIA

Media, short for *mass media*, covers methods of communicating information to large numbers of people. It includes television, Web sites, and books.

The substance that an artist uses to make a picture—for example, oil paint or crayon—is called a medium. The word *medium* (plural, *media*) applies to any method of communication. A telephone is a medium, as is a postcard. When people discuss "the media," they are usually referring to the way we experience mass communication and entertainment. The "media industry" covers broadcasting, publishing, advertising, and the Internet.

Early media

Communication of literature, art, and ideas to large audiences became possible with the invention of the printing press in the 1400s. Books became less expensive to produce over the following centuries. The telegraph and telephone, both invented in the 19th century, made it quicker and cheaper to send information over long distances.

However, the media, as we understand it now, did not exist until the late 19th and early 20th centuries. By this time, the expansion of education in Europe and North America meant that most people were able to read and write. Public libraries allowed people to borrow and read more books than they could afford to buy. Magazines and newspapers were able to react quickly to events by publishing news and opinion. Beginning in the 1920s, radio and then, from the late 1940s, television brought news, sports, and music "live" into people's homes. Today the World Wide Web has become a separate publishing medium, providing the very latest news and electronic versions of some paper publications.

Passengers in a railroad station in Seoul, South Korea, watch television as news breaks of an historic visit by their president to North Korea.

Forms of media

At first, different forms of media were very separate. For example, newspaper publishers and radio stations provided their own products. Now, however, the difference between media products is less obvious. A movie or a sports team might have its own Web site to promote it. A rock band will produce a video to be shown on TV. Some large companies have interests in different forms of media. News Corporation publishes more than 175 different newspapers and owns the Fox TV network and movie studios, *TV Guide* magazine, HarperCollins book publishers, and many other companies.

One area of the media that crosses all these boundaries is advertising. This is where companies and other organizations buy space in media for their message. A campaign to launch a new candy bar or for a presidential candidate might include TV and radio commercials, space in newspapers and magazines, or banners on Web sites. It is important for the advertiser to match the message to the medium. There would be little point in placing an advertisement for a presidential candidate in a magazine read mostly by young teenagers, who cannot vote.

Interactive media

For many years, editors and publishers decided what went into newspapers and magazines. The only way the readers could influence content was by not buying a publication if they did not like the opinions it expressed. The development of communication technology has changed this. Talk radio has opened the airwaves to anyone with a telephone. Interactive television means that viewers can vote for the winner of a talent show.

The most important change in recent years has been the expansion of the World Wide Web. Users can join Internet chat rooms and exchange views with people around the world. Software allows individuals to set up their own websites.

The Cable News Network (CNN) center in Atlanta, Georgia. CNN broadcasts news around the world in a large number of languages.

City centers around the world display large advertisements, such as this one on the Nasdaq building in Times Square, New York.

The power of the media

The modern media can be a powerful force for good. Educational programs can be broadcast to remote areas by radio and television. Governments can use the media to make important announcements. Great historical moments, such as the first moon landing in 1969 or the fall of the Berlin Wall in 1989, united viewers in all countries around their television screens.

The media also have a great responsibility. They must make wise use of their power to influence people's thoughts and attitudes. This becomes even more crucial as the world's major media outlets come increasingly under the control of a small number of organizations.

SEE ALSO: Communication; Internet; Newspapers and Magazines; Printing; Radio; Telecommunications; Television

✳ MEDICINE

Medicine is the use of science to cure disease and maintain good health. There are four aspects: prevention, diagnosis, treatment, and rehabilitation.

Doctors are men and women who use medicine to treat illnesses. Most people visit them only when they are unwell, but doctors do not only treat the sick: They try to keep people from becoming sick in the first place. They do so by increasing health awareness—teaching people about cleanliness, good food, and immunization (vaccination) against infectious diseases, and encouraging them to seek medical advice at the right times. This is called prevention, or preventive medicine.

Diagnosis

Diagnosis is the identification of illness. When patients visit a doctor, they expect to be told what is wrong with them and to be given the prognosis (the doctor's view of their chance of recovery).

No two illnesses and no two patients are ever exactly alike. When making a diagnosis, the doctor looks at three things—the case history, the symptoms, and the signs. A patient's case history includes his or her pattern of disease, personal details about health habits, family, and job, and how the patient feels at the moment. A symptom is evidence of illness that the patient can detect, such as pain, loss of weight, or unusual tiredness. A sign is evidence of something abnormal, such as a tumor, that the doctor finds during the course of examination.

The doctor's experience and observation are often enough to provide a diagnosis without any special equipment. However, there are many devices that assist in diagnosis. Some are very simple. A stethoscope is two pieces of rubber

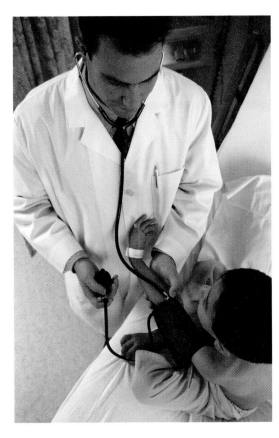

A doctor takes the blood pressure of a child in his care.

tubing with earpieces at one end and a flat metal disk at the other. A doctor uses it to hear the heart and lungs inside the patient's chest. A thermometer can tell the doctor if the patient has a fever.

More complicated equipment includes the electrocardiograph (EKG), which can reveal whether the heart is behaving normally. The ultrasonoscope uses sound to make a picture of organs inside the body. It is also used to observe the development of unborn babies. X-rays enable doctors to see inside the body without having to cut it open. They are useful for diagnosing disease and identifying broken bones. ➡

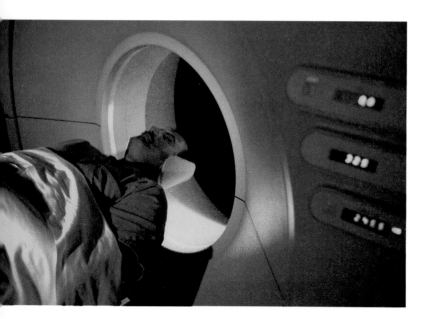

Rehabilitation begins after the severe part of the patient's illness is over. Its aim is to help the patient recover completely; but if that is impossible, it tries to keep pain and loss of function to a minimum.

Doctors' qualifications
To become a doctor in the United States, a person must study for at least seven years after graduation from high school and then serve a year's internship (practical experience) in a hospital. Doctors who start practicing right after that are called general practitioners. They may have to deal with any illness. Other student doctors continue training and eventually become specialists in a particular illness or part of the body.

Surgery
Surgery is a branch of medicine in which specially trained doctors, called surgeons, treat patients by operating on them. The removal of an appendix is a fairly common example of a surgical treatment. Surgery is sometimes combined with

Computerized axial tomography (CAT) scans help medical diagnosis by producing stereoscopic (three-dimensional) pictures of the inside of the body.

Treatment
Treatment, or therapy, is the method used to help the patient recover from his or her illness. It may involve taking prescribed medicines; a course of action, such as exercising and losing weight; or quitting an unhealthy activity, such as cigarette smoking.

This sculpture from the fourth century B.C. shows the ancient Greek Amphiaraus healing a patient.

other treatments, such as drugs or chemotherapy (used on tumors). Machines, such as a special viewing camera called a laparoscope, have enabled surgeons to see inside the body as they perform operations. This technique means that the surgeon needs to make only a small incision, or cut, in the body. The patient has very little pain afterward and recovers much more quickly as a result.

Medical professionals

In addition to doctors, there are many other people who work to fight sickness and injury. Large groups of specialists work in hospitals, clinics, pharmacies, and nursing homes. Nurses have a great deal of medical knowledge and assist doctors and surgeons. Anesthesiologists administer anesthetics, which provide the patient with a safe, pain-free sleep during an operation. Researchers and technicians work in laboratories, testing samples of blood and other body products. Technicians with training in mechanics and electronics look after medical equipment.

The science dealing with the properties of drugs and the way they act on particular organs in the body is called pharmacology. People working in the pharmaceutical industry develop new drugs and give out existing drugs to the sick. Clerical and support workers, who do not have medical or scientific training, provide doctors with administrative backup.

History

From the earliest times, people have had ways of making themselves and others feel better, but modern medicine began only when people started testing various treatments. Ancient people did not really understand what caused disease, and it was often thought to have been brought about by evil spirits or black magic. Cures involved magic and spells, as well as

IMPORTANT FIGURES IN MEDICINE

The following are just a few of the people who made important advances in medical knowledge. There have been many others.

Hippocrates (about 460–377 B.C.)
Ancient Greek doctor who provided the basis for modern Western medicine.

Avicenna (Ibn Sina) (A.D. 980–1037)
Persian who wrote two important books on medicine that were used by doctors for centuries after his death.

Vesalius, Andreas (1514–64)
Belgian doctor who wrote a major book on anatomy, correcting many mistaken beliefs about the structure of the body.

Harvey, William (1578–1657)
English doctor who discovered the circulation of the blood.

Rush, Benjamin (1745–1813)
American doctor who reformed the treatment of mental illness. He was also one of the signers of the Declaration of Independence.

Jenner, Edward (1749–1823)
English doctor who developed vaccination.

Laënnec, René-Théophile-Hyacinthe (1781–1826)
French doctor who invented the stethoscope.

Long, Crawford Williamson (1815–78)
American surgeon who first used ether as an anesthetic.

Lister, Joseph (1827–1912)
English doctor who developed germ-free, or antiseptic, surgery.

Röntgen, Wilhelm Conrad (1845–1923)
German doctor who discovered the medical uses of X-rays in 1895.

Mayo, William James (1861–1939), and **Mayo, Charles Horace** (1865–1939)
American brothers who founded the first modern medical clinic.

Landsteiner, Karl (1868–1943)
Austrian-born American doctor who discovered blood groups.

Salk, Jonas Edward (1914–95)
American microbiologist who developed the first polio vaccine.

Barnard, Christiaan (Neethling) (1922–2001)
South African surgeon who performed the first successful human heart transplant.

medicines made from olive oil, honey, herbs, and other ingredients. Almost all medicines were made from plants.

India and China have very ancient traditions of medicine. The Western use of alternative or complementary treatments based on these traditions has grown since the 1960s. The first people in the West to approach medicine as a science were the ancient Greeks, most notably Hippocrates, who insisted that diseases were caused by natural forces.

The Romans made great advances in health care. They used taxes to pay for hospitals, improved drainage, and sewer systems. They were pioneers in public health policy. Claudius Galen (about A.D.

A Malaysian woman in Sarawak picks Tuba aka, a medicinal plant that is used to cure fever. ▷

129–199), the greatest of Rome's medical teachers, wrote the first study of anatomy (the structure of living things) and described many surgical procedures.

After the fall of the Western Roman Empire in the fifth century A.D., people lost interest in scientific medicine, and superstition took over. When a plague called the Black Death killed millions of Europeans during the Middle Ages, many thought it was a punishment from God.

It was not until the 1400s that European scientists rediscovered Greek and Roman medical authors, whose writings had been ignored in the West for so long that they survived only in Arabic translations.

18th century to today

From the mid-1700s, as industry became mechanized, many people moved from the countryside to the cities to work in factories. That caused overcrowding and illness. As scientists began to understand how bacteria spread diseases, social reformers campaigned for improved sanitation and clean water supplies.

In the 1800s, new anesthetic techniques meant that surgeons could carry out operations such as the removal of limbs while the patient was unconscious.

In many Western nations, alternative or complementary treatments based on Eastern medicine have become popular in recent years. These include herbal remedies, massage, and acupuncture.

SEE ALSO: Blood; Diseases; Fleming, Alexander; Greece, Ancient; Health; Hospitals; Human Body; Pasteur, Louis; Psychology; Roman Empire; Surgery; X-rays

✻ MELVILLE, HERMAN (1819–91)

Herman Melville is best known for his novels of the sea. The greatest of these, *Moby Dick*, is an exciting adventure story and a complex novel of ideas.

Herman Melville was born in New York City. His father died in 1832, and Melville tried to earn money by working in a bank and later as a teacher. In 1839 he went to seek his fortune at sea.

In 1841 Melville sailed on a whaling ship. When the ship docked on the Polynesian island of Nuku-Hiva, Melville jumped ship and fled into the jungle. He lived there for a short while and then sailed on to Tahiti and Hawaii. He reached home in 1844.

Melville immediately began to write about his experiences as a sailor. When he published *Moby Dick*, a story about a great white whale, in 1851, the book

disappointed readers who preferred the simpler style of Melville's previous novels. It is now regarded as a masterpiece. Although he was upset by the book's commercial failure, Melville continued to write. The manuscript for *Billy Budd*, a short novel, was discovered among Melville's papers after his death in 1891. It was published in 1924.

Herman Melville based his writing on his experiences at sea.

SEE ALSO: Literature

✻ MERCURY

Mercury is the second-smallest planet in the solar system. Its orbit, or path, around the sun is the shortest and fastest of any planet.

Mercury is not easy to see clearly from the earth, even with a telescope. Most of what scientists know about the planet has been gathered from 2,700 photographs sent back by the spacecraft *Mariner 10* during its three voyages to the planet in 1974 and 1975.

Structure
Astronomers now believe that the interior of Mercury consists of a core of iron and nickel. It is probably surrounded by a rocky zone about 360 miles (580 km) thick and a light crust no thicker than 40 miles (65 km). The core of Mercury may be larger than Earth's moon. Because of the iron in its core, Mercury has a magnetic field, but it is not as strong as that of Earth. ➡

Mercury is named for the messenger of the gods in ancient Roman mythology. This is a reference to the speed with which the planet orbits the sun.

KEY FACTS

POSITION IN THE SOLAR SYSTEM:
Closest planet to the sun

AVERAGE DISTANCE FROM THE SUN:
35,900,000 mi. (57,800,000 km)

SOLAR ORBIT:
88 Earth days

DIAMETER:
3,032 mi. (4,880 km)

MASS:
330 quintillion tons

ATMOSPHERE:
Almost none

AXIAL ROTATION:
59 Earth days

SEE ALSO:
Astronomy;
Comets,
Meteors, and
Asteroids;
Planets;
Solar
System;
Space
Exploration

Surface

The images transmitted by *Mariner 10* revealed that Mercury looks a lot like Earth's moon. The surface has thousands of craters caused by meteorites crashing into the planet. The largest crater is the Caloris Basin, which is over 800 miles (1,290 km) in diameter. It was formed billions of years ago when a huge object, perhaps as much as 100 miles (160 km) in diameter, crashed into Mercury.

Mercury's surface is also covered with many flat, dark plains. They are known as seas because early astronomers thought they might contain water. Scientists now know that there is no water on Mercury. The features are made of lava (hot, liquid rock that pours out of a volcano and then turns solid).

Mercury has a series of cliffs, called scarps, hundreds of miles long. They were probably formed early in the planet's history. The interior cooled and expanded, forcing sections of the planet's crust to split, creating the cliffs.

The lack of atmosphere on Mercury means that there are no natural forces to erode (wear away) the surface. Craters and other surface features have remained unchanged for millions of years.

✳ METALS

Metals are a group of chemical elements. Metals such as gold are valued for their beauty, and metals such as iron are mined for use in industry.

At room temperature, metals are solid, with the exception of mercury. When they are polished, metals reflect light. This sheen is called luster. Metals can be pulled and stretched into wires—this quality is called ductility. Metals are also malleable—in other words, they can be hammered into sheets. Most metals allow heat and electricity to pass through them, a property called conductivity. Silver and copper are particularly good conductors.

A few metals, such as gold and platinum, occur naturally in a pure form in the earth. Most metals, however, are found combined with other elements and have to be isolated by chemical means.

Metals combined with oxygen are called oxides. Metals combined with sulfur are called sulfides. Any geological material that contains a metal is called an ore. When ores are mined, the metals in them are separated and processed into forms that can be used in industry. The science of separating and processing metals is called metallurgy.

Alloys

Sometimes a metal does not have all the properties needed for a particular purpose. Metallurgists fill the gap by combining two metals or combining a metal with a nonmetal to form an alloy. Iron, for

Molten gold is poured into a mold. When the metal cools, it will resolidify into a bullion bar.

example, is a cheap and useful metal, but it tends to rust. If iron is combined with carbon (a nonmetallic element), the result is steel. Steel does not rust and withstands heat better than pure iron.

Extraction processes

Once an ore has been mined, the metal has to be extracted from it. The ore is first crushed and then passed through filter screens to remove as much waste material, such as sand, soil, and rock, as possible. Strong magnets attract metals such as iron to separate it from nonmagnetic material. Other ores are separated in water. Some metals rise to the top, others sink to the bottom. Early gold prospectors shook pans containing ore under running water. The waste washed away, and the heavier gold sank to the bottom.

Refining metals

When a metal has been extracted from its ore, it still may not be pure. The process of removing impurities is called refining. In a process called smelting, the ore is melted in a furnace. The impurities float to the top of the furnace, and the molten (liquid) metal flows out of the base. Zinc, iron, lead, and copper are the main metals extracted through smelting. Chemicals or electric current are also used in refining.

Once the metal has been extracted and refined, it can be worked or shaped as required. Metal can be worked cold or hot. The oldest method is hot forging, when the metal is heated until it becomes soft and is hammered between two flat surfaces, such as an anvil and a hammer.

Modern methods use machines to form sheets, tubes, or bars. When the metal is cold, it can be worked again to harden and strengthen it or to give it luster. Metals can also be reduced to powder and poured into a mold. The powder is then compressed and heated until it forms the desired shape. ➡

This figure of the ancient god Ba'al dates from about 2000 B.C. It is made of bronze covered with gold and silver leaf.

Using metals

The discovery of how to extract and work metal was one of the keys to the development of human civilization. By about 8000 B.C., people in several parts of the world had learned to shape nuggets (pure lumps) of copper and gold into ornaments and simple tools.

In about 6000 B.C., people in western Asia and southeastern Europe discovered how to smelt copper and gold in the kilns (ovens) they used for pottery. However, copper and gold are soft metals that are not suitable for making tools or weapons.

When people discovered how to make a hard alloy called bronze from copper and tin, they were able to make tools and weapons. Bronze was first made in the Middle East in about 3500 B.C. and gradually spread across Europe and Asia.

In about 2000 B.C., people discovered how to smelt iron. One of the first peoples to do this were the Hittites, who lived in Anatolia (part of modern Turkey). Iron weapons were more effective than bronze, so the Hittites were able to win many battles and enlarge their empire. Iron replaced bronze for most uses, and it is still one of our most important metals. Silver was not mined until about 600 B.C. because its smelting and refining processes are quite complex.

SEE ALSO:
Ancient Civilizations;
Chemistry;
Electricity;
Elements;
Minerals and Gems;
Natural Resources;
Tools;
Warfare

This comb from about 1000 B.C. is made of bronze, an alloy of copper and tin.

---

*METEORS ⟶ *COMETS, METEORS, AND ASTEROIDS

---

* MEXICO

Mexico is bordered by the United States to the north, Guatemala and Belize to the south, the Pacific Ocean to the west, and the Gulf of Mexico to the east.

Mexico's national flag

The United Mexican States is the southernmost country of North America. It is the third most populous country in the Western Hemisphere after the United States and Brazil.

Land and climate

The central upland region, known as the Mexican plateau, contains most of the population and most of the important cities. The plateau is roughly triangular, with its base along the U.S. border and its tip extending south to Mexico City.

High, rugged mountain ranges border the plateau. On the west is the Sierra Madre Occidental, which has several spectacular volcanoes. A second range, the Sierra Madre Oriental, lies along the plateau's eastern edge. Near Mexico City, the two mountain ranges meet at the country's highest peak—the snowcapped volcano of Citlaltepetl, or Pico de Orizaba, 18,405 ft. (5,610 m) high.

The climate varies from tropical and wet to temperate and dry. The coastal plains

OFFICIAL NAME:
Estados Unidos Mexicanos

AREA:
756,066 sq. mi.
(1,958,210 sq. km)

POPULATION:
98,881,000

CAPITAL & LARGEST CITY:
Mexico City

MAJOR RELIGION:
Roman Catholicism

MAJOR LANGUAGES:
Spanish (official), various Indian languages

CURRENCY:
Peso

are hot and humid, with heavy rainfall. The north is dry, with extremes of temperature, while the region around Mexico City has a pleasant climate. Only the coast and parts of the central region get enough rainfall for farming.

Plants and animals
Forests cover nearly a quarter of Mexico's land. Animal life throughout the country is enormously varied and includes wolves, jaguars, tapirs, monkeys, and colorful birds such as parrots and macaws.

People
Most Mexicans are mestizos—that is, people of mixed Indian and European ancestry. About 30 percent of the population is of Indian ancestry.

Economy
Only about 13 percent of the land is suitable for farming. Mexico has rich mineral resources. It is the world's largest producer of silver, and its land contains many other valuable metals. Mexico's biggest export is oil. After oil, tourism is Mexico's largest source of income.

History
The Aztec Indians ruled central Mexico from the 1300s to the 1500s. The Spanish under Hernán Cortés (1485–1547) invaded the country in 1519 and conquered it in under two years. For the next 300 years, Mexico was ruled as a Spanish colony.

For many years, Indians and mestizos fought the Spanish. Spain was forced

The Zócalo is the main square in the center of Mexico City. This view shows the Metropolitan Cathedral and the National Palace.

to sign a treaty in 1821 granting Mexico independence. But the country still had no real government, and its progress to nationhood was slow and difficult.

Between 1846 and 1848, Mexico was at war with the United States over disputed territory. In 1848 the United States paid Mexico $15 million for all of California, Utah, and Nevada, and most of Arizona and New Mexico.

A monarchy was established in 1864, but overthrown in 1867. President Benito Juárez laid the foundation for Mexico's industry and its transportation and communications systems. When he died in 1872, Mexico had finally become a full-fledged nation.

Porfirio Díaz, one of Juárez's generals, seized power in 1876 and ruled Mexico for nearly 35 years. He brought stability, built

railroads, improved harbors, and increased agricultural output. However, his iron rule led to revolution in 1910.

In 1934 Lázaro Cárdenas established the Institutional Revolutionary Party (PRI), which stayed in power until 2000. He nationalized the oil industry and the railroads and gave land to the poor.

In 1942 Mexico joined World War II (1939–45) on the side of the Allies. Demand for oil during the war stimulated Mexico's industrial growth. In the 1980s and 1990s, the economy suffered. In 2000 Vicente Fox Quesada of the National Action Party (PAN) became president.

SEE ALSO: Aztecs; Conquistadors; North America, Geography

❋ MICHELANGELO (1475–1564)
Painter and sculptor Michelangelo is most famous for his paintings of biblical scenes on the ceiling of the Sistine Chapel in the Vatican City.

A self-portrait of Michelangelo painted in 1522.
▽

Michelangelo di Lodovico Buonarroti Simoni was born near Florence, Italy. At the age of 13, he began studying with a Florentine painter who trained him in the art of frescoes—paintings on wet plaster. He started studying sculpture when he was 16 and tried to create perfect human forms in marble, just as the ancient Greek sculptors had.

In 1496 Michelangelo went to Rome, where he carved his first major sculpture, called the *Pietà*. Returning to Florence, he then carved a magnificent marble statue of the biblical

character David. The statue was so popular that he was asked to produce far more work than he could complete. Pope Julius II commissioned Michelangelo to build him a tomb and to paint the ceiling of the Sistine Chapel in the Vatican.

In 1547 Michelangelo became chief architect for the rebuilding of St. Peter's Cathedral in the Vatican City and designed its famous dome. He continued working until his death at age 89.

SEE ALSO: Architecture; Art and Artists; Renaissance

✳ MICROSCOPES

Microscopes use lenses to produce enlarged images of small objects, especially details that are too small to be seen by the naked eye.

The most common type of microscope is the light microscope, or optical microscope, which uses light and lenses to magnify images. If light waves reflected off an object pass through a lens in a certain way, they will refract, or bend. The refracted light waves are spread out and appear to be coming from a bigger object. The simplest light microscope is the magnifying glass, a lens that can magnify an image up to 25 times.

Compound light microscopes—the type most often found in schools—contain two magnifying lenses: the objective lens and the eyepiece, or ocular, lens. Visible light reflected from the mirror on the base passes first through a condenser lens, then the specimen, and then into the objective lens, forming a magnified primary image. The primary image is further magnified as it passes through the eyepiece lens. The final image is projected onto the retina of the viewer's eye. Most compound microscopes give a choice of objective lenses mounted on a rotating disk, each lens providing a different magnification of up to 50 times.

Electron microscopes

The most powerful microscopes create magnified images by passing electrons through the specimen to be viewed. The most advanced electron microscopes can magnify objects up to a million times.

Microscopes help scientists study body cells and microorganisms that are too small to view with the unaided eye. In the early 1800s, microscopes brought huge advances in medicine by revealing that

INSIDE A COMPOUND MICROSCOPE

This diagram shows the path of light (red lines) past an adjustable mirror, through a condenser lens, then through the specimen (which is placed on a glass slide), and up the lens tube via the objective lens to the eyepiece, or ocular, lens and the eyepiece itself.

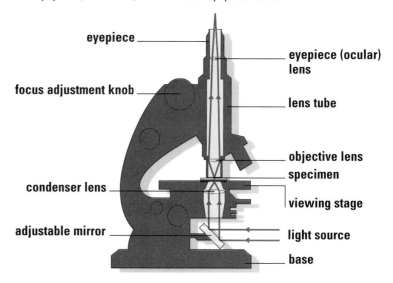

many diseases were caused by bacteria that had previously been invisible.

Microscopes are also used in other fields. Engineers use them to study metals. Forensic scientists use them to analyze hair, fabric, and other materials found at crime scenes. Microscopes are also used to check the safety and quality of products in the service, manufacturing, and pharmaceutical industries.

SEE ALSO: Biology; Crime and Law Enforcement; Diseases; Eyes and Vision; Human Body; Medicine; Scientific Instruments

* MIDDLE AGES

The Middle Ages were the period of European history from the fall of the Roman Empire in A.D. 476 to 1453, when the Ottoman Turks captured Constantinople.

At its height the Roman Empire controlled most of western Europe. However, in A.D. 395 the empire finally split in two—the Western Empire ruled from Rome, and the Eastern, or Byzantine, Empire ruled from Constantinople (modern Istanbul, in Turkey).

Germanic tribes, whom the Romans called barbarians, were settling in western Europe. They removed the last western Roman emperor from the throne in 476. The Eastern Empire continued to flourish.

A French book illustration by the Limburg brothers, dating from about 1416, of the grape harvest in September. In the background is the Château de Saumur. The castle was rebuilt throughout the 1200s and 1300s and is typical of medieval architecture.

The Middle Ages were once known as the Dark Ages. People thought of them as a time of ignorance, but in fact artists, craftsmen, and scholars thrived. Towns and cities grew, and trade routes reached as far as India and China.

Kings and nobles

The barbarian tribes that overran the Roman Empire were led by chiefs or kings. Their power was based on their ability to win battles and reward their supporters with goods.

For three centuries after 476, there were only small states and kingdoms. Then Charlemagne (about 742–814) became king of the Franks in 771. He built an empire that extended across western and Central Europe, and set up Christian schools to encourage learning. Nobles were given land in exchange for military support. Charlemagne's empire crumbled after his death, but he is often considered to be the true founder of the Holy Roman Empire, which later ruled much of Europe.

In the early Middle Ages, kings struggled to control their nobles. In many cases, the nobles were more powerful than the king. In France and England, the power of the king slowly increased until the king was the most powerful of the princes. In some areas, like Germany, a single king did not emerge. It was not until the end of the 14th century that the modern idea took shape of a state governed by a ruler whose authority came from the people.

Between the 9th and 12th centuries in England and northwestern Europe, kings and lords gave grants of land, called fiefs or fiefdoms, to their nobles. In return the nobles owed the lords loyalty and military service. Similarly, nobles granted land to peasants (small farmers) in return for services, such as labor. Historians later gave this system of loyalties and services the name of feudalism.

The church
The Catholic Church grew powerful during the Middle Ages. It was governed by bishops and archbishops under the authority of the pope at Rome. The church was also served by monks and nuns. Monks were men who lived together in a house called a monastery. They devoted their lives to the service of God. Nuns were women who followed a similar life in houses usually called convents.

During the Middle Ages, monasteries were the main centers of learning and education in western Europe. Monks hand-copied books until printing was invented in the 15th century, and ran schools that taught reading, writing, and Latin. Bishops also established schools, known as cathedral schools. In the 12th century, some of the cathedral schools became great centers of learning called universities.

Islam
Shortly after Muhammad founded the Islamic religion in 610, Muslim armies began to conquer new land. By 750 the Islamic Empire stretched from India in the east to Spain and Morocco in the west. Islam was usually tolerant of other religions, and Muslim scholars preserved and transmitted the learning of ancient Greece and Rome to western Europe.

Christianity and Islam clashed between 1096 and 1291 in a series of wars called the Crusades. The Crusaders' aim was to protect the holy sites of Christianity and recapture Palestine (modern Israel, Lebanon, and Syria) from the Muslims. Christians also fought to regain the Iberian Peninsula (modern Spain and Portugal) from Muslim control. They finally succeeded in 1492.

The late Middle Ages
Great changes swept Europe during the late Middle Ages. Between 1337 and 1453, France and England fought the Hundred Years' War. In the late 1340s, the Black Death, a terrible plague, killed about one-third of Europe's population. Farmland stood idle, with few laborers to work it. The peasants who survived the plague were able to demand more freedom from the nobles as well as payment in wages.

The church's power started to fade. In its place came a new spirit of freedom in art, science, and learning. This period came to be known as the Renaissance, meaning "rebirth," because people went back for their ideas to ancient Greece and Rome.

In 1453 France and England made peace. That same year, Constantinople fell to the Muslim Ottoman Turks, giving them control of the main trade route between the Mediterranean Sea and Asia.

▲

An illumination (illustration) from a French manuscript showing Louis VI founding an abbey. The king— nicknamed "Louis the Fat"—ruled France from 1108 until his death in 1137.

SEE ALSO: Byzantine Empire; Castles; Central Europe; Charlemagne; Christianity; Crusades; France; Germany; Islam; Italy; Knights and Chivalry; Printing; Renaissance; Roman Empire; United Kingdom

✳ MIDDLE EAST

The Middle East is the cradle of some of the world's earliest civilizations and of three great religions—Judaism, Christianity, and Islam.

Land, climate, and economy

The Middle East is a geographical area that includes the nations of Southwest Asia, the Arabian Peninsula, and eastern North Africa. High mountains rise to the north of the region. Others extend along the eastern Mediterranean coast and along the west and south of the Arabian Peninsula. Huge deserts stretch across the inland regions.

The Middle East is hot and dry for much of the year except in the highest mountains. In the deserts, the daytime temperature often rises above 125°F (52°C), yet at night the deserts are cool or even cold. There is little rainfall, and fresh water is scarce. Although fertile land suitable for farming is limited to the river valleys, agriculture is the most important economic activity. More than half of the world's known oil reserves are found in the Middle East, bringing great wealth to parts of the region.

A traditional souk (market) in the narrow alleyways of Dubai in the United Arab Emirates. ▼

Cities

The largest city of the Middle East is Cairo, Egypt. Founded by Arab conquerors in 641, it was originally known as Al-Fustat. The older Egyptian port of Alexandria was rebuilt by the Macedonian leader Alexander the Great in the fourth century B.C.

Damascus, Syria, was founded about 5,000 years ago. Baghdad, Iraq, was founded in the 700s A.D. Jerusalem, in Israel, contains places holy to Jews, Christians, and Muslims.

People

The fertile regions of the Middle East are densely settled, while other parts, especially the deserts, are empty of human life. There are three main ethnic groups: Arabs, Turks, and Iranians. Smaller groups include Armenians, Kurds, Pakistanis, Jews, Indians, and Greeks, who live mainly on the island of Cyprus. The major languages are Arabic, Turkish, and Persian (or Farsi). Most Middle Easterners are Muslims—followers of Islam. About half of the region's population lives in cities.

History

Wandering tribes first settled and grew crops beside the Tigris and Euphrates rivers more than 8,000 years ago. The world's first known civilizations, notably Sumer, arose in the fertile valleys.

Before the Christian era began 2,000 years ago, the Middle East had seen the rise and fall of many powerful peoples. Among them were the Egyptians, Hittites, Babylonians, Assyrians, and Persians.

Alexander the Great brought Greek culture to the region when he invaded it in the fourth century B.C. The Romans invaded in the first century B.C. While the Western Roman Empire fell in the fifth century A.D., the Eastern, or Byzantine, Empire, based in Constantinople (modern Istanbul in Turkey), lasted another thousand years.

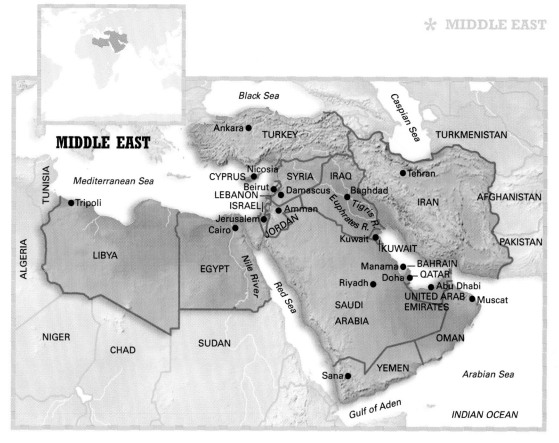

MIDDLE EAST

KEY FACTS

AREA:
3,500,000 sq. mi.
(9,065,000 sq. km)

POPULATION:
246,000,000

COUNTRIES:
17

LARGEST COUNTRY:
Saudi Arabia

SMALLEST COUNTRY:
Bahrain

RELIGIONS:
Islam, Christianity, Judaism

LANGUAGES:
Arabic, Turkish, Persian (Farsi), Kurdish, Hebrew, English, French

In the 600s, the Arabs, newly converted to Islam by the prophet Muhammad, swept out of the Arabian Peninsula and created a vast empire that stretched from India in the east to Spain in the west. The last great empire of the region was that of the Ottoman Turks, who by the 1500s ruled most of the Middle East. Their empire fell after their defeat in World War I (1914–18).

After the war, Britain and France governed large areas of the Middle East. Saudi Arabia and Iraq were created in 1932, and other nations won their independence during or after World War II (1939–45). Israel was created in 1948 as a homeland for the Jews. This led to five Arab–Israeli wars between 1948 and 1982, as well as ongoing terrorist attacks. Between 1980 and 1988, there was a war between Iran and Iraq. Iraq invaded Kuwait in 1990 but was driven out by the United States and its allies in 1991. In 2003 Iraq was attacked by a U.S.-led coalition that aimed to remove President Saddam Hussein from power.

A panoramic view across the rooftops of Damascus, the capital of Syria.

SEE ALSO:
Alexander the Great; Ancient Civilizations; Asia; Christianity; Egypt; Iran; Iraq; Islam; Israel; Judaism; North Africa; Palestine; Persian Gulf War; Turkey and the Caucasus

✳ MIGRATION

Migration is the movement of animals from one area to another to find food or shelter, or to raise young. It usually takes place as the seasons change.

Many birds migrate. For example, waterfowl move from nesting areas in the north-central United States and southern Canada to spend the winter along the warm coast of the Gulf of Mexico. Other birds move from high up in the mountains down to valleys where winters are milder.

Butterflies

Monarch butterflies migrate north from Mexico to Canada. The first to set off lay eggs along the way, then die. The adults that hatch from these eggs continue to migrate. By the end of summer, successive generations of butterflies have reached Canada. The new butterflies head south again in fall. No one knows how they navigate.

Wildebeests cross the Mara River during their annual migration across Kenya.

▼

Sea migrations

Several marine animals migrate. Pacific gray whales migrate between their warm breeding bays off Mexico and the food-rich

waters off Alaska. Northern fur seals and elephant seals often swim thousands of miles between their ocean feeding areas and the breeding islands and beaches to which they return every year. Sea turtles make similar journeys. Salmon hatch in shallow streams and then migrate to the oceans. Years later they return to the same streams in which they hatched to lay eggs.

Land animals

Very few land animals migrate. Exceptions include large hoofed mammals, such as caribou in North America and wildebeests in East Africa.

Navigation

Migrating animals use several methods to navigate. Some follow familiar landmarks, such as mountains and lakes. Many are able to sense Earth's magnetic field and use it as a compass. Others use the sun or stars as a guide to direction. Another method of navigation involves learning the smells or tastes of each place along the route. Salmon, for example, recognize the scent of their home river.

Arctic terns have the longest of all migrations. They nest in the far north. In winter they fly south to the Antarctic, where it is summer. Then they return for the northern spring, a round-trip of about 18,600 miles (30,000 km).

SEE ALSO: Birds; Butterflies and Moths; Fish; Hibernation; Magnetism; Mammals; Whales and Dolphins

MILLIPEDES AND CENTIPEDES

Millipedes and centipedes are animals with long, thin bodies and many legs. They are close relatives of spiders and insects.

Myriapods

Millipedes and centipedes belong to a group of invertebrates (animals without a backbone) called myriapods.

They have between 15 and 200 pairs of legs (*centipede* means "hundred feet or legs"; *millipede* means "thousand feet or legs"). Their bodies are made up of many segments (parts). The head has long antennae (feelers), and some species have eyes. A hard shell covers the soft body parts and serves as a skeleton. The outer layer of the shell is shed from time to time as the animal grows. Holes in the segments allow the animal to breathe. The tubelike heart pumps blood from one end of the body to the other.

Millipedes

There are about 10,000 species of millipedes. Most have about 35 segments, each with two pairs of legs. Millipedes generally feed at night on dead, rotting plants or animals. By day they hide under logs or leaves. When disturbed, these slow-moving animals coil up or roll into a ball. Many have poison or stink glands along each side of the body that they use to repel enemies. Millipedes lay eggs in groups of 25 to 50.

Centipedes

There are about 2,800 species of centipedes. The body is flatter in shape than a millipede's, with one pair of legs on each segment. The two front legs are hollow fangs primed with venom. Most centipedes are fast-moving hunters. They use the venom to kill their prey—usually slugs, earthworms, and insects. The bite may cause pain, but it cannot kill people. Centipedes are most common in damp places, especially in warm, tropical parts of the world. They hide during the day under stones or in rotten logs and become active at night. Some centipedes bear live, wriggling young. Most others lay eggs.

AMAZING FACTS!

A variety of millipede found in California, the *Luminodesmus sequoiae*, lights up.

The largest centipede, *Scolopendra gigas*, lives on an island in the West Indies. It may grow to a length of 12 in. (30 cm). It feeds mostly on insects, but it sometimes captures and eats mice and lizards.

The millipede defends itself by rolling into a ball when it is disturbed. Many kinds have poison glands along the sides of their bodies. The glands give off a substance that repels insects and other enemies.

SEE ALSO: Insects; Spiders and Scorpions

✳ MINERALS AND GEMS

Minerals are the most common solid substances on Earth. They occur in rock, sand, soil, and even in the air. Gems are minerals valued for their beauty.

A mineral is any natural material that originates on or in the ground. It may be a single element, such as copper, gold, or diamond; a compound, such as rock salt (sodium chloride) or chalk (calcium carbonate); or a mixture, such as petroleum, coal, peat, and asphalt. Some minerals are found not only in the earth's crust but also in planetary bodies, such as the moon, Mars, and meteorites.

A human-made product is not a mineral, even though it may be practically identical to a natural mineral. An example is synthetic (human-made) diamond.

Emerald is a gem that has been treasured for its attractive green color for thousands of years. There are many references to the mythical properties of the emerald in philosophy, religion, and literature.

Identifying minerals

The surest ways to identify a mineral are by chemical and X-ray analysis. However, these tests can be expensive and time-consuming, so mineralogists usually decide which minerals are which by looking at their physical features.

One of the most easily determined physical features of any mineral is its hardness, which depends on the strength of the bonds that hold its atoms together in a crystal structure. Some minerals, such as talc, are so soft that rubbing them between the fingers will break the bond. At the other extreme is diamond, which is so strongly bonded that the only natural substances that can scratch it are other diamonds.

The hardness of any mineral is determined by the ease of scratching one of its smooth surfaces with the sharp edge of a mineral of known hardness. In 1812 the German mineralogist Friedrich Mohs proposed that 10 common minerals be used as a scale. Each mineral can scratch those with the same or a lower rating, but cannot scratch higher-numbered minerals. The Mohs scale is the most common way of rating mineral hardness.

Symmetry

Other important distinguishing features of minerals are the aspects of their external appearance that reflect their internal structure—in some cases this is the only distinguishing feature. If a solid body is turned through a full circle in any direction and the same shape is seen more than once during the rotation, the body is said to display symmetry. On the basis of their symmetry, crystals can be grouped into seven different crystal systems.

DID YOU KNOW?

The diamond has become a symbol of faithful love and is a favorite stone for engagement rings. But the great hardness of this sparkling gem makes it very useful for industrial purposes, too. Diamonds that are not good enough to make into gems may be added to drill tips or saw blades for cutting through hard rock and concrete, to liquid polish, or to grinding wheels for sharpening metal tools.

The mineral quartz is made up of silicon and oxygen. These two chemical elements are the components of silica, which has been found in nearly every kind of rock.

The jewels in the English monarch's crown date from Charles II's coronation in 1661 or earlier. Since then there have been many additions and alterations to the original jewels.

Minerals are most accurately classified by their chemical composition. The most common class of minerals is the silicate group, because silica is the most abundant component of the earth's crust (about 60 percent). Among the other important classes are native (single) elements, carbonates, oxides and hydroxides, phosphates, sulfates, and sulfides.

Ores

Ores are minerals that are mined to provide a particular material, usually a metal. Examples are bauxite, the most important ore of aluminum; chalcopyrite, the main source of copper; galena, an ore of lead; and hematite, an iron-rich mineral.

Gems

A gem is a mineral that happens to be valued for its beauty or rarity. Few generalizations can be made about gems because each specimen is judged and priced on its own merits. As a result, not even all diamonds are precious—those that lack clarity and sparkle are used as scraping and cutting tools in industry.

Some ordinary minerals have gem varieties. Corundum, for example, is not a gem but may take the form of precious ruby or sapphire.

The finest gems are cut to increase their beauty and can be worn as jewelry. They can also be made into combs, jewel cases, and other decorative items.

SEE ALSO: Elements; Geology; Metals; Natural Resources

MOLECULES see ✷ATOMS AND MOLECULES

MOLLUSKS see ✷SNAILS AND OTHER MOLLUSKS

✳ MONEY

Money can be anything that is generally accepted as payment for goods or services. Today's money is bills and coins, but other materials have also been used.

The currency of this Nigerian money changer includes cowrie shells, Kissi pennies, bracelets, and anklets.

Before the invention of coins, people exchanged one thing for another, a practice called barter. For example, one person might offer some grain to another in return for a fish. Barter still takes place in some societies, but it is not a perfect system. People may not agree on how much grain equals a herring, for example.

Many ancient civilizations used grain or metal in exchange for other goods. In ancient China and Africa, seashells were used as currency. Native Americans used shell beads, called wampum, as trading counters. Each bead had a certain value.

Coins and notes

The first coins were made at about the same time, around 600 B.C., in three different parts of the world—India, Lydia (part of modern Turkey), and China. In about A.D. 1024, the Chinese issued the world's first paper money. Early Roman coins were made in the temple of the goddess Juno, also called Moneta. That is the origin of the English word *money*.

It took hundreds of years for coins to replace barter and other forms of money. In the 13th century, as trade routes expanded, coins became more widespread. They were usually made of metal, especially gold or silver, and their value was determined by their weight. Governments controlled the supply of coins, and people who counterfeited— copied coins illegally—were punished.

Paper money and credit cards

Paper money was cheaper to make and easier to carry around than coins. Coins could be minted only if there was enough gold and silver available, but paper money could be produced in almost unlimited quantities. At first governments tried to limit the creation of paper money by insisting that it be backed by gold or silver. In the United States, for example, people were once entitled to exchange a dollar bill for a set amount of gold. However, governments eventually found this requirement too limiting. In 1972 the nations of the world abandoned the system known as the Gold Standard.

Today many people use credit cards instead of money. The card provider (a firm such as MasterCard or Visa) pays the retailer, and the customer later pays back the card provider. Credit cards can now be used to buy almost anything in nearly all parts of the world.

SEE ALSO: Banking; Economics; Native Americans; Stock Markets

✳ **MONKEYS** 👀 ✳ **APES, MONKEYS, AND PRIMATES**

✳ MOON
A moon is any natural object that orbits, or circles, a planet. However, the word is most often used for the only natural satellite of Earth.

Scientists have a number of theories about how the moon came into being. One idea is that it originally orbited the sun but was captured by Earth's gravitational pull. Another is that Earth and the moon were once a single mass of material. As the mass grew, it formed a bulge that broke away into space and became the moon. A more recent theory is that the moon formed when a giant object crashed into Earth. Some of the debris that broke off became a satellite orbiting the planet.

Size and structure
The moon has a diameter of 2,160 miles (3,475 km), about one-quarter the size of Earth. It travels at an average speed of 2,237 mph (3,600 kph). It speeds up when it gets closer to Earth because of gravitational pull.

Like Earth, the moon's surface is not smooth. It has mountainous areas, with some peaks as high as Mount Everest. There are also millions of depressions called craters. There are dark patches known as seas because early astronomers thought they contained water. However, they are areas of lava (solidified molten rock). There is no water on the moon.

Inside the moon
Scientists know a little about the interior of the moon thanks to instruments placed by astronauts who landed there in the 1960s and 1970s. The moon has a crust, with an average thickness of 40 miles (64 km). Beneath is a mantle of about 435 miles (700 km), but no one knows what is under the mantle.

DID YOU KNOW?
The moon has no light of its own—moonlight is sunlight that is reflected off the moon's surface. Sometimes we can see the entire lighted side of the moon. At other times, we see only a portion of it lit, so the moon appears to change its shape from night to night. These changes occur because the earth's shadow blocks sunlight from reaching the moon.

There is almost no atmosphere on the moon. There is no air to breathe and nothing to filter out radiation. The temperature varies between 250°F (120°C) and –255°F (–160°C). People can survive on the moon only wearing special suits and using breathing equipment.

SEE ALSO: Astronauts; Astronomy; Earth; Gravity; Planets; Satellites; Solar System; Space Exploration

This view of the moon was taken from the spacecraft Galileo as it flew by in December 1992. The photograph is made up of 18 images.

✳ MORRISON, TONI (1931–)

Toni Morrison is one of the great American writers of her generation. She has won the Pulitzer Prize and the Nobel Prize for literature.

Toni Morrison's novels explore the relationship between racism and self-discovery in American life.

Morrison was born Chloe Anthony Wofford in Lorain, Ohio, on February 18, 1931. After graduating from Howard and Cornell universities, she became a book editor and taught at several universities.

Morrison writes fiction and nonfiction. Her novels deal with the effects of racism on American life. Her first novel, published in 1969, is *The Bluest Eye*. It is about a young black girl who longs for the white idea of beauty. Morrison's most famous book is *Beloved* (1987), which won her the

Pulitzer Prize. It deals with an escaping slave who kills her own child rather than see her grow up in slavery.

Morrison's other books include *Song of Solomon*, *Tar Baby*, and *Jazz*. In 1993 she was awarded the Nobel Prize for literature.

SEE ALSO: African Americans; Literature; Nobel Prize; Slavery

---

✳ **MOTHS** 🔎 ✳ **BUTTERFLIES AND MOTHS**

✳ **MOTORCYCLES** 🔎 ✳ **BICYCLES AND MOTORCYCLES**

✳ MOUNTAINS AND VALLEYS

A mountain is a landform that rises at least 1,000 ft. (300 m) above its surroundings. A valley is a long, natural depression in the surface of the earth.

The theory of plate tectonics explains how mountains form. Earth's surface is made up of huge slabs, or plates, of rock that are constantly moving. Sometimes plates collide. The immense forces of these slow collisions last for millions of years. Mountain ranges are thrust up along the plate boundaries as pressure causes layers of rock to crumple and fold.

There are four main types of mountains: folded mountains, fault-block mountains, volcanoes, and erosion mountains. When two plates collide, they sometimes crumple. The plates fold up, forming

mountains and valleys. The Alps in Europe and the Appalachians in the United States are examples of folded mountains. Sometimes the plates do not fold, but the rock cracks, forming a fault. Rocks on either side of the fault move against each other, forming peaks and valleys. The Sierra Nevada in California and the Ruwenzori mountain range in Africa include fault-blocks.

Volcanoes form when molten rock from deep inside the earth rises to the surface. Unlike other types of mountains, volcanoes can form in days or weeks.

AMAZING FACTS !

Mount Everest, Asia, is the world's highest mountain at 29,078 ft. (8,863 m).

The Andes, South America, are the longest mountain range on land, at 4,500 miles (7,240 km).

The Mid-Atlantic Ridge is a submerged mountain chain over 10,000 miles (16,000 km) long.

Mauna Kea, Hawaii, is 33,408 ft. (10,183 m) high when measured from its base under the Pacific Ocean. Only 13,796 ft. (4,205 m) is above sea level.

The Great Rift Valley stretches about 4,000 miles (6,440 km) from the Jordan Valley in Syria along the Red Sea into Ethiopia, Kenya, Tanzania, Malawi, and Mozambique.

The movement of water or wind can cut through flat layers of rock over thousands of years. This process is called erosion. The Catskill Mountains in New York State were formed by erosion.

Mountain ranges

Mountains are formed along lines, such as faults or folds in the earth's tectonic plates, so groups of mountains tend to be long and narrow. They are called mountain ranges. The San Juan Mountains in Colorado and the Wind River Mountains in Wyoming are mountain ranges.

Valleys

Erosion also forms long depressions in the surface of the earth. Water drains from a mountain or other high place, cutting through land over thousands of years. The depression it forms is a valley.

The mountainous landscape of central Nepal, with Machapuchare Mountain in the background.
▼

As an erosion valley lengthens, the volume and speed of water increases. This makes the valley deeper. Sometimes the water also causes material to fall away from the sides, widening the valley.

Canyons are the result of rapid erosion by a river. Deepening of the valley is usually much faster than erosion of the sides, so the canyon has steep sides. Valleys also form when folded or fault-block mountains develop. Just as parts of the earth's plates are pushed upward, some are pushed downward. When part of the earth's crust sinks below the surrounding area, the depression is called a rift valley. The best known is the Great Rift Valley in Africa and the Middle East.

SEE ALSO: Earth; Geology; Plate Tectonics; Volcanoes

---

*MOVIES see *FILMS

---

* MOZART, WOLFGANG AMADEUS (1756–91)
Many people believe that Mozart is the greatest composer of all time. His operas, symphonies, and other pieces are still performed all over the world.

This portrait of Mozart was painted in 1766–67, when he was about 10.

Wolfgang Amadeus Mozart was born on January 27, 1756, in Salzburg, Austria. The son of a composer, he was writing his own music by the age of five, and at eight years old he wrote his first symphony. He became concertmaster to the archbishop of Salzburg when he was just 13. In 1781 he quarreled with the archbishop and was dismissed. Mozart decided to settle in Vienna.

In 1782 Mozart married Constanze Weber. Although he had many troubles, including the deaths of four of his children and his wife's ill health, his greatest works were written during his years in Vienna. They included the operas *The Marriage of Figaro* and *Cosi fan tutte* and his last three symphonies, which he wrote in less than seven weeks.

In 1791 Mozart began to suffer from fevers and headaches. One rumor is that another composer, who was jealous of his genius, poisoned him. It is actually believed that he died of kidney failure. Mozart's final opera, *The Magic Flute*, had its first performance in September. When Mozart died, on December 5, 1791, his last great work, the *Requiem*, was unfinished. Mozart died penniless, and because he had no money, his body was buried in an unmarked grave.

SEE ALSO: Music

---

*MUMMIES see *EGYPT, ANCIENT

MUSCULAR SYSTEM

Muscles are the body's movers. They are tough elastic tissues that make up nearly half the weight of the body. Humans have more than 650 muscles.

There are three main types of muscles. Skeletal muscles—those joined directly to bones—move arms, legs, and other body parts. They are attached to the bones by hard, ropelike tissues called tendons. Usually, skeletal muscles work in groups. Simply taking a single step involves the use of about 200 muscles. Skeletal muscles are called voluntary muscles, because we can control what they do.

The walls of the heart, the organ that pumps blood around the body, are formed of cardiac muscle. The cardiac muscle expands and contracts to keep the blood pumping. Because we cannot control its work consciously, the cardiac muscle is known as an involuntary muscle.

Smooth muscles are also involuntary. They are found in many parts of the body and are not attached to bones. Among other things, smooth muscles propel food through the digestive tract.

How muscles work
Muscles work by contracting—becoming shorter—and then relaxing. When a skeletal muscle shortens, it pulls on the tendons that are attached to the bone, and the bone moves. Muscles pull but they cannot push, so they must work in pairs. If you bend your arm, one set of muscles contracts and pulls your forearm up. To straighten your arm, you relax the first set of muscles. A second set pulls in the opposite way, straightening your arm.

Some muscles are controlled by electrical messages from the brain that are passed through nerve cells. Others are controlled by chemical messengers called hormones.

The energy that gives muscles the power to move comes from food. The muscles store chemicals called ATP (adenosine triphosphate) and glycogen. These chemicals are good for quick bursts of power, but for more sustained work the muscles need fuel from the blood supply.

Muscles need regular exercise. Exercise causes the muscle fibers to grow stronger. If muscles are not used for a long time, they begin to waste away, or atrophy, becoming small and weak.

SEE ALSO:
Brain and Nervous System; Heart and Circulatory System; Human Body; Stomach and Digestive System

MUSCULAR SYSTEM

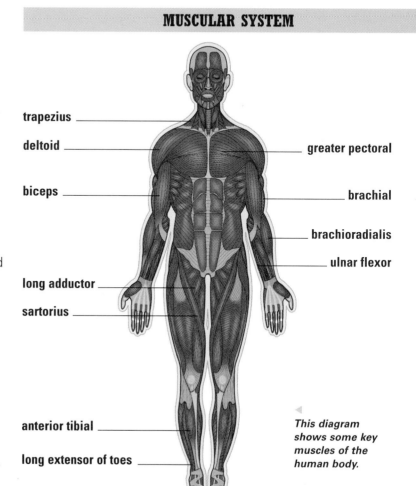

trapezius
deltoid
biceps
long adductor
sartorius
anterior tibial
long extensor of toes

greater pectoral
brachial
brachioradialis
ulnar flexor

This diagram shows some key muscles of the human body.

413

✷ MUSIC

From ancient times, people have sung and played music. Each culture developed its own style of singing and its own instruments.

Music contains certain basic elements, such as melody, rhythm, and harmony. A single musical sound is called a tone. When music is written, tones are represented by symbols called notes. Most music is a combination of tones chosen from a set of tones called a scale.

In Western music, most scales have seven tones. If you have a keyboard, you can play a scale by starting on C (the white key immediately to the left of two black keys), and playing each of the next seven white keys up to C again (see diagram below).

The interval between two notes of the same letter (C to C, D to D, and so on) is called an octave. The distance between adjacent tones can be either a whole step or a half step. A whole step is called a tone; a half step is called a semitone. A chromatic scale contains all 12 notes of the octave, black and white, each a semitone apart from its neighbor.

Melody is a tune that can be whistled or sung. A beat is the underlying pulse of the music, while the way notes are played or grouped in patterns gives music its rhythm. Two or more tones played at the same time make up a harmony, giving each piece of music its particular mood and texture.

Written music

Music is written in a special way known as notation. Notes are written on a staff—five parallel lines and the spaces between them. The shape of a note shows how long it lasts, as shown on the diagrams below.

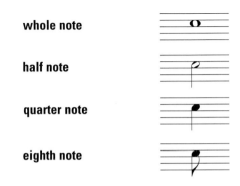

whole note	
half note	
quarter note	
eighth note	

The position of a note on the staff shows its pitch—how high or low it is. A sharp sign (#) in front of a note raises its pitch by half a tone; a flat sign (♭) lowers it by half a tone. A clef sign appears at the beginning of the staff. The two most common clef signs are the treble clef and the bass clef (see below).

treble clef   bass clef

The treble clef is used to indicate that the notes are in the higher range. The bass clef shows that the music should be played in the lower range. The group of sharp or flat signs at the beginning of each staff (up to seven of each, always in the same arrangement) shows the key signature (see opposite). This tells the

musician the key (or scale) in which
the music is written.

sharps   **flats**

Vertical lines on the staff divide it
into measures, or bars, which each
contain a certain number of beats.
They look like this:

bars

The time signature at the beginning of
a piece shows how many beats there
are in each measure. It consists of
two numbers, one above the other.
For example, 3/4 indicates three quarter-
notes in each bar, 6/8 indicates six eighth-
notes, and 4/4 indicates four quarter-notes
(see below).

time signature

Classical music

The structured music of Western tradition
is called classical music. The earliest form
was chant, or plainsong, which was used
in church music in the Middle Ages. It
consisted of a single line of sung melody
without instrumental accompaniment.
When a simple form of notation developed
beginning in about the ninth century,
plainsong became more elaborate.
Composers—people who create pieces of
music—began to write two or more
melodies to be sung at the same time,
creating harmonies.

Church music was important during the
15th and 16th centuries, but composers

FAMOUS COMPOSERS

This is a list of some famous
classical composers. The "see
also" box (next page) indicates
entries on others, but there
are many more.

Purcell, Henry (1659–95)
English composer who wrote
operas, theater music,
songs, and church anthems.
Unsurpassed for setting the
English language to music.

Vivaldi, Antonio (Lucio)
(1678–1741)
Italian composer and violinist
who wrote over 500 concertos.
Known as "the Red Priest"
because of his red hair.

Handel, George Frideric
(1685–1759)
German-born English composer
(below) who wrote many
famous operas in Italian, and
oratorios in English.

Haydn, (Franz) Joseph
(1732–1809)
Austrian composer who
developed the string quartet
and the symphony, earning
him the title "father of
the symphony."

**Verdi, Giuseppe (Fortunino
Francesco)** (1813–1901)
Italian composer whose
operas, such as *Rigoletto* and
La traviata, are still the core
works of opera houses all over
the world.

Brahms, Johannes (1833–97)
German composer who wrote
chamber music, numerous
works for piano, four
symphonies, and more than 100
songs and choral works.

Ives, Charles (Edward)
(1874–1954)
American composer who used
new, experimental techniques,
but who took his inspiration
from the popular music of
his childhood.

Stravinsky, Igor (Fyodorovich)
(1882–1971)
Russian-born American
composer whose revolutionary
rhythms and harmonies greatly
influenced 20th-century music.

Copland, Aaron (1900–90)
The leading American classical
composer of the 20th century.
His works include music for the
ballet *Appalachian Spring* and
the orchestral piece *Fanfare
for the Common Man*.

also began writing secular (nonchurch) music. The 17th and 18th centuries saw many new musical forms, including the sonata, concerto, symphony, opera, and oratorio. The sonata is usually for a solo instrument and consists of three or four movements. The concerto is a piece for solo instrument (often piano or violin) and orchestra, and has three movements. The symphony is a longer work for orchestra, usually with four movements. An opera is a dramatic piece for solo singers, chorus, and orchestra, staged in a theater with costumes and scenery. An oratorio is a musical setting of a dramatic, usually religious, text, performed in a concert hall.

In the 19th century, composers used their music to express emotions. Songs and short pieces for the piano conveyed the composer's feelings, while orchestral music became more dramatic. In the 20th century, some composers began to use a new system of harmony called the 12-tone system, which uses all the notes of the chromatic scale instead of major (full tone) and minor (semitone) keys. Others used clashing harmonies and irregular rhythms.

Important composers in the Western tradition include Claudio Monteverdi (1567–1643), who wrote the first major opera in 1607; Johann Sebastian Bach (1685–1750), who wrote church and instrumental music; Wolfgang Amadeus Mozart (1756–91), who composed many operas and concertos; Ludwig van Beethoven (1770–1827), who wrote symphonies and chamber music; and Richard Wagner (1813–83), who created grand operas on mythological subjects.

Other types of music
In the 20th century, music from the southern United States became very influential, giving rise to many different popular styles. First, black musicians from New Orleans began to play a slow, intense, improvised music in small groups. They called this the blues, and it led to jazz, a faster-paced music. Jazz was very popular, particularly from the 1920s to the 1940s.

Rock 'n' roll
In the 1950s, rhythm and blues—a louder, faster, simpler style of music—developed. This was the start of rock music. Elvis Presley was its major star in the 1950s. In the 1960s, groups like the Beatles (from England) brought their own style to rock music. Another important musician of the time was Bob Dylan, who used folk music to express political and social ideas. At the same time, soul music—a mix of rhythm and blues with a style of black church music called gospel—was at its height. By the 1970s, soul had developed into the intense rhythms of funk, and then disco.

Country music, developed mostly by white musicians in the southern United States from the folk music of the British Isles, was popular during the 20th century. It became integrated with other commercial popular music as the century progressed.

In the late 1970s, an energetic form of rock music called punk became popular. Later in the decade, black New York musicians and dj's used heavy beats and spoken rhymes to create hip-hop and rap.

SEE ALSO: Armstrong, Louis; Bach, Johann Sebastian; Beethoven, Ludwig van; Chopin, Frédéric; Ellington, Duke; Fitzgerald, Ella; Gershwin, George; Guthrie, Woody; Mozart, Wolfgang Amadeus; Musical Instruments; Orchestras; Rodgers, Richard; Sound Recording; Sousa, John Philip

IMPORTANT POPULAR MUSICIANS

These are some of the popular musicians who have established a lasting reputation. The "see also" box (opposite page) indicates entries on others, but there are many more.

Waters, Muddy (McKinley Morganfield) (1915–83)
American singer-songwriter, guitarist, and harmonica player who was a pioneer of the electric blues style that began in Chicago, IL, in the 1940s.

Berry, Chuck (Charles Edward Anderson) (1926–)
American singer and guitarist who wrote some classic rock 'n' roll songs.

Cash, Johnny (1932–2003)
American singer, songwriter, and guitarist who was a leading influence in both country and rock music.

Presley, Elvis (Aaron) (1935–77)
Hugely influential American singer (below left). One of the first white rock 'n' roll performers.

The Beatles
English four-piece band. Their worldwide popularity throughout the 1960s was known as "Beatlemania." The best-selling and most important pop group of all time.

Dylan, Bob (Robert Allen Zimmerman) (1941–)
American songwriter who began as a protest singer, then brought folk and country elements to rock music.

The Beach Boys
American band whose complex harmonies and songs celebrating surfing, cars, and girls presented a classic image of California to the world.

Hendrix, Jimi (James Marshall) (1942–70)
American singer-songwriter whose innovative guitar work influenced heavy rock and funk musicians.

Franklin, Aretha (1942–)
American singer who brought gospel music to a mainstream pop and soul audience.

The Rolling Stones
English band that combines blues and rock 'n' roll with an outrageous stage act. The band continues to tour 40 years after forming.

Marley, Bob (Robert Nesta) (1945–81)
Jamaican singer-songwriter of reggae—songs of social protest with a throbbing beat—who became an international superstar.

Parton, Dolly (Rebecca) (1946–)
American country singer-songwriter and actress.

Springsteen, Bruce (1949–)
American singer and guitarist who writes songs about working-class life.

Wonder, Stevie (Steveland Judkins Morris) (1950–)
American singer-songwriter, producer, and multi-instrumentalist, who has been blind since birth. He had his first hit at age 12.

Jackson, Michael (1958–)
American singer-songwriter who became a child star in a pop group with his brothers. His 1982 album *Thriller* is the biggest-selling recording in history.

Madonna (Louise Veronica Ciccone) (1958–)
American singer-songwriter and actress (below) who is famed for her ever-changing appearance.

LL Cool J (James Todd Smith) (1968–)
American rapper and actor who made hip-hop popular.

Jones, Norah (1979–)
American singer-songwriter and pianist who won five Grammy Awards in 2003. She is the daughter of Indian musician Ravi Shankar.

✳ MUSICAL INSTRUMENTS
Musical instruments are devices used to produce musical sounds. Instruments are grouped in "families" according to the way they make sound.

▲ *A band playing traditional musical instruments in a park in Beijing, China.*

When a musical instrument is played, it produces vibrations, or sound waves, in the air, which is how we hear it. Every instrument gives off its own pattern of sound waves, which is how we tell the sound of one instrument apart from another. The instrument families are stringed instruments, woodwind instruments, brass instruments, and percussion instruments.

Stringed instruments
Stringed instruments consist of one or more strings stretched over a sound box (such as the body of a violin) or soundboard (as in a piano), which helps to amplify the sound. The strings are made to vibrate by plucking, striking, or playing with a bow.

One of the oldest instruments is the harp, which is played by plucking the strings with the fingers. Other plucked

instruments include the lute, guitar, banjo, and the Indian sitar. For all these, the player's left-hand fingers press the strings against a fingerboard to alter the length of the string and therefore its pitch, while the fingers of the right hand pluck the strings.

Instruments of the violin family (violin, viola, cello, and double bass) are usually played with a bow, although they can also be plucked with the hand (a method called pizzicato). They produce a rich, mellow tone and are the basis of the modern symphony orchestra.

Some stringed instruments are operated from a keyboard. The strings of a harpsichord are plucked by a quill when the keys are pressed. In the piano, a felt-covered hammer strikes a string when a key is pressed.

Woodwind instruments
Woodwind instruments are played by blowing into or across a hole at the end of a tube, making a column of air vibrate and so producing sound. Flutes, oboes, clarinets, saxophones, and bassoons are all woodwind, so called because most of them were once made from wood, though some are now made from metal or plastic.

Woodwind instruments have one of three different kinds of mouthpiece. The clarinet and saxophone both have a single reed attached to the mouthpiece, while the oboe and bassoon both have a double reed. When the player blows across a reed, it vibrates and moves the air inside the instrument. Flutes have a hole near one end at their side, which the player blows across, vibrating the air inside the

The wall of an Egyptian tomb dating from the 15th century B.C. The painting shows female musicians playing a harp and other stringed instruments.

flute. To produce different notes in woodwind instruments, the player's fingers cover and uncover holes along the length of the tube, changing the length of the column of air that vibrates inside the instrument.

Brass instruments

Brass instruments also make sound when the player blows into a tube. However, their mouthpieces are shaped like a funnel. Cornets, trumpets, horns, trombones, and tubas are all brass instruments, so called because they are made from metal. Most brass instruments have valves that can be opened and closed to alter the length of the tube and so change the note. Trombones use a slide mechanism to get the same result.

Percussion instruments

Percussion instruments are struck with the hands or fingers, or sticks, to produce a musical sound. The best known are drums, cymbals, triangles, xylophones, and glockenspiels.

Drums are found all over the world. They are usually made by stretching an animal skin tight across one or both ends of an open cylinder. (In modern orchestral instruments, plastic "skins" are used.) The skin is struck with the hand or a drumstick

to make it vibrate and produce a sound. The pitch of the note can be changed by altering the tension of the skin across the cylinder—the tighter the skin, the higher the note.

Cymbals are brass plates that are clashed together to make an exciting sound. The triangle is a bent rod of steel that is hit with another, smaller rod, making a sweet-toned high sound. The xylophone is a row of wooden bars that produce a dry, eerie sound when played. The glockenspiel has metal bars that give a ringing, magical sound. Xylophones and glockenspiels are played with round-ended wooden mallets.

SEE ALSO: Music; Orchestras; Sound Recording

Some of the musical instruments used to play bluegrass, a type of music that originated in Kentucky. The instrument on the left is an autoharp.

✳ MYTHS AND LEGENDS

A myth is a story that is not true but conveys an important truth about life. A legend is based on fact, even if many of the details are imaginary.

► *This wood carving represents the myth of the separation of Rangi the Sky Father and Papa the Earth Mother. It was made by the Maori people in New Zealand.*

Myths and legends are often passed on from generation to generation through the spoken word before being written down. That process is called an oral tradition.

► *Amaterasu appears from the cave. In Japanese myth, Amaterasu, the goddess of the sun, hid in a cave after being insulted by her brother. The other gods performed a dance to entice her out. When she left the cave, she brought light back to the world.*

Most of the stories developed many different versions as they were retold.

Myths

Myths often came about when people wanted to explain the world around them. How did life begin? Why do trees grow? Where does the sun go at night? Why do people die? The Maori people of New Zealand, for example, have a myth that tells how animals argued about whether life was better on land or in the sea. Unable to agree, some went off to the sea and became fish, while others headed inland and became land animals. One group, although having sea parents, also decided to head inland: They are the lizards. This story provides an explanation not only of why there are both fish and animals on Earth, but also why lizards, although land animals, resemble fish.

Myths also teach people the values and beliefs of the culture in which they live. Some myths are unique to one society, while others are found in many societies. Myths with similar themes occur in cultures throughout the world.

Many myths deal in some way with origins. Among the most fascinating origin stories are those that tell of the beginnings of Earth and the universe. Other myths explain crucial events in human life, such as conflicts and death.

Many societies had or have a number of myths familiar to everyone. They might be related, containing the same cast of gods and other characters. This collection of myths is called a mythology. Greek mythology, for example, contains many different stories about gods, such as Zeus and Aphrodite, and heroes, such as Hercules and Achilles. The ancient Greeks thought of their gods as a family, living on Mount Olympus in northern Greece. At the head of the family were Zeus and his wife, Hera.

Homer

In the 700s B.C., a Greek poet known to us as Homer put many of the myths about the Trojan War into a single long poem. It was called the *Iliad*. It tells the story of

OLYMPIAN GODS

This is a list of the most famous Greek gods. The Romans gave the gods their own names; these are given in parentheses.

Zeus (Jupiter)
King of the gods and god of the sky and of justice. His favorite weapon was the thunderbolt, the supreme weapon in the universe.

Hera (Juno)
Queen of the gods and Zeus's sister and wife. She was the goddess of women in the various stages of their life, from girlhood to widowhood.

Athena (Minerva)
Goddess of wisdom and of female arts, such as weaving, and also goddess of war (right). She was born from the head of Zeus as a fully grown maiden. The city of Athens is named for her.

Ares (Mars)
A son of Zeus and Hera. He was a god of war, but sometimes he himself was a coward.

Hermes (Mercury)
Another son of Zeus. He was the messenger of the gods, and his winged sandals allowed him to fly through the air with great speed.

Poseidon (Neptune)
A brother of Zeus. He was god of the waters (especially the seas), horses, and earthquakes.

Hephaestus (Vulcan)
Son of Hera. He was the blacksmith god of fire and crafts.

Aphrodite (Venus)
The beautiful goddess of love. In some accounts she is called a daughter of Zeus, while in others she is said to have sprung from the sea. Her son Eros (Cupid) was a winged, mischievous boy. An arrow from his bow made a human or god fall in love.

Apollo
Son of Zeus and the goddess Leto (Latona). An archer, he was also god of music, prophecy, and healing.

Artemis (Diana)
Sister of Apollo and goddess of the hunt.

Dionysus (Bacchus)
Son of Zeus and a human mother named Semele. He was god of vines, and so was the patron of wine and drinking.

Demeter (Ceres)
Sister of Zeus and goddess of agriculture. Her daughter Persephone (Proserpina) was seized by Hades, god of the dead.

how the war came about when Paris, a son of King Priam of Troy, stole Helen, the wife of Menelaus, the king of Sparta, and took her back to Troy. The Greeks fought the Trojans for 10 years until Odysseus (also known by his Latin name, Ulysses) brought it to an end with his plan for the Trojan Horse. In a second poem, the *Odyssey*, Homer describes Ulysses' journey home after the war, which, because of many adventures and delays, took another 10 years.

Legends

Legends are usually concerned with people who actually lived. However, legendary subjects range from the entirely imaginary hero to the real historical figure.

A 15th-century woodcut of the Romanian prince Vlad Tepes, or Vlad the Impaler (1431–76). He is thought to be the basis for the legend of Count Dracula.
▶

There are four basic types of legends: historical, personal, supernatural, and modern, or contemporary.

Historical legends are stories that are based on historical events. For example, historians believe that in about A.D. 500 there was a British ruler who in later centuries came to be called King Arthur, but that the stories about Camelot, his knights, and the Round Table are fiction. Little is known about King Arthur other than the legends, and these vary. In the oldest legends, Arthur is a godlike warrior, but in later legends he is a king.

Personal legends recount the events in the life of a real person, although some of the details may be fictional. Davy Crockett (1786–1836), for example, was a famous frontiersman, but many of the stories told about him are probably untrue.

Supernatural legends involve ghosts, haunted houses, werewolves, or people who return from the dead. They are less easy to trace to historical fact. Although the vampire in Bram Stoker's 1897 novel *Dracula* is fictional, the character is thought to be based on a Romanian prince who lived in the 1400s.

Modern legends are usually spread through newspapers, television, or the Internet, as well as by word of mouth. Their setting is often the city, so they are called urban legends. Modern legends that have become widely told include stories about alligators in sewers, strange behavior of celebrities, and bizarre medical occurrences or causes of death.

SEE ALSO: Ancient Civilizations; Greece, Ancient; Literature; Pirates and Outlaws; Religions

N

✳ NAPOLEON (1769–1821)

Napoleon Bonaparte ruled as emperor of France from 1804 to 1814. A military genius, he also wrote a new code of laws that protected people's rights.

Napoleon was born on the French island of Corsica. He joined the army in 1785. At the time France was at war with much of Europe. In 1796 Napoleon took command of the French army in Italy and led it to a number of major victories.

In 1799 Napoleon returned to Paris. He and his followers overthrew the unpopular French government on November 9, and Napoleon took control as First Consul.

In 1804 Napoleon helped write the Napoleonic Code, a set of laws that is still widely used. That year he made himself emperor. A series of brilliant campaigns in Europe, known as the Napoleonic Wars, followed. By 1807 his armies held Europe from Spain to the borders of Russia.

In 1812 Napoleon failed to conquer Russia. He was forced to give up his throne in 1814 and was exiled to the island of Elba. In 1815 he led France again, but he was finally defeated at Waterloo in June. He was imprisoned on the island of St. Helena until his death.

SEE ALSO: Europe; France; Warfare

As well as being an outstanding military leader, Napoleon Bonaparte modernized the French government, giving more power to the citizens. This sketch was drawn by Jacques-Louis David in 1799.

✳ NATIVE AMERICANS

Native American people were the first inhabitants of North America. Today they make up fewer than 1 percent of the population.

Some archaeologists believe that the first people to inhabit America traveled from Siberia to Alaska as early as 40,000 years ago. While looking for food, some of these people moved down the Pacific coast. When their descendants reached what is now California, they spread inland. As groups settled in various areas, they adapted to different ways of life suited to the land and climate. Major cultures developed in four broad regions:

the East (peoples from the Mississippi and Missouri rivers to the Atlantic coast, and from the St. Lawrence River to Florida); the Great Plains (peoples on the prairies from the Canadian provinces of Alberta, Manitoba, and Saskatchewan south to Texas and New Mexico); the Southwest (peoples from Arizona, New Mexico, and southern California); and the Northwest (peoples who spread along the Pacific coast from Alaska to California).

An ornamental bird's foot made from mica by the Hopewell people. The Hopewell lived in Ohio and Midwest America between about 100 B.C. and A.D. 400. They made many objects out of mica, a fragile, glasslike material.

Early Native American peoples in the East included the Mound Builders, named for their burial mounds. The mounds were built over a period of 2,500 years by the Adena, Hopewell, and Mississippians, based in the Ohio and Mississippi valleys.

Towns appeared in the Southwest about 2,000 years ago. The Hohokam people lived in houses that they built around public squares. Also in the Southwest, the Anasazi began building towns in about A.D. 700. By 1000 they were building apartment blocks that became known as pueblos, the Spanish word for "towns." The name was also used to describe the people who lived there.

In the East

Before European settlement, there may have been about 10 million Native Americans in North America. Soon after Columbus's discovery of the New World in 1492, many European nations sent explorers to the unfamiliar lands.

In the East after 1501, boats regularly sailed from Europe to fish and hunt whales off Newfoundland in Canada. The boats stopped at the mouth of the St. Lawrence River before going home. There Native Americans would trade furs for steel tools. Most of the St. Lawrence Valley was occupied by the Five Nations of the Iroquois—the Mohawk, Oneida, Onondaga, Cayuga, and Seneca. European trade sparked quarrels among the nations and brought new diseases that wiped out thousands of Native Americans. In the 1700s, the Iroquois helped the British fight the French. After Americans won their independence from the British, they took land from the Iroquois, who moved to reservations.

To the north and south of the Iroquois were smaller nations speaking Algonquian languages. Algonquians were the first to meet the English colonists, but in 1637 Massachusetts colonists turned on their neighbors in the Pequot War. A second war followed between 1675 and 1676.

Algonquian peoples of the Southeast included the Powhatan League, who met the Jamestown colonists in 1607. Other groups in this region spoke Muskogean, Siouan, or Caddoan languages.

During the 1500s and 1600s, Spain, France, and England took control of the southeastern United States. They treated Native Americans badly and seized their land. But by the 1700s, Southeastern peoples had built up trade with the English. This included selling other Native Americans into slavery. By the 1800s, some Southeastern Native Americans had become wealthy farmers.

The Removal Act of 1830 allowed the U.S. government to take Native American lands within the settled states in return for territories not yet settled by whites. Native Americans in the East were forced to vacate their land and march hundreds of miles to "Indian Territory" in Oklahoma. So many of them died on the march that it came to be called the Trail of Tears.

On the plains and prairies

Native Americans had lived on the plains and prairies of North America since prehistoric times. For about 5,500 years, hunting bison supplied them with food and hides. Some plains peoples were nomads, or wandering people. In time trading towns developed along major rivers. Spanish settlers brought horses to North America, and by 1750 all the plains and prairie peoples used them. After the Civil War (1861–65), the U.S. Army forced the plains peoples off their land. Many of them resisted the white invaders.

The last Native American victory was the battle of the Little Bighorn on June 25, 1876. The Sioux and the Cheyenne had tried to stop whites prospecting for gold on their land in Dakota. Lieutenant Colonel George Armstrong Custer led an attack on a Sioux camp beside the Little Bighorn River in Montana. Custer and all his men were killed in the battle.

In the Southwest
In 1540 the Spanish began to organize the Pueblo groups in northern Mexico and New Mexico. They treated the Pueblos harshly. In 1680 a Pueblo rebellion drove

DID YOU KNOW?

During the 1880s, the plains peoples began to practice the Ghost Dance religion. They prayed that the Creator might send the European settlers away and bring back their ancestors and the bison. The religion spread rapidly among the Lakota Sioux. The government feared that the Lakota might try to win back their old land. On December 15, 1890, the police tried to arrest Sitting Bull, a Sioux leader. In the scuffle he was shot and killed. Hundreds of angry Lakota gathered in South Dakota for a council with Big Foot, another chief. On the morning of December 29, 1890, soldiers went into the Lakota encampment at Wounded Knee Creek and asked the natives to hand over their guns. Shooting broke out. Two hours later more than 200 Lakota lay dead on the snowy ground, along with Chief Big Foot.

the Spanish out of New Mexico, but the invaders returned in 1692. From 1821 Mexico ruled the area. After the Mexican War (1846–48), the United States took it over. In 1924 Congress passed a law to protect Pueblo lands.

Another major Southwestern group is the Apache, which includes the Navajo. The Apache came south from western Canada after A.D. 1000. They moved in among Pueblo villages in Arizona and New Mexico. While under Spanish rule, small bands of Apache captured and sold other Native Americans as slaves.

In 1863 U.S. troops destroyed Navajo settlements. The next year, 8,000 Navajo were forced to resettle in New Mexico. The Navajo were given a reservation on the New Mexico–Arizona border. During the 1930s, the government destroyed nearly half their livestock when it built the Hoover Dam on the Colorado River. Since the 1950s, the Navajo reservation has been polluted by mining.

In the Northwest
For centuries the Native Americans of the Northwest lived as hunters and gatherers. Unlike Eastern peoples, they did not set up towns and villages, but mixed with other Native American groups along trade

Dressed in colorful feathered Sioux costumes, Native Americans of the plains perform a dance for tourists.
▼

425

This mask was made by the Kwakiutl, a Northwest Native American people who live on Vancouver Island and in neighboring mainland British Columbia, Canada.

routes that ran along the Pacific coast. Europeans came to the Northwest in the 1700s. They brought diseases that wiped out native villages. But they also brought trade, such as fishing and lumbering. However, these industries suffered during the Great Depression. Many Native Americans lost land and jobs to new industries.

The Great Basin, from the northern Rockies west to the Pacific, was the last region of North America to be settled by Europeans. Native Americans there moved from one food resource to the next, rather than settle. In California, Native Americans lived in villages. During the 1800s, California Native Americans were enslaved or killed by the thousands. In the 1900s, they were allowed to stay on reservations. During and after World War II (1939–45), Native Americans from the plains and the Southwest moved to California cities.

Native Americans today
Today Native American populations are growing. One problem they face is a lack of job opportunities owing to the location of many reservations. Prejudice toward Native Americans still exists, but America is their true homeland, and their cultures must be preserved or they will disappear. A map showing the major historical locations of Native Americans is at the end of the encyclopedia.

SEE ALSO: American Revolution; Canada; Chief Joseph; Civil War; Colonial America; Crazy Horse; French and Indian Wars; Osceola; Pocahontas; Sacajawea; Sitting Bull; United States of America; West, The American

* NATURAL RESOURCES
Anything that occurs naturally on Earth becomes a natural resource when people use it to supply their needs or serve their wants.

Air and water are vital natural resources—people need both to live. Land is a natural resource if people can use it to grow food or dig minerals out of it. But our most basic natural resource is the sun's energy. Plants change this energy to sugar and produce oxygen. Animals need oxygen to survive. Some animals eat plants and use their sugars. Some of these creatures are then eaten by other animals. As plants and animals die and decay, bacteria and fungi convert them into chemicals. The chemicals enter the soil and nourish plants. In a broad sense, all elements of this energy cycle are natural resources.

Usefulness to people is very important in deciding whether a material is considered a natural resource. The mineral bauxite was not known as a natural resource until the 1880s, when a cheap way was found to refine it to produce aluminum.

How people affect resources
Scientific progress increases our ability to improve natural resources. But people can also change the environment so that resources are destroyed or reduced in value. Automobiles and factories cause pollution, making the air unfit to breathe. And we often use resources wastefully.

Renewable resources

We can increase the usefulness of natural resources and reduce their loss by substituting a nonrenewable resource with a renewable one. Fossil fuels—natural gas, petroleum, and coal—are nonrenewable. There is only a certain amount of each fuel in the earth. If we continue to use them in the same amounts, there will eventually be none left.

In contrast, sunlight is constantly being renewed. We have learned to convert solar energy into energy that we can use for heating, transportation, and power.

Wind power and waterpower are other renewable resources that we can use to produce electricity. Wood—used to make paper and build houses—is another renewable resource. If we manage forests sensibly, we can grow trees as quickly as we use them.

SEE ALSO: Atmosphere; Conservation; Ecology; Energy; Environment; Food Chains; Fossil Fuels; Pollution; Sun; Water

▲
This is a solar power plant, where sunlight is converted to heat energy and used to generate electricity.

✴ NAVIGATION

Navigation is the science of finding your way. Many birds and animals have a built-in sense of direction, but people have to learn to navigate.

The English word *navigation* comes from the Latin words meaning "ship" and "move." Today the word means finding your way on or under the sea, on land, in the air, or even in space.

History of navigation

The first navigators were sea travelers. They stayed close to familiar coasts and used landmarks, such as islands, to figure out where they were. This technique, called piloting, is very useful when a ship is close to shore because the navigator can tell the distance between the craft and rocks or other dangers. Buoys and lighthouses also help navigators guide their ships safely.

Navigators also use charts—maps of sea areas—to help them. Compasses, with metal needles that always point to the magnetic North Pole, help the navigator decide on the right direction to steer.

When people began to explore farther out to sea, where there are no landmarks, they used the positions of the sun and stars to find their way. By

▷
A compass is an instrument for finding direction. The magnetized needle swings freely on a pivot to point toward magnetic north.

about the second century B.C., mapmakers had devised a system of imaginary lines that covered the earth and helped sailors plot their position more accurately than ever before.

The first and longest of these imaginary lines is the equator. The equator circles Earth midway between the North and South poles, where its circumference is about 25,000 miles (40,000 km). Its name comes from the Latin word *aequare*, meaning "to make equal." The equator divides the earth into two equal halves, known as the Northern and Southern hemispheres.

Latitude

Lines of latitude are shown on maps and globes as lines or circles parallel to the equator. Latitude is measured in degrees, with the equator at zero degrees (0°). Any point north of the equator is said to be in north latitude; any point south of the equator is said to be in south latitude. For example, Miami, Florida, has a latitude of 26 degrees north, or 26°N; Buenos Aires, Argentina, has a latitude of about 35 degrees south, or 35°S. The farther a place is from the equator, the higher the number of degrees in its latitude—the North and South poles are at 90°.

Longitude

Longitude indicates the number of degrees any place is to the east or west of an imaginary straight line drawn from the North Pole to the South Pole through Greenwich, London, England. This line is called the prime meridian. For example, New York City's longitude is 74 degrees west (of Greenwich), or 74°W. The longitude of Tokyo, Japan, is 140 degrees east (of Greenwich), or 140°E.

Celestial navigation

When a ship is on the equator, certain stars will seem to be overhead. If the ship sails north, these stars appear to move lower in the sky. By measuring the distance between the stars and the horizon, a navigator can judge the ship's latitude. For centuries navigators used a device called a sextant, a telescope fixed on a metal scale, to measure the distance between the sun and the horizon.

To judge longitude, navigators needed a clock to tell them the exact time in Greenwich. In 1735 John Harrison, an Englishman, made the first accurate clock, or chronometer, for use at sea. By observing the sun, a navigator found the time it was aboard the ship. Then, by comparing the ship's time with Greenwich time, the navigator could figure out the ship's longitude. If the

Conservationists in Sumatra, Indonesia, use the GPS to determine whether illegal logging is being carried out within a restricted area in which tree felling is banned.

ship's time was earlier than Greenwich time, its longitude had to be west of Greenwich. If the ship's time was later than Greenwich time, the ship's longitude had to be east. It is 15 degrees east or west for each hour's difference in time.

Using these two systems for determining latitude and longitude, skilled navigators were able to figure out their exact position anywhere in the world. This method is called celestial navigation.

Electronic navigation

Today navigators can use electronic equipment to find their positions. Radar uses radio waves to provide a "picture" of the surrounding area and can also identify ships, airplanes, or other craft.

A recent development in navigation is the global positioning system, or GPS. It is a group of 24 satellites around the earth that send signals to receivers, giving them their precise location. As well as ships and airplanes, many cars are now equipped with GPS receivers. Even people on foot can find their way by using handheld receivers of this type.

Space navigation

Electronic navigation is also important to space travel. But because of the danger of computer error, astronauts still need to understand celestial navigation in order to figure out where they are and the direction in which they are traveling.

SEE ALSO: Exploration and Explorers; Geography; Maps; Radio; Satellites; Time

✳ NEPTUNE

The planet Neptune is so far away from Earth that very little was known about it until recently. It cannot be seen from Earth without a telescope.

Neptune is about four times larger than Earth. The planet revolves around the sun in a huge elliptical (oval-shaped) orbit about 30 times greater than that of Earth. Since its discovery in the 1840s, Neptune has not yet completed a single revolution of the sun.

In 1989 the planetary space probe *Voyager 2* flew past Neptune. The pictures it took revealed some remarkable facts about the planet and its moons.

Blue gas giant

Unlike Earth, which has a rocky crust with an interior of molten rock, Neptune has a deep, thick atmosphere of hydrogen and helium gases, together with traces of methane gas, surrounding an ocean of water, methane, and ammonia. About 10 percent of Neptune's mass is made up of hydrogen and helium. The remaining 90 percent of its mass consists mostly of heavier elements, such as carbon, nitrogen, and oxygen. In contrast, Jupiter's mass is about 96 percent hydrogen and helium.

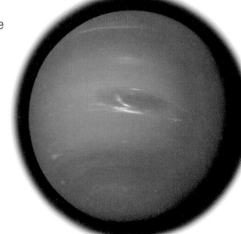

This picture of Neptune was taken by the Voyager 2 *space probe when it was 4.4 million miles (7 million km) away from the planet.*

KEY FACTS

POSITION IN THE SOLAR SYSTEM: Eighth planet from the sun	**DIAMETER:** 30,800 mi. (49,600 km)
AVERAGE DISTANCE FROM THE SUN: 2,800,000,000 mi. (4,500,000,000 km)	**MASS:** 103 sextillion tons
	ATMOSPHERE: Hydrogen, helium, methane
SOLAR ORBIT: 165 Earth years	**AXIAL ROTATION:** 16 hours, 5 minutes

absorbs six spectral colors but reflects blue, which is why Neptune appears that color when it is hit by light from the sun. Thin, wispy clouds floating in the upper atmosphere are above most of the methane, so they appear to be white. The upper atmosphere of Neptune is very cold, but temperatures increase closer to the center of the planet. Within Neptune, astronomers think there may be a rocky core about the size of Earth. The temperature at the core may reach 15,000°F (8,000°C).

All white light is made up of a spectrum of seven colors—red, orange, yellow, green, blue, indigo, and violet. Objects appear to be one color or another because their surfaces absorb the other colors. Methane

SEE ALSO: Astronomy; Light; Planets; Solar System; Space Exploration

---

*NERVOUS SYSTEM see *BRAIN AND NERVOUS SYSTEM

---

* NETHERLANDS, BELGIUM, AND LUXEMBOURG

The Netherlands, Belgium, and Luxembourg are small countries in northwest Europe. Together they are sometimes known as the Low Countries.

Netherlands' national flag

Belgium's national flag

Luxembourg's national flag

Netherlands

The Netherlands is often called Holland, after the province (now divided in two) that has long been the political and economic center of the country. The people and language are known as Dutch.

Most of the country is very low and flat. More than one-quarter lies below sea level and has been reclaimed from the North Sea over many years. Dikes were built around flooded areas, and the water was pumped out with windmills. The drained areas are called polders. With its many rivers and canals, the Netherlands has the densest network of waterways in the world.

Farming, fishing, shipping, and trade have traditionally been the main economic activities. The country's location on the North Sea has made it a natural trade center, and in the 17th century, Dutch merchants and sea captains made this small nation a leading world power, with colonies in Asia, Africa, and the Americas. Today Rotterdam is the largest port in Europe and one of the largest in the world.

The area that is now the Kingdom of the Netherlands has been ruled by the Romans, the Franks, the French dukes of Burgundy, and the Spanish. In 1648 Spain recognized the independence of the Dutch Republic. In 1795 the Netherlands was

King Leopold II of Belgium (ruled 1865–1909) claimed a huge expanse of land in Africa's Congo River basin as his own personal colony.

NETHERLANDS, BELGIUM, AND LUXEMBOURG

Frisian Islands

NETHERLANDS

North Sea

■ Amsterdam

■ The Hague
● Rotterdam

Rhine River

● Antwerp

BELGIUM

GERMANY

■ Brussels

Meuse River

FRANCE

LUXEMBOURG
■ Luxembourg

occupied by the French. It regained independence in 1813 as a monarchy and united with Belgium between 1815 and 1830. During World War II (1939–45), the country was occupied by Germany. After the war, the Netherlands became one of the first countries to campaign for cooperation among European states.

Belgium

The Kingdom of Belgium is a nation of two peoples. Flemings, who live in a region in the north called Flanders, make up about 60 percent of the population. They speak Flemish. The French-speaking Walloons, who live in Wallonia in the south, form about 30 percent of the population. About 60,000 German speakers live in the east.

Like the Netherlands, Belgium was part of the Roman Empire and later came under Spanish and then French rule. It was united with the Netherlands between 1815 and 1830.

Germany invaded the country during World War I (1914–18) and World War II (1939–45), causing great devastation. Today Belgium is a highly industrialized nation, and Belgian products are sold all over the world.

Luxembourg

Luxembourg is a tiny country, smaller than the state of Rhode Island. Its official name is Grand Duchy of Luxembourg, and its head of state is a grand duke or grand duchess. It is a very prosperous nation,

The castle at Vianden in Luxembourg dates from the ninth century, but has been restored to its 18th-century appearance.

▼

with one of the highest standards of living in the world. The traditional language is Letzeburgisch, a dialect of German. French and German are also widely spoken.

Luxembourg was first an independent state in 963, when Count Siegfried of Ardennes took over an old Roman fortress on the Alzette River. In 1443 Duke Philip of Burgundy conquered Luxembourg, and several European powers fought over the area for the next four centuries. It became independent again in 1839, but was invaded by Germany in both world wars.

European unity
In 1948 Belgium, the Netherlands, and Luxembourg set up an economic union called Benelux. In 1957 they joined with France, Germany, and Italy to form the European Economic Community (now the European Union). Its administrative center is in Brussels, Belgium.

SEE ALSO: Europe; Roman Empire; World War I; World War II

✳ NEWSPAPERS AND MAGAZINES
Newspapers are publications that provide information and opinions on current events. Magazines often give readers more specialized information.

History of newspapers
In ancient Rome, handwritten notices were posted in public places to inform citizens of the latest events. Newsletters were also sent by courier to far reaches of the empire. The invention of the printing press in the 1400s made mass communication possible. Newspapers, as we now know them, began to appear in Europe in the 1500s. The first newspaper in America was published in 1690, but the colonial authorities soon closed it down. By the end of the 1700s, there were more than 200 American newspapers, of which 24 were printed daily. Many of today's newspapers, including *The New York Times*, were first published in the 1800s.

Since the 1950s, newspapers have had to compete with radio and television, which can report news as it happens. The number of daily newspapers has dropped, and many of the remaining newspapers belong to corporations that own several newspapers. Currently most cities and towns have one newspaper rather than several competing ones. In 1982 *USA Today*, the first national newspaper in the United States, was launched.

Newspapers today
Although there are differences between big, internationally known newspapers and local publications, they share certain features. The most important part of any

This newsstand in Lisbon, Portugal, sells a range of newspapers and magazines.

newspaper is news. Reporters are the people responsible for getting news stories. Some reporters are specialists, concentrating on sports, politics, or other subjects. Others are general reporters, who cover any story. Newspapers may take their stories from a news agency, such as Reuters, whose reporters supply many different publications.

Editors decide which subjects get covered and how much space they should take up on the pages. A large newspaper may have many editors, covering the main areas of importance. On a small paper one person might make all the decisions. But there will always be a single person, often called the editor in chief, who will have the final say about content.

In addition to news, newspapers contain photographs and illustrations that help explain stories and add impact. A really good front-page photo can greatly increase the number of papers sold.

On the inside pages there are articles of serious comment about events, lighter pieces that take an amusing look at life, cartoons, comic strips, and crosswords. There are also reviews of movies, books, and exhibitions, as well as readers' letters.

Other important jobs on a newspaper include distribution—the physical process of getting the paper to the customer—and selling space for advertising.

Magazines

The word *magazine* means "storehouse" or "treasury." Magazines are sometimes called periodicals because they are published regularly—often once a week or once a month—at specific times. The first magazine, *The Review*, was a weekly. It was started in England in 1704. In 1741 Benjamin Franklin and Andrew Bradford, two rival printers, published the first American magazines. Today in the United States there are 9,000 magazines that are published at least four times a year. ➡

Magazines are divided into general- or special-interest magazines, also called consumer magazines, and business magazines, also called trade magazines. In addition there are scholarly journals, which report on research in various fields. Many special-interest magazines deal with a single subject, such as photography. Some are published for a specific readership, such as teenagers or African Americans. Some readers pay a subscription to have their favorite magazine delivered regularly.

SEE ALSO: Cartoons and Animation; Communication; Media; Photography; Printing

✳NEW TESTAMENT ᵴₑₑ ✳BIBLE

✳ NEWTON, ISAAC (1642–1727)

Isaac Newton was one of the most important scientists in history. His ideas about gravity, motion, and other subjects still influence modern science.

This portrait of Newton was made after he had been knighted (become Sir Isaac Newton) by Queen Anne of England in 1705.

Isaac Newton was born on Christmas Day, 1642, in the small town of Woolsthorpe in eastern England. A dreamy, impractical boy, he left school to work on his mother's farm. He was such a failure that she sent him back to school. At age 18 he went to study at Cambridge University, where he showed great interest in mathematics and physics.

At the age of 22, Newton worked out a basic formula, called the binomial theorem, that has been used by mathematicians ever since. In 1669 he became a professor of mathematics at Cambridge.

Newton's studies of light and color led him to make the first reflecting telescope. He also developed the theory of gravity.

In 1687 Newton published his great work, *The Mathematical Principles of Natural Philosophy*, often known as the *Principia*. Many people think of this as the most important scientific book of all time. It included his three laws of motion and his law of universal gravitation. Newton's ideas explain why a ball falls to the ground when it is thrown in the air, and why drivers jerk forward when their cars stop suddenly. Newton was buried at Westminster Abbey in London, where there are tombs of many famous Britons.

SEE ALSO: Astronomy; Colors; Force and Motion; Gravity; Light; Mathematics; Physics; Scientists; Telescopes

✳NEW ZEALAND ᵴₑₑ ✳AUSTRALIA AND NEW ZEALAND

NIGERIA

Nigeria is a federal republic of 36 states in West Africa. It has the largest population on the continent and is rich in natural resources, especially oil.

Land and climate

Nigeria takes its name from the Niger River, which flows through the west of the country. About one-third of the country, mostly the south, is tropical forest. To the north, grassland, or savanna, is more common. The climate is tropical. In December and January, a dry wind called the harmattan blows dust and sand in from the Sahara Desert to the north.

People and economy

There are more than 250 different ethnic groups in Nigeria, each with its own language and customs. The Hausa are the largest group in the north. The Yoruba and the Igbo dominate the south.

Islam is the main religion in the north, while Christianity is prevalent in the south. However, many Nigerians also take part in traditional African religious ceremonies.

Oil accounts for 95 percent of Nigeria's exports. Iron, tin, and coal are also important resources. Cocoa and palm oil are the main crops.

History

The earliest known civilization of the savanna region, the Nok, dates back to 500 B.C. After that time, several great empires developed in what is now Nigeria. Around A.D. 1000 the rulers of the Kanem-Borno state were the first Nigerians to adopt the Islamic faith.

The first Europeans to arrive were the Portuguese in the 1400s. The area became a major center for the slave trade. In 1861 the British created the colony of Lagos, which became the colony of Nigeria.

Pressure for self-government grew after World War II (1939–45), and Nigeria became independent in 1960. There was a military coup in 1966, and the eastern part of Nigeria declared independence as the Republic of Biafra. Civil war continued until Biafra's surrender in 1970. Democratic rule returned in 1979, but economic problems led to the military returning to power.

President Sani Abacha died in 1998, and free elections were held the following year. The new president, Olusegun Obasanjo, had to deal with corruption, economic inequality, and tension between Muslims (followers of Islam) and Christians.

Nigeria's national flag

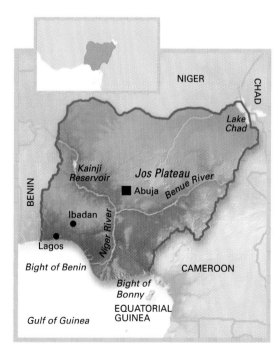

SEE ALSO: Africa; West Africa

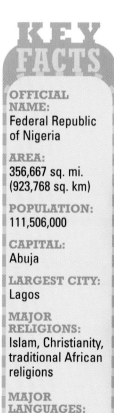

435

✳ NOBEL PRIZE

Nobel Prizes are awards for major achievements in specific fields. They commemorate Alfred Nobel, the inventor of dynamite.

The Swede Alfred Bernhard Nobel (1833–96) made his fortune from the invention of dynamite and other explosives, as well as artificial fabrics. When he died, he left most of his fortune to fund annual awards to the men and women who had made the greatest contribution to humanity in the fields of physics, chemistry, medicine, literature, and peace. An individual award can be shared or can be given to an organization. Since 1969 experts in economics have also been eligible to receive prizes.

Choosing a winner

Expert committees in Norway and Sweden, Nobel's homeland, decide each year who will win prizes. Sometimes there is controversy over an award. For example, the Russian Boris Pasternak (1890–1960), author of the novel *Dr. Zhivago*, was awarded the literature prize in 1958, but was forced by the Soviet authorities—who had banned the book—to refuse it.

In 2001 the Nobel Peace Prize was won jointly by the United Nations and its secretary-general, Kofi Annan.

Each winner receives about $1 million, a gold medal, and a diploma. However, the value of the prize is greater than this—Nobel Prize winners have made great contributions to the human race.

SOME FAMOUS NOBEL PRIZE WINNERS

These are just a few of the best-known Nobel Prize winners.

Curie, Marie (Poland/France): physics, 1903; chemistry, 1911

Einstein, Albert (Germany): physics, 1921

King, Martin Luther, Jr. (United States): peace, 1964

Mother Teresa (Albania): peace, 1979

Mandela, Nelson, and **de Klerk, F. W.** (South Africa): peace, 1993

Morrison, Toni (United States): literature, 1993

Naipaul, V. S. (Britain/Trinidad): literature, 2001

Carter, James E. (Jimmy) (United States): peace, 2002

SEE ALSO: Curie, Marie and Pierre; Einstein, Albert; King, Martin Luther, Jr.; Mandela, Nelson; Morrison, Toni; United Nations

NORTH AFRICA

The countries of North Africa are, from west to east, Morocco (including Western Sahara), Algeria, Tunisia, Libya, Egypt, and Sudan.

Land and climate

The Atlas Mountains cross the northwest corner of North Africa. Along the northwestern coast high rainfall has created a strip of fertile land. The region is dominated by the world's largest desert, the Sahara, where the annual average rainfall is only 3 in. (76 mm). The Nile River flows north through Sudan and Egypt, providing a slender ribbon of life in the northeastern deserts. There are swamps and rain forests in the south of Sudan.

People and economy

Most of the north is inhabited by Arabs and Berbers, although southern Sudan is home to black Africans. Tribes of Berber-speaking nomads called the Tuareg wander the deserts as they have done for centuries, trading goods and tending their flocks. But this way of life is dying out. Today most North Africans live in towns or cities, where modern offices mix with ancient ruins and winding market streets.

Mining for minerals and gems is a major industry. Petroleum and natural gas are important sources of income, especially to Libya. Tourism brings millions of visitors to the region each year.

History

Egypt is unique among North African nations. It was home to a civilization that flourished more than 5,000 years ago. Many ancient Mediterranean peoples invaded and settled North Africa, including the Phoenicians and their successors, the Carthaginians. Later the Romans conquered the Carthaginians and ruled North Africa from Egypt to Morocco.

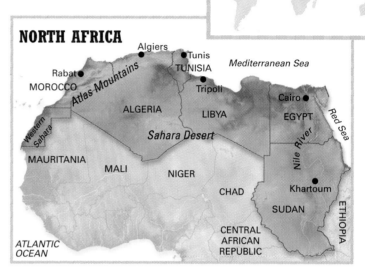

NORTH AFRICA

Algiers · Tunis · TUNISIA · Mediterranean Sea · Rabat · MOROCCO · Atlas Mountains · Tripoli · Cairo · ALGERIA · LIBYA · EGYPT · Red Sea · Western Sahara · Sahara Desert · Nile River · MAURITANIA · MALI · NIGER · Khartoum · CHAD · SUDAN · ETHIOPIA · ATLANTIC OCEAN · CENTRAL AFRICAN REPUBLIC

In the middle of the seventh century, Arabs from the Middle East swept into the region and brought a new religion—Islam. Today most North Africans are Muslims (followers of Islam).

In the 15th century, the Ottoman Turks conquered North Africa. It took nearly four centuries to drive them out. In the 19th century, France took control of Algeria and Tunisia, while Great Britain, Spain, and Italy claimed other parts of the region. Egypt gained its independence in 1922, and the other North African nations followed between 1951 and 1962. The Western Sahara has been claimed by Morocco, which controls the area, although many of its peoples want independence.

SEE ALSO: Africa; Deserts; Egypt; Islam; Roman Empire

✳ NORTH AMERICA, GEOGRAPHY

The continent of North America is made up of three large countries—Canada, the United States, and Mexico.

Land and climate

North America is the world's third-largest continent in area, after Asia and Africa. It is bordered by the Pacific Ocean in the west; the Arctic Ocean in the north; the Atlantic Ocean in the east; and Central and South America in the south. The landscape is one of huge variety, with great rivers, towering mountains, dense forests, rugged plateaus, and broad stretches of plains.

The continent's greatest length from north to south is about 5,300 miles (8,500 km). Its greatest width from east to west is about 4,000 miles (6,400 km). It has a varied climate that ranges from polar in the north to tropical in the south.

Along with Canada, the United States, and Mexico, North America is sometimes said to include Central America and numerous islands, including Greenland (a territory of Denmark) and the Caribbean Islands.

Major regions

The major regions of North America are the North American Cordillera, the Appalachian Highlands, the Great Central Plain, and the Canadian Shield.

The North American Cordillera is a great mountain system that stretches across western North America. It includes the Rocky Mountains, the Alaska Range, the Coast Mountains, the Cascade Range, the Sierra Nevada, and the mountains of the Sierra Madre. The Rocky Mountains span about 3,000 miles (4,800 km) in the United States and Canada. The great ridge of the Rockies, called the Continental Divide, separates river systems that flow to opposite sides of the continent. The Sierra Madre is the chief mountain system of Mexico. Its highest peak is the volcano Citlaltepetl, or Pico de Orizaba.

The Bow River flows through Banff National Park in the Canadian Rockies.

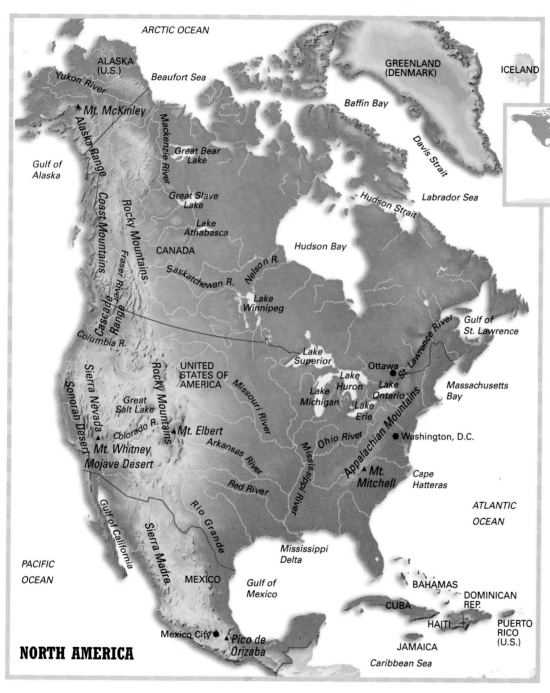

ARCTIC OCEAN

ALASKA
(U.S.)
Yukon River
Beaufort Sea

GREENLAND
(DENMARK)
ICELAND

▲ Mt. McKinley

Baffin Bay

Gulf of
Alaska

Davis Strait

Mackenzie River

Great Bear
Lake

Labrador Sea

Alaska Range

Coast Mountains

Great Slave
Lake

Hudson Strait

Rocky Mountains

Lake
Athabasca

Hudson Bay

CANADA

Fraser River

Abitibi

Saskatchewan R.

Nelson R.

Columbia R.

Lake
Winnipeg

Lake
Superior

Gulf of
St. Lawrence

St. Lawrence River

Sierra Nevada

Rocky Mountains

UNITED
STATES OF
AMERICA

Missouri River

Lake
Huron

Ottawa

Lake
Ontario

Massachusetts
Bay

Great
Salt Lake

Lake
Michigan

Lake
Erie

Sonoran Desert

Colorado R.

▲ Mt. Elbert

Appalachian Mountains

▲ Mt. Whitney
Mojave Desert

Arkansas River

Ohio River

● Washington, D.C.

Mississippi River

▲ Mt.
Mitchell

Cape
Hatteras

Red River

ATLANTIC
OCEAN

Gulf of California

Rio Grande

Sierra Madre

Mississippi
Delta

PACIFIC
OCEAN

MEXICO

Gulf of
Mexico

BAHAMAS

DOMINICAN
REP.

CUBA

HAITI

PUERTO
RICO
(U.S.)

Mexico City ●

▲ Pico de
Orizaba

JAMAICA

NORTH AMERICA

Caribbean Sea

The Appalachian Highlands consist of a broad plateau with several mountain ranges, including the Green Mountains in Vermont, the White Mountains in Maine and New Hampshire, and the Blue Ridge Mountains, which run from Pennsylvania to Georgia. The highest point in the Appalachians is Mount Mitchell, at 6,684 ft. (2,037 m).

The Great Central Plain lies between the Cordillera and the Appalachians. A low ridge that extends from Newfoundland to the Rocky Mountains divides it into northern and southern sections.

The Canadian Shield extends over much of eastern and northern Canada. It contains the oldest and hardest rocks in North America. The action of glaciers dotted the region with a large number of lakes. It also has many bogs and swamps.

Rivers and lakes

North America has five major river systems. The Arctic system includes the Mackenzie, the Saskatchewan, and the Nelson rivers. In the Atlantic system, the major river is the St. Lawrence. The Gulf system includes the great Mississippi and all its tributaries and the Rio Grande and Colorado. In the Pacific system, the Columbia and the Fraser rivers are the most important. The inland system is made up of streams that do not drain into the sea.

North America has more lakes than any other continent. The five Great Lakes, four of which are shared by the United States and Canada, are some of the largest bodies of water in North America. Lake Superior is the world's largest freshwater lake. Other major lakes, all in Canada, are Great Bear Lake, Great Slave Lake, Lake Athabasca, and Lake Winnipeg. Lake Chapala is the largest lake in Mexico.

Major Physical Features

DESERTS
- Sonoran 120,000 sq. mi. (310,800 sq. km)
- Mojave 25,000 sq. mi. (64,750 sq. km)

MOUNTAIN RANGES & HIGHEST POINTS
- Alaska Range 20,320 ft. (6,194 m) at Mt. McKinley
- Sierra Madre 18,405 ft. (5,610 m) at Citlaltepetl (Pico de Orizaba)
- Sierra Nevada 14,494 ft. (4,418 m) at Mt. Whitney
- Rocky Mountains 14,433 ft. (4,399 m) at Mt. Elbert

RIVERS
- Mississippi-Missouri 3,741 mi. (6,019 km)
- Mackenzie 2,635 mi. (4,240 km)
- Yukon 1,979 mi. (3,184 km)

LAKES
- Lake Superior 31,820 sq. mi. (82,414 sq. km)
- Lake Huron 23,010 sq. mi. (59,596 sq. km)
- Lake Michigan 22,400 sq. mi. (58,016 sq. km)
- Great Bear Lake 12,275 sq. mi. (31,792 sq. km)

Niagara Falls forms part of the border between the United States and Canada. ▶

SEE ALSO:
Canada;
Caribbean Islands;
Central America;
Greenland;
Mexico;
United States Geography

NUCLEAR POWER

The center, or nucleus, of an atom contains the strongest source of energy in the universe. This energy has many uses.

All matter, such as a solid piece of wood, is made up of atoms. Atoms are made up of smaller subatomic particles. The nucleus (plural, *nuclei*) consists of two kinds of particles, named protons and neutrons. Clouds of particles called electrons surround the nucleus. Each electron carries a negative electrical charge. Each proton carries a positive charge. (Neutrons have no charge.) Opposite electrical charges attract each other, and this attraction joins the electrons and the nucleus as an atom.

A group of atoms bound together is called a molecule. The atoms join by sharing or exchanging electrons. Their nuclei remain unchanged. The forms of energy we use most result from reactions that involve electrons. For example, when wood burns, molecules in the wood come apart. Their atoms are combined with oxygen from the air, and chemical energy is released.

Nuclear energy, however, involves changes in the nucleus itself. Certain elements, such as uranium, have very large nuclei with many positively charged protons. The protons repel each other to overcome the so-called strong force that holds protons and neutrons together. The nuclei become unstable and break down into smaller nuclei and individual particles until they become stable. In this way, uranium gradually changes into lead, which is a more stable element. This process is called radioactivity.

Fusion and fission

Radioactivity is a spontaneous nuclear reaction because it takes place without the action of any outside force. Scientists discovered that similar reactions can be made to happen. They found that after a nuclear reaction occurs, the total mass of the particles left was less than the mass of the original nucleus. The missing mass had been converted into energy.

In the same way that heavy nuclei can break apart, light nuclei can join together. In both cases, the nuclei are seeking to

The Diablo Canyon Power Plant in California is one of the most important nuclear power facilities in the United States. It supplies electricity to more than two million Californians every day.

become more stable. And in both cases, small amounts of mass can be converted to large amounts of energy. So nuclear energy can be released in two types of reactions: fusion (when nuclei join) and fission (when a nucleus is split).

In nuclear fusion, two light nuclei join to form a heavier nucleus. Fusion is the source of energy of the sun and other stars. To create this reaction in the laboratory requires high pressure and temperature. At extreme temperatures, matter breaks down into plasma. This type of fusion is called thermonuclear fusion. It is the principle behind most modern nuclear weapons.

In nuclear fission, a nucleus splits into two nuclei of lighter elements. A small amount of mass creates a huge amount of energy. The neutrons released by fission can cause other nuclei to break up. This is called a chain reaction, and it can be designed to produce continuous, controllable energy. Nuclear reactors use fission to create electrical power.

In a nuclear power plant, the energy to drive the generators that produce electricity comes from a nuclear reactor. The central part of a reactor is the core. It contains fuel—generally uranium—formed into small pellets inside long, metal rods.

Technicians refueling the core at the Comanche Peak Nuclear Plant in Texas.

They are surrounded by a moderator. This is a substance that slows the speed of the free neutrons that are released in fission. This increases the chance that they will be absorbed by the fuel and cause fission. In the United States, water is the most common moderator. The core also contains a coolant, also usually water. This provides steam that drives the turbines.

Nuclear safety

If there is too much fission, the reaction may run out of control. If a reactor fails and releases radioactive material, radiation could harm people, animals, and crops over a wide area. A famous nuclear accident occurred at the Chernobyl power plant in the Ukraine (part of the former Soviet Union) in 1986. More than 30 people died and hundreds more suffered from radiation poisoning. Nuclear power is an inexpensive way to produce energy, but concerns about safety have slowed its development.

Nuclear weapons

During World War II, the United States financed research to create a nuclear bomb. The only time these weapons have been used in war was when they were dropped on the Japanese cities of Hiroshima and Nagasaki in 1945. Nuclear weapons create radioactive fallout that causes sickness and death. The dangers of nuclear weapons have led to many attempts to persuade governments to reduce their stock of them.

SEE ALSO: Atoms and Molecules; Einstein, Albert; Elements; Energy; Matter; Physics; Pollution; World War II

✳NUTRITION ᵴᵉᵉ ✳HEALTH

*OCEANIA see *AUSTRALIA AND NEW ZEALAND/
PACIFIC ISLANDS/PACIFIC OCEAN/
PACIFIC RIM

* OCEANS AND SEAS

Seawater covers more than 70 percent of Earth's surface. Oceans and seas contain valuable resources for human life, such as food and energy.

Most scientists today agree that the continents were created when the plates forming Earth's crust slid apart. The gaps between the continents form the areas of Earth's oceans. No one knows for certain how these gaps filled with water. One theory is that the planet was surrounded by a cloud layer that cooled, releasing huge quantities of rain. Another idea is that water vapor was released by hot rocks in Earth's crust.

Sometimes, the word *ocean* is used to refer to all areas of seawater. But geographers generally use the term to define the four largest bodies of water—the Arctic, Atlantic, Indian, and Pacific oceans. There is disagreement about whether the seas around the Antarctic should be considered a fifth ocean. Other areas, such as the Caribbean and the Mediterranean, are called seas.

Seawater

The measure of salt in water is called salinity. Seawater usually has a salinity level of about 35 parts per thousand—in other words, 1,000 ounces of water contain 35 ounces of dissolved salt.

Seawater also contains dissolved carbon dioxide and oxygen, which are necessary

As the world's oceans and seas pound the coasts, they alter the shape of the surrounding land.

THE WORLD'S LARGEST OCEANS & SEAS

Pacific Ocean	96,658,638 sq. mi. (250,345,000 sq. km)
Atlantic Ocean	53,785,890 sq. mi. (139,305,000 sq. km)
Indian Ocean	42,598,723 sq. mi. (110,330,000 sq. km)
Southern Ocean	12,630,612 sq. mi. (32,713,000 sq. km)
Arctic Ocean	8,220,740 sq. mi. (21,292,000 sq. km)
South China Sea	1,848,330 sq. mi. (4,787,200 sq. km)
Caribbean Sea	1,710,634 sq. mi. (4,430,500 sq. km)
Mediterranean Sea	1,555,292 sq. mi. (4,028,200 sq. km)
Bering Sea	1,409,394 sq. mi. (3,650,300 sq. km)
Gulf of Mexico	958,714 sq. mi. (2,483,100 sq. km)

to maintain plant and animal life in the sea. Many other substances, such as dissolved nitrates and phosphates, are also present.

DID YOU KNOW?

The highest ocean waves are caused not by powerful winds but by sudden movements in Earth's crust. These waves are known as tsunamis. The word *tsunami* is Japanese in origin and means "harbor wave." Although they are sometimes called tidal waves, they have nothing to do with tides. They happen as a result of earthquakes, volcanic eruptions, and underwater landslides. Tsunamis can reach heights of up to 30 ft. (9 m) and speeds of almost 600 mph (965 kph). Although rare, they occur most commonly in the Pacific Ocean. The huge waves move across the ocean very rapidly, and can cause serious damage when they reach the shore, killing people and devastating property.

Waves, currents, and tides

The waters in the oceans and seas are constantly moving. Winds cause movements on the surface called waves. Some movements are continuous and in a single direction—they are called currents. Currents carry warm water into cold regions and cool water into tropical regions. This mix of temperatures creates many kinds of weather patterns. Tides are rhythmic rises and falls in the level of the sea. They are caused by the gravitational pull of the moon and the sun.

Life in the sea

Thousands of different species of plants and animals live in the seas and oceans. One of the biggest groups of organisms is plankton. Most plankton are so small that they can be seen only under a microscope. They float in the water and are carried along by the tides and currents. Phytoplankton contain a green pigment known as chlorophyll. Like green plants on land, they use chlorophyll in the presence of sunlight to combine water and carbon dioxide to make their own food. They produce oxygen in this process, which is called photosynthesis. Small animals known as zooplankton feed on phytoplankton. These animals provide food for larger animals, which may in turn become food for people. Thus all the living things in the oceans and seas depend on plankton for food and oxygen.

SEE ALSO: Antarctica; Arctic; Atlantic Ocean; Corals and Coral Reefs; Crabs; El Niño; Fish; Jellyfish; Pacific Ocean; Photosynthesis; Plate Tectonics; Seashores; Starfish and Other Echinoderms; Water; Weather

✳OIL ▶see▶ ✳FOSSIL FUELS

✳ O'KEEFFE, GEORGIA (1887–1986)
One of the most original American artists, Georgia O'Keeffe portrayed nature simply but dramatically, with precise lines and glowing colors.

Georgia O'Keeffe was born on a farm in Sun Prairie, Wisconsin, in 1887. She studied art in Chicago and New York City. Some of her drawings were exhibited in 1916 by the photographer Alfred Stieglitz. In 1918 O'Keeffe moved to New York to paint. In 1924 she married Stieglitz. By the 1920s, she had developed her unique style of painting, and some of her most famous works, including flower studies such as *Black Iris*, date from this period. She also painted many views of the New York City skyline. After Stieglitz died in 1946, O'Keeffe moved to New Mexico, where she lived until her death. The stark desert landscape inspired her later work.

This photograph of Georgia O'Keeffe was taken in August 1960, when she was 72 years old.

SEE ALSO:
Art and Artists

✳ OLD TESTAMENT ⇒see ✳ BIBLE

✳ OLYMPIC GAMES
The Olympic Games draw athletes from all over the world. The modern Olympics began in 1896, but the idea is much older.

No one knows when the first Olympics took place, but there are records of games honoring the god Zeus in 776 B.C. They were held at Olympia in ancient Greece.

For many centuries, Greek cities competed against one another in events that included running, wrestling, jumping, discus, and javelin. Warring city-states even stopped fighting while the games took place. Interest in the games spread, and foreign athletes came to Greece to compete. When Rome conquered Greece in the first century B.C., Olympic standards began to decline. The Roman emperors demanded prizes and cheated in order to win. The early Olympic Games were stopped in A.D. 394.

The modern Olympics
In the late 1800s, Baron Pierre de Coubertin, a Frenchman, became interested in the ancient Olympics. He believed that sports and exercise were a vital part of young people's education. He also believed that people should take part in sports without financial and commercial pressures, so the games were for

amateur sportspeople only. In 1896 Coubertin organized the first modern Olympic Games in Athens, Greece. They have been held in different places around the world every four years since then, except in 1916, 1940, and 1944, when world wars prevented them.

Organization

Coubertin founded the International Olympic Committee (IOC), and this organization continues to run the games. Each country has its own national Olympic committee, and each sport has an international federation to oversee the selection of athletes for the games.

Cities compete for the honor of hosting the games. Every four years, thousands of athletes, coaches, officials, and spectators come to one place, and millions more watch on television. A modern Summer Olympic Games requires many different facilities for the various sports, and they are often spread through an entire city and the surrounding area. Track-and-field

events need an open-air arena. Weight lifting, gymnastics, and combat sports, such as boxing and judo, take place in covered spaces. The swimmers and divers need pools; other water sports, such as canoeing, are held outdoors.

One of the most challenging events is the marathon, a running race of 26 miles 385 yards (42.12 km), which usually takes place on the streets of the host city, finishing in the main stadium. The race was included in the 1896 Olympics to commemorate the run Pheidippides was said to have made to Athens to tell the citizens of their army's victory at the battle of Marathon in 490 B.C.

Ceremonies

The Olympics have changed greatly since their origins, but some aspects remain the same. Most important, there is no prize money for competitors. Athletes who claim first, second, or third place win medals—gold, silver, or bronze. The games always begin when the Olympic torch

Runners compete in the women's 1,500-meter semifinal in the 2000 Olympics in Sydney, Australia.
▶

AMAZING FACTS!

At the 2000 Games in Sydney, Australia, 10,651 athletes from 199 nations competed in 300 events.
The Olympic torch was first lit at the 1928 games in Amsterdam, Netherlands.
At the 1904 games in St. Louis, MO, Fred Lorz (USA) was the first marathon runner to cross the line. However, he was disqualified when it turned out that he had covered most of the course in a car.

for the duration of the games. The games begin and end with elaborate ceremonies celebrating the history and culture of the home nation and the Olympic ideals of fair play. The Olympic symbol of five colored rings is often used in these ceremonies.

Winter Olympics

The first Winter Olympic Games were held at Chamonix, France, in 1924. They took place in the same year as the Summer Games until 1992. Since 1994 the Winter Games are held two years before and after the Summer Games. The cold-weather sports of today's Winter Olympic Games could never have developed in the warm climate of Greece.

enters the main stadium. Athletes running in relays have carried the torch from Olympia. An athlete from the home nation uses the torch to light a flame that burns

SEE ALSO: **Greece, Ancient; Hockey; Sports**

✳ ORCHESTRAS

Orchestras are large groups of musicians playing their instruments together. They are usually made up of strings, woodwind, brass, and percussion.

Orchestras can have as few as 10 members or more than 100. A group of about 15 to 30 players is known as a chamber orchestra—so called because it is small enough to play in a small hall or chamber. Much early music was composed for such an orchestra. A military or concert band may be as large as an orchestra but does not use stringed instruments. A string orchestra is made up of only the stringed instruments of the symphony orchestra.

Symphony orchestras

The typical modern symphony orchestra—so called because they often play pieces called symphonies—contains about 60

string players, about 12 woodwind and 12 brass players, and about 6 percussionists. Their performance is directed by a conductor, who stands at the front in clear view of all the players, keeping time with a short stick called a baton and giving directions to the players with his hands.

The orchestra's seating is arranged so that the loudest instruments (the percussion) are at the back and the quietest (the strings) are at the front. The strings are arranged in a fan shape, all the players looking toward the conductor. The violins are split into two groups (first and second violins, each playing different parts of the music) and are seated on the left of the

THE ORCHESTRA

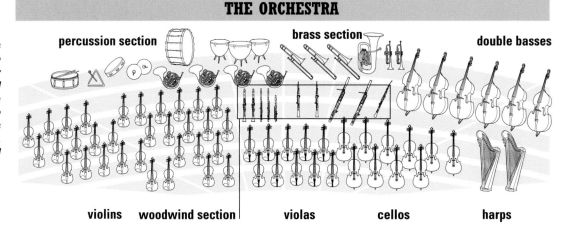

percussion section   brass section   double basses

violins   woodwind section   violas   cellos   harps

The various sections of the orchestra as they are arranged onstage for a performance. The conductor stands in front of them, visible to all the players.

stage. The violas are in front of the conductor, and the cellos and double basses to the right. Behind the strings sit the woodwind, and behind them the brass section. The timpani (kettledrums) are at the back of the orchestra with the rest of the percussion section. The conductor interprets the music, deciding how fast or slow it should be, and how loud or soft. Conductors tell the players how they would like them to play the music during rehearsals. Rehearsals can take many hours each day, and preparations for a single performance can begin several weeks in advance.

SEE ALSO: Music; Musical Instruments

✱ OSCEOLA (ABOUT 1800–38)

Osceola was a Native American warrior who gathered together a band of followers and fought against European settlers in Florida.

Osceola was born among the Creek people of Georgia or Alabama; when he was a boy, his mother joined the Seminole people of Florida.

In 1832 some of the Seminole leaders signed a treaty with the Europeans agreeing to move their people west of the Mississippi River. Osceola, who opposed the treaty, gathered bands of followers to fight against resettlement. According to legend, at one meeting in 1835 between Native American and white leaders, Osceola plunged his knife into a document, shouting, "This is the only treaty I will make with the whites!" He was imprisoned but soon released. He then murdered General Wiley Thompson, a U.S. Native American agent. The conflict known as the Second Seminole War began. Osceola took his men deep into the Everglades and led raids on the Army for two years. In 1837, bearing the white flag of truce, he met to negotiate with General Thomas Jesup. But Jesup ordered Osceola's capture and imprisonment. He died at Fort Moultrie, South Carolina.

Osceola at about 30 years of age. He was not born a chief, but he led the Seminole people into battle.

SEE ALSO: Native Americans; West, The American

*PACIFIC ISLANDS

There are about 25,000 islands in the Pacific, most of them in the southern ocean. Often called Oceania, the islands are divided into three main groups—Polynesia, Melanesia, and Micronesia.

Pacific Community's flag

◀

The shore of American Samoa, one of the groups of islands that make up Polynesia.

The Pacific Islands are of two main types—continental and oceanic. Continental islands rise from the continental shelves, the underwater areas surrounding most continents. These islands are the tips of the long chains of mountains and volcanoes that border the Pacific Basin.

Two processes formed the Pacific's oceanic islands—volcanism and subsidence. Volcanic islands form when lava (molten rock) pours out from Earth's interior, then cools. Hawaii is the largest Pacific island created in this way. In subsidence, the weight of the volcanic mass forces the crust of the ocean basin to sink, or subside. The older an island is, the more it will have sunk, and therefore the lower it appears in the ocean.

As a volcanic island subsides, colonies of small organisms called corals, living just below the surface of the water,

ISLANDS

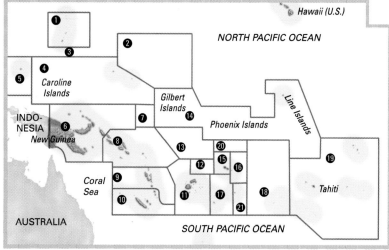

Micronesia

The 2,000 tiny islands of northwestern Oceania are known as Micronesia, meaning "small islands." Many of them are coral atolls. Four island chains— the Carolines, the Gilberts, the Marianas, and the Marshalls—dominate the region. Johnston Atoll and the islands of Nauru and Wake are also in Micronesia. So too is Midway, the scene of a crucial battle during World War II (1939–45). Micronesia is divided into five independent nations, eight U.S. territories, and one U.S. commonwealth.

sometimes attach themselves to it. In time the volcanic material may disappear beneath the ocean. But the corals go on building upward, forming reefs. If sand, made by erosion of the coral rock, collects on top of the rock, a low, sandy island results. If this sandy island is shaped like a ring, it is called an atoll. The water enclosed by an atoll is a lagoon. Many of the islands of Tonga formed in this way.

Polynesia and Melanesia

Polynesia, meaning "many islands," is a large triangle of islands in the central and southeastern ocean. Major island groups in Polynesia include Hawaii, Tonga (the Friendly Islands), Tuvalu (formerly the Ellice Islands), Samoa and American Samoa, and part of Kiribati, including Christmas Island. Also in Polynesia is Easter Island, which is famous for its mysterious giant carved heads. The Maoris, the original inhabitants of New Zealand, are Polynesians.

The islands of the southwestern Pacific are called Melanesia. The word means "black islands." Melanesia includes Papua New Guinea, Fiji, New Caledonia, the Solomon Islands, and Vanuatu (formerly the New Hebrides).

Economy

Most Pacific Islanders are subsistence farmers, growing food for themselves and their families. Some of the higher volcanic islands produce pineapples, sugarcane, and bananas for export. The lower coral islands have little fertile soil, and copra, the dried flesh of coconuts, is the only cash crop. There are few mineral resources. Some islands earn money from tourism, but most are too remote for easy access. Many islanders worry that tourism will damage their culture. They also fear that global warming will raise the level of the oceans and cover low-lying islands.

SEE ALSO: Australia and New Zealand; Corals and Coral Reefs; Islands; Pacific Ocean; Pacific Rim; Volcanoes; World War II

PACIFIC OCEAN

The Pacific is the largest and deepest of the world's oceans. It covers just under one-third of Earth's surface and plunges to more than 7 miles (11 km) in one area.

The Pacific extends from the Arctic to the Antarctic, a distance of more than 9,000 miles (14,480 km). Along the equator, it extends about 11,000 miles (17,700 km), from the west coasts of the Americas to the east coasts of Asia and Australia. The equator divides the North and South Pacific. Because of its enormous area, the Pacific Ocean is often considered to be Earth's principal physical feature.

The Pacific is linked to the Indian Ocean by the Strait of Malacca between Indonesia and Malaysia. The two oceans also join south of Australia. The Bering Strait connects the Pacific with the Arctic Ocean, and at Cape Horn (at the southern tip of South America), the Pacific merges with the Atlantic Ocean.

The Pacific's greatest known depth is in the Challenger Deep of the Mariana Trench, which is located off the island of Guam in the western Pacific. Plunging 36,198 ft. (11,033 m)—over 7 miles (11 km)—below the ocean's surface, this is the deepest point on Earth known to man.

At certain times of the year, the ocean experiences many intense tropical storms, known in the western Pacific as typhoons. These often cause severe coastal flooding, damage to property, and loss of life.

Pacific Islands

There are about 25,000 islands in the Pacific, most of which are found in the southern ocean, particularly its western reaches. New islands, coral reefs, and atolls (sandy islands) continue to be created by volcanic action. Scientists mapping the ocean floor in 1993 found more than 1,000 volcanoes in an area of the South Pacific. It was thought to be the largest known concentration of active volcanoes on Earth.

Ice floes floating on the sea in the most northerly stretches of the Pacific Ocean near the Bering Strait between Alaska and Siberia, Russia.

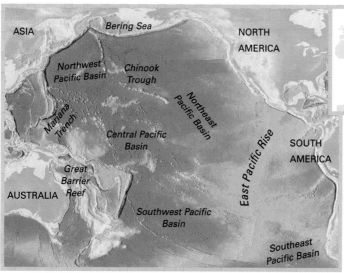

ocean during his attempt to sail around the world. He found its waters especially calm and so named it Pacific, meaning "peaceful." In the 1760s and 1770s, the English explorer James Cook became the first European to see and map many of the islands. American and British whaling ships also began to stop at the islands. Planters, traders, and missionaries followed them and settled. Some islands became important as naval bases.

By the end of the 1800s, Britain, France, Germany, and the United States had established themselves as colonial powers in the Pacific. In 1918, after defeat in World War I, Germany lost its colonies, some of them to Japan.

During World War II (1939–45), the Pacific Ocean was the site of many battles, especially between the United States and Japan. After the war, Japan was forced to give up its islands. Since the 1960s, most of the Pacific states have become independent.

Discovery and history

The earliest inhabitants of the Pacific Islands probably migrated thousands of years ago, when there was a land bridge from Southeast Asia. Successive waves of migration from west to east followed, reaching the easternmost islands by about 1,000 years ago.

The peoples of the Pacific are often divided into three major groups: the Melanesians, in the southwest Pacific; the Micronesians, in the northwest; and the Polynesians, in the central and southeast Pacific. However, only the Polynesians form a distinct ethnic group. Polynesian navigators from the Society Islands sailed north to reach Hawaii, and south to New Zealand, the largest of the islands in the Pacific. The settlers of New Zealand became known as the Maoris.

European exploration

The first European known to have seen the Pacific was the Spanish explorer Vasco Núñez de Balboa. After crossing the Isthmus of Panama in 1513, he sighted the great ocean, which he called the South Sea. In the 1520s, the Portuguese navigator Ferdinand Magellan crossed the

SEE ALSO: Australia and New Zealand;
Balboa, Vasco Núñez de; Corals and Coral
Reefs; El Niño; Exploration and Explorers;
Hurricanes and Typhoons; Oceans and Seas;
Pacific Islands; Pacific Rim; Volcanoes;
World War II

✳ PACIFIC RIM

The Pacific Rim is a term for all land on the coast of the Pacific Ocean. It includes the east coast of Asia and Australia and the west coast of the Americas.

Until World War I (1914–18), the most important trade routes were between Europe and its overseas colonies. During the 1900s, the United States played an increasingly important role in international economics and politics. Its west coast faced the Pacific with its trade routes. In the 1950s, Japan's economy began to recover from World War II (1939–45). In the 1970s, the Chinese government began to adopt a more competitive (capitalist) economy, and the economies of other East Asian nations also grew. These countries, such as Taiwan and Singapore, became known as "tiger economies" because of their power and energy.

An Asian man sells seafood in the Chinatown district of Vancouver, British Columbia, Canada.

Economy

The first big boost to the Asian nations of the Pacific Rim came in the 1960s when Japan, Taiwan, South Korea, and Hong Kong began to export cheap consumer goods, including radios and televisions. From the 1970s, computer companies flourished on the west coast of the United States. By the 1980s, some of the world's most successful companies were based

around the Pacific Rim. Japan ranks among the top world industrial powers.

Culture

Increased business links also brought a new cultural closeness among the peoples of the Pacific Rim. Immigrants from East Asia moved to cities such as Vancouver, British Columbia. Many businesspeople from North America and Australia relocated to Japan and Hong Kong. One of the most obvious signs of cultural exchange was the development of "fusion cuisine"—restaurant dishes that combined ingredients and styles from Asian areas with European food traditions.

East Asia suffered economic problems in the 1990s, which had a bad effect on the whole of the Pacific Rim. Political problems, such as tension between Taiwan and China, make the future uncertain. However, the growth of the area into a key trading zone in only a few years has been remarkable.

> **DID YOU KNOW?**
>
> The key Pacific Rim areas are: Australia; British Columbia, Canada; California, U.S.; Chile; China, including Hong Kong and Macao; Hawaii, U.S.; Indonesia; Japan; Malaysia; Mexico; New Zealand; Papua New Guinea; Peru; Philippines; Singapore; South Korea; Taiwan; Thailand; Vietnam; Washington, U.S.

SEE ALSO:
Asia;
Australia and New Zealand;
Canada;
Chile; China;
Economics;
Indonesia;
Japan; Korea;
Malaysia;
Mexico;
North America, Geography;
Pacific Ocean; Peru;
Philippines;
Southeast Asia; Trade;
United States Geography

✳ PAINE, THOMAS (1737–1809)

Thomas Paine was an 18th-century political writer and revolutionary. He was both admired and hated for his radical ideas.

▲
Paine was a skilled writer, but his beliefs turned many people against him.

Thomas Paine was born into a poor family in England. He left home at 19 and spent 17 years doing different jobs in various towns. In London he met the American statesman Benjamin Franklin. Franklin was impressed by Paine's beliefs and gave him letters of introduction to Americans.

Paine emigrated to America in 1774. In 1776 he published *Common Sense*, a pamphlet that argued powerfully for American independence from England. It was widely read. During the American Revolution, Paine fought with George Washington's army.

Paine supported the French Revolution of 1789. After publishing *The Rights of Man* in England in 1791, he was forced to flee to France. He fell out with France's new leaders and was jailed for 10 months. The first part of Paine's *Age of Reason* was published in 1794. It was unpopular because it rejected organized religion. Paine spent his final years in poverty in America.

American Revolution; Declaration of Independence; Franklin, Benjamin

✳ PALESTINE

Palestine is a region of southwestern Asia at the eastern end of the Mediterranean Sea. Christians, Jews, and Muslims all consider the area to be holy.

Palestine's flag

Palestine takes its name from that of the Philistines, one of many ancient peoples who lived in the area. In about 2000 B.C., the Hebrews, who followed the Jewish religion, settled in Palestine. They controlled the area until the eighth century B.C., when the Assyrians and then the Babylonians forced them into exile. In the following centuries, Palestine fell under the control of the Persians and then of Alexander the Great. In 167 B.C., Judah Maccabaeus led a revolt that reestablished a Jewish kingdom that lasted until 63 B.C.

For the next 700 years, Palestine was part of the Roman and then the Byzantine empires. During this time, Jesus Christ began his ministry in Palestine and was crucified by the Romans. Shortly after

A.D. 630, the Arabs, who followed the new faith of Islam, conquered the area. Muslims (followers of Islam) believe that their prophet Muhammad went to heaven from Jerusalem, Palestine's main city. The region also contains many places that are described in the Bible, such as Bethlehem.

Zionism and the Palestinian Arabs
From the 1500s, the Turkish Ottoman Empire ruled Palestine. At the end of World War I (1914–18), the area became a British protectorate. Zionism became popular with European Jews. Zionists wanted Palestine to be a homeland for the Jewish people. After World War II (1939–45), many Jewish survivors of persecution in Europe wanted to move to Palestine. Muslim Arabs who lived there

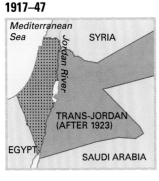

1917–47

Mediterranean Sea · Jordan River · SYRIA · TRANS-JORDAN (AFTER 1923) · EGYPT · SAUDI ARABIA

1948

SYRIA · GAZA STRIP · JORDAN · EGYPT · SAUDI ARABIA

1967–82

GOLAN HEIGHTS · SYRIA · GAZA STRIP · WEST BANK · JORDAN · SINAI · EGYPT · SAUDI ARABIA

Today

GOLAN HEIGHTS · SYRIA · GAZA STRIP · WEST BANK · JORDAN · EGYPT · SAUDI ARABIA

- ▪ British mandate
- ⣿ Palestine (after 1923)

- ⣿ Occupied by Egypt
- ⣿ Occupied by Jordan
- ▪ Israel

- ▪ Israel
- ⣿ Occupied by Israel after Six-Day War, 1967

- ▪ Israel
- ▫ Occupied territories

did not want the area to become a Jewish state. In 1948 the State of Israel declared independence. It was attacked by its Arab neighbors but defeated them. Thousands of Arabs left their homes.

After another Arab–Israeli war in 1967, Israel occupied more Palestinian land. In 1996 Palestinians living in two of the occupied areas—the Gaza Strip and the West Bank—elected their own National Authority. Some Palestinian groups continue to use terrorist tactics to try to force Israel to let them govern themselves.

In 1917 the area controlled by Britain and known as Palestine extended from the Mediterranean Sea to east of the Jordan River. In 1923 the British divided the area. In 1948 the State of Israel was established. After the 1967 war, Israel occupied the Gaza Strip, the West Bank, Sinai, and the Golan Heights. Sinai was returned to Egypt in 1982, but Syria's Golan Heights remain under Israeli control.

SEE ALSO: Alexander the Great; Byzantine Empire; Christianity; Egypt; Holocaust; Islam; Israel; Judaism; Middle East; Roman Empire

✻ PANAMA

Panama is a small nation in Central America. A canal linking its Pacific and Atlantic coasts makes the country important to world trade.

Land and climate
Panama lies on the Isthmus of Panama, the thinnest part of Central America, which is about 32 miles (51 km) wide at its narrowest part. A long mountain range divides the country into Caribbean and Pacific sides. Jungles and rain forests cover much of the land. The rest is thinly wooded grassland called savanna.

The climate is tropical, and rainfall is heavy, especially on the Caribbean coast.

People and economy
Most Panamanians are mixed-race descendants of early Spanish settlers and American Indians. Immigrants from the Caribbean, the United States, and Africa added to the rich cultural mix.

Farming, fishing, and logging employ many workers, but the Panama Canal and its related businesses are the top money earners. The major industries are oil refining and the processing of petroleum products.

Panama's national flag

✱ PASTEUR, LOUIS (1822–95)

French scientist Louis Pasteur's discoveries about the causes of disease have improved food hygiene and saved countless lives worldwide.

▲
Pasteur's work has saved many lives.

Louis Pasteur was born in Dôle, Jura, eastern France. He became a professor of chemistry at the universities of Strasbourg and, later, Lille. He used his knowledge to help France's wine makers keep their wine from spoiling. He discovered that there were tiny living things— microorganisms—floating in the air. They could cause chemical changes that spoiled the wine. Pasteur showed that many of the microorganisms could be killed by heating wine and then cooling it.

This process is now called pasteurization. Pasteur also showed that milk would last longer after it had been pasteurized.

Pasteur proved that diseases are caused by harmful microorganisms called germs. When he injected a dose of weakened anthrax germs into animals, the animals became protected against the disease. He used this method, called vaccination, to protect people from the rabies virus.

SEE ALSO: Chemistry; Diseases; Human Body; Medicine; Scientists

✱ PEARY, ROBERT E. (1856–1920)

The American Robert Peary was credited with leading the first successful expedition to the North Pole in 1909. He became a national hero.

▲
Peary aboard a ship on its way to the North Pole.

Robert Edwin Peary was born in Cresson, Pennsylvania, and raised in Maine. In 1881 he became an engineer for the United States Navy in Washington, D.C.

Peary made his first Arctic expedition in 1886. After two failed attempts to reach the North Pole, in 1893–94 and 1905–06, he set out again in 1908. With only his African-American aide, Matthew Henson, and four Inuit guides, Peary finally reached the pole on April 6, 1909.

It took five months for the team to return and break their news to the world. However, days before Peary cabled his message, explorer Frederick A. Cook

announced that he had reached the pole in April 1908. Cook's claim was generally dismissed, but for decades it cast a shadow over Peary's counterclaim. Nevertheless, Peary returned home to great praise. He was buried with military honors in Arlington, Virginia, in 1920.

In 1989 the National Geographic Society concluded that Peary actually came within 5 miles (8 km) of the North Pole.

SEE ALSO: Arctic; Exploration and Explorers

1917–47

1948

1967–82

Today

| | British mandate |
| | Palestine (after 1923) |

	Occupied by Egypt
	Occupied by Jordan
	Israel

| | Israel |
| | Occupied by Israel after Six-Day War, 1967 |

| | Israel |
| | Occupied territories |

did not want the area to become a Jewish state. In 1948 the State of Israel declared independence. It was attacked by its Arab neighbors but defeated them. Thousands of Arabs left their homes.

After another Arab–Israeli war in 1967, Israel occupied more Palestinian land. In 1996 Palestinians living in two of the occupied areas—the Gaza Strip and the West Bank—elected their own National Authority. Some Palestinian groups continue to use terrorist tactics to try to force Israel to let them govern themselves.

In 1917 the area controlled by Britain and known as Palestine extended from the Mediterranean Sea to east of the Jordan River. In 1923 the British divided the area. In 1948 the State of Israel was established. After the 1967 war, Israel occupied the Gaza Strip, the West Bank, Sinai, and the Golan Heights. Sinai was returned to Egypt in 1982, but Syria's Golan Heights remain under Israeli control.

SEE ALSO: Alexander the Great; Byzantine Empire; Christianity; Egypt; Holocaust; Islam; Israel; Judaism; Middle East; Roman Empire

✳ PANAMA

Panama is a small nation in Central America. A canal linking its Pacific and Atlantic coasts makes the country important to world trade.

Land and climate
Panama lies on the Isthmus of Panama, the thinnest part of Central America, which is about 32 miles (51 km) wide at its narrowest part. A long mountain range divides the country into Caribbean and Pacific sides. Jungles and rain forests cover much of the land. The rest is thinly wooded grassland called savanna.

The climate is tropical, and rainfall is heavy, especially on the Caribbean coast.

People and economy
Most Panamanians are mixed-race descendants of early Spanish settlers and American Indians. Immigrants from the Caribbean, the United States, and Africa added to the rich cultural mix.

Farming, fishing, and logging employ many workers, but the Panama Canal and its related businesses are the top money earners. The major industries are oil refining and the processing of petroleum products.

Panama's national flag

COSTA RICA

Caribbean Sea

Panama Canal

Colón ●

Mosquito Gulf

Tabásará Mountains

Panama City

PACIFIC OCEAN

Azuero Peninsula

Gulf of Panama

Darién National Park

COLOMBIA

KEY FACTS

OFFICIAL NAME:
República de Panamá

AREA:
29,761 sq. mi.
(77,081 sq. km)

POPULATION:
2,856,000

CAPITAL & LARGEST CITY:
Panama City

MAJOR RELIGION:
Roman Catholicism

MAJOR LANGUAGES:
Spanish (official), English

CURRENCIES:
Balboa, U.S. dollar

History
Spanish explorers arrived in Panama in 1501 and soon overpowered the Native American Indians. In the 1800s, South American countries fought to end Spanish rule. Panama, at first loyal to Spain, later took sides with Colombia, which won independence in 1821.

In 1903 the United States helped Panama become independent from Colombia. In return, the Americans were allowed to build the Panama Canal across the country. The canal, which opened in 1914, reduced the long journey between the Pacific and Atlantic oceans by 7,000 miles (11,200 km). About 12,000 ships make the 8-hour, 51-mile (82-km) crossing every year. In 1999 the ownership of the canal passed from the United States to Panama.

SEE ALSO: Central America; Canals; Wonders of the World

✳ PARAGUAY
Paraguay is a landlocked country in the heart of South America, bordered by Brazil, Argentina, and Bolivia. It is slightly smaller than California.

Paraguay's national flag

Land and climate
The Paraguay River divides the country into two parts and provides a water route to the Atlantic Ocean. Eastern Paraguay, known as the Región Oriental, is fertile. The western two-thirds of the country are known as the Gran Chaco. During the dry season, this plain is a parched wasteland.

Paraguay has a subtropical climate, with humid conditions in the east and dry, tropical savanna conditions in the west. It rains all year everywhere other than in

parts of the Gran Chaco. The rainy season is the hottest time of year.

People and economy
Paraguay has a smaller population than most other South American countries. Nearly all the people live in the eastern area of the country. Most Paraguayans are of mixed Guaraní (indigenous Indian) and Spanish ancestry. Traditionally the economy of Paraguay was based on agriculture and forestry. Since the

Guacurús and Payaguás lived in the Gran Chaco; the Guaraní lived in the east. Jesuit missionaries came to Paraguay in 1587, but they were driven out in 1767. Paraguay declared independence from Spain in 1811 and was ruled by dictators.

In a war against Brazil, Argentina, and Uruguay from 1865 to 1870, Paraguay lost more than half its population and a quarter of its land. Another war (1932–35) against Bolivia won Paraguay the Gran Chaco but cost more than 90,000 lives.

In 1954 General Alfredo Stroessner took control of the government in a military coup. His dictatorship brought political stability and some economic growth but at the cost of individual rights. In 1989 he was removed from power in a coup. In 1993 Paraguay held its first free elections.

completion of two huge dams along the Paraná River in the 1970s, Paraguay has been one of the world's largest producers of hydroelectricity.

History
At the time of the Spanish conquest in the early 1500s, Paraguay was inhabited by three main Indian groups. The

SEE ALSO: South America

KEY FACTS

OFFICIAL NAME:
República del Paraguay

AREA:
153,398 sq. mi. (397,300 sq. km)

POPULATION:
5,496,000

CAPITAL & LARGEST CITY:
Asunción

MAJOR RELIGION:
Roman Catholicism

MAJOR LANGUAGES:
Spanish, Guaraní (both official)

CURRENCY:
Guaraní

✳ PARKS, ROSA (1913–)

On December 1, 1955, in Montgomery, Alabama, Rosa Louise (McCauley) Parks made history by refusing to give up her seat on a bus to a white man.

Rosa Parks helped to launch the modern civil rights movement.
▼

At the time Rosa Parks made her historic gesture, buses in Montgomery were segregated—black people had to sit at the back and were expected to give up their seats to white people. Parks was arrested, sparking a boycott of (refusal to use) the city's transportation system.

The boycott, led by Martin Luther King Jr., was widely reported and encouraged African Americans to press for equal rights in other fields. In November 1956 the Supreme Court ruled that segregation on the buses of Montgomery was illegal.

As a result of Parks's courageous act, she and her husband Raymond lost their jobs and had to move to Detroit, where they had some difficult years. Parks continued to campaign for civil rights. In 1996 she was awarded the Presidential Medal of Freedom, and in 1999 she received the Congressional Gold Medal.

SEE ALSO: African Americans; Civil Rights; King, Martin Luther, Jr.; Supreme Court

✳ PASTEUR, LOUIS (1822–95)

French scientist Louis Pasteur's discoveries about the causes of disease have improved food hygiene and saved countless lives worldwide.

▲
Pasteur's work has saved many lives.

Louis Pasteur was born in Dôle, Jura, eastern France. He became a professor of chemistry at the universities of Strasbourg and, later, Lille. He used his knowledge to help France's wine makers keep their wine from spoiling. He discovered that there were tiny living things— microorganisms—floating in the air. They could cause chemical changes that spoiled the wine. Pasteur showed that many of the microorganisms could be killed by heating wine and then cooling it.

This process is now called pasteurization. Pasteur also showed that milk would last longer after it had been pasteurized.

Pasteur proved that diseases are caused by harmful microorganisms called germs. When he injected a dose of weakened anthrax germs into animals, the animals became protected against the disease. He used this method, called vaccination, to protect people from the rabies virus.

SEE ALSO: Chemistry; Diseases; Human Body; Medicine; Scientists

✳ PEARY, ROBERT E. (1856–1920)

The American Robert Peary was credited with leading the first successful expedition to the North Pole in 1909. He became a national hero.

▲
Peary aboard a ship on its way to the North Pole.

Robert Edwin Peary was born in Cresson, Pennsylvania, and raised in Maine. In 1881 he became an engineer for the United States Navy in Washington, D.C.

Peary made his first Arctic expedition in 1886. After two failed attempts to reach the North Pole, in 1893–94 and 1905–06, he set out again in 1908. With only his African-American aide, Matthew Henson, and four Inuit guides, Peary finally reached the pole on April 6, 1909.

It took five months for the team to return and break their news to the world. However, days before Peary cabled his message, explorer Frederick A. Cook

announced that he had reached the pole in April 1908. Cook's claim was generally dismissed, but for decades it cast a shadow over Peary's counterclaim. Nevertheless, Peary returned home to great praise. He was buried with military honors in Arlington, Virginia, in 1920.

In 1989 the National Geographic Society concluded that Peary actually came within 5 miles (8 km) of the North Pole.

SEE ALSO: Arctic; Exploration and Explorers

✴ PEI, I. M. (1917–)

The Chinese-American architect I. M. Pei has designed some of the most imaginative public buildings in recent years.

Ieoh Ming Pei was born in Guangzhou (Canton), China. He moved to the United States in 1935 to study architecture and became a U.S. citizen in 1954. He opened his own architectural firm in New York City in 1955. He first gained widespread notice that same year for his design for the Mile High Center in Denver, Colorado.

Pei's buildings are distinctive for their bold geometric shapes. He is also noted for designs that fit unusual or difficult sites. The East Wing of the National Gallery of Art in Washington, D.C. (1978), for example, is made of two connecting triangles. Other Pei buildings in the United States include the John Hancock Tower in Boston, Massachusetts (1973), and the Jacob K. Javits Convention Center in New York City (1986).

One of Pei's most famous designs is a glass and steel pyramid, 65 ft. (20 m) tall, that forms the entrance to the Louvre Museum in Paris, France. His 70-story Bank of China building in Hong Kong opened in 1989.

I. M. Pei during the building of the glass pyramid at the Louvre Museum, Paris. His designs have won many awards.

SEE ALSO: Architecture

✴PERCUSSION 👀 ✴MUSICAL INSTRUMENTS

✴ PERSIAN GULF WAR

The Persian Gulf War was a conflict that took place from January to March 1991. It was fought between Iraq and a large coalition of nations.

The anti-Iraqi forces were led by the United States, which provided the largest number of troops, aircraft, ships, and arms; the coalition also included the United Kingdom, France, and Italy. The cause of the war was the invasion and occupation of Kuwait by Iraq. The conflict took its name from the location of the two countries on the northwestern shore of the Persian Gulf.

Background

The discovery of oil in the 1930s had transformed Kuwait into one of the world's richest countries. In the spring of 1990, Saddam Hussein, Iraq's leader, began voicing grievances against Kuwait. These were mostly connected with the price and overproduction of oil, which Iraq saw as a danger to its own oil-based economy. On August 2, 1990, the day after walking out of negotiations, Iraq invaded and quickly overran Kuwait.

International reaction against Iraq's aggression was strong and included most Arab nations. The United Nations (UN) Security Council passed resolutions that condemned Iraq's action, imposed economic sanctions, and finally authorized

A U.S. soldier in action in Kuwait during Operation Desert Storm.

the use of force. When the UN deadline for Iraq's withdrawal from Kuwait passed on January 15, 1991, without action, the war—code-named Operation Desert Storm—began.

Course of the war

The Allied forces were commanded by U.S. General H. Norman Schwarzkopf. The first phase of the war consisted entirely of air bombardment of Iraqi military facilities. Iraqi forces made no move to withdraw. The second phase was a large-scale ground offensive. It resulted in the complete liberation of Kuwait, and the war was formally ended on March 2, 1991.

SEE ALSO: Iraq; Middle East; United Nations

✳ PERU

Peru is the third-largest country in South America after Brazil and Argentina. It lies on the west coast of the continent and is bounded by the Pacific Ocean.

Peru's national flag

Land and climate

Much of Peru lies in the Andes Mountains. Because of the great variations in height between the tallest peaks and the Pacific shore, Peru has many different climate zones. Most of the cities and farms are in coastal valleys, where the weather is hot and dry in the north and cool and humid farther south. The densely forested interior plains form part of the Amazon Basin.

People and economy

Most Peruvians are descendants of either the Incas and other Indian people, or are mestizos, people of mixed Indian and Spanish ancestry. About 10 to 15 percent of the people are of pure Spanish origin. The remainder of the population includes the descendants of black African slaves and immigrants from China, Japan, Italy, Germany, and Britain.

Traditionally a few wealthy families owned most of the land. They grew cotton, rice, and sugarcane on plantations along the coast and crops for export in the highlands. The rest of the people were very poor. After 150 years of conflict, the government passed a land reform act in 1969 that broke up the haciendas (estates) and turned many of them into cooperatives. Mining, fishing, and textile manufacture are important industries.

KEY FACTS

OFFICIAL NAME:
República del Perú

AREA:
496,222 sq. mi.
(1,285,215 sq. km)

POPULATION:
25,662,000

**CAPITAL &
LARGEST CITY:**
Lima

**MAJOR
RELIGION:**
Roman Catholicism

**MAJOR
LANGUAGES:**
Spanish, Quechua
(both official)

CURRENCY:
Nuevo sol

History

Peru was the center of the vast Inca Empire until the 1500s, when it was conquered by the Spanish, who ruled for 300 years. War with Chile (1879–83) left the country bankrupt.

The political situation in Peru has been unstable since the mid-20th century. There has been civilian rule since 1980, but terrorism and corruption have both caused problems. Peru and Ecuador settled a longstanding border dispute in 1998.

SEE ALSO: Chile; Conquistadors; Ecuador; Incas; South America

✴ PHILIPPINES

The Philippines is an island nation lying off the southeastern coast of Asia. It is in the Pacific Ocean, northeast of Borneo and south of Taiwan (Formosa).

Land and climate

The Philippines is made up of more than 7,000 islands that form a chain, or archipelago, stretching 1,100 miles (1,800 km). The three main groups are Luzon and Mindoro, the central group, and Mindanao and the Sulu Archipelago.

Temperatures average between 75 and 85°F (24–29°C). There are about 80 in. (2,030 mm) of rain a year. Typhoons occur between July and November. The area is also prone to earthquakes.

People

Most Filipinos (people of the Philippines) are of Malay ancestry and are related to the people of Malaysia and Indonesia. Many Filipinos also have some Spanish, American, or Chinese ancestry.

Most people live on the 11 largest islands. The biggest island is Luzon, where about half the population live. The majority of Filipinos live in rural areas, although large numbers have moved to the cities in recent times.

**Philippines'
national flag**

461

Economy

The Philippines is still mainly an agricultural nation. About 40 percent of the labor force works in agriculture or related industries. Rice is the most important food crop. Corn is also important. Copra (dried coconut meat), sugarcane, and abaca (a fiber used to make ropes) are the chief cash crops.

Recently, by taking advantage of cheap labor, the economy has expanded rapidly. Major industries include textiles, food processing, chemicals, machinery, and electronic products. The Philippines is a major exporter of skilled labor to the United States, the Middle East, and Europe. Money sent home from Filipinos working abroad is an important source of foreign currency.

In the Philippines, rice has been grown on terraces such as these since before the birth of Christ.
▼

History

The first people to live in the Philippines probably migrated there from Southeast Asia about 50,000 years ago. In 1521 the explorer Ferdinand Magellan claimed the islands for Spain. They were later named for King Philip II.

The Philippines remained a Spanish colony for more than 300 years until the Spanish–American War of 1898. It then came under the control of the United States. Japan occupied the islands during World War II (1939–45). The people of the Philippines finally gained complete independence in 1946.

President Ferdinand Marcos held power from 1965 to 1986. During his first term, more roads and schools were built and rice production increased. After Marcos's

reelection, however, the country suffered civil unrest and economic problems. Amid mounting charges of corruption, Marcos lost the presidential election in 1986 and was forced into exile in Hawaii.

Corazon Aquino became president in 1987. She was the widow of Benigno Aquino, who had been Marcos's chief opponent and was killed in 1983. Many people held Marcos responsible for his death.

SEE ALSO: Asia; Earthquakes; Hurricanes and Typhoons; Southeast Asia; Spanish–American War

✳ PHILOSOPHERS

Philosophers study truth, wisdom, and the nature of knowledge—why we think what we think, and how we know what we think we know.

The English word *philosophy* comes from the ancient Greek meaning "lover of wisdom." A philosopher is someone who is devoted to the pursuit of knowledge for its own sake rather than its practical use.

Today philosophy has both a popular and a technical meaning. In the popular sense, it is any set of beliefs about human beings, nature, society, and God. Everyone who has wondered about the meaning of life and found an answer that is satisfying has a philosophy. In its technical sense, philosophy means a highly disciplined and rational method of criticizing beliefs to make them clearer and more reliable.

The earliest philosophers were ancient Greeks in the sixth century B.C. who studied the underlying causes of natural phenomena such as birth and death.

Analytical method
Another Greek, Socrates, was more concerned with human society. His motto was "Know thyself." He was the first to use the analytical method of reasoning, which tries to define central ideas such as virtue, justice, and knowledge. It also explores the reasons for beliefs that most people accept

▶ *Plato (left) and Aristotle as imagined by the Italian artist Raphael (1483–1520) in his painting* **The School of Athens**.

463

FAMOUS PHILOSOPHERS

The following are just a few of the world's most influential philosophers. There are many others.

Lao-tzu (sixth century B.C.)
Chinese philosopher who founded Taoism, which had a great influence on the Buddhist religion.

Confucius (K'ung Ch'iu) (551–479 B.C.)
Chinese philosopher who placed great emphasis on society and values.

Socrates (about 470–399 B.C.)
Ancient Greek who believed that understanding ignorance led to wisdom, and that question-and-answer study led to knowledge.

Plato (about 427–347 B.C.)
Ancient Greek who believed that certain ideas could be understood by the use of reason.

Aristotle (384–322 B.C.)
Ancient Greek philosopher. Western culture is based on his broad understanding of the world of humans, nature, and science.

Hobbes, Thomas (1588–1679)
Englishman who claimed that humans are naturally violent and need to be kept under control.

Descartes, René (1596–1650)
Frenchman who believed in two separate worlds—mind and body. He distrusted knowledge and, like Plato, attached great importance to Rationalism—the use of reason.

Locke, John (1632–1704)
Englishman who disputed Hobbes's ideas, believing instead that humankind's natural state is happiness. Supported Empiricism (understanding through experience), not Rationalism.

Kant, Immanuel (1724–1804)
German who separated the world of objects as we see them from the world of objects as they really are. He encouraged people to act as if their behavior were ruled by universal laws.

Hegel, Georg Wilhelm Friedrich (1770–1831)
German who claimed that we can understand our continually developing and changing reality only if we see it as one big idea.

Russell, Bertrand (Arthur William) (1872–1970)
Englishman who attacked what he saw as wrong in society and contributed to the understanding of math.

without question, such as the idea that pleasure, wealth, and power are the best things in life.

Synthetic method

Socrates' pupil Plato founded a school called the Academy. Its most gifted student was Aristotle. He organized every field of human knowledge into a unified view of nature and humankind. This is called synthetic philosophy.

Synthetic philosophy has become more difficult to carry out as human knowledge has increased. Today's philosophers set themselves more limited goals. They connect psychology with biology in explaining the relation between the mind and the body. They relate science to religion in order to try and explain how the world began and how life grew out of inanimate (nonliving) matter.

Lao-tzu was the founder of Taoism, a philosophy that advocates a simple life and advises against interference in the course of natural events.
▼

Philosophy is now divided into smaller areas according to the type of problems investigated. Ethics is the study of the standards for judging whether things are "good" or "bad." It investigates the meaning of terms such as *justice*, *virtue*, *morality*, and *responsibility*. Epistemology tries to define truth, logic, and perception. It investigates the ways in which knowledge is acquired. Metaphysics deals with the nature of reality: What is real, and what only seems to be real? Aesthetics tries to define art and beauty.

In addition to these wide areas of study, each field of scholarship has to define its own subject matter and methods of procedure. That is why people talk about, for example, the philosophy of physics, the philosophy of religion, and the philosophy of history.

SEE ALSO: Greece, Ancient; Psychology; Religions

✳ PHOTOGRAPHY

A photograph is a picture made through the action of light. The English word *photography* comes from the Greek words meaning "light" and "writing."

To take a photograph, you need light and a camera. Traditional cameras use film. The film is made of transparent (see-through) plastic coated with a chemical that changes when light shines on it. When you take a picture, light rays reflected from your subject enter the camera and create a hidden image on the film. When the film is treated with chemicals, the image is made visible, and a print can be made from it.

Modern digital cameras do not use film. They have sensors that convert the light into electrical charges so that the image can be stored on a computer.

All cameras are made up of four basic parts—body, lens, shutter, and viewfinder. The body of a camera is a box that keeps out all light except the light that passes through the lens. The lens is a piece of glass or plastic with curved surfaces. The lens concentrates the light rays as they enter the camera to make a sharp image of the photographed object on the film.

It is important that you focus on a subject before shooting the picture. Otherwise, the picture may be blurry. When a picture is in focus, it is sharp and clear. Some cameras have a fixed-focus lens, but others have a lens that you can focus on subjects at almost any distance. With a telephoto lens, you can photograph a distant scene or even the moon. With a close-up lens, you can photograph a flower or an insect.

The shutter is a mechanical device behind the lens. It opens and closes to let the light into the camera. By releasing a button on the outside of the camera, the photographer opens the shutter. A simple camera has only one shutter speed, but in many cameras you can change the speed at which the shutter opens and closes.

This early camera was manufactured in England in the 1890s.

➡

FAMOUS PHOTOGRAPHERS

These are some of the people who have captured the qualities of the natural world or human life in photographs.

Cameron, Julia Margaret (1815–79)
British woman who took portraits of famous people.

Atget, Eugène (1856–1927)
Frenchman who photographed the buildings and people of Paris.

Emerson, Peter Henry (1856–1936)
Englishman who was one of the first to turn photography into an art form.

Stieglitz, Alfred (1864–1946)
American who pioneered artistic photography. He married artist Georgia O'Keeffe.

Salomon, Erich (1886–1944)
German photojournalist (a journalist telling news stories through photographs) and portraitist.

Ray, Man (Emmanuel Radnitzky) (1890–1976)
American photographer, filmmaker, and artist.

Lange, Dorothea (1895–1965)
American who photographed the suffering caused by the Great Depression.

Brassaï (Gyula Halász) (1899–1984)
Hungarian-born Frenchman who photographed Paris by night.

Adams, Ansel (Easton) (1902–84)
American who was famous for photographing landscapes.

Edgerton, Harold E. (1903–90)
American who pioneered high-speed photography.

Siskind, Aaron (1903–91)
Influential American teacher known for his abstract photographs.

Karsh, Yousuf (1908–2002)
Canadian who was born in Armenia, Turkey. He took portraits of famous people such as artists and musicians.

Cartier-Bresson, Henri (1908–)
French pioneer of documentary photojournalism. He helped found the Magnum Photos agency in 1947.

Capa, Robert (Andrei Friedmann) (1913–54)
Hungarian-born American war photographer who also helped found Magnum.

Arnold, Eve (1913–)
American photojournalist who was the first female photographer to work for Magnum.

DeCarava, Roy (1919–)
American celebrated for his portraits of black Americans. He works primarily in New York City.

Ansel Adams photographing the Pacific coast at Big Sur, California.

If the shutter opens and closes quickly, little light enters the camera. If the shutter is set to stay open longer, more light enters. In bright sunlight, the photographer can set the shutter at a fast speed since there is plenty of light to make an image on the film. A fast shutter speed lets you take pictures of moving subjects without blurring. On gloomy days or in dim light, the shutter can be set at a slower speed. That allows more light to enter the camera.

The viewfinder shows you the scene that the lens will focus on the film. Some viewfinders are glass windows, and some make use of lenses. Others are reflecting prisms that show the actual image coming through the lens.

History

The early ancestor of today's camera was the camera obscura (Latin for "dark chamber"), a dark room with a tiny hole in one wall. Light came through the hole and produced an image on the opposite wall of whatever was outside.

For about 500 years, the camera obscura was used mostly for watching eclipses of the sun. Artists and mapmakers gradually invented smaller, more handy versions of the device, but people had not learned how to capture the images produced.

In 1727 Johann Schulze, a German doctor, discovered that a chemical, silver nitrate, turned black when he shined light on it. This discovery led to photographic film. In 1839 Louis Daguerre developed the first permanent photographic process. In the 1880s, George Eastman invented the first handheld camera and the roll of film that went in it. He founded the Eastman Kodak Company in Rochester, New York. The company also processed the film, so anyone could take photographs.

In 1924 the Leica camera was introduced in Germany. It used a filmstrip 35 mm wide. Much smaller than other cameras, it gave photographers new flexibility.

Digital camera technology dates from the 1960s, when NASA spacecraft sent digital images home from space. The first popular digital, or filmless, cameras were made in the 1970s and 1980s.

SEE ALSO: Astronomy; Inventors and Inventions; Light; O'Keeffe, Georgia

✷ PHOTOSYNTHESIS

Photosynthesis is the process by which green plants use the sun's energy to turn water and carbon dioxide into food. In doing so, they give off oxygen.

The word *photosynthesis* comes from two Greek words meaning "putting together with light." If plants are kept in the dark, photosynthesis stops. Photosynthesis occurs only in the plant kingdom. Animals cannot use the sun's energy directly to make their own food. Instead they eat plants or other animals that eat plants. This means that nearly all life depends on the sun.

How photosynthesis works

Plants can make use of the sun's energy if their leaves possess a green chemical substance called chlorophyll. The word *chlorophyll* comes from Greek words meaning "green leaf." Plant leaves and often plant stems are green because of their chlorophyll content. When chlorophyll absorbs sunlight, it gains energy through a series of chemical reactions. That energy is used to split apart water molecules in the plant. Water is absorbed by the plant from the soil.

Water molecules consist of atoms of hydrogen and oxygen bound tightly together. When they are split apart, some of the hydrogen and oxygen atoms recombine into water. The leftover hydrogen atoms combine with carbon dioxide molecules, which have been absorbed from the air through the leaves, to form glucose. Glucose is an important sugar present in all living things. The molecules of glucose combine to form

HOW PHOTOSYNTHESIS WORKS

Most plants make their own food by photosynthesis, a process in which energy from sunlight is captured by chlorophyll in their leaves and stems. The plant uses the energy to take carbon dioxide from the air and nutrients and water from the soil. It turns them into sugars that are used for growth. It also releases oxygen back into the air.

▶

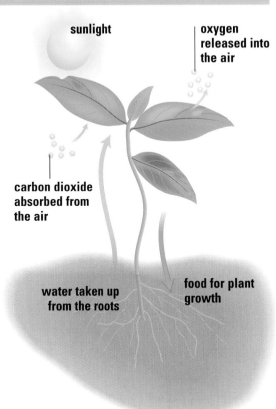

sunlight

oxygen released into the air

carbon dioxide absorbed from the air

water taken up from the roots

food for plant growth

large molecules of starch (which is used to make new plant cells) or even larger molecules of cellulose (which trees use to make wood). In addition, glucose combines with minerals that the plant has absorbed from the soil to form complicated molecules of protein. The remaining oxygen atoms, meanwhile, are expelled through the leaves into the atmosphere.

By taking in carbon dioxide and expelling oxygen, plants do the opposite of animals, which breathe in oxygen and expel carbon dioxide. In this way, plants and animals are in balance, each recycling the other's waste product. There is enough oxygen in the natural world for animal life and enough carbon dioxide for plant life.

SEE ALSO: Atoms and Molecules; Biology; Botany; Corals and Coral Reefs; Energy; Food Chains; Fungus; Plants; Trees

✳ PHYSICS

Physics is the study of matter and energy. Matter is the basic substance of which everything is made; energy is what makes matter move and change.

Physics is the science that studies the structure of matter. Physicists study all aspects of nature. They want to know what forces hold atoms together, how gases change to liquids, why metals conduct electricity, and how stars evolve. Physics can be loosely divided into two categories: classical physics and modern physics. Classical physics deals with fields of study that were well developed before the 1900s. It includes mechanics, heat, sound, light, and electromagnetism, which is the relationship between electricity and magnetism.

Mechanics

The science of mechanics looks at the effects of forces on bodies at rest or in motion. For example, Earth's gravity is a force. When you throw a ball, gravity pulls it toward the ground. On a larger scale, the sun's gravity acts on Earth, holding it in orbit. Isaac Newton described such effects in his laws of motion in 1687.

Heat

Heat is a form of energy. It can be produced from other forms of energy. You can make heat energy by rubbing your hands together. Heat can also make other forms of energy. It is turned into kinetic (movement) energy in a steam engine. The way one kind of energy changes to another is an important area of study.

Sound

Sound is caused when the atoms that make up a substance are made to vibrate, or move back and forth, very rapidly. Sound travels in waves—through air, water, or other substances—to our ears. Because sound is caused by motion, it can be explained by Newton's laws.

Light

Light is also a wave. James Clerk Maxwell, a Scottish physicist, proved that in 1865. A light wave travels in an electromagnetic field—a force in space that is both electrical and magnetic. The wave radiates (sends out) energy as light. Light is only one form of electromagnetic radiation. Other forms include radio, radar, microwaves, and X-rays.

Electromagnetism

The study of electromagnetism developed in the 1800s. Hans Christian Oersted in Denmark and Michael Faraday in England experimented with electricity and magnetic fields. Maxwell later showed that they were in fact two aspects of the same force: electromagnetism. He predicted that the force moved at the speed of light—186,000 miles (300,000 km) per second.

Modern physics

By the late 1800s, it seemed that little remained to be discovered in physics. At the start of the 1900s, however, scientists saw things that could not be explained, and so modern physics was born. In 1911 the British physicist Ernest Rutherford found that the center of every atom

contained a nucleus with a positive electrical charge. This led to the science of nuclear physics, which studies the properties of the nucleus, and to the study of smaller parts of atoms called subatomic particles. Nuclear physics has led to new ways of generating power and treating cancer, as well as nuclear weapons.

Beginning in 1905 the German scientist Albert Einstein developed the theory of relativity—a series of laws about energy, mass, space, time, and the speed of light that changed almost everything that physicists believed or understood. His discoveries led to the age of atomic bombs and nuclear power. His ideas also made it possible to explain how the planets move in time through outer space.

Quantum theory

Together with another German scientist, Max Planck, Einstein also developed quantum theory, a complicated area of study that describes how light does not always behave as a smooth wave should. Sometimes it behaves like a

▲
Accelerators, or atom smashers, increase the kinetic energy of subatomic particles. Physicists use them to study the nature and behavior of materials and to develop nuclear fusion devices.

stream of tiny, separate "grains," or particles, of matter.

Quantum physics is gradually unlocking the world's deepest secrets. It has led to new ideas about atoms, matter, and motion, and paved the way for computers and laser beams. Scientists now know that there are even smaller particles than the nucleus, and that is giving them new ideas about how stars are made.

Modern physics covers the study of everything that exists, from this book to the most distant galaxies. The universe is larger than we can imagine, yet scientists think it is still growing. Will it go on growing forever or will it shrink back into nothing? The answer to this question will come from future discoveries in physics.

SEE ALSO: Astronomy; Atoms and Molecules; Einstein, Albert; Electricity; Energy; Force and Motion; Gravity; Heat; Lasers; Light; Machines; Magnetism; Matter; Newton, Isaac; Nuclear Power; Sound

Physicist Hans Christian Oersted discovered the principle of the electromagnet.

✳PIANOS 👉see ✳MUSICAL INSTRUMENTS

✳ PICASSO, PABLO (1881–1973)

Pablo Picasso was one of the most imaginative artists of the 20th century. He is famous for developing the Cubist style of painting.

Pablo Picasso experimented with sculpture, collage, ceramics, and printmaking, as well as painting.

Pablo Ruiz y Picasso was born in Málaga, Spain. His family later moved to Barcelona. He visited Paris and settled in a studio on the Left Bank in 1904. His early work there was painted in gray-blue colors with long, thin, sad figures. This is known as Picasso's blue period.

Picasso and the French artist Georges Braque (1882–1963) visited an exhibition of Paul Cézanne (1839–1906) in 1907. Cézanne tried to paint the geometric lines that he saw in nature. Influenced by Cézanne and by their interest in the simple shapes and lines used in African art,

Picasso and Braque developed a style called Cubism. Instead of showing only the visible side of an object, they tried to paint all the sides at once using forms such as cubes and cones.

One of Picasso's most famous works was influenced by the bombing of the city of Guernica during the Spanish Civil War (1936–39). His mural *Guernica* (1937) vividly shows the brutality of war.

After World War II (1939–45), Picasso moved to the south of France, where he continued to produce work into old age.

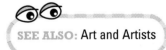

SEE ALSO: Art and Artists

PIRATES AND OUTLAWS

Pirates commit robbery or violent actions at sea.
Outlaws are also criminals, especially ones who are
running away from the law.

Pirates

For thousands of years, piracy was a common hazard of sea travel. The ancient Greeks and Romans often risked having their cargoes stolen as they sailed the Aegean and Mediterranean seas. Centuries later, Viking pirates began attacking ships in the Baltic Sea and English Channel.

Beginning in the 1300s, bands of seafaring criminals known as corsairs established settlements along the coast of North Africa. For hundreds of years, they attacked European, and later American, trading vessels. By the 1500s, it had become common for rulers of one nation to give privately owned vessels the right to carry arms and attack the ships of enemy countries. The crew of these ships were known as privateers.

After the first settlements in the New World began to flourish, piracy became popular in the Caribbean Sea and the Spanish Main (the northeastern coast of South America). Pirates there were called buccaneers, from the *boucan*, a wooden grill on which they cured their meat. They attacked not only the Spanish galleons that traveled between Spain and its colonies, but also the colonies themselves. It was not until the middle of the 1800s that the navies of the United States and several European countries rid the Mediterranean and Caribbean seas of pirates.

Outlaws

The most famous outlaw of medieval times was Robin Hood. According to legend, he and his followers lived in Sherwood Forest, England, robbing from the rich to give to the poor. It is uncertain whether Hood really existed, or whether he is simply a legendary figure who stood up for the rights of the people against unjust laws.

The outlaws of the American frontier during the 19th century were more violent, although fictional accounts have glamorized the careers of Jesse and Frank James and Butch Cassidy and the Sundance Kid (Robert LeRoy Parker and Harry Longabaugh).

When the gold rush to the West began in the mid-1800s, stagecoaches and trains carrying gold and money were targeted by outlaws, and bank robberies multiplied. After the Civil War (1861–65), stealing cattle and horses occurred frequently, as ranges grew in Texas and neighboring states. By the end of the 19th century, major crime had moved to the cities. Organized crime spread in the 1920s with the introduction of Prohibition (a ban on alcohol).

Robin Hood, the legendary English hero who was said to have robbed the rich to give to the poor, was probably a fictional character. Attempts to prove his identity, based on people who lived between the 1100s and 1400s, have failed. This woodblock of Robin Hood dates from about 1600.

SEE ALSO: Crime and Law Enforcement; Myths and Legends; Vikings; West, The American

✷ PLANETS

There are nine known planets that circle the sun. They are Mercury, Venus, Earth, Mars, Jupiter, Saturn, Uranus, Neptune, and Pluto.

The word *planet* comes from the Greek for "wandering star." The ancient Greeks noticed that there were five special points of light in the night sky. All the other points of light always kept the same positions relative to one another. These were the stars. The constellations that they formed remained the same year after year. The five points of light were different because, from week to week and month to month, they slowly moved among the stars. The Greeks named the planets for their gods: Hermes, Aphrodite, Ares, Zeus, and Chronos. Instead of using the names of the Greek gods, we call these planets by the names of the equivalent Roman gods: Mercury, Venus, Mars, Jupiter, and Saturn.

In addition to the five planets known since ancient times, three more (Uranus, Neptune, and Pluto) have been discovered since the invention of the telescope.

A planet is very different from a star. A star is a huge ball of gases that gives off light. A planet gives off no light of its own. A planet that shines in the night sky is simply reflecting the sun's light.

Planetary orbits and gravitation
Today we know that the planets "wander" in the sky because they are traveling at different speeds around the sun. They travel in paths called orbits. The German astronomer Johannes Kepler (1571–1630) discovered that the orbits of all the planets are ellipses, or flattened circles, rather than perfect circles. This means that the distance between a planet and the sun varies as the planet travels along its orbit.

Kepler also found that a planet travels fastest when it is closest to the sun and slowest when it is farthest from the sun.

Mercury is the closest planet to the sun. Pluto is often the most distant, but at certain times the shape of Pluto's orbit brings it inside the orbit of Neptune. When this happens, Neptune is farther away from the sun than Pluto.

The laws of planetary motion developed by Kepler did not explain why the planets move as they do. In the late 1600s, the English scientist Isaac Newton (1642–1727) proved that the same force—gravity—that pulls an object to Earth also holds the moon in its orbit around Earth and keeps the planets moving in their

DID YOU KNOW?

Astronomers are gathering information to prove that other planets orbit stars beyond our sun. These so-called extrasolar planets are almost impossible to see. The stars they orbit give off so much light that the glare hides the planets from view. However, astronomers have been able to see wobbles in the motion of these stars that they think are caused by the gravitational pull of huge planets. The planets found so far are not like Earth; they are similar to the gas giant Jupiter. Astronomers hope to view these planets more closely using special telescopes based in space. They may then be able to tell if other solar systems have planets that support life.

COMPARING THE PLANETS

	Discovery	Position in the solar system	Average distance from the sun	Solar orbit	Diameter	Satellites
Mercury	Ancient times	Closest planet to the sun	35,900,000 mi. (57,800,000 km)	88 Earth days	3,032 mi. (4,880 km)	None
Venus	Ancient times	Second planet from the sun	67,200,000 mi. (108,200,000 km)	224.7 Earth days	7,519 mi. (12,100 km)	None
Earth	Formed about 4.6 billion years ago	Third planet from the sun	93,000,000 mi. (150,000,000 km)	365.25 Earth days	7,923 mi. (12,751 km)	1
Mars	Ancient times	Fourth planet from the sun	142,000,000 mi. (228,000,000 km)	687 Earth days	4,200 mi. (6,760 km)	2
Jupiter	Ancient times	Fifth planet from the sun	483,000,000 mi. (778,000,000 km)	11.9 Earth years	89,000 mi. (143,000 km)	39
Saturn	Ancient times	Sixth planet from the sun	885,500,000 mi. (1,400,000,000 km)	29.5 Earth years	74,500 mi. (120,000 km)	30
Uranus	1781 by British astronomer William Herschel	Seventh planet from the sun	1,800,000,000 mi. (2,900,000,000 km)	84 Earth years	32,000 mi. (51,500 km)	21
Neptune	1840s by English and French astronomers John Couch Adams and Urbain Leverrier	Eighth planet from the sun	2,800,000,000 mi. (4,500,000,000 km)	165 Earth years	30,800 mi. (49,600 km)	8
Pluto	1930 by American astronomer Clyde Tombaugh	Ninth planet from the sun	3,700,000,000 mi. (5,900,000,000 km)	247.7 Earth years	1,400 mi. (2,250 km)	1

orbits around the sun. Without gravity, a planet in motion would travel through space forever in a straight line.

Satellites of the planets

Apart from Mercury and Venus, all the planets in the solar system have satellites, or moons that revolve around them. Our moon is one of these satellites. Some of the satellites travel at great speeds. For example, Phobos, one of Mars's satellites, orbits the planet completely in about 7½ hours. Since Phobos's orbital period is less than a day on Mars (24 hours, 37 minutes), the satellite moves from west to east in the Martian sky. Other satellites have longer orbital paths. Just like the planets orbiting the sun, the farther a satellite is from a planet, the longer it takes to circle the planet.

SEE ALSO: Astronomy; Comets, Meteors, and Asteroids; Earth; Gravity; Greece, Ancient; Jupiter; Mars; Mercury; Moon; Neptune; Newton, Isaac; Pluto; Satellites; Saturn; Solar System; Space Exploration; Stars; Telescopes; Universe; Uranus; Venus

✳ PLANTS

There are more than 500,000 plant species. They make oxygen and remove carbon dioxide from the air—without them there would be no life on Earth.

Ferns have compound, or multipart, leaves called fronds. Here they are in the process of unfurling, when they are known as fiddleheads.

A plant is a living, growing organism made of many tiny cells. It does not eat food and cannot move around by itself. It usually grows in a medium provided by soil, water, or another plant, such as the branch of a tree.

Parts of a plant

Most plants have roots, a stem, and leaves. The roots grow into the ground, absorb water and dissolved minerals from the soil, and support the plant. The stem also supports the plant and carries nutrients. The leaves usually manufacture food. Other plant parts include the flowers, fruits, and seeds, which are used in making new plants.

The cells of plants usually have tough walls made of cellulose. Most plants contain chlorophyll (green pigment) and can make their own food from sunlight during the process of photosynthesis. Sunlight and moisture are most abundant in tropical regions, and that is where the greatest number of plants are found.

Classification

People classify plants in different ways. One way is according to growth: Plants over 8 ft. (2.4 m) tall are trees; low, woody plants are shrubs; and plants with tender stems are herbs. A second classification is according to life cycles. Annuals sprout, flower, and die within a year. Biennials complete their life cycle in two years. Perennials live for over two years.

Scientists arrange the plant kingdom in order from the simplest to the most complex. The simplest plants are algae, which include seaweeds. All other plants are either vascular or nonvascular. Vascular plants have special tissues in them, called xylem and phloem, to carry water and food around the plant. Nonvascular plants, such as mosses, liverworts, and hornworts, lack these food-carrying tissues.

The most successful vascular plants are the seed plants. Seed plants are separated into gymnosperms—plants with naked seeds—and angiosperms, or flowering plants—plants with seeds enclosed in fruit. The fruit may be soft, like a strawberry, or hard, like a pecan nut. The principal gymnosperms are the conifers.

Reproduction and defense

Plants reproduce either sexually or asexually. In sexual reproduction, a male sex cell (sperm, produced by pollen) and a female sex cell (egg) join to produce a seed. This takes place within a flower. The ripe seed parts from the plant and enters the soil, where it puts out roots and a leafy shoot. From this point, growth usually continues by photosynthesis.

In asexual reproduction, there is no joining of separate sex cells. Instead a new plant forms from some part of the old plant—the root, for example, or a stem.

Plants have many enemies. They are eaten by all kinds of animals from insects to cattle. They are attacked by diseases and destroyed by frost, fire, and high winds. Plants defend themselves with weapons that include bad-tasting juices, unpleasant odors, thorns and burrs, deep roots, and thick seed coverings. Many plants, such as foxglove, contain poisons that can either make grazing animals sick or kill them.

Plants live in communities made up of other plants and animals. Often these species rely on one another. Many plants need insects, for example, to help their

Conifers are gymnosperms. The seeds lie on the scales of female cones. Male cones produce pollen.
▼

sex cells mingle and reproduce. Animals use plants for food and shelter. Plant roots also help stop rain and wind from removing topsoil.

Humans are totally dependent on plants. They use them for food and fuel, and to make clothing, paper, and medicines. About 20 species of plant supply nearly 90 percent of the world's food. The most important food crops are wheat, rice, and corn, which are specially bred grasses.

▲
The paw paw tree is an angiosperm. It produces purple flowers, and its seeds are embedded in its edible fruit.

SEE ALSO: Biomes; Botany; Evolution; Flowers; Forests; Fruit; Fungus; Grasslands; Insects; Photosynthesis; Pollination; Trees; Vegetables; Wetlands

* PLASTIC
Plastic is a moldable, lightweight material that is used to make many items, from toys and fabrics to car bodies and bullet-resistant jackets.

▲
Plastic bottles such as these will never break down naturally, or decompose, and so burying them in great holes in landfill sites damages the environment. The best way to deal with waste plastic is to recycle it so that it is used for other purposes.

Plastics are artificial, or human-made, materials that consist of polymers—long molecules made of smaller molecules joined in chains. Not all polymers are artificial—wood and cotton are types of a natural polymer called cellulose, but they are not considered plastics because they cannot be melted and molded.

Plastics have many advantages over other materials. They do not rust, like steel, or rot, like wood. They can be transparent, as in eyeglass lenses, or they can be colored by adding pigments when the plastics are melted. They can be very slippery and smooth, making them ideal for moving parts like artificial hip joints.

Compact disks (CDs) have a plastic layer that stores recorded music in patterns of tiny pits. Even though there are millions of these pits on every CD, they can be made in a single step using plastic molding.

Plastics are relatively lightweight and can be used to make products that are easy to handle and transport. Low weight is important for portable appliances, such as laptop computers, for sporting goods, like football helmets, and for automobile parts, since lighter cars use less fuel.

Plastics and the environment
Most plastics are made from petroleum products, such as oil or natural gas, but plastics can save more energy than is used in making them. That is especially true in the case of plastic insulation used in buildings and domestic appliances, such as refrigerators.

Plastics can cause problems when they are discarded. Old plastic products take up landfill space, which is an expensive form of disposal. Once buried, most plastics will not degrade, or break down. Plastic litter can be a problem for wildlife, which can get entangled in plastic fishing lines and can holders. Many products are therefore made from plastics that break down into harmless substances when exposed to sunlight or to microorganisms in the soil. Most discarded plastics can be burned but this also creates unwanted byproducts. A popular way to treat plastic waste is to recycle it. For example, plastic milk cartons can be recycled into plastic lumber for outdoor structures such as playground equipment.

SEE ALSO: Conservation; Natural Resources; Pollution; Sound Recording

PLATE TECTONICS

The earth beneath our feet seems solid, but it is constantly moving and changing. The process that explains these changes is called plate tectonics.

The earth is made up of three main layers. At the center is the molten core. Around that is the mantle. The topmost layer is the crust.

Within the mantle, temperatures and pressures are so high that rocks become soft. Just as warm air rises in the atmosphere, the hotter rocks rise, and the cooler rocks sink.

Earth's crust, like the mantle, consists of solid rock. The thickness of the crust varies from only about 3 miles (4.8 km) under the oceans to an average of 22 miles (35 km) under the continents. The crust and the uppermost part of the mantle are made up of several major sections, or plates, and numerous smaller ones. Each large plate is several thousand miles across.

How the plates move

The changes of temperature in the earth's mantle create pressure on the plates above it, which makes them move.

Sometimes the movement of the plates is very gradual. About 200 million years ago, the east coast of the Americas and the west coast of Europe and Africa were joined together. The coasts slowly moved apart, and the space between them became the Atlantic Ocean. This process is continuing—the Atlantic becomes about 2 in. (5 cm) wider each year.

The first person to notice that the two coastlines might once have fitted together was the Englishman Francis Bacon (1561–1626) in 1620. But it was not until the German meteorologist Alfred Wegener

(1880–1930) developed the theory of continental drift in 1912 that scientists began to consider how the surface of the earth has moved over time. By the 1960s, Wegener's ideas had led to the theory of plate tectonics.

When plates move apart, the space between them fills with new crust formed of molten rock from the mantle. This is the way ocean basins have formed. Plates also move closer together. When two plates carrying continents collide, the force slowly thrusts up great mountain ranges. This process takes place over many thousands of years. At other times, the movement of plates can be violent. The strain created by two plates rubbing together can cause earthquakes. The pressure of molten substances in the mantle can erupt in volcanoes. Plate movements beneath the oceans can result in massive waves called tsunamis.

▲ *The volcanic country of Iceland sits on the Mid-Atlantic Ridge. This ridge, caused by movement of the earth's plates, is creating cracks, or rifts, in the earth's surface.*

SEE ALSO: Atlantic Ocean; Continents; Earth; Earthquakes; Geology; Mountains and Valleys; Oceans and Seas; Volcanoes

477

✳ PLUTO

Pluto is the outermost of the nine planets that orbit the sun. It is also the smallest, and some scientists prefer to think of it as a large rock.

After the discovery of Neptune in the 1840s, astronomers noticed that the gravity of an unseen force was pulling the planet a little out of its normal orbit around the sun. They began to suspect that there was a ninth planet. But it was not until 1930 that Clyde Tombaugh, an astronomer in Arizona, found a tiny unidentified light in the sky. The "missing" planet was named Pluto for the Greek god of the underworld, a mythical place of cold and darkness.

Pluto was full of surprises. Its distance from the sun varied during orbit from about 2.8 billion miles (4.5 billion km) to 4.6 billion miles (7.4 billion km). Its orbit was more elliptical (noncircular) than that of the other planets. At two points during its orbit, Pluto came closer to the sun than Neptune. Little more was learned about Pluto for years because it is so far away.

Pluto (top) and Charon (bottom), are so close together and so similar that some astronomers think that they may be two planets rather than one planet and a moon.
▼

Charon

In 1978 the American astronomer James Christy discovered Pluto's only known moon. He named it Charon for the ferryman of the underworld in Greek mythology. Between 1987 and 1990, Pluto and Charon eclipsed (blocked the sun's light from) one another a number of times, enabling astronomers to see them both more clearly.

With a diameter of 1,400 miles (2,250 km), Pluto is less than twice the size of Charon, which is 746 miles (1,200 km) across. No other moon in the

KEY FACTS

POSITION IN THE SOLAR SYSTEM:
Ninth planet from the sun

AVERAGE DISTANCE FROM THE SUN:
3,700,000,000 mi. (5,900,000,000 km)

SOLAR ORBIT:
247.7 Earth years

DIAMETER:
1,400 mi. (2,250 km)

MASS:
14.7 quintillion tons

ATMOSPHERE:
Methane

AXIAL ROTATION:
6 Earth days, 9 hours, 18 minutes

solar system is so large in relation to its planet. Neither is any moon closer to its planet—Charon and Pluto are only 12,200 miles (19,630 km) apart. Pluto is made of rocky materials and ice. It is bitterly cold—it receives a thousand times less light and heat from the sun than does Earth. Pluto has a thin atmosphere of methane. The methane is a gas when Pluto is close to the sun, but freezes over when the planet moves farther away.

The origin of Pluto

When the sun formed millions of years ago, it was surrounded by many lumps of rock and ice. The lumps spun through space, collided with one another, and formed planets. Astronomers think that Pluto is the sole survivor of this period—a lone lump that never collided with another.

SEE ALSO: Astronomy; Gravity; Planets; Solar System

✱ POCAHONTAS (ABOUT 1596–1617)

Pocahontas, also known as Matoaka, was a Native American who helped improve relations between her Algonquian people and English colonists.

Pocahontas was the daughter of Powhatan, who ruled a group of Algonquians. In 1607, when English settlers arrived in Jamestown, Virginia, there was hostility between the two groups, but Pocahontas became friendly with the colonists.

In December 1607 Powhatan's followers captured the leader of Jamestown, Captain John Smith. According to Smith's own account, Pocahontas saved him from execution, although most historians believe this event never happened.

In 1613 Captain Samuel Argall captured Pocahontas. She married the colonist John Rolfe and had a child. In 1616 they sailed to England. Just before she was due to return to Virginia, she died suddenly. She is buried at Gravesend, in southeast England.

When Pocahontas married John Rolfe, she took the name Rebecca.

> SEE ALSO: Colonial America; Native Americans

✱ POE, EDGAR ALLAN (1809–49)

Edgar Allan Poe was one of America's most famous poets and short-story writers. He is credited with the invention of the modern detective story.

Poe was born in Boston, Massachusetts. His father deserted the family, and his mother died in 1811. John and Frances Allan of Richmond, Virginia, took Edgar into their home. In 1826 Poe entered the University of Virginia, but gambling debts forced him to drop out. He moved to Boston, where his first volume of poetry was published in 1827.

Penniless, Poe enlisted in the army. In 1829 he published another volume of poetry. He entered West Point Military Academy, but he deliberately neglected his duties and was expelled in 1831.

Poe struggled to make a living as a writer. In 1833 he won a short-story contest. By 1935 he was editor of the *Southern Literary Messenger* in Richmond. His

writing attracted attention, and he later wrote for journals in Philadelphia and New York City.

Among Poe's best-known stories are "The Fall of the House of Usher" (1839) and "The Murders in the Rue Morgue" (1841), which is considered to be the first detective story. In 1844 Poe moved to New York City. His last volume of poetry, *The Raven and Other Poems*, appeared in 1845. He continued to write, but his wife's death in 1847 was a severe blow. He died two years later.

The American author and poet Edgar Allan Poe was the pioneer of the modern detective story.

> SEE ALSO: Literature

✳ POLAND

Poland covers part of a vast plain that extends across much of eastern central Europe. It takes its name from the Slavic word *pole*, meaning "field."

Poland's national flag

Land and climate

Most of the country consists of a low plain dotted with small lakes and forests. The land rises toward the south, reaching its greatest height in the Carpathian Mountains on the border with Slovakia. Winters are cold and frequently snowy. The average January temperature near the German border is about 30°F (–1°C). In the east it is colder. Summers are mild.

Economy

Before World War II, Poland's economy was mainly agricultural. Today less than one-third of the workforce is employed in agriculture, although meat products remain a leading export. One of the main industries is the production of metals.

History

Poland's recorded history dates from A.D. 966. It was once one of the largest kingdoms in Europe, but in later centuries it was invaded and occupied by other countries. Between the late 1700s and early 1900s, Poland disappeared altogether after being divided among its neighbors. The nation regained its independence at the end of World War I (1914–18). It was invaded by Germany at the outbreak of World War II (1939–45).

Poland suffered badly during World War II. After the war, the eastern territory was given to the Soviet Union. In return Poland received part of Germany. Many Poles from the eastern territory moved to settle in these new lands.

After the war, a Communist government took power. In 1980 workers, led by Lech Walesa, won the right to form Solidarity—the first free labor union in a Communist country. In 1990 Poland held its first fully democratic elections since World War II, and Lech Walesa became president.

SEE ALSO: Eastern Europe; Europe; Labor; World War II

KEY FACTS

OFFICIAL NAME:
Rzeczpospolita Polska

AREA:
120,725 sq. mi. (312,678 sq. km)

POPULATION:
38,765,000

CAPITAL & LARGEST CITY:
Warsaw

MAJOR RELIGION:
Roman Catholicism

MAJOR LANGUAGE:
Polish

CURRENCY:
Zloty

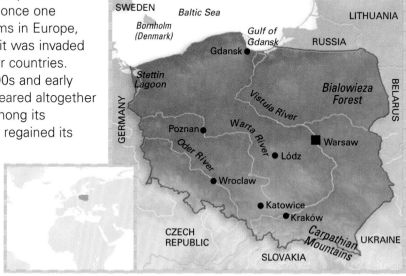

✳POLICE ᵴₑₑ➤ ✳CRIME AND LAW ENFORCEMENT

POLLINATION

Pollination is part of the process by which seed plants reproduce. Pollen grains from the male part of the plant are transferred to the female part.

Pollen grains are formed in the stamen, which is the male reproductive structure of seed-producing plants. The grains produce the male sex cells, or sperm. The female reproductive structure, the pistil, is made up of three parts. The base is called the ovary. It encloses the ovules, which hold the female sex cells, or eggs. The ovary is connected to the stigma, a sticky tip at the top of the pistil, by a thin stalk called the style. When a pollen grain lands on the stigma, it forms a tube that grows down into the ovules through the style. An ovule develops into a seed when a sperm cell fuses with an egg cell—this is called fertilization.

Some plants are able to pollinate themselves by a process named self-pollination. This occurs in so-called perfect flowers, which have both male and female parts, when the pollen from a stamen lands on the stigma of the same flower.

Cross-pollination

Many plants rely on cross-pollination, which occurs when pollen from one flower lands on the stigma of another flower of the same species. For this process to happen, an outside agent, such as an insect or a bird, is required to transport the pollen from one flower to another. These agents are called pollinators.

As the pollinator visits a flower, searching for sweet nectar to eat, it rubs against the sticky pollen grains and picks them up on its body. It then carries the pollen to the stigma of the next flower that it visits. Most flowers are pollinated by flying insects, such as bees, wasps, moths, and butterflies. A few are pollinated by hummingbirds, bats, and other small mammals.

Pollen is also scattered by the wind. Many grasses, conifers, and deciduous trees are adapted to this method of pollination. The flowers of these plants produce huge amounts of pollen, which wafts on the wind.

DID YOU KNOW?

Color and odor are important in deciding which animal pollinators visit particular flowers. Flowers that are red or yellow and have little odor tend to be pollinated by birds. Flowers that are yellow or blue and have sweet odors tend to be pollinated by bees, while flowers that are white or neutral in color with unpleasant odors tend to be pollinated by beetles. Many night-blooming flowers are white to make them visible to moths, which are active during the evening hours.

SEE ALSO:
Birds;
Butterflies
and Moths;
Flowers;
Insects;
Plants

By taking nectar, bees feed themselves and also help cross-pollination.

✳ POLLUTION

Air and water are essential to life on Earth. Human activity, however, can sometimes damage their purity and make them polluted, or dirty.

Children in Turin, Italy, protest traffic pollution by wearing face masks. Exhaust fumes from automobiles are a major source of pollution.

Air is considered to be polluted when it contains enough harmful impurities to affect the health, safety, or comfort of living things. Clean air is made up of the gases nitrogen and oxygen, together with water vapor and smaller amounts of carbon dioxide and other gases.

Some impurities in the air are natural, such as plant pollen. Pollution, however, usually means damage to the environment caused by human activity. Vehicles, such as cars and airplanes, give out exhaust fumes. Factories burn chemicals and fossil fuels, such as coal and oil, and release waste matter into the air. When people use fossil fuels, carbon dioxide and other gases are released into the air. These gases act like the glass in a greenhouse, trapping heat from the sun. This "greenhouse effect" causes the atmosphere to warm and world temperatures to rise.

Artificial pollutants can sometimes combine with natural weather conditions. Smoke, for example, can combine with fog to create smog. This is especially dangerous to people who suffer from breathing disorders, such as asthma, bronchitis, and emphysema. Sometimes high temperatures above an area can trap pollutants on the earth's surface. This is called temperature inversion and is a common occurrence in cities like Los Angeles and Mexico City.

AMAZING FACTS!

The United States has only 5 percent of the world's population, but it produces 25 percent of the greenhouse gases that cause global warming.

Water pollution

Water, like air, is polluted when it contains harmful impurities that affect living things. Water pollution can have natural causes. Storms can cause soil and other debris to dissolve in water. But human activity causes the most damage to water. Factories release harmful chemicals into rivers and lakes. Sewage—household waste from toilets, sinks, and bathtubs—pumps into the oceans. Even if polluted water is not dangerous, excess chlorine and other chemicals can make it unpleasant to drink. Waste material on land can also pollute groundwater—the water contained in soil and among rocks. Dangerous material can pass into the food cycle through crops or animal feed.

Acid rain

When certain pollutants mix with water vapor, they cause a particular form of pollution called acid rain. Acid rain is mostly the result of industrial processes. When rainwater contains sulfuric or nitric acids, it can alter the composition of soil and damage plants. If the acid reacts with aluminum in the soil, it releases poisons. Acid rain pollutes lakes and rivers, killing fish. It can also damage buildings and statues.

Stopping pollution

Most scientists agree on the main causes of pollution. However, it is harder to agree on solutions. Harmful emissions from motor vehicles have fallen since the introduction of catalytic converters and unleaded gas. Legislation requires government and industry to take action to remove pollutants from fuel and other materials. International restrictions on the use of harmful chemicals called CFCs (chlorofluorocarbons) have slowed down the loss of the ozone layer—the vital strip in the atmosphere that protects Earth from the sun's harmful rays.

Some big companies say that too many controls on pollution will harm the economy. In 1997 many nations met in Kyoto, Japan, and agreed to restrict pollution. But in 2001 the United States withdrew its support for the agreement, saying that it was bad for industry.

Everyone can take steps to protect the environment from pollution in easy ways, such as by making fewer car journeys, using less electricity, and throwing away less garbage. However, major changes need to come from big industrial companies and governments.

SEE ALSO:
Atmosphere;
Conservation;
Environment;
Fossil Fuels;
Health;
Natural
Resources;
Water

Oil spilled from tankers at sea washes ashore. It soaks the feathers of birds, making them unable to fly.

✳ POPULATION AND CENSUSES

The total number of people living in a country or a region is called its population. Most countries carry out a regular census—a count—of their population.

Newborn babies in a maternity hospital in China.

About 2,000 years ago, the total population of Earth was around 250 million people. This is fewer than the number of people in the United States today. Better nutrition, medical care, and sanitation meant that by 1750 there were 800 million people on the planet. Within 250 years, the figure had multiplied to over six billion.

The areas of high population have also changed. Today six of the ten most populous countries are in Asia. Populations within individual countries change because of three factors. The birthrate represents the number of children born per 1,000 people. The death rate represents the number of people who die. And the migration rate shows the number of people who enter or leave the country.

Overpopulation

An increase in population seems like a good thing. It shows that fewer children are dying in infancy and that people are living longer. However, more people require more food and housing. As cities and towns grow, they destroy the natural environment. Unless the growth in population slows down, the earth may not be able to meet all humanity's needs.

Census

Governments need to know how many people live in their countries. They need to know their ages and whether some areas are more crowded than others so that they can plan for the future. Countries often carry out a census to discover these facts. It is a survey of a country's population, done every five or ten years.

The results are vital to a government's planning. If the number of older people is increasing, the government might need to provide special health care. More people being born means that more housing is needed, and more young people means that schools must be built.

AMAZING FACTS❗

The most rapidly growing populations in the world are in Africa, which is doubling in population every 24 years. The population of Europe doubles only every 240 years.

At its present rate of growth, the total population of the world will double in about 40 years.

More than 60 percent of the world's people live in just 10 countries.

SEE ALSO: Housing; United States Government

☀ PORTUGAL

Portugal shares the Iberian Peninsula with its larger neighbor, Spain. It directly faces the Atlantic Ocean and is the westernmost country in mainland Europe.

Land and climate

The Tagus River divides Portugal in half. The north is mountainous. The Serra da Estrela is the major mountain range. The land south of the river is flat. The climate is cooler and rainfall heavier in the north than in the south.

The Atlantic islands of Madeira and the Azores belong to Portugal, but each has its own elected legislature.

People and economy

The first inhabitants of the peninsula were Iberians. Around 1000 B.C., Celtic peoples settled in the north. At the same time, Phoenicians, a people from the eastern Mediterranean, and later Greeks and Carthaginians founded cities and colonies in the south. The Romans conquered the area in the first century A.D. When the Western Roman Empire collapsed in the fifth century, two Germanic tribes fought for control of the region. Muslims, followers of Islam, invaded in the 700s, conquering most of Spain and more than half of Portugal.

Agriculture and fishing were traditionally important to the economy. Recently the emphasis has been on developing industry and tourism. Textiles and clothing are the chief manufactured products.

History

In 1179 Portugal became a kingdom under Alfonso Henriques. Later kings conquered more land, and by 1270 the country had its modern boundaries. Henry the Navigator (1394–1460) encouraged voyages of discovery. He started the process that led to the Portuguese sailing around Africa and building an overseas empire. The new trade routes brought wealth to the country.

Portugal's national flag

From 1932 to 1968 António de Salazar ruled as a dictator. In 1976 democratic government was restored. In 1999 Portugal returned its last overseas territory, Macao, to China.

SEE ALSO: China; Europe; Exploration and Explorers; Islam; Spain

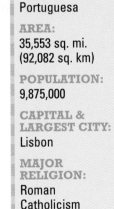

KEY FACTS

OFFICIAL NAME:
República Portuguesa

AREA:
35,553 sq. mi.
(92,082 sq. km)

POPULATION:
9,875,000

CAPITAL & LARGEST CITY:
Lisbon

MAJOR RELIGION:
Roman Catholicism

MAJOR LANGUAGE:
Portuguese

CURRENCY:
Euro

✳ PREHISTORIC PEOPLES

Prehistoric means "before written history." People have lived on Earth for about seven million years. Most of this time was before written history.

Scientists believe that humans developed from early primates, mammals that were also ancestors to apes such as gorillas, chimpanzees, and orangutans. Over many thousands of years, primate species changed and adapted to new environments through a process called evolution. Originally scientists saw human evolution as a ladder with simple steps from ape ancestor to modern humans, but now they see it as a branching tree with many unclear connections.

Fossil finds

Scientists have formed their ideas about prehistoric people from finding fossilized bones and teeth. New finds mean that scientists keep having to revise their opinions about the origins of humans. In 1974 scientists found a fossil skull, which they called Lucy, in East Africa. It dated from about 3.2 million years ago. In 1998 they discovered a skeleton in South Africa dating from about 3.5 million years ago. In September 2002 French scientists located a skull in Chad, in Central Africa, that is almost seven million years old.

These early humans are called hominids—primates that walk on two legs. By 2.3 million years ago, at least one form had developed a slightly larger brain and more skillful hands, enabling it to make stone tools. This species is called *Homo habilis*, or "handy person." Scientists consider it to be the first human. *Homo habilis* lived in open grassland and ate wild plants and meat killed by other animals.

About 1.8 million years ago, a new human form appeared in Africa. This species had a more upright posture, and scientists call it *Homo erectus*, or "person who stands erect." Over the next 1.5 million years, *Homo erectus* spread into Asia and Europe. They still ate wild plants, but they also used wooden spears to kill animals for meat.

Neanderthals and *Homo sapiens*

By 200,000 years ago, some hominids had developed larger brains. Scientists called them Neanderthals because they found the first skeleton of the type in the Neander Valley, Germany. Neanderthals lived in caves, wore skins, used fire, hunted animals, made and used stone tools and wooden spears, and buried their dead.

For many years, scientists thought that Neanderthals were the direct ancestors of modern humans, but many now believe that, although Neanderthals and modern humans shared a common ancestor, the two lines separated between 550,000 and 690,000 years ago.

Scientists do not agree on the exact origins of modern human beings, known as *Homo sapiens sapiens*, a subspecies of *Homo sapiens*, meaning "people who are wise." Most believe that the first people

In 2002 scientists discovered a skull in the Central African country of Chad that is almost seven million years old. They nicknamed the hominid Toumai, which means "hope of life" in the local language. Toumai was like an ape in some ways. Its brain was the size of a chimp's and the skull had a big ridge over the eyes, like a gorilla. But Toumai's teeth put it in the human family. Its face was also flatter than a chimp's and more humanlike.

Archaeologists can learn a great deal about prehistoric life by studying cave paintings. These paintings at Tassili n'Ajjer in southern Algeria date from about 4500 B.C. Whereas today the Sahara is a dry desert, the cave paintings show it as a moist area full of animal life and the home of hunters and herdsmen.

like ourselves appeared in Africa between 100,000 and 200,000 years ago, then spread rapidly elsewhere. Others argue that *Homo sapiens sapiens* appeared in Africa, Asia, and Europe about the same time.

By 32,000 years ago, only modern human beings lived in Europe. By this time, modern people had also settled in Central Asia and Siberia, China, and Southeast Asia. The earliest modern Europeans are known as the Cro-Magnons, named after a rock shelter in southwestern France where their skeletons were first found in 1868. They lived between 10,000 and 40,000 years ago and were among the first humans to develop art. Their cave paintings and engravings, which depict animals, are believed to have had deep spiritual meaning.

The first Americans

Some scientists believe that people crossed from Siberia to Alaska as early as 40,000 years ago. Most argue for a much later settlement, about 15,000 years ago. Low sea levels, caused by an Ice Age,

meant that people could walk from Asia to America. By 12,500 years ago, small groups of hunter-gatherers had spread as far south as Chile in South America.

Farming

Beginning about 15,000 years ago, Earth's climate began to warm rapidly. People settled by lakes and rivers and developed fishing techniques. By about 7000 B.C., some groups in Asia had learned to plant crops, such as wheat. Instead of hunting animals, they kept herds of cattle.

Civilization

From about 8000 B.C., trade developed between farming communities. Some villages between the Tigris and Euphrates rivers in Mesopotamia (modern Iraq) became small towns. Similar communities grew up along the banks of the Nile River in Egypt. Most historians regard this as the beginning of civilization.

About 3000 B.C., the first examples of writing appeared in Mesopotamia, and people began to leave written records about how they lived their lives.

SEE ALSO:
Agriculture;
Ancient
Civilizations;
Apes,
Monkeys,
and
Primates;
Archaeology;
Art and
Artists;
Evolution;
Fossils;
History;
Tools;
Writing

✳ PRESIDENCY, THE

The men who wrote the Constitution were against an all-powerful head of state, but today the leader of the United States is the most powerful man in the world.

▲
President George W. Bush in the White House Oval Office.

The president is elected every four years. Since Franklin D. Roosevelt (president 1933–45), none has been allowed to serve more than two terms. All presidents still swear the same oath on their inauguration day as that taken by the first president, George Washington: "I do solemnly swear [or affirm] that I will faithfully execute the Office of President of the United States, and will to the best of my ability, preserve, protect, and defend the Constitution of the United States."

Changing role

Since the first president was inaugurated in 1789, the obligations and duties implied in the oath have changed enormously. The key to the change lies in the words *the Office of President*. The framers of the Constitution believed that with the presidency they had created an office of prestige but little power. They provided for three separate branches of government—legislative, executive, and judicial—because they did not think all governmental powers should rest with one body. The president heads the executive branch of government. He is elected by the entire country and is responsible for carrying out the laws approved by the legislative branch of government, Congress. The president has the power to appoint and remove important officials, including cabinet members, federal judges, military and naval officers, heads of agencies, attorneys, and marshals. He is also commander in chief of the armed forces.

With each new president, the machinery of government has become more complex. The earliest presidents were able to carry out their duties with little assistance. When George Washington was president, his staff consisted of a secretary, one or two clerks, and household servants. But with the growth in the president's power, the office now employs more than 1,500 people. The role of the president has grown from that of a largely honorary officer to a powerful leader in national and international affairs.

A list of U.S. presidents can be found at the end of the encyclopedia.

SEE ALSO: Congress; Constitution, United States; States and State Governments; Supreme Court; United States Government; Vice Presidency, The

✳**PRIMATES** 👀➡ ✳**APES, MONKEYS, AND PRIMATES**

✳**PRIME MERIDIAN** 👀➡ ✳**NAVIGATION**

PRINTING

Until the invention of printing, it could take years to create a book. Now thousands of books, newspapers, and magazines roll off the presses every hour.

The earliest known recorded information is in the form of European cave paintings more than 30,000 years old. About 5,000 years ago, people in Mesopotamia (modern Iraq) and Egypt began carving records on stone. The Chinese invented paper about 2,000 years ago. They also used woodblocks to print books.

Printing press

Printing as we know it dates from the mid-1400s, when Johannes Gutenberg built the first printing press in Germany. He molded individual letters from metal and used them to print a Bible.

Until this time, books were very rare and expensive. Each one was handwritten by specially trained scribes. Very few people were able to read. Even with Gutenberg's invention, only rich people could afford books. However, within a few decades most families in Europe and North America had Bibles. Newspapers began to appear in the 1500s. Cheaply printed "primers" made it easier to teach children basic reading and writing.

From the 1800s, industrial developments began to influence printing methods. The process of putting the characters together to make pages is called typesetting. Automatic techniques for using images and color meant that books could be produced more cheaply and quickly, and the finished products looked more interesting than ever before. The advent of computers means that books, newspapers, and other publications can be put together, say, in New York, sent to China electronically, and immediately printed.

Easy access to photocopiers and cheap printers means that anyone with an idea can publish a book.

The printing process

Printing has changed greatly since Gutenberg, but some principles remain the same. Most printed material begins with type. Each type character represents a letter, number, or other mark. The characters can be made of solid material, such as metal, or they can be photographic or in digital form on a computer.

Once type has been set, it is combined with illustrations, such as photographs and diagrams, and put into position on the page. This process is called layout. The design is checked, or proofed; once it is correct, a plate is made. The plates print text and images onto paper or other material, and the sheets are then folded, cut, and bound to make a book, magazine, or other publication.

Printing methods

There are many different printing methods. The oldest is letterpress, or relief printing. It is the method that Gutenberg used for

A reconstruction of the first printing press, originally built by Johannes Gutenberg (about 1390–1468).

A color press machine in a modern printing factory. From here the pages are taken to a bindery, where they are turned into books.

his Bible. The image to be printed is carved or molded so that it is raised from the surface around it. When ink is rolled over the area, it sticks to the raised surface only. Rubber stamps also use this technique. Flexography, a form of letterpress using rubber plates, is increasingly used for printing newspapers.

Lithography is done from a flat printing surface, using photographic negatives on aluminum plates. When the plates are dampened, the unexposed areas reject ink. The ink sticks to the image, which is transferred to a rubber blanket, and then onto paper.

Gravure printing is done from images carved into a metal plate. Ink sinks into the grooves left by the carving and transfers to the paper. In screen printing, artists place a stencil on a mesh screen, then squeeze ink through the screen onto paper, canvas, or cloth. Photocopying uses static electricity on a rotating cylinder to transfer black powder onto paper. A photocopier can make hundreds of copies in a matter of minutes.

SEE ALSO: Communication; Media; Newspapers and Magazines; Photography; Writing

BASIC LITHOGRAPHY

Lithography is based on the principle that grease and water do not mix. The original procedure, first developed in 1798, is shown below. In the 1900s, lithography was improved when the flat stone was replaced by a light-sensitive metal plate, and the images were transferred onto paper.

First draw a letter on a flat stone with a greasy crayon, then wipe the stone with a damp sponge, leaving water on the areas that are not covered in crayon.

Cover the stone with ink, which does not mix with water, and will therefore stick only to the area that has been marked with crayon.

Press a sheet of paper onto the top of the stone. When the paper is removed, it will be marked with a reversed image of what was originally drawn in crayon.

PRISONS

A prison is a place where people are confined after they commit a crime. Prisons exist to punish offenders, to help them reform, and to protect society.

Until the 1500s, the normal punishments for criminals were execution, exile, and corporal punishment—inflicting pain. The first houses of correction—an early term for prisons—were built in England and the Netherlands.

Until the 1700s, prisoners were housed in large, open rooms. Men, women, and children were held together, and there was no distinction between convicted criminals and those awaiting trial. This was also the system used in the American colonies.

Beginning in the late 1700s, reformers such as John Howard, Elizabeth Fry, and Walter Crofton worked to make prisons more humane places. They believed that prisons should make criminals better citizens through education and training.

Prisons such as Auburn, New York, and the Western Penitentiary in Pittsburgh, Pennsylvania, were built with a single cell for each prisoner. Separate institutions were created for women, children, and people with mental health problems.

Types of prisons

Prison is a general term for any place of confinement. But there are many types of institution that serve this purpose. In the United States, a prison, or penitentiary, is officially defined as an institution that holds people serving sentences of a year or more. Prisons are run either by the federal government or by individual states. Jails and detention centers hold people who have committed minor offenses, such as disorderly conduct. They also hold

Prisoners spend much of their time in cells, but they may be allowed to take part in activities during the day.

people who have been accused of a crime but have not yet been tried. Training schools are institutions that hold young offenders and prepare them for life after they have served their sentences.

Life in prison

Most prisoners follow a similar routine. They sleep in simple cells that are usually furnished with only a bed, a washbasin, and a toilet. Prison guards control all their activities. Various times are allocated to work, education, meals, and recreation. By about 9:00 P.M., the prisoners are locked up in their cells for the night.

SEE ALSO: Crime and Law Enforcement; Law

DID YOU KNOW?

In the United States today, there are more than two million people serving time in federal or state prisons and local jails. Most prisoners are male high school dropouts between the ages of 18 and 29. They have committed violent crimes against people (such as murder), property crimes (such as burglary), or "white-collar" crimes (such as tax evasion or embezzlement). More than 6 percent of federal and state prison convicts are women.

*PSYCHOLOGY

Psychology is the study of the mind—the ways in which people learn, think, and feel—and human behavior.

▲
Sigmund Freud is widely known as the father of psychoanalysis. Much of his work was based on the analysis and interpretation of dreams.

Everyone is interested in why people think, say, and do certain things. A psychologist uses scientific methods to study these questions. Some psychologists work in the medical health field. They help people with mental problems, such as depression or phobias (unreasonable fears). Others work in areas such as business, advertising, or politics. They use their skills to explain why people make certain choices in behavior. Other psychologists work in education—for example, helping children who are unhappy in school. An important educational psychologist was the American John Dewey (1859–1952), who argued that children learn better when they are interested in subjects.

Psychologists usually have four stages in their work. The first is description. This requires observing what, when, and how people think, feel, or act in a particular situation. It might involve anything from describing the behavior of someone with mental health problems to studying the voting patterns of electors.

The next stage is explanation. The psychologist uses his or her training to decide why people think or behave the way they do. This is followed by prediction—working out how people will behave in the future. The final step is modification, which means helping people to change their behavior. This might involve helping a patient improve his or her mental health, or persuading electors to vote for a particular candidate.

Ideas in psychology

Psychology did not properly develop as a separate science until the late 1800s. But the ideas at its heart go back to ancient Greek philosophy. For example, some psychologists believe that people are born with a certain level of intelligence and other qualities. Others feel that environment, education, and upbringing are more important. The debate between these positions, usually called "nature versus nurture," dates back to the philosophers Plato and Aristotle nearly 2,500 years ago, and still goes on today.

An important 20th-century development was led by the Austrian Sigmund Freud (1856–1939). He believed that childhood experiences influence people's later development, even if they do not remember these experiences. This idea is called the unconscious, and is important in the branch of psychology that Freud founded, called psychoanalysis.

Brain and Nervous System; Medicine; Philosophers

*PYRAMIDS see *EGYPT, ANCIENT

✳ RADIO

Radio is an electronic technology used in many areas. It makes communication possible between two points without connecting wires.

A girl tunes in to a radio station and listens using headphones. Radio stations broadcast on different frequencies.

Radio waves are electromagnetic waves moving at about 186,000 miles (300,000 km) per second (the speed of light). They are created when an electrical current flows through a metal wire or rod—the transmitting antenna. When the waves reach a receiving antenna, they produce a current that is converted into sound. Each radio wave has a high point (a crest) and a low point (a trough). The distance between one crest and the next is called the wavelength. The number of complete waves, or cycles, in a second is called the frequency. It is measured in kilohertz (kHz), or thousands of cycles per second.

A radio station broadcasts on a unique frequency. By setting a radio receiver to the correct frequency, the listener can pick up the radio station that he or she wants. Some frequencies are restricted to specific uses for emergency services, the military, and other organizations.

No single person invented the radio. In 1865 the Scottish scientist James Clerk Maxwell used mathematics to predict the existence of radio waves. It was a German, Heinrich Hertz, who proved they existed, in 1888. (The unit of frequency is named in his honor.) The British scientist Ernest Rutherford sent the first radio

AMAZING FACTS!

The tallest radio tower ever built was 2,120 ft. (646 m) tall. It was built in Poland in 1974 and fell down in 1991.

signal, while the Englishman Oliver Lodge, figured out the basic principle of the tuner. Guglielmo Marconi (1874–1937), an Italian based in England, created the first practical radio transmitter. In 1901 he sent and received a series of dots and dashes—like those used in telegraphy—across the Atlantic Ocean. His wireless was used for signaling to ships at sea.

In 1904 another Englishman, John A. Fleming, created a vacuum tube that made it possible to send sounds—speech and music—by radio. An American, Lee DeForest, improved on this in 1906, adding a grid to the tube. This was the earliest loudspeaker. That same year, R. A. Fessenden made the first voice and music broadcast from his home in Massachusetts. Over the next few decades, sales of radios increased rapidly, and broadcasting stations began setting up in North America, Europe, and beyond.

Guglielmo Marconi at Signal Hill, St. John's, Newfoundland, just after receiving the first wireless signal to cross the Atlantic from England on December 12, 1901.

An important development came in 1948, when the transistor was invented at Bell Telephone Laboratories. The transistor is a small device that replaced tubes in radios. This meant that radios could be smaller and more portable.

Frequency modulation (FM) and digital radio have added to the quality and variety of radio broadcasts. A big boost for FM radio was stereophonic sound, or stereo. In a stereo system there are two speakers. But the principle remains the same as it was when Marconi made his first broadcasts—the transmission of information without restrictive wires.

Two-way radio

Many radios are both receivers and transmitters, enabling two-way communication. Police officers communicate with one another through two-way radios. Fire departments, ambulance services, and taxi companies use radio to keep track of their vehicles. Safe airplane travel would be impossible unless pilots could communicate with air traffic control. Radio waves can even travel beyond the atmosphere and back, as astronauts keep in touch with Earth.

Radio waves do not only carry sounds. Radar is a form of radio. It works by producing short radio pulses that bounce off an object as echoes. The echoes appear on an indicator as bright spots known as blips. They show how far away the object is. Pagers also use radio waves to send alerts or text messages.

SEE ALSO: Communication; Electricity; Electronics; Sound; Telecommunications

∗**RAILROADS** see ∗**TRAINS AND RAILROADS**

✽ RAIN FORESTS

Rain forests are jungles that receive over 59 in. (1,500 mm) of rain evenly through each year. The largest rain forests are found in tropical regions.

Tropical rain forests are found close to the equator from the Brazilian Amazon and Central America to Southeast Asia, northeast Australia, and equatorial Africa. The average annual temperature in these rain forests is 77°F (25°C). Rain forests farther from the equator are cooler and receive less rain. Known as temperate rain forests, they grow in the Pacific Northwest of the United States, southeast Australia, New Zealand, and Chile.

Tropical rain forests

Rain-forest trees usually have tall trunks and grow close to one another. Their leafy crowns form an almost solid canopy, like a ceiling, up to 150 ft. (45 m) above ground. The canopy takes nearly all the sunlight. Vines and creepers reach up the tree trunks to the canopy, and branches are covered with plants whose roots absorb water from the humid air. Plants of the lower understory have broad leaves that capture as much light as possible.

On the ground, fungi and invertebrates, such as ants and millipedes, break down fallen leaves into nutrients. Tree roots quickly absorb the nutrients.

Most rain-forest animals, such as sloths, flying squirrels, and various monkeys, live in the canopy and seldom visit the ground. Colorful birds of the rain forest include toucans, hornbills, and parrots.

The importance of rain forests

Rain forests contain more plant and animal species than any other habitat. People living in rain forests have long depended on the forest for food, shelter, and

medicine. Rain forests are a source of many agricultural crops. They provide rubber, coffee, and cacao for chocolate. They help control Earth's temperature and rainfall by absorbing carbon dioxide (a gas that traps the sun's heat) and capturing water in the atmosphere. Today the rain forests are destroyed for timber and to make room for mining and farmland.

Many people and organizations are working to protect the rain forests from destruction. One way to achieve this is to avoid buying rain-forest products that have been harvested and not replaced.

SEE ALSO: Biomes; Botany; Climate; Conservation; Environment; Forests; Fungus; Natural Resources; Plants; Pollution; Trees

✳ REFORMATION

The Reformation was a religious movement that attempted to reform the Roman Catholic Church, but resulted in the establishment of Protestant churches.

Martin Luther was the most important leader of the movement known as the Reformation, and the founder of the Protestant religion.

Although the Reformation began in Europe in the early 1500s, two earlier reformers had paved the way. The Englishman John Wycliffe (about 1330–84) and the Czech Jan Hus (about 1372–1415) were both highly critical of the power and wealth of the Roman Catholic Church. They preached a form of Christianity that emphasized poverty, purity, and strong religious devotion. In particular, they protested the church's practice of raising money by selling indulgences—official documents that promised forgiveness for sins.

Martin Luther

In 1517 the German priest Martin Luther (1483–1546) drew up 95 theses (statements) outlining what he thought was corrupt about the Catholic Church. He nailed them to a church door in Wittenberg, Germany, on October 31. This was an accepted way to invite debate.

Luther was a professor of theology (religious thought) who believed that much of the elaborate structure of the church was unnecessary, and that the individual believer could be in direct contact with God through Christ. This contradicted the teachings of the church, and in 1521

Luther was excommunicated (banned from church membership). After that he established his own church.

The Lutheran Church held services in the local language instead of the traditional Latin. Luther's mixture of new and traditional ideas soon became popular throughout Germany. The conflict between Lutheranism and Catholicism caused many wars of religion over the following years.

Calvinism

Other reformers followed Luther, principally John Calvin (1509–64), who set up a reformed church in Geneva, Switzerland. It was run by ministers chosen by their congregations and a group of elders who were elected laymen (nonclergy). Calvinism spread to Germany, the Netherlands, and Great Britain. In France, Calvin's followers became known as Huguenots.

John Knox (1513–72) was strongly influenced by Calvin. He led the Reformation in Scotland, creating Presbyterianism, a form of Christianity that attaches great importance to the views of religious laymen.

All the new forms of Christianity that emerged during the Reformation and were not Roman Catholic became known as Protestantism. The people who follow them are known as Protestants.

SEE ALSO: Bible; Christianity; Middle Ages; Religions; Renaissance

RELIGIONS

Religions take many different forms and are found in almost every culture, past and present. They can unite people, but they can also be a cause of wars.

What is a religion?

There are thousands of types of religions throughout the world, and it is not easy to identify elements common to all of them. However, they usually include a set of beliefs about what is most important in life; a community of believers; a series of rituals and practices, such as the Christian baptism; sacred texts, such as the Islamic Koran; and rules by which followers should live. Many religions involve worshiping a supreme being, or other spiritual forces. There is often a belief in some kind of life after death. This may be in the form of an afterlife, or reincarnation, where a dead person's identity comes back in another living form.

Religion can unite people with similar beliefs and require them to behave in a way that benefits others. In ancient civilizations, all people followed the same religion. The ruler was often both a political and a religious leader. This is still the case in some parts of the world.

In most parts of the modern Western world, people from different religious backgrounds and people with no religious beliefs live close together. This can be very rewarding, as people learn about their neighbors' ways of life. But some people are intolerant of different religions. This intolerance has led to many conflicts.

Types of religion

There are several ways to classify religions. One is to group them according to their beliefs about a deity (a god or goddess). Followers of some religions believe in one god. That is called monotheism. Followers of other religions believe in more than one god. That is known as polytheism.

Also, the faiths in each group may be related to one another because they all developed in the same part of the world or because they have beliefs, prophets, or sacred texts in common. For example, Buddhism, Hinduism, and Sikhism, which all began in India and spread throughout Asia, share a belief in reincarnation. Christianity, Judaism, and Islam, which all began in the Middle East, are monotheistic.

Individual religions may have several different divisions. Followers share core beliefs, but might differ over styles of worship or the interpretation of sacred texts. For example, most Christians are Roman Catholic, Protestant, or Orthodox. Islam is divided into Sunni, Shi'ite, and Sufi groups.

Major religions

There are entries on Buddhism, Christianity, Hinduism, Islam, and Judaism in the encyclopedia. The following list details other important world religions.

Sikhism

Sikhism is a monotheistic religion that arose in northwest India (present-day Pakistan) in the 1500s as an alternative to

In the 11th century, the Christian church in Europe became divided between east and west. This bishop is a member of the eastern Russian Orthodox Church.

497

A Shinto priest bangs a drum during a religious ceremony in Kyoto, Japan.

Islam and Hinduism. Sikhs use meditation (quiet, concentrated thought) in order to communicate with their god. Male Sikhs wear turbans—lengths of cloth wrapped around the head. There are about 23 million Sikhs worldwide.

Confucianism
Confucianism is a philosophy that was founded in China in the 500s B.C. by Confucius. He taught that people should live in harmony with others, behaving with honesty, courage, and courtesy. Many people combine Confucianism with other beliefs. Today there are an estimated 160 million Confucians.

Taoism
Taoism is based on the writings of Lao-tzu, a Chinese philosopher who died in 531 B.C. Taoists believe that the Tao, a form of energy, is the source of everything in the universe, and consists of two complementary aspects, yin and yang, that need to be balanced. Today there are about 20 million Taoists, mainly in China and Taiwan.

Shinto
Shinto is the ancient religion of Japan. Its sacred books, dating from the 700s, are collections of myths about a time when the world was young and the gods mingled with Japanese people. At its core is the belief in *kami* (the sacred power), which is present in many animals and objects and helps connect humans with the natural world. Today there are about four million followers of Shinto in Japan.

The Nihang Singhs are warrior Sikhs who live in the Punjab area of India. Five symbols are particularly important to Sikhs: uncut hair, a special comb, "drawers" or trousers, a saber (sword), and a bracelet of steel.

SEE ALSO: Bible; Buddhism; Christianity; Hinduism; Islam; Judaism; Koran; Myths and Legends; Philosophers; Torah

✳ REMBRANDT VAN RIJN (1606–69)

One of the greatest European painters, the Dutch artist Rembrandt van Rijn is noted for his handling of shade and light, especially in portraits.

Rembrandt Harmensz van Rijn was born in Leiden, Holland. His father was a miller. As soon as Rembrandt was old enough, he set up as a portrait artist. In about 1632, he moved to Amsterdam to paint wealthy customers. He quickly became successful and lived with his wife, Saskia, in a grand home.

In 1642 Saskia died, leaving Rembrandt with a son, Titus. By now his portraiture style was out of fashion, but that did not trouble him. Until then he had painted people in the midst of dramatic action, as in the great group portrait *The Night Watch*. Now he became more interested in people's inner feelings. He painted new

subjects, such as Bible stories. His last years, although spent as a poor man, marked the most creative period of his life.

Rembrandt's paintings, drawings, and prints cover many subjects, but his work can often be identified by its contrasts of light and dark or the golden-brown haze surrounding his figures. He was the first artist to make self-portraiture a specialty.

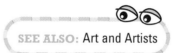

SEE ALSO: Art and Artists

▲ **Rembrandt painted** Self-Portrait as a Young Man *between 1633 and 1634.*

✳ RENAISSANCE

The Renaissance was a period in European history that saw a rebirth of interest in the learning and arts of ancient Greece and Rome.

The spirit of the Renaissance took many other forms. It was a time of discovery and growth. Europeans developed new scientific ideas and inventions, produced new literature and art, and discovered new lands and trade routes.

The word *renaissance* means "rebirth." The Renaissance began in Italy in the 1300s and gradually spread to other European countries. At that time, Italy was divided into independent city-states, the most powerful of which were Florence, Milan, and Venice. Their rulers supported artists and scholars by commissioning (ordering) new buildings and works of art. This encouraged new ideas to flourish.

The humanists

The learned scholars who revived interest in ancient Greek and Roman culture were known as humanists. For hundreds of years before the Renaissance, art had concentrated mainly on religious themes. The new generation, however, studied the history of antiquity and admired its literature, which told of human deeds and feelings rather than the glory of God. The humanists modeled their own works on those of the ancient authors, concentrating on the joys of this world rather than the rewards of the next.

Humanists wrote mostly in Latin, the scholarly language of the time, but some started writing in the vernacular, the everyday language of the people. The Italian poet Petrarch wrote many poems in Italian, and Boccaccio wrote a collection of stories in Italian entitled the *Decameron*. Other writers started writing in their own languages, and the development of printing meant that ideas spread rapidly.

Some scholars felt that the Bible should be translated into European languages rather than being in Latin, which most people could not understand. In the 14th century, an English translation was made, and in the early 1500s, Martin Luther made a German translation. People could read the Bible in their own language, and this helped the Protestant Reformation—a religious movement to reform the Catholic Church—spread in Germany.

Art and architecture

Renaissance artists turned for inspiration to the classical (ancient) world. They borrowed classical forms and used them in new ways. Medieval artists had focused on religious subjects; Renaissance artists looked to the world around them.

Painters and sculptors often drew their subject matter

from Greek and Roman mythology. Although that subject matter was old, the way of painting it was new. To give the appearance of reality, painters studied the human body, the interplay of light and shade, and perspective (the method of creating the illusion of depth on a flat surface). They also painted worldly subjects, such as portraits of powerful patrons. When a Renaissance artist painted a religious painting, he made the people in the painting look like real people rather than the stylized characters of medieval art.

Renaissance architects used the domes, round arches, and columns of the buildings of antiquity to create a new kind of architecture based on ideas of harmony and geometry. Renaissance architects often based their designs on circles or squares, because they were considered perfect shapes.

Exploration and science

The Renaissance was a time when Europeans made many discoveries about the physical world. Explorers found sea routes to Asia and to the Americas. Their voyages were made possible by improvements in navigational aids. There were important developments in mining, trade, and commerce. Coinage was standardized to meet the growing needs of bankers, traders, and merchants.

In scientific matters, there was a new emphasis on direct observation and experiment, rather than relying on the traditional knowledge of the past. The Swiss-born physician Paracelsus used chemical remedies rather than the old plant-based remedies, laying the foundations of modern chemistry. The Belgian anatomist Andreas Vesalius dissected human bodies and produced the first authoritative book on human anatomy.

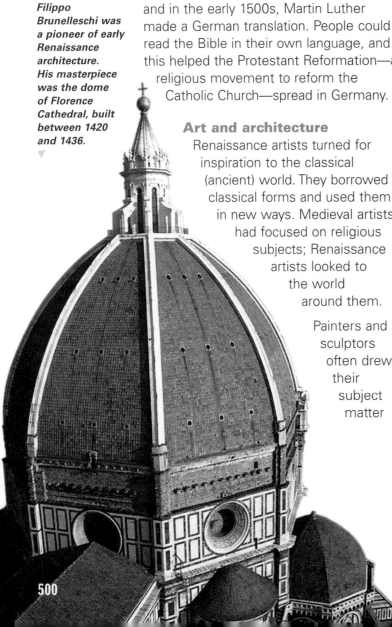

Filippo Brunelleschi was a pioneer of early Renaissance architecture. His masterpiece was the dome of Florence Cathedral, built between 1420 and 1436.

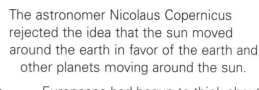

The astronomer Nicolaus Copernicus rejected the idea that the sun moved around the earth in favor of the earth and other planets moving around the sun.

Europeans had begun to think about the world in new and different ways. By the end of the 1500s, the ideas of the Renaissance were being replaced by even newer ideas, but this period marked the beginning of the modern world.

Michelangelo was skilled at representing the human body. His sculpture Pietà *was completed in 1499.*

SEE ALSO: Architecture; Art and Artists; Astronomy; da Vinci, Leonardo; Exploration and Explorers; Literature; Medicine; Michelangelo; Middle Ages; Reformation

✳ REPRODUCTIVE SYSTEM

Reproduction is the process by which living things create new beings. In humans, the male and female body parts are specially adapted for this process.

There are two main types of reproduction. In one type—known as asexual reproduction—the young come from a single parent. For example, some worms and many single-celled creatures reproduce by dividing in half.

The other main type of reproduction is sexual reproduction. The young are created from two different parts of the same parent, or, more usually, by two parents. The process begins when a male reproductive cell, called a sperm, joins with a female reproductive cell, called an ovum, or egg. The joining of the egg and sperm is called fertilization. The fertilized egg grows and develops into a new individual combining the characteristics of both parents. In some organisms—for example, mammals—fertilization takes place inside the body; in others—for example, fish—it is external.

Human reproductive system

In males, the reproductive structures include the testes (singular, *testicle*), two oval-shaped structures that hang between the legs. The testes produce and store sperm. Sperm travel through a narrow tube, called the vas deferens, to the penis. The penis is used for both transporting sperm into the female reproductive system and eliminating urine.

REPRODUCTIVE SYSTEM

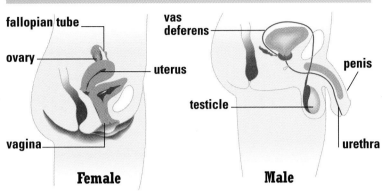

fallopian tube

ovary

vagina

Female

vas deferens

uterus

testicle

penis

urethra

Male

▲
These diagrams show the male and female body parts involved in the reproductive process.

In females, the reproductive structures include the ovaries (which produce the egg) and the uterus (which is where babies grow until they are ready to be born). Women have two ovaries. Each ovary is connected to the top of the

uterus by a small tube called the fallopian tube. At the bottom of the uterus, a canal-like structure called the vagina opens to the outside of the body.

Women usually release one egg a month. As the egg develops, changes occur in the uterus. It is preparing a place for a baby to grow. The lining of the uterus thickens and forms new blood vessels. If the egg is not fertilized, the uterus sheds this inside layer. This is called menstruation.

SEE ALSO: Animals; Biology; Endocrine System; Evolution; Human Body; Mammals; Plants; Pollination; Worms

✳ REPTILES
Reptiles form a group of egg-laying vertebrates (animals with backbones) with scaly skin. There are about 6,000 different species of reptiles.

Alligators, snakes, turtles, and lizards are all reptiles. Reptiles share a number of characteristics. They all have internal skeletons. They are covered in dry, scaly skin. They breathe air through their lungs.

All reptiles are ectothermic, or cold-blooded. This means that their body temperature is entirely dependent on the temperature of their environment. Reptile species have various ways to control their temperatures. Some move to shady areas or burrow in sand when it gets too hot. Others change their skin color to absorb or reflect heat.

Most reptiles, except for snakes and some lizards, have four legs, each ending in a foot with five clawed toes. Most females lay eggs that hatch outside the body, although some lizards give birth to live

young. Reptile eggs dry out easily, so females lay them in damp places. Newborn reptiles resemble their parents—they do not go through stages of development like insects or amphibians do.

The first reptiles evolved about 300 million years ago. Most scientists believe that reptiles are the ancestors of birds and mammals. The dinosaurs were among the reptilian species that are now extinct. Reptiles exist throughout the temperate and tropical parts of the world, although they are more common in warmer areas.

Alligators and crocodiles
Alligators, crocodiles, caimans, and gavials belong to a group called the crocodilians. The crocodilians have long tails and large jaws, and live in or near water.

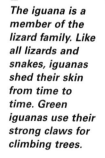

AMAZING FACTS !

A tortoise named Tui Mala died in 1965, aged at least 188. It belonged to the royal family of the Pacific nation of Tonga. The Cairo Zoo in Egypt claims that one of its Galápagos tortoises is more than 260 years old.

The Gila monster of the Southwestern United States and its close relative, the beaded lizard of Mexico, are poisonous. Their bite can kill other animals, but it is rarely fatal to people.

They feed mainly on fish and birds, but larger crocodilians can attack dogs, cattle, and people.

Snakes

Snakes are long, slender reptiles that have no legs. There are about 3,000 species. Most live in warm climates. Some snakes have special glands in their mouth that produce venom (poison), which they inject into their prey through hollow fangs.

Turtles and tortoises

Reptiles with hard, bony shells are called chelonians. Those that live on water are usually called turtles, and those that live on land are called tortoises. The Native American name *terrapin* usually refers to small freshwater turtles, especially those used for food. There are about 250 species of turtles. They range in size from tiny bog turtles, about 3 in. (7.6 cm) long, to massive leatherbacks that can reach almost 9 ft. (2.7 m) in length and weigh 1,500 lb. (680 kg).

A chelonian's shell is made of two parts joined by bony bridges. The upper part is called the carapace; the lower part is called the plastron. The animal uses the shell for protection, drawing its head and legs inside when in danger. Some species, such as mud turtles, can shut their shells completely. Others squirt out unpleasant fluids, or bite and claw their enemies.

Most turtles can move slowly on land. Strangely, freshwater turtles can move faster on land than most tortoises.

Lizards and tuataras

Chameleons, iguanas, skinks, monitors, anoles, and geckos are all types of lizards. Most lizards have four legs, although some have two, or even none. All lizards have shoulder bones, which snakes lack. The skulls of lizards are also more complex than those of snakes.

Most lizards are less than 16 in. (40 cm) long, but the largest, the Komodo dragon, can grow to 10 ft. (3 m) in length and reach weights of 300 lb. (136 kg). Some geckos are less than ¾ in. (2 cm) long, making them the smallest reptiles.

Scientists classify the tuatara, found only on islands off the coast of New Zealand, as a separate group, although it looks similar to a lizard. In common with some lizards, it has a third eye, on top of its head. It can remain active at 52°F (11°C),

The iguana is a member of the lizard family. Like all lizards and snakes, iguanas shed their skin from time to time. Green iguanas use their strong claws for climbing trees.

The diamondback terrapin is native to the salt marshes of the East Coast of the United States. Its meat is eaten as a delicacy.

a temperature that is too cold for most reptiles. It is the last surviving member of a reptilian group that was common in prehistoric times.

SEE ALSO: Alligators and Crocodiles; Animals; Dinosaurs; Evolution; Snakes

*RESPIRATORY SYSTEM *LUNGS AND RESPIRATORY SYSTEM

* REVERE, PAUL (1735–1818)

Paul Revere was a hero of the American Revolution (1775–81). His midnight ride is one of the great legendary acts in the history of the United States.

Portrait of Paul Revere, *painted by John Singleton Copley. Revere took an active part in the American Revolution and the events leading up to it.*

Paul Revere was born in Boston, Massachusetts. His father died when Paul was 19, and he took over the family silversmith business. He built up a reputation as one of the best silversmiths in America.

Revere joined in anti-British protests against the Stamp Act of 1765, which placed a tax on newspapers, business papers, and other items. He also took part in the Boston Tea Party of 1773—a protest against a tax on tea.

In 1775 patriots, fearing an attack by British soldiers, stored ammunition and supplies in Concord, Massachusetts. If the British attacked, they planned to warn other patriots by hanging lanterns in the steeple tower of Boston's North Church.

On April 18 colonists in Boston found out that the British governor was planning an attack on Concord. Revere alerted the

church deacon, who lighted the lanterns. Revere then took a boat across the Charles River to Charlestown. Alerted by the lanterns, patriots had a horse ready for him. Revere rode through the night warning patriots from Medford to Lexington. William Dawes and Samuel Prescott joined Revere at Lexington, and together they rode on to Concord. Halfway there Revere was captured and Dawes was unhorsed, but Prescott continued to Concord. Later that night the British released Revere but kept his horse. As he walked into Lexington, the first shots of the Revolution were being fired.

When the war ended, Revere returned to his work as a silversmith. In 1863 Henry Wadsworth Longfellow commemorated his feat in the poem "Paul Revere's Ride."

SEE ALSO: American Revolution

RHINOCEROSES

Rhinoceroses are large, thickset mammals with one or two horns. They live in Africa and Asia, but they may become extinct due to hunting.

Rhinoceroses, or rhinos, have heavy bodies with four short legs. They are hoofed animals, related to horses. Each of their feet has three toes.

Rhinos are herbivores, which means that they eat only grass and other plants. They move slowly and are usually quiet in temperament. But if they are cornered, they may become very fierce and can charge at speeds of about 30 miles (50 km) per hour. A charging rhinoceros can be very dangerous.

Horns

A rhinoceros's horns are just above its nostrils. The horns can be as long as 3 ft. (1 m) or more. They are made up of masses of tough hair packed very closely together. Rhinos are hunted for their horns because in some cultures rhino horn is thought to have magical powers.

Apart from hair on the tail and around their ears, rhinos are usually hairless. They have very tough, thick skin, which has no sweat glands. They have to cool themselves by bathing in water, mud, and dust.

Different species

There are five different species of rhinoceros. The black rhinoceros and the white rhinoceros live in Africa. Both of these species have two horns. The other three species—Indian, Javan, and Sumatran—live in Asia. Indian and Javan rhinos have one horn and deep folds that divide their skin into great, shieldlike sections. The Sumatran rhino has two horns, and its skin is not so deeply folded. Its body has a covering of short hair.

The Sumatran is the smallest rhino. It usually weighs less than 1 ton. At the shoulder, it measures about 3 ft. (1 m) high. The African white rhinoceros is the largest species. It weighs about three times more than the Sumatran and is about twice as high at the shoulder.

Families

Rhinoceroses usually live alone, but they are sometimes found in small family groups. Female rhinos give birth to one calf at a time. The calf is born about 18 months after mating and stays with the mother for several years.

A male Sumatran rhinoceros eating leaves. Rhinoceroses do not hunt other animals for food. They eat only grass and other plants.

SEE ALSO: Animals; Endangered Species; Mammals

505

✳ RIVERS

A river is a natural stream of freshwater that flows in a definite channel. Rivers range in length from tiny streams to the mighty Nile and Amazon.

A river estuary in northwestern Madagascar. The soil is not fertile, and salt marshes have formed.
▶

When rain falls, some of it flows downhill. Sometimes water gouges a gully out of the ground as it moves. If there is enough water to provide a constant flow, and if it moves quickly enough to cut a channel, then a river often forms. Some rivers start high up in the mountains, where melted snow combines with rain to create fast-flowing rivers.

The place where a river begins is called its source. Every river flows through a river valley. The place where the river ends is called a mouth—this is usually the place where it flows into another river, a lake, or the sea.

The water of most rivers picks up soil and other matter as it flows. If the river ends at a quiet sea or lake, it will deposit this matter at the mouth. This deposit is called a delta, and it usually includes plenty of fertile soil. When tides at the mouth of the river are strong, however, they carry away the soil and no delta is formed. Some rivers end in estuaries. They have drowned mouths, where the land sank and the oceans rose, submerging the lowest parts of the river.

The importance of rivers

Rivers can be rich in life, especially in fish and plants. They are also valuable areas for recreation and transportation. River barges carry heavy cargoes on rivers such as the Illinois, Mississippi, Ohio, and Hudson. River deltas often provide rich farming areas. Increasingly the energy of rivers is harnessed to create electricity.

THE WORLD'S LONGEST RIVERS	
Nile, Africa	4,145 mi. (6,670 km)
Amazon, South America	4,007 mi. (6,447 km)
Chang Jiang (Yangtze), Asia	3,915 mi. (6,299 km)
Mississippi-Missouri, North America	3,741 mi. (6,019 km)
Yenisey-Angara, Asia	3,442 mi. (5,538 km)
Huang He (Yellow River), Asia	3,395 mi. (5,463 km)
Ob, Asia	3,230 mi. (5,197 km)
Paraná-Río de la Plata, South America	3,032 mi. (4,878 km)
Congo, Africa	2,920 mi. (4,700 km)
Lena, Asia	2,734 mi. (4,399 km)

SEE ALSO: Dams; Egypt; Floods; Geography; Lakes; Mountains and Valleys; Natural Resources; United States Geography; Water

ROADS

A well-planned, well-built network of roads is vital to modern society. Building a modern road requires planning and many people working together.

Thousands of years ago, people found their way through forests by following the tracks of wild animals. Later they filled ruts with soil and laid logs over wet spots. This was the beginning of road construction.

Many of the great ancient civilizations built roads, but the most impressive constructions were those of the Romans. They built more than 50,000 miles (80,500 km) of roads throughout their empire, some of which still exist today.

After the end of the Western Roman Empire in the fifth century, the quality of roads declined. It was not until the 1700s that French and English engineers began to construct high-quality, long-lasting roads for the increasing amount of traffic.

In the 1900s, as cars became the most popular form of transportation, good road networks became vital to the world's economies. For many people, the interstates and freeways of the United States symbolize progress and freedom.

Modern roads

The first step in building a modern road is planning the route. Surveyors, engineers, and government representatives consider the amount of traffic that a road might take now and many years into the future. This will determine the road's width, the number of lanes, and the strength of the surface. Builders have to determine how well the soil drains on the proposed routes and must consider what the road will displace. New roads sometimes cut through areas such as forests, and there are environmental considerations, such as

A Roman road in Petra, Jordan. The Romans built roads to link the different parts of their empire.

the destruction of wildlife habitats. If the route runs through private property, the owners will have to be paid.

After the planning, construction can begin. Bulldozers clear a path for the foundation, or roadbed. Earth and stones, called fill, are laid down, and large rollers press down the fill to make it level. Pipes are laid to drain away water. The next step is to put down two or more layers of rocks and stones. The bottom layer consists of large stones; the next layer has smaller stones, and so on. The surface layer of the road must be strong and watertight. This pavement layer is made of either concrete or a material such as asphalt or tar.

SEE ALSO: Cars; Roman Empire

✳ ROBOTS

A robot is a machine capable of being set up and programmed to perform a wide variety of tasks for which it must physically move itself or other objects.

For hundreds of years people fantasized about creating artificial forms of life clever enough to perform tasks. The first use of the word *robot* was by the Czech dramatist Karel Capek in 1921 in his play *R.U.R.* (for Rossum's Universal Robots). The play was about a man who creates humanlike machines to work in his factory. Capek coined the word *robot* from the Czech word *robota*, meaning "work" or "slavery."

The first robot was developed by American inventors George Devol and Joseph Engelberger in 1958. General Motors purchased the first industrial robot and installed it in a Trenton, New Jersey, automobile factory to lift and stack hot pieces of metal.

"Asimo" the robot has been designed to perform basic tasks, such as walking up and down stairs and greeting people.

Use of robots today

Today commercial robots are available in two basic types: manipulator and mobile. A robot manipulator looks like a mechanical arm and may range in length from 12 in. (30 cm) to 12 ft. (3.7 m) or longer. Most robots used today are manipulators. Mobile robots roll on wheels from place to place. So far they have only a few practical applications. However, mobile robots are being developed in many research laboratories. Researchers have built a humanoid (humanlike robot) that can walk slowly, turn, and climb stairs.

Robots have "brains" that are computers programmed for the jobs they do. Some robots have powerful computers, but they cannot think in the way that people can. It is possible to program a robot to perform the exact motions needed to dust a room, for example, but it cannot decide whether or not the room needs dusting.

Many robots today can recognize objects using a special computer that translates a television picture into a form the robot's brain can understand. Others can "talk" using a device called a voice synthesizer. Industrial robots perform tasks that people find difficult, dangerous, or boring, such as welding, pouring hot metal, and spraying paint. Robots are very accurate and precise. They are also important in space exploration. In 1997, for example, a robotic rover explored the surface of Mars, studying its soil and rocks.

Robots are also used in medicine. One kind of robot responds to a surgeon's voice by moving a small video camera inserted inside the patient's body through a tiny incision, or cut. This allows the surgeon to operate through small incisions while watching a video monitor. Small cuts heal much more quickly than large ones.

Scientists are continually improving robot technology. Some people fear that as robots become more useful, people will not be able to find jobs. Others believe that the robot industry will open up new and more interesting jobs for people.

SEE ALSO: Computers; Manufacturing; Mars; Space Exploration; Surgery; Technology

✱ ROCKETS

A rocket is a device used to propel a vehicle, often a spacecraft. However, rockets can also be used to move cars, boats, and aircraft.

In its simplest form, a rocket is a tube of fuel that is closed at one end and open at the other. As the fuel burns, it creates hot gases that expand and rush out of the open end. This action is called thrust, and it causes the rocket to move in the opposite direction from the hot gases. The expanding gases are released through a chemical reaction. The chemicals that produce this reaction are called propellants. Rocket propellants can be either liquid or solid.

Rockets are suitable for use in outer space for two main reasons. First, in order to burn, fuels must combine with a chemical known as an oxidizer. Large quantities of oxygen, which is the most common oxidizer, are present in the air, but there is almost no oxygen in outer space. Rockets, however, carry their own oxidizer, so they do not need oxygen from the air in order for their fuel to burn. Also, when a rocket moves through air, the air creates friction, or drag, which causes the rocket to slow down. Because there is no air in outer space, there is almost no drag against the rocket to slow it down.

History

The first rockets were invented in the 1200s by the Chinese. These early rockets were made by stuffing gunpowder into sections of bamboo tubing. They were used as weapons, to send signals, or to create fireworks displays. However, it was not until the mid-1900s that the principles of rocket propulsion were understood well enough for them to be used for journeys into space. Russian inventor Konstantin Tsiolkovsky developed the ideas that made space travel in rockets possible. He published his theories in 1903. Another important step came in 1917, when German scientist Hermann Oberth proposed using a liquid fuel for rockets. The first liquid-fuel rocket to fly successfully was launched by American scientist Robert Goddard in 1926.

During World War II (1939–45), German scientist Wernher von Braun led a team of scientists in the development of the V-2 rocket, which became the first long-range guided missile. After the war, he and other German scientists worked in the United States developing other missiles and rockets, including the *Saturn V* rocket that launched U.S. astronauts to the moon in 1969. Since then, rockets have become more powerful and efficient. They are still an essential part of space travel.

▲ *The space capsule Friendship 7, launched in 1962, was the first manned U.S. rocket-propelled vehicle to orbit the earth.*

SEE ALSO: Spacecraft; Space Exploration

✳ RODENTS

Rodents are mammals that gnaw. About 50 percent of all mammal species are rodents. They include squirrels, rats, mice, and porcupines.

The word *rodent* comes from a Latin word that means "to gnaw." The easiest way to identify a rodent is to study the animal's teeth. Every rodent has four gnawing teeth, called incisors. They are shaped like chisels. They keep growing throughout the animal's lifetime, but they wear against each other, which means that they remain a constant length. All rodents eat plants. Some also eat eggs, insects, and other small animals. Many rodents have cheek pouches in which they transport food to storage places.

Scientists group rodents into three main divisions: squirrels and their relatives; rats and mice; and porcupines and their relatives.

Squirrels and their relatives

Tree squirrels have thick, plumed tails that can aid balance and warm the animal as it sleeps. They live in holes in trees or in leaf nests. Flying squirrels have membranes of skin joining their front and rear legs. They use them to glide from tree to tree, covering up to 150 ft. (46 m) in one leap.

Chipmunks, marmots, and prairie dogs are members of the same group. Chipmunks are ground squirrels common in North America. Marmots, including groundhogs, or woodchucks, are large, heavy-bodied relatives of squirrels. They have short legs and tails. The slightly smaller

Kangaroo rats and their relatives play an important part in the growth of Indian rice grass, whose seeds provide their food.

prairie dog looks very similar. Chipmunks, marmots, and prairie dogs live in burrows that they dig underground.

Rats and mice

Rats and mice are the most abundant of all rodents. The house mouse and the brown rat have populated most areas of the world. Both species breed very quickly throughout the year. The brown rat is one of the most destructive creatures on the planet. It destroys millions of dollars' worth of food every year and spreads serious diseases.

Kangaroo rats and their close relatives, on the other hand, are responsible for the production of the food that they live on. They bury thousands of Indian rice-grass seeds during the brief growing season, but often do not return to dig up and eat the seeds. Many of the seeds sprout and grow the following year.

Field mice, or voles, live in fields and woodlands, and can do great damage to crops. Lemmings, their close relations, live in the far northern areas of the world. In favorable weather conditions, lemmings breed very quickly. They migrate in great hordes, sometimes numbering many millions, in search of less crowded areas. Their enemies—foxes, wolves, and hawks—follow the hordes and feast on them. If the lemmings come to a sea cliff, they plunge over, and many drown in the water below. Finally the lemming population drops sharply. Other varieties of mice and rats include the muskrat, which lives in ponds and marshes, and the golden hamster, a popular household pet.

Beavers spend most of their lives near water. They build dams across small streams to form ponds.

AMAZING FACTS!

The largest rodent is the South American capybara. Some specimens are more than 4 ft. (1.2 m) long and weigh 100 lb. (45 kg).

The quills on the neck and back of crested porcupines from Africa and Asia can be as long as 20 in. (50 cm).

A beaver can fell trees as thick as 2 ft. (0.6 m) in diameter. Their dams can be more than 100 ft. (30 m) long and up to 10 ft. (3 m) high.

Porcupines and their relatives

The third group of rodents—porcupines—has only a few species. Unlike most rodents, the young of these species are born fully furred with their eyes open.

The porcupine's most obvious characteristic is its dense covering of sharp quills. An adult North American porcupine can be 3 ft. (1 m) long, weigh 30 lb. (14 kg), and have up to 30,000 quills. The quills are loosely attached and come out on contact with an attacker's skin. Each quill has many tiny barbs at its tip. If these dig their way deep into the attacker's face or mouth, the animal may be unable to eat and may die as a result.

Porcupines live in wooded areas and make homes in burrows or hollow trees. Their main food is tree bark.

Beavers are members of the same group of rodents. They are easily recognized by the flat, scaly tails that help them swim. Beavers use their incisors to cut trees to make their homes, or lodges, and dams to stabilize the water level of their habitat.

Guinea pigs, coypus, capybaras, and chinchillas also belong in this group. All these rodents originated in the Americas. Guinea pigs are still eaten in parts of South America, and coypus and chinchillas are bred for their fur.

SEE ALSO: Animals; Mammals; Migration

* RODGERS, RICHARD (1902–79)

Richard Rodgers composed theater music. With his partner, Oscar Hammerstein II (1895–1960), he created some of the best-loved musicals of all time.

Richard Rodgers composed many famous songs.

Richard Charles Rodgers was born in New York City. His early success came with the musical comedies he wrote in partnership with lyricist Lorenz Hart (1895–1943). These included *A Connecticut Yankee* (1927) and *Pal Joey* (1940).

When Hart died, Rodgers collaborated with Oscar Hammerstein II. Their first musical, *Oklahoma!* (1943), combined Rodgers's musical comedy talent with Hammerstein's operetta (a form of light musical theater) to produce one of the first true musical plays. The many successes that followed in the 1940s and 1950s included *Carousel* (1945), *South Pacific* (1949), and *The King and I* (1951). Rodgers and Hammerstein won many awards for their musicals.

After Hammerstein's death, Rodgers continued to write. His first solo project, *No Strings* (1962), won two awards. He also worked on a number of film and television projects. He died in 1979 at the age of 77. In 1990 the 46th Street Theatre on Broadway was renamed in his honor.

SEE ALSO: Films; Music

* ROMAN EMPIRE

The ancient city of Rome was the heart of one of the longest-lasting empires in history. It began as a small city-state in about 500 B.C.

At its height, the Roman Empire stretched from western Asia to Britain and Spain, and from the Danube River in Central Europe to the edge of the Sahara Desert in North Africa. The empire in the west lasted to A.D. 476, while in the east it endured another thousand years.

In creating their empire, the Romans were often ruthless. They destroyed entire cities and enslaved whole populations. However, they also brought peace, an advanced culture, and the rule of law. The many different peoples in the empire were united by common citizenship. They enjoyed free trade and travel over good roads and safe waterways, a high level of public services, and a uniform law code, government, and system of money.

The ruins of the Colosseum, which was ancient Rome's largest amphitheater, or public arena. On public holidays Romans enjoyed watching men, called gladiators, fight one another.

Latin, the Roman language, spread to all parts of the Western Empire. Even after the fall of the empire in the west, Latin remained a common language of educated people as well as the language of the Catholic Church, the law, medicine, and science. It is the ancestor of modern French, Italian, Spanish, Portuguese, and Romanian, which are known as the Romance languages.

Roman Empire at its greatest extent

North Sea

BRITANNIA

ATLANTIC OCEAN

GAUL

GERMANIA

Cologne

DACIA

CRIMEA

ASIA

Caspian Sea

Black Sea

IBERIA

CORSICA

ITALIA

Adriatic Sea

Rome

MACEDONIA

Byzantium

SARDINIA

GREECE

Athens

ANATOLIA

SYRIA

Carthage

SICILY

CYPRUS

MAURETANIA

CRETE

Mediterranean Sea

Jerusalem

Persian Gulf

AFRICA

Sahara Desert

EGYPT

Alexandria

ARABIA

Red Sea

Arabian Desert

The extent of the Roman Empire at its height in A.D. 116.

The republic

According to legend, the city of Rome was founded in 753 B.C. by Romulus, who became its first king. The last king was overthrown in 509 B.C., when a republic was established. It was ruled by popular assemblies of male citizens; the Senate, made up of wealthy nobles; and two chief magistrates, called consuls. The republic had an efficient and well-trained army, which by the end of the third century B.C. had conquered much of Italy. It then went on to conquer many of the lands bordering the Mediterranean Sea.

In the first century B.C., Julius Caesar became dictator (an all-powerful ruler). Many Romans were unhappy at having a single ruler, and Caesar was assassinated in 44 B.C. A struggle for power developed between Caesar's adopted son, Octavian, and Mark Antony. Octavian became the first emperor of Rome in 27 B.C., taking the name Augustus.

The empire

Under Augustus and later emperors, the Roman Empire expanded and enjoyed a period of prosperity and peace for 200 years. Roads were built to link all parts of the empire, and aqueducts carried water to the cities. The provinces were well governed, and many people in the provinces rose through the ranks of the army or civil service to become Roman citizens. Wealthy citizens built luxurious homes with central heating, and their households and farms were worked by slaves. However, poorer people lived crowded together in apartment houses.

As the empire grew, the old gods of Greece and early Rome no longer seemed relevant. People began to worship the emperors and to become interested in religions from the eastern part of the empire. Christianity began in the Roman province of Palestine. Early Christians were unpopular with the authorities and were often persecuted. However, the religion gradually spread throughout the empire and was eventually made legal in A.D. 313 by Emperor Constantine.

The empire's size made it increasingly difficult to defend all its borders. In the third century, Germanic peoples attacked Roman provinces in the north, and the

DID YOU KNOW?

The Roman army consisted of legions, each containing about 5,000 men. A soldier, or legionary, carried a spear, short sword, and shield, and wore a metal helmet, tunic (robe) and chest piece, shin guards, and sandals. When the army was on the move, it built a new camp every night. A soldier marched about 20 miles (32 km) in five hours before stopping to build another camp.

Sassanid kings of Persia (modern Iran) attacked the empire in the east. In 330 Emperor Constantine moved his capital to the old Greek city of Byzantium, which was renamed Constantinople for him. It is now Istanbul in Turkey. In 395 the empire was formally split into two—the Western Empire, with its capital in Rome, and the Eastern Empire, with its capital in Constantinople. The Western Empire was increasingly invaded by tribes from Asia and Germany. In 476 the last Western emperor, Romulus Augustulus, gave up the throne. The Eastern Empire survived as the Byzantine Empire until 1453.

SEE ALSO: Ancient Civilizations; Byzantine Empire; Caesar, Julius; Christianity; Cleopatra; Italy; Languages; Roads

✻ ROSETTA STONE

The Rosetta Stone is a large slab of granite dating from 196 B.C. Its discovery was the key to reading hieroglyphs—an ancient Egyptian form of writing.

King George III gave the Rosetta Stone to the British Museum in London in 1802.

The Rosetta Stone was found in the town of Rashid (Rosetta), Egypt, in 1799 by French soldiers. The stone's text had been written by priests to honor the pharaoh, or ruler. Three scripts were in use in Egypt at that time. The first was hieroglyphic. It was used for important documents or monuments. The second was demotic, the common script of Egypt. The third was Greek, the language of the rulers of Egypt.

Knowledge of how to read and write hieroglyphic script had been lost. In 1822 a French scholar called Jean-François Champollion finally managed to decipher hieroglyphs by using the Rosetta Stone.

He could read both Greek and Coptic (a script that combined the Greek alphabet with characters derived from hieroglyphs). He figured out what the demotic signs were in Coptic and what they stood for. He then traced the demotic signs back to hieroglyphic signs. By working out what some hieroglyphs stood for, Champollion was able to translate the other signs. His discovery meant that archaeologists could learn a lot more about ancient Egypt from old hieroglyphs.

SEE ALSO: Alphabet; Egypt, Ancient; Writing

RUSSIA AND THE BALTIC STATES

Until 1991 Russia was the dominant part of the Soviet Union, which also included the now independent Baltic states of Estonia, Latvia, and Lithuania.

Land

Russia—officially known as the Russian Federation—is the largest country in the world, comprising more than one-tenth of the earth's land surface. It extends over two continents—Europe and Asia. Within its borders there are vast plains, called steppes, and the Ural and Caucasus mountain ranges.

People

About 80 percent of the population is made up of ethnic Russians, who are descended from East Slavs. The Slavs probably first appeared in Europe about 2,000 years ago. Russia also has a number of non-Slavic minorities, including people of Turkic origins, such as the Tatars, and the Finno-Ugric, who live along the border with Finland. The Russian language is written in the Cyrillic alphabet, which is based on Greek letters.

Although religion was banned during Soviet rule, Russians have traditionally belonged to the Eastern Orthodox Church. Today about 40 percent of ethnic Russians consider themselves Orthodox Christians.

History

Over many centuries, the Goths, Huns, Vikings, Mongols, and others ruled over what is now called Russia. From 1462 the most important ruler was Grand Prince Ivan of Moscow. He was the first Russian leader to call himself *czar*, a word derived from the Roman title "caesar." Ivan greatly expanded the territory under Moscow's control.

In 1613 the Russian nobles elected Michael Romanov as czar, and his family ruled for the next 300 years. Under the Romanovs, the Russian Empire more than tripled in size. But Russia had a medieval labor system in which the peasants, or serfs, were bound by the law to the land owned by wealthy landowners. Nicholas II, the last czar, was forced to abdicate (give up his throne) during the Russian Revolution in 1917. He was later murdered.

Communism

After the revolution, Russia adopted Communism, a system of government based on the abolition of private property. The first leader of the Communist Party was Vladimir Lenin (1870–1924). He established the Union of Soviet Socialist

Russia's national flag

Latvia's national flag

Estonia's national flag

Lithuania's national flag

KEY FACTS

AREA: 6,700,000 sq. mi. (17,353,000 sq. km)	**SMALLEST COUNTRY:** Estonia
POPULATION: 154,357,000	**RELIGIONS:** Eastern Orthodoxy, Lutheranism, Roman Catholicism, Islam, Judaism
COUNTRIES: 4	
LARGEST COUNTRY: Russian Federation	**LANGUAGES:** Russian, Lithuanian, Latvian, Estonian, Polish, Tatar, Chuvash

St. Basil's Cathedral, with its distinctive onion-shaped domes, stands in Red Square at the heart of the Russian capital, Moscow.

Republics, also known as the USSR, or Soviet Union. After Lenin died, power went to Joseph Stalin (1879–1953), whose government murdered at least 20 million people and put many more in labor camps.

After 1945 the world was divided between the Soviet Union and its allies, and the West, especially the United States. This period was known as the Cold War. The last political leader of the Soviet Union was Mikhail Gorbachev (1931–). He introduced radical reforms, but he was unable to solve economic problems or control nationalist forces. When he stepped down as president in 1991, the Soviet Union had already ceased to exist. The former Soviet republics broke away from Russian domination and declared independence. Since then, Russia has suffered many problems, including inflation, racial unrest, and unemployment.

Estonia

Estonia is the smallest of the three Baltic countries. The land is mainly rolling plains, broken up by thousands of small rivers and lakes. Manufacturing is the most important economic activity, followed by farming and fishing. The capital is Tallinn.

Estonia was ruled by Germans, Danes, and Swedes until it became part of the Russian Empire in the 1700s. Estonia declared independence in 1918, but the Soviet Union invaded in 1940. Estonia remained a Soviet republic until 1991.

Latvia

Like Estonia, Latvia was ruled by other European powers until a brief period of independence between 1918 and 1940. It regained independence from the Soviet Union in 1991.

Latvia had one of the most effective economies of the Soviet states, and industry and agriculture are still strong. About half the population lives in or around the capital, Riga.

Lithuania

The largest and most populous of the Baltic countries, Lithuania is heavily industrialized, with two-thirds of its people living in cities. Unlike Estonia and Latvia, Lithuania was an independent state for many centuries. It united with Poland in 1569, and became part of the Russian Empire in 1795. Like its neighbors, it gained independence in 1918, was annexed by the Soviet Union in 1940, and became independent again in 1991.

SEE ALSO: Asia; Central Asia; Communism; Eastern Europe; Economics; Europe; World War II

✳ SACAJAWEA (ABOUT 1787–1812)

Sacajawea (or Sacagawea) was a Native American of the Shoshone Nation who accompanied the Lewis and Clark Expedition of 1804–06.

Sacajawea was born in what is now Idaho. She was captured by a Hidatsa raiding party when she was about 11 and taken to their village in present-day North Dakota. Later the Hidatsa sold her to a French-Canadian fur trader, Toussaint Charbonneau, who made her his wife.

In the fall of 1804, the expedition to the Pacific led by Meriwether Lewis and William Clark arrived in North Dakota. They hired Charbonneau as an interpreter and guide. It was agreed that Sacajawea would accompany the party. In February 1805 she gave birth to a boy, and, when the expedition set out again in April, she carried him on her back. She collected edible plants for the explorers, and when

the party met the Shoshone on August 17, she was able to negotiate for horses. Her presence reassured suspicious Native Americans that the party had peaceful intentions. Sacajawea and Charbonneau stayed with the expedition to the Pacific. On the return journey, they remained in North Dakota. Most historians believe that Sacajawea died in 1812 in South Dakota. However, some believe that she rejoined the Shoshone and died in 1884 in Wyoming.

SEE ALSO: Lewis, Meriwether; Native Americans

In 2000 the U.S. Mint put Sacajawea's portrait on the new dollar coin.

✳ SATELLITES

A satellite is an object that orbits a planet. Some, like the moon, are natural. Thousands of others are artificial. They improve our knowledge of space.

Earth's moon is a natural satellite, as are the moons that circle other planets. Most natural satellites contain large amounts of water or other liquids. Unusually, Earth's moon is made up of very dry rocks.

Artificial satellites are ones that have been designed and built on Earth, then launched into space. In 1957 the Soviet

Union launched the first artificial satellite, *Sputnik I*. Since then the designs have become more sophisticated. Satellites continue to provide information about space and Earth.

Many human-made satellites are used for astronomical research. On the ground we can see visible light coming from the

DID YOU KNOW?

Of the planets in the solar system, only Mercury and Venus have no known satellites.

The International Space Station *as seen from the* Discovery *spacecraft in 1999. The land below is part of China.*

stars, galaxies, and other objects in space. We cannot detect other types of radiation, such as X-rays, ultraviolet radiation, and microwaves, because they are absorbed by Earth's atmosphere. Satellites can detect these types of radiation and reveal important information about what is happening in the universe.

Satellites are also used to collect information about Earth. Some, such as the *Landsat* satellites, take pictures of the earth's surface and collect data about the oceans, natural resources, and changes in the environment. Others gather information about the weather. They help scientists give advance warning of hurricanes and other severe storms.

Many communication satellites orbit Earth. Since *Echo 1* was launched in 1960, satellites have transmitted radio and television programs around the world. In the 1990s, satellites were launched to form networks that cover the entire globe and provide

almost total worldwide access to telephone services and computers.

The military uses satellites for spying or for guiding missiles. Automobiles, ships, and airplanes can also use satellites as navigation aids.

A special type of satellite is the orbiting space station, where people live for months conducting research. The United States launched its first space station, *Skylab*, in 1973. Crew members on the Soviet *Mir* space station, launched in 1986, set a record by remaining in space for more than a year. In 1998 the United States, with other countries, began assembling the largest satellite to date, the *International Space Station*.

SEE ALSO: Communication; Earth; Geography; Moon; Navigation; Planets; Solar System; Spacecraft; Space Exploration; Warfare; Weather; X-rays

✳ SATURN

Saturn is the second-largest planet in the solar system. It is nine times larger than Earth and is made mainly of gases.

The most notable feature of Saturn is its ring system. Through a telescope, the rings appear as one gleaming white hoop, but a closer look reveals that they are, in fact, in three sections—an outer ring, a brighter middle ring, and the innermost ring, which is faint and almost transparent.

Saturn is more than nine times farther from the sun than Earth and takes much longer than Earth to complete a revolution, or orbit. Its axis of rotation is tilted. This causes it to be seen from different angles

on Earth during its orbit. For half of each revolution, astronomers see the northern side of Saturn, and for the other half they see the southern side.

Most of the planet consists of hydrogen and helium gas. Its outer atmosphere has clouds and haze caused by small amounts of ammonia, methane, and possibly water. The atmosphere gets denser and hotter toward the interior of the planet.

Astronomers now know that Saturn's ring system is made up of trillions of chunks of

▷ *Between 1996 and 2000 Saturn and its rings were photographed in greater detail than ever before by the Hubble Space Telescope, an astronomical observatory that orbits Earth.*

ice, some as small as a grain of sand, others larger than a house. Each chunk of ice orbits Saturn separately, but together they appear as an enormous ring encircling the planet. The ring system begins about 4,200 miles (6,800 km) above the cloudy surface of the planet.

Unsolved mysteries

Astronomers have plotted the orbits of 30 satellites, or moons, orbiting Saturn. There may be even more. Saturn emits more heat than it receives from the sun, and

astronomers have yet to discover what causes the intense heat at the center of the planet. They also do not know how Saturn's ring system was formed. To answer some of those questions, the *Cassini* space probe was launched in 1997. It is programmed to reach Saturn in 2004.

SEE ALSO: Astronomy; Planets; Solar System; Space Exploration

✱ SCANDINAVIA

The lands of the Vikings, in northwestern Europe, are now home to five thriving modern nations: Denmark, Finland, Iceland, Norway, and Sweden.

Denmark's national flag

Finland's national flag

Iceland's national flag

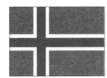
Norway's national flag

Sweden's national flag

The monarchies of Denmark, Norway, and Sweden form the geographical region of Scandinavia. In addition, the republics of Finland and Iceland are usually considered part of Scandinavia. All five countries cooperate on political, economic, and

cultural matters as members of the Nordic Council, formed in 1953. Denmark, Iceland, and Norway are members of the North Atlantic Treaty Organization (NATO). Denmark, Finland, and Sweden are members of the European Union (EU).

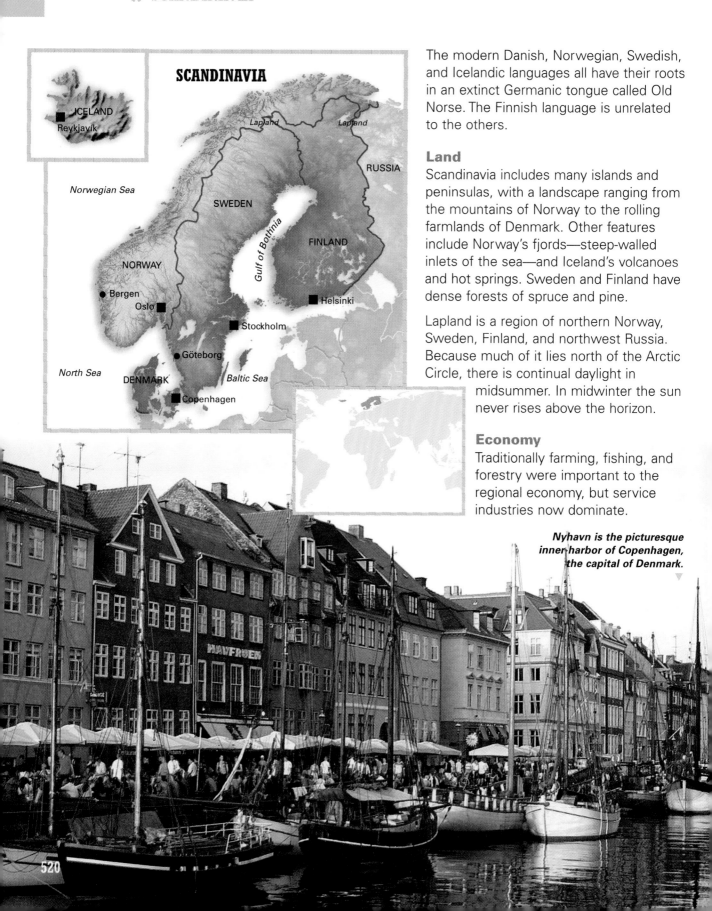

SCANDINAVIA

ICELAND
Reykjavík

Norwegian Sea

Lapland   Lapland

RUSSIA

SWEDEN

FINLAND

Gulf of Bothnia

NORWAY

Bergen
Oslo

Helsinki

Stockholm

Göteborg

North Sea

DENMARK   Baltic Sea

Copenhagen

The modern Danish, Norwegian, Swedish, and Icelandic languages all have their roots in an extinct Germanic tongue called Old Norse. The Finnish language is unrelated to the others.

Land

Scandinavia includes many islands and peninsulas, with a landscape ranging from the mountains of Norway to the rolling farmlands of Denmark. Other features include Norway's fjords—steep-walled inlets of the sea—and Iceland's volcanoes and hot springs. Sweden and Finland have dense forests of spruce and pine.

Lapland is a region of northern Norway, Sweden, Finland, and northwest Russia. Because much of it lies north of the Arctic Circle, there is continual daylight in midsummer. In midwinter the sun never rises above the horizon.

Economy

Traditionally farming, fishing, and forestry were important to the regional economy, but service industries now dominate.

Nyhavn is the picturesque inner harbor of Copenhagen, the capital of Denmark.

Scandinavians have very high standards of living, with access to high-quality, state-funded education and health care.

People and history

In the eighth century A.D., the Vikings and other Scandinavian warriors began to terrorize the coasts of Britain, Ireland, and France. Over the next 300 years their voyages took them as far west as North America. After 1100 a German union, the Hanseatic League, prevented expansion by Scandinavian powers into Europe.

In the 1300s, both Norway and Iceland came under the control of Denmark. In 1397 the Danish queen, Margaret, established the Kalmar Union, which joined Denmark, Norway, and Sweden under a single crown. Sweden left in 1523 and pushed the Danes out of the Swedish mainland in 1660, establishing the present boundary between the two countries. Sweden lost Finland to Russia in the early 1800s, during the Napoleonic Wars, but

later won control of Norway from Denmark. Norway declared independence from Sweden in 1905, and Finland became independent from Russia in 1917. Iceland was recognized as an independent country in 1918, but it remained linked to Denmark until 1944. Greenlanders have had self-rule since 1979, although the Danish monarch is their head of state.

KEY FACTS

AREA:
485,313 sq. mi.
(1,256,960 sq. km)
(excluding
Greenland)

POPULATION:
24,125,000

COUNTRIES:
5

**LARGEST
COUNTRY:**
Sweden

**SMALLEST
COUNTRY:**
Denmark

RELIGION:
Evangelical
Lutheranism

LANGUAGES:
Danish, Finnish,
Icelandic,
Norwegian,
Swedish

SEE ALSO:
Arctic;
Europe;
Exploration
and
Explorers;
Greenland;
Iceland;
Russia and
the Baltic
States;
Vikings

✳ SCIENTIFIC INSTRUMENTS

You can perform some experiments with just a notebook, a pencil, and your own observation. But most scientific work needs special instruments.

The instruments that scientists need depend on the work they are doing. Astronomers use telescopes to study the stars, planets, and other celestial objects. Chemists and biologists are more likely to use microscopes that enable them to see small objects in great detail. A research scientist at a large university laboratory will have different instruments from those in an elementary school.

Many scientific instruments are used to measure properties such as length, temperature, mass, or sound. Others provide heat or an electrical charge in

order to set off some kind of reaction. Some, such as test tubes and flasks, simply store substances.

Thermometers

Scientists often need to judge if something is getting hotter. They could do this by touching it. But what if the change in temperature is so small that the scientist cannot detect it? Scientists use thermometers to measure temperature.

Some thermometers contain gas or mercury—these substances expand, or get bigger, as they become hotter, and

A meteorologist measures the temperature at a climate station in Finland.

contract, or get smaller, as they become colder. The exact change in temperature can be gauged by looking at a scale of degrees Fahrenheit or Celsius that has previously been marked on the side of the column that contains the substance. Electrical thermometers measure electrical properties that change with temperature, such as the electrical resistance of metals. Radiation thermometers measure electromagnetic radiation.

Weighing machines

Scientists also need to be able to measure mass (the amount of matter in an object) accurately. They might want to find out whether animal or plant specimens have grown, or to measure the amount of water that has evaporated during a chemical reaction.

The earliest form of weighing machine was the balance, or scale. Some modern balances can register the mass of a tiny hair. Spring scales measure mass according to the pull on a vertical spring. The heavier the load, the further the spring stretches. Fan scales show the mass of the load in a small window. Modern scales often use computers to measure the mass of an object. They can give readings that are accurate to the tiniest fraction of a gram.

Heating instruments

There are many ways to heat a substance or an object. In a scientific experiment, it is often necessary to ensure that the heating device produces a constant supply of heat. It must also be safe to use. The Bunsen burner, first built in 1855, uses natural gas to produce a clean, hot flame that can be controlled safely and easily. Another source of heat is the incubator. It maintains a constant temperature for biological specimens such as unhatched eggs. A thermostat controls the temperature.

Thermometers are used by doctors to measure the body temperature of their patients.

AMAZING FACTS !

An electronic balance made in Germany can measure weight as small as that of the ink in the period at the end of this sentence.

Microscopes and magnifiers
Scientists often have to study small things. They use a magnifying glass or, for more detailed work, a microscope.

Computers and science
Scientists use computers to perform calculations quickly and accurately. Even instruments that have been in use for years, such as balances, are controlled by computerized microprocessors.

THE MICROMETER GAUGE

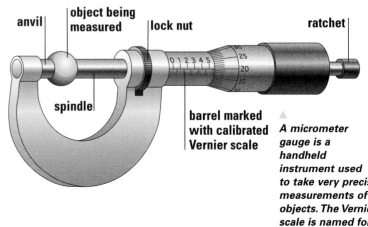

anvil | object being measured | lock nut | ratchet

spindle

barrel marked with calibrated Vernier scale

▲ *A micrometer gauge is a handheld instrument used to take very precise measurements of objects. The Vernier scale is named for its inventor, the French scientist Pierre Vernier (about 1580–1637).*

SEE ALSO: Computers; Heat; Matter; Microscopes; Scientists; Telescopes

✳ SCIENTISTS
Scientists are people who study or practice any of the subjects classified as sciences. Some do research; others find practical uses for new discoveries.

◄ *Linus Pauling (1901–94) won the Nobel Prize in chemistry in 1954 and the Nobel Peace Prize in 1962. He is the only person to have won two unshared Nobel Prizes.*

IMPORTANT SCIENTISTS

The following are just a few of the world's greatest scientists. The "see also" box indicates entries on some others.

Thales of Miletus (about 625–547 B.C.)
Ancient Greek who concluded that physical forces, rather than the gods, caused natural phenomena such as weather.

Copernicus, Nicolaus (1473–1543)
Polish astronomer who first figured out that the earth revolves on an axis and orbits the sun.

Bacon, Francis (1561–1626)
English philosopher who defined the scientific method of observation and experimentation.

Kepler, Johannes (1571–1630)
German astronomer who explained how the planets move.

Volta, Alessandro (Giuseppe Antonio Anastasio) (1745–1827)
Italian physicist who developed the first electric battery. Volt, the unit of electrical measurement, is named for him.

Lovelace, Ada Byron (1815–52)
English mathematician and scientist who wrote the first computer program.

Ehrlich, Paul (1854–1915)
German bacteriologist whose discoveries about the spread of diseases led to chemical agents being used as treatment.

Planck, Max (Karl Ernst Ludwig) (1858–1947)
German physicist who proposed the quantum theory of energy, later verified by Albert Einstein (1879–1955).

Hamilton, Alice (1869–1970)
American toxicologist who investigated industrial poisons, and the first woman professor at Harvard Medical School.

Fermi, Enrico (1901–54)
Italian-born American physicist whose research helped create the first atomic reactor.

Hawking, Stephen (William) (1942–)
English astrophysicist and mathematician who developed new theories about how the universe was formed.

English chemist Dorothy Crowfoot Hodgkin (1910–94) at work in her laboratory in 1964, the year she was awarded the Nobel Prize in chemistry.

A scientist is anyone whose job or area of study concerns the nature or behavior of the material or physical universe. Although scientists usually specialize in one area of either the physical sciences (for example, astronomy, chemistry, meteorology, and physics) or the life, or biological, sciences (botany and zoology), all scientists work in much the same way. They observe, measure, and experiment.

The English word *scientist* comes from the Latin *scientia*, which means "knowledge." Yet although all science is knowledge, not all knowledge is science. Learning a foreign language, for example, is not a science because it does not involve scientific method—an investigation in which a problem is first identified, and then observations, experiments, and other relevant information are used to form theories that aim to solve the problem. By contrast, linguistics—the study of the development of languages and the ways people learn them—is a science.

Theory and practice

There are two types of research. Basic research tries to uncover new knowledge that has no immediate practical use. Applied research seeks knowledge that can be used to create new products or in other practical ways.

Scientists carrying out new research may be astronomers looking for new bodies in space or doctors trying to find cures for illnesses. Scientists in different fields use their own approaches and instruments to investigate problems. The most famous scientists are those who have made big breakthroughs leading to discoveries and inventions. Yet not all research need be original. For example, school pupils who use litmus paper to tell whether a substance is acid or alkaline are carrying out a form of research. They are using scientific method to determine facts through their own observations, rather than taking information on trust.

Many scientists work in industry. They make sure that established products are made in the right way, safely, and according to valid scientific principles. For example, pharmaceutical chemists may prepare thousands of capsules and pills every day. It is their responsibility to ensure that every product contains the same materials in the correct proportions.

SEE ALSO: Carson, Rachel; Curie, Marie and Pierre; Darwin, Charles; Einstein, Albert; Fleming, Alexander; Galilei, Galileo; Newton, Isaac; Nobel Prize; Pasteur, Louis

✳SCORPIONS see ✳SPIDERS AND SCORPIONS
✳SEAS see ✳OCEANS AND SEAS

✳ SEASHORES
The seashore is land alongside the edge of an ocean or sea. It is usually rocky or sandy. The ocean tides have a major impact on the appearance and ecology of seashores.

Seashores can vary greatly. They can be covered in rocks and broken shells, dotted with tidal pools and with areas covered in moss and seaweed. Or they can consist of yellow-white sand as far as the eye can see, fringed with palm trees and other exotic plant life. But seashores also have something in common—the fact that the ocean moves back and forth against them.

Tides
A tide is the regular rise and fall in the level of the sea. This is usually easy to see on a seashore, because the amount of land covered by water changes through the day. The time when the sea is at its highest level on the shore is called high tide, or high water. The time when the sea is at its lowest level, and the most land is exposed, is called low tide. The time difference between high and low tide is about 6 hours and 13 minutes. So, in most places, two high and two low tides take place in just over one day.

The difference in length between the points where high and low tide reach is called the tidal range. There may be vast differences in tidal ranges.

Elephant seals are found in coastal waters from southeastern Alaska to Baja California, and around Argentina.

➡

For example, in the Bay of Fundy, in eastern Canada, the tidal range can reach 50 ft. (15 m). In the Gulf of Mexico, it can be as small as 1 ft. (30 cm).

Tides are caused by the gravitational pull of the moon. Because the moon orbits Earth, it is nearer to different parts of Earth at different times, and its gravitational pull also differs. As it moves, it causes the ocean surface to bulge, forming a high tide. The moon takes about 24 hours and 50 minutes—a lunar day—to circle Earth, and in this time there are usually four tides.

The constant movement of the water against the land means that the seashore is constantly changing shape. The tide can wear away rock and other material—this is called erosion. It can also bring new deposits onto the seashore. These changes are usually very gradual.

Life on the seashore
Because the environment of the seashore changes each day, a wide variety of animal and plant life lives there. Typical inhabitants include crabs and other crustaceans; mollusks, such as snails and squids; and many varieties of seaweed. But the wildlife varies according to the climate, water temperature, and the composition of the shore. For example, the rocky shores of the North American Pacific coast are home to many animal species, such as acorn barnacles, sea urchins, octopuses, and starfish; and plants such as seaweeds, kelp, and algae. By comparison, the sandy areas on the Atlantic coast have much less diversity. Clams and crabs are among the most common species there.

Both coasts include bays and estuaries lined with marshland. Marsh plants include pickleweed and cord grass; oysters often live on the lower edge of the marshes, and the mud is full of worms and small shrimps.

Humans and the seashore
Many people live and work close to the sea. Sea fishermen moor their boats in harbors, to be within easy reach of their catch. Lighthouses are near cliffs to warn boats of rocky areas.

On some seashores, especially those covered by sandy beaches, leisure pursuits are an important part of the economy. People go there to swim, surf, sail, play beach volleyball, or simply to relax on the sands. In some areas, developers have changed the natural seashore, by replacing rocks with sand or by adding or removing trees. These alterations can have dangerous effects on the local ecology. Seashores can also be the sites of outlets for sewage and other waste products, which has a negative impact on nearby sea life.

A view of Highway 101 and Pistol River State Park from Cape Sebastian, Oregon, on the Pacific coast.

NATIONAL SEASHORES

In the United States, 10 areas of seashore are administered by the federal government because of their natural beauty or importance to the environment and wildlife. They are:

Assateague Island, MD/VA

Canaveral, FL

Cape Cod, MA

Cape Hatteras, NC

Cape Lookout, NC

Cumberland Island, GA

Fire Island, NY

Gulf Islands, FL/MS

Padre Island, TX

Point Reyes, CA

The chambered nautilus is a marine mollusk found in tropical Indo-Pacific waters. The brightly colored coiled shell is lined with mother-of-pearl and consists of about 36 chambers. The animal occupies the largest chamber in the front.

SEE ALSO: Corals and Coral Reefs; Crabs; Ecology; Fish; Gravity; Jellyfish; Moon; Oceans and Seas; Snails and Other Mollusks; Starfish and Other Echinoderms; Wetlands; Whales and Dolphins

✳ SEASONS

The four periods of the year called seasons—spring, summer, fall, and winter—are caused by the tilt of Earth's axis and Earth's revolution around the sun.

Once every 24 hours, Earth completes one rotation on its own axis, an imaginary line through the center of the planet between the North and South poles. Earth's rotation on its axis is what causes day and night—at any one time about half the earth faces the sun and is therefore in daylight; the other half faces away from the sun and is therefore in darkness.

Once each year, Earth completes one revolution in its orbit, or path, around the sun. Seasonal changes occur because Earth's axis is tilted at an angle of 23.5 degrees to the plane of its orbit around the sun. Because of this tilt, the Northern Hemisphere is closer to the sun than the

On Christmas Day, Greenland (top) is covered in snow, while natives of Australia (below) relax on the beach in the mid-summer heat. This seasonal contrast between the Northern and Southern hemispheres is caused by the earth's tilted axis.

Southern Hemisphere for one-half of the year. While it is spring and summer in North America, it is fall and winter in Australia. For the other half of the year, the situation is reversed.

In most places, the seasons bring changes in the length of daylight, temperature, and weather. The sun shines longer each day in spring and summer than in fall and winter. There is almost continuous night during fall and winter at both poles.

Some regions experience fewer seasonal changes than others. Areas near the equator receive about the same amount of sunlight throughout the year and have little change in temperature. Although the polar regions are always cold, temperatures there fluctuate on a seasonal basis.

Seasonal datelines

Scientists have worked out specific dates for when the seasons begin and end. From about March 21 to September 22, more of the Northern than the Southern Hemisphere faces toward the sun and is warmed by it. So, beginning on March 21 in the Northern Hemisphere, the seasons run as follows: spring, March 21–June 20; summer, June 21–September 22; fall, September 23–December 21; and winter, December 22–March 20. The seasons are reversed in the Southern Hemisphere, with spring beginning about September 23.

SEE ALSO: Climate; Earth; Sun

---

*SEEDS ⮞ *PLANTS

---

* SEUSS, DR. (1904–91)

Dr. Seuss was one of the world's best-loved children's authors and illustrators. He wrote more than 40 books with many fantastic characters.

Dr. Seuss wrote in a style that revolutionized books for beginning readers.

Theodor Seuss Geisel was born in Springfield, Massachusetts. After graduating from college and studying at Oxford University in England, he became an advertising illustrator.

His first children's book, *And to Think That I Saw It on Mulberry Street*, was published in 1937 under the name Dr. Seuss. His picture books combined nonsense and rhyme to tell a moral. One of his most popular stories, *The Cat in the Hat* (1957), uses only 175 words to tell a story easy enough for first-graders to read on their own. Other favorites for young readers are *Green Eggs and Ham* (1960) and *Hop on Pop* (1963).

Dr. Seuss also designed and produced animated cartoons. In 1950 he won an Academy Award for his animated film *Gerald McBoing-Boing*. The book *How the Grinch Stole Christmas!* (1957) became a television cartoon and later a movie.

In 1980 Dr. Seuss received the Laura Ingalls Wilder Medal for his contribution to children's literature. Millions of copies of his books have been sold worldwide.

SEE ALSO: Cartoons and Animation; Children's Authors; Wilder, Laura Ingalls

* SHAKESPEARE, WILLIAM (1564–1616)

William Shakespeare is widely regarded as the world's greatest playwright. He was born in England during the reign of Queen Elizabeth I.

William Shakespeare's birthplace was the small town of Stratford-on-Avon. He was taught at the local school. When he was 18, he married Anne Hathaway, and they had three children. By 1592 he was working in London as an actor and had written several plays.

In 1592 London theaters were closed due to a plague, and Shakespeare began to write poetry. When the theaters reopened, he joined a company of actors called the Chamberlain's Men (later the King's Men, for King James I). They were so successful that they built their own theater, named the Globe. Most of Shakespeare's plays were first performed there.

Shakespeare wrote 36 dramas, including history plays such as *Henry V*, comedies such as *As You Like It*, and tragedies such as *Hamlet*. He spent most of his last years in Stratford. He was buried in the local church.

Shakespeare may have played the Ghost in the first production of Hamlet.

SEE ALSO: Literature; Theater

* SHARKS

Sharks, skates, and rays are sleek hunters of the seas. Their skeletons are made of cartilage, while the skeletons of most other fish are made of bone.

Sharks, skates, and rays are found worldwide. Most species live in warm, shallow waters in or near the Tropics, but they may roam great distances. A few species are found in freshwater.

There are about 250 species of sharks. Some are less than 8 in. (20 cm) long. The whale shark, up to 60 ft. (18 m) long, is the largest of all fish.

Skates and rays number about 340 species. The "wings" of the largest, the manta ray, may span 23 ft. (7 m). It swims near the surface, but skates and most other rays lurk on the bottom.

A shark has rough, scaly skin. It usually has eight fins, including two winglike chest (pectoral) fins. Skates and rays have smoother skin and fewer fins. Their pectoral fins are joined to their heads.

The strong jaws of these fish are lined with many teeth, which are arranged in rows. As the outer row of teeth wears out, the next row comes into use. Dogfish and most rays use several rows of teeth at the same time.

Skates, rays, and most sharks have five gill openings behind each eye. Some sharks have six or seven gills. Gills take oxygen from the water.

Lifestyle
Sharks, skates, and rays feed mainly on bony fish, squid, and

The blue shark is one of the most common and wide-ranging sharks. It eats mainly squid and fish, but has been known to attack humans.

crustaceans, or shellfish. Whale sharks, basking sharks, and manta rays sieve tiny animals from mouthfuls of seawater. Using their superb sense of smell, sharks can track prey from afar. The teeth of sharks are extremely effective for capturing and eating prey. Skates and most rays lie in ambush on the seabed, waiting for prey. Torpedo and electric rays stun their victims with electric charges. Stingrays have venomous spines for defense.

Skates and some sharks lay leathery eggs in the sea. Most young sharks and rays, however, develop inside the mother before being "live-born," like mammals.

SEE ALSO: Animals; Fish

* SHIPS AND BOATS

For thousands of years people have used ships and boats to trade goods, fight their enemies, and explore the world. They are also used for pleasure.

A ship or boat is a watertight, waterborne vessel usually powered by oars, sails, steam turbines, or internal-combustion engines. The back of a ship or boat is called the stern; the front is the bow. The body of the boat is called the hull. Facing forward, the left side is known as port and the right side as starboard.

Types of ships
Ships are large seagoing craft such as cargo vessels, oil tankers, warships, and cruise liners. The word *boat* is normally used to describe smaller craft, ranging from yachts and motor cruisers to racing dinghies and open rowboats.

Some vessels have unusual designs. Aircraft carriers serve as oceangoing airstrips. Submarines can travel under the water and are used mostly as warships or for exploration. Hydrofoils skim over the water on skilike struts designed so that their hulls can lift clear out of the water at high speeds. Hovercraft sail on a cushion of air a few inches above the surface of the water. Catamarans have two hulls; trimarans have three hulls.

History
The earliest craft were probably hollowed-out logs, bundles of reeds, and rafts made with animal skins. By 3000 B.C., ancient Egyptians had built the first boats made of wooden planks. They were propelled by oars and a single square sail.

The Chinese were the first to invent the rudder (a fixed underwater device that steers a ship), in the fourth century B.C.;

bulkheads (solid planked walls) that divide the hull into separate sections; and slatted sails. Their ships, called junks, were much more maneuverable than Western boats.

The age of sail

From the 13th century onward, larger ships were built to carry more cargo over greater distances. Instead of one mast with a single sail, ships had numerous sails on two or three masts. Dividing the sails in this way made them easier to handle. Open ships were replaced by decked ships. Many ships had several decks built on top of each other.

Warships carried oars as well as sails. Their crews used the oars in battle to get close to enemy ships. By the late 1500s, warships fought under sail, firing cannons at each other from a distance.

The American colonies built ships for sailing to Europe, ferrying goods, and whaling. After winning independence, the young American nation built armed frigates to protect shipping from pirates. The frigate *United States*, launched in 1797, was the first ship of the U.S. Navy.

The first scheduled sailing-ship service across the Atlantic began in 1816. The ships were called packet ships because they carried packets of mail as well as passengers and cargo. They took several weeks to cross the ocean.

The greatest of all sailing ships were the clippers. Built from the finest wood, these giants carried more sails than any ships before them. They were sleek, beautiful, and fast. In 1852 the clipper *Challenge* sailed across the Pacific in 18 days.

Steam power and metal

In the early 1800s, steam power began to take over from sail. The first steamships were propelled by twin paddle wheels.

Steam power was more reliable than sail power, since it did not depend on the winds. Another important development was the iron hull. Iron is stronger and longer-lasting than wood. In the late 1800s, steel replaced iron, screw propellers replaced paddle wheels, and new high-speed turbines were developed. The diesel engine replaced steam power during the early 1900s. This was the dawn of the age of the luxury liner, huge ships that carried passengers in style across the oceans. Mighty battleships and huge freighters were also launched at this time.

New developments

Modern cargo vessels include container ships—large, flat-decked craft that can be stacked high with sealed freight containers. The cargo may be loaded on and off railroad flatcars at the ports, or the containers may be rolled directly on and off the ship by trucks. The largest ships in the world are oil-carrying supertankers.

Powered by onboard nuclear reactors, modern submarines and aircraft carriers can sail for months without refueling. ➥

Launched in Japan in 1979, the world's largest ship was sunk by Iraqi jets in 1986, then salvaged and restored in 1990. Now named Jahre Viking, *it carries oil between the Middle East and the United States.*

AMAZING FACTS!

The world's largest ship is the oil supertanker *Jahre Viking*. It is 1,504 ft. (458 m) long and, when laden, displaces more than half a million tons of water. It will be dwarfed, however, by *Freedom*, a megaship planned by Florida engineer Norman L. Nixon. His "floating city," with apartment space for 70,000 people, will measure 4,320 ft. (1,317 m) and displace 2.7 million tons.

Hydrofoils and hovercraft are used for fast, short-range passenger services.

Air travel has taken many passengers away from ships because it is a quicker form of transport. However, cruise liners remain popular as "floating hotels," and ships continue to carry millions of tons of cargo every year.

SEE ALSO: Ancient Civilizations; China; Egypt, Ancient; Engines; Navigation; Pirates and Outlaws; Submarines; United States Armed Forces; Warfare

---

*SIGHT ➤ *EYES AND VISION

---

* SITTING BULL (ABOUT 1831–90)

Sitting Bull was a great and respected leader of the Hunkpapa Sioux tribe. His Native American name was Tatanka Iyotake.

Sitting Bull in 1885, when he joined Buffalo Bill's famous traveling Wild West Show for a few months.

▼

Sitting Bull was born on the Grand River in present-day South Dakota. He joined his first war party at the age of 14 and earned a reputation for courage. He helped extend Sioux hunting grounds westward. In 1863 he fought his first battle with white soldiers. For the next five years, the Sioux clashed with soldiers who invaded their hunting grounds. In 1867 Sitting Bull was made chief of the entire Sioux Nation.

Along with two other warriors, Crazy Horse and Gall, Sitting Bull fought to prevent the whites from mining gold in the Black Hills of South Dakota in the mid-1870s. He was a key figure in planning the defeat of Lieutenant Colonel George Custer at the Little Bighorn River in Montana in 1876.

White settlers killed the bison that provided food for the Sioux. In 1877, to avoid starvation, Sitting Bull led his people to Canada, but the Canadian government was unable to supply them with food. After four years Sitting Bull was forced to surrender and return to the United States. He was imprisoned for two years and then confined on the Standing Rock Reservation in South Dakota. In 1890 Sitting Bull was shot and killed by reservation police while resisting arrest for allegedly encouraging the Sioux to practice the Ghost Dance religion.

SEE ALSO: Crazy Horse; Native Americans

SKELETAL SYSTEM

The human skeleton supports other body structures. Bones also work with muscles to allow body parts to move. And they protect delicate organs.

The parts of the skeleton that let bones move are called joints. Bones fit together at joints and are held fast by tough straps, called ligaments. The joint surfaces are covered with gristly cartilage, which cushions the contact with other bones.

Bone is made up of two types of living tissue. The outer layer is hard, compact bone; the inner layer is cancellous, or spongy, bone. The holes in the spongy tissue and the hollows inside long bones are filled with marrow, inside which blood cells are formed. The outside of the bone is covered with a thin skin. It holds the blood vessels that carry food to the bone.

SECTION OF A BONE

A cutaway diagram of the human femur (thighbone).

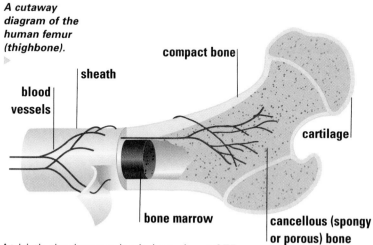

SKELETAL SYSTEM

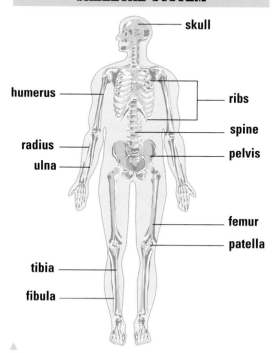

skull, humerus, ribs, spine, radius, ulna, pelvis, femur, patella, tibia, fibula

The human skeleton provides support so that we can stand upright and move about freely. It also protects internal organs from injury.

At birth the human body has about 275 bones; but as the body develops, many of these bones fuse together. The normal adult total is 206. They include 26 bones called vertebrae in the spinal column. The skull consists of eight bones that form the bowl-shape cranium covering the brain.

The humerus is the bone in the upper arm between the shoulder blade and the elbow. The forearm contains two bones— the radius and the ulna. The hand is made up of 27 bones—8 carpals (wrist bones), 5 metacarpals (palm and knuckles), and 14 phalanges, 2 for each thumb and 3 for each finger.

The largest bone in the human body is the thighbone, or femur. It joins the pelvis (hipbone) to the tibia (shinbone). The joint between the femur and the tibia is protected by the patella, or kneecap. The lower leg contains a fibula. The ankle and foot have 26 bones—7 tarsals, 5 metatarsals, and 14 phalanges.

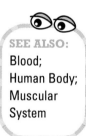

SEE ALSO:
Blood;
Human Body;
Muscular
System

533

✳ SKYSCRAPERS

Skyscrapers are very tall buildings with many stories. They are a practical way of accommodating large numbers of people in limited ground space.

SKYSCRAPER CONSTRUCTION

Rooftop access
Some skyscrapers have helipads on their roofs.

Steel frame
Long pieces of metal (girders) are bolted together for strength.

Reinforced concrete foundations
They are built deep in the ground.

Services
Electricity and water supplies are stored either between floors or on a special service floor.

Elevator shafts
They are usually deep in the building, where daylight is not needed.

Revolving doors
They minimize the effects of high winds.

▲
A typical modern skyscraper.

Construction of the earliest skyscrapers began in Chicago, Illinois, after the Great Fire of 1871 destroyed much of the city. The idea of tall buildings was not new, but they had never been built before because of the difficulties of getting people up and down hundreds of steps to their offices. The problem was solved after 1857, when American inventor Elisha Graves Otis installed the first passenger elevator in a five-story building in New York City. The electric elevator was introduced in 1889.

Skyscrapers can be built to great heights because their frameworks are made from steel. This metal is lighter and stronger than bricks and mortar, and can be used to support the floor, walls, and roof of each level independently. It also enables the building to withstand high winds. The stone exterior of the modern skyscraper is no more than a curtain wall—a wall that supports only its own weight. In conventional structures made of brick or stone, the walls—known as bearing walls—support the beams, which in turn support the floors and roof. This restricts the height of a building.

Onward and upward

The world's first skyscraper was the 10-story Chicago Home Insurance Building, completed in 1885. The first skyscraper to break the 100-story barrier was the Empire State Building in New York City, which opened in 1931.

Skyscrapers have mostly been built as offices, but some structures are more like minicities. For example, the John Hancock Center in Chicago, a 100-story building standing 1,127 ft. (344 m) high, contains apartments, restaurants, banks, theaters, and an observatory. In 1998 the Petronas Towers in Malaysia became the tallest skyscrapers, at 1,483 ft. (452 m). Union Square, in Hong Kong, is scheduled for completion in 2007. It will be 1,575 ft. (480 m) high.

SEE ALSO: Architecture; World Trade Center

SLAVERY

A slave is a person who is owned by and forced to work for another without payment or rights. Slavery goes back to ancient times.

Slavery flourished in the ancient civilizations of Egypt, Greece, and Rome, and in the Middle East and Asia. Although slavery went into decline in Christian Europe during the Middle Ages (about A.D. 500–1500), it was reintroduced at the beginning of the modern age, when colonial empires needed large numbers of laborers. That led to the African slave trade, which, over a period of about 300 years, subjected approximately 10 million black Africans to forced labor.

Slaves from Africa

The African slave trade began in the mid-1400s. Portuguese sea captains exploring the west coast of Africa began to bring back black people to be sold as slaves in Portugal and Spain. Early in the 1500s, African slaves were shipped to Hispaniola in the West Indies as labor when local Indians died from European diseases.

Slaves were first imported to the English settlements in the New World in the early 1600s. At first slaves there faced a limited period of slavery—21 years, or sometimes less. But by 1663 Virginia and Maryland had passed laws stating that slaves should serve for life, and that children born to slaves should also belong to the master. By 1715 there were about 23,000 slaves in Virginia and similar numbers in Maryland and the Carolinas.

There were fewer slaves in New England than in the South, but New Englanders were deeply involved in the slave trade. Slave ships were built in their shipyards, and New England rum was important in the "triangular trade" between New

England, Africa, and the West Indies. Rum and other goods were traded for slaves in Africa; the slaves were sold and traded in the West Indies for sugar and molasses, which were needed to supply the British, African, and American rum trade. Because the transport of the slaves across the Atlantic Ocean was the second stage of this three-stage process, it became known as the Middle Passage.

George Washington said that one of his first wishes after the American Revolution was to see slavery wiped out. In 1777 Vermont abolished slavery, followed in 1783 by Massachusetts. Pennsylvania, Connecticut, and Rhode Island all provided for the gradual abolition of slavery. In 1808 a law came into effect to end the slave trade. Slaves could no longer be imported, but slavery continued in the South. ➡

This picture shows European traders gathering slaves on the coast of West Africa in the late 1700s.

Slavery in the Cotton Kingdom

The South's economy relied on cotton, tobacco, and sugarcane. Free slave labor meant huge profits for plantation owners. Most slaves worked in the fields and were called field hands. Thousands more served as domestic staff, and a few did skilled work such as carpentry. The field hands were the most cruelly treated. A rebellion led by Nat Turner in 1831 scared slave owners into inflicting harsher punishments.

Southern cotton planters needed new land, so they used their political power to promote the spread of slavery westward. By 1848 the area under cotton cultivation, known as the Cotton Kingdom, stretched from South Carolina to Texas. However, most Northerners called for a ban on slavery in all the newly acquired territories.

War for emancipation

Eventually most Southerners felt that the only way to maintain their independence and their self-proclaimed right to own slaves was to secede (withdraw) from the United States. One by one, the Southern states seceded, and on April 12, 1861, forces of the new Confederate States of America attacked Fort Sumter, a U.S. Army post in South Carolina, starting the Civil War (1861–65).

On January 1, 1863, President Abraham Lincoln issued the final version of the Emancipation Proclamation, which decreed that slaves in the Confederate states were free. But it was not until 1865, when the 13th Amendment was passed, that slavery was formally abolished in the United States.

SEE ALSO: Abolition Movement; African Americans; Ancient Civilizations; Civil War; Confederacy; Douglass, Frederick; Emancipation Proclamation; Tubman, Harriet; Underground Railroad

The workers in this 19th-century picture of a Mississippi cotton plantation are all slaves.

✳ SLEEP ➡️ ✳ HEALTH

✳ SMELL ➡️ ✳ TASTE AND SMELL

SNAILS AND OTHER MOLLUSKS

Snails are the most familiar members of a group of animals called mollusks. Slugs, clams, octopuses, and squids are also mollusks.

Mollusks are invertebrates—animals without backbones. Their soft bodies are made of a boneless substance called the visceral mass. The visceral mass contains internal organs and is protected by a skinlike organ called the mantle. In some mollusks, the mantle produces a hard substance that forms a shell. All mollusks have some kind of muscular foot.

Snails

Snails belong to a class of mollusks called gastropods. A snail has a head, with a mouth, eyes, and tentacles, and a shell, usually in the shape of a spiral coil. Many species have a plate of hard material on the foot, and this plate closes like a door when the snail retreats into the shell. Snails can be male, female, or hermaphroditic—that is, possessing both male and female sex organs.

Different species of snails live on land and in fresh- and saltwater. Some species live less than a year, but European escargot snails can live for 35 years. Some snails carry disease and can be garden pests.

But they are an important part of the food chain. Other gastropods include slugs, which resemble snails without shells. Whelks, abalones, and conchs are also kinds of saltwater gastropods.

Other mollusks

Bivalves form the second-largest class of mollusks. They include clams, scallops, oysters, and mussels. They have flat bodies inside two hinged shells. Many bivalves provide food for humans.

Cephalopods include some of the largest species of mollusks. In this group, which includes octopuses and squids, the muscular foot has evolved into tentacles, which help the animal to catch prey. Other classes include scaphopods, which are mollusks with long, tubelike shells and a powerful foot that they use to burrow into the seabed, and polyplacophorans, or chitons, which are mollusks with a broad, sticky foot and a flat, oval body covered by eight overlapping shell plates. They usually cling to rocks and other hard surfaces.

Snails belong to the largest class of mollusks—the gastropods. Several species can be eaten by humans.

AMAZING FACTS!

The largest snail is the Australian trumpet snail, which can reach a length of about 30 in. (76 cm).

The largest mollusk is the giant squid, which can measure 57 ft. (17 m) in length, including its tentacles, and weigh more than 2 tons.

SEE ALSO: Animals; Seashores

✳ SNAKES

Snakes are reptiles that have long, slender bodies with no arms or legs. There are around 3,000 species of snakes.

Snakes are found in nearly all parts of the world, both in the water and on land. Most snakes live in tropical regions, although some have been found as far north as the Arctic Circle.

Characteristics

Snakes do not have movable eyelids, which gives them a glassy, unblinking stare. Their eyes never close. Like other reptiles, snakes have scaly skins and cannot regulate their body temperature from within. They therefore spend a lot of time seeking conditions that help them maintain a comfortable body temperature. They can raise their temperature by basking in the sun. And they can lower their temperature by moving into the shade or underground.

Many people think that snakes have slimy skins. However, like most reptiles, a snake's skin is dry to the touch. It does not grow with the animal, and has to be shed regularly. Snakes shed their skins all at once, leaving a hollow skin that is an exact copy of their body surface except that it is inside out, or inverted.

Snakes have more vertebrae (backbones) than other animals. This means that they can move in flexible ways that other animals cannot. Because snakes have no limbs, they use special techniques for movement. The most common way of moving is undulation. The snake presses different points of its body against fixed points, such as rocks, and the muscles that run along the length of its body contract alternately. This makes the snake move forward in an S-shaped motion.

Diet

Snakes are carnivores, or meat-eaters. They eat only other animals and their eggs. Snakes swallow their prey whole without chewing. They have powerful digestive systems that can dissolve bones. A snake's jaws are able to stretch so that it can eat prey larger than its head. After a big meal, many snakes can go for long periods without eating.

Snakes use two main approaches for killing their prey—constriction and poisoning with venom. Constrictors, such as boas and pythons, squeeze their prey very tightly by coiling their body around it and suffocating it to death.

Venomous snakes

Other snakes produce venom in special glands, which they inject into victims through grooves in their fangs. Large pit vipers and some cobras can deliver a bite that will kill a rat in seconds.

The emerald tree boa is found in South America. It gives birth to live young rather than laying eggs. When they are young, the boas are a dull orange color, but they turn green as they mature.
▼

In the United States there are four main types of venomous snakes—rattlesnakes, copperheads, cottonmouths, and coral snakes. Rattlesnakes, copperheads, and cottonmouths are pit vipers. Coral snakes belong to the cobra family and are found mainly in the southern states. Except for Maine, Alaska, and Hawaii, all states have at least one venomous snake species. But venomous snakes make up fewer than 20 percent of the snake species found in the United States, and lethal bites to humans from snakes are rare.

Snake senses

Snakes have several well-developed senses. Many snakes have good vision. Although they have no external ears or ear openings, some snakes seem sensitive to vibrations transmitted on the ground or through water.

Snakes use their forked tongues to detect smells in the air and pick up chemical molecules from surfaces. When the tips of the tongue are touched against a sense organ in the roof of the mouth known as Jacobson's organ, a snake is able to identify smells and use them to determine another animal's direction of travel.

Some snakes, including pit vipers and some boas and pythons, have a sense not known in other animals. They can detect small changes in heat. To do this, they use facial pits found either between the eye and the nostril or on the lips. This sense allows a snake to track prey in total darkness by detecting their body heat.

Life cycle

Some snakes give birth to live young, but most lay eggs. Snakes that live in temperate zones usually hatch in the late summer or early autumn. Snakes remain dormant during winter throughout most of North America. Snakes in colder mountainous areas often migrate to underground dens for winter.

In many parts of the world, snakes are in danger due to loss of their habitat, pollution, and overhunting. Some snakes are hunted for their skins. Others are collected for the pet trade.

▲ *An Egyptian cobra adopts a threatening posture. To scare off its enemies, it tries to appear bigger than it is by rising up and flaring its hood.*

SEE ALSO: Animals; Reptiles

✳ SOCCER

Soccer, or association football, is a ball game played by two teams. Each team tries to score points by putting the ball in the opposing team's goal.

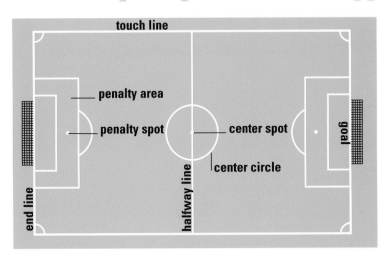

A soccer field diagram labeled: touch line, penalty area, penalty spot, center spot, center circle, goal, halfway line, end line.

A soccer field may be between 100 and 130 yards (90–120 m) long, and 50 to 100 yards (45–90 m) wide, but must be longer than it is broad. Goals are 8 yards (7.3 m) wide and 8 ft. (2.4 m) high.

SEE ALSO:
Olympic Games;
Sports

Kicking a ball around is a pastime that dates back thousands of years. Modern soccer began in England in the mid-1800s. It is now played by more than 150 million people worldwide and is an Olympic sport.

The field and players

The lines on the long sides of a soccer field are called touch lines. Those on the short sides are called end lines. The goals are in the center of the end lines. A team is made up of a goalkeeper and 10 other players used as forwards, defenders, and midfielders. The forwards, or strikers, are usually the goal scorers. The goalkeeper and defenders try to prevent the opposing team from scoring. The midfielders feed the ball between the

defenders and the forwards. After a goal, the team that is scored against kicks off to restart play. Professional games consist of two 45-minute halves with a 15-minute break at halftime.

Each team tries to move the ball toward the opponents' goal. When in a position to do so, a player kicks or heads the ball at the goal. If the ball crosses a touch line or an end line, the team that last touched it loses possession. A member of the other team returns the ball to the field.

No player except the goalkeeper is allowed to touch the ball with the arms or hands. Any other part of the body may be used. Free kicks are given to a team when an opposing player commits a violation, or foul. The main fouls are handling the ball, obstruction, and dangerous play. If a foul is committed by the defending team in the penalty area, a penalty kick is awarded to the attackers. The ball is kicked from the penalty spot with only the goalkeeper to stop it. Other players stand at least 10 yards away (outside the penalty area and the semicircular line at its edge).

World Cup

Soccer's biggest prize is the World Cup, held every four years between the world's top 24 teams. All nations belonging to the International Federation of Association Football (FIFA) can compete for a place in the championship.

Ronaldo was the leading forward for Brazil when it won the World Cup in 2002. Brazil has won the cup more often than any other country.

☀ SOIL

Soil is a thin layer of loose material on the surface of the earth. Beneath it is solid rock. The depth of soil can range from a few inches to several feet.

Soil is a mixture of rock and mineral particles, air, water, organisms, and the remains of once-living creatures. It began to form millions of years ago, as wind and rain wore down the rock on the earth's surface in a process called erosion. Tiny fragments of rock combined with material from dead animals and plants. Eventually this loose mixture covered much of the solid rock.

There are many different types of soil, depending on the amount of minerals they contain, the climate and location, the way humans use the soil, and the size of the rock particles. If most of the particles are very small, dense, and sticky, the soil is known as clay. Slightly larger particles make a silt soil. Even larger particles make sand. A soil mixture of sand, clay, and silt is called loam.

The decaying matter in soil is known as humus. It is important for soil fertility. It separates tightly packed rock particles to let in more air and water. It provides food for microorganisms in the soil and forms substances that plants use for growth.

In addition to microorganisms, many animals live in the soil. Some mammals, such as rabbits, make their burrows there. Their tunnels allow in more water and air. Earthworms act like tiny plows, turning over the soil to improve it in many ways.

Effects of human activity
Soil is vital to human life. Farmers and gardeners use it to grow crops, which provide food for people and for animals, such as cows, that supply humans with dairy products and meat. However, much of the soil on farmlands is damaged. Chemical fertilizers have killed the living matter in the soil. Intensive farming has taken out many minerals—soil needs periods of rest. Fertile soil has been worn away to leave rocks on which few plants can grow.

Recently some farmers have gone back to using natural fertilizers, such as compost. They do not try to squeeze such a high volume of crops from every square foot of soil. This will help maintain good soil for future generations.

▲
The soil surface of this wheat field in Washington State has been eroded—worn away by the action of wind and water.

SEE ALSO:
Agriculture;
Earth; Ecology;
Environment;
Geology;
Plants; Worms

☀ SOLAR POWER 🔜 ☀ ENERGY

✳ SOLAR SYSTEM

The solar system consists of the sun and all the planets and other bodies that revolve around it. It is shaped like a disk with the sun at its center.

THE PLANETS

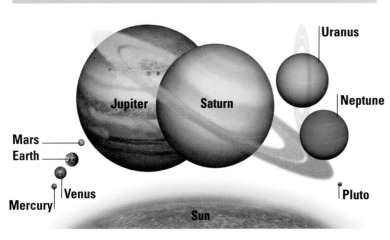

Uranus

Jupiter Saturn Neptune

Mars
Earth

Venus

Mercury Sun Pluto

▲
In this diagram, the nine known planets of the solar system and part of the sun have been brought closer together to give an idea of their relative sizes.

The largest objects orbiting the sun are the planets: Mercury, Venus, Earth, Mars, Jupiter, Saturn, Uranus, Neptune, and Pluto. Most planets have moons—natural bodies that revolve around them.

Asteroids and comets
Other planetary bodies orbiting the sun include thousands of tiny objects called asteroids and comets—chunks of ice, rock, and dust. The solar system also contains dust and gases left over from when it was formed.

All the planets and most asteroids revolve around the sun in nearly circular orbits (paths) that are in almost the same plane. They all move in counterclockwise orbits, as seen from above. Some moons have clockwise motion.

Theories about the solar system
Five planets—Mercury, Venus, Mars, Jupiter, and Saturn—are regularly visible from Earth and have been known since

ancient times. Around 300 B.C., some ancient Greek scientists suggested that the sun was the center of the solar system. Until the mid-1500s, however, most people believed that Earth was the center of the solar system and that everything else revolved around it. Then, in 1543 the Polish astronomer Nicolaus Copernicus (1473–1543) figured out that Earth and the other planets move through space in orbits around the sun.

By 1618 further discoveries by the German astronomer Johannes Kepler (1571–1630) led to what became known as Kepler's three laws of planetary motion. The English scientist Isaac Newton (1642–1727) used a form of math called calculus to show that gravity, the force that holds objects to Earth, also holds the planets in their orbits around the sun.

Distance from the sun
The German astronomer Johannes Bode (1747–1826) discovered a mathematical relationship in the distances of the planets from the sun. In 1781, when the German-born British astronomer William Herschel (1738–1822) discovered Uranus, it fit into Bode's pattern, as did many asteroids when they were discovered. Astronomers discovered Neptune in the 1840s and Pluto in 1930.

SEE ALSO: Astronomy; Comets, Meteors, and Asteroids; Earth; Galilei, Galileo; Gravity; Jupiter; Mars; Mercury; Moon; Neptune; Newton, Isaac; Planets; Pluto; Satellites; Saturn; Sun; Universe; Uranus; Venus

SOUND

Sounds are made by vibrations that pass through the air as sound waves. If the waves are detected by a receiver, like an ear, they are translated into sound.

Very fast, back-and-forth motions called vibrations are the source of all sounds. You can feel these vibrations if you pluck the string of a guitar or another stringed instrument. If you touch the string lightly, you can feel it moving. When the vibration stops, the sound stops.

Sound travels from a vibrating object to the ear by means of a carrier, or medium. The medium may be a solid, a liquid, or a gas. The most common carrier is air, which is a mixture of several gases.

Sound travels from its source in the form of waves. When pushed by a vibrating object, the molecules that make up the medium—for example, molecules of air—bunch up, or compress, and then expand. The effect is passed along to neighboring molecules, setting a compression wave in motion. The waves travel out in all directions, gradually becoming weaker until they die out.

The speed of sound is slower than the speed of light. That is why we hear thunder several seconds after seeing the lightning that caused the sound. Sound travels at different speeds depending on the medium through which it is passing. It travels four times faster in water than it does in air, and even faster in solids. Temperature also has an effect: Sound travels faster in warm air than in cold air. But at a given temperature, all sounds in the same medium have the same speed.

Wavelength, pitch, and frequency
The distance between one compression and the next is called the wavelength of a sound wave. Humans can hear sounds whose wavelengths in air are between about ¾ in. (2 cm) and about 69 ft. (21 m) long.

Pitch is the rate at which vibrations are produced. An object that vibrates 500 times per second causes a sound wave that vibrates at the rate of 500 cycles per second. (One cycle is a complete vibration back and forth.) This rate is usually expressed in hertz (Hz). The unit is named for the German scientist Heinrich Hertz (1857–94). The number of Hz is the frequency of the sound. The higher the frequency of a sound, the higher its pitch.

There is also a relationship between wavelength and frequency. Sounds with a high frequency, where there are many vibrations in a second, tend to have short wavelengths. Long wavelengths have a low frequency.

WAVES OF SOUND

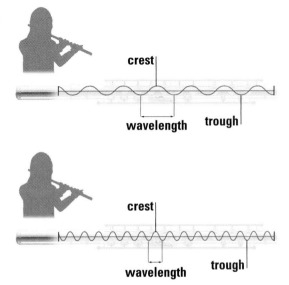

Sound waves repeat over and over. Waves have crests (peaks) and troughs (hollows between the peaks), with regular spacing between them. If a sound wave has a long wavelength, as in the upper diagram, a low note is produced. If the crests are closer together, as in the lower diagram, the note is higher.

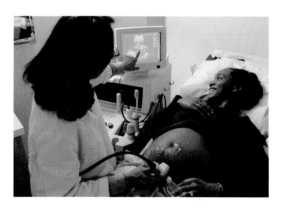

A doctor uses high-frequency sound waves—ultrasonography—to produce an image of an unborn child. It enables the doctor to monitor the baby's growth.

Loudness

As a sound wave moves, it disturbs the particles of the medium through which it travels.

The distance each particle moves is called the amplitude of the sound wave. Usually, the greater the amplitude, the louder the sound. However, loudness depends on the listener's sense of hearing. Two people listening to the same sound may not experience the same loudness.

Because of this, scientists cannot measure loudness. They can, however, measure the intensity of a sound—the amount of energy it produces. In most cases, the more intense a sound is, the louder we hear it.

Scientists work out the intensity of a sound by measuring the amplitude of the sound wave. Intensity is measured in units called decibels. A whisper that you can just hear from 5 ft. (1.5 m) away registers about 20 decibels. A noisy rock band is about 100 decibels. For most people, sounds of above 120 decibels become uncomfortable.

Echoes and sonar

Sound waves often bounce when they strike something. If you shout toward a wall on the other side of an empty space, you might hear an echo—the result of the sound waves that your shout created coming back to your ears.

Scientists have used echo to develop SOund NAvigation Ranging, or sonar. This technology uses sound signals to detect objects underwater. Operators bounce the

signals off objects. By measuring the time it takes for the echo to bounce back, they can calculate how far away the object is.

Ultrasound

The sound waves used in sonar are usually ultrasonic—this means that they have such a high frequency (over 20,000 Hz) that humans cannot hear them. Other species, such as dogs, can hear sounds at high frequencies. Dolphins and bats have a kind of built-in sonar system: They produce ultrasonic squeaks that are echoed back to them from solid objects like walls, allowing them to find their way underwater or in darkness.

Ultrasonic holography is a method of producing three-dimensional pictures with ultrasound. Using this technique, medical professionals can see live images inside a body. This is especially useful for studying unborn babies.

SEE ALSO: Bats; Dogs, Wolves, and Other Wild Dogs; Ears and Hearing; Music; Radio; Sound Recording; Whales and Dolphins

SOUND RECORDING

Sound recording is a means of preserving sound in a permanent form so that it can be reproduced at a later time.

◄ *At the dawn of the talking movie era in 1929, Leo the lion is filmed and recorded for the opening sequence of MGM films. Sound for a motion picture is recorded on special magnetic tape and transferred to the edge of the film as a series of light and dark areas. When the film is played, a beam of light from the projector passes through the film. It varies as the light and dark regions pass by, and the variations are converted back into sound.*

Cassettes, compact disks, and vinyl records are all methods of storing sound recordings. Machines, such as record players, tape recorders, and CD players, turn the recordings back into sound.

The oldest method of sound recording, the phonograph record, was invented by Thomas Alva Edison in 1877. Early recordings were acoustic—direct from the sound without converting it into any other form. The person making the recording spoke or sang loudly into a megaphone. Attached to the narrow end was a tightly stretched membrane, or diaphragm, that vibrated when hit by the sound waves made by the person's voice. The vibrations were transferred to a needle, or stylus, that engraved a rotating cylinder with grooves. The cylinder was later replaced by the flat phonograph disk. Playback was the reverse of the recording process. The playback needle vibrated the diaphragm, and the resulting sound was amplified (made louder) by the megaphone. From the 1920s, megaphones were replaced by microphones that converted sound waves into electrical waveforms.

At playback, the recorded patterns are converted back to electrical waveforms nearly identical to the originals. These waveforms are amplified and sent to a loudspeaker or headphones, where they produce sounds that are close imitations of the originals. ➡️

A *magnetophone was an early reel-to-reel tape recorder, first produced in the 1930s. Reel-to-reel tapes were replaced by cassette tapes, which contain both reels in a plastic housing.*

Magnetic recordings are made on thin plastic tape coated on one side with tiny metal particles. The tape passes over an electromagnet called the recording head. The head magnetizes the particles weakly or strongly depending on the electronic signals it receives. These variations form magnetic patterns on the tape. This is known as analog recording.

To play back the recording, the tape is rewound and passed over the playback head—another electromagnet. It reads the magnetic patterns and produces faint signals that are amplified and then changed back into sound by loudspeakers.

One problem with analog recordings is that they can be changed by repeated use. The playback head gradually wears away the magnetic particles on the tape, which means the sound heard becomes less like the sound recorded.

In digital recording, the analog signal from the microphone is converted into binary numbers—a series of 0s and 1s. During playback, the digital signal passes through a converter that changes the digital 0s and 1s back to an analog signal. Because the same series of numbers is used to make up the sound each time the recording is played, it always sounds the same as when it was first recorded.

Compact disks (CDs) were first produced in 1982. They produce better sound and are more long-lasting than any other form of recording. The signals are recorded as a spiral track containing millions of tiny pits. Inside a CD player, a laser scans the spiral track. The beam is reflected from the pits onto a photodetector that sends out a signal when light hits it and remains off when there is not enough light. These ons and offs produce a digital signal that matches the original recorded signal. It is decoded by a converter into the original analog signal, which is converted back to sound by the loudspeakers.

SEE ALSO: Computers; Edison, Thomas Alva; Electricity; Electronics; Films; Lasers; Magnetism; Music; Radio; Sound; Tongue and Speech

COMPOSITION OF A CD

A Sony Walkman® for playing CDs on the move.

Aluminum
The plastic is covered with a thin, reflective layer of aluminum.

Label
The label is printed onto the acrylic.

Plastic
The plastic is printed with tiny pits containing the data.

Acrylic
A thin acrylic layer protects the aluminum.

A cross section showing the layers that make up a CD.

* SOUSA, JOHN PHILIP (1854–1932)

John Philip Sousa was a bandleader, conductor, and composer. He wrote some of the most popular marches in American musical history.

John Philip Sousa was born in Washington, D.C. His father was a trombonist. At age 13, John Philip joined the U.S. Marine Corps as an apprentice musician. He left the Marines in 1875 to conduct theater orchestras and perform on the violin. He returned to the U.S. Marine Band in 1880 to become its bandmaster. He left in 1892 to form the Sousa Band, which successfully toured the United States and Europe several times.

Sousa composed waltzes, comic operas, and other pieces, but he is best known for his stirring marches, of which he wrote about 140. His most famous composition is "The Stars and Stripes Forever," which

is the national march of the United States. Others include "Semper Fidelis," "The Washington Post," and "Liberty Bell." Sousa also developed a kind of bass tuba that eventually became known as the sousaphone. He died at age 77 in Reading, Pennsylvania.

Bands across the United States still play many of the tunes that earned John Philip Sousa his nickname, "March King."
▶

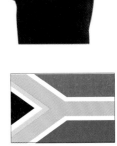

SEE ALSO: Music; Orchestras

* SOUTH AFRICA

The Republic of South Africa is at the southern tip of Africa. It is the richest and most industrialized country on the continent.

South Africa's national flag

Land and climate
There are areas of fertile farmland in the south of the country, while farther north there are plateaus (flat highlands). The High Veld, still farther north, is grassland. The land then changes to wooded savanna and forests. The climate is mild, with the heaviest rainfall in the east.

People and economy
About 75 percent of South Africa's people are black Africans. Tribes include Xhosa, Zulu, Sotho, and Tswana. They speak a variety of Bantu languages. People of white European descent make up nearly 14 percent of the population. The main groups are the English, descended from

the settlers who arrived in the early 1800s, and the Afrikaners, descended from the Dutch who arrived in the 1600s. French and German Protestants joined the Dutch.

Manufacturing, especially steel products, is important for the economy. South Africa produces more than half the world's gold and large quantities of diamonds.

History

In 1652 Dutch settlers founded a colony at the Cape of Good Hope. The British took over Cape Province from the Dutch in 1815. The Dutch, who called themselves Boers (meaning "farmers"), moved northward during the 1830s to establish their own republics outside British rule. Discoveries of diamonds and gold in the late 1800s brought more British settlers. The Boers declared war on the British in 1899, but were defeated in 1902. In 1910 the country became independent as the Union of South Africa, composed of the former British colonies and Boer republics.

In 1948 the Nationalist Party, dominated by Afrikaners, came to power. Under a system called apartheid, only white people had the vote. The apartheid laws sparked violent protests by blacks. In 1990 the black leader Nelson Mandela was released after almost 26 years in prison and in 1994 became the country's first black president.

KEY FACTS

OFFICIAL NAME:
Republic of South Africa

AREA:
441,444 sq. mi.
(1,143,340 sq. km)

POPULATION:
40,377,000

CAPITALS:
Cape Town (legislative), Pretoria (administrative)

LARGEST CITY:
Johannesburg

MAJOR RELIGIONS:
Christianity, traditional African religions, Hinduism, Islam, Judaism

MAJOR LANGUAGES:
Afrikaans, English, various Bantu languages

CURRENCY:
Rand

SEE ALSO: Africa; Mandela, Nelson; Southern Africa

✳ SOUTH AMERICA

The continent of South America contains 12 countries and amazing natural features, such as the world's longest mountain range and the largest river basin.

South America ranks fourth in area and fifth in population among the world's continents. It makes up most of the larger cultural region known as Latin America, which also includes Mexico, Central America, and many of the islands of the Caribbean Sea. These three regions, although geographically part of North America, share a common heritage and historical experience with South America. South America also includes two territories that belong to European countries: French Guiana, an overseas department of France, and the Falkland Islands, a British crown colony.

Land and climate

South America has three main geographical regions. In the west the Andes, the longest mountain range on any continent, run down the entire length of South America. The Eastern Highlands include the Brazilian and Guiana highlands. A vast interior lowland contains the Amazon Basin and a cool, dry, windswept area, called Patagonia, in the southern part of the continent. The interior lowland is drained by three great river systems: the Amazon, the Paraná-Río de la Plata (consisting of the Paraguay, Paraná, Uruguay, and Río de la Plata rivers), and the Orinoco.

South America does not have the extremes of temperature found in North America. Its northern bulge lies on or near the equator, giving the area a hot, humid climate, with heavy rain and temperatures averaging 80°F (27°C). The coldest regions are Tierra del Fuego and the Andes, where temperatures can fall below 32°F (0°C). The highest temperatures occur in the Gran Chaco, with readings above 100°F (38°C) common in summer.

Plants and animals

More than 40 percent of South America is forested. About 30 percent is grassland, which is ideal for raising cattle. Animal life includes jaguars, mountain lions, capybaras (the world's largest rodent), vampire bats, giant armadillos, and many snakes and insects. The llama, alpaca, guanaco, and vicuña—all related to the camel—are used as pack animals and are prized for their wool. South America is home to many species of fish, including the meat-eating piranha. It also has more species of birds than any other continent.

KEY FACTS

AREA:
6,883,000 sq. mi.
(17,827,000 sq. km)

COUNTRIES:
12 (excluding
French Guiana
and the Falkland
Islands)

**LARGEST
COUNTRY:**
Brazil

**SMALLEST
COUNTRY:**
Suriname

POPULATION:
345,782,000

RELIGIONS:
Roman Catholicism,
traditional
African religions

LANGUAGES:
Spanish,
Portuguese,
Indian languages,
English, Dutch,
French

People

South America covers about 12 percent of the world's land surface but contains fewer than 6 percent of its people. However, the population is increasing more quickly than that of any continent except Africa. About 75 percent of the people live in or near cities. Many areas are too densely forested, mountainous, or barren for human settlement.

The people are chiefly of Indian, Spanish, and Portuguese descent, but there are significant numbers with other European, African, and Asian origins. Spanish and Portuguese are the continent's dominant languages.

(continued on page 551)

A Quechua woman tends her alpacas in the mountains of Peru. Alpacas are raised mainly for their soft wool.
▼

549

ATLANTIC OCEAN

Caracas
Lake Maracaibo
Orinoco River
GUYANA
VENEZUELA
Georgetown
Paramaribo
Cayenne
Bogotá
Guiana Highlands
Mt. Roraima
SURINAME
FRENCH GUIANA (FRANCE)
Llanos
COLOMBIA
Negro River
Mouths of the Amazon
Quito
ECUADOR
Amazon River
Magdalena River
PERU
Selvas
Madeira River
Araguaia River
Tocantins River
São Francisco River
Huascarán
Lima
BRAZIL
Lake Titicaca
La Paz
Brasília
BOLIVIA
Pico da Bandeira
Lake Poopó
Sucre
Brazilian Highlands
PARAGUAY
Atacama Desert
Andes
Gran Chaco
Paraguay River
Paraná River
PACIFIC OCEAN
Salado River
Asunción
Paraná River
Uruguay River
Aconcagua
URUGUAY
Santiago
Buenos Aires
Montevideo
CHILE
Colorado River
Pampas
Río de la Plata
ARGENTINA
ATLANTIC OCEAN
Patagonia
FALKLAND ISLANDS (UK)
Tierra del Fuego
Cape Horn

SOUTH AMERICA

Major Physical Features

DESERTS
- Atacama 70,000 sq. mi. (181,300 sq. km)

MOUNTAIN RANGES & HIGHEST POINTS
- Andes 22,834 ft. (6,960 m) at Aconcagua and 22,205 ft. (6,768 m) at Huascarán
- Brazilian Highlands 9,482 ft. (2,890 m) at Pico da Bandeira
- Guiana Highlands 9,094 ft. (2,772 m) at Mt. Roraima

RIVERS
- Amazon 4,007 mi. (6,447 km)
- Paraná-Río de la Plata 3,032 mi. (4,878 km)
- São Francisco 1,811 mi. (2,914 km)
- Orinoco 1,700 mi. (2,735 km)
- Araguaia 1,632 mi. (2,626 km)

LAKES
- Maracaibo 5,100 sq. mi. (13,210 sq. km)
- Titicaca 3,205 sq. mi. (8,300 sq. km)
- Poopó 977 sq. mi. (2,530 sq. km)

Economy

South America is rich in natural resources. Brazil is one of the world's largest producers of iron ore and a major producer of manganese and bauxite (aluminum ore). Chile possesses the world's largest copper reserves. Bolivia is among the world's top tin producers. Venezuela has South America's largest petroleum deposits and is a major oil exporter. Colombia is the world's foremost producer of emeralds.

Agriculture has always played the most important role in South America's economy. Corn is the most widely grown food crop. Major commercial crops include coffee, bananas, sugarcane, wheat, and cacao (or cocoa beans). Brazil and Argentina are the continent's major cattle-raising countries. Fish are important both as a source of food and as an export.

The tropical rain forests are a source of valuable hardwoods, chiefly mahogany and rosewood, which are used to make fine furniture. Other important forest products include rubber, nuts, tannin (used to tan leather), palm oil, waxes, and chicle (the base for chewing gum).

History

The first people to live in South America, the ancestors of the Indians, probably came from North America. The most sophisticated Indian civilization that emerged was that of the Incas, who lived in the Andean highlands of what are now Peru, Bolivia, and Ecuador.

The first European known to have reached South America was Christopher Columbus, who landed at the mouth of the Orinoco River in 1498. Spanish adventurers known as conquistadors, drawn to the region by the lure of gold and silver, overcame the native peoples. Although relatively few in number, the Europeans were better armed, and the Indians were weakened by new European diseases and by disputes. Roman Catholic priests arrived with the first colonists to convert the Indians to Christianity. The Catholic Church is still a powerful force.

By the early 1800s, South Americans were unhappy about being ruled by the Europeans. The leaders in the struggle for independence, such as Simón Bolívar, suffered defeats against the Spanish before victory was first achieved in 1824.

Lauca National Park in northern Chile has one of the world's highest lakes.

Maracaña Stadium in Rio de Janeiro, Brazil, is the world's largest soccer stadium.

frequently torn by political conflict. Unstable governments led to the rise of military rulers. Uneasy relations between countries led to several long and bloody wars. During the 1950s and 1960s, ineffective governments were often overthrown by the military. A pattern of military regimes alternating with civilian rule lasted until the early 1990s, when democratically elected governments were restored throughout the continent. South America's continuing problems include the growing population, poverty, a shortage of schools, and a huge foreign debt.

Only Brazil won independence peacefully, from Portugal in 1822. By 1830, 10 of today's 12 South American nations had formed. Guyana gained independence in 1966 and Suriname in 1975. But unlike Brazil, which was a monarchy until 1889 and was relatively stable, the 19th-century Spanish-speaking republics were

SEE ALSO: Argentina; Bolívar, Simón; Bolivia; Brazil; Chile; Colombia; Columbus, Christopher; Conquistadors; Ecuador; Incas; Paraguay; Peru; Uruguay; Venezuela

✳ SOUTHEAST ASIA

After centuries of poverty, war, and foreign exploitation, the nations of Southeast Asia are now beginning to prosper as independent states.

Land

Five of the 11 countries of Southeast Asia—Vietnam, Laos, Cambodia, Thailand, and Myanmar (formerly Burma)—are on the Asian mainland. Four are island nations—the Philippines, Indonesia, East Timor, and the city-state of Singapore. Malaysia holds territory on both the mainland and the islands. Brunei is situated on the island of Borneo, which it shares with Indonesia and Malaysia.

Vast parts of the mainland and islands of Southeast Asia are blanketed with tropical forests. There are many mountain ranges, plateaus, plains, and broad stretches of grasslands. Southeast Asia also has many

great rivers, such as the Mekong, which are important transportation systems.

Climate

Rainfall is heavy throughout Southeast Asia. Near the equator there are no distinct seasons, and there are brief downpours almost every afternoon. In much of the area, the weather is controlled by the monsoon winds, which blow from a single direction for months at a time. The northeast monsoons, which are generally dry, begin in October. In late spring, strong winds begin to blow across the ocean from south of the equator. For the next few months, during the main growing season, there is rain almost daily.

People

Southeast Asia is home to many different peoples. It has a population of more than 518 million, which is growing at about 1.6 percent each year. There are ethnic Chinese throughout the region. More than 75 percent of Singaporeans and about one-third of Malaysians are of Chinese ancestry. People from India and Europe also live throughout Southeast Asia. English is the most common second language.

SOUTHEAST ASIA

Buddhism is the main religion of Laos, Myanmar, Thailand, Cambodia, and Vietnam. Islam is the major religion of Indonesia and Malaysia. Hinduism is practiced on Bali. In the Philippines most people are Christians.

Economy

Southeast Asia was once one of the poorest regions of the world. Until the 1970s, most people earned their living from farming. Rice is the main crop. Most people still work in agriculture, but several countries are rapidly industrializing. Myanmar, Laos, and Cambodia are still poor. Singapore, Malaysia, and Thailand are the most developed countries. Brunei has huge oil and natural gas reserves in the South China Sea and is extremely wealthy. Many international companies have opened factories in Southeast Asia because costs there are lower and labor is plentiful. The electronics industry is well established in Thailand, Malaysia, the Philippines, and Singapore.

History

People first settled in Southeast Asia about 500,000 years ago. Great kingdoms flourished after A.D. 900, but today their cities and temples lie in ruins.

The Portuguese and Spanish were the first Europeans to arrive, in the 1500s. The Dutch and British soon followed. ➡

A woman steers a boat through the Mekong River Delta in the south of Vietnam.
▼

In a series of wars during the 1800s, Britain made Burma a colony, and France made colonies of Vietnam, Laos, and Cambodia. The United States took the Philippines from Spain in 1898. During World War II (1939–45), Japan briefly conquered all of Southeast Asia. The Philippines won independence in 1946. Between 1948 and 1963, the British left Burma, Malaya, Singapore, Sabah, and Sarawak (Malaya, Sabah, and Sarawak formed Malaysia). The Dutch finally quit Indonesia in 1949. In 1954, after the defeat of France in the First Indochina War, Vietnam was divided into Communist North Vietnam and non-Communist South Vietnam. This led to the Second Indochina War, which lasted 20 years and became known as the Vietnam War. The United States backed South Vietnam, while North Vietnam received aid from the Soviet Union and China. The war later spread into Laos and Cambodia. North and South Vietnam were unified under a Communist government in 1976. East Timor won independence from Indonesia in 2002.

SEE ALSO: Asia; Indonesia; Malaysia; Philippines; Vietnam War

✳ SOUTHERN AFRICA

The countries of Southern Africa are Angola, Botswana, Lesotho, Malawi, Mozambique, Namibia, South Africa, Swaziland, Zambia, and Zimbabwe.

Land

Dominating the interior of Southern Africa is a high plateau that descends in shelves toward the southeastern lowlands. The Drakensberg Mountains, which divide the plateau from the lowlands, rise to 11,425 ft. (3,482 m). Although Southern Africa has areas of fertile soil, it also contains the Kalahari Desert in southern Botswana and the Namib Desert in Namibia.

People

People have lived in Southern Africa for at least half a million years. Beginning about 2,000 years ago, black African peoples gradually swept south, pushing out other native peoples. The newcomers all spoke languages belonging to the Bantu group.

Today most Southern Africans still speak a Bantu language. Other major languages are English, Portuguese, and, in South Africa, Afrikaans. Christianity is the major religion, along with various folk beliefs.

History

Southern African kingdoms and chiefdoms farmed and traded long before Europeans arrived. The most powerful pre-European empire was based at Great Zimbabwe, in southeastern Africa, during the 11th to 15th centuries. Beginning in the late 15th century, settlers from Portugal came to Southern Africa. They founded cities along the coasts, where they traded in gold and slaves. Angola and Mozambique were Portuguese colonies until 1975.

From the 1860s onward, Britain controlled what are now Botswana, Lesotho, Malawi, and Swaziland. It also controlled Northern and Southern Rhodesia (modern Zambia and Zimbabwe). In the 1960s, all British-controlled countries became independent, but Rhodesia stayed under white control until 1980, when it became Zimbabwe.

Since the 1600s, South Africa has been home to the Afrikaners, or Boers, whose ancestors came from the Netherlands. The Boers came into conflict with the British at the end of the 1800s, when diamonds and gold were discovered. In 1948 the white government developed a system of laws called apartheid. It withheld many basic human rights from blacks until it was dismantled in 1994.

SOUTHERN AFRICA

SEE ALSO: Africa; Mandela, Nelson; Slavery; South Africa

* SPACECRAFT

A spacecraft is any human-made vehicle that travels in space. Spacecraft can be manned or unmanned. They include space probes, shuttles, and stations.

Space probes

Most spacecraft are sent into space without astronauts or scientists on board. Many of them are space probes sent to study distant objects in the solar system. The artificial satellite *Sputnik I*, launched in 1957 by the Soviet Union, is usually considered the first space probe, even through it only orbited the earth. By the mid-1960s, space probes had landed successfully on the moon.

The American *Mariner 2*, launched in 1962, was the first probe to reach another planet, Venus. *Mariner 9*, the first probe to

orbit a planet, reached Mars in November 1971. Later, the *Pioneer* and *Voyager* probes became the first spacecraft to travel beyond the outer planets of our solar system.

Space shuttles

The first astronauts traveled in spacecraft that could be used only once. Because each mission required a new spacecraft and new rockets, space flight was very expensive. In 1981 the United States launched the space shuttle *Columbia*, the first reusable space vehicle.

The space shuttle Atlantis *was launched on March 24, 1992, for its eleventh flight. It had twin solid rocket boosters and three main engines. On board was a crew of seven astronauts.*

A shuttle launches with the aid of two rocket boosters and a fuel tank. These separate from the shuttle after launch. When the shuttle starts orbiting, it is self-powered. It returns to Earth and lands like an airplane, on a runway. This distinguishes it from other manned spacecraft, which crash-land in the ocean. Shuttles make transport easier to and from space stations. However, the *Challenger* and *Columbia* shuttles were involved in two of the worst disasters in human spaceflight in 1986 and 2003, respectively. Seven astronauts died on each occasion.

Space stations

The orbiting space station is a special type of satellite that allows people to live in space for long periods. The first one, *Salyut 1*, was launched in 1971 by the Soviet Union. The United States launched its first space station, *Skylab*, in 1973. An important recent venture is the *International Space Station*, or *ISS*, a joint project between the United States, Russia, and 14 other countries. The station should be complete by 2006.

SEE ALSO: Astronauts; Planets; Rockets; Satellites; Space Exploration; Universe

✳ SPACE EXPLORATION

People used to dream of traveling through space to visit the moon and explore other planets and stars. Some of these dreams have now become a reality.

Earth's atmosphere extends for hundreds of miles around the planet. Beyond that is space. Scientists do not know where, or if, space ends. The greatest distance that humans have traveled in space is 250,000 miles (400,000 km) to the moon. The star nearest our sun is 25 trillion miles (40 trillion km) away; in space that is a relatively small distance. There are billions of galaxies, each containing billions of stars. Space probes and astronomers have collected much information from space, but there is still a lot that we do not know.

Science-fiction authors began imagining journeys into space in the 1800s. For decades technology did not have the means to make a spacecraft. To escape Earth's gravity, a craft needs to reach a speed of about 7 miles per second (11 km/s), or 25,000 mph (40,000 km/h). This is called escape velocity. Long-range rockets, built for use in World War II (1939–45), provided the answer. By the 1950s, scientists in the United States and the Soviet Union were making rockets that could travel beyond Earth's atmosphere.

The space race

The space age truly began on October 4, 1957, when the Soviet Union launched the first artificial satellite, *Sputnik I*, into orbit. The first man in space was the Soviet cosmonaut Yuri Gagarin. His spacecraft,

Vostok 1, made a single orbit of Earth on April 12, 1961. The Soviet Union also had the first woman in space—Valentina Tereshkova, in 1963—and the first man to walk outside his orbiting craft—Alexei Leonov, in 1965. The first American in space was Alan Shepard, on May 5, 1961.

Scientists and politicians in the United States were concerned that their rivals were advancing more quickly. At the time, the two countries were the most powerful states in the world. Many people thought that space exploration could have military advantages.

Moon landing

On July 16, 1969, the *Apollo 11* spacecraft was launched from Cape Kennedy, Florida. Aboard were Neil Armstrong, Edwin

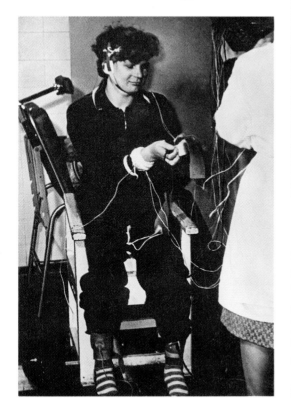

Valentina Tereshkova trains for a spaceflight. She became the first woman in space on June 16, 1963, in the Soviet spacecraft **Vostok 6.**

"Buzz" Aldrin, and Michael Collins. Four days later Armstrong and Aldrin descended in the lunar module of the spacecraft. Armstrong was the first human to walk on the moon. He and Aldrin spent about two and a half hours there. Many people around the world watched them on television. There were five more successful moon landings up to 1972.

Stations, shuttles, and satellites

In 1971 the Soviet Union launched the first space station, *Salyut 1*. It was a craft that orbited Earth permanently, with enough

Astronaut Buzz Aldrin walks on the moon during the Apollo 11 space mission in 1969. This photograph was taken by Neil Armstrong, the first astronaut to step on the moon's surface.

room for astronauts to remain there for months. The first United States space station was *Skylab*, launched in 1973. In 1998 the first modules of the *International Space Station*, or *ISS*, were joined in

AMAZING FACTS!

On March 22, 1995, Russian cosmonaut Valery Polyakov returned to Earth after orbiting in the *Mir* space station for a record-breaking 438 days. During his mission, he circled Earth about 7,000 times.
In 1962 John Glenn was the first American to orbit Earth. In 1998, at the age of 77, he became the oldest person ever to go into space.

space. Built by 16 nations, it will act as an orbiting laboratory for up to seven astronauts. In 1981 the United States launched the first space shuttle. It was a reusable spacecraft that returned to Earth by touching down on a runway.

Although humans have not yet traveled farther than the moon, space probes have sent back messages from beyond Earth's solar system. People have not yet achieved all the feats that science-fiction writers imagined, but they have made great progress since the space age began.

SEE ALSO: Astronauts; Astronomy; Atmosphere; Galaxies; Gravity; Moon; Planets; Rockets; Satellites; Solar System; Spacecraft; Stars; Sun; Universe

✳ SPAIN

Spain is situated on the Iberian Peninsula in southwestern Europe. It had a leading role in the exploration and colonization of the New World.

Spain's national flag

Land and climate
Spain is the fourth-largest country in Europe. It has rugged mountains and high plateaus. The coastal areas are fertile and densely populated. The country also includes two major island groups, the Balearics in the Mediterranean Sea and the Canaries in the Atlantic Ocean. Tenerife, in the Canary Islands, includes Spain's highest point, Pico de Teide—12,198 ft. (3,718 m). Major rivers include the Ebro, the Guadalquivir, and the Tagus. The British colony of Gibraltar is on Spain's southern coast.

The climate in northern and western Spain is moderate, with heavy rainfall. Farther

south, the climate is Mediterranean, with hot, dry summers and mild winters.

People
The Spanish are descendants of many peoples. The oldest group is the Iberians, who also inhabited what is now Portugal. Over the years the Phoenicians, from the eastern Mediterranean, the Greeks, and the Romans all settled in Spain. Visigoths from Central Europe arrived after the Western Roman Empire fell in the fifth century A.D., followed later by Muslims and Jews from North Africa. The Basques of northern Spain have a culture and language unlike any other Europeans. Their origins remain a mystery.

Economy

Service industries provide about half of Spain's total wealth. Tourism is one of the country's main sources of income. Each year more than 30 million people visit Spain's beaches and historic cities. Manufacturing employs more than one-third of the population. Agriculture is less important than in the past, but Spain is still a major producer of oranges, olives, wine, and cork.

History

In the third century B.C., Spain became a key part of the Roman Empire. The Visigoths then ruled Spain until A.D. 711, when Muslims from North Africa defeated the Visigoth King Roderick. The Muslim Umayyad dynasty ruled until 1031.

Spanish Christians, led by the kingdom of Castile, began to drive the Muslims out of Spain, moving southward. By 1248 the southern kingdom of Granada was the only part of Spain that was still in Muslim hands. Granada finally fell to the Christians in 1492.

The two largest kingdoms in Spain united in 1479, when Isabella of Castile married Ferdinand of Aragón. They were the monarchs who sent Christopher Columbus on his voyages to the New World and later

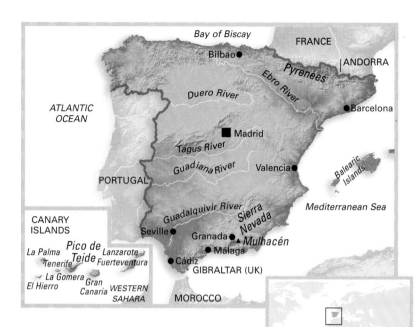

ruled over vast areas in North and South America, as well as colonies in North Africa and Asia.

Ferdinand and Isabella's daughter married into Austria's Hapsburg dynasty in 1496. Her grandson, Philip II (1527–98), took Spain to its highest level of power and military strength. Spain ruled Portugal, the area that is now Belgium and the Netherlands, and much of Italy, as well as its vast overseas empire.

Philip II was a devout Catholic who tried hard to stop the spread of the Protestant

Segovia Cathedral took more than 50 years to build. Work on it started in the 1520s after the old cathedral was destroyed by fire. It is an example of the Gothic style of architecture that was popular in Europe during the 16th century.

KEY FACTS

OFFICIAL NAME:
Reino de España

AREA:
194,896 sq. mi.
(504,781 sq. km)

POPULATION:
39,630,000

CAPITAL & LARGEST CITY:
Madrid

MAJOR RELIGION:
Roman Catholicism

MAJOR LANGUAGES:
Castilian Spanish (official), Catalan, Galician, Basque

CURRENCY:
Euro

religion. However, in 1566 the Dutch rose up against Spanish rule in Holland, one of its richest lands. The Dutch Revolt proved costly to Spain and led to the formation of the Dutch Republic in 1581. In 1588, while attempting to invade the British Isles, the great Spanish fleet known as the Armada was defeated by Britain's naval forces.

Decline of Spanish power
From the 1700s, Spain declined in power. It lost most of its American possessions in the early 1800s and then, in 1898, suffered defeat by U.S. forces in the Spanish–American War.

In the 19th century, Spain suffered a series of civil wars and rebellions known as the Carlist Wars. In 1931 King Alfonso XIII was forced to leave the country, and a republic was proclaimed.

In 1936 a new government threatened the interests of the Catholic Church and landowners. Army units revolted, beginning a civil war that lasted until

1939. One million Spaniards were killed or wounded in the conflict, and a further million fled the country. The Nationalists, who opposed the republican government, won the Civil War, and General Francisco Franco (1892–1975) ruled as a dictator (supreme ruler). After Franco's death, Alfonso XIII's grandson, Juan Carlos, became king.

Under King Juan Carlos, Spain quickly reestablished a democratic government and in 1977 held the first free elections since before the Civil War. Spain became a member of the European Community—now the European Union (EU)—in 1986. In 1999 the Spanish adopted the euro, the EU's common currency, as a further step toward European economic integration.

SEE ALSO: Columbus, Christopher; Europe; Exploration and Explorers; Portugal; Spanish–American War

* SPANISH–AMERICAN WAR

In the Spanish–American War of 1898, which freed Cuba from Spanish rule, the United States acquired possessions in the Pacific and Latin America.

The battle of Manila in 1898 started the Spanish–American War. All the Spanish ships in Manila Bay were destroyed without the loss of any U.S. ships or sailors.

Cuba was a colony of Spain from the 1500s. In 1895 the Cubans began fighting their colonial rulers for independence. Spain brutally put down the rebellion, killing many innocent people as well as the rebels. American newspapers printed reports of Spanish cruelty and stirred up war fever in the United States. Spain granted limited self-government to Cuba.

In January 1898 the U.S. battleship *Maine* was sent to Cuba to protect American citizens there. On February 15, while anchored in the harbor in the capital,

Havana, the ship exploded, killing 260 crewmen. It was widely suspected that it had been blown up by the Spanish. In fact, we know today that the explosion was an accident. Anti-Spanish feeling ran high in the United States. Congress recognized Cuba's independence on April 19 and a few days later declared war on Spain.

The first battle was fought in the Philippine Islands, a Spanish possession in the Pacific Ocean. On May 1, a U.S. fleet attacked and destroyed the Spanish fleet in Manila Bay. At the end of May, the Americans trapped a fleet of Spanish ships in Santiago harbor in Cuba. About 18,000 American troops landed near the city in June. On July 3, the Spanish ships tried to slip past the blockade, but they were sunk by the American warships. Deprived of reinforcements, the Spanish troops in Cuba surrendered on July 17.

On July 25 the Americans captured Puerto Rico. In the Philippines, U.S. troops took Manila on August 13, unaware that an armistice signed with Spain had ended the war the previous day. Under the terms of a peace treaty, Spain gave the Philippines, the Pacific island of Guam, and Puerto Rico to the United States. Cuba came under the control of the U.S. military until 1902, when it became independent.

SEE ALSO: Cuba; Philippines; Spain

✳**SPEECH** 👉 ✳**TONGUE AND SPEECH**

✳ SPIDERS AND SCORPIONS

Spiders and scorpions are among the 74,000 different species of arachnids, a class of animals that also includes mites, ticks, and daddy longlegs.

Arachnids resemble insects, but they are different in several ways. They have eight jointed legs, rather than six. Their bodies are divided into two parts, not three, and they do not have wings or antennae.

Spiders

There are more than 30,000 species of spiders. Most range from about ⅕ in. (5 mm) to 3½ in. (8.9 cm) in size. The biggest ever found was a tarantula in South America, which measured 10 in. (25 cm) with its legs outstretched.

Most spiders eat insects, although some feed on frogs, fish, and small animals. Some species chase their prey; others spin webs to capture insects. Spiders kill or paralyze their prey by injecting venom (poison) through their fangs.

Spiders have abdominal glands that produce silk. The silk comes out as a liquid thread that hardens on contact with the air. All spiders make a silk used for binding up prey. Most females produce another type of silk for wrapping up their eggs. Some spiders have two or more kinds of silk for making webs.

Different species of spider make different kinds of webs. Grass spiders make large funnels in tall grass or under a rock; the purseweb spider creates tubes under stones and on the sides of trees; the

DID YOU KNOW?

The bola spider has an unusual use for its silk thread. It fires a sticky spitball at its prey. The saliva is attached to a length of silk, and when it sticks to an insect, the spider reels it in, like a fisherman.

The black and yellow garden spider is sometimes known as the writing spider because it weaves a line of white X's down the center of its web.

A scorpion with its young on its back in the tropical dry forest of Costa Rica.

common garden spider spins a web that resembles a spoked wheel. Webs are a mixture of dry silk, which provides the structure, and sticky material, which traps the prey. A spider has oily feet to stop it from sticking to the threads. The feet are very sensitive to vibrations. Although a spider has eight eyes, its vision is poor.

Most spiders also make a fine kind of silk known as a dragline. The line acts as a safety rope, allowing the spider to climb or swing from danger. The silken thread is incredibly strong—it can support 4,000 times the weight of the spider.

Young spiders use their silk to catch the wind and carry them away. Some spiders have traveled more than 200 miles (322 km) by this method, known as ballooning.

Scorpions

There are more than 1,200 species of scorpions. They can be up to 7 in. (18 cm) long, although they are usually 1½ to 3 in. (4–7 cm) in length. They tend to live in desert and tropical regions. They are nocturnal, hunting at night and taking shelter during the day.

A scorpion has a tapered body and a long tail arching over its back. The tail is tipped with a venomous stinger. The poison can be painful to humans, but is not usually fatal. Like other arachnids, a scorpion's body is divided into two parts, but these sections are made of further segments— seven at the front, five at the back.

Scorpions feed on insects and other arachnids. A scorpion seizes its prey using clawlike pincers alongside the jaw, injects it with poison from its stinger, and crushes it. It then spits a digestive fluid over the animal to dissolve it. It sucks the resulting liquid up into its mouth.

Because scorpions' reflexes are so good, mating can be dangerous. If a male approaches a female, he may be mistaken for prey or an aggressor. Because of this, scorpions have developed complicated courtship rituals, sometimes known as the scorpion waltz. The male clutches the female's claws and follows a specific set of movements. The waltz can sometimes last for an hour before mating begins. After mating, the female sometimes kills and eats the male.

Unlike spiders, scorpions give birth to live young, rather than laying eggs. Young scorpions ride on their mothers' backs until they can fend for themselves.

SEE ALSO: Animals; Insects

SPORTS

People have been playing sports for thousands of years. More recently, sports have become organized, with fixed rules and international competitions.

The earliest sports were based on skills that people needed to survive. Good hunters and warriors needed to be able to run fast and to fight. The ancient Greeks held sporting events to honor their gods. The earliest recorded Olympic Games took place in 776 B.C. The Romans enjoyed watching chariot races and fights to the death between gladiators—fighters who were usually slaves or prisoners of war.

By about A.D. 1200 people in Europe played games similar to soccer and field hockey. When Europeans reached the New World, they found Native Americans playing a form of lacrosse, and the Aztecs and Mayans playing games similar to basketball.

Modern sports

Organized sports, with written rules, became common in the 1800s, especially in England. New sports were created in North America, where people played football, baseball, and basketball.

The modern Olympic Games began in Greece in 1896. In 1930 the first soccer World Cup began in Uruguay. Soccer quickly became the most popular team sport in the world.

In recent years, television and sponsorship have made great changes in sports. Sport stars can make millions of dollars in a year.

At the same time, many amateur sportspeople take part simply for fun and fitness. The majority of athletes make no money from sports.

Track and field

The early Olympics tested athletes' abilities at running, jumping, and throwing. These skills still form the basis of track and field events. There are races at various distances, as well as walking, relay, hurdling, and steeplechase events. Field events include long jump, pole vault, discus, and javelin. Decathlon and heptathlon test athletes' abilities in a number of events.

Ball sports

In some ball sports players use only hands or feet to propel the ball. These include football, soccer, bowling, and volleyball. In others they use implements, such as bats or rackets. Baseball, golf, lacrosse, and tennis are examples of this kind of ball sport. All these sports require fitness, accuracy, and coordination.

Water sports

The simplest water sport is swimming. A competitive swimmer uses one of four swimming strokes. These are crawl, breaststroke, backstroke, and butterfly.

The crawl is the fastest and most popular stroke in competitive swimming.

FAMOUS SPORTSPEOPLE

Here are just a few of North America's top sportspeople.

Ruth, George Herman "Babe" (1895–1948)
American baseball player who hit 714 home runs in 8,399 times at bat.

Owens, James Cleveland "Jesse" (1913–80)
American track-and-field athlete. He set three world records and equaled a fourth in one day in 1935 and won four Olympic gold medals in 1936.

Zaharias, Mildred Ella "Babe" (1914–56)
American all-around athlete, born Mildred Didrikson. She was an All-American as a high school basketball player, set world records in four different track-and-field events, won three Olympic medals, and won 55 professional golf tournaments.

Ali, Muhammad (1942–)
American boxer (below right), born Cassius Clay. He was the first boxer to become world heavyweight champion three times.

Spitz, Mark (Andrew) (1950–)
American swimmer who won seven Olympic gold medals in 1972.

Griffith Joyner, (Delorez) Florence "Flo-Jo" (1959–98)
American sprinter. She set new world records for 100 and 200 meters in 1988 that still stand today.

Gretzky, Wayne (Douglas) (1961–)
Canadian hockey player, known as the "Great One." He holds NHL and Stanley Cup career points records.

Jordan, Michael (Jeffrey) (1963–)
American basketball player. He holds a record average of 30.12 points per NBA game.

Armstrong, Lance (1971–)
American cyclist. He won the Tour de France in five consecutive years (1999–2003) after surviving cancer.

Woods, Eldrick "Tiger" (1975–)
American golfer who dominated world golf at the beginning of the 21st century.

Williams, Venus (1980–), and **Williams, Serena** (1981–)
American tennis players. In 2002 they became the first sisters to hold the top two world rankings.

Other water sports include synchronized swimming, diving, and water polo. There are also many forms of racing in boats, including rowing, yachting, and canoeing.

Combat sports
Wrestling and boxing are based on unarmed combat. Most martial arts also involve combat without weapons. Fencing is based on sword skills used by soldiers until the 1800s. Target shooting and archery are also based on military skills.

Winter sports
Skiing, snowboarding, and tobogganing are popular in cold, mountainous areas. Ice sports, such as hockey and skating, began on frozen lakes. They now usually take place on artificial rinks.

Disability sports
Athletes with similar disabilities play against one another. The Paralympics, an international event for disabled sportspeople, is held every four years in the same venue as the Summer Olympics.

SEE ALSO:
Baseball;
Basketball;
Football;
Hockey;
Olympic Games;
Soccer

STARFISH AND OTHER ECHINODERMS

Starfish, also known as sea stars, are echinoderms, a group of sea creatures that also includes sea urchins and sea cucumbers.

Echinoderms first appeared on Earth over 500 million years ago. There are 6,000 living species, inhabiting the seabeds of every ocean.

An echinoderm's body consists of a central disk with arms radiating outward. It has a tough internal skeleton of calcium carbonate, which protects its inner organs. There is also a network of water-filled tubes, branching out from the center. At the tips of the tubes are small, suckerlike feet. The echinoderm uses these to move and to touch.

Starfish

There are about 1,800 species of starfish. They range in size from ⅜ in. (1 cm) to 30 in. (75 cm) across the arms. They live in all temperatures of seawater. Many live quite close to shore, but some have been found at depths of 19,800 ft. (6,035 m).

Most starfish have five arms, but some species have as many as 50. They can regenerate—if an arm breaks off, a new one grows. Some species can even grow a new animal from a single arm. However, most starfish mate to create new animals. Males and females release sperm and eggs into water at the same time, water currents bring them together, and many of the eggs are fertilized. Most young starfish develop away from their parents. The eggs hatch tiny larvae, which drift along, feeding on microscopic sea creatures. The larvae anchor themselves to the ocean bottom and change into their adult form.

Adult starfish mainly eat mollusks. Some, such as the crown of thorns starfish, also eat live coral. As a result, many coral reefs have been badly damaged or destroyed.

Other echinoderms

Brittle stars and basket stars resemble starfish. They have five long, thin, fragile arms. Sea urchins are rounded and bristle with spines, some of which can contain poison. They nibble seaweed off the surface of rocks. Sand dollars look similar but are flatter, with short spines.

Sea lilies get their name because they look like plants. They usually attach themselves by a stalk to the sea floor. Sea cucumbers, despite their name, are also echinoderms. They are long, finger-shaped creatures with tentacles at one end.

SEE ALSO: Oceans and Seas; Seashores

The crown of thorns starfish eats live coral. It can grow to over 30 in. (75 cm) and has up to 21 arms.

✷ STARS

From Earth, stars appear to be very faint, but they are actually large, extremely bright balls of gas that give out enormous amounts of light and heat.

The earth's sun is a star. Unlike other stars, it is relatively close to Earth—about 93 million miles (150 million km) away. Other stars are so far away that their distance from Earth is measured in light-years rather than miles. One light-year is the distance that light travels in one year—nearly six trillion miles (9.6 trillion km).

▲ *One of the densest clusters of stars in the Milky Way galaxy. It is located about 28,000 light-years from Earth. All the stars are about 15 billion years old, and the bright red ones are nearing the ends of their lives.*

AMAZING FACTS !

The chemical elements that make up stars are the same as those that make up humans and other objects on Earth. But the elements in the stars exist in a physical state different from those on Earth. The atoms of the elements on Earth combine to form water, carbon dioxide, and the complex molecules that make up humans. In stars the temperatures are so hot that molecules such as these cannot exist. Instead the atoms in stars exist as a hot gas called plasma. About 90 percent of the atoms in a star are hydrogen.

Light from the sun takes about eight minutes to reach Earth. The nearest star to Earth after the sun is Alpha Centauri, which is about 4 light-years away. The brightest star in the sky is Sirius, which is about 8 light-years away. Although Sirius is larger and hotter than the sun, it appears much smaller and dimmer because it is so far away.

Formation of stars

Stars are created in vast clouds of dust and gases that drift through space. The particles begin to condense, exerting a strong gravitational pull on nearby dust and gases in space, causing all of these materials to form a large mass. The center of this mass becomes hotter and hotter, eventually reaching a temperature so great that the mass begins to generate its own energy, and a star is born.

Stars give off enormous amounts of energy in the form of heat, light, and other types of radiation. This energy is generated by nuclear reactions taking place between the nuclei, or centers, of the hydrogen atoms that make up the star. Stars like the sun have enough hydrogen to last about 10 billion years. When stars grow old, they explode and spread different elements throughout space. These elements become the building blocks of new stars and planets.

SEE ALSO: Astronomy; Atoms and Molecules; Earth; Elements; Galaxies; Light; Nuclear Power; Planets; Sun; Universe

STATES AND STATE GOVERNMENTS

Each state has its own government, with a constitution and laws. States provide education, health care, police protection, and other services.

The state legislature in Nebraska during a session. It is the only legislature in the nation that has a single chamber. The other state legislatures all have two parts, similar to the United States Senate and House of Representatives.

The United States of America is a federal republic. This means that it is a union of individual states. The first to join the union were those eastern states that fought in the American Revolution. By the beginning of the 1800s, there were just 16 states. During the next 100 years, an additional 29 states joined the country. In 1959 Hawaii took the number of states to 50.

State and federal government

The federal government in Washington, D.C., sets laws and policies that affect the whole country. However, the 50 individual states also have many powers within their own borders. The roots of the division between state and federal powers lie with the founding of the nation.

The state governments existed long before the federal government was created. Before the United States was established, each colony was governed under the laws of its own charter. When the Founders drafted the Constitution in 1787, they gave many powers to the federal government. But they also wanted to ensure that each state's government retained some authority over its citizens. This issue was not resolved before the Constitution was ratified. As a result, in 1791 Congress drafted and adopted the 10th Amendment to the Constitution as part of the Bill of Rights. The amendment specifies that any powers not specifically given to the federal government belong to the states or the people.

▶ *President Eisenhower signs the proclamation of Hawaii's statehood on August 21, 1959, in Washington, D.C. Hawaii was the last state to join the Union.*

State constitutions and laws

Each state has a written constitution that provides the framework for its government. It defines the basic laws and duties of the state government and gives specific details of its operation. A state's constitution may not conflict with the Constitution of the United States or with federal laws. Every act of a state's legislature, order of its governor, or local law must agree with the terms of the state's constitution. The municipal, or local, governments must operate under the authority of the state.

If the people of a state want to change their constitution, an elected convention draws up an amendment. Except in Delaware, the people then have to approve the amendment.

How state government works

State governments are organized in much the same way as the federal government. Power is divided among three branches—legislative, executive, and judicial. This system is called the separation of powers.

The head of the executive branch is the governor. The governor's position in a state is similar to that of the president in the whole country. He or she is responsible for making sure that the laws of the state are carried out. Governors are elected by the state's voters. Elections take place every four years in most states.

The legislatures make the basic decisions for the states. They are responsible for policies dealing with schools, parks, roads, courts, hospitals, policing, and banking. Money for these services comes mainly from taxes. Taxes must be approved by a majority vote in the state legislatures.

All state legislatures except Nebraska have two chambers, generally known as the senate and the house of representatives.

Each state has its own court system, or judiciary. Cases go first to a trial court, and then parties can take them to higher courts on appeal. The highest state court is the supreme court. In more than half of the states, supreme court judges are elected by the people.

👀

SEE ALSO: Congress; Constitution, United States; Supreme Court; United States Government; United States of America

✳ STEINBECK, JOHN (1902–68)

John Steinbeck was one of America's greatest writers. His work showed great sympathy with the poor and disadvantaged.

John Ernst Steinbeck was born in Salinas, California. His father was a government official and his mother was a teacher. Steinbeck went to Stanford University between 1919 and 1925 but left without a degree. While there, he wrote poems and prose for university magazines.

Steinbeck had a number of jobs after leaving Stanford, including one as caretaker of an estate in the High Sierras. In 1929 he published his first novel, *Cup of Gold*. His first best-seller, *Tortilla Flat*, was published in 1935. It humorously describes the life of the Mexican American inhabitants of a California town.

Steinbeck's 1939 novel, *The Grapes of Wrath*, presents a bleak picture of poverty and despair for the "Okies" who, evicted from their farms in Oklahoma, tried to resettle in California. It was one of the most important and controversial novels of the time and won the Pulitzer Prize in 1940. Steinbeck's other famous novels include *Of Mice and Men* (1937) and *East of Eden* (1952). Several of his books have been made into movies.

In 1962 Steinbeck was awarded the Nobel Prize for literature. He died in New York City in 1968.

SEE ALSO: Literature

John Steinbeck photographed in about 1930. He is known especially for his novels about agricultural workers.

✳ STOCK MARKETS

A stock market, or stock exchange, is an organized market for selling and buying stock in a company.

A company may decide to raise money by issuing stocks. These are shares in the ownership of a company. People buy stock that they believe will increase in value. Someone who owns stock in a company is called a stockholder. The management of the company has a responsibility to the stockholders to run the business efficiently and profitably. A stockholder has a say in how the company is run and receives dividends—a proportion of the profits of the company.

Stocks are bought and sold at a stock market, or stock exchange. Brokers usually arrange the deals on behalf of their clients. Buying and selling stocks first took place face-to-face, but now millions of dollars' worth of stocks can be exchanged by pressing a single key on a computer.

The value of individual stocks can go up or down. If many people want to buy stocks in a company, the value rises; if many want to sell, the value goes down. This can have many causes. If a company is very successful, people will want to invest (buy shares) in it. Or it might not do so well, which will put investors off. Changes in an entire industry, such as oil, can affect all companies in a sector. Changes in the economy can affect the value of stock. The Great Depression began with the stock market crash of October 1929. Many

The New York Stock Exchange is the largest stock market in the world.

people decided to sell stock at the same time, and stock prices fell dramatically. Stockholders panicked and tried to sell their stock before the value fell again. The value of stocks dropped by billions of dollars in a few days.

New York Stock Exchange
In 1792 a group of New York City brokers and merchants began to meet daily to trade stocks. They made a pact, the Buttonwood Tree Agreement, out of which the New York Stock Exchange (NYSE) developed. At first it was very easy for a company to have its stock traded on the NYSE, but now it is usually just the largest, most well-established businesses that qualify to trade there.

SEE ALSO: Banking; Economics; Great Depression; Money

✱ STOMACH AND DIGESTIVE SYSTEM
Food must pass through the digestive system before the body can use it for energy. The stomach is one of the organs that breaks down food.

DIGESTIVE SYSTEM

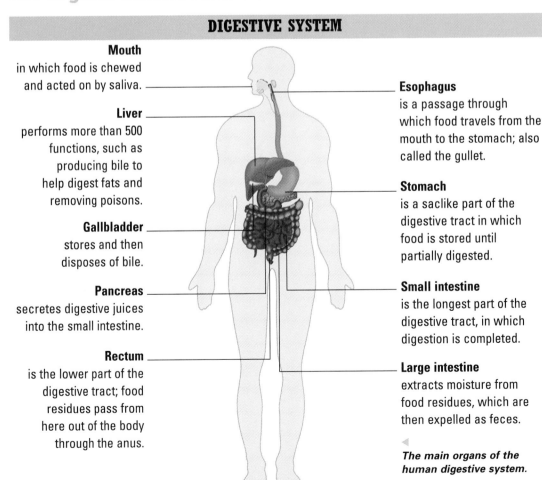

Mouth
in which food is chewed and acted on by saliva.

Liver
performs more than 500 functions, such as producing bile to help digest fats and removing poisons.

Gallbladder
stores and then disposes of bile.

Pancreas
secretes digestive juices into the small intestine.

Rectum
is the lower part of the digestive tract; food residues pass from here out of the body through the anus.

Esophagus
is a passage through which food travels from the mouth to the stomach; also called the gullet.

Stomach
is a saclike part of the digestive tract in which food is stored until partially digested.

Small intestine
is the longest part of the digestive tract, in which digestion is completed.

Large intestine
extracts moisture from food residues, which are then expelled as feces.

The main organs of the human digestive system.

Food contains certain essential chemicals, called nutrients, that enable the body to function normally: proteins, carbohydrates, fats, vitamins, minerals, and water. The body can absorb some nutrients, but it has to break down, or digest, others in order to use them for energy.

In humans, digestion begins when food or drink is put in the mouth. Teeth tear and grind the food into smaller pieces. The mouth produces a fluid called saliva that contains enzymes. The enzymes break down carbohydrates into sugars.

Stomach and small intestine

After chewing, food is swallowed and passes down a tube called the esophagus to the stomach. Water, salts, and some sugars are absorbed directly into the bloodstream through the stomach wall. The remaining food is mixed with acid and an enzyme called pepsin. It becomes a soupy substance called chyme. The chyme moves from the stomach into the small intestine. It mixes with juices from the liver and pancreas. Starches are broken down into sugars. Proteins are split into smaller particles. Fats are changed to fatty acids. The digested materials pass into the bloodstream through the intestinal cells.

Whatever food is left undigested moves into the colon, then the rectum. These two parts of the body form the large intestine. Waste leaves the body as feces through a hole called the anus. Some waste is also processed by the kidneys and removed as urine through the bladder and urethra.

SEE ALSO: Health; Human Body; Teeth

✱ STONEHENGE

Stonehenge, a huge stone structure in England, is one of the world's most famous prehistoric monuments.

Stonehenge was built toward the end of the Stone Age on Salisbury Plain in southern England. It was once thought to be a temple of the pagan Druid religion. It is now generally assumed to have had some ceremonial or religious purpose.

Stonehenge was built and rebuilt in three stages over a period of 2,000 years. The first stage began about 3100 B.C. as a round ditch with a high inner bank. Inside the bank were 56 pits, named Aubrey holes for John Aubrey, the first scholar to investigate the stones. A thousand years later, about 2150 B.C., two circles of bluestone pillars were placed in the center of the original circle but were never completed. The entrance path and the bluestones were lined up so that it would be possible to see the sunrise at summer solstice (around June 21). The third stage of Stonehenge began around 2000 B.C. and ended about 1100 B.C. This is when it took its familiar form. The stones were transported great distances by sea and over land. Huge groups of people, led by skilled engineers, must have carved the stones and labored hard to raise them into place to complete their incredible task.

SEE ALSO: Archaeology; Astronomy; Religions; Wonders of the World

While some people believe that Stonehenge was built to measure the heavens, its exact purpose remains a mystery.

✱STRING INSTRUMENTS 👀see 👀 ✱MUSICAL INSTRUMENTS

✻ SUBMARINES
People have tried to develop underwater ships since ancient times. The first safe and practical submarines were built in the late 1800s.

Many submarines are used for military purposes. However, they are also used for underwater scientific exploration, such as mapping the ocean floor and investigating wrecked ships.

In the 300s B.C., the Macedonian ruler Alexander the Great was lowered into the sea in a barrel with glass portholes. This was the first recorded attempt at building an undersea vessel.

Early submarines
By 1620 the Dutchman Cornelius van Drebbel had sailed a self-propelled submarine—a wooden boat covered in greased leather—in England. But it was not until John Holland (1840–1914), an Irish-American inventor, improved the design and efficiency of submarines that they became practical military craft.

The U.S. Navy bought its first submarine from Holland in 1900. During the 1900s, submarines played a major role in both world wars, particularly World War II. Submarines on both sides inflicted great damage on enemy shipping. Only depth charges—special explosives set to go off underwater—could stop them.

Modern submarines
A submarine must have a very strong hull to cope with the enormous pressure it encounters as it descends underwater. It also has special ballast tanks. These fill with water, making the submarine heavier, when it needs to descend toward the sea bottom. When it needs to rise to the surface, the tanks are emptied. There are rudderlike fins called hydroplanes on the submarine's bow and stern to keep it at a certain depth and guide its course.

There are two main types of naval submarines—conventional and nuclear-powered. Conventional submarines have large diesel engines. These need air to operate. They only work when the submarine is on the ocean surface, or when it uses a snorkel, or air tube, to reach the surface. When the submarine descends below about 30 ft. (9 m), batteries supply its power. Conventional submarines must resurface frequently to refuel and recharge their batteries. Nuclear submarines, however, can go for months without refueling. They can cruise for 400,000 miles (about 650,000 km) and stay underwater for three months or more.

SEE ALSO: Alexander the Great; Civil War; Nuclear Power; Ships and Boats; United States Armed Forces; World War I; World War II

DID YOU KNOW?

The first submarine to make a successful attack on an enemy ship was the Confederate craft *Hunley*, during the U.S. Civil War. It was powered by a hand-cranked propeller turned by eight men. In 1864 the submarine rammed a bomb into the hull of the Union gunboat *Housatonic*. It destroyed the gunboat, but the submarine was also sunk in the explosion.

☀ SUN

The sun is a star. It is a huge ball of hot gases that gives off intense light and heat. The sun's light and heat are necessary to all life on Earth.

At a distance of about 93 million miles (150 million km), the sun is the star nearest to Earth. The next closest star, Alpha Centauri, is more than 250,000 times farther away. Light from the sun takes about 8 minutes to reach Earth; light from Alpha Centauri takes 4 years. Because the sun is so close to Earth, astronomers can study it more easily than other stars. That allows them to learn more about stars in general. Astronomers also study the sun with great interest because of its importance to Earth. Any changes in the amount of light and heat the sun produces could have tremendous consequences for everything on Earth.

Observing the sun

Although it is possible to look directly at the stars at night because they are so far away, it is very dangerous to look directly at the sun. Its intense brightness can injure people's eyes. Astronomers use special telescopes, called solar telescopes, that spread out the light from the sun instead of concentrating it. Astronomers have been able to analyze the chemical elements in the sun. They now know that the sun is made up mostly of hydrogen and helium, and that it also contains traces of other elements found on Earth.

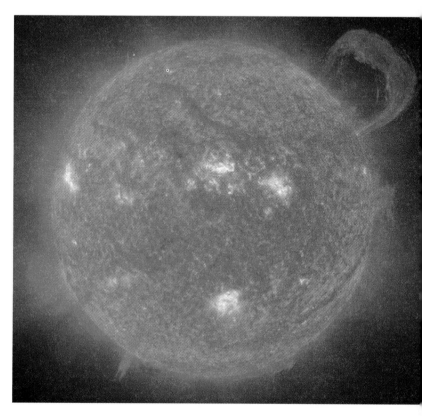

This photograph of the surface of the sun was taken from a high-powered modern telescope. An immense cloud of glowing gas, called a prominence, extends outward at top right.

Scientists estimate that the sun is about 4.55 billion years old, almost the same age as Earth and the other planets in the solar system. In comparison, scientists think that the universe is up to 15 billion years old. By studying how similar stars are formed today, scientists now think that the sun condensed out of a swirling cloud of dust and gases. The particles formed a large mass with a temperature so great that it began to generate its own energy.

AMAZING FACTS !

The sun is 10 times wider than the largest planet, Jupiter. More than a million Earths would fit inside the sun.

SEE ALSO: Earth; Light; Solar System; Stars; Telescopes; Universe

✳ SUPREME COURT

The Supreme Court is the most powerful court of law in the United States. It decides whether laws are in agreement with the Constitution.

Completed in 1935, the Supreme Court building stands across the street from the U.S. Capitol in Washington, D.C. Above its columns is the inscription "Equal Justice Under Law."

The Supreme Court heads the judicial branch of the federal government. It shares power with the legislative branch (Congress) and the executive branch (headed by the president). The Founders believed that combining the legislative, executive, and judicial powers would lead to an oppressive government. By making the judicial branch independent, they protected the court from domination by either Congress or the president.

The court was authorized by the Constitution of the United States. Article III, Section 1 of the Constitution declares that "the judicial Power of the United States, shall be vested in one supreme Court, and in such inferior Courts as the Congress may from time to time ordain and establish." The Supreme Court was established by the Judiciary Act of 1789.

John Marshall was chief justice of the Supreme Court for 34 years. He established the principle of judicial review.

Judicial review

The court's most important function is to decide whether local, state, and federal laws are in agreement with the Constitution. Its interpretation of the meaning of the Constitution and of laws is final and authoritative. Its decisions serve as guidelines for every other court in the land. It has the authority to overturn any act of government (local, state, or federal) that the presiding justices determine violates the Constitution. This power is called judicial review. It was asserted for the first time in the case of *Marbury v. Madison* (1803). Chief Justice John Marshall (1755–1835) described the Constitution as the "superior, paramount law." Since the early 1800s, the court has used the power of judicial review more than 1,000 times. In about 90 percent of these cases, the court has invalidated state laws.

How the Supreme Court works

The Supreme Court consists of nine experienced lawyers, called justices, one of whom is appointed chief justice. Congress fixed this number in 1869. The president nominates justices to the court, but the Senate has to approve his decision. Once appointed, a justice can remain with the court for the rest of his or her life, unless found guilty of serious wrongdoing.

The court usually operates from early October until late June. Most of the cases that it hears come from lower courts, mainly the state supreme courts and the U.S. appellate (appeal) courts. Parties might disagree with a decision made by one of those courts and wish to take the matter to a higher authority. Thousands of cases are presented to the Supreme Court every year. The court considers fewer than 250 cases—fewer than 5 percent of those submitted—in a session.

Once the court agrees to consider a case, the justices examine the evidence. The parties involved argue their case in court and present detailed written summaries.

The justices then discuss the matter among themselves and reach a decision. Often they do not all agree, in which case the court's decision reflects the view of the majority of justices. Justices who disagree may issue a dissenting opinion, but this does not affect the court's ruling.

The Supreme Court usually hands down its decisions on Mondays during the last few weeks of the term. The judges' opinion explains this decision. Once the court has made a decision, even the president cannot overturn it. Only an amendment to the Constitution can change a Supreme Court ruling.

Important cases
The Supreme Court has made decisions on many important issues in American history. In the "Dred Scott" case of 1857, Chief Justice Roger Taney declared that African Americans could not become citizens of the United States and that Congress did not have the authority to outlaw slavery in United States territories. President Abraham Lincoln attacked this decision as unconstitutional.

In the 1930s, the court overruled many aspects of President Franklin D. Roosevelt's New Deal program. Roosevelt was so annoyed by the constant blocking that he tried to appoint more justices in order to win a majority. The Senate defeated Roosevelt's attempt.

JUSTICES OF THE U.S. SUPREME COURT, 2003	
William Hubbs Rehnquist (1924–)	Appointed 1971 by President Richard Nixon; chief justice since 1986
Stephen Gerald Breyer (1934–)	Appointed 1994 by President Bill Clinton
Ruth Bader Ginsburg (1933–)	Appointed 1993 by President Bill Clinton
Anthony McLeod Kennedy (1936–)	Appointed 1988 by President Ronald Reagan
Sandra Day O'Connor (1930–)	Appointed 1981 by President Ronald Reagan; the first woman ever chosen
Antonin Scalia (1936–)	Appointed 1986 by President Ronald Reagan
David Hackett Souter (1939–)	Appointed 1990 by President George Bush
John Paul Stevens (1920–)	Appointed 1975 by President Gerald Ford
Clarence Thomas (1948–)	Appointed 1991 by President George Bush

In recent years, there has been much debate about how the Supreme Court should interpret the Constitution. Activists argue that the Constitution is a living document whose guidelines should be adapted to the needs of the times. Traditionalists take a more conservative view, basing their judgments on the precise language of the Constitution. They believe that it is the court's duty to try to determine what the views of the Founders would be, and then interpret matters accordingly. Today most Supreme Court justices tend to hold traditionalist views.

▲
Ruth Bader Ginsburg was a court of appeals judge for the District of Columbia before she was appointed to the Supreme Court.

SEE ALSO: Congress; Constitution, United States; Law; Presidency, The; States and State Governments; United States Government

✳ SURGERY

Surgery is a branch of medicine in which specially trained doctors called surgeons treat patients by repairing or removing parts of the body.

Even in the Stone Age, primitive healers performed operations using knives made of flint stone. An early procedure called trepanation involved cutting a hole into the skull. Prehistoric people probably practiced trepanation in order to let out evil spirits that they believed caused illness. In time surgeons developed special instruments to aid their work. Ancient Greeks and Romans used early forms of scalpels (surgical knives) and forceps (gripping instruments). They also used special saws for amputating, or removing, limbs.

Problems of pain and infection

Although there were many surgical instruments by the 1700s, pain and infection greatly limited surgery. Until 1846 alcohol and drugs, such as opium, were the only pain relief available during an operation, and they were not very effective. Surgeons had to work quickly, which was at times dangerous for the patient. In the 1840s, a method was discovered of putting patients to sleep using gases known as anesthetics.

However, many patients continued to die after operations due to infection. The French chemist Louis Pasteur (1822–95) discovered that bacteria could spoil wine and beer. In 1867 the English surgeon Joseph Lister (1827–1912) used Pasteur's findings to prove that bacteria could also cause infection in human tissue. By spraying the chemical carbolic acid on wounds, he was able to kill bacteria and stop infection. This made possible many new operations much deeper into the body, such as the abdomen and chest.

Today new technology allows more complicated procedures to be performed and makes recovery quicker and less painful for patients. For example, surgeons use special cameras called laparoscopes to see deep inside the body while they are operating. This enables them to make only a small incision (cut) in the body.

Most surgeons specialize in a particular problem. For example, a patient with a heart problem sees a cardiac surgeon. Sometimes surgery, such as the removal of the appendix, is the only treatment for a problem. But an operation can also be combined with other treatments, such as chemotherapy, which is a special drug therapy for cancer.

Surgeons perform an operation with the help of onscreen images produced by a laparoscope inside the patient's body.

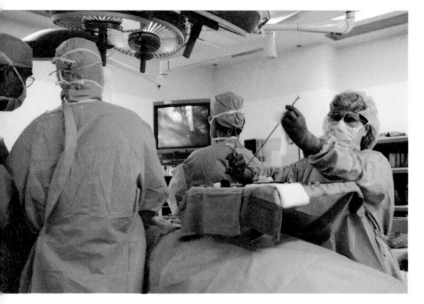

SEE ALSO: Diseases; Health; Hospitals; Medicine; Pasteur, Louis; X-rays

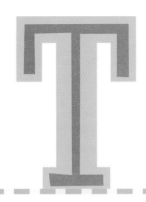

✳ TASTE AND SMELL
Taste and smell are two senses that work closely together. The most important organs for taste and smell are the tongue and the nose.

Taste

The tongue has many small bumps, called papillae (singular, *papilla*), on its surface. They contain taste buds that are activated by the chemical reaction that occurs when food is dissolved in saliva in the mouth. Taste buds send messages to the brain about whether the flavor of the food is sweet, sour, bitter, or salty.

Taste helps people enjoy food. But it has a more important function. Many poisons and other dangerous substances have a strong, bitter taste. Food that is spoiled often tastes sour. If something tastes bad, we can spit it out before swallowing and it is less likely to do harm.

The tastes that people enjoy can vary greatly. Some people like very sweet foods, while others prefer saltiness. Different cultures have different ideas about what tastes good.

Smell

Anything that has an odor gives off tiny particles of gas that mix with the air. By breathing, we draw these particles into our noses, where nerve cells sense the particles and send a message to the brain, which can then identify the smell.

Smell stimulates the appetite, but it can also protect against danger. Some harmful substances, such as natural gas, give off bad smells.

Smell affects taste. That is because food in the mouth also gives off gases that reach the smell receptors. If something happens to restrict the sense of smell—for example, a cold—the sense of taste is also dulled.

▲ *In the storeroom of a cheese factory in Parma, Italy, a cheesemaker tests the quality of a piece of Parmesan cheese by smelling it.*

AMAZING FACTS❗

An adult human has about 10,000 taste buds in the tongue, palate, and cheeks. **A human** has about 40 million receptor cells to identify odors, whereas a rabbit has 100 million, and a dog has 1 billion.

SEE ALSO: Brain and Nervous System; Food; Human Body

✳ TECHNOLOGY

Technology is the term for all the many different methods that people use to make products or perform tasks in order to improve their lives.

▲
This experiment demonstrates the insulating property of aerogel. Despite the concentrated flame, aerogel prevents the wax crayons from melting. Aerogel is the lightest solid material known. It was first developed in the 1930s. Today it is used in space research.

Almost every part of our lives is touched by technology, from the food we eat to the way we spend our leisure time. Technology is not the same as science, but the two subjects are connected. Scientists help us to understand the technologies we use, and they develop new ideas. Technology gives scientists different ways of making and doing things.

Technology is changing all the time. For example, humans learned long ago to build houses and sow crops, but research still continues in construction and agriculture. Today we can build energy-efficient homes and grow disease-resistant soybeans.

Sometimes a change in one area of technology leads to change in others. Radar, developed to spot enemy aircraft, now helps control air traffic at busy airports. Materials developed for space travel have found many uses on Earth.

The pace of technological change was once much slower than it is today. The Chinese, for example, were making paper by about A.D. 100, but it took more than 1,000 years for this technology to reach western Europe. By contrast, only a century has passed since the Wright brothers first flew their powered airplane, and yet today jet airliners carry more than a billion passengers a year.

Technological change sped up after the Industrial Revolution, which began in Europe in the 1700s. Textiles and other goods began to be produced by machine rather than by hand. Factories were built to house the machines, and people began to produce goods faster and in greater quantities than ever before.

The 20th century saw great leaps in technology. Computers now control many machines and have become basic tools of research, education, communication, and business. Rockets have launched humans into space. Communications satellites circle the planet, watching the world, foretelling the weather, and transmitting information. With nuclear technology, people have developed new sources of energy—and powerful new weapons.

TECHNOLOGY TIMELINE

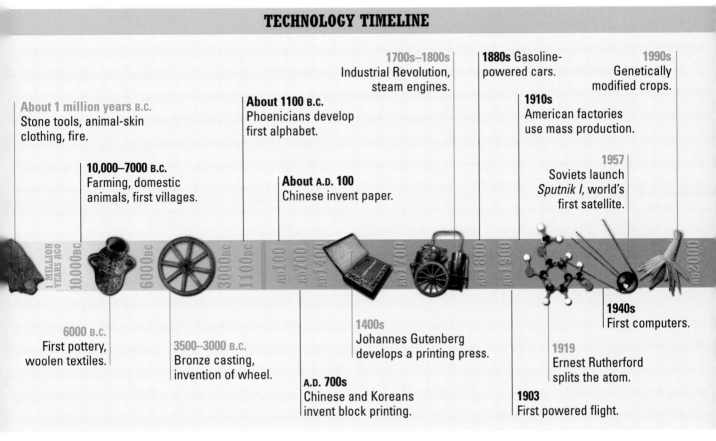

1700s–1800s
Industrial Revolution, steam engines.

1880s Gasoline-powered cars.

1990s
Genetically modified crops.

About 1 million years B.C.
Stone tools, animal-skin clothing, fire.

About 1100 B.C.
Phoenicians develop first alphabet.

1910s
American factories use mass production.

10,000–7000 B.C.
Farming, domestic animals, first villages.

About A.D. **100**
Chinese invent paper.

1957
Soviets launch *Sputnik I*, world's first satellite.

1 MILLION YEARS AGO · 10,000BC · 6000BC · 3000BC · 1100BC · AD100 · AD700 · AD1400 · AD1700 · AD1800 · AD1900 · AD2000

1940s
First computers.

6000 B.C.
First pottery, woolen textiles.

3500–3000 B.C.
Bronze casting, invention of wheel.

1400s
Johannes Gutenberg develops a printing press.

1919
Ernest Rutherford splits the atom.

A.D. **700s**
Chinese and Koreans invent block printing.

1903
First powered flight.

Effects of technology

Some societies are more technologically advanced than others. They have become richer, while less-developed societies remain poor. Also, technology can bring harmful as well as helpful effects. For example, improvements in transportation have allowed people to travel farther and faster than ever before, but automobiles cause many highway deaths and pollute the air. Mass production uses up natural resources, and mass consumption of goods causes large amounts of trash that must be disposed of in some way.

However, technology can provide ways to solve these problems. Materials can be recycled, for example. This preserves raw materials and saves energy. New synthetic materials are being developed to replace natural materials that are in short supply.

Technology can also provide better ways to limit pollution. The challenge for the future is to make sure that the benefits of technological change outweigh the harmful effects.

▲
This timeline shows some of the key inventions in the history of technology.

SEE ALSO: Agriculture; Aircraft; Alphabet; Ancient Civilizations; Cars; Communication; Computers; Electronics; Energy; Engines; Fabrics and Cloth; Genetics; Industrial Revolution; Internet; Inventors and Inventions; Machines; Manufacturing; Matter; Medicine; Metals; Nuclear Power; Pollution; Printing; Robots; Rockets; Satellites; Ships and Boats; Spacecraft; Space Exploration; Telecommunications; Telephones; Television; Tools; Wright, Orville and Wilbur

✳ TEETH

Healthy teeth are an important part of overall good health. They also help us to speak clearly and to chew food properly.

PARTS OF A TOOTH

▷ *A human tooth consists of a crown and one or more roots. The crown is covered by very hard enamel and is visible above the gum. The roots are embedded in the jawbone. The central part of the tooth—the pulp—contains nerves and blood vessels.*

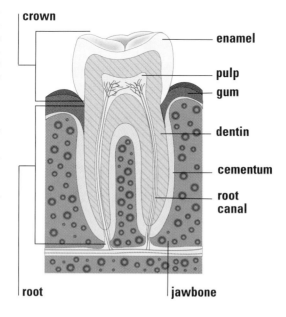

crown
enamel
pulp
gum
dentin
cementum
root canal
root
jawbone

Parts of a tooth

Human teeth are made up of a crown and one or more roots. The crown grows above the gums, and the root grows in a socket in the jawbone. The crown is coated in a hard substance called enamel. The root has an outer, bonelike layer called cementum. A third hard substance, called dentin, forms a continuous shell beneath the enamel and the cementum. The dentin makes up most of the body of the tooth. The inside of the tooth is filled with a soft tissue called dental pulp. The pulp contains blood vessels and nerves that cause pain when they are irritated by, for example, tooth decay.

Caring for teeth

Pain in a tooth is a sign that you may have tooth decay, or cavities. A cavity is a hole in the enamel surface of the tooth. Cavities are caused by the bacteria that are always present in the mouth. These bacteria live on the cooked starch and sugar present in food. The bacteria turn these foods into acid, which slowly causes the tooth's enamel to dissolve.

The best way to protect your teeth against cavities is to brush and floss them after each meal to remove bacteria and food particles. You should also limit the amount of sugary and starchy food in your diet, such as cookies, candies, and soft drinks, and have regular dental examinations.

Human beings grow two sets of teeth. The first set are known as primary teeth; the second set are known as secondary, or permanent, teeth. The primary teeth start to come through the gum between six months and a year after a baby is born. By the age of three, a child has 20 teeth. At about six years of age, the permanent teeth start to push out the first teeth. Most children have their permanent teeth by the age of 11. In the permanent set, there are 32 teeth.

There are different types of teeth, each performing a different function. For example, incisors are the eight sharp-edged teeth in the front of the mouth used to cut food. Molars are the teeth at the back of the mouth used for grinding.

SEE ALSO: Health; Stomach and Digestive System; Tongue and Speech

TELECOMMUNICATIONS

Technology that allows people to communicate with one another, frequently over great distances, is called telecommunications.

People use many different devices to communicate. These include telephones, fax machines, radio, television, and, increasingly, computers. Many computers, telephones, and other machines are linked in networks. These enable people to share large amounts of information.

Using electricity

The telegraph, invented by Samuel Morse in 1837, was an early device that used the flow of electricity to transmit messages from sender to receiver. Operators tapped on keys to spell out messages in combinations of long and short electrical pulses, called dots and dashes. These corresponded to letters and numbers in a system known as Morse code. The pulses traveled over wires to other telegraph machines, where operators translated the code back into the original message. Alexander Graham Bell worked out how to transmit the human voice over telegraph wires in the 1870s, and the long-distance telephone service was developed.

Facsimile, or fax, machines are able to send and receive documents. Early systems enabled newspapers to exchange photographs of events around the world. Faster and cheaper machines became common during the 1980s. By the 1990s, faxes could be sent and received using computers connected to telephone lines.

Using radio waves and light waves

In 1901 Guglielmo Marconi sent a message in dots and dashes across the Atlantic Ocean using radio waves. Radio broadcasts of voices and music became a source of entertainment, but radio also

provided a vital link for ships and planes because it allowed them to communicate without wires. A popular application of radio today is cellular telephones. These are portable devices connected to telephone networks through a series of radio transmitter–receivers that cover small areas, or cells.

Inventors began to experiment with broadcasting moving pictures over radio waves in the early 1900s. Television was widely available by the middle of the century. Today it is the leading source of news and entertainment around the world.

Microwave and satellite relay systems are used to transmit radio signals over long distances. Microwaves are radio waves with very short wavelengths. They travel in narrow, straight lines and carry signals between towers spaced many miles apart. Satellites are positioned above the earth

Optical fibers are threads of glass or plastic that transmit signals in the form of light pulses. They carry much more information than copper cables or microwaves, and are used in telephone, computer, and cable-television networks.

and circle the planet at the same rate as it rotates, remaining fixed over one spot. As they receive microwave transmissions from ground stations, they relay the transmissions to other stations.

Fiber optics use pulses of light generated by a tiny laser. The pulses are transmitted over thin strands of glass called optical fibers. A device detects the light and converts the signal into electrical pulses.

Digital communications

The biggest change in telecommunications in recent times has been the move from analog to digital signals. Analog signals are electrical currents or electromagnetic waves that change smoothly in their amplitude (height) or frequency. Digital signals represent the original signals in strings of 1s and 0s. These bits (short for "binary digits") correspond to "on" and "off" electrical pulses and can represent a sound wave's changing amplitude and frequency, or the letters and numbers of computer data. Digital information is transmitted at great speed.

The first computer network was developed in the 1960s in order for scientists at a few U.S. universities to share information. It later grew to connect millions of computers across the world in what is now called the Internet. One of the earliest uses of the Internet was electronic mail, or e-mail. A recent use of the Internet is the World Wide Web. It is a method of sharing information on "pages" that can be viewed on a computer screen. Collections of pages are called websites.

SEE ALSO: Bell, Alexander Graham; Communication; Computers; Electricity; Internet; Inventors and Inventions; Media; Radio; Satellites; Telephones; Television

✳ TELEPHONES

Telephones use an electric current to carry sound over a great distance so that people who are far apart can talk to each other.

A CARBON-GRANULE MICROPHONE

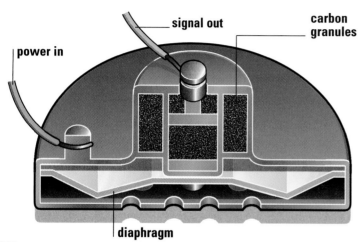

power in

signal out

carbon granules

diaphragm

A telephone has three main parts: the transmitter (or microphone), the receiver (or speaker), and the connecting wires. The transmitter and receiver are in the handset, the part of the telephone that you hold. A dialing mechanism is located either in the handset or in a base unit. When you speak into the transmitter, the sound waves of your voice meet a thin piece of metal called the diaphragm,

◄

The microphone in a telephone converts sound into electrical signals that are then sent along wires. The diaphragm moves when hit by sound waves. That compresses the carbon granules, producing a varying electrical signal.

causing it to vibrate. The vibrations are converted into an electrical current. Changes in the electrical current form an electrical pattern of your voice. When your call reaches another telephone, its receiver changes the current carrying your voice back into sound waves.

Telephone networks

A telephone call may travel in a variety of ways. Older long-distance telephone cables consist of thousands of copper wires or of special pipelines called coaxial cables. Each wire or pipeline can handle a number of calls at the same time. Calls do not interfere with each other because each one is transmitted at a slightly different frequency, or rate of vibration. In many areas, copper and coaxial cables are being replaced by fiber-optic cables. These

cables carry light, and although they are no thicker than a finger, they can carry tens of thousands of calls at one time.

In a fiber-optic system, the electrical signal produced by your voice is changed into a code made up of 1s and 0s, like the code that operates computers. This binary, or two-digit, code switches a tiny laser on and off thousands of times a second. Pulses of laser light travel down the optical fiber to their destination, where they are changed back into electrical signals and sound.

SEE ALSO: Bell, Alexander Graham; Communication; Computers; Electricity; Lasers; Sound; Telecommunications

✳ TELESCOPES

A telescope is an instrument used to make distant objects appear nearer and more distinct. *Telescope* comes from the Greek words for "far" and "see."

OPTICAL TELESCOPES

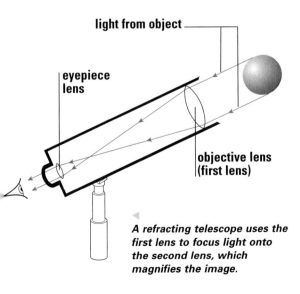

light from object

eyepiece lens

objective lens (first lens)

A refracting telescope uses the first lens to focus light onto the second lens, which magnifies the image.

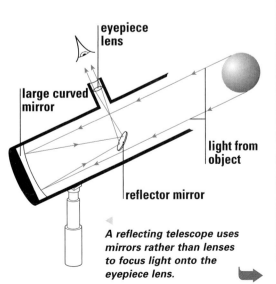

eyepiece lens

large curved mirror

light from object

reflector mirror

A reflecting telescope uses mirrors rather than lenses to focus light onto the eyepiece lens.

Telescopes gather and focus light, radio, infrared (heat), and X-ray waves to create close-up images. Optical telescopes, which use light, are the most common type. There are three main kinds: refractors, which use lenses; reflectors, which use mirrors; and catadioptrics, which use both lenses and mirrors. Each has a different way of gathering light.

The world's largest telescopes are reflectors because it is easier and less expensive to create a big mirror than it is to create a big lens. The world's largest optical telescopes are in the astronomical observatory on Mauna Kea, Hawaii.

Radio telescopes

Besides visible light, many stars send out other kinds of radiation, some of it in the form of radio waves. Astronomers can detect these waves with radio telescopes. A radio telescope works in a way similar to a reflector, but it has an antenna instead of a mirror. The antenna is often a huge metal dish, fitted on a movable stand so that it can be pointed at any part of the sky. The antenna detects radio waves and sends them to a receiver that amplifies (strengthens) them. The amplified waves are changed to electrical pulses, or signals, that are recorded by a computer.

Telescopes in space

The thick blanket of atmosphere around Earth prevents most forms of radiation from reaching the ground. Astronomers place telescopes sensitive to invisible energies on board spacecraft that orbit Earth. The Hubble Space Telescope, launched in 1990, can detect visible light as well as ultraviolet and infrared radiation coming from objects in space. It has helped astronomers study distant galaxies.

SEE ALSO: Astronomy; Atmosphere; Galaxies; Galilei, Galileo; Light; Newton, Isaac; Radio; Scientific Instruments; Stars; Universe; X-rays

❋ TELEVISION

Television (TV) is a means of sending images and sound over distances. It is one of the most important methods of communication in the modern world.

A television camera splits incoming light into three colors—red, green, and blue. The light strikes special silicon chips called charge-coupled devices (CCDs) that convert it into electrical signals. Sound waves enter a microphone, where their vibrations are also converted into electrical signals. In a live broadcast, the picture and sound are transmitted at once, but more often they are recorded on tape.

The signals travel from the camera to a transmitter, which combines the signals with electromagnetic waves. Transmitting towers relay the waves over distances up to about 50 miles (80 km), to an antenna connected to a receiver—a television set. Today signals are often carried by underground cable or bounced off satellites orbiting the earth.

Once the signals reach the television set, a complex electronic circuit processes the sound and video information. It sends the video information to the screen, where it is reconstructed into the original image.

The inside of the television screen is coated with thousands of tiny phosphors,

◀
A photograph of rows of televisions taken in the 1990s. Television is a major source of entertainment for most Americans. It also enables people to keep up-to-date with news and sports. In the United States, more than 98 percent of homes have at least one TV set.

substances that emit light when struck by electrons. Each phosphor is responsible for reproducing either the color red, green, or blue. Three electron guns, one for each color, shoot a beam of electrons, line by line, through a screen pierced with thousands of holes. The holes direct the beams to hit the phosphors, so that when each dot is hit, it glows with its respective color. Because the dots are so close together, the viewer's eyes see the mix of primary colors as the whole range of colors that were in the original scene. The sound signals are sent to loudspeakers, where the electrical signals are converted back into sound in the same way that the microphone first recorded the sound.

History

In the late 1800s, scientists discovered that electrical signals could be transmitted through air as electromagnetic waves. This led to the invention of radio. Inventors tried to send images in the same way, but

INSIDE A TELEVISION

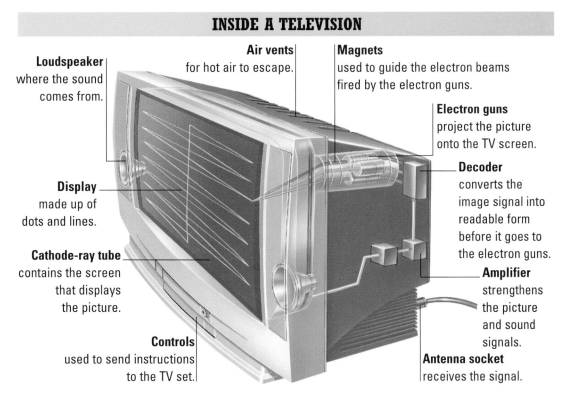

Loudspeaker
where the sound comes from.

Air vents
for hot air to escape.

Magnets
used to guide the electron beams fired by the electron guns.

Electron guns
project the picture onto the TV screen.

Display
made up of dots and lines.

Cathode-ray tube
contains the screen that displays the picture.

Controls
used to send instructions to the TV set.

Decoder
converts the image signal into readable form before it goes to the electron guns.

Amplifier
strengthens the picture and sound signals.

Antenna socket
receives the signal.

The television is a complex piece of equipment that converts electrical signals into sounds and pictures.
◀

the problem was how to "scan" a scene line by line in order to turn it into electrical signals. In 1926 the Scot John Logie Baird (1888–1946) demonstrated a mechanical system, using spinning disks with holes in them. In the 1930s, Philo T. Farnsworth and Vladimir K. Zworykin, both working in the United States, developed different electronic systems, using glass vacuum tubes and electron beams, that could scan many lines very quickly. In 1941 the National Television Systems Committee (NTSC) set up a system that combined elements of both systems. In the NTSC system, television pictures are made up of 525 horizontal lines each, displayed at a speed of 30 frames (pictures) per second. At that speed, the frames blend smoothly.

Color broadcasts began in the 1950s. Around the same time, videotape recorders were invented, although the technology was not available to home users until the 1970s. Sending programs through cable and satellite, which began in the 1980s, made it possible for a set to receive hundreds of channels. In the late 1990s, digital high-definition television (HDTV) appeared. It converts sound and pictures into electronic pulses that stand for the digits 1 ("on") and 0 ("off")—the same code used by computers. HDTV allows broadcasters to send pictures that are up to four times sharper than conventional television pictures. Digital signals can also carry better color and reproduce movie-quality sound.

SEE ALSO: Colors; Electronics; Light; Media; Radio; Satellites; Sound Recording; Telecommunications; Video Recording

* THEATER

A theater is a place in which actors perform for an audience. The word *theater* also describes the whole process of producing and performing drama.

A performance of a Greek tragedy. The actors are wearing traditional masks to show grief.

A typical theater building has a stage, which is where the actors perform, and an auditorium, where the audience sits. Backstage (behind the stage) are the actors' dressing rooms, as well as stored scenery and props—items used onstage.

Theater people

The playwright, or dramatist, writes the play. The producer selects the play, and the director is responsible for the whole process of presenting the play. The director works with the actors and the rest of the company to turn the playwright's words into drama. The stage manager helps the director and is in charge backstage during the performance.

Actors take on the roles of characters in the play. Theirs is an ancient tradition, dating back thousands of years to when the first actors danced, chanted, and sang in religious ceremonies. Actors need to be able to speak clearly, to take on the

T

personality of their characters, and to show feelings with their facial expressions and body movements.

Other members of the theater company include set designers, lighting and sound designers, costume designers, and makeup artists. They are assisted by the backstage crew, who carry props and operate equipment.

Theater around the world

Theater is a worldwide art form. In most countries the government helps pay for at least one major national theater. New York City's theaters are clustered in a theater district called Broadway. In England many theaters are located in a part of London called the West End. France's most famous theater, the Comédie-Française in Paris, began in 1680. Russia's Moscow Art Theater was founded by Konstantin Stanislavsky in 1898.

The two most famous forms of Japanese drama are Noh and Kabuki. Noh plays use ancient language and are performed very slowly. Kabuki plays, which were written in the 1500s and 1600s, have more action, and their language is more modern.

SEE ALSO: Dance; Literature; Nobel Prize; Shakespeare, William

✳TIGERS see ✳CATS AND BIG CATS

✳ TIME

Time cannot be seen or touched, but measuring it is important. Being able to tell the time helps daily life run efficiently.

Time is invisible, but we can observe its passing. The growth of a flower and the darkening night sky show that time has passed. However, it is useful to be able to measure progress from one day, hour, or minute to the next. Ancient civilizations kept time by studying the movement of tides, planets, and stars. Clocks and watches are more convenient, but the hours they mark still follow the rhythms of nature—in particular, Earth's rotation.

Time around the world

As Earth spins from west to east on its polar axis, each point on the planet moves into and then out of the sun's light. Dawn therefore arrives earlier in New York than in San Francisco.

Because Earth rotates a full 360 degrees every 24 hours, the surface of the globe is divided into 24 different time zones, each 15 degrees wide—one time zone for each hour of Earth's rotation. Anywhere in that zone, and in that zone only, the time is the same, or "standard."

AMAZING FACTS!

The U.S. Naval Observatory's atomic clock loses or gains less than 0.0000000001 seconds between one day and the next. Check your watch against it at http://tycho.usno.navy.mil/cgi-bin/timer.pl

The lower 48 states are divided into four time zones, each one hour apart. Traveling eastward, they are Pacific, Mountain, Central, and Eastern. There are two more zones—Alaska, one hour behind Pacific time, and Hawaii, two hours behind. In summer all the states except Arizona and Indiana set their clocks ahead by one hour. This provides one more hour of daylight in the evening rather than in the morning, so it is called daylight saving time. In the fall, clocks turn back an hour to standard time. This is common practice in many other parts of the world. A world time zone map can be found at the end of the encyclopedia.

The midpoint of each zone is indicated by a vertical line, called a meridian, that runs from one pole to the other. The meridian that runs through Greenwich, England, is at 0° longitude. All other meridians are either east or west of Greenwich. New York, for example, is five meridians west of London so it is five hours behind. The time at Greenwich is called Universal Time.

The meridian on the opposite side of the world from Greenwich, through the Pacific Ocean, is the International Date Line. The date changes as travelers cross the line, so it is December 31 on one side and January 1 on the other.

SEE ALSO: Astronomy; Clocks and Watches; Mathematics; Navigation

---

✳TOADS ⟨see⟩ ✳FROGS AND TOADS

✳TONGUE AND SPEECH

Humans have a very complex communication system. We produce speech using a number of organs in the throat and mouth, including the tongue.

The organs of speech in the mouth and throat are the larynx, pharynx, tongue, teeth, and lips.

The larynx is a muscular tube in the throat. It contains the vocal cords that are the source of sound in the voice. Sound begins when air passes over the vocal cords and makes them vibrate. When the vocal cords are pulled tight by muscles in the larynx, the vibrations produce a high-pitched sound. When the vocal cords are loosened, they produce a lower tone. The cavities of the throat (pharynx) help

reinforce the sound coming from the vocal cords. The teeth, tongue, and lips all help shape the sound into syllables (units of sound in a word) and words.

In order to speak, you must be able to make different sounds. The consonant sounds P, B, and M are all made with the lips. Vowel sounds are made by changing the positions of the jaw, lips, and tongue. For the ee sound in "mean," the tongue is high in the front of the mouth. For the oo sound in "moon," the tongue is low in the back of the mouth.

Speech disorders

People who have a problem with their speech that interferes with communication are said to have a speech disorder. Speech disorders include lisping (a problem with *s* sounds) and stuttering (difficulty in getting sounds out). Speech therapists can usually help with these and similar problems.

Tongue

The tongue is a muscular organ covered in receptors that allow us to taste. Its rough surface assists in chewing and swallowing. It is also vital to the ability to speak. Many speech disorders occur because the tongue does not move properly. Physical therapy or, in some cases, surgery can help give the tongue full mobility.

SEE ALSO: Communication; Human Body; Languages; Sound; Taste and Smell; Teeth

HUMAN SPEECH ORGANS

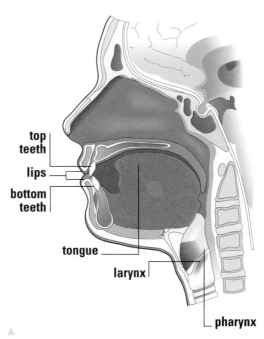

top teeth
lips
bottom teeth
tongue
larynx
pharynx

Speech is produced by muscular structures in the throat and mouth. The larynx contains vocal cords that vibrate to make sound.

DID YOU KNOW?

A tongue twister is a group of words that is difficult to repeat rapidly several times. Most tongue twisters are just for fun, but they have also been used to improve speech or to help people with speech problems. "Black bug's blood" is a well-known example of a difficult tongue twister.

✳ TOOLS

A tool is a device used to carry out a task. The ability to make and use tools is an important difference between humans and other animals.

Some animals use sticks and stones to carry out simple tasks, but that is the extent of their tool use. People have been devising tools since prehistoric times.

Anything from a paintbrush to a computer could be called a tool. Usually, however, the term describes hammers, drills, and other such implements that are used to make and mend objects. Tools can be divided into hand tools, hand power tools, and machine tools.

Some of the many hand tools include hammers and mallets (for pounding), axes, chisels, and saws (cutting), planes and files (shaping), drills (boring), wrenches (turning), pliers (holding), and rules (measuring).

Powered hand tools, which are driven by small electric motors, are light, fast, and powerful. One of the most versatile hand power tools is the electric drill. It not only drills holes but can also screw, brush, polish, sand, rasp, and cut. Other useful power tools include routers (for cutting moldings and channels in wood) and saws (for cutting wood). ➡

Beginning about 9000 B.C., people made blades from pieces of stone. They were used to scrape flesh from animal skins.

▶ **The Building of Noah's Ark,** *painted in 1423 by an unknown artist. The workmen are using hammers, drills, planes, axes, and saws.*

History

Humans probably used sticks and stones as simple tools about one million years ago. But it was not until about 9000 B.C. that people began to make tools similar to those of today.

In the New Stone Age, or Neolithic Period (started about 9000 B.C. in some parts of the world), tools were made from wood, bone, ivory, and shell as well as stone. Hammers were simple hand-sized stones. Scrapers—stones chipped on one side to create a sharp edge—were used to skin animals. Bone awls (spikes) were used to make holes in a skin in order to stitch it into clothing. The first drills were stones shaped into sharp points, which were twisted back and forth.

During the Bronze Age (about 3300–1500 B.C. in some parts of the world), people discovered how to use fire to separate copper ore from rock. By pouring molten copper into clay molds, they created metal tools. Later they added tin to copper to make bronze, a stronger, harder metal. Metal tools were easier to handle and produced finer work.

During the Iron Age (about 1500 B.C. to the A.D. 400s), iron replaced copper and bronze in toolmaking. Tools made from iron had sharper edges. The Romans used many iron tools and introduced iron nails.

During the Middle Ages (about 500–1500), tools changed little, although planes,

Machine tools include lathes (for turning wood and metal), drills, grinders, and mechanical saws. They are large, stationary devices that are designed to do much of the same type of work as hand tools. Because of their size and power, they can do a job much faster than a worker with hand tools, and the results are more consistent and precise. Machine tools can also handle much larger pieces of work, and since they can produce hundreds of identical parts, they are used for mass production. Some machine tools are small enough to be used in home workshops.

which had been developed during the Iron Age, were modified for special uses. During the 1600s and 1700s, toolmaking became a separate trade, requiring years of training. Lathes for turning metal appeared and were first used by clockmakers. Steel, which holds a sharp edge longer than iron, was widely used.

Before the Industrial Revolution, hand tools were used to produce goods. The invention of steam meant that goods were produced by power-driven machines that could only be manufactured by machine tools. Electricity also brought huge changes to tool use. Today factory production is largely automated—controlled by computers and robots.

SEE ALSO: Agriculture; Ancient Civilizations; Engines; Industrial Revolution; Machines; Manufacturing; Metals; Robots; Technology

✳ TORAH

The Torah is the first five books of the Hebrew Bible. In a broader sense, it refers to a body of learning that is central to Judaism.

In Hebrew *Torah* means "instruction." In its narrowest sense, the word *Torah* refers to the Pentateuch ("the books of the law")—the first five books of the Hebrew Bible. These are Genesis, Exodus, Leviticus, Numbers, and Deuteronomy. They are considered an exact record of the word of God that was given to Moses on Mount Sinai. The books describe the creation of the world, the origins of the Jewish people, their exile and slavery in Egypt, their redemption, and the giving of the Torah to Moses.

The written Torah is kept in all Jewish synagogues on handwritten scrolls of parchment. The scrolls are housed in the Ark, a large, elaborately decorated cabinet. Readings from the Torah are an important part of worship in the synagogue. The Torah portions are divided in such a way that the entire Torah is read during the course of a year. The reading is completed and a new one begun on the day following the end of Sukkoth, a fall harvest festival. Orthodox, or strict, Jews do not allow women to read from the Torah.

Oral traditions

The word *Torah* is also sometimes used to refer to the whole Hebrew Bible. Some Jews consider the laws passed down through oral traditions to be part of God's revelation to Moses. They make up the "oral Torah." In this sense, Torah stands for both the written law and the oral law.

Some Jews treat the scholarly commentaries on and interpretations of oral and written law as an extension of

A father and son hold the Torah in front of the Western Wall in Jerusalem, Israel, after the boy's Bar Mitzvah service. When boys turn 13 years old, they read from the Torah as a part of the Bar Mitzvah ceremony.

oral tradition. The study and interpretation of Jewish oral traditions is recorded in a large body of literature known as the Talmud. Its compilation was begun by rabbis—the teachers of Judaism—in the first and second centuries A.D. So, in its widest sense, Torah refers to the entire body of Jewish laws and customs.

◄

A Torah procession in Brooklyn, New York City. Processions are held when new Torah scrolls are carried into a synagogue for the first time. The Torah is paraded through the streets under a canopy called a chuppah.

SEE ALSO: Bible; Holocaust; Israel; Judaism; Religions

✳ TORNADOES

A tornado is a violent windstorm in which a rotating column of air forms at the base of a thunderstorm and extends toward the ground in a funnel shape.

Tornadoes can happen almost anywhere in the world, but they mostly occur in the United States, where they are sometimes known as twisters. There are about 1,000 tornadoes a year in the United States, especially in the Midwest. Most of them occur between March and June.

How tornadoes form

A tornado usually begins with an area of low pressure (a region in which warm, light air is rising into the atmosphere). Winds bring warm, humid air from one direction and cold, dry air from another. When the streams of air meet around an area of low pressure, storms can occur. In some conditions, massive thunderstorms can extend 50,000 ft. (15,240 m) or more into the atmosphere. At times these storms develop a rotation (turn in circles),

and smaller rotations, or tornadoes, may form within the larger rotation. These conditions occur most frequently in an area of the United States called Tornado Alley, which runs northeastward from northern Texas into Illinois.

Characteristics of tornadoes

Most tornadoes begin as a funnel-shaped cloud extending from the base of a thundercloud. Sometimes this funnel reaches the ground; at other times, it simply dangles from the bottom of the thundercloud. If the circulating air of the tornado has already reached the ground, the only clue to its presence may be dust swirling on the ground.

The rotating winds of tornadoes can range from about 40 mph (64 kph) to more than

300 mph (480 kph). The extremely high winds of some tornadoes can cause enormous destruction, flattening everything in their path, sometimes picking up people, animals, vehicles, and even small buildings and carrying them long distances.

Tornadoes are classified according to the Fujita scale, depending on their wind speeds and damage. The largest tornadoes, classified F4 and F5, can be more than a mile (1.6 km) wide, last up to an hour or more, and travel over paths averaging 30 to 35 miles (48–56 km) long.

A tornado can be a very frightening experience. Meteorologists—experts who study the weather—can predict when a tornado might occur and issue warnings. People in areas that receive tornado warnings should seek shelter immediately and follow tornado safety rules.

SEE ALSO: Climate; Hurricanes and Typhoons; Weather; Wind

As a tornado picks up soil and debris, it becomes brown, gray, or black in appearance.

✱ TOUCH

Touch is the sense that reacts to pressure applied to the surface of the body. Nerve cells in the skin send signals to the brain about the effect of the touch.

The sense of touch is created by electronic messages that are sent to the brain from fine nerve endings all over the surface of the body, in the skin, and in hair shafts. Some parts of the body—the fingertips, tongue, and lips—have particularly large collections of nerve cells.

The sense of touch is vital to humans. Without it even simple tasks, such as fastening a shirt, would be very difficult because we would not be able to feel the buttons. Touch is very important for people who have lost another sense, especially sight. Braille, the system of printing for blind people, uses raised dots that are "read" by touching them with the fingers.

Temperature and pain

The various nerve endings of the skin respond differently to changes in temperature. People become aware of warmth or cold only if something that is hotter or colder than normal skin temperature—about 77°F (25°C)—is applied to their skin. Once the brain has been informed of such changes in temperature, it can trigger physical responses, such as shivering, perspiration, or the raising of hairs on the skin.

If the temperature becomes more than 68°F (20°C) above or below normal, the brain cannot always tell whether the sensation is too hot or too cold. That is

The Braille alphabet is used by blind people. Each letter has its own special arrangement of raised dots. ▶

why, for example, when you touch a block of ice, you sometimes experience a burning sensation.

The reaction to extreme temperature is very similar to a pain reaction. The pain reaction is a special kind of touch sensation that protects people from harm. If you touch something that hurts, you immediately pull your hand away in an automatic response—you do not think before you do it. People often think of pain as a bad thing, but it is useful because it tells the brain that something is wrong. Pain might warn of injury, infection, or illness. It can also alert people to get away from danger.

SEE ALSO: Brain and Nervous System; Human Body

✱ TOWNS AND VILLAGES

Towns are urban communities that are smaller than cities. Villages are even smaller settlements, sometimes within the borders of a town.

Towns

Cities are large towns that have been granted a special document confirming their importance. By contrast, there is no real definition of a town. Towns tend to be smaller and less crowded than cities, but generally have at least 1,000 inhabitants. They usually have stores, movies, and hospitals, but not business headquarters or institutions such as embassies.

Before the foundation of the United States, towns in North America were colonial taxing units. Through taxes a town paid for its own roads, education, and relief for the poor. Several towns paid toward the costs of a county court.

Modern towns may still provide these and other services, such as fire and police protection, and libraries. Each town has a chief officer to plan the budget and supervise the various departments. The chief officer may be the town supervisor, town manager, town board, or, in the New England states, the town meeting.

Villages

In Europe villages developed as small pockets of community in rural areas. Before the 1800s, most people lived in such settlements. Each village had a church and maybe a few tradespeople, such as blacksmiths. The nearest stores were in the local market town, which could be several miles away.

Villages are generally smaller than a town, but larger than a hamlet (a settlement with several families and some form of commerce, but no more than 50 people). Most villages in the United States today are communities located within a town. They developed when clusters of people began to need specific services of their own. A village may have an elected mayor and a board of trustees. Village residents use the town facilities for some services.

SEE ALSO: Cities; Colonial America; States and State Governments

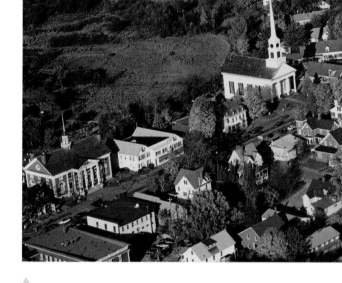
▲
The first settlement at Stowe, Vermont, was in 1793, and the town developed during the early 1800s. Skiing was introduced in 1913 by Swedish families, and Stowe has become a popular center for winter sports.

★ TRADE

Trade is the exchange of one product for money, a service, or another product. Since ancient times, it has been the cornerstone of wealth and civilization.

The exchange of goods and services to satisfy the needs of consumers is known as trade or commerce. *Trade* usually refers to the exchange of a particular product. For example, people might say that a country's main trade is in coffee, tea, or sugar. The word *commerce* covers all aspects of trading.

History

The earliest trading was bartering—the simple exchange of one type of goods for another, such as grain for cloth, cloth for a knife, and so on. But bartering was not practical because traders could not always find other traders with the kind of goods they wanted. People began to exchange their goods for money, which they could use to buy anything they wanted.

For thousands of years, traders traveled from place to place to exchange goods. Most international trade was in luxuries—goods that people could not get at home. At the height of the Roman Empire, the market stalls in Rome sold spices from the Middle East, silks from the Far East, precious stones from Egypt, ivory from Africa, and tin from Britain.

After the Western Roman Empire fell in the fifth century A.D., trading declined. The people of Europe returned to bartering or growing their own produce until the Crusades in the 11th to 13th centuries revived the trade in Eastern luxuries.

The discoveries of America and a sea route to Asia around Africa's Cape of Good Hope brought new life to world trade. ➡

Many cities on the coast of the Baltic Sea, such as Lübeck, Germany, prospered through international sea trade during the Middle Ages (about 500–1500).
▶

A spice seller at his shop in Aswan, Egypt.
▶

Many people left Europe for the New World and Asia to set up plantations (large farms) growing sugar, tea, tobacco, and coffee. Traders formed powerful associations, such as the Hanseatic League in Baltic Europe, to increase their share of the international market.

The 19th century brought railroads and steamships that could carry goods rapidly from one place to another. It also heralded the age of heavy machinery, which could produce goods cheaply and quickly in large factories. Different regions began to specialize in producing different kinds of goods. The modern system of trade and commerce is based on this specialization.

Trade and commerce today
Specialization helps a nation make best use of its natural resources (such as coal, forests, or farmland), capital goods (tools, machines, and factories), and labor

(workers). Not every country has the same resources. Saudi Arabia, for example, has about 25 percent of the world's known oil reserves; petroleum exports provide almost all of the country's income. But it has to import about 70 percent of its food to make up for its lack of farmland.

There are special organizations that help control trade. The World Trade Organization (WTO), founded in 1995, took over from the General Agreement on Tariffs and Trade (GATT), founded in 1947. Both were set up to encourage international trade. Many countries have a government department that is responsible for trade.

SEE ALSO: Ancient Civilizations; Columbus, Christopher; Crusades; Economics; Exploration and Explorers; Industrial Revolution; Manufacturing; Money; Natural Resources; Roman Empire

DID YOU KNOW?

In ancient times, the spices of Eastern lands, such as cinnamon, ginger, and cloves, were in great demand in the West. Merchants, in particular Arab traders, took spices from east to west across Asia, each charging a little extra as they passed them on. The cost of trade duties at wealthy ports such as Alexandria and Venice added to the price of the spices. By the time the spices reached the markets of western Europe, they had become very expensive.

It was to cut out the "middlemen" that 15th-century European explorers sailed west in search of the spice islands of the East. They discovered America instead, which opened a new chapter in trade. Eventually, in the late 1400s, explorers found a sea route around the tip of Africa that gave Europe's merchants the east–west shortcut they had long sought.

* TRAINS AND RAILROADS

Railroads played a vital role in opening up the American frontier. They are still an important means of moving freight and passengers.

A railroad is a form of transportation in which wheeled vehicles called trains run on tracks. The tracks are two parallel lines of metal a set distance apart. Most tracks around the world have a standard gauge— the distance between the rails—of 4 ft. 8½ in. (1.4 m). The wheels have projecting rims, or flanges, on their inner edges to keep the trains on the rails.

Rails are made of steel. They are made in 1,500-ft. (460-m) lengths that are welded together. Rails are fastened to crossties, which support the track, hold it together, and keep the rails parallel. Crossties are

made of hard wood, concrete, or steel. They sit on a layer of crushed rock called ballast. The ballast forms a sturdy base for crossties and track. It allows water to drain away from the track, and it helps control the growth of grass and weeds.

Trains cannot climb steep slopes, or grades, so the roadbed—the smooth, hard-packed ground over which the track is laid —must be as level as possible. Workers fill in dips and flatten areas where the grade rises. If the hills and valleys are too big, engineers have to construct tunnels and bridges to carry the railroad.

Locomotives

Locomotives are self-propelled vehicles that pull railroad cars along the rails. They use various types of energy to pull their loads. The earliest locomotives were powered by steam. They carried large supplies of coal that fueled an onboard furnace. The furnace heated water that produced steam to move pistons, which in turn moved the wheels.

Diesel locomotives use diesel engines with electric traction motors to drive the wheels. Diesel locomotives are the most common types of locomotives and are capable of pulling the largest loads. They are cheaper to run, more efficient, and need far less maintenance than steam locomotives.

Electric locomotives are most often used to pull high-speed passenger trains. The power comes from either electrified rails or overhead wires. Most underground railroads and subways also use electric locomotives because they do not create exhaust fumes, which could poison people.

In 2003 the world's first magnetic levitation (maglev) trains for public use entered service in China. The

trains reach speeds of over 250 mph (400 kph). The maglev's motor produces an electromagnetic field. The force of this field lifts the train a fraction of an inch above the track and sends it forward. Because the train does not touch the track, there is no friction to slow it down.

Railroad cars

A train is made up of one or more locomotives and a series of cars that serve several purposes. On passenger trains, most cars are coaches that contain seats. These trains might also have dining cars, sleepers, observation cars, and cars for mail or baggage.

The Rocket, built in 1829, was the most famous of the steam locomotives designed by the British engineer George Stephenson.
▶

There are also various kinds of freight cars. A common type is the boxcar, which has large sliding doors on each side to load and unload goods. Other cars include tank cars for liquids, refrigerator cars for foodstuffs, and stock cars for live animals.

History

In England in the 1600s, mining railroads were built that consisted of horse-drawn wagons whose wheels rode along channel-like rails. In 1785 William Jessop (1745–1814) invented the first metal rails for flanged wheels. In 1804 Richard Trevithick (1771–1833) built the first steam locomotive. By 1825 George Stephenson (1781–1848) had built the first locomotive to pull a passenger train.

The first U.S. railroads began operation in 1827. By the 1850s, railroads were aiding the expansion to the American West. In 1869 crews building the Union Pacific Railroad across the Great Plains met those constructing the Central Pacific route through the Sierra Nevada. This meeting, at Promontory Summit in Utah, cut the six-month cross-country journey to five days. By 1900 there were seven rail lines linking Chicago and the Pacific Ocean.

Railroads remained an important mode of passenger transport until the mid-1900s, after which most people traveled by car or airplane. However, trains still carry goods across the country. Elsewhere, such as in Europe and India, the passenger train continues to be a popular way to travel.

SEE ALSO: Bridges; Engines; Magnetism; Tunnels; West, The American

✳ TREES

A plant is called a tree if its stem is at least 15 ft. (4.5 m) long when mature. Trees play a vital role on Earth, absorbing carbon dioxide and releasing oxygen.

All trees grow from seeds. A seed soaks up moisture from the ground, its shell splits, and two shoots appear. One shoot grows down into the soil to become the root of the tree. The other shoot grows up to become the trunk and leaves.

Roots

Roots anchor a tree in the ground, holding it firmly in place. As well as being strong, roots are sensitive; they are able to grow around an obstacle. If a root becomes trapped in a rock, it can split the rock and grow through to the soil beneath.

Trees often have a long main root, or taproot, with hundreds of other roots and feathery rootlets branching from it in every

A woman harvests latex, used for making rubber, at a plantation near Pakidie, Ivory Coast, Africa.

Palm trees grow in warm coastal areas. The trunk can grow up to 200 ft. (60 m) tall.

direction. There is actually more growth belowground than above. Tree roots help prevent soil erosion by holding the soil in place. Each root has millions of tiny root hairs growing near its tip. They soak up water and minerals from the soil. The water travels up into the trunk and then to the branches and leaves.

Trunks

The outer layer of the trunk is its bark. As a tree grows thicker and taller, its bark stretches and sometimes splits. Although the rough outer bark on a tree trunk is dead, it protects the living tissue beneath. Underneath the bark is the cambium, which forms two new cell layers each year. They are the inner bark, which carries food made in the leaves down to the roots, and the sapwood. Sapwood is made of cells that form pipes that carry water and nutrients, known as sap, up from the roots. Some trees are tapped for their sap—for example, sugar maples for maple syrup. The sap of rubber trees is known as latex. As pipes in the sapwood fill up with waste and become darker than the new wood, they form the heartwood, which gives the tree strength.

Leaves

Each leaf on a tree takes in carbon dioxide from the air and water and minerals from the soil. The green pigment of the leaf, called chlorophyll, absorbs energy from the sun and uses it to change the carbon dioxide and water into sugar. This process is known as photosynthesis. The sugar made in the leaves is the tree's basic food.

Only a small fraction of the water that flows up through the sapwood pipes is used to make food. Most of the rest evaporates through millions of tiny holes on the surface of the leaves. The water vapor rises and forms clouds. Eventually the water that was soaked up from the ground by the tree's roots returns as rain.

In winter, when the ground freezes, a tree's water supply is cut off. Trees prepare by stopping the flow of sap to their leaves. As photosynthesis slows down, the leaves lose their green chlorophyll, and other pigments—yellows, reds, and oranges—show through. Their stalks become brittle, and the leaves fall. Some types of trees, such as pines and firs, do not shed their leaves in fall; they are called evergreens. Their needle-shaped leaves have a waxy covering that prevents water evaporation. Other types of trees, such as palms, grow only in places where winters are warm.

Buds

While preparing for winter, trees also get ready for spring by making buds. Buds contain leaves, stems, and flowers packaged inside scales to keep them dry. Most of the buds along the sides of a branch produce only leaves. Buds at the tips of a branch produce leaves and new shoots. Some trees wrap their leaves and flowers in the same package. Others have separate buds for flowers.

Flowers and seeds

When the flowers open, pollen from the male flowers is carried by wind or insects to the female flower, and a seed begins to form inside. Many evergreens grow their seeds in cones, which is why their scientific name is conifer, or "cone-bearer."

AMAZING FACTS !

Redwood trees sometimes grow 350 ft. (107 m) tall.

Giant sequoias have trunks so thick that 20 people standing with their arms outstretched can barely circle them.

Some sequoias in northern California were saplings, or young trees, 3,500 years ago, when ancient Egyptian pharaohs (kings) were building temples along the Nile River.

Each kind of tree has its own way of spreading seeds. If seeds fell directly to the ground beneath the tree, few would live. The tree would take up all the water in the soil, and its leaves would shade the seedling too much for it to grow.

Coconuts, the largest tree seeds, fall from a coconut palm. If the tree is growing on a sloping beach, the coconuts roll across the sand to float away on the sea. The hard shell protects the seed until it is washed ashore.

Uses of trees

Almost every part of a tree can be put to use in some product. The fruit of many trees, such as bananas, is a source of food. The trunk may be cut up into lumber or made into pulp for papermaking. Wood also yields many useful chemicals. Wood cellulose is used to make certain plastics and synthetic fibers.

SEE ALSO: Flowers; Forests, Fruit; Photosynthesis; Plants; Rain Forests; Soil

✳ TUBMAN, HARRIET (ABOUT 1821–1913)

Harriet Tubman was a former slave who helped more than 300 other fugitives reach freedom and safety. She was called the "Moses of her people."

Harriet Tubman was born into slavery in Dorchester County, Maryland. In 1849, fearing that she was about to be sold farther south, she decided to escape to the North, where she would be free. She reached Philadelphia and found work as a cook. Friends told her of the Underground Railroad, a secret network of people who helped fugitive slaves reach the North.

Tubman determined that she would return to the South and rescue as many of her people as possible. She made a total of 19 trips in about a dozen years. In 1857 she succeeded in freeing her own parents. Slaveholders offered rewards for her capture, but she was never caught.

Tubman became a popular speaker at antislavery meetings. During the Civil War (1861–65), she was a spy in the South and encouraged slaves to join the Union army. After the war, she lived in Auburn, New York, where she set up a home for poor black people. After her death, the people of Auburn put up a monument in her honor.

Harriet Tubman used the North Star as a guide as she led groups of slaves to freedom.
▶

SEE ALSO: Abolition Movement; African Americans; Civil War; Slavery; Underground Railroad

✳ TUNNELS

Tunnels are passages built under the ground, under the water, or through a mountain and used by cars and trains. They also deliver water to cities.

The first step in building a tunnel is to plan its exact route. Surveyors make maps showing how deep in the ground or how far below a body of water the tunnel must be dug. Geologists try to learn about the materials through which the tunnel will pass. They drill deep holes and bring up samples of what lies beneath the surface—this could be hard rock, soft soil, wet soil, clay, or sand.

Rock tunnels

There are two main ways of building tunnels through rock. One is to blast the rock into pieces with explosives. Another is to use a machine called a mechanical mole, which has a number of cutting wheels with steel teeth that grind the rock into small pieces. In order to keep bits of rock from falling off the walls, tunnels may be lined with bricks, blocks of stone, or a mixture of cement and water.

Soft materials

When digging through soft material such as soil, there is a danger of the tunnel collapsing. The soil can be hardened by pumping a mixture of cement and chemicals into it. In another technique, a pipelike steel shield is driven through the soil. Workers digging at the tunnel face stand inside the shield. Powerful machines push the shield forward so that the workers are always protected.

To help the workers breathe, large fans keep the tunnel ventilated. They force fresh air in and draw contaminated air out. Finished tunnels also need ventilation.

History

The first permanent tunnels were built about 3,000 years ago, not for the passage of people but to carry water to towns or dry areas. Tunnels through rock were made by building a fire close to the rock face and then throwing cold water on the heated rock until it cracked and could be broken up. Another method involved driving wooden wedges into holes or cracks in the rock. The wedges were kept wet until they swelled enough to put pressure on the rock and split it into bits.

These ancient tunneling methods were used until the 1700s, when factories first required large-scale transportation of goods and people. Tunnels through hills and mountains were built using powerful new explosives, new equipment, and new methods. The first underwater tunnel was dug under the Thames River in London, England, and opened in 1843.

Opened in 1994, the Channel Tunnel provides a train link between the United Kingdom and the rest of Europe. It is 31 miles (50 km) long.
▼

SEE ALSO: Geology; Roads; Soil; Trains and Railroads

TURKEY AND THE CAUCASUS

Turkey lies on two continents—Europe and Asia.
Armenia, Azerbaijan, and Georgia are south of the
Caucasus Mountains, which divide Europe and Asia.

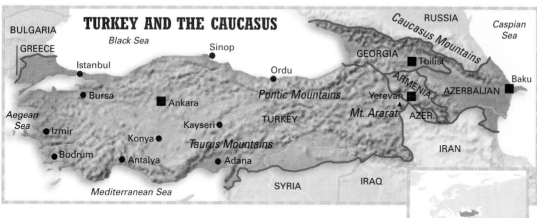

TURKEY AND THE CAUCASUS

BULGARIA
GREECE
Black Sea
Istanbul
Bursa
Aegean Sea
Izmir
Bodrum
Konya
Antalya
Ankara
Kayseri
Taurus Mountains
Adana
Mediterranean Sea
SYRIA
Sinop
Ordu
Pontic Mountains
TURKEY
Caucasus Mountains
RUSSIA
Caspian Sea
GEORGIA
Tbilisi
ARMENIA
Yerevan
Mt. Ararat
AZER.
AZERBAIJAN
Baku
IRAN
IRAQ

Turkey's national flag

Armenia's national flag

Azerbaijan's national flag

Georgia's national flag

Land

European Turkey is separated from Asian Turkey by a narrow waterway connecting the Aegean and Black seas. The Caucasus is a great mountain system between the Black and Azov seas, and the Caspian Sea. The region south of the range is called Transcaucasia.

People and economy

Turks, who came from Central Asia in the 11th century, dominate Turkey's population. Armenia's residents live on a tiny corner of their ancient homeland, most of which is now in Turkey. Most of Azerbaijan's people are Azeris descended from an ancient Central Asian people. Georgians trace their roots in this region back over 3,000 years. Cotton and tobacco are major export crops in Turkey. Mining and manufacturing are important throughout the region. Azerbaijan is a leading oil producer.

History

In about the 1200s B.C., Greeks began to establish states along the coasts. In the 600s B.C., the Greek city of Byzantium was founded. In A.D. 330 it was renamed

Constantinople (modern Istanbul), when it became the capital of the Eastern Roman Empire, later the Byzantine Empire. The Byzantine Empire became a great world power. During the 1000s, the first Turkish tribes, the Seljuks, came from western Central Asia. They attacked the Byzantine Empire and set up a Muslim state in what is now central and eastern Turkey. By 1360 the Ottomans, a group of Muslim tribes from Central Asia, had conquered most of what is now Turkey. The modern Republic of Turkey was founded in 1923.

Thousands of years ago Armenia, Azerbaijan, and Georgia were divided into numerous kingdoms that later fell to the Ottoman Turkish, Persian, and Russian empires. They came under Soviet control in 1920–21, but gained independence in 1991 with the breakup of the Soviet Union.

SEE ALSO: Asia; Byzantine Empire; Greece, Ancient

✱ TUTANKHAMUN (ABOUT 1357–1339 B.C.)

Tutankhamun is the most famous of the pharaohs—
the rulers of ancient Egypt—because of the
treasures discovered in his tomb in 1922.

The gold coffin that contained the remains of Tutankhamun.

Little is known about Tutankhamun's life. He was born about 1357 B.C. and may have been the son of the pharaoh Akhenaten. He became king when he was about nine years old and died in his late teens. The cause of his death is unknown, but he may have been murdered.

Tutankhamun was buried in the Valley of the Kings, the main burial ground of the pharaohs between 1550 and 1070 B.C. The valley is located on the eastern bank of the Nile River, close to present-day Luxor.

The English archaeologist Howard Carter discovered Tutankhamun's tomb in 1922, after many years of searching. The tomb had four rooms, or chambers. The largest room, the antechamber, contained nearly 700 objects, including chariots and couches. The annex housed furniture and objects such as jars of wine and game boards. The treasury held many religious objects.

In the burial chamber lay the mummy—the preserved body—of Tutankhamun. It was covered with a solid gold mask and encased in a golden coffin. The tomb and its contents were meant to accompany the king into the afterlife. Today most of the artifacts are on display in Cairo, but Tutankhamun is at rest inside his tomb.

👀 **SEE ALSO:** Archaeology; Egypt, Ancient

✱ TWAIN, MARK (1835–1910)

Mark Twain is regarded as one of America's
greatest writers. His stories and novels are
among the best loved in American literature.

Samuel Langhorne Clemens wrote under the name Mark Twain.

Mark Twain was born Samuel Langhorne Clemens. His family lived on the banks of the Mississippi River, and he became fascinated with river life.

Twain set out for the western frontier in 1861. He got a job with a newspaper in Nevada after writing humorous sketches about his adventures. He moved to San Francisco in 1864, and became famous after a New York magazine published one of his short stories. Twain began lecturing and traveling abroad. In 1869 his comic letters, published as *The Innocents Abroad*, earned him worldwide fame. When he married, he settled in Hartford, Connecticut. Twain's most important works are *The Adventures of Tom Sawyer* (1876) and *The Adventures of Huckleberry Finn* (1884).

👀 **SEE ALSO:** Literature

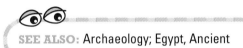

✱**TYPHOONS** 👓➡ ✱**HURRICANES AND TYPHOONS**

UNDERGROUND RAILROAD

The Underground Railroad was a network of hiding places in the United States to help slaves escape from the South in the years before the Civil War (1861–65).

The Underground Railroad was operated by abolitionists, people who wanted to see an end to slavery. In 1808 a law came into effect that made it illegal to import slaves from Africa. This gave the slaves already in the United States greater value and increased the demand for slaves to work on the cotton and sugar plantations in the South. Many slaves were sold and separated from their families. More and more slaves tried to escape to the North, to states where slavery had been outlawed.

How the Railroad started

The Underground Railroad is said to have got its name around 1831, when a slave catcher remarked, "He must have gone on an underground road," after a slave vanished from sight. The word *railroad* was substituted later. The people who helped the runaways used a code based on railroad terms. Guides were known as "conductors," hiding places were "stations," and escape was known as "catching the next train." Runaways usually moved at night and hid during the day. Sheltering a runaway slave was very dangerous; slave catchers did not hesitate to use the guns they carried. The Fugitive Slave Law, passed by Congress in 1850, declared that anyone who helped a fugitive could be fined or imprisoned.

In this engraving entitled A Brave Stroke for Freedom, *slaves shoot slave catchers who try to pursue them as they escape in a covered wagon.*

Quakers, members of the Religious Society of Friends, were particularly active in the Underground Railroad. Levi Coffin (1789–1877), who was known as the president of the Underground Railroad, was a devout Quaker. Many escaped blacks, such as Harriet Tubman, returned to help others. Around 40,000 slaves escaped to the North between the 1820s and 1861.

SEE ALSO: Abolition Movement; African Americans; Civil War; Emancipation Proclamation; Slavery; Tubman, Harriet

✳ UNITED KINGDOM

The United Kingdom is an island nation in northwest Europe. Although it is a relatively small country, it has had a huge influence on world history.

United Kingdom's national flag

The United Kingdom consists of four distinct parts: England, Scotland, Northern Ireland, and Wales. England, Scotland, and Wales together make up the island of Great Britain. Northern Ireland occupies a small area on the island of Ireland, which it shares with the Republic of Ireland.

Land and climate

Scotland has three major land regions. They are the Highlands in the north, the Central Lowlands, and the Uplands of southern Scotland. Its highest peak is Ben Nevis, which rises to 4,406 ft. (1,343 m).

The low mountains of the Pennine chain extend like a backbone from the Scottish border to central England. To the east of the Pennines are the moors and dales of Yorkshire, and to the west is the Lake District. The Midlands, the industrial heartland of England, lies to the south. London is in southeast England.

Wales occupies the land on the western edge of Great Britain. Most of its interior is hilly, with Snowdon, the highest peak, rising to 3,560 ft. (1,085 m).

Northern Ireland makes up about one-sixth of the island of Ireland. It has a varied landscape with low mountains, rolling plains, and deep valleys.

The United Kingdom has a temperate climate. Temperatures rarely rise above 75°F (24°C) in summer or fall below 23°F

Tower Bridge in London, England, is one of many bridges spanning the Thames River. The two halves of the roadway part and lift to let tall ships, cruise liners, and large craft pass through. ▶

(–5°C) in winter. Annual rainfall ranges from over 100 in. (2,540 mm) in some areas to about 26 in. (660 mm).

People
Despite its size, the United Kingdom is one of the most densely populated countries in Europe. England is the largest and most populous of the four parts of the kingdom. The Welsh, Scots, and Northern Irish have maintained their individual cultures. Both Gaelic and Welsh, Celtic languages that were spoken by the early Britons, are still in use. Many British cities are home to immigrants from former colonies in Africa, Asia, and the Caribbean, providing a rich mix of different cultures.

Economy
Britain was once the wealthiest nation in the world and is still one of the most important trading nations. In 1973 the United Kingdom was admitted to the European Economic Community, which became the European Union (EU) in 1993.

Service industries are now the largest sector of the economy, employing more than two-thirds of the labor force. London, in particular, is an international center of finance and commerce. Tourism is also a major source of income.

History
Britain's island location, close to the European mainland but separated from it by water, has played an important role in its history. In the first century B.C., Britain became part of the Roman Empire. In the eighth and ninth centuries, Vikings raided the coasts. In 1066 William of Normandy, France, conquered England.

Between the late 1700s and the mid-1900s, Britain was the world's leading naval power. British explorers, traders, and colonists sailed to most of the world.

Many of the world's nations modeled the structure of their governments on the British parliament. English is the world's most widely used language, and English literature is one of the world's best known.

The Industrial Revolution began in Britain in the mid-1700s, when the age-old agricultural economy first gave way to the growth of factories. Along with the growth of its industry, Britain acquired a vast empire. In the early 1900s, one-quarter of the world's land and about one-fifth of its people were governed by Britain or according to British laws. During the 25 years after World War II (1939–45), most of Britain's colonies became independent.

SEE ALSO: Europe; Industrial Revolution; Ireland, Republic of; Vikings; World War I; World War II

KEY FACTS

OFFICIAL NAME:
United Kingdom of Great Britain and Northern Ireland

AREA:
94,242 sq. mi. (244,087 sq. km)

POPULATION:
58,830,000

CAPITAL & LARGEST CITY:
London

MAJOR RELIGIONS:
Church of England, Roman Catholicism, Church of Scotland

MAJOR LANGUAGE:
English

CURRENCY:
Pound sterling

✳ UNITED NATIONS

The United Nations was formed in 1945 to maintain international peace. Today it has 191 member countries. Its headquarters are in New York City.

United Nations' flag

The first plans for the United Nations (UN) were made during World War II (1939–45). In 1944, at the Dumbarton Oaks conference in Washington, D.C., the Soviet Union, the United Kingdom, the Republic of China, and the United States agreed on proposals for an international organization to work for world peace and security. The UN Charter came into force on October 24, 1945.

The United Nations is made up of many specialized agencies, but there are six main bodies. The General Assembly is made up of one representative from each member nation. Each country casts one vote in every decision, so smaller nations have equal influence.

The UN Security Council meets following the terrorist attacks on the United States on September 11, 2001. The council passed a resolution requiring all member nations to deny money, support, and protection to terrorists.
▼

The Security Council has five permanent members—the United States, the Russian Federation, France, the United Kingdom, and China—and 10 members that each serve two years. The council's chief role is to keep international peace and security.

The Economic and Social Council has 54 nonpermanent members and deals with concerns such as economic development.

The Trusteeship Council oversaw the former colonies of European nations before they became fully independent or self-governing. It rarely meets now.

The International Court of Justice settles disputes submitted by nations for final decision and advises UN agencies. It meets at The Hague in the Netherlands.

The Secretariat is the administrative body of the United Nations. It is headed by the secretary-general. Every member nation is represented on the Secretariat staff.

United Nations in action

The United Nations has successfully negotiated cease-fires between warring nations and ended civil wars in, for example, Mozambique and Angola. UN peacekeepers have also been active in Bosnia and Somalia. However, the UN has not always been able to ensure the peaceful resolution of disputes.

Various UN programs work to improve economic and social conditions in developing countries. They include UNICEF, which fosters the well-being of children, and the World Food Program, which provides food aid.

Aside from maintaining peace, one of the UN's main objectives is to safeguard basic human rights. The Universal Declaration of Human Rights sets standards for human rights, but it is not legally enforceable.

SEE ALSO: Human Rights; Iraq; Korean War; Labor; World War II

UNITED STATES ARMED FORCES

The United States armed forces exist to protect U.S. citizens. The three major branches are the Army, the Air Force, and the Navy. Other branches include the Marine Corps and the Coast Guard.

A sergeant in the United States Air Force uses radar to track civilian and military aircraft, making sure that they stay a safe distance apart.

The president of the United States is the commander in chief of the armed forces. He commands the forces through the Department of Defense (DOD), which has its headquarters at the Pentagon, in Arlington, Virginia. The head of the department is the secretary of defense. The DOD has three lower departments, one each for the Army, Air Force, and Navy. The president, the secretary of defense, and the heads of departments are civilians (nonmilitary people).

Each department also has a chief of staff, who is a military officer. The chiefs of staff of the Army and the Air Force, the chief of naval operations, and the commandant of the Marine Corps (which operates under the authority of the Navy) are together called the joint chiefs of staff, or JCS. They are responsible for military operations.

There are about 1.4 million people on active duty in the armed forces. About 35 percent are in the Army; 27 percent in the Navy; 26 percent in the Air Force; and 12 percent in the Marines. In addition, there are 1.3 million people in the National Guard and reserves, and 672,000 civilian employees of the Department of Defense.

United States Army

The United States Army began as the Continental Army, created in 1775 by the Continental Congress to fight in the American Revolution. Its first general was George Washington. The Army must be ready at all times to defend the nation against enemy attacks. In peacetime it concentrates on training its combat forces. Its other duties include providing disaster relief and controlling civil disturbances.

➡️

▲
This U.S. soldier was part of the peacekeeping force in Bosnia-Herzegovina in 1999.

Marines raise the Stars and Stripes in 1945 on Iwo Jima, a small island 660 miles (1,062 km) south of Tokyo. It is estimated that more than 20,000 Japanese defenders lost their lives during the two-month battle for the island. The Iwo Jima Memorial in Arlington, Virginia, was built to remember all Marines who have died in battle.
▷

The Army's forces are organized into several categories. Soldiers in the combat arms do the actual fighting; combat support soldiers provide operational assistance in battle; and members of combat service support provide assistance to the Army as a whole.

The Army has seven combat arms, or branches. Infantry soldiers fight on foot or from vehicles and use handheld weapons such as rifles. The armor branch uses tanks and other armored vehicles. The artillery fights with large cannons, rockets, and missiles. The air defense artillery uses surface-to-air missiles (SAMs). Special forces train the allies of the United States and carry out guerrilla operations. Engineers provide construction assistance and also fight as infantry soldiers. Army aviation scouts for enemy positions and provides aerial gunfire and airlifts.

Combat support personnel include the Signal Corps, Military Intelligence, and Military Police. The combat service support branches include medical, supply, and administrative services. Women may belong to all branches of the Army, except for infantry, armor, and special forces.

United States Air Force
The Army created an Aeronautical Division in 1907. The Army Air Forces played an important role in World War II (1939–45). It was not until 1947 that the United States Air Force (USAF) became a separate military service of the U.S. armed forces.

The Air Force performs its military operations using aircraft and missiles. In peacetime it works with other military and civilian agencies to develop and improve aircraft, rockets, and missiles, and explore outer space. In wartime the Air Force seeks to destroy enemy air forces, ground targets, and supplies; surveys enemy territory to gain strategic information; and supports the other armed service forces in battle.

There are nine Air Force major commands, or units, each responsible for certain tasks. They include Air Combat Command, which organizes and trains the tactical air forces; the Pacific Air Forces; and the U.S. Air Forces in Europe. Women can serve in any job in the Air Force except those involving combat.

United States Navy
The Continental Congress created the Continental Navy in 1775. Its first steel battleships were introduced in the late 1800s. The Navy patrols the seas in peacetime, transporting emergency relief to

disaster areas, as well as supplies to U.S. troops stationed overseas. In wartime the Navy's task is to destroy enemy ships and submarines and prevent attacks by sea.

The Navy is divided into three parts: the Navy Department, which deals with administration; the Operating Forces, also called "the fleet," which carry out naval operations; and the Shore Establishment, which supports the fleet through commands such as telecommunications, engineering, and supplies. Women in the Navy may not serve on submarines or in naval special operations units.

United States Marine Corps

The Navy also maintains its own air and ground forces, called the Marine Corps. In 1775 the Continental Congress created two battalions of Marines to fight in the American Revolution, but it was not until 1798 that the Corps became a permanent branch of the U.S. armed forces.

In peacetime Marines guard naval bases and U.S. embassies and consulates. The fighting units of the Marine Corps are called the Fleet Marine Forces. In wartime their role is to capture and defend bases for the Navy and to engage in amphibious warfare (fighting that takes place both on land and at sea). Women Marines may serve in all military jobs except infantry, artillery, and armor.

United States Coast Guard

The Coast Guard provides law enforcement and safety in U.S. waters and on the high seas. In peacetime it is part of the Department of Homeland Security, but it becomes part of the Operating Forces of the Navy during wartime. It was founded in 1790 by Alexander Hamilton as the Revenue Marine. It joined with the Life Saving Service in 1915, when it took its present name. It became a permanent branch of the armed forces in 1949.

Important tasks of the Coast Guard include search-and-rescue missions for nonmilitary vessels in distress, weather information, and the control of drug smuggling.

United States Merchant Marine

In wartime the Navy also controls the ships and personnel of the United States Merchant Marine. The Merchant Marine is made up of all the ships in the United States that are privately owned by Americans and operate for commercial profit. The DOD may call up any number of these ships for service.

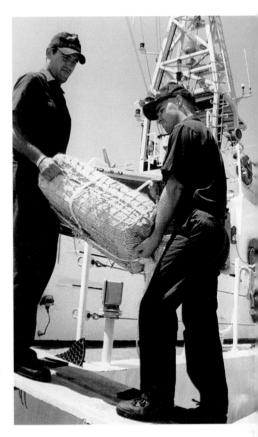

These two coastguardsmen in Miami, Florida, are unloading illegal drugs that have been confiscated.

SEE ALSO: Aircraft; American Revolution; Civil War; Korean War; Ships and Boats; Spanish–American War; Submarines; United States of America; Vietnam War; War of 1812; World War I; World War II

✳ UNITED STATES GEOGRAPHY

The United States has a wide variety of geographical features, from mountains to lowlands and prairies, and dry deserts to lush forests and swamps.

Land

Forty-eight of the 50 states of the union are conterminous—they have borders with one or more of the other states. They are sometimes known as the "Lower 48." The exceptions are Alaska, in the far northwest of the North American continent, bordering Canada, and Hawaii, 2,400 miles (3,900 km) off the West Coast, in the Pacific Ocean.

The Lower 48 extend for nearly 3,000 miles (4,800 km) between the Pacific and Atlantic oceans. They border Canada in the north and Mexico in the south.

This huge area can be divided into three major regions: the eastern highlands, the central plains, and the western mountains. These regions are divided into many smaller landforms. They include the Coastal Plain, the Appalachian Highlands, the Central Lowland, the Great Plains, the Rocky Mountains, the Intermountain Plateaus, and the Pacific Mountain System.

At the far east, bordering the Atlantic Ocean and the Gulf of Mexico, the Coastal Plain stretches from southeastern Massachusetts to eastern Texas. This land is low and often marshy. It rises to the west, where it meets the Piedmont, the foothills of the Appalachian Highlands.

The Appalachian Highlands stretch from the Gulf of St. Lawrence to central Alabama. The highest point is Mount Mitchell in North Carolina, at 6,684 ft. (2,037 m). To the west lies the Central Lowland, including most of the Great Lakes, and several highland regions.

Next to these lie the Great Plains, vast areas of grassland and the source of most of the nation's wheat. The Plains are largely flat, but include mountainous areas, such as the Black Hills of South Dakota. To the west of the Plains lies the country's largest mountain system, the Rocky Mountains. The Rockies, covering eight western states, are important locations for minerals and forests.

The Columbia and Colorado plateaus and the Basin and Range are to the west of the Rockies. They form a region called the Intermountain Plateaus. The Colorado Plateau includes the Grand Canyon. The

Fireweed provides a carpet of color in the Tongass National Forest of southeastern Alaska. In the distance is the Mendenhall Glacier.

(continued on page 614)

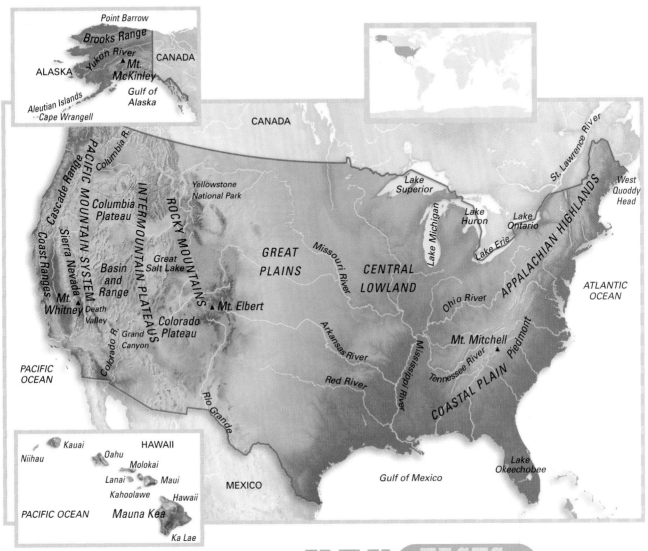

Point Barrow

Brooks Range

Yukon River

▲ Mt. McKinley

ALASKA

CANADA

Aleutian Islands

Cape Wrangell

Gulf of Alaska

CANADA

Lake Superior

St. Lawrence River

West Quoddy Head

Lake Michigan

Lake Huron

Lake Ontario

Lake Erie

APPALACHIAN HIGHLANDS

ATLANTIC OCEAN

PACIFIC MOUNTAIN SYSTEM

Columbia R.

Cascade Range

Columbia Plateau

ROCKY MOUNTAINS

Yellowstone National Park

Coast Ranges

Sierra Nevada

INTERMOUNTAIN PLATEAUS

Basin and Range

Great Salt Lake

GREAT PLAINS

Missouri River

CENTRAL LOWLAND

Mt. Whitney ▲ Death Valley

Colorado R.

Grand Canyon

Colorado Plateau

▲ Mt. Elbert

Arkansas River

Ohio River

Mississippi River

Mt. Mitchell ▲

Piedmont

Tennessee River

COASTAL PLAIN

PACIFIC OCEAN

Red River

Rio Grande

MEXICO

Gulf of Mexico

Lake Okeechobee

Kauai

HAWAII

Niihau

Oahu

Molokai

Lanai

Maui

Kahoolawe

Hawaii

PACIFIC OCEAN

Mauna Kea

Ka Lae

KEY FACTS

NORTHERNMOST POINT:
Point Barrow, AK

SOUTHERNMOST POINT:
Ka Lae, HI

EASTERNMOST POINT:
West Quoddy Head, ME

WESTERNMOST POINT:
Cape Wrangell, Attu Island, AK

HIGHEST POINT:
Mt. McKinley, AK, 20,320 ft. (6,194 m)

LOWEST POINT:
Badwater, Death Valley, CA, 282 ft. (86 m)
below sea level

CHIEF RIVERS:
Mississippi, Missouri, Arkansas, Colorado,
Rio Grande (partly in Mexico), Red, Columbia
(partly in Canada), Ohio, St. Lawrence (partly
in Canada), Tennessee, Yukon

CHIEF LAKES:
Superior, Erie, Ontario, Huron, Michigan,
Great Salt, Okeechobee

CHIEF MOUNTAIN PEAKS:
Mt. McKinley, Mt. Whitney, Mt. Elbert

Basin and Range is the home of Utah's Great Salt Lake. The Cascade Range and the Sierra Nevada border these areas. The Cascade Range includes the nation's deepest lake, Crater Lake, and volcanoes such as Mount St. Helens. Mount Whitney, the highest peak in the Lower 48 at 14,494 ft. (4,418 m), is in the Sierra Nevada. These two ranges, together with the Pacific Coastal Region, form the Pacific Mountain System.

Alaska, which covers 615,230 sq. miles (1,593,446 sq. km), is by far the largest state in the union. Its coastline is greater than the nation's entire Atlantic coastline. It includes the Aleutian Islands, one of the longest volcanic island chains in the world. Many volcanoes in the Aleutians and on the Alaska Peninsula are still active. Mount McKinley, part of the Alaska Range, is the highest point in North America. It rises 20,320 ft. (6,194 m).

Hawaii is made up of a long chain of volcanic islands that stretch a distance of more than 1,500 miles (2,400 km). There are eight main islands, seven of which are inhabited, and many scattered islets, shoals, and reefs. The highest peak is Mauna Kea, on the island of Hawaii, at 13,796 ft. (4,205 m).

Forests and woodlands cover about 30 percent of all the land in the United States. Permanent pasture accounts for another 25 percent, and croplands about 19 percent. The remainder, including urban areas, makes up 26 percent.

Climate

The nation's climate varies enormously. The north of Alaska, inside the Arctic Circle, can be very cold, while southern Florida and Hawaii are semitropical. High areas, such as the Appalachians and the Rockies, are usually cool. The Gulf of

Death Valley National Park, California, is a memorial to the early pioneers who died trying to cross the desert. It is thought to be the hottest and driest spot in the United States.

Mexico states, Georgia, and South Carolina, tend to be hot and humid. The deserts of California and Arizona are among the driest parts of the world. The northwest Pacific coast has heavy rainfall.

Rivers and lakes

There are natural water supplies in most parts of the Lower 48, apart from the western deserts. The longest river system, at 3,741 miles (6,019 km), is the Mississippi-Missouri, which drains into the Gulf of Mexico. It has 2,500 tributaries. Many rivers are important for the irrigation or hydroelectric power that they provide.

The largest lakes are the Great Lakes in the north (Michigan, Superior, Huron, Erie, and Ontario), although only Lake Michigan is entirely in the United States. These huge expanses of water cover an area of 94,710 sq. miles (245,300 sq. km). There are many other natural lakes, particularly in northern parts of Michigan, Wisconsin, and Minnesota.

The longest river in Alaska is the Yukon, which winds through 1,200 miles (1,930 km) of the state. The largest lake is Iliamna, covering about 1,000 sq. miles (2,590 sq. km). Hawaii has no rivers or large lakes, although many small streams drain into the Pacific Ocean.

National Parks

Many geographical features in the United States are of great scientific and environmental importance, or are major tourist attractions. To protect and promote these aspects of American heritage, the federal government operates the National Park System.

The first National Park was Yellowstone, in northwestern Wyoming, which opened in 1872. One of its main attractions is the geyser "Old Faithful," which spouts hot water 140 ft. (43 m) into the air.

▲ *The Pearl River meanders through Mississippi toward the Gulf of Mexico.*

Today there are over 350 National Parks, covering a total area of 80 million acres (32 million ha). The largest is the Wrangell-St. Elias National Park and Preserve in southeastern Alaska. It covers more than 8.3 million acres (3.4 million ha) and contains the largest group of glaciers in North America.

Other important features now contained in National Parks include the giant redwoods and sequoias, the biggest trees in the world; Yosemite Falls in Yosemite National Park, the nation's highest waterfall at 2,425 ft. (739 m); and northern Arizona's awe-inspiring Grand Canyon, 277 miles (446 km) long and 1 mile (1.6 km) deep.

👀

SEE ALSO: Arctic; Atlantic Ocean; North America, Geography; Pacific Islands; Pacific Ocean; United States of America

✳UNITED STATES GOVERNMENT

The government of the United States is a complex organization that serves to improve the lives and protect the interests of all American citizens.

Many terms describe the government of the United States. First of all, it is a democracy, which means that the people rule. It is a representative government because the people elect leaders who will represent their views when making decisions. It is a republic, which means that the chief of state (in this case, the president) is elected by the people. It is a constitutional government because it operates according to laws and principles outlined in the Constitution. It is a federal government, which means that the national government shares responsibility with state and municipal governments.

In 1787 the founders of the United States decided to limit the power of government by dividing authority among three separate but equally powerful branches: the legislative (writes the laws), the executive (carries out the laws), and the judicial (reviews the way the laws are applied).

The legislative branch

There are two legislative bodies—the House of Representatives and the Senate. Together they are called the Congress. Its main powers are to raise money and to decide how to spend it. It may also bring charges against a member of the executive branch suspected of a crime.

The House of Representatives has 435 voting members who serve two-year terms. The states with the smallest populations each have one representative; the state with the largest population (California) has 53. Additionally, each state has two senators elected to a six-year term in the Senate.

The executive branch

The executive branch consists of the president and advisers whom he appoints to head up various departments (see opposite). Presidents are elected to four-year terms. The president's job is to manage the executive branch and to make sure the laws of the nation are enforced. The president is also chief of state. In this capacity, he performs ceremonial duties. The president also has certain legislative and judicial powers: He may suggest legislation to Congress and veto (reject) legislation. He recommends candidates for the position of attorney general and nominates Supreme Court justices, federal court judges, and U.S. district attorneys. The president is the head of the diplomatic corps and commander in chief of the armed forces.

The judicial branch

The highest court in the United States is the Supreme Court. It is made up of one chief justice and eight associate justices.

The Supreme Court has the power to declare laws unconstitutional. This enables it to check the activities of the other two branches of the federal government and those of the state governments. The Supreme Court mostly hears cases that come on appeal from the lower courts.

SEE ALSO: Congress; Constitution, United States; Presidency, The; States and State Governments; Supreme Court; Vice Presidency, The

STRUCTURE OF GOVERNMENT

THE CONSTITUTION OF THE UNITED STATES

THE LEGISLATIVE BRANCH

THE EXECUTIVE BRANCH

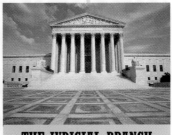

THE JUDICIAL BRANCH

The House of Representatives	The Senate	The President	The Supreme Court

Congress

Architect of the Capitol
Congressional Budget Office
General Accounting Office
Government Printing Office
Library of Congress
Stennis Center for Public Service
U.S. Botanic Garden

The Executive Office of the President

Council of Economic Advisers
Council on Environmental Quality
Domestic Policy Council
National Economic Council
National Security Council
Office of Administration
Office of Faith-Based and
  Community Initiatives
Office of Global Communications
Office of Homeland
  Security
Office of Management and
  Budget
Office of National AIDS Policy
Office of National Drug Control
  Policy
Office of Science and
  Technology Policy
Office of the United States Trade
  Representative
President's Critical Infrastructure
  Protection Board
President's Foreign Intelligence
  Advisory Board
USA Freedom Corps
White House Military Office

Lower Courts
  U.S. Bankruptcy Courts
  U.S. Court of Appeals for the
    Federal Circuit
  U.S. Judicial Circuit Courts of
    Appeals
  U.S. Court of International
    Trade
Special Courts
  U.S. Court of Appeals for the
    Armed Forces
  U.S. Court of Appeals for
    Veterans Claims
  U.S. Court of Federal Claims
  U.S. Tax Court
Administrative Office of the United
  States Courts
Federal Judicial Center
U.S. Sentencing Commission

On the road to the White House: Republican candidate George W. Bush makes a speech during the 2000 presidential election campaign.

The chamber of the House of Representatives, a legislative body that contains 435 elected members. There are viewing galleries for the public.

Cabinet Departments

State	Treasury	Defense	Justice	Interior	Agriculture	Commerce	Labor
Health and Human Services	Housing and Urban Development	Transportation	Energy	Education	Veterans Affairs	Homeland Security	

✳ UNITED STATES OF AMERICA

The United States is the wealthiest and most powerful nation in the world. It has the third-biggest population and is the fourth-largest country in area.

United States of America's national flag

British forces surrender after the battle of Trenton, New Jersey, in December 1776. It was one of George Washington's great victories in the American Revolution.

Land and people
Forty-nine of the 50 U.S. states are on the continent of North America. Hawaii is located far to the west in the Pacific Ocean. The capital, Washington, D.C., is not part of any state but occupies its own federal district, the District of Columbia. New York City is the banking and business center and is the most populous city.

About three-quarters of the population is classified as white. More than 12 percent of Americans are black. The fastest-growing minority group is Hispanics. Hispanics may belong to one or more races. Asians, Native Americans, Inuit, Aleuts, and Hawaiians and other Pacific Islanders complete the population.

Government and economy
The nation is a constitutional democracy, led by a president who is elected to serve a four-year term of office. Individual states draw up their own body of laws, but all American citizens must also obey federal (central government) laws.

By the end of the 20th century, the United States had become the world's only superpower. It has an economic strength at least twice that of any other nation.

History
Native Americans, belonging to many different peoples, lived on the land that is now the United States many thousands of years ago. European exploration of the Americas began in the 1490s with the voyages of Christopher Columbus. Spanish and French colonists were followed by English, Dutch, and Swedes.

The first of England's 13 colonies was established at Jamestown, Virginia, in 1607. The colonies planted crops, such as rice and tobacco, to be sent back to Europe. The exports were especially

important to the Southern colonies, where slaves provided a steady supply of labor on large farms called plantations.

Relations between colonists and Native Americans were uneasy, and there were frequent fights. French and English settlers also came into conflict. In the French and Indian wars (1689–1763), Britain won most of Canada, plus the Ohio and Mississippi valleys.

By the mid-1700s, life in the 13 colonies was relatively peaceful. But when Britain imposed a new set of taxes, many American colonists rebelled. The American Revolution broke out in 1775. With the Declaration of Independence in 1776, Americans hardened their resolve to throw off British rule. The war continued for another five years. Britain formally accepted American independence in the Treaty of Paris of 1783. The Constitution under which the country is now governed

was drafted in 1787. George Washington was elected first president of the United States in 1789. The first ten amendments to the Constitution, known as the Bill of Rights, were added in 1791.

In 1803 the nation bought France's vast American territories, which stretched from present-day Louisiana to Canada, doubling the area of the United States. It is known as the Louisiana Purchase. Between 1804 and 1805, the Lewis and Clark expedition followed the Missouri River to the Rockies and then crossed to the Pacific Coast.

In the early 1800s, when Britain was at war with France, British warships stopped American merchant vessels, seizing their cargoes and crews. In 1812 the United States declared war on Britain; Americans also hoped to conquer Canada, which at that time was a colony of Britain. U.S. troops won a battle at New Orleans in 1815 after a peace treaty had been signed.

Settlers travel through the Barlow Cutoff near Mount Hood, Oregon, in about 1865. In the mid-1800s, thousands of families journeyed west on the Oregon Trail to farm in the Willamette Valley.

Union forces at Yorktown, Virginia, during the Civil War (1861–65). The development of heavy artillery meant that the conflict became a war of sieges. The Union troops had larger guns, which helped them win the war.

KEY FACTS

OFFICIAL NAME:
United States of America

AREA:
3,717,796 sq. mi. (9,629,092 sq. km)

POPULATION:
281,421,906 (2000 census)

CAPITAL:
Washington, D.C.

LARGEST CITY:
New York

MAJOR RELIGIONS:
Protestantism, Roman Catholicism, Judaism, Islam

MAJOR LANGUAGE:
English

CURRENCY:
U.S. dollar

Immigration and expansion

The United States continued to grow, acquiring Florida from the Spanish in 1819. Newly invented machines for farming cotton, spinning textiles, and the mass production of other goods boosted the nation's industrial strength. Steamboats regularly sailed inland waterways, and after 1830 railroads began to connect towns. Immigrants flocked from Europe to start new lives. To create space for white settlers, more than 60,000 Native Americans were forced to move to lands west of the Mississippi River during the 1830s. About 15,000 died on the journey.

Americans looked to new lands in the West. Settlers had been moving to Texas, a Mexican province, since the 1820s. In 1836 Texas won independence from Mexico. It joined the Union in 1845. The United States bought part of the Oregon Territory from Britain in 1846, but Mexico refused to sell California. War broke out between Mexico and the United States. Mexico's defeat in 1848 gave California to the United States, as well as present-day Utah and Nevada, most of Arizona, and parts of New Mexico, Colorado, and Wyoming.

Secession and Civil War

By the mid-1800s, Americans were in dispute over slavery. The Union was more or less evenly divided between the "free" states of the North, in which slavery was banned, and those states in the South in which it was permitted. The Fugitive Slave Law of 1850 made it illegal to help a slave escape in the North or the South.

In 1860 Abraham Lincoln, who opposed slavery, was elected president. This angered the Southern states. Many of them seceded (withdrew) from the Union and set up their own nation—the Confederate States of America. Lincoln was determined to preserve the Union. In 1861, when civil war broke out between Confederate and Union states, he tried to recapture the South. In 1863 he issued the Emancipation Proclamation, after which all slaves in the Confederacy were considered free. The North finally emerged victorious in 1865.

A nation shattered by civil war turned to rebuilding itself in a period known as Reconstruction. Southern states were gradually allowed back into the Union.

Growth of the nation

As settlers continued to push westward, Native Americans lost even more of their homelands, along with vast herds of bison. Alaska was bought from Russia in 1867. Meanwhile, the steady flow of immigrants from Europe caused huge growth in the industrial cities. By 1890 the nation had more than doubled its pre–Civil War population and had become one of the world's leading industrial countries.

In 1898 the United States took control of Hawaii. It also waged a brief war with Spain in order to free Cuba from Spanish rule. After the war, Spain yielded Puerto Rico, the Philippines, and the Pacific island of Guam to the United States.

War and peace

The 20th century saw the United States emerge as a world power. In 1914 World War I broke out in Europe. In 1917 the United States sent a force of some two million men, which helped end the war in 1918. President Woodrow Wilson then set about rebuilding postwar Europe.

The 1920s were a time of prosperity—of jazz music, the growth of the automobile industry, and the start of a golden age for Hollywood's movie studios; but excessive risk-taking led to the collapse of the stock market in 1929. America entered the Great Depression as businesses went bankrupt and unemployment soared. In the 1930s, President Franklin D. Roosevelt introduced the New Deal, a program of economic and social reforms.

World War II began in 1939, when Germany invaded Poland. The United States entered the conflict at the end of 1941, when Japan launched an air attack on the U.S. naval base at Pearl Harbor, Hawaii. The war in the Pacific was brought to an end when American planes dropped two atomic bombs on Japan in 1945. The economic boost from the war effort had revived the United States so much that it became the world's most powerful nation.

Cold War and civil rights

After the war, the Soviet Union installed Communist governments in Eastern European nations that it had freed from German occupation. This led to a long period of hostility between the United States and the Soviet Union that became known as the Cold War. The two sides never came into actual conflict, but there was constant tension as both built nuclear missiles with which to threaten each other. American soldiers went to fight in Korea (1950–53) and Vietnam (1965–72) in attempts to contain Communism.

Unjust laws in the South still denied African Americans their full rights as citizens. A growing protest movement overthrew these laws with the Civil Rights Acts of 1964 and 1968.

The modern era

President Lyndon B. Johnson spoke of creating a "Great Society," and much was done by later presidents to build that society despite wars in the Persian Gulf and Afghanistan and a continuing gap between rich and poor at home. After the terrorist attacks on New York City and Washington, D.C., on September 11, 2001, President George W. Bush declared a "war on terrorism." In 2003 the United States led an invasion of Iraq.

In 1917 an American soldier bids farewell to his family before going off to fight in Europe in World War I (1914–18).

SEE ALSO: Abolition Movement; African Americans; American Revolution; Asian Americans; Bill of Rights; Civil Rights; Civil War; Colonial America; Confederacy; Congress; Constitution, United States; Declaration of Independence; Ellis Island; Emancipation Proclamation; French and Indian Wars; Great Depression; Hispanic Americans; Immigration; Korean War; Louisiana Purchase; Native Americans; North America, Geography; Persian Gulf War; Presidency, The; Slavery; Spanish–American War; Supreme Court; Underground Railroad; United States Armed Forces; United States Geography; United States Government; Vice Presidency, The; Vietnam War; War of 1812; West, The American; World Trade Center; World War I; World War II

✳ UNIVERSE

The vast expanses of space, and all the planets, stars, galaxies, and other matter contained there, are known as the universe, or the cosmos.

We usually think of a journey around Earth as being a great distance, but Earth is just one of the nine known planets in our solar system, all revolving around the sun. The sun is just one of more than 100 billion stars in the Milky Way galaxy, and there are many other galaxies in the universe, some of them bigger than the Milky Way.

Size and age of the universe

Scientists disagree about the size of the universe, or the number of stars in it. Many think that it is infinite—that it has no end. If it does have an end, our most advanced space probes and telescopes have not discovered it.

Since the 1960s, many astronomers and physicists have come to believe the Big Bang theory. This states that the universe began in a massive explosion, perhaps 10 or 15 billion years ago. The early universe was so hot that matter could not exist, only radiation. The universe began to expand rapidly, a process that continues today. The stars that make up the galaxies, and the galaxies themselves, are shifting their positions in the universe.

Not all scientists agree with this theory. And even those who do support the Big Bang idea do not agree on what will happen in the future. Some believe that the universe will keep expanding into infinite space and time. Others think that the universe will eventually begin to contract, leading to a massive implosion, or a Big Crunch. If this does occur, it will be many millions of years from now.

Studying the universe

The most important tool of astronomers for hundreds of years has been the telescope. Optical telescopes use lenses and mirrors to gather visible light from distant objects and create a magnified image of planets, moons, stars, and other bodies in the universe.

However, Earth's atmosphere blocks or distorts most forms of radiation that could give us information about the universe. Our ideas about what exists beyond Earth have developed greatly since the first space telescopes were launched in the 1970s. They can pick up infrared, ultraviolet, gamma, and X-rays that planets and stars give off. These cannot be seen from Earth, but computers can interpret data from the telescopes and convert it into a visual form. This allows us to "see"

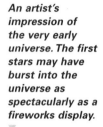

An artist's impression of the very early universe. The first stars may have burst into the universe as spectacularly as a fireworks display.

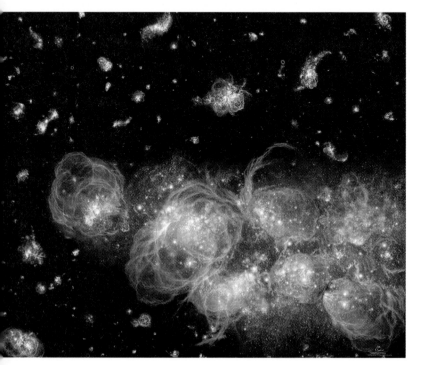

stars and planets many billions of miles away—much farther than the range of the most powerful Earth-based telescope.

In the 1990s, the National Aeronautics and Space Administration (NASA) began launching space telescopes called Great Observatories. The first of these was the Hubble Space Telescope (HST), named for the American astronomer Edwin Hubble (1889–1953). The HST orbits Earth at a height of about 370 miles (600 km). Its cameras can detect galaxies 10 billion light-years away. A light-year is the distance that light travels in one year—about six trillion miles (9.6 trillion km).

Life beyond Earth

One aspect of the universe that the greatest space telescopes have not been able to pick up is life on other planets. Many people tell stories of seeing strange lights in the sky, meeting aliens, or being taken to alien spaceships, but there is no hard, scientific evidence.

Researchers on a project called SETI— Search for Extraterrestrial Intelligence— use radio telescopes to detect radio-wave and microwave signals from space. They use computers to detect patterns that

might indicate an extraterrestrial presence attempting to make contact. The SETI@home project sends this data to thousands of computers across the world. Researchers can then analyze huge amounts of data much more quickly in an attempt to determine the big question—is there anybody out there?

SEE ALSO: Astronomy; Big Bang Theory; Galaxies; Planets; Solar System; Space Exploration; Telescopes

▲

The Hubble Space Telescope (HST) is berthed in the cargo bay of the space shuttle Endeavour *for repair by astronauts. The HST's cameras are designed to view objects so faint or so distant that they are invisible on Earth.*

✳ URANUS

Four times the size of Earth, Uranus is the third-largest planet in the solar system. Like Jupiter, Saturn, and Neptune, it is made mainly of gas.

In 1781 the British astronomer William Herschel surveyed the sky with a telescope he had built himself, examining every star and looking for something unusual. One night he found a tiny shining disk that was clearly not a star. At first he thought it was a comet, but other astronomers soon realized that he had discovered a new planet. They named it Uranus, for the Greek god of the heavens.

This image of Uranus, taken by the Hubble Space Telescope, shows the planet and its elaborate ring system.

Rotation and revolution

At a distance of 1.8 billion miles (2.9 billion km), Uranus is the seventh planet from the sun. It revolves around the sun once in every 84 years in a large oval orbit that is 19 times larger than the orbit of Earth. Uranus rotates once on its axis about every 17 hours. Its tilt on its axis at 98° from the plane of its orbit is unique in the solar system. This might be because the planet was struck by a large object during its formation, causing it to tip sideways.

Gas giant

The atmosphere of Uranus is composed mainly of hydrogen and helium, with traces of methane and other gases. Unlike the other gas giants Jupiter, Saturn, and Neptune, which have bands of clouds that can be seen clearly in their atmospheres, Uranus appears to be an almost featureless blue-green sphere. The clouds lower down in the planet's atmosphere are hidden from view by a smoglike haze in the outermost layers. The temperature at the upper layers of Uranus's atmosphere is extremely cold, typically about −355°F (−215°C). Beneath the outer layer of haze lies a vast ocean of water, ammonia, and methane.

Ring system

Uranus is surrounded by a complex system of rings that are much narrower and darker—and therefore harder to see—than those of Saturn. These rings are made up of tiny particles of ice and rock.

Many moons

Uranus has 21 known moons. The largest are named Miranda, Ariel, Umbriel, Titania, and Oberon. Miranda is unlike any other moon in the solar system. Cliffs, canyons, and ancient craters are mixed with much younger features. Scientists think that Miranda must have been broken apart by a collision and then put together again by gravity—perhaps several times.

KEY FACTS

POSITION IN THE SOLAR SYSTEM: Seventh planet from the sun	**DIAMETER:** 32,000 mi. (51,500 km)
AVERAGE DISTANCE FROM THE SUN: 1,800,000,000 mi. (2,900,000,000 km)	**MASS:** 87 sextillion tons
	ATMOSPHERE: Hydrogen, helium, methane
SOLAR ORBIT: 84 Earth years	**AXIAL ROTATION:** 17 hours

SEE ALSO: Astronomy; Planets; Solar System

✳ URUGUAY

Uruguay lies on the eastern coast of South America, between Brazil to the north, Argentina to the west, and the Atlantic Ocean to the south and east.

Land and climate

Uruguay is the second-smallest country among the independent nations of South America, after Suriname. It is the only country on the continent with no large uninhabited areas. Much of the land is made up of gently rolling grassy plains and broad valleys. The most important river is the Uruguay. In the southwest is the broad estuary (mouth) of the Río de la Plata, a huge river that carries the combined flow of the Paraná and Uruguay river systems to the Atlantic Ocean.

Uruguay lies between two climatic regions, the mild Argentine pampas and the hot, rain-soaked Brazilian Highlands. Summers are long and winters are short. Temperatures average between 50 and 72°F (10–22°C).

People

The early people of the region were native Indians. They were known by a variety of names, including the Charrús, Chanáes, and Guaranís. Spanish explorers arrived in 1516, but another century passed before any Spanish settlement began. At the beginning of the 19th century, most people were of mixed Spanish and Indian (mestizo) ancestry, although Spanish culture was dominant. However, toward the end of the century, many people emigrated to Uruguay, mostly from Spain and Italy. Smaller numbers of Germans, East Europeans, and Britons also settled in the early 20th century. As a result, most Uruguayans today are of European descent. About 10 percent of the people are of mestizo or African ancestry.

Uruguay is the most urban of the Latin American republics, with over 90 percent of the population living in urban areas. Spanish is the official language, although the Spanish spoken in Uruguay has been heavily influenced by Italian. Some people also speak Portunol or Brazilero, a mixture of Portuguese and Spanish spoken on the Brazilian border. About two-thirds of the people are Roman Catholics, although, unlike other Latin American countries, less than half of the population attends church regularly.

Uruguay's national flag

A view toward the harbor at Montevideo. The old part of the city stands on a tiny peninsula that reaches out into the Río de la Plata. This was the site of the first permanent Spanish settlement in Uruguay in 1726.

ARGENTINA

BRAZIL

Uruguay River

● Salto

● Paysandú

Negro River

Lake Rincón del Bonete

Laguna Mirim

● Fray Bentos

Río de la Plata

Montevideo

ATLANTIC OCEAN

KEY FACTS

OFFICIAL NAME:
República Oriental del Uruguay

AREA:
67,035 sq. mi.
(173,621 sq. km)

POPULATION:
3,337,000

CAPITAL & LARGEST CITY:
Montevideo

MAJOR RELIGION:
Roman Catholicism

MAJOR LANGUAGE:
Spanish

CURRENCY:
Uruguayan peso

Economy

Since the 1870s, when refrigerated ships began to carry cargoes of frozen beef to Europe, Uruguay's economy has been based on the export of cattle and sheep products. The government encourages farmers today to grow more crops, such as grains and citrus fruits. It also supports the growth of tourism, offshore fishing, and manufacturing.

History

The first European to visit the territory now called Uruguay was the Spanish navigator Juan Díaz de Solís (1470–1516), who landed in 1516. Native Indians killed him and drove his followers away. For the next three centuries, few settlers went to Uruguay. From time to time, the Portuguese, who then ruled Brazil, invaded the region, but they were driven back by Spanish forces from Argentina.

In the early 1800s, Uruguay and Argentina rebelled against Spain. But Uruguay's struggle for independence faced difficulties. The Portuguese wanted the territory to become part of Brazil, while the Argentinians thought it should be a province of Argentina. In 1811 José Gervasio Artigas (1774–1850) organized an army of gauchos (cowboys) to drive out both powers. He and his supporters were defeated by the Portuguese in 1820.

Uruguay finally won its independence in 1828. But until the beginning of the 20th century, the new nation was troubled by foreign intervention, civil wars, and revolts. The turning point came when José Batlle y Ordóñez (1856–1929) was elected president. Batlle was one of the great political figures of the Americas, and as president from 1903 to 1907 and 1911 to 1915, he introduced many social reforms.

In the late 1960s and early 1970s, Uruguay was faced with growing economic problems and antigovernment terrorism. In 1973 the army was brought into the government. Three years later, the army leaders took full control of the country. A gradual return to constitutional rule under a civilian government began in the 1980s. In 1999 Jorge Batlle, the grandnephew of José Batlle y Ordóñez, was elected president. He faced the challenge of securing economic growth for Uruguay.

Gauchos—or cowboys—drive cattle along a rough track near the city of Salto.
▶

SEE ALSO: Argentina; Brazil; South America

*VALLEYS 👀 *MOUNTAINS AND VALLEYS

* VAN GOGH, VINCENT (1853–90)

Vincent van Gogh was an important artist. His style of painting, which used bold patterns of color, reflected his intense personality.

Vincent van Gogh was born in Groot-Zundert, in the Netherlands. He tried various careers, including training to be a clergyman, but by 1880 he had decided to concentrate on his art.

Vincent's brother Theo worked for an art dealer in Paris, and Vincent joined him there in 1886. Theo introduced him to the Impressionists, a group of artists who tried to reproduce the effect of light striking solid objects. Although Vincent learned much from Impressionism, he developed his own unique style, applying bright color in swirling brushstrokes.

In 1888 van Gogh moved to Arles, in southern France, where he painted many of his most famous works. He suffered a mental breakdown and cut off part of his left ear. After some time in an asylum, Vincent moved to Auvers, near Paris, to be closer to his brother. Despite Theo's encouragement, Vincent sank deeper into despair. He shot himself and died on July 29, 1890.

Vincent van Gogh painted many self-portraits, such as this one, as well as scenes of the people and countryside of southern France.

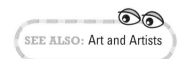

SEE ALSO: Art and Artists

* VEGETABLES

Vegetables are herbaceous (nonwoody) plants with edible parts—for example, roots, leaves, and stems. They supply us with vitamins and minerals.

Early humans probably gathered wild pod-bearing plants, such as peas, and root plants, such as carrots. The ancient Egyptians grew vegetables such as beans, lettuce, cabbage, radishes, and onions by the Nile River. The Greeks and later the Romans also grew these vegetables, as well as cucumbers, asparagus, and celery. When European explorers reached the New World, they found vegetables, such as potatoes, that were unknown in Europe. They took seeds and tubers back home, but many of these vegetables did not become popular until the 1800s. ➡️

In the 19th century, farmers started using better farming methods to improve their crops. The invention of the train, and then the automobile, meant that vegetables could be transported quickly from farm to market.

Cultivation

Climate and soil type are the two main factors that determine which vegetables farmers grow. Farmers use machinery to sow and harvest many of their vegetables. However, for certain crops, much of the work is still done by hand to avoid damaging delicate leaves.

Most vegetables reach the stores within a few days of picking and need to be eaten while they are fresh. However, modern

Historians believe that cabbages were grown in gardens over 4,000 years ago.

AMAZING FACTS!

The largest vegetable is the tropical yam. The edible tubers can grow to lengths of over 8 ft. (2.4 m) and weigh over 130 lb. (59 kg). These vegetables are not the same as sweet potatoes, which are sometimes called yams in North America.

methods of preserving, such as freezing and canning, mean that vegetables can last months or even years.

Vegetables that are out of season in one part of the world can be grown in another and shipped in refrigerated containers or transported by air, enabling people to enjoy them all year.

SEE ALSO: Agriculture; Ancient Civilizations; Food; Fruit; Health; Plants

* VENEZUELA

Venezuela is a nation on the northern coast of South America. It is the world's largest oil producer outside of the Middle East.

Venezuela's national flag

Venezuela means "Little Venice" in Spanish. The country was given its name in the 1400s by the explorer Alonso de Ojeda. The native houses built on stilts over Lake Maracaibo reminded him of the houses along the canals in Venice, Italy.

Land and climate
Venezuela has many plateaus and mountains in the north and south. The highest point is Pico Bolívar, at 16,427 ft.

(5,007 m). Other important areas include the lowlands around Lake Maracaibo and the huge, grassy plains called the llanos, which have long been used for grazing cattle. Native animals include pumas, jaguars, ocelots, sloths, anteaters, monkeys, and many colorful birds.

Venezuela is bordered in the north by the Caribbean Sea. The most important waterway is the Orinoco, one of the largest river systems in South America.

The spectacular Angel Falls, in the Guiana Highlands, is the world's highest waterfall, with a drop of 3,212 ft. (979 m).

Venezuela lies entirely within the tropics. There are only slight seasonal changes in temperature, but temperatures vary greatly with changes in altitude (height). The lowlands are hot and humid, with cooler and more variable conditions on high ground. Pico Bolívar and other nearby peaks remain snowcapped year round.

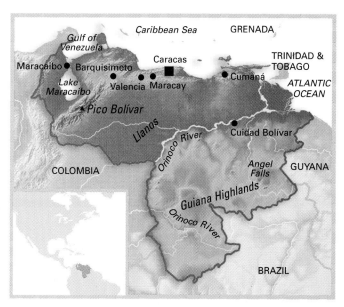

People

About 70 percent of Venezuelans are mestizos, or people of mixed European and native Indian descent. The rest of the population is mostly of European, African, or Indian descent. Most people are Roman Catholics. Spanish is the official language.

Most of the major cities are in the valleys. The capital city, Caracas, was founded by Spanish settlers in 1567. It is the most populous city, with one in every six Venezuelans living in the city area. Other cities include Maracaibo and Valencia.

Economy

Petroleum products make up more than 80 percent of Venezuela's export earnings. Other important resources include natural gas, bauxite, and iron ore. More than two-thirds of workers are employed in service industries. Farmers grow corn, sugarcane, rice, and bananas. Coffee, grown on large estates, is the chief commercial crop.

History

The first inhabitants of Venezuela were Carib and Arawak Indians. Christopher Columbus landed in 1498, and the first permanent European settlement on the mainland was at Cumaná in 1523. Venezuela was a Spanish colony for nearly 300 years. Many explorers went to Venezuela in search of El Dorado, a legendary city of gold believed to be situated by the Orinoco River. But only small amounts of gold were ever found.

Venezuela played a major role in South America's long struggle for independence from Spain. In the early 1800s, Francisco de Miranda led two revolts against Spanish rule. Although these revolts failed, they inspired Simón Bolívar, known as *El*

KEY FACTS

OFFICIAL NAME:
República Bolivariana de Venezuela

AREA:
352,143 sq. mi. (912,050 sq. km)

POPULATION:
24,170,000

CAPITAL & LARGEST CITY:
Caracas

MAJOR RELIGION:
Roman Catholicism

MAJOR LANGUAGES:
Spanish (official), Indian languages

CURRENCY:
Bolívar

The Venezuelan capital, Caracas.

629

Libertador (the liberator), to take up the cause. In 1811 Venezuela declared its independence, but Spanish troops still occupied most of the country. Bolívar invaded Venezuela and defeated the Spanish at Boyacá, Colombia, in 1819. He finally liberated Venezuela in 1821. Venezuela, Colombia, and Ecuador were briefly united as the Republic of Gran (Greater) Colombia, with Bolívar as president. Venezuela became fully independent in 1830. José Antonio Páez was the first president. He remained the most important figure in the country for nearly 20 years.

For many years political instability and dictatorship dominated the country. In the early 1900s, President Juan Vicente Gómez, known as the Tyrant of the Andes because of his harsh treatment of opponents, arranged contracts with foreign oil companies. Venezuela became one of the world's leading oil exporters.

The election of Rómulo Betancourt in 1959 ended the years of dictatorship. During his years in office (1959–64), Betancourt introduced many democratic reforms. However, corruption and natural disasters still made governments unstable. Floods and mudslides killed thousands of people in the north in 1999 and 2000. In 2002 the already weakened economy was further damaged by a nationwide strike by opponents of President Hugo Chávez Frías.

SEE ALSO: Bolívar, Simón; Colombia; Columbus, Christopher; Ecuador; South America

A variety of birds such as the crested oropendola are found in Venezuela's tropical areas and also throughout South America.

* VENUS

The closest planet to Earth, Venus can be seen before sunrise, when it is called the morning star, and after sunset, when it is called the evening star.

Venus is sometimes called Earth's twin because it is similar to our planet in size and mass. It has the most circular orbit (path around the sun) of any planet in the solar system. It turns very slowly on its axis. A "day" on Venus is 243 Earth days. Venus rotates from east to west; most other planets revolve in the opposite direction.

Hundreds of radar images taken by the Magellan space probe in the early 1990s have been used to create a computer-simulated view of Venus.

Cloud-covered planet

Venus is always surrounded by a thick, dense layer of gleaming white clouds. The first space probes to fly through them revealed that they are made of carbon dioxide plus tiny droplets of sulfuric acid.

The clouds end about 30 miles (48 km) above the surface of Venus. Strong winds blow the cloud layers around the planet. Moving at a speed of about 225 mph (362 kph), the clouds circle Venus in about four Earth days.

The atmosphere of Venus consists of about 97 percent carbon dioxide and 3 percent nitrogen, with small amounts of sulfur dioxide, argon, carbon monoxide, and oxygen. The atmosphere is densest near the surface of the planet, where the temperature is about 900°F (480°C).

KEY FACTS

POSITION IN THE SOLAR SYSTEM:
Second planet from the sun

AVERAGE DISTANCE FROM THE SUN:
67,200,000 mi. (108,200,000 km)

SOLAR ORBIT:
224.7 Earth days

DIAMETER:
7,519 mi. (12,100 km)

MASS:
4.9 sextillion tons

ATMOSPHERE:
Carbon dioxide, nitrogen

AXIAL ROTATION:
243 Earth days

Surface

Space probes sent to Venus since the late 1970s have used radar to "look through" the clouds and reveal that the planet has a dry, desertlike surface. More than 60 percent of it is covered with low-lying plains. Rising above the plains are two high, mountainous regions. Venus also has several large volcanic regions covered with hundreds of volcanoes more than 12 miles (19 km) in diameter, and tens of thousands of smaller volcanoes.

SEE ALSO: Astronomy; Planets; Solar System; Space Exploration

✶ VICE PRESIDENCY, THE

The Vice Presidency of the United States is the office occupied by the person who is next in line for the presidency if anything happens to the president.

If the president should die, resign, or be impeached (have formal charges brought against him if he has been accused of misconduct or a criminal offense), the vice president would take over the office of president. If the president should be disabled in any way, the vice president would take over the president's duties only as "acting president."

There have been eight instances of death in the history of the presidency, four of them assassinations. The first vice president to succeed to the presidency was John Tyler in 1841. He became president upon the death in office of William Henry Harrison. Probably the best-known case of a vice president succeeding to the presidency was after the assassination of President John F. Kennedy in 1963, when Lyndon Baines

Johnson took the oath of office as president of the United States only hours after Kennedy's death.

The Founders of the Constitution created the office of vice president for just such occasions. The vice president is also president of the Senate—the upper chamber of the national legislature—and presides over their daily sessions. The Constitution gave only one power to the president of the Senate. It is used if there is a tie vote. At such a time, the vice president can make what is called a casting vote.

How the vice president is elected
Originally the Constitution said that the person who lost, or came second, in the presidential election would be vice president. The 12th Amendment to the

Dick Cheney, George W. Bush's vice president, has previously served in three presidential administrations.

Constitution, added in 1804, changed this. It stated that electors had to vote for president and vice president separately. The office of vice president then became less important. The office has been vacant 16 times for a total of more than 37 years. The office of vice president is vacant when the vice president succeeds to the presidency; the office is also vacant if the vice president dies.

Since the death of President Kennedy, there has been more concern if the office of vice president is vacant. The 25th Amendment, ratified in 1967, states that when there is a vacancy in the vice presidency, the president nominates a vice president who takes office upon confirmation of a majority vote of Congress. The first vice president to take office under this amendment was Gerald R. Ford in 1973.

A list of U.S. vice presidents can be found at the end of the encyclopedia.

SEE ALSO: Congress; Constitution, United States; Presidency, The; States and State Governments; Supreme Court; United States Government

✳VIDEO RECORDING

With the technology of video recording, it is possible to record a TV program, make a record of a family occasion, or watch a movie at home.

Video recording is the transfer of sight and sound images onto a magnetic tape (videotape) or onto a special kind of disk (videodisk). Most video recording is done on magnetic tape. The tape is wound on two small reels within a plastic holder called a cassette.

History

The earliest attempts at video recording were made in the 1940s, but the Ampex corporation developed the first successful videotape technology in the 1950s. By the late 1970s, VCRs (videocassette recorders) were widely available for home use. People could rent or buy prerecorded cassettes of movies and other material. They could also record programs from the television, even if the television set was turned off or they were watching a program on a different channel. The portable VCR (also called VTR, for videotape recorder) and color video camera were developed soon after. They allowed people to make their own recordings of vacations, sports, business meetings, and other events.

The television broadcasting industry continues to make wide use of video recording. Television studios make video recordings of many shows which can then be broadcast at any future time. Videotape is easy to edit and can be erased and used over and over. In contrast, movie film can be used only once. Videotape can be played back immediately after it records, but film must go through a development process. Videotape has changed television news programs in particular. Because there is no waiting time for film to be developed, news stories can be broadcast very shortly after they are recorded.

Videotape also allows an exciting action at a sports event to be shown over and over again on television just after it happens.

Modern video cameras are lightweight and easy to use. Video recording events such as a family holiday is a popular hobby.

This is known as instant replay. The videotape can be sped up, slowed down, reversed, and stopped for what is called freeze-frame, then played back one frame at a time. Instant replay allows us to study, for example, pitching and batting motions in baseball that take place too quickly for the eye to see completely.

Videodisks

From the 1980s, various methods for putting video images on disks were marketed. Early videodisks could hold only two hours of information. They were also expensive. The DVD (digital versatile disk) has been more successful; the picture quality is better, and a single disk can store more information.

Digital video images can also be stored on computers and then transmitted over the Internet. New technology includes a type of video recorder/player that can download images direct from a television, without the need for tapes or disks. A recent development is "interactive" video recording. With the help of a computer, the user of a video recorder will be able to ask questions, receive answers, and be guided to further information within the recorded material.

How video recording works

Videotape is coated in particles that can be magnetized. Recording generates a magnetic field that corresponds to the signal coming from the television, or from the image entering the camera. The particles arrange themselves in patterns similar to this field. When the tape is played back, electronics convert these patterns into a standard broadcast signal. DVDs and other disk formats convert the data into digital form. The playback equipment converts a signal consisting of a series of 1s and 0s into pictures and sound.

Video-recording technology is changing rapidly. Today's modern equipment may seem out of date, and even primitive, in 10 years' time.

SEE ALSO: Computers; Films; Internet; Magnetism; Sound Recording; Technology; Television

✳ VIETNAM WAR
War devastated the Southeast Asian country of
Vietnam between about 1957 and 1975. From 1965
the United States fought on the side of South Vietnam.

In the mid-1800s, France started to build a
colonial empire in Southeast Asia. By the
end of the century, it controlled what was
known as French Indochina (present-day
Vietnam, Cambodia, and Laos).

In 1940, during World War II (1939–45),
Japanese troops occupied Vietnam. In
1941 the Communists, led by Ho Chi
Minh, formed the Vietminh, or League for
the Independence of Vietnam, to fight the
Japanese and oppose the continuation of
French rule.

When the war ended, France reestablished
control in the south. The Vietminh seized
power in the north and proclaimed the
Democratic Republic of Vietnam.

The Indochina War
The French accepted the republic as a free
state within the French Union, but they
planned to reestablish their colonial rule
eventually. In December 1946, fighting
broke out between the French and the
Vietminh, beginning what became known
as the Indochina War.

The conflict lasted eight years. It cost the
French colonial forces 74,000 dead and
more than 150,000 casualties. The
Vietminh perfected what is called guerrilla
warfare. They focused on ambushes and
usually avoided large-scale conventional
fighting. They controlled the countryside
and kept effective lines of communication
and supply through dense rain forests.

*Helicopters fly
over two
American soldiers
in 1967 during an
attack on South
Vietnam.*

In 1954 the Vietminh overran a French fortress at Dien Bien Phu. This led to a peace settlement drawn up at Geneva, Switzerland. Vietnam was divided into two separate zones at the 17th parallel. The capitals were Hanoi in the north and Saigon (now Ho Chi Minh City) in the south. According to the agreements, the partition was temporary, and nationwide elections were promised, but they never took place. In the north, Ho Chi Minh created a tightly controlled Communist government. President Ngo Dinh Diem established the Republic of Vietnam in the south. The United States supported Diem with financial aid and military advice.

Vietnam War begins

What is known as the Vietnam War began in 1957 when Communist guerrillas in the south, called the Vietcong, began to attack village officials. Diem asked for increased U.S. aid. The United States felt that the Communists had broken the Geneva agreements and feared that the whole of Southeast Asia might fall to communism. But the South Vietnamese army was so badly organized and corrupt that U.S. aid was of little help. Meanwhile, North Vietnam sent more guerrilla forces and regular troops south.

In 1963 and 1964 there were two military coups in the south. General Nguyen Khanh took power. The South Vietnamese government remained unstable throughout the war. U.S. military advisers secretly began to take part in the fighting and to lead South Vietnamese forces.

America joins the war

In August 1964 North Vietnamese patrol boats attacked the U.S. destroyer *Maddox* in the Gulf of Tonkin. U.S. Navy planes bombed North Vietnamese targets in retaliation. In 1965 President Lyndon B. Johnson sent the first U.S. ground troops

to South Vietnam and increased bombing of the North. By 1968 there were 550,000 U.S. troops in Vietnam.

In early 1968 the Communists launched the Tet Offensive—a series of attacks on cities in the south (so-called because the attacks took place during the Vietnamese New Year period known as Tet). The Communists suffered heavy losses, but the attacks proved that in three years of fighting, U.S. troops had not managed to defeat the Vietcong.

Peace talks began in Paris, France, in May 1968, but progress was slow. The war was becoming increasingly unpopular in the United States, which was spending nearly $30 billion a year on the conflict. The bombing of North Vietnam had become a moral issue and harmed the reputation of the United States throughout the world.

Failed peace agreement

Richard M. Nixon became president in 1969. He announced that U.S. troops would begin to withdraw from Vietnam, leaving the fighting to the South Vietnamese. The last U.S. ground troops left Vietnam in 1972. A peace treaty was signed in 1973, but neither side kept to its terms. In 1974 North Vietnam invaded the South. The South Vietnamese government surrendered in 1975. The country was united under Communist rule in 1976.

Some 58,000 Americans died or disappeared during the war. More than a million Vietnamese lost their lives. Vietnam was devastated economically. The destruction also affected the neighboring countries of Cambodia and Laos.

SEE ALSO: Communism; Southeast Asia; Warfare

✳ VIKINGS

Between the eighth and 11th centuries, Scandinavian warriors traveled throughout Europe and sailed to Greenland and the North American continent.

A fleet of Viking longships races across the North Sea toward England.

The Vikings originally lived in the lands that are now called Norway, Denmark, and Sweden. They worshiped the Norse gods, including Odin and Thor. Their history and legends were recorded in long poems called sagas, which were not written down but passed by word of mouth from one generation to another. In their own lands, the Vikings were farmers and traders. They were also expert sailors. By the late 700s, they had built fast boats for war, called longships or dragon-ships.

Exploration and invasion

In the late 700s, Vikings began to raid England, taking away many treasures and capturing people to sell as slaves. Over the next 250 years, they carried out raids on Scotland, Ireland, the Netherlands, and France, and as far south as Spain and Italy.

However, they were not simply violent robbers. From 862 Swedish Vikings under Rurik traveled eastward and established a kingdom in what is now Russia. In 911 the Viking Hrolfr, or Rollo, became the first duke of Normandy, in northern France. Many of his followers settled there. Norwegian and Danish Vikings built settlements in northeastern England and in Ireland. The Danish king Canute ruled England between 1017 and 1035.

By the 800s, the Vikings had also begun to settle Iceland. In 982 an Icelandic Viking named Eric the Red was banished from the island and colonized Greenland. His son, Leif Eriksson, explored farther west and landed on Newfoundland, in Canada.

Christianity eventually replaced Viking beliefs and culture in Scandinavia and other areas of Viking influence. The last Viking invasion of England took place in 1066, just weeks before it was conquered by the Normans, who were themselves descendants of Viking settlers in France.

SEE ALSO: Exploration and Explorers; Greenland; Iceland; Scandinavia

VOLCANOES

A volcano is a place where molten (melted) rock, solid pieces of hot rock, and hot gases formed inside the earth erupt through its surface.

Heat in the earth's interior continually escapes toward the surface. As the heat rises, it warms rock, which begins rising slowly. This molten rock, or magma, usually cools within the earth. Sometimes, however, magma continues to push upward. It absorbs water in the ground and heats it to produce steam, which is a gas. Gas-filled magma is lighter and can rise through a series of conduits, or channels, toward the surface. When it reaches a vent, or opening, in the surface, it spews out. Magma that erupts from a vent is called lava. During eruption it reaches temperatures of about 2,000°F (1,100°C). Cooled lava and other material, such as ash and rock, build up to form the cone of a volcano.

Most volcanoes are located near the edges of continents, where the huge plates that form the earth's crust collide, forcing one plate to slide beneath the other. Rocks in the plate are pushed toward the earth's interior, where they melt. The melted rock rises as magma, forming volcanoes near where the plates meet. Volcanoes also occur where plates are spreading apart.

Types of volcanoes

Volcanologists, the scientists who study volcanoes, divide them into four types. Stratovolcanoes get their name from the different layers, or strata, of ash and lava that form them. Most are irregular in shape, and they usually have large, circular depressions at their summits. Depressions less than 1 mile (1.6 km) wide are called craters. Larger depressions are called calderas.

Mount St. Helens volcano in Washington State erupts. The explosion on May 18, 1980, created a cloud of gas and ash over 15 miles (24 km) high. Much of the mountain was destroyed, and about 60 people were killed. Scientists monitor the volcano for possible further eruptions.

637

The largest volcanoes are shield volcanoes. They form when large flows of lava spread rapidly from central vents. They have broad bases and gentle slopes. The island of Hawaii is made of five overlapping shield volcanoes. The largest is Mauna Loa.

Small volcanoes, called cinder cones, dot the landscape in volcanic regions. There are more cinder cones than any other type of volcano. They form when small explosions of magma occur many times from one vent, leaving chunks of ash and lava on the surface.

- vent
- side vent
- conduit
- conduit
- layers of lava and ash
- magma chamber

The most powerful eruptions are produced by ashflow calderas. The magma and other material blow so far from the vent that almost no mountain is built up. A large caldera forms, surrounded by low hills of ash deposits.

Types of eruptions

Scientists use special terms for the different kinds of eruption. The gentlest are Hawaiian eruptions, which are nonexplosive. Strombolian eruptions, named for a volcano in Italy, have many weak eruptions. Vulcanian eruptions produce a lot of ash but little lava. Peléean eruptions are named for Mount Pelée, on the Caribbean island of Martinique. They are violent explosions, with rapid flows of ash, rock, and gases. The most powerful eruptions are Plinian eruptions. Named after Pliny the Elder, a Roman scholar killed when Mount Vesuvius erupted in A.D. 79, they hurl plumes of ash many miles into the sky.

Scientists also classify volcanoes by how often they erupt. Extinct volcanoes have not erupted for many thousands of years. Dormant volcanoes have also been inactive for many years, but might erupt in the future. Active volcanoes either erupt constantly or they have erupted sometime in the last 10,000 years. Volcanologists monitor active volcanoes. Earthquakes and the emission of gases may signal that a volcano is about to erupt.

◄

A volcano is a complex system of conduits (channels), storage areas, and rock deposits that transports heat from deep inside the earth to its surface.

SEE ALSO: Earth; Earthquakes; Geology; Mountains and Valleys; Plate Tectonics

✳ WARFARE

As far back in history as we have evidence, humans have fought wars. Regardless of its rights and wrongs, warfare is an important human activity.

Early peoples fought with clubs or bows and later with axes, spears, and swords. Battles were tiring and probably lasted only a few hours. A vital part of warfare was attacking enemy villages and fortifying them as defense.

Nomads (wandering peoples) in Central Asia started riding horses about 4,500 years ago. In about 1850 B.C., they built chariots, two-wheeled carts that served as stable fighting platforms. Chariots were eventually replaced by cavalry— skilled riders who charged at the enemy.

Foot soldiers
Not every commander depended on cavalry. Although the ancient Greeks and Alexander the Great (356–323 B.C.) used cavalry, the core of their armies remained units of foot soldiers. The Roman army, the finest fighting force of its day, developed much larger units of soldiers called legions. Legionaries were foot soldiers armed with spears, javelins (throwing spears), and short swords. Superior tactics, discipline, and organization gave them an advantage even over a mounted enemy.

After the fall of the Western Roman Empire in A.D. 476, cavalry dominated warfare in Europe and Asia. The cavalry armies of the Mongol Genghis Khan

(about 1167–1227) conquered the largest land empire the world has ever seen. In India armies fought mounted on elephants.

By the mid-1300s in Europe, English infantry armed with powerful longbows inflicted defeats on French cavalry. In the battles of Crécy (1346) and Agincourt (1415), English archers rained arrows down on heavily armored French knights.

Firearms
By then, however, a revolutionary new substance—gunpowder—had reached Europe from the East. Large cannons

▲
This mosaic (a picture made from small stones) is thought to show the battle of Gaugamela in 331 B.C. For the Greeks, led by Alexander the Great, it was an important victory against the Persians, led by King Darius III (in the chariot).

Dutch and English ships fight against the Spanish Armada in 1588. This painting dates from 1608.

named siege guns helped Turkish forces capture Constantinople in 1453. The use of firearms spread swiftly. The 1600s and 1700s saw the rise of paid, uniformed infantry armed with muskets and bayonets. Battles were precisely planned. Armies drew up in lines facing one another so that each man could use his musket.

New, lightweight cannons named field guns, of the late 1700s, arrived in time for the French emperor Napoleon Bonaparte. He favored flexible tactics, concentrating his forces at the point where they would cause the most damage to the enemy.

In the American Civil War (1861–65), traditional tactics were no longer possible because advancing lines of uniformed troops would be cut down in a hail of gunshot. The need for infantry to seek cover and the arrival of railroads greatly extended the scale of battles. Napoleon had been defeated in a day at Waterloo (1815); the battle of Gettysburg (1863) lasted three days. In World War I (1914–18), machine guns pinned troops in trenches. Many soldiers died for the sake of a few miles of ground.

Aircraft
World War I saw the arrival of two new weapons of war—the tank and aircraft. Tanks could roll over defensive trenches and were impervious to bullets. Aircraft

were used to spy on enemy forces, to drop bombs, and to "dogfight" with enemy planes. Tanks and aircraft played an even more important part in World War II (1939–45). Two atomic bombs dropped on Japan by U.S. airplanes in 1945 helped end the war—and heralded a new era.

The atomic age
From 1945 to 1990 the United States and the Soviet Union, two victors of World War II, faced each other in a tense standoff known as the Cold War. Neither side dared attack the other because both had atomic and then thermonuclear weapons.

Today's armed forces use guided missiles, satellite surveillance, and jet fighters. The line between war and peace is not always clearly defined, and terrorist organizations form "invisible" worldwide armies—that is, members conceal their identities and activities because they operate unlawfully.

SEE ALSO: Aircraft; Alexander the Great; American Revolution; Ancient Civilizations; Civil War; Genghis Khan; Knights and Chivalry; Korean War; Napoleon; Roman Empire; Ships and Boats; Spanish–American War; United States Armed Forces; Vietnam War; War of 1812; World War I; World War II

⚹ WAR OF 1812

The War of 1812 was the last conflict between the United States and Britain. It is also known as the Second War of Independence.

The United States became independent from Britain in 1783. However, tensions remained between the new nation and its old colonial ruler. Britain was at war with France and seized U.S. merchant ships to prevent America trading with its enemy. The British even forced American seamen to serve in the British navy. Some U.S. politicians called for an invasion of Canada, which was then a British colony. After much debate in Congress, President James Madison signed a declaration of war on June 18, 1812.

Course of the war

The British captured Detroit and defeated the United States in battles along the Canadian border in the winter of 1812–13. In September 1813 a U.S. fleet took control of Lake Erie. In October the Americans were victorious at the battle of the Thames. Nevertheless, most of Canada remained under British control.

The mighty British navy suffered some defeats in the early months of the war, but after the European war ended in 1814, the British devoted more resources to North

America. They planned to invade New York from Canada and New Orleans from the Caribbean. They captured Washington, D.C., forcing the president to flee. However, a U.S. naval victory at Lake Champlain in September halted the British invasion from the north.

The U.S. victory at the battle of New Orleans in 1815 took place after a peace treaty had been signed, but the news was slow to arrive. Even though the United States failed to conquer Canada or force Britain to recognize its neutral trading rights, British failures late in the war enabled the Americans to claim victory.

Peace and the last battle

In December 1814 a treaty was signed in Ghent (now in Belgium) that gave no advantages to either side. However, this news did not reach the United States for some weeks. The British fleet was approaching New Orleans, defended by General Andrew Jackson, and the battle of New Orleans, on January 8, 1815, resulted in a great victory for the United States.

DID YOU KNOW?

The British attempted—and failed— to capture Baltimore, Maryland, in 1814. The sight of the American flag still flying above Fort McHenry in Baltimore harbor inspired Francis Scott Key to write a poem. As "The Star-Spangled Banner," it was set to music and later became the national anthem of the United States.

SEE ALSO: American Revolution; Canada; United Kingdom; United States of America; Warfare

✳ WATER

Water is the most common substance on Earth, covering almost three-quarters of the planet's surface. All living things depend on it for survival.

Children in Udaipur, India, draw water from a well. In the developing world, water sources such as wells are not always clean and may cause disease.

Water is composed of two chemical elements, hydrogen (H) and oxygen (O). Each molecule of water consists of two hydrogen atoms and one oxygen atom. Chemists write this formula as H_2O.

At normal temperatures, water is a liquid. However, it also appears as a solid and as a gas. When its temperature falls below 32°F (0°C), it expands and becomes a solid called ice. When its temperature is raised above 212°F (100°C), water becomes a gas, called vapor or steam. These temperatures are, respectively, the freezing and boiling points of water.

The amount of water on Earth remains constant, but its form is always changing—from solid to liquid, from liquid to gas, and back again. It moves in a pattern called the water cycle. Heat from the sun causes water in oceans, lakes, and rivers to evaporate into vapor. Further vapor is given off by plants and animals. As the vapor rises, it condenses into tiny droplets that form clouds. Water in the clouds gathers to form raindrops, snowflakes, or hailstones that fall back to Earth.

Water use

Only 3 percent of water is fresh (not salt water). Two-thirds of that freshwater is frozen in glaciers and ice caps. People now use over half of the freshwater available. If the world's population keeps growing at its current rate, people could be using over 90 percent of all available freshwater within 25 years, leaving just 10 percent for all other living things. Almost three-quarters of the freshwater used by humans is for agriculture. It takes a huge amount of water to produce crops.

Water and health

During the 20th century, the world's human population tripled, and water use increased sixfold. In the same period, half the world's wetlands disappeared, and many freshwater fish became endangered. Agriculture uses more water to meet the demands of a growing population, while other users have less and less water. About five million people die every year from diseases caused by water pollution or lack of water.

In 1972 the Clean Water Act was passed in the United States. Before then only one-third of U.S. streams, lakes, and coastal waters were clean enough for fishing and swimming. Now two-thirds of our waters are safe.

SEE ALSO: Agriculture; Dams; Floods; Glaciers; Lakes; Matter; Natural Resources; Oceans and Seas; Rivers; Pollution; Population and Censuses; Weather; Wetlands

✳ WEATHER

Weather is the continually changing conditions of the air around us. These changes can take many different forms, including wind, rain, and snow.

Changes in the weather influence how we live from day to day. When it rains or snows, we are often forced to be indoors. Weather affects our choice of clothes. We wear light clothes when the weather is hot, and thick, close-fitting clothes when it is cold. Fierce storms can damage property or even take people's lives.

No one can change the weather, but scientists can try to predict it so that we can be prepared for it. The study of weather is called meteorology. Weather experts, called meteorologists, try to understand the forces that control weather and how to predict it.

Where does weather come from?
Heat, air, and water act together to affect weather. Variations in the heat of the earth's surface make air rise to different levels. That causes changes in air pressure. Scientists measure air pressure in millibars (mb) or kilopascals (kPa) using an instrument called a barometer. An area of high or rising pressure usually means that the weather will be fair. Low or falling pressure tends to mean bad weather.

Movement of air between high- and low-pressure areas causes wind. Because of the earth's rotation, wind tends to move in a circular motion around the high- and low-pressure areas. If the difference between air pressure is great, storms such as hurricanes and tornadoes develop.

Clouds, rain, and snow
The surface waters of oceans, lakes, and rivers are constantly evaporating. This means that the water changes from a liquid to a gas, called water vapor. Warm air laden with water vapor rises and cools. Its water vapor comes into contact with dust and other particles in the air. The vapor condenses (turns into a liquid), and a droplet of water forms around each tiny particle. Clouds are collections of millions of water droplets or ice crystals. By the time the air is cool enough for clouds to form, the water vapor has usually been carried high up by the rising air. This is

This picture shows a series of thunderstorms located over southern Brazil. Storms of this size can drop large amounts of rain in a short period of time, causing floods.

A flooded street in Hanoi, Vietnam. Floods occur when heavy rain or storms cause the banks of rivers, lakes, and streams to overflow or if the land is too hard or frozen to absorb any excess rainfall.

why clouds are usually seen high above Earth's surface. When clouds form at ground level, we see fog, or mist.

Inside a cloud, the droplets or ice crystals bump into one another and grow in size. When they are large enough, they fall to the ground below. If the air below a cloud is warm, any crystals will melt and reach the ground as rain; if the air is colder, they will fall as snow. If water droplets are carried up into a thunderstorm cloud and freeze, they become balls of ice called hailstones. If rain refreezes before it reaches the ground, it is called sleet. If strong winds and snow combine, the result is a blizzard.

The shapes of the three main forms of clouds—cumulus, stratus, and cirrus—are clues to predicting the weather. Cumulus clouds are puffy with broad, flat bases. A few small cumulus clouds are a sign of fair weather, but tall, bulky cumulus clouds, known as cumulonimbus clouds, can produce thunderstorms. Stratus clouds are flat, sheetlike clouds and usually mean warm, possibly wet weather. Cirrus clouds

are wispy clouds found at great heights. They are full of ice crystals. These clouds often mean stormy weather.

Weather forecasts

Weather conditions high above Earth's surface alter conditions near the ground. Meteorologists can observe the conditions by using satellites. These are spacecraft orbiting high above Earth that take detailed pictures of the planet, its oceans, and its atmosphere.

Both a record of weather conditions over a long period of time and a record of current weather conditions over the whole planet are needed to create an accurate forecast. Around 10,000 weather stations across the world gather observations. Four times a day, each station forwards data to one of three meteorological centers in Australia, Russia, and the United States. These centers process the information and send it back around the world. Meteorologists can then make local weather forecasts.

SEE ALSO: Atmosphere; Blizzards; Climate; El Niño; Floods; Hurricanes and Typhoons; Satellites; Tornadoes; Water; Wind

✳ WEST, THE AMERICAN

In the 19th century, American pioneers pushed west of the Mississippi River and braved harsh conditions in search of a better life.

The settlement of the lands west of the Mississippi River began around 1815. The lands in the east were becoming crowded. Explorers and fur trappers, meanwhile, told romantic stories of the West: the Great Plains, the Rocky Mountains, the Southwestern deserts, and the Pacific Coast. The West seemed to be a place of promise and opportunity, prompting newspaper editor Horace Greeley (1811–72) to coin the phrase "Go west, young man."

Westward bound
A steady flow of pioneers set off west in wagon trains. Many were farmers, but others hoped to earn a living as storekeepers, reporters, preachers, even actors. Gold and silver were discovered in California and the Rockies in the 1840s and 1850s. Many miners hurried to the mountains. They lived in violent mining towns without any laws or sheriffs.

The growth of mining and trade spurred the construction of the railroad. In 1869 a line linked the East and West coasts. Telegraph lines also spread across the country, connecting East and West.

Cattle country
The last great region to be settled was the Plains, home to the most famous figures of the West, the cowboys. After the Civil War (1861–65), ranchers in Texas began to drive their longhorn cattle north to graze the grasslands of Kansas, Nebraska, Colorado, Wyoming, Montana, and the Dakotas. The ranchers hired cowboys to drive the herds to "cow towns," such as Dodge City and Abilene, Kansas, where the cattle were loaded onto

A cowboy in South Dakota during the late 1880s. Despite the romantic image later created by Hollywood, cowboys spent most of their time doing work that was difficult, dirty, and often boring.

645

The Western outlaw gang known as the Wild Bunch. Left to right: Harry Longabaugh (the "Sundance Kid"); William Carver; Ben Kilpatrick (the "Tall Texan"); Harvey Logan ("Kid Curry"); Robert LeRoy Parker ("Butch Cassidy").

Western land at no cost. (A homestead is an area of land granted to a settler.) Thousands of people took up the government offer. They went west with hopes of a better future, but were often disappointed by the tough prairie soil and the savage climate. Homes were often miles apart, and the work was hard.

Many homesteaders found themselves facing gunmen hired by wealthy cattle ranchers. The cattlemen regarded the newcomers as rustlers (thieves). They did not want homesteaders to fence in the range where their herds grazed. Fighting broke out in the so-called "range wars" in Wyoming and Montana. Yet by the end of the 19th century, the homesteaders had won. The open range had gone forever.

End of the wild frontier

In 1890 the director of the census declared that "there can hardly be said to be a frontier line" remaining in the United States. Today the spirit of the West lives on in popular culture, especially movies. They show the "Wild West" as a land of cowboys, Indians, and gunfighters. The heroes and heroines are depicted as quiet, honest, and independent. But the truth is less romantic—life in the West was a hard, lonely struggle in a difficult environment.

Today museums, such as the National Cowgirl Museum and Hall of Fame in Texas, honor some of the outstanding pioneers of the West. Yellowstone, which was established as the world's first national park in 1872, preserves a small part of the West's wide, open spaces.

railroad cars and shipped to stockyards in the eastern cities. Life in the cow towns was rowdy. Town marshals and county sheriffs were appointed to keep the peace, but many of the lawmen were corrupt. During the 1890s and early 1900s, there were many criminals in the West— among the most famous were Butch Cassidy and the James brothers.

The settlers faced many dangers, including attack by Native Americans who tried to protect their lands from the newcomers. For example, the spread of miners into the Black Hills of the Dakotas in 1874 was resisted by the Sioux. At the battle of the Little Bighorn in 1876, the Sioux killed 200 cavalry led by Lieutenant Colonel George A. Custer. But even the Sioux were later overwhelmed. Native Americans were eventually confined to reservations.

Homesteaders

A new wave of settlers began to arrive in the West in the 1860s, enticed by the 1862 Homestead Act, which allocated

SEE ALSO: Chief Joseph; Crazy Horse; Native Americans; Pirates and Outlaws; Sitting Bull; United States of America

✱ WEST AFRICA

West Africa is made up of 16 different countries, which give the region a diverse mixture of people and customs.

The countries of West Africa are Benin, Burkina Faso, Cape Verde, The Gambia, Ghana, Guinea, Guinea-Bissau, Ivory Coast (Côte d'Ivoire), Liberia, Mali, Mauritania, Niger, Nigeria, Senegal, Sierra Leone, and Togo.

Land and climate

The Sahara Desert occupies the interior of much of West Africa, an area that gets almost no rain. A broad lowland strip surrounds the coast of the region. Here the tropical climate supports a dense blanket of rain forests, palm groves, and mangrove swamps. Farther inland, the land rises to a plateau of rolling grassland, or savanna, which is ideal for farming.

People and economy

West Africa's mix of peoples reflects its history as a trading crossroads linking Africa, Europe, and the Americas. Islam is the chief religion across much of the region, followed by Christianity and folk religions. French and English are also widely spoken, along with local African languages.

West Africa includes some of the world's poorest countries, due to barren land, a difficult climate, and political problems. Many countries grow cash crops, such as peanuts, cacao (for cocoa and chocolate), palm oil, and coffee.

History

Long ago African states fought for control over West Africa. The greatest, which flourished between about 1000 and 1600, included the Soninke, Benin, Songhai, and Mali empires.

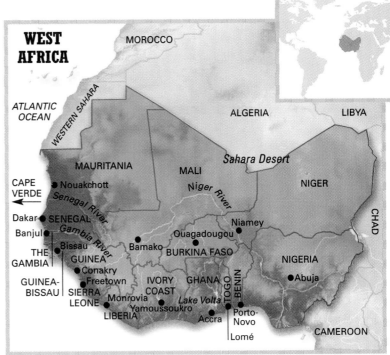

The Portuguese set up colonies in Guinea-Bissau and the Cape Verde Islands in the 15th century. They were followed by other Europeans, who came to trade gold and ivory or to seize slaves. By the end of the 19th century, France and Great Britain controlled much of West Africa. All these nations became independent between the 1950s and 1970s. Liberia was settled in 1822 by freed American slaves. In 1847 it became an independent republic, but it continued to rely on American financial aid. Civil war (1989–96) further damaged the economy.

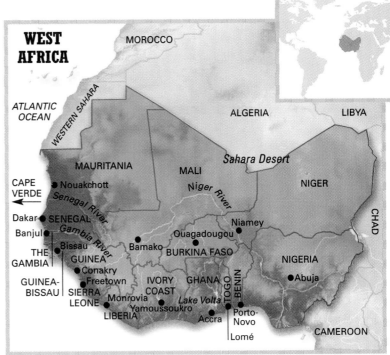

SEE ALSO: **Africa; Ghana; Islam; Nigeria; Slavery**

✳ WETLANDS

A wetland is an area where the soil is saturated (wet through) with water or covered by shallow pools of water for long periods of time.

Cypress Creek National Wildlife Refuge in Illinois provides a habitat for many animals that are in danger of becoming extinct (dying out). ▶

Wetlands cover 6 percent of the earth's land surface and are found in all countries and in all climates. They include swamps, bogs, and marshes. The type of water in a wetland (whether it is freshwater or salt water), its amount, and how it moves, distinguish a wetland environment from other water habitats, such as rivers and lakes. The amount of water in a wetland is always changing due to tides, rainfall, and dry weather.

Swamps

Swamps are forested wetlands. In shallow-water swamps, the ground stays moist all year. Deep-water swamps form along rivers and often flood. Along the seacoasts of tropical areas, saltwater swamps sometimes develop. Some trees in swamps grow right out of the water; others grow on small islands called hummocks. The animal and plant species that thrive in swamps vary. Hemlock and willow trees are both suited to wet ground. Mangrove trees can survive in both salty and freshwater environments.

Bogs

Bogs are usually found in northern regions in the depressions left by glaciers (rivers of ice). Water settles in the depressions, and plants take root. Because of poor drainage, plant matter does not decay fully. Moss grows on the surface of the water. A brown, spongy material called peat builds up below the surface. Wood frogs and small mammals thrive in bogs.

Marshes

The main vegetation in marshes is soft-stemmed plants called emergents. Saw grass, wild rice, and rushes are examples. Emergents grow with part of their stems below the water and the tops above the surface. Marshes are an important habitat for many kinds of fish, birds such as herons, and otters and beavers.

The importance of wetlands

Most wetlands provide habitats for a wide variety of wildlife. Next to rain forests, they are the richest communities on Earth. Humans also benefit from wetlands by raising fish and growing crops such as rice. Wetlands control flooding and prevent erosion. Laws have protected some wetlands as conservation areas, but people have already destroyed about half of the world's wetlands. They have been drained and built over or used as dumping grounds for sewage and other waste.

SEE ALSO: Biomes; Ecology; Environment; Glaciers; Lakes; Rivers; Water

WHALES AND DOLPHINS

Whales and dolphins belong to a group of aquatic mammals called cetaceans. Some of these creatures are the largest animals in the world.

Leaving the land

Millions of years ago a group of mammals moved from the land to live in the water. They developed short, flat forelimbs for steering and broad, flat tails to propel them through the water. No one knows how or why the whale's ancestors first took to water. It may have been to escape from predators or to find food.

Most sea mammals develop a thick layer of fatty tissue, or blubber, beneath the skin to keep them warm in water. They are intelligent creatures. Most species live and feed in groups. They swim and dive well, but they must return regularly to the surface to breathe air.

Whales

Whales are the largest cetaceans. There are two main groups of whales: toothed whales and baleen whales. Most toothed whales belong to the delphinid family. Most delphinids are dolphins, but some—including pilot whales and killer whales—reach such a large size that they are called whales. The killer whale is the only cetacean that hunts other warm-blooded prey, such as seals and penguins. It is among the fiercest creatures in the sea but, as far as scientists know, it does not attack humans. The other families of toothed whales include sperm whales, white whales and narwhals, and about 12 species of bottlenose whales.

When people speak of whales, they usually mean the baleen whales. The largest animals ever to live on Earth belong to this group. The blue whale, a species of fin whale, can be 100 ft.

(30 m) long and weigh more than 130 tons. Even the biggest dinosaurs did not reach this size.

Baleen whales are named for the curtains of baleen that hang from the roof of the mouth. The baleen, a substance like stiff hair, filters small animals from mouthfuls of seawater. Right whales, fin whales (or rorquals), gray whales, and humpback whales are all baleen whales.

Dolphins

The smaller members of the cetacean group are called dolphins or porpoises. There are 50 known species in total. The main difference between dolphins and porpoises is in the shapes of their snouts

The humpback whale produces the longest and most varied songs in the animal world. They range from high-frequency whistles to low rumbles in long and organized patterns.

and teeth. The difference between a whale and a dolphin or porpoise is basically one of size. Dolphins range in length from 4 to 12 ft. (1.2–3.6 m). Some species live in freshwater, but most inhabit the deep seas or coastal waters.

Intelligent creatures

The word *dolphin* comes from the Greek word *delphis*, which probably referred to the shape of the dolphin's long snout. Dolphins and porpoises have been known since ancient times as playful, intelligent creatures. Unlike most wild animals, dolphins will voluntarily associate with people. They sometimes follow ships and boats, and even play with bathers. Because dolphins are easily trained and can carry out complex actions, they are popular attractions at ocean aquariums.

The gray and white bottlenose dolphin is the best-known dolphin. It can frequently be seen in bays, harbors, and aquariums.

▼

Most of what we know about dolphin behavior was learned from a study of a colony of bottlenose dolphins at Marineland in Florida from 1938. Dolphins have a highly developed sense of touch and good vision. But hearing is their most important sense. Like many bats, dolphins use echolocation to navigate and to find prey. They make sounds, then listen to the echoes that bounce back from other objects in the water around them.

Conservation

Water pollution is affecting all sea mammals. In the past most whales have been hunted, and some are still, despite legal protection. Dolphins are snagged in fishing nets during tuna fishing or caught for use as bait. Like whales, dolphins are legally protected, and fishing nets have been designed so that dolphins can escape while the tuna remain inside.

SEE ALSO: Animals; Conservation; Endangered Species; Mammals; Sound

✱ WHITE, E. B. (1899–1985)

E. B. White was an American poet, essayist, and children's author. He wrote *Charlotte's Web*—one of the most popular children's books of all time.

Elwyn Brooks White was born in Mount Vernon, New York. He graduated from Cornell University in 1921, and tried various jobs before joining the staff of *The New Yorker* magazine in 1926.

White's first two books, one of them a book of poems called *The Lady is Cold*, were published in 1929, and he married a *New Yorker* editor, Katherine Sergeant Angell, the same year. In 1937 the couple moved to Maine, where White continued to write magazine columns, poetry, and essays. In 1960 he received the gold medal for essays and criticism from the National Institute of Arts and Letters.

White wrote three classic fantasies for children—*Stuart Little* (1945), *Charlotte's Web* (1952), and *Trumpet of the Swan* (1970). *Charlotte's Web* is about an unlikely group of animal friends, including a pig called Wilbur and a spider named Charlotte. White was awarded the Laura Ingalls Wilder Medal for his children's writing in 1970. He died in Maine in 1985.

▲
E. B. White wrote for both adults and children.

SEE ALSO: Children's Authors; Wilder, Laura Ingalls

✱ WHITMAN, WALT (1819–92)

Walt Whitman was one of America's greatest poets. His work celebrated America and its people in a unique language and style.

Walt Whitman was born in West Hills, New York. He had little formal education, but he loved reading. At the age of 12, Whitman became apprenticed to a newspaper printer on Long Island. In 1836 he began teaching, and by the time he was 19, he was both a teacher and a newspaper writer and editor.

In 1855 Whitman published a book of 12 poems called *Leaves of Grass*. The first edition of the book was not popular. Whitman broke with tradition by writing in free verse, meaning that the poetry did not have a regular rhythm or rhyme. Whitman issued new editions of *Leaves of Grass* throughout the rest of his life. His most famous poem, "Song of Myself,"

appeared in every edition. His work praised democracy, the beauty of nature, and the force of love.

When his brother was wounded during the Civil War (1861–65), Whitman moved to Virginia to care for him. He worked in the army hospitals in Washington, D.C., until the end of the war. His war poems were published as *Drum-Taps* in 1865.

In 1873 Whitman had a stroke. He moved to New Jersey to stay with his brother. He died there in 1892.

▲
Walt Whitman wrote about nature and human relationships.

SEE ALSO: Civil War; Literature

* WILDER, LAURA INGALLS (1867–1957)

Laura Ingalls Wilder was the author of the "Little House" series of books on American pioneer life. She received many awards and honors for her books.

Laura Ingalls Wilder wrote about her family's adventures on the American frontier.

The Ingalls family lived in a log cabin in Wisconsin. Laura was the second of four sisters. From 1869 to 1879 the family traveled by covered wagon throughout the Midwest in search of land on which they could build a homestead (farmland given to people by the government). They finally settled in South Dakota in 1880.

When she was in her forties, Wilder started writing for regional magazines and newspapers. At the age of 65, she published her first novel, Little House in the Big Woods, taken from her memories of her girlhood. Popular demand led her to write eight more books based on the story of the family's adventures.

Wilder's books made her internationally famous. They were widely used in schools to teach about frontier life. A children's literature award was created in her honor in 1954. She died at her Missouri farm at age 90.

A popular television series in the 1970s and 1980s, Little House on the Prairie, was loosely based on Wilder's stories. All her former homes have been restored to honor her life and work.

SEE ALSO: Children's Authors; White, E. B.

* WIND

Wind is air in motion. Air moves because of several factors. One is related to temperature; another is related to uneven air pressure.

A tornado strikes Phuket Island, Thailand. The fierce winds of a tornado are very destructive.

Warm air is lighter than cold air, so it rises like a hot-air balloon. Regions of warm and cold air near one another form what is called a circulation cell: Cold air flows in to replace rising warm air, and warm air cools and sinks to replace cold air. Circulation cells can cause local or global patterns of air movement.

Air pressure is the weight of air above Earth's surface. When two nearby places have different levels of air pressure, air is drawn from the high-pressure area to the low-pressure area. The greater the difference in pressure between the two areas, the stronger the wind will blow between them.

AMAZING FACTS !

One of the world's fastest winds was recorded at Mount Washington, NH, on April 12, 1934. It reached a speed of 231 mph (372 kph).

Wind systems

Winds blow in patterns called wind systems. Small-scale winds are driven by local temperature differences. Sea and land breezes, for example, are caused by the movement of warm and cold air near coastlines. Some small-scale winds are violent. For example, tornadoes are spiraling winds produced by rotating thunderstorms. Large-scale wind systems include monsoons. Monsoons are often caused by seasonal temperature differences between the air over the continents and the air over the oceans. Prevailing wind systems, such as the trade winds—strong, steady winds that blow over the tropics toward the equator—determine Earth's overall weather patterns.

Winds are classified by speed. Winds between 32 and 63 mph (51–101 kph) are called gale force. At speeds of over 74 mph (119 kph), a wind is at hurricane force. Strong winds and storms can cause massive destruction. Winds combined with cold weather can create an effect called wind chill, which can kill people.

However, winds can also make Earth more habitable for people and other species. They also increase the evaporation of water from oceans and lakes. In recent years, people have used winds to provide energy. Large groups of windmills produce electricity in California and other areas. This is a renewable energy source, since the supply can never be exhausted.

SEE ALSO:
Blizzards;
Climate;
Electricity;
Energy;
Floods;
Hurricanes
and Typhoons;
Natural
Resources;
Tornadoes;
Water;
Weather

✳WOLVES 👀 ✳DOGS, WOLVES, AND OTHER WILD DOGS

✳ WOMEN'S RIGHTS

For most of history, women have not enjoyed the same rights as men. The first campaigns for women's rights began in the 1800s.

Until the early 1900s, women in most Western countries were treated as second-class citizens. They could not vote. It was very difficult for them to enter college or a profession. If they married, all their property belonged to their husbands.

One of the earliest supporters of equality for women was Mary Wollstonecraft (1759–97). She argued that women should have equal educational and social rights.

The campaign for women's rights in the United States began in 1848 at a meeting at Seneca Falls, New York. The organizers presented a "Declaration of Rights and Sentiments." It was based on the Declaration of Independence but announced that "all men and women are created equal."

Susan B. Anthony, Elizabeth Cady Stanton, Lucretia Mott, and Lucy Stone led the U.S. women's movement. They pressured state legislatures to reform voting and property laws. Many campaigners were also involved in the struggle to abolish slavery.

Englishwoman Mary Wollstonecraft was one of the first feminist writers.

▸

Campaigners for women's right to vote, known as suffragists, march in front of the Capitol in Washington, D.C., in 1913.

Women gradually began to win property rights and the right to attend college. They could also vote in some states. By the early 1900s, many other countries had overtaken the United States in granting rights to women.

In 1913 Alice Paul (1885–1977) formed the Congressional Union for Woman Suffrage (later the National Woman's Party, or NWP). The NWP organized protest marches and picketed the White House. Women were finally guaranteed the right to vote in 1920 when the 19th Amendment to the Constitution was ratified.

The battle for equality

Alice Paul continued to campaign for equality for women. In 1923 she proposed an Equal Rights Amendment to the Constitution. It stated simply: "Men and women shall have equal rights throughout the United States and every place subject to its jurisdiction." It was introduced to Congress but did not pass.

By the mid-1900s, women had the vote in most democratic countries, but they were not treated as equal to men. Employers could pay women less than men for doing the same job. Some professions remained closed to women. Women were expected to stop working when they had children.

The campaign for full equality between men and women became a major force throughout the world during the 1960s.

DID YOU KNOW?

New Zealand gave women the vote in 1893. World War I (1914–18) was a major turning point. Many women worked in factories, performing "male" jobs. They argued that if they could be equal with men in industry, they should have equal voting rights. By 1919, 15 countries had given women the vote, including the United Kingdom, Canada, Germany, and Russia.

The first female political leaders of nations took power in Sri Lanka and India. Writers such as Simone de Beauvoir, Germaine Greer, and Betty Friedan led the campaign. People began to use a new word for their ideas—*feminism*.

President John F. Kennedy ordered federal agencies to treat men and women equally in employment. In 1963 he signed the Equal Pay Act, which required that men and women receive the same wages for the same work.

The 1964 Civil Rights Act outlawed racial discrimination. Campaigners successfully fought for it also to prohibit discrimination against women. The Equal Employment Opportunity Commission was set up to enforce these laws. The campaign to pass the Equal Rights Amendment (ERA) into law was renewed in 1970. The ratification

deadline passed in 1982. Since then, the ERA has been reintroduced into every Congress, but it has still not been ratified by enough states to become law.

Women's rights around the world
In North America, Europe, and other parts of the world, women's rights are now guaranteed by law. But in many countries, religious or economic restrictions mean that women are still second-class citizens. Campaigners disagree about whether the West should force these countries to accept women's rights—or whether this is forcing Western ideas onto other cultures.

SEE ALSO: Abolition Movement; Anthony, Susan B.; Constitution, United States

✳ WONDERS OF THE WORLD
Ancient travelers listed seven wonders of the world as the greatest examples of human creativity. Our world is still full of wonders, both natural and humanmade.

Wonders of the ancient world
Ancient writers, such as Antipater of Sidon and Philo of Byzantium, have left us a list of seven wonders that existed in the centuries before the birth of Christ.

The pyramids of Egypt, at Giza, are the oldest of the wonders and the only ones that survive. The largest pyramid, the Great Pyramid, was the tomb of Khufu, or Cheops, who ruled about 2700 B.C. It contains nearly 2.5 million stone blocks.

The Hanging Gardens of Babylon were created more than 2,500 years ago, probably by King Nebuchadnezzar II. Babylon was in Mesopotamia, near present-day Baghdad, Iraq. Workers built

an artificial hill 350 ft. (107 m) high. They pumped water from the Euphrates River to the top of the hill; from there it flowed down through miniature waterfalls, over terraces of trees, lawns, and flowers.

The Statue of Zeus stood in the temple dedicated to the king of the gods at Olympia in Greece. The sculptor Phidias completed it in about 456 B.C. The statue, a wooden form covered in gold plate, jewels, and ivory, rose to a height of 40 ft. (12 m). It was moved to Constantinople (modern Istanbul) in the A.D. 400s and was destroyed by fire about 475.

The Temple of Artemis was dedicated to the Greek goddess of the moon, known to

The Pharos of Alexandria in Egypt was a lighthouse. Horse-drawn wagons carried fuel up a spiral ramp that led to the ever-burning light.

This 18th-century engraving shows the Colossus of Rhodes. The Colossus was a bronze statue of the Greek sun god, Helios.

the Romans as Diana. It was built in the 300s B.C. at Ephesus, a city in present-day Turkey. The temple was made of white marble, enriched with gold and silver, and precious jewels were stored beneath it.

The Mausoleum at Halicarnassus was a marble tomb built in the 300s B.C. for King Mausolus by his wife, Artemisia. The tomb, at a height of 140 ft. (43 m), overlooked the port of Halicarnassus in present-day western Turkey. It was made of white marble, decorated with many statues, and topped with a golden chariot containing likenesses of Mausolus and Artemisia. The word *mausoleum* now means a type of burial place.

The Colossus of Rhodes was a bronze statue of the sun god Helios. It stood over 100 ft. (30 m) tall above the harbor of Rhodes, an island in the Aegean Sea. The Colossus, built by the Greek Chares of Lindos, was completed in 280 B.C. However, only 56 years later it collapsed in an earthquake. The huge bronze plates lay there for centuries until, in the A.D. 600s, they were sold as scrap metal.

The Pharos of Alexandria was a lighthouse, built between 285 and 247 B.C. by Sostratus of Cnidus on the island of Pharos near Alexandria, Egypt. It stood around 400 ft. (122 m) high. At the top was a platform supporting a brass pan in which a fire burned day and night. A huge mirror reflected the light so that it could be seen far out at sea. The Pharos was destroyed by an earthquake in the 1300s.

The wonders of our world
A list of modern wonders of the world—either natural or built by humans—would be endless. Anyone can make up a list of great wonders, and no two lists would be exactly the same. Some people might consider wonders to include only ancient

changed our lives. Or are the great achievements of our time less visible? The eradication of deadly diseases like polio and smallpox, the development of transplant surgery, and the decoding of the human genome are all wonders in their own way.

Natural wonders

The creativity of human beings often seems insignificant compared to the natural world. Think of the sheer size of the Grand Canyon in Arizona, or Niagara Falls in New York. Mount Everest in the Himalayas, the world's highest peak, challenges climbers to this day. Australia's Great Barrier Reef is amazing in terms of its size and the wildlife it supports. Nature has provided many other wonders.

and often mysterious constructions, such as Stonehenge in England, the stone figures of Easter Island, or the Inca city of Machu Picchu in Peru.

But there are also more modern wonders that are great feats of architecture and engineering, such as the Suez and Panama canals and the great skyscrapers of Chicago and New York City. Technology such as television, automobiles, and artificial satellites could also be considered wonders because of the way they have

SEE ALSO: Ancient Civilizations; Archaeology; Egypt, Ancient; Myths and Legends; Skyscrapers; Stonehenge

A natural wonder: The Grand Canyon was formed millions of years ago by the Colorado River as it cut its way through the rocks of northern Arizona.

✶ WORLD GOVERNMENT

Every one of the world's independent nations has its own government, which runs that country's affairs. There are many different forms of government.

Since early human history, people living together have needed rules to regulate their daily lives. At first societies were run by chiefs or other leaders who made and enforced rules. As cultures developed, people wanted to be more involved in making the laws that governed them. They developed the idea of choosing leaders who would draw up laws that the people thought suitable. People set up systems for enforcing these laws. They had learned how to create a government.

The power of government

The governments that people establish can influence their lives in many ways. Governments regulate relations with other countries (foreign policy) and can declare war. They decide such matters as what kinds of property should be publicly owned (that is, owned by the state in the name of the people) rather than privately owned, and how much each person must pay in taxes. They can set educational requirements, place limits on immigration, and conscript (draft) citizens into military service. The availability of public libraries, museums, hospitals, and parks depends at least in part on government decisions.

In most modern nations, there are agreements between the government and the governed. One basic form of agreement is a constitution, which defines what a government can do. Constitutions can be written or unwritten. Unwritten constitutions are usually based on established laws and customs.

Autocracy

An autocracy is a government in which one person has unlimited power. A monarchy is a government with a single ruler—a king or queen—who inherits his or her position and rules for life. An absolute monarchy refers to a monarch who rules without checks on his or her power. Absolute monarchies exist today only in some of the states of the Arabian Peninsula. At one time, some monarchs believed that they ruled by divine right, meaning that God, not the people, had given them the right to rule.

Modern democracy

The term *democracy* comes from the Greek words *demos*, meaning "common people," and *kratos*, "rule." Most modern

▶ *The state opening of Parliament, a ceremonial event at which the king or queen of the United Kingdom outlines the government's plans for the next year. Britain is a constitutional monarchy.*

democracies are republics in which the people do not take a direct role in governing but choose representatives to express their views. A democratic government exists when representatives are freely elected by the people.

Democratic governments have other standards by which they can be measured. One is freedom of speech, under which people may criticize the government without fear of persecution and form political parties in opposition to the government. Another is the peaceful transfer of political power when new leaders are elected to office.

Today there are two main types of democratic government—parliamentary and presidential. Parliamentary government, also known as cabinet government, is modeled on the British parliamentary system. The government is headed by a prime minister, or premier, who is usually the leader of the political party that has won a majority of seats in elections to the parliament. The prime minister and cabinet form the government but are responsible to the parliament, of which they are members. No government of this type may rule for longer than a certain period without calling an election.

Presidential government, such as that of the United States, is based on the separation of powers. Power is distributed among three branches of government—the executive (the president), the legislative (Congress), and the judicial (the Supreme Court and other courts). This system of checks and balances serves to limit the power of government, which is defined by a written constitution.

A constitutional monarchy is a democratic government in which the monarch is the ceremonial head of state but has little or no political power. Constitutional

monarchies evolved from absolute monarchies, whose powers were gradually reduced and whose functions are now limited by a constitution. Probably the best-known constitutional monarchy is that of the United Kingdom, which has an unwritten constitution.

Totalitarianism

Totalitarianism is a nondemocratic form of government. The term is often used interchangeably with *dictatorship*. A totalitarian government has total control over all aspects of its citizens' political and economic activities.

Two dictators of the 20th century: Nazi leader Adolf Hitler (right) with his Italian counterpart, Benito Mussolini, in 1937.

The term *totalitarianism* was first used in the 1920s and 1930s to describe regimes such as those of Fascist Italy, ruled by Benito Mussolini (1883–1945), and Nazi Germany, ruled by Adolf Hitler (1889–1945), that had a distinct set of beliefs. Later it was applied to the governments of the Soviet Union and the Communist states of Eastern Europe.

Revolution

Revolution is the overthrow by force of one government or ruler and its replacement with another. Revolutions often take place in countries where ordinary people have been suffering under a cruel leadership. People may eventually feel that their only choice is to bring down the leadership and replace it with a fairer system. However, violence is frequently a part of revolutions, and it is not easy to establish a stable government amid the chaos. The revolutionary war that began in

America in 1775 obtained independence from Great Britain and led to a new form of government that inspired revolution in other nations, especially in Spain's South American colonies. The French Revolution of 1789 and the Russian Revolution of 1917 violently overthrew old regimes in the name of social and economic equality.

Imperialism

Imperialism is the term that describes one nation's dominance over another nation or territory. Nations often built empires for political prestige, economic opportunity, or military advantage. Some imperialists simply believed that they had a duty to spread their forms of government, religion, and culture to nations that they considered less advanced or civilized. The best known of the ancient empires is the Roman Empire. In the 1700s, Britain became a leading imperial power. By the end of the 19th century, the British Empire comprised almost one-quarter of the world's land surface.

▶ *Russian revolutionary Vladimir Ilich Lenin leads the people in* Long Live the Revolution, *painted by Pavel Kuznetsov.*

SEE ALSO: Citizenship; Communism; Law; United States Government

WORLD TRADE CENTER

The twin towers of the World Trade Center dominated the skyline of New York City, until they were destroyed in the terrorist attacks of 2001.

The World Trade Center was a complex of seven buildings, covering a 16-acre (6.5-ha) site in lower Manhattan. It was officially opened in 1973. The complex was owned and operated by the Port Authority of New York and New Jersey. The architect was Minoru Yamasaki, in cooperation with Emery Roth and Sons.

At the time of their completion, the 110-story twin towers were the world's tallest buildings. At the top of the North Tower was a luxury restaurant. Observation decks were located at the top of the South Tower.

The center included other office buildings and a hotel. Beneath the central plaza was a mall with shops and restaurants. The office space was intended to be used by many small companies involved in world trade, but it gradually came to be occupied by large companies, such as banks.

Attacks on the towers

On February 26, 1993, a bomb exploded in an underground garage in the center. Six people died, and more than 1,000 were injured. Six men were convicted of the attack. They were linked to terrorist groups in the Middle East.

On September 11, 2001, terrorists hijacked four airliners. They flew two of them into the twin towers of the World Trade Center. Within hours both towers collapsed, and almost 3,000 people lost their lives. The third airliner caused serious damage to the Pentagon in Arlington, Virginia. The fourth plane crashed in a field in Pennsylvania after passengers fought the hijackers. It was the most destructive terrorist act in

history. On September 20, President George W. Bush announced a "war on terrorism" to bring the organizers to justice. The mastermind of the attacks was believed to be Osama bin Laden, head of the Al Qaeda network, an international terrorist organization. Its members believe all people should follow their radically orthodox interpretation of the Koran, the holy book of the Muslim religion.

There are plans to rebuild on the site of the World Trade Center and to include a memorial to the victims of the attacks.

The North Tower of the World Trade Center (with the antenna) was 1,368 ft. (417 m) tall; the South Tower was 1,362 ft. (415 m) tall. The twin towers were specially designed to withstand strong winds. They were the world's tallest buildings until the Sears Tower in Chicago broke the record in 1974.

SEE ALSO: Architecture; Skyscrapers; United States of America

✳ WORLD WAR I

World War I (1914–18) involved more than 30 nations. It claimed more than 14 million lives, devastated Europe, and toppled kings and emperors.

The origins of World War I can be traced back at least as far as a war between France and Germany in 1871. Tensions remained, and both countries sought allies. By the 1900s, Europe formed two hostile camps—France, Russia, and Britain on one side, and Germany, Italy, and Austria-Hungary on the other. Germany's kaiser (emperor), Wilhelm II, wanted a great empire to rival that of Britain and was prepared to take it by force.

The spark for war came in the Balkans. On June 28, 1914, a Serbian student assassinated Archduke Franz Ferdinand, heir to the throne of Austria-Hungary. The assassin was part of a terrorist group that wanted to free Bosnia from Austrian rule and unite it with Serbia. Austria declared war on Serbia on July 28. Russia was allied to Serbia, and Russia's ally France also prepared for war. Germany

▷ *An American soldier and his horse wear gas masks to protect them against poison gas, which caused suffocation.*

sided with Austria and declared war in early August. When German troops marched into neutral Belgium, Britain entered the war. Japan later joined the Allies (France, Britain, and Russia).

Western front, 1914

In the west, the German plan was to sweep through Belgium into France. The Belgians fought bravely, but the Germans pressed on and advanced almost to Paris, the French capital, by early September. They were stopped at the battle of the Marne. By Christmas the fighting had reached a stalemate. The front (the zone of fighting) was a shell-cratered maze of trenches and barbed wire stretching 475 miles (765 km). Already more than 1.5 million soldiers had died.

The wider conflict

In the east, the Germans had driven back Russian attacks in August and September 1914. In October the Ottoman (Turkish) Empire joined the Central Powers, headed by Germany and Austria-Hungary. The Turks prevented supplies from reaching Russia via the Black Sea, and they defeated all Allied attempts to reopen the route. In 1915 Bulgaria joined the Central Powers and Italy joined the Allies, while in 1916 Romania and Greece also joined the Allied side. Fighting would later spread into the Middle East and Africa.

Western front, 1915–17

The fighting in the west during 1915 was marked by futile offensives by both sides. Men fell by the thousands, cut down by machine guns or choked by a deadly new

German weapon—poison gas. However, the front lines did not advance more than 3 miles (5 km) in any direction. The British tried without success to draw pressure off the French by advancing along the Somme River in 1916, using a new weapon of their own—the tank. At the battle of the Somme around 1.2 million men died for the sake of 5 miles (8 km) of land.

The year 1917 was another dark one for the Allies. Attempts to break through the German positions in northern France failed. At the second battle of the Aisne, parts of the French army mutinied (refused to obey orders). At the battle of Passchendaele, months of fighting cost the British some 300,000 men.

Russia and the United States

In 1916 Russia launched a grand offensive against Austria, but after early successes the onslaught ground to a halt, with more than one million Russian casualties. In March 1917 the Russian people overthrew their czar (emperor), Nicholas II, and in November the Communists swept to power. Their leader, Vladimir Lenin, took Russia out of the war in December 1917.

So far the United States had kept out of the fighting. However, in April 1917, after many months of protesting against Germany's unrestricted submarine warfare, President Woodrow Wilson declared war on Germany, and in June the first American troops landed in France.

Final stages

By 1918, with Russia out of the war, Germany transferred more than a million troops from the eastern front to the west. On March 21, the Germans launched the enormous "Michael" offensive. Once again they were halted, after terrible loss of life on both sides. By May, however, American troops were at last tipping the

balance in the Allies' favor, and bit by bit the German army weakened until it was decisively defeated in the fall.

On September 30, Bulgaria surrendered. Turkey followed on October 30, and Austria on November 3. Finally, on November 11, Germany signed a truce. The war was over.

Aftermath

World War I changed the map of Europe and sowed the seeds for World War II. The Ottoman Empire broke up. The Austro-Hungarian Empire crumbled, giving rise to new states, including Czechoslovakia, Yugoslavia, and Poland. Finland, Estonia, Latvia, and Lithuania broke free from the Russian Empire. Through the Treaty of Versailles, signed in France in 1919, the Allied powers blamed Germany for the war, stripped it of land, and ordered it to pay billions of dollars.

▲

British soldiers advance toward German trenches in 1918. The killing power of machine guns changed the nature of warfare. The guns pinned their targets down in whatever cover could be found or made. This meant that the front lines of the two sides were often separated by only a short distance.

SEE ALSO: Central Europe; Eastern Europe; Europe; Greece and the Balkans; Warfare; World Government; World War II

✳ WORLD WAR II

World War II (1939–45) was the most destructive war in history. It involved all the world's great powers and many of the smaller nations.

After the bloodshed of World War I (1914–18), the world's most powerful countries signed treaties that they hoped would create a lasting peace. But economic problems and political tensions between the traditional ruling groups, the middle classes, and revolutionary Communist parties ravaged much of Central Europe.

In 1933 an ambitious ex-soldier, Adolf Hitler, came to power in Germany. He blamed Germany's defeat in World War I on a Jewish plot. He ruled as a dictator (leader with total power) at the head of the National Socialist, or Nazi, Party and steadily built up Germany's armed forces.

Other brutal dictators also rose to power after World War I: Benito Mussolini in Italy, and military leaders in Japan, including Tojo Hideki. Italy and Japan would fight alongside Germany as the major Axis powers.

War breaks out
Hitler, Mussolini, and Japan's leaders all wanted to build great empires. During the 1930s, Japan invaded eastern China, and Italy invaded Ethiopia in East Africa. Germany swallowed up the Rhineland, its neighbor Austria, and Czechoslovakia. When Hitler invaded Poland in September 1939, Britain and France declared war on Germany. But Germany swiftly conquered Poland, helped by the Soviet Union, which was led by Joseph Stalin.

▶
Supplies arrive for U.S. Marines on the Japanese island of Iwo Jima. The island was of vital importance in the battle between the United States and Japan in 1945.

Hitler's armies were the finest in Europe. Their fighting tactics were called Blitzkrieg ("lightning war"). In spring 1940, they overran Norway, Denmark, Belgium, the Netherlands, and Luxembourg. Winston Churchill became prime minister of Britain on May 10. Three days later the Germans invaded France. Only the British Royal Air Force and Royal Navy stopped Germany from crossing the English Channel and attacking England.

Mussolini, meanwhile, had invaded Albania in 1939. In 1940 he attacked British-held Egypt from his colony in Libya, but the Italians were fiercely opposed by British forces, and Hitler was forced to send German military support.

The eastern front
In spring 1941 Germany attacked the Balkans, and then on June 22, 1941, invaded the Soviet Union. German troops and armor rolled victoriously across the vast land until the fall, when rain made their progress slower. They reached the suburbs of Moscow in December 1941.

Russian counterattacks and the winter cold halted them. By the fall of 1942, German forces had reached the city of Stalingrad.

America and the Pacific

The United States had lent warships to Britain to help defeat the U-boats (German submarines) that were sinking Allied supply ships in the North Atlantic Ocean. Otherwise it had deliberately kept out of the conflict. Then, on December 7, 1941, Japanese aircraft attacked the U.S. Pacific Fleet at its base in Pearl Harbor, Hawaii. The next day the United States entered the war.

Japan mounted offensives in the Pacific and controlled much of Southeast Asia by May 1942. From that point, however, U.S. naval forces began to hit back. The battles of the Coral Sea in May and Midway in early June severely damaged Japan's vital aircraft carrier fleet.

Europe and North Africa

By 1943 the tide had begun to turn against Hitler in Europe. Allied aircraft were pounding Axis factories and supply routes. Soviet troops had surrounded and destroyed the German Sixth Army at Stalingrad. Axis troops in North Africa were finally defeated in May 1943.

The Allies invade Europe

From July 1943 Allied troops invaded and fought their way up through Italy, finally taking Rome in June 1944. On June 6, "D-Day," American, British, and Canadian forces landed in Normandy, France. Weeks of bitter fighting followed. They freed Paris on August 25 and pressed on to reach the German border by October. The Soviet Red Army, which had been steadily advancing west, reached the outskirts of Berlin in April 1945. Hitler committed suicide on the 30th. Two days earlier Italian freedom fighters had shot

Mussolini, and Italy's war was over. Germany surrendered on May 7.

War still raged in the Pacific between the Allies and the Japanese. To end the bloodshed swiftly, President Harry S. Truman gave the order to drop atomic bombs on the Japanese cities of Hiroshima and Nagasaki on August 6 and 9, 1945. The two explosions killed more than 150,000 people. Japan surrendered on September 2. Truman's decision to use the bombs is still very controversial.

Aftermath

World War II has been called a "total war." Civilians were deliberately killed. Perhaps the worst aspect of the war on civilians was the attempt by the Nazis to wipe out Europe's Jewish population, called the Holocaust. The use of atomic weapons took the political world into a dangerous new age. The United States and the Soviet Union emerged as the world's superpowers. Europe, which had once ruled the world, lay in ruins. In the years to come, European colonies in Africa and Asia would rush to claim independence.

British aircraft, known as Spitfires, flying in formation at over 300 mph (480 kph).

SEE ALSO:
Germany;
Holocaust;
Italy; Japan;
Russia and
the Baltic
States;
United
Kingdom;
United States
Armed
Forces;
United States
of America;
Warfare;
World
Government;
World War I

✳ WORMS

Worms are invertebrates—animals without backbones—with soft, long bodies. They can live on land, in water, and even in other animals.

Annelids

The most familiar type of worm is the earthworm. It is an annelid, a word meaning "little rings"—the body of an annelid is divided into small segments, or rings. An earthworm has no eyes or ears and spends most of its time underground. It burrows through the ground, taking soil into an inner digestive tube that runs the length of its body. It takes nutrition from plant and animal matter in the soil, and discards the rest. This process improves the soil by turning it to let in air and water.

The largest group of annelids are bristle worms. They are found mainly in salt water. Their segments have feetlike structures, sometimes with bristles attached, which they use to wriggle along the sand or swim through water in search of food. Most bristle worms live in tubes made in the sand or mud. Leeches are also annelids. Leeches are found mainly in freshwater and damp earth. They have smooth bodies with a sucker at each end. They attach themselves to live animals and suck out blood for food. This is called parasitism.

Roundworms

Roundworms, or nematodes, have digestive tubes inside an outer body tube, like annelids. However, the body is not segmented.

The brandling worm is an annelid with small rings, or segments. They are used by gardeners to make compost heaps and by fishermen as bait. ▼

DID YOU KNOW?

In the past doctors used leeches to suck blood from patients in the belief that this would cure the patient. Today leeches are making a medical comeback. They secrete an anticoagulant—a substance that prevents scabs from forming. That allows wounds to heal from the inside outward. Leeches also produce a natural painkiller and an antihistamine—a substance that acts against allergic reactions.

Most roundworms are tiny, although some can grow to 3 ft. (0.9 m) long. Many live in soil or water, but some, such as the hookworm, can enter the human body. Hookworms are parasites, entering the intestines and sucking blood.

Flatworms

Most flatworms are small and thin. There are three types: planarians, flukes, and tapeworms. Planarians can be found under stones in freshwater or gliding over the sand in shallow salt water, feeding on tiny animals. Flukes and tapeworms are parasites. They feed on the body fluids and tissues of their hosts such as a sheep or a pig, but they can also enter and live in the human body, causing damage to the internal organs.

SEE ALSO: Animals

✳ WRIGHT, FRANK LLOYD (1867–1959)

Frank Lloyd Wright was one of the most important architects in history. His buildings still influence modern designers.

Frank Lloyd Wright was born in Richland Center, Wisconsin. His mother gave him wooden blocks and shaped cards to play with, and that gave him an early interest in building things. Wright's career began in Chicago, where he worked for the architect Louis Sullivan. In 1893 he opened his own office.

When designing buildings, Wright followed the principle that "form follows function." This means that the needs of a building's users, not rules laid down by architects in the past, should determine its structure. He created houses in what came to be called prairie style—they were long and flat, so they seemed to grow out of the landscape. Eventually buildings designed by Wright were constructed in 36 states. Some of the finest include Fallingwater, Pennsylvania; the Johnson Wax Company offices and research tower, Wisconsin; and the Guggenheim Museum, New York City.

SEE ALSO: Architecture

Frank Lloyd Wright designed more than 400 buildings, including his own homes and studios in Arizona and Wisconsin.

✳ WRIGHT, ORVILLE (1871–1948) AND WILBUR (1867–1912)

The Wright brothers invented the first power-driven airplane. In 1903 they made the first successful powered flight in a heavier-than-air craft.

Wilbur Wright was born in Millville, Indiana, in 1867, and Orville was born in Dayton, Ohio, in 1871. From childhood the brothers were greatly interested in mechanics. They worked first with printing machines and bicycles, but what really fascinated them was flight. They built a glider and took it to Kitty Hawk, North Carolina, in the fall of 1900. The brothers glided about a dozen times there, but did not have complete control of the glider. Back home they experimented further. They replaced the glider's tail fins with a single movable rudder, and then they built their own engine.

On the morning of December 17, 1903, the brothers made history by getting their plane to fly just under 120 ft. (37 m) in 12 seconds. Later that day Wilbur managed to stay airborne for 59 seconds.

In 1909 the brothers formed their own company to manufacture airplanes. Wilbur died in 1912. Orville continued to experiment with aviation, and he lived long enough to know that a plane could fly faster than the speed of sound.

SEE ALSO: Aircraft; Inventors and Inventions

Wilbur (left) and Orville Wright made the world's first successful airplane flight at breezy Kitty Hawk off the North Carolina coast.

*WRITING

Writing is the ability to convey information, ideas, and experiences to other people in a physical form. It is a very important means of communication.

People first learned to communicate with one another using speech or gesture. But such direct communication could take place only at one time and over a short distance. When people began to write, messages could be seen at a later time and in a different place from when and where they were first written.

Learning to write at school is just the beginning. We use writing in our everyday lives— for example, writing essays, reports, records of meetings, and letters, or keeping a diary.

Writing began as pictographs. These were very simple drawings that represented objects. Gradually the drawings came to represent ideas associated with the objects. A picture of the sun, for example, might mean "day." These ideograms, as they were called, made it possible to express more complicated messages.

Cuneiform and hieroglyphs

About 3000 B.C. in Mesopotamia (modern Iraq), the ancient Sumerians developed cuneiform, a system of wedge-shape signs pressed into wet clay with the end of a reed. The ancient Egyptians invented a system of signs, called hieroglyphs, for inscribing stone monuments and writing important documents on papyrus. Both cuneiform and hieroglyphs were used to express individual words or sometimes sounds rather than ideas and meanings.

The next step was to invent a written language in which each symbol stood for a single sound instead of a whole word. We call this system an alphabet. In about

DID YOU KNOW?

What you write can be read by another person only if it is legible—that is, if the letters are formed clearly. Errors due to illegible handwriting can be costly. The U.S. Postal System handles billions of pieces of mail each year. But about one million of these end up in the "dead letter file" because poor handwriting makes delivery impossible.

1100 B.C., the Phoenicians developed a system of 22 symbols, or letters, that stood for the sounds of the consonants in their language. The ancient Greeks added symbols that meant vowel sounds. More than 2,000 years ago, the Romans developed the alphabet that we still use in the Western world.

Among the few people in medieval Europe who could read and write were monks. They made copies of books by writing on parchment with pens made from quills (large feathers). These were manuscript books. (The word *manuscript* comes from the Latin for "written by hand.") But even after writing developed, pictures remained an important means of communication. Paintings and stained-glass windows in churches told biblical stories, while murals (paintings on walls) and tapestries depicted battles and other events.

SEE ALSO: Alphabet; Ancient Civilizations; Communication; Languages; Rosetta Stone

*X-RAYS

X-rays are a form of energy similar to light. But there is one important difference—X-rays can penetrate many materials that will stop most kinds of light.

X-rays are beamed through an object to a sheet of photographic film. The image of the inner structure of the object is recorded on the film. The material in one part of the object may be penetrated by many more X-rays than the material in another part. This difference will show on the film, revealing the inner structure of the object. X-rays can be used to inspect machinery for flaws, but the best known use of X-rays is in medicine.

Doctors use X-rays to reveal inner parts of the body. X-rays distinguish between bone, soft tissues (muscles, blood vessels, and major organs), fat, and air (in the lungs). An X-ray picture of an arm shows the bones because the X-rays do not pass through them as easily as through the muscles. A chest X-ray shows the heart surrounded by air in the lungs.

In the late 1960s, scientists developed an X-ray machine called a computerized axial tomography (CAT) scanner. The machine produces cross-section views of the body, and is especially useful for viewing the brain, chest, and abdomen.

History
X-rays were discovered accidentally by the German scientist Wilhelm Conrad Röntgen in 1895, when he was

HOW X-RAYS WORK

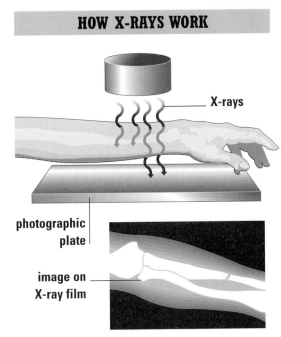

X-rays

photographic plate

image on X-ray film

The best-known use of X-rays is in medicine. The beam of X-rays is sent through the patient's body onto a plate of photographic film. Bones absorb a large amount of the X-rays and show up as white shadows on the film. Other tissues absorb fewer X-rays, so they show up as gray areas. The branch of medicine that uses X-rays is called radiology.

experimenting with a special kind of lamp called a cathode-ray tube. Röntgen learned how to produce the new rays and became familiar with their characteristics, but he never found out exactly what they were. For this reason he called them X-rays, *X* standing for unknown.

SEE ALSO: Light; Medicine; Scientific Instruments; Scientists

Z

✳ ZOOLOGY

Zoology is the branch of science that deals with all aspects of animal life. The word comes from the Greek for "knowledge of animals."

▲
A zoologist tags a loggerhead sea turtle at the Archie Carr National Wildlife Refuge in Florida, where the habitat and nesting areas of the turtles are being protected.

Humans have long been interested in the study of animals. Aristotle, in ancient Greece, developed a system of animal classification. Pliny the Elder, in Rome, wrote a major work on natural history.

In the 15th and 16th centuries, Leonardo da Vinci and Andreas Vesalius dissected (cut up) animals in order to discover more about the human body. In the 1700s, Carolus Linnaeus created the modern system of classifying animals, which uses a different Latin name for each species.

In the mid-1800s, the English scientist Charles Darwin published his theory of evolution—that animal species adapt to their environments over generations. The 1900s saw discoveries about inheritance involving genes and DNA. These developments increased our knowledge about all forms of life, including animals. In recent years, zoologists have taken a more active role in protecting animal life by campaigning against human activity that puts animals at risk.

Work of modern zoologists

Some zoologists observe animals in their natural habitat. They may be researching animal behavior or seeking ways to protect endangered species. Others work in zoos or safari parks. Many species of animals would now be extinct (have died out) if they had not been bred in captivity. Zoologists who work in natural history museums also use their knowledge to inform the public.

Many zoologists carry out research in universities or laboratories. They study live animals and cell samples. Their scientific discoveries often benefit humans as well as other animals.

SEE ALSO: Animals; Biology; Botany; Darwin, Charles; da Vinci, Leonardo; Endangered Species; Evolution; Extinction; Genetics; Scientists

FOR FURTHER REFERENCE

MAP OF THE WORLD

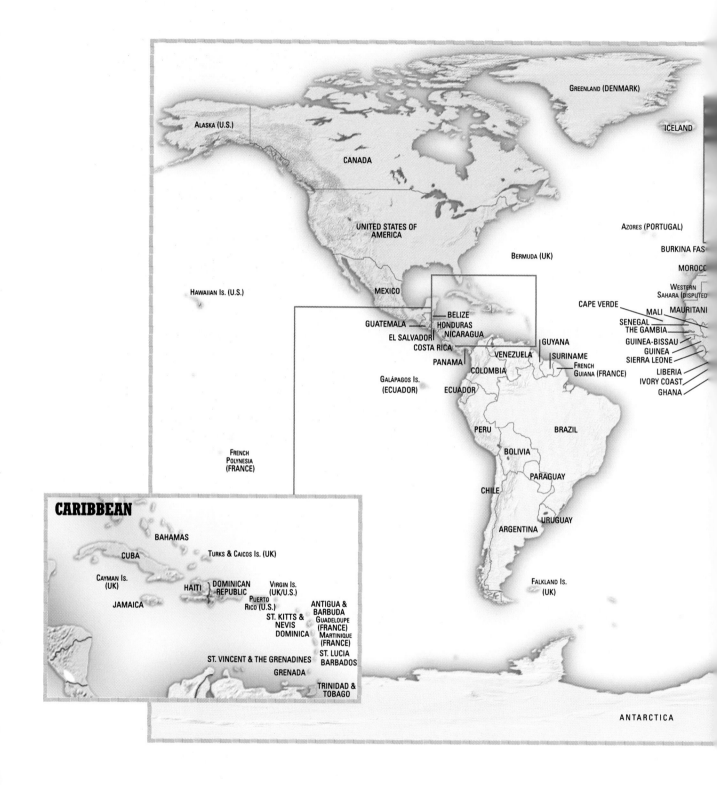

ALASKA (U.S.)

CANADA

GREENLAND (DENMARK)

ICELAND

UNITED STATES OF
AMERICA

AZORES (PORTUGAL)

BERMUDA (UK)

BURKINA FAS

MOROCC

HAWAIIAN IS. (U.S.)

MEXICO

WESTERN
SAHARA (DISPUTED)

CAPE VERDE

MALI   MAURITANI

BELIZE

SENEGAL

GUATEMALA

HONDURAS

THE GAMBIA

EL SALVADOR   NICARAGUA

GUINEA-BISSAU

COSTA RICA

GUYANA

GUINEA

PANAMA

VENEZUELA

SURINAME

SIERRA LEONE

COLOMBIA

FRENCH
GUIANA (FRANCE)

LIBERIA

GALÁPAGOS IS.
(ECUADOR)

ECUADOR

IVORY COAST

GHANA

FRENCH
POLYNESIA
(FRANCE)

PERU

BRAZIL

BOLIVIA

PARAGUAY

CHILE

URUGUAY

ARGENTINA

FALKLAND IS.
(UK)

CARIBBEAN

BAHAMAS

CUBA

TURKS & CAICOS IS. (UK)

CAYMAN IS.
(UK)

HAITI

DOMINICAN
REPUBLIC

VIRGIN IS.
(UK/U.S.)

JAMAICA

PUERTO
RICO (U.S.)

ST. KITTS &
NEVIS

DOMINICA

ANTIGUA &
BARBUDA

GUADELOUPE
(FRANCE)

MARTINIQUE
(FRANCE)

ST. VINCENT & THE GRENADINES

ST. LUCIA

BARBADOS

GRENADA

TRINIDAD &
TOBAGO

ANTARCTICA

RUSSIA

KAZAKHSTAN

ARMENIA

AZERBAIJAN

KYRGYZSTAN

UZBEKISTAN

GEORGIA

TURKMENISTAN

TAJIKISTAN

TURKEY

CYPRUS

MONGOLIA

NORTH KOREA

SOUTH KOREA

JAPAN

TUNISIA

LEBANON

ALGERIA

ISRAEL

SYRIA

JORDAN

IRAQ

IRAN

AFGHANISTAN

CHINA

KUWAIT

PAKISTAN

NEPAL

BHUTAN

LIBYA

EGYPT

BAHRAIN

QATAR

INDIA

TAIWAN

TOGO

SAUDI
ARABIA

UNITED
ARAB
EMIRATES

MYANMAR

LAOS

HONG
KONG
(CHINA)

NORTHERN MARIANA IS.
(U.S.)

NIGER

OMAN

THAILAND

GUAM
(U.S.)

BENIN

CHAD

SUDAN

ERITREA

YEMEN

VIETNAM

PHILIPPINES

PALAU

MARSHALL
ISLANDS

IGERIA

DJIBOUTI

BANGLADESH

CAMBODIA

FEDERATED STATES OF
MICRONESIA

CENTRAL AFRICAN
REPUBLIC

ETHIOPIA

SRI LANKA

BRUNEI

KIRIBATI

CAMEROON

SOMALIA

MALDIVES

MALAYSIA

NAURU

GABON

UGANDA

SINGAPORE

INDONESIA

SOLOMON
ISLANDS

TUVALU

DEMOCRATIC
REPUBLIC
OF CONGO

KENYA

RWANDA

BURUNDI

PAPUA
NEW
GUINEA

TANZANIA

SEYCHELLES

EAST TIMOR

SAMOA

REPUBLIC OF
CONGO

MALAWI

COMOROS

VANUATU

FIJI

AMERICAN
SAMOA
(U.S.)

ANGOLA

ZAMBIA

MOZAMBIQUE

ZIMBABWE

MADAGASCAR

NEW CALEDONIA
(FRANCE)

TONGA

NAMIBIA

MAURITIUS

RÉUNION
(FRANCE)

BOTSWANA

AUSTRALIA

SWAZILAND

SOUTH
AFRICA

LESOTHO

NEW
ZEALAND

SÃO TOMÉ &
PRÍNCIPE

EQUATORIAL
GUINEA

EUROPE

1 SLOVENIA
2 CROATIA
3 BOSNIA-HERZEGOVINA
4 SERBIA & MONTENEGRO

SWEDEN

FINLAND

NORWAY

ESTONIA

DENMARK

LATVIA

RUSSIA

LIECHTENSTEIN

LITHUANIA

RUSSIA

UNITED
KINGDOM

BELARUS

REPUBLIC
OF IRELAND

NETHERLANDS

GERMANY

POLAND

BELGIUM

LUXEMBOURG

CZECH
REPUBLIC

UKRAINE

SLOVAKIA

FRANCE

AUSTRIA

HUNGARY

MOLDOVA

SWITZERLAND

1

ANDORRA

MONACO

2

3

4

ROMANIA

SAN MARINO

ITALY

BULGARIA

SPAIN

VATICAN
CITY

ALBANIA

MACEDONIA

PORTUGAL

GREECE

MALTA

WORLD TIME ZONE MAP

It would not be practical for it to be noon everywhere at the same time, especially if it were nighttime on half of the earth. So Earth is divided into 24 time zones by imaginary lines, called meridians, that run through the North and South poles. On a flat map, these look like vertical lines. The distance between the meridians is called degrees of longitude. Each zone is about 15 degrees wide, and it takes one hour for the earth to rotate 15 degrees of longitude.

The zones are numbered from the Greenwich Meridian—which runs through Greenwich, England—and each extends 7½ degrees on either side of the meridian. The zones are zigzagged so that large cities do not have two different times. Some countries use half-hour time zones of 7½ degrees. As we travel east, time is later in the day. As we travel west, it is earlier. Exactly halfway around the earth from the Greenwich Meridian is the International Date Line. This means you have traveled one full day of time zones. When the date line is crossed going westward, the date must be advanced one day. If it is crossed moving eastward, we move back one day.

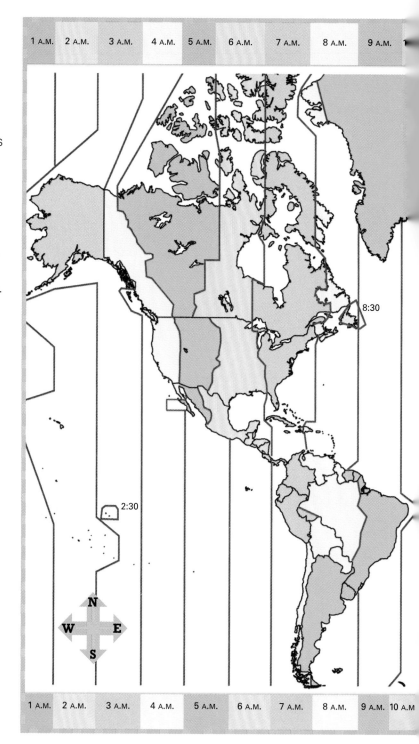

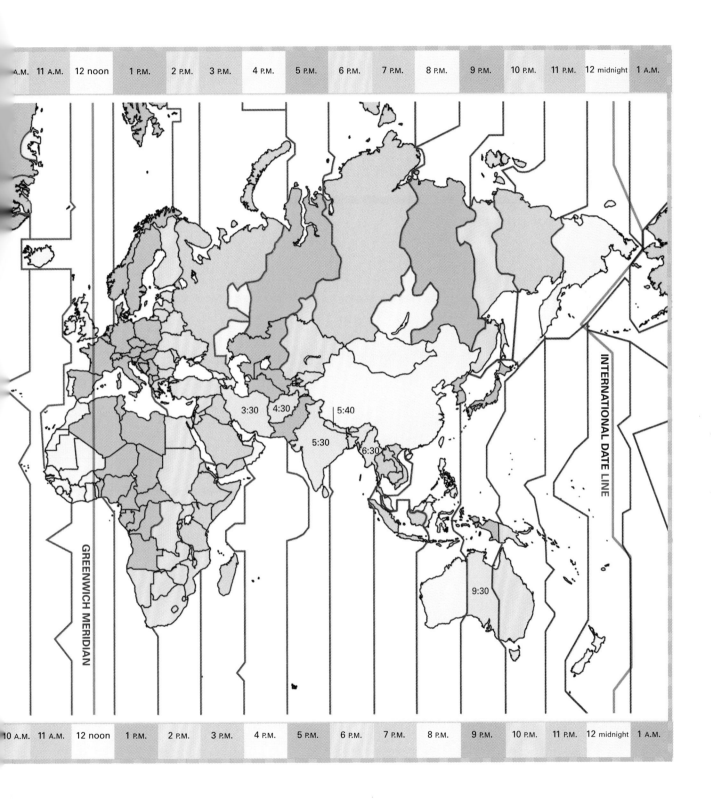

MAP OF THE UNITED STATES

WASHINGTON
Olympia

Columbia River

Salem

OREGON

IDAHO

Boise

MONTANA
Helena

NORTH DAKOTA

Bismar

Snake River

WYOMING

SOUTH DAKOTA

Pierre

CALIFORNIA

NEVADA

Cheyenne

NEBRAKSA

Sacramento

Carson City

Salt Lake City

UTAH

Denver

Linc

COLORADO

KANSAS

Colorado River

PACIFIC OCEAN

ARIZONA

Santa Fe

Oklahoma

OKLAHOM

Phoenix

NEW MEXICO

Red River

Rio Grande

TEXAS

MEXICO

ALASKA

CANADA

PACIFIC OCEAN

Honolulu

HAWAII

Bering
Sea

Juneau

Gulf of Alaska

Austin

NOTE: Alaska is not in
position.

NOTE: Hawaii is not in
position.

CANADA

L. Superior

NNESOTA

St. Paul

WISCONSIN

Madison

L. Huron

L. Michigan

MICHIGAN

Lansing

L. Ontario

L. Erie

VERMONT

Montpelier

Concord

MAINE

Augusta

NEW
HAMPSHIRE

Albany

NEW YORK

Boston

MASSACHUSETTS

Providence

Hartford

RHODE
ISLAND

CONNECTICUT

IOWA

Des Moines

ILLINOIS

Springfield

INDIANA

Indianapolis

Ohio River

OHIO

Columbus

PENNSYLVANIA

Harrisburg

Trenton

NEW JERSEY

Annapolis

Dover

DELAWARE

MARYLAND

Missouri River

peka

Jefferson
City

MISSOURI

WEST
VIRGINIA

Charleston

Frankfort

KENTUCKY

VIRGINIA

Richmond

Washington, D.C.

Raleigh

ARKANSAS

Arkansas River

Little Rock

Nashville

TENNESSEE

NORTH CAROLINA

MISSISSIPPI

Mississippi River

SOUTH CAROLINA

Atlanta

Columbia

ALABAMA

Jackson

Montgomery

GEORGIA

ATLANTIC OCEAN

LOUISIANA

Baton
Rouge

Tallahassee

FLORIDA

Gulf of Mexico

BAHAMAS

MAP OF NATIVE AMERICAN NATIONS

Makah
Nootka
Duwamish
Nisqualli
Tillamook
Chinook
Columbia River
Yakima
Palouse
Warm Springs
Flathead
Blackfeet
Nez Percé
Cre
Lake Winnipe
Shasta
Yuki
Northern Paiute
Snake River
Bannock
Shoshone
Crow
Sioux
Mandan
Missouri River
Si
Great Salt Lake
Arapaho
Arikara
Io
Pomo
Ute
Brea
Pawnee
Omaha
Oto
Paiute
Cheyenne
Wichita
Walapai
Hopi
Osage
Serrano
Mojave
Navajo
Taos
Pawnee
Colorado River
Yuma
Zuni
Pueblo
Cochimi
Tohono O'Odham
Apache
Comanche
Caddo
Río Grande
Atakapa
Lagunero
Aztec

PACIFIC OCEAN

Bering Sea
Haida
ALASKA
Tlingit
Yukon River
Tsimshian
Gulf of Alaska

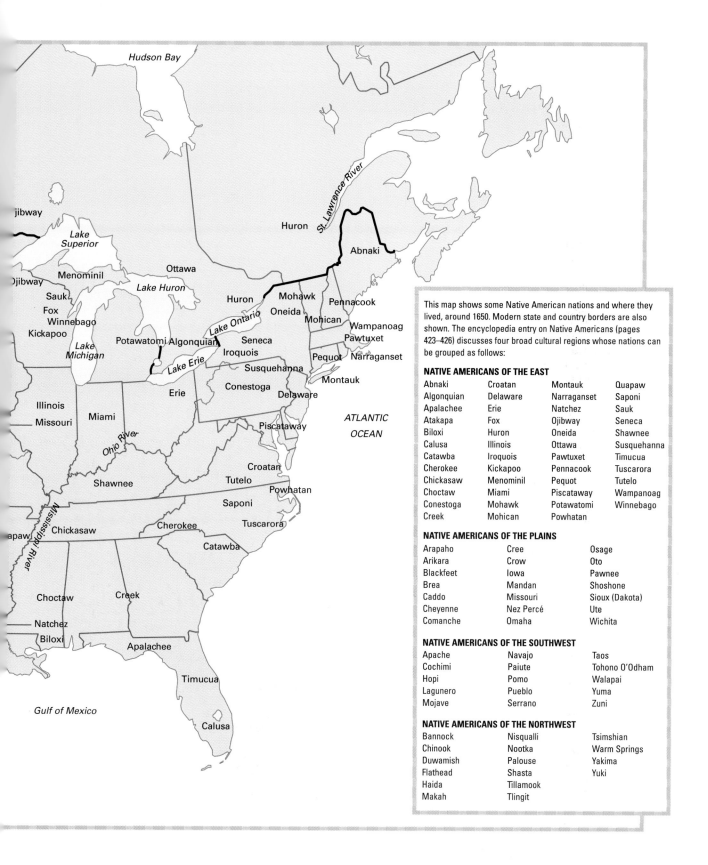

Hudson Bay

Ojibway

Lake Superior

Menominil

Ojibway

Sauk
Fox
Winnebago
Kickapoo

Lake Michigan

Ottawa

Lake Huron

Huron

Lake Ontario

Potawatomi Algonquian

Seneca
Iroquois

Erie

Lake Erie

St. Lawrence River

Huron

Abnaki

Mohawk
Oneida

Pennacook

Mohican

Wampanoag
Pawtuxet

Pequot   Narraganset

Montauk

Illinois

Missouri

Miami

Ohio River

Conestoga

Delaware

Susquehanna

Piscataway

ATLANTIC
OCEAN

Shawnee

Mississippi River

Chickasaw

Cherokee

Croatan

Tutelo

Powhatan

Saponi

Tuscarora

Catawba

Choctaw

Creek

Natchez

Biloxi

Apalachee

Timucua

Gulf of Mexico

Calusa

apaw

This map shows some Native American nations and where they lived, around 1650. Modern state and country borders are also shown. The encyclopedia entry on Native Americans (pages 423–426) discusses four broad cultural regions whose nations can be grouped as follows:

NATIVE AMERICANS OF THE EAST

Abnaki	Croatan	Montauk	Quapaw
Algonquian	Delaware	Narraganset	Saponi
Apalachee	Erie	Natchez	Sauk
Atakapa	Fox	Ojibway	Seneca
Biloxi	Huron	Oneida	Shawnee
Calusa	Illinois	Ottawa	Susquehanna
Catawba	Iroquois	Pawtuxet	Timucua
Cherokee	Kickapoo	Pennacook	Tuscarora
Chickasaw	Menominil	Pequot	Tutelo
Choctaw	Miami	Piscataway	Wampanoag
Conestoga	Mohawk	Potawatomi	Winnebago
Creek	Mohican	Powhatan	

NATIVE AMERICANS OF THE PLAINS

Arapaho	Cree	Osage
Arikara	Crow	Oto
Blackfeet	Iowa	Pawnee
Brea	Mandan	Shoshone
Caddo	Missouri	Sioux (Dakota)
Cheyenne	Nez Percé	Ute
Comanche	Omaha	Wichita

NATIVE AMERICANS OF THE SOUTHWEST

Apache	Navajo	Taos
Cochimi	Paiute	Tohono O'Odham
Hopi	Pomo	Walapai
Lagunero	Pueblo	Yuma
Mojave	Serrano	Zuni

NATIVE AMERICANS OF THE NORTHWEST

Bannock	Nisqualli	Tsimshian
Chinook	Nootka	Warm Springs
Duwamish	Palouse	Yakima
Flathead	Shasta	Yuki
Haida	Tillamook	
Makah	Tlingit	

THE COUNTRIES OF THE WORLD

This table lists the world's independent countries. Population figures for the United States and Canada are based on the 2000 U.S. Census and the 2001 Canadian Census. Population figures for other countries are based on mid-2000 estimates provided by the United Nations.

COUNTRY	FLAG	CAPITAL	POPULATION (2000)
Afghanistan		Kabul	22,720,000
Albania		Tiranë	3,113,000
Algeria		Algiers	31,471,000
Andorra		Andorra la Vella	78,000
Angola		Luanda	12,878,000
Antigua and Barbuda		St. John's	68,000
Argentina		Buenos Aires	37,032,000
Armenia		Yerevan	3,520,000
Australia		Canberra	18,886,000
Austria		Vienna	8,211,000
Azerbaijan		Baku	7,734,000
Bahamas		Nassau	307,000
Bahrain		Manama	617,000
Bangladesh		Dhaka	129,155,000
Barbados		Bridgetown	270,000
Belarus		Minsk	10,236,000
Belgium		Brussels	10,161,000
Belize		Belmopan	241,000
Benin		Porto-Novo	6,097,000
Bhutan		Thimphu	2,124,000
Bolivia		La Paz, Sucre	8,329,000
Bosnia-Herzegovina		Sarajevo	3,972,000
Botswana		Gaborone	1,622,000
Brazil		Brasília	170,115,000
Brunei		Bandar Seri Begawan	328,000
Bulgaria		Sofia	8,225,000
Burkina Faso		Ouagadougou	11,937,000
Burundi		Bujumbura	6,695,000
Cambodia		Phnom Penh	11,168,000
Cameroon		Yaoundé	15,085,000
Canada		Ottawa	31,081,900 (2001)

COUNTRY	FLAG	CAPITAL	POPULATION (2000)
Cape Verde		Praia	428,000
Central African Republic		Bangui	3,615,000
Chad		N'Djamena	7,651,000
Chile		Santiago	15,211,000
China, People's Republic of		Beijing	1,277,558,000
Colombia		Bogotá	42,321,000
Comoros		Moroni	694,000
Congo, Democratic Republic of		Kinshasa	51,654,000
Congo, Republic of		Brazzaville	2,943,000
Costa Rica		San José	4,023,000
Croatia		Zagreb	4,473,000
Cuba		Havana	11,201,000
Cyprus		Nicosia	786,000
Czech Republic		Prague	10,244,000
Denmark		Copenhagen	5,293,000
Djibouti		Djibouti	638,000
Dominica		Roseau	71,000
Dominican Republic		Santo Domingo	8,495,000
East Timor		Dili	885,000
Ecuador		Quito	12,646,000
Egypt		Cairo	68,470,000
El Salvador		San Salvador	6,276,000
Equatorial Guinea		Malabo	453,000
Eritrea		Asmara	3,850,000
Estonia		Tallinn	1,396,000
Ethiopia		Addis Ababa	62,565,000
Fiji		Suva	817,000
Finland		Helsinki	5,176,000
France		Paris	59,080,000
Gabon		Libreville	1,226,000

COUNTRY	FLAG	CAPITAL	POPULATION (2000)
Gambia, The		Banjul	1,305,000
Georgia		Tbilisi	4,968,000
Germany		Berlin	82,220,000
Ghana		Accra	20,212,000
Greece		Athens	10,645,000
Grenada		St. George's	94,000
Guatemala		Guatemala City	11,385,000
Guinea		Conakry	7,430,000
Guinea-Bissau		Bissau	1,213,000
Guyana		Georgetown	861,000
Haiti		Port-au-Prince	8,222,000
Honduras		Tegucigalpa	6,485,000
Hungary		Budapest	10,036,000
Iceland		Reykjavík	281,000
India		New Delhi	1,013,662,000
Indonesia		Jakarta	212,107,000
Iran		Tehran	67,702,000
Iraq		Baghdad	23,115,000
Ireland, Republic of		Dublin	3,730,000
Israel		Jerusalem	6,217,000
Italy		Rome	57,298,000
Ivory Coast		Yamoussoukro	14,786,000
Jamaica		Kingston	2,583,000
Japan		Tokyo	126,714,000
Jordan		Amman	6,669,000
Kazakhstan		Astana	16,223,000
Kenya		Nairobi	30,080,000
Kiribati		Bairiki	83,000
Korea, North		Pyongyang	24,039,000
Korea, South		Seoul	46,844,000
Kuwait		Kuwait	1,972,000
Kyrgyzstan		Bishkek	4,699,000
Laos		Vientiane	5,433,000

COUNTRY	FLAG	CAPITAL	POPULATION (2000)
Latvia		Riga	2,357,000
Lebanon		Beirut	3,282,000
Lesotho		Maseru	2,153,000
Liberia		Monrovia	3,154,000
Libya		Tripoli	5,605,000
Liechtenstein		Vaduz	33,000
Lithuania		Vilnius	3,670,000
Luxembourg		Luxembourg	431,000
Macedonia		Skopje	2,024,000
Madagascar		Antananarivo	15,942,000
Malawi		Lilongwe	10,925,000
Malaysia		Kuala Lumpur	22,244,000
Maldives		Male	286,000
Mali		Bamako	11,234,000
Malta		Valletta	389,000
Marshall Islands		Dalap-Uliga-Darrit	64,000
Mauritania		Nouakchott	2,670,000
Mauritius		Port Louis	1,158,000
Mexico		Mexico City	98,881,000
Micronesia		Palikir	119,000
Moldova		Chisinau	4,380,000
Monaco		Monaco	34,000
Mongolia		Ulaanbaatar	2,662,000
Morocco		Rabat	28,351,000
Mozambique		Maputo	19,680,000
Myanmar		Yangon	45,611,000
Namibia		Windhoek	1,726,000
Nauru		Yaren	12,000
Nepal		Kathmandu	23,930,000
Netherlands		Amsterdam, The Hague	15,786,000
New Zealand		Wellington	3,862,000
Nicaragua		Managua	5,074,000
Niger		Niamey	10,730,000

COUNTRY	FLAG	CAPITAL	POPULATION (2000)	COUNTRY	FLAG	CAPITAL	POPULATION (2000)
Nigeria		Abuja	111,506,000	Spain		Madrid	39,630,000
Norway		Oslo	4,465,000	Sri Lanka		Colombo	18,827,000
Oman		Muscat	2,542,000	Sudan		Khartoum	29,490,000
Pakistan		Islamabad	156,483,000	Suriname		Paramaribo	417,000
Palau		Koror	19,000	Swaziland		Mbabane	1,008,000
Panama		Panama City	2,856,000	Sweden		Stockholm	8,910,000
Papua New Guinea		Port Moresby	4,807,000	Switzerland		Bern	7,386,000
Paraguay		Asunción	5,496,000	Syria		Damascus	16,125,000
Peru		Lima	25,662,000	Taiwan (Republic of China)		Taipei	22,100,000
Philippines		Manila	75,967,000	Tajikistan		Dushanbe	6,188,000
Poland		Warsaw	38,765,000	Tanzania		Dar es Salaam	33,517,000
Portugal		Lisbon	9,875,000	Thailand		Bangkok	61,399,000
Qatar		Doha	599,000	Togo		Lomé	4,629,000
Romania		Bucharest	22,327,000	Tonga		Nuku'alofa	99,000
Russia		Moscow	146,934,000	Trinidad and Tobago		Port of Spain	1,295,000
Rwanda		Kigali	7,733,000	Tunisia		Tunis	9,586,000
Saint Kitts and Nevis		Basseterre	38,000	Turkey		Ankara	66,591,000
Saint Lucia		Castries	154,000	Turkmenistan		Ashgabat	4,459,000
Saint Vincent and the Grenadines		Kingstown	114,000	Tuvalu		Fongafale	12,000
Samoa		Apia	180,000	Uganda		Kampala	21,778,000
San Marino		San Marino	27,000	Ukraine		Kiev	50,456,000
São Tomé and Príncipe		São Tomé	147,000	United Arab Emirates		Abu Dhabi	2,441,000
Saudi Arabia		Riyadh	21,607,000	United Kingdom		London	58,830,000
Senegal		Dakar	9,481,000	United States		Washington, D.C.	281,421,906
Serbia and Montenegro		Belgrade	10,640,000	Uruguay		Montevideo	3,337,000
Seychelles		Victoria	77,000	Uzbekistan		Tashkent	24,318,000
Sierra Leone		Freetown	4,854,000	Vanuatu		Port-Vila	190,000
Singapore		Singapore	3,567,000	Vatican City		Vatican City	1,000
Slovakia		Bratislava	5,387,000	Venezuela		Caracas	24,170,000
Slovenia		Ljubljana	1,986,000	Vietnam		Hanoi	79,832,000
Solomon Islands		Honiara	444,000	Yemen		Sana	18,112,000
Somalia		Mogadishu	10,097,000	Zambia		Lusaka	9,169,000
South Africa		Cape Town, Pretoria	40,377,000	Zimbabwe		Harare	11,669,000

THE 50 UNITED STATES

This table lists the 50 states that make up the United States of America. The population figures are based on the U.S. Census for the year 2000.

STATE	STATE FLAG	POSTAL ABBREVIATION	NICKNAME(S)	CAPITAL	YEAR OF ADMISSION	POPULATION (2000 CENSUS)
Alabama		AL	Heart of Dixie	Montgomery	1819	4,447,100
Alaska		AK	Last Frontier	Juneau	1959	626,932
Arizona		AZ	Grand Canyon State	Phoenix	1912	5,130,632
Arkansas		AR	Natural State	Little Rock	1836	2,673,400
California		CA	Golden State	Sacramento	1850	33,871,648
Colorado		CO	Centennial State	Denver	1876	4,301,261
Connecticut		CT	Constitution State	Hartford	1788	3,405,565
Delaware		DE	First State	Dover	1787	783,600
Florida		FL	Sunshine State	Tallahassee	1845	15,982,378
Georgia		GA	Empire State of the South, Peach State	Atlanta	1788	8,186,453
Hawaii		HI	Aloha State	Honolulu	1959	1,211,537
Idaho		ID	Gem State	Boise	1890	1,293,953
Illinois		IL	Prairie State	Springfield	1818	12,419,293
Indiana		IN	Hoosier State	Indianapolis	1816	6,080,485
Iowa		IA	Hawkeye State	Des Moines	1846	2,926,324

STATE	STATE FLAG	POSTAL ABBREVIATION	NICKNAME(S)	CAPITAL	YEAR OF ADMISSION	POPULATION (2000 CENSUS)
Kansas		KS	Sunflower State	Topeka	1861	2,688,418
Kentucky		KY	Bluegrass State	Frankfort	1792	4,041,769
Louisiana		LA	Pelican State	Baton Rouge	1812	4,468,976
Maine		ME	Pine Tree State	Augusta	1820	1,274,923
Maryland		MD	Free State, Old Line State	Annapolis	1788	5,296,486
Massachusetts		MA	Bay State	Boston	1788	6,349,097
Michigan		MI	Great Lake State, Wolverine State	Lansing	1837	9,938,444
Minnesota		MN	Gopher State, North Star State	St. Paul	1858	4,919,479
Mississippi		MS	Magnolia State	Jackson	1817	2,844,658
Missouri		MO	Show Me State	Jefferson City	1821	5,595,211
Montana		MT	Treasure State	Helena	1889	902,195
Nebraska		NE	Cornhusker State	Lincoln	1867	1,711,263
Nevada		NV	Silver State	Carson City	1864	1,998,257
New Hampshire		NH	Granite State	Concord	1788	1,235,786
New Jersey		NJ	Garden State	Trenton	1787	8,414,350
New Mexico		NM	Land of Enchantment	Santa Fe	1912	1,819,046
New York		NY	Empire State	Albany	1788	18,976,457
North Carolina		NC	Old North State, Tar Heel State	Raleigh	1789	8,049,313

STATE	STATE FLAG	POSTAL ABBREVIATION	NICKNAME(S)	CAPITAL	YEAR OF ADMISSION	POPULATION (2000 CENSUS)
North Dakota		ND	Peace Garden State	Bismarck	1889	642,200
Ohio		OH	Buckeye State	Columbus	1803	11,353,140
Oklahoma		OK	Sooner State	Oklahoma City	1907	3,450,654
Oregon		OR	Beaver State	Salem	1859	3,421,399
Pennsylvania		PA	Keystone State	Harrisburg	1787	12,281,054
Rhode Island		RI	Little Rhody, Ocean State	Providence	1790	1,048,319
South Carolina		SC	Palmetto State	Columbia	1788	4,012,012
South Dakota		SD	Mount Rushmore State	Pierre	1889	754,844
Tennessee		TN	Volunteer State	Nashville	1796	5,689,283
Texas		TX	Lone Star State	Austin	1845	20,851,820
Utah		UT	Beehive State	Salt Lake City	1896	2,233,169
Vermont		VT	Green Mountain State	Montpelier	1791	608,827
Virginia		VA	Old Dominion	Richmond	1788	7,078,515
Washington		WA	Evergreen State	Olympia	1889	5,894,121
West Virginia		WV	Mountain State	Charleston	1863	1,808,344
Wisconsin		WI	Badger State	Madison	1848	5,363,675
Wyoming		WY	Equality State	Cheyenne	1890	493,782

PRESIDENTS OF THE UNITED STATES

PRESIDENT	PARTY	BORN	DIED	TERM(S)
1 George Washington	Federalist	February 22, 1732	December 14, 1799	1789–97
2 John Adams	Federalist	October 30, 1735	July 4, 1826	1797–1801
3 Thomas Jefferson	Democratic-Republican	April 13, 1743	July 4, 1826	1801–09
4 James Madison	Democratic-Republican	March 16, 1751	June 28, 1836	1809–17
5 James Monroe	Democratic-Republican	April 28, 1758	July 4, 1831	1817–25
6 John Quincy Adams	Democratic-Republican	July 11, 1767	February 23, 1848	1825–29
7 Andrew Jackson	Democratic	March 15, 1767	June 8, 1845	1829–37
8 Martin Van Buren	Democratic	December 5, 1782	July 24, 1862	1837–41
9 William Henry Harrison	Whig	February 9, 1773	April 4, 1841	1841
10 John Tyler	Whig	March 29, 1790	January 18, 1862	1841–45
11 James Knox Polk	Democratic	November 2, 1795	June 15, 1849	1845–49
12 Zachary Taylor	Whig	November 24, 1784	July 9, 1850	1849–50
13 Millard Fillmore	Whig	January 7, 1800	March 8, 1874	1850–53
14 Franklin Pierce	Democratic	November 23, 1804	October 8, 1869	1853–57
15 James Buchanan	Democratic	April 23, 1791	June 1, 1868	1857–61
16 Abraham Lincoln	Republican	February 12, 1809	April 15, 1865	1861–65
17 Andrew Johnson	National Union	December 29, 1808	July 31, 1875	1865–69
18 Ulysses S. Grant	Republican	April 27, 1822	July 23, 1885	1869–77
19 Rutherford Birchard Hayes	Republican	October 4, 1822	January 17, 1893	1877–81
20 James Abram Garfield	Republican	November 19, 1831	September 19, 1881	1881
21 Chester Alan Arthur	Republican	October 5, 1829	November 18, 1886	1881–85
22 Grover Cleveland	Democratic	March 18, 1837	June 24, 1908	1885–89
23 Benjamin Harrison	Republican	August 20, 1833	March 13, 1901	1889–93
24 Grover Cleveland	Democratic	March 18, 1837	June 24, 1908	1893–97
25 William McKinley	Republican	January 29, 1843	September 14, 1901	1897–1901
26 Theodore Roosevelt	Republican	October 27, 1858	January 6, 1919	1901–09
27 William Howard Taft	Republican	September 15, 1857	March 8, 1930	1909–13
28 Woodrow Wilson	Democratic	December 28, 1856	February 3, 1924	1913–21
29 Warren Gamaliel Harding	Republican	November 2, 1865	August 2, 1923	1921–23
30 Calvin Coolidge	Republican	July 4, 1872	January 5, 1933	1923–29
31 Herbert Clark Hoover	Republican	August 10, 1874	October 20, 1964	1929–33
32 Franklin Delano Roosevelt	Democratic	January 30, 1882	April 12, 1945	1933–45
33 Harry S. Truman	Democratic	May 8, 1884	December 26, 1972	1945–53
34 Dwight David Eisenhower	Republican	October 14, 1890	March 28, 1969	1953–61
35 John Fitzgerald Kennedy	Democratic	May 29, 1917	November 22, 1963	1961–63
36 Lyndon Baines Johnson	Democratic	August 27, 1908	January 22, 1973	1963–69
37 Richard Milhous Nixon	Republican	January 9, 1913	April 22, 1994	1969–74
38 Gerald Rudolph Ford	Republican	July 14, 1913		1974–77
39 James "Jimmy" Earl Carter Jr.	Democratic	October 1, 1924		1977–81
40 Ronald Wilson Reagan	Republican	February 6, 1911		1981–89
41 George Herbert Walker Bush	Republican	June 12, 1924		1989–93
42 William "Bill" Jefferson Clinton	Democratic	August 19, 1946		1993–2001
43 George Walker Bush	Republican	July 6, 1946		2001–

VICE PRESIDENT(S)	DID YOU KNOW?
John Adams	He was the only president elected unanimously.
Thomas Jefferson	He was the first president to occupy the newly built White House.
Aaron Burr, George Clinton	About 6,000 books from his private library were purchased to help start the Library of Congress.
George Clinton, Elbridge Gerry	He completed a four-year course in two years at what is now Princeton University.
Daniel D. Tompkins	The U.S. Marine Band played at his 1821 inauguration and at every inauguration since.
John C. Calhoun	He was the first president to have his photograph taken.
John C. Calhoun, Martin Van Buren	He was the first president to ride on a railroad train.
Richard M. Johnson	He was the first president born in the United States.
John Tyler	President for the shortest time, he died of pneumonia 31 days after his inauguration.
None	He was the first president whose wife died while he was in office.
George M. Dallas	He was the first president to govern a United States that extended from the Atlantic Ocean to the Pacific Ocean.
Millard Fillmore	He kept his old army horse, Whitey, on the White House lawn.
None	He established the first permanent library in the White House.
William R. King	A brilliant courtroom lawyer, he was such a good speaker that he was able to deliver his inaugural address from memory.
John C. Breckinridge	He was the first and only president who never married.
Hannibal Hamlin, Andrew Johnson	He was the first president to be assassinated.
None	His wife taught him to write.
Schuyler Colfax, Henry Wilson	He was born Hiram Ulysses Grant but was registered as Ulysses S. Grant at military academy, and he never corrected the error.
William A. Wheeler	He was the first president to visit the West Coast while in office.
Chester A. Arthur	He juggled clubs to build up his muscles.
None	He was nicknamed "Elegant Arthur" because he had 80 pairs of pants, which he changed several times daily.
Thomas A. Hendricks	He was the only president married in the White House.
Levi P. Morton	He was the grandson of a former president (William Henry Harrison).
Adlai E. Stevenson	He was the only president to serve two nonconsecutive terms.
Garret A. Hobart, Theodore Roosevelt	He always wore a red carnation in his lapel for good luck.
Charles W. Fairbanks	He was the first American to win a Nobel Prize, when he was awarded the Nobel Peace Prize in 1906.
James S. Sherman	He later became chief justice of the Supreme Court.
Thomas R. Marshall	He was the first president to hold a press conference.
Calvin Coolidge	He was the first president to speak over the radio.
Charles G. Dawes	His nickname was "Silent Cal" because he was a man of few words.
Charles Curtis	He spoke Chinese with his wife in the White House to protect themselves against eavesdroppers.
John N. Garner, Henry A. Wallace, Harry S. Truman	He was the only president elected to more than two terms.
Alben W. Barkley	The "S" did not stand for any name; it was a compromise between the names of his two grandfathers.
Richard M. Nixon	Camp David was named after his grandson.
Lyndon B. Johnson	He was the youngest man elected president, at age 43.
Hubert H. Humphrey	He was the first president sworn in by a woman.
Spiro T. Agnew, Gerald R. Ford	He was the first president to resign his office.
Nelson A. Rockefeller	He was the first president to serve without having been elected president or vice president.
Walter F. Mondale	He studied nuclear physics and served aboard one of the first nuclear submarines.
George H. W. Bush	He was the oldest man elected president, at age 69.
J. Danforth Quayle	He was a former director of the Central Intelligence Agency (CIA).
Albert Gore Jr.	He decided to enter politics after meeting President John F. Kennedy.
Richard B. Cheney	He was the first president to have fathered twins.

CLASSIFICATION OF PLANTS AND ANIMALS

There are many different kinds of living things, or organisms, in the world. Scientists name and classify (place in related groups) organisms according to their similarities and differences. The branch of biology that deals with how organisms are named and classified is called taxonomy.

The ancient Greek philosopher Aristotle (384–322 B.C.) compiled detailed descriptions of organisms and divided them into two kingdoms—plants and animals. Most scientists now use five kingdoms—Monera (simple single-celled organisms such as bacteria and blue-green algae), Protista (more complex single-celled organisms), Fungi, Plantae (plants), and Animalia (animals).

Scientists divide each kingdom into smaller groups. In the animal kingdom the largest divisions are phyla (singular, *phylum*). In the plant kingdom these are called divisions. Each phylum or division is subdivided into classes, the classes into orders, and the orders into families. Families are divided into genera (singular, *genus*), and each genus is divided into species. A species is a group of organisms with similar features that are able to breed with one another. Different species do not normally interbreed.

Every organism has a scientific name taken from Latin words. The name has two parts, comprising the genus and the species. For example, the scientific name for the lion is *Panthera leo*—*Panthera* is the genus and *leo* is the species. This system was developed by the Swedish scientist Carolus Linnaeus (1707–78).

These sample classifications show the groups to which the common sunflower and the domestic dog belong:

CLASSIFICATION OF THE COMMON SUNFLOWER (*HELIANTHUS ANNUUS*)

kingdom	Plantae (plants—multicellular organisms that are able to make food by a process called photosynthesis; cannot move about freely)
division	Anthophyta, or Magnoliophyta (flowering vascular seed plants)
class	Magnoliopsida (dicotyledons, or dicots—flowering plants with two seed leaves)
order	Asterales (flowers are grouped together on a head)
family	Asteraceae (Aster family)
genus	*Helianthus* (meaning "sunflower")
species	*annuus* (meaning "annual," "yearly")

There can be many subdivisions between these seven ranks, such as subphylum, superdivision, and subclass. For example, the domestic dog (see table on right) belongs to the subphylum Vertebrata (vertebrates—chordates with a backbone).

CLASSIFICATION OF THE DOMESTIC DOG (*CANIS FAMILIARIS*)

kingdom	Animalia (animals—multicellular organisms that must eat other organisms for energy; most are able to move about freely)
phylum	Chordata (chordates—animals that at some stage in their development have a notochord, a rodlike structure that is replaced by a spinal cord and backbone in some animals)
class	Mammalia (mammals—warm-blooded chordates that are covered in hair and feed their young with milk produced by the mother's mammary glands)
order	Carnivora (carnivores—meat-eating mammals that have strong jaws with teeth that grip or slice flesh)
family	Canidae (canids—carnivores with long, slender legs and muscular bodies that are adapted for running and chasing prey)
genus	*Canis* (meaning "dog")
species	*familiaris* (meaning "belonging to a household")

PLANTAE—THE PLANT KINGDOM

Plants are multicellular organisms that make their own food by a chemical process called photosynthesis. Unlike animals, they do not have the ability to move independently. There are more than 500,000 plant species. Scientists organize the plant kingdom into divisions depending on how simple or complex a plant is. The divisions can be arranged into four general groups based on differences in the plant's structure. More complex plants usually have vascular tissues—tissues that transport water (xylem) and food (phloem) around the plant.

PLANTAE—PLANTS

MULTICELLULAR ALGAE

a primitive group of plants that live in water; they have no roots, stems, or leaves

NONVASCULAR LAND PLANTS

a general grouping of small, flat plants that grow close together in moist, shady places; they have simple stems and leaves, but no true roots; they reproduce by producing spores in a capsule

VASCULAR SEEDLESS PLANTS

a general grouping of land plants that have specialized tissues to transport water and food; most have true roots, stems, and leaves; they reproduce by means of spores

VASCULAR SEED PLANTS

a general grouping of plants that have vascular tissues and reproduce by producing seeds

DIVISION: ANTHOCEROTOPHYTA (hornworts)

DIVISION: BRYOPHYTA (mosses)

DIVISION: HEPATOPHYTA (liverworts)

GYMNOSPERMS

a general name for plants with seeds that lie exposed, usually on the scales of cones

ANGIOSPERMS

a general name for plants with seeds that are enclosed in fruit

DIVISION: EQUISETOPHYTA (horsetails)

DIVISION: LYCOPHYTA (club mosses and spike mosses)

DIVISION: PSILOPHYTA (whisk ferns)

DIVISION: PTERIDOPHYTA (ferns)

DIVISION: CONIFEROPHYTA (conifers)

DIVISION: CYCADOPHYTA (cycads)

DIVISION: GINKGOPHYTA (ginkgo)

DIVISION: GNETOPHYTA (gnetophytes)

DIVISION: ANTHOPHYTA, OR MAGNOLIOPHYTA (flowering plants)

CLASS: LILIOPSIDA (monocotyledons, or monocots)

plants with one seed leaf, such as grasses, lilies, orchids, and palms

CLASS: MAGNOLIOPSIDA (dicotyledons, or dicots)

plants with two seed leaves, such as beans, foxgloves, oaks, and roses

ANIMALIA — THE ANIMAL KINGDOM

ANIMALIA—THE ANIMAL KINGDOM

Animals are multicellular organisms that are able to move independently and that can sense their surroundings. Unlike plants, animals are unable to make their own food, so they must eat either plants or other animals. There are more than one million named species. This chart shows the most general groupings used in animal classification. Within the

ANIMALIA — ANIMALS

PHYLUM:
ANNELIDA (annelids)
round, segmented worms such as earthworms, sandworms, and leeches

PHYLUM:
ARTHROPODA (arthropods)
animals that have an external skeleton, jointed limbs, and segmented bodies

PHYLUM:
CHORDATA (chordates)
animals that have symmetrical bodies and, at some stage in their development, have a notochord—a rodlike structure that in some animals is replaced by a spinal column and backbone

SUBPHYLUM:
CHELICERATA (chelicerates)

SUBPHYLUM:
CRUSTACEA (crustaceans)
arthropods, such as crabs, lobsters, and shrimps, that mostly live in water and breathe with gills; they typically have three major body regions that are divided into segments, each with a pair of appendages; they have two pairs of antennae

SUBPHYLUM:
UNIRAMIA (uniramians)

SUBPHYLUM:
VERTEBRATA (vertebrates)
animals with a backbone

CLASS:
ARACHNIDA (arachnids)
arthropods, such as mites, scorpions, spiders, and ticks, that usually have a two-part body, two pairs of appendages that are used for grasping, biting, and touching, and four pairs of walking legs

CLASS:
CHILOPODA (centipedes)
arthropods with long bodies of many segments, most with a pair of legs

CLASS:
DIPLOPODA (millipedes)
arthropods with long bodies of many segments, most with two pairs of legs

CLASS:
INSECTA (insects)
arthropods, such as beetles, butterflies, and mosquitoes, that usually have a three-part body, a pair of antennae, two pairs of wings, and three pairs of walking legs

CLASS:
CHONDRICHTHYES (cartilaginous fish)
cold-blooded vertebrates, such as sharks and rays, that live in water; they have streamlined bodies covered in scales; they use fins to move and breathe with gills

ORDER:
MARSUPIALIA (marsupials)
mammals, such as kangaroos, koala bears, and opossums, that give birth to tiny young that develop in a pouch outside the mother's body

ORDER:
MONOTREMATA (monotremes)
mammals, such as platypuses, that lay eggs but produce milk for their young when born

ORDER:
CARNIVORA (carnivores)
meat-eating mammals, such as bears, cats, and weasels, that have strong jaws with teeth that grip or slice flesh

kingdom, phyla are the broadest categories. They are based on the structure of the animal's body. The chart shows only the major phyla; there are more than 30 phyla in total. Large phyla are subdivided into subphyla. Phyla or subphyla contain classes; classes are made up of orders. Some of the most familiar classes and orders are shown here.

**PHYLUM:
CNIDARIA
(cnidarians, or coelenterates)**
soft-bodied invertebrates (animals without a backbone), such as corals, jellyfish, and hydra, that are radially symmetrical; they live in water; many have tentacles with stinging cells

**PHYLUM:
ECHINODERMATA
(echinoderms)**
invertebrates, such as sea cucumbers and starfish, that are radially symmetrical and have an internal skeleton made of plates or spines of calcium carbonate; they live in water

**PHYLUM:
MOLLUSCA (mollusks)**
invertebrates, such as clams, octopuses, slugs, and snails, with soft, unsegmented bodies and a muscular foot; some have a shell

**PHYLUM:
NEMATODA (nematodes)**
thin, round worms, such as hookworms; some are parasites (animals that live on or inside another animal)

**PHYLUM:
PLATYHELMINTHES
(flatworms)**
unsegmented worms, such as tapeworms; some are parasites

**PHYLUM:
PORIFERA (sponges)**
very simple animals without tissues that live in water

**CLASS:
OSTEICHTHYES
(bony fish)**
cold-blooded vertebrates, such as eels, pikes, and salmon, that live in water; most have streamlined bodies covered in scales; they use fins to move and breathe with gills

**CLASS:
AMPHIBIA
(amphibians)**
cold-blooded vertebrates, such as frogs, toads, and newts, that usually have smooth, moist skin; as adults they breathe with lungs; most live on land but return to water to breed and lay eggs

**CLASS:
REPTILIA
(reptiles)**
cold-blooded vertebrates, such as crocodiles, snakes, and turtles, with scaly skin; most lay eggs

**CLASS:
AVES (birds)**
warm-blooded vertebrates, such as eagles, sparrows, and penguins, that have wings and a beak with no teeth; their bodies are covered with feathers; they lay eggs

**CLASS:
MAMMALIA
(mammals)**
warm-blooded vertebrates that are covered in hair and feed their young with milk produced by the mother's mammary glands

**ORDER:
CETACEA (cetaceans)**
mammals, such as whales and dolphins, that spend their lives in water, breathing air into their lungs through one or two blowholes

**ORDER:
INSECTIVORA (insectivores)**
small mammals, such as hedgehogs, moles, and shrews, with long snouts, that feed on invertebrates, especially insects, mollusks, and worms

**ORDER:
RODENTIA (rodents)**
mammals, such as mice, rats, and squirrels, that have special teeth adapted for gnawing

**ORDER:
PRIMATES**
intelligent mammals, such as apes, humans, and monkeys, that have good vision and hands and feet adapted for grasping

MEASUREMENTS

To measure is to find the amount or size of some quality of an object. The quality might be length, volume, area, or weight.

We measure a quality by comparing it with an established unit. Most of the world's countries use a system of measurement known as the metric system, or International System of Units. It is also known by its French name—*Système International d'Unités*, or SI. The United States is one of the few countries that use a different system, known as the customary system. Although an act was passed in 1988 that declared the metric system to be the preferred system of measurement for trade and commerce in the United States, the changeover from customary to metric is proceeding slowly.

The conversion tables on these pages show how to change units of the customary system to metric units, and vice versa.

LENGTH AND DISTANCE

Customary system
12 inches (in.) = 1 foot (ft.)
3 feet = 1 yard (yd.)
1,760 yards = 1 mile (mi.)

Metric system
10 millimeters (mm) = 1 centimeter (cm)
100 centimeters = 1 meter (m)
1,000 meters = 1 kilometer (km)

To convert	multiply by
inches to millimeters	25.4000
inches to centimeters	2.5400
feet to meters	0.3048
yards to meters	0.9144
miles to kilometers	1.6090
millimeters to inches	0.0394
centimeters to inches	0.3937
meters to feet	3.2810
meters to yards	1.0936
kilometers to miles	0.6214

VOLUME AND CAPACITY (liquid)

Customary system
27 cubic feet (cu. ft.) = 1 cubic yard (cu. yd.)
8 U.S. pints (pt.) = 1 U.S. gallon

Metric system
1,000 cubic millimeters (cu. mm) =
  1 cubic centimeter (cu. cm) or 1 milliliter (ml)
1,000 cubic centimeters or 1,000 milliliters =
  1 cubic decimeter (cu. dm) or 1 liter (l)
1,000,000 cubic centimeters or 1,000 liters =
  1 cubic meter (cu. m)
1,000,000,000 cubic meters =
  1 cubic kilometer (cu. km)

To convert	multiply by
fluid ounces to milliliters	29.5735
cubic inches to cubic centimeters	16.3900
cubic feet to cubic meters	0.0283
cubic yards to cubic meters	0.7646
cubic inches to liters	0.0163
U.S. pints to liters	0.4732
U.S. gallons to liters	3.7853
milliliters to fluid ounces	0.0338
cubic centimeters to cubic inches	0.0610
cubic meters to cubic feet	35.3100
cubic meters to cubic yards	1.3080
liters to cubic inches	61.0300
liters to U.S. pints	2.1134
liters to U.S. gallons	0.2642

AREA

Customary system
9 square feet (sq. ft.) = 1 square yard (sq. yd.)
4,840 square yards = 1 acre
640 acres = 1 square mile (sq. mi.)

Metric system
100 square millimeters (sq. mm) = 1 square centimeter (sq. cm)
10,000 square centimeters = 1 square meter (sq. m)
10,000 square meters = 1 hectare (ha)
100 hectares = 1 square kilometer (sq. km)

To convert	multiply by
square inches to square centimeters	6.4520
square feet to square meters	0.0929
square yards to square meters	0.8361
square miles to square kilometers	2.5900
acres to hectares	0.4047
square centimeters to square inches	0.1550
square meters to square feet	10.7600
square meters to square yards	1.1960
square kilometers to square miles	0.3861
hectares to acres	2.4710

WEIGHT AND MASS

Customary system (avoirdupois)
16 ounces (oz.) = 1 pound (lb.)
2,000 pounds = 1 short ton

Metric system
1,000 milligrams (mg) = 1 gram (g)
1,000 grams = 1 kilogram (kg)
1,000 kilograms = 1 metric ton (tn)

To convert	multiply by
ounces to grams	28.3500
pounds to grams	453.6000
pounds to kilograms	0.4536
short tons to kilograms	907.1848
short tons to metric tons	0.9072
grams to ounces	0.0353
grams to pounds	0.0022
kilograms to pounds	2.2046
kilograms to short tons	0.0011
metric tons to short tons	1.1023

TEMPERATURE CONVERSIONS

There are several sets of temperature units. The two in most common use are the Celsius system and the Fahrenheit system. The Celsius system—in which water freezes at 0 degrees Celsius (0°C) and boils at 100°C—is used by scientists and in everyday life in most countries of the world. Temperatures on the Fahrenheit scale—in which water freezes at 32 degrees Fahrenheit (32°F) and boils at 212°F—can be converted to Celsius, and vice versa.

To convert Fahrenheit to Celsius:
Celsius = (Fahrenheit − 32°) x 5/9

To convert Celsius to Fahrenheit:
Fahrenheit = (Celsius x 9/5) + 32°

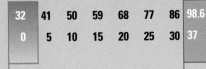

Fahrenheit	32	41	50	59	68	77	86	98.6	104	113	122	131	140	149	158	167	176	185	194	203	212
Celsius	0	5	10	15	20	25	30	37	40	45	50	55	60	65	70	75	80	85	90	95	100

freezing point of water   *temperature of human body*   *boiling point of water*

INDEX

694

PHOTO CREDITS

b = bottom; c = center; l = left; r = right; t = top

Airport Authority Hong Kong: 14
AKG: 40t, 42br, 52, 61t, 63, 98b, 99, 132b, 152t, 160b, 299, 301, 324b, 345, 398, 400, 415, 423, 431, 458t, 465, 471, 496, 596t, 640, 660, British Library 344, 590, S. Domingie 133, Suzanne Held 498t, Erich Lessing 9b, 41, 112, 195b, 276t, 293, 390b, 396, 419t, 489, Jean-Louis Nou 403, VISIOARS 72t, 401, /British Museum 16
Ardea: Pascal Goetgheluck 95t, Francois Gohier 263
Art Explosion: 62tl, 219, 233, 314, 321, 334, 500, 525
Artineed.com: 251b, 300, 559, 563, 600, 606
Artville: 405, Burke/Triolo 320, 537
Australian Tourist Commission: 2

BASF Corporate Archives: 546
British Airways plc: 13b
Brown Reference Group: 333, 421, 512b
Bruce Coleman Collection: Jane Burton 21, John Cancalosi 250, 562b, Alain Compost 505, Derek Croucher 328, Joe McDonald 380, Pacific Stock 449, 526, Andrew Purcell 255, John Shaw 208, Mark Taylor 330, Staffan Widstrand 411, Gunter Ziesler 68
Bureau of Reclamation: 173

Centers for Disease Control: 181
CERN Geneva: 469
Chandra X-Ray Center: 53cl
Corbis: 53b, 352b, 524, 535, 601, 605, Paul Almasy 143b, Archivo Iconografico, S.A. 18, 26t, 111t, 281, 499, 656b, Tony Arruza 433, Yann Arthus-Bertrand 266, Asian Art & Archaeology Inc. 420b, William A. Bake 114, Tiziana & Gianni Baldizzone 83, David Ball 315, Bass Museum of Art 361l, Tom Bean 34, Morton Beebe 136, Lester V. Bergman 203, Bettmann 7b, 15, 26b, 97, 106t, 123b, 139, 164, 175b, 253t, 290b, 295, 305, 393t, 523, 545, 564, 568, 652t, 667b, Bowers Museum of Cultural Art 117r, Gary Braasch 615, Burstein Collection 40b, 110b, Christie's Images 82b, Dean Conger 304, Richard A. Cooke 424, Gianni Dagli Orti 25, 122b, Darama 633, Araldo De Luca 501, 639, Duomo 67, Ecoscene 78b, Macduff Everton 238, 477, Najlah Feanny 631, Jack Fields 336b, Kevin Fleming 243, Owen Franken 459, 577, Freelance Photographers Guild 504b, Gallo Images/Diana Frances Jones 7t, Arvind Garg 23, Raymond Gehman 192, Daniel Geller 552, Annie Griffiths Belt 453, Jeremy Horner 288, Kit Houghton 39t, Hanan Isachar 507, Robbie Jacks 586, Catherine Karnow 211t, 329, 585, Layne Kennedy 358, Alain Le Garsmeur 104, Charles & Josette Lenars 353, Michael S. Lewis 527c, Chris Lisle 498b, Wally McNamee 296t, Buddy Mays 425, David Muench 91, 150t, Mug Shots 594, Museum of the City of New York 141t, Richard T. Nowitz 35l, Charles O'Rear 155b, 395t, Papilio/Clive Druett 22b, Clay Perry 239, Carl & Ann Purcell 119b, Steve Raymer 49, 201, Roger Ressmeyer 240, 339, 441, 466, 493, Lynda Richardson 22t, Galen Rowell 516, 549, Ted Spiegel 463, Hubert Stadler 84, Sygma/Philippe Caron 602, /Jerome Favre 188, /Brooks Kraft 617bl, /Rick Maiman 137, Peter Turnley 350b, Underwood & Underwood 108t, Gian Berto Vanni 289t, Sandro Vannini 142t, 604t, Brian A. Vikander 27t, Nik Wheeler 169t, 291, Nevada Wier 225

Corbis Royalty Free: 57, 200, 248, 249t, 249b, 427t, 491, 529b, 565, 628

Daimler Chrysler: 73t, 267t
Digital Vision: 211b, 476, 483, 495, 581, 642, 650, 652b, Jeremy Horner 397, Jeremy Woodhouse 629

Egyptian State Tourist Office: 197
Empics: Neal Simpson 446

FEMA: Dave Gatley 207t, Dave Saville 235b

Getty Images: 1, 9t, 20b, 48, 61b, 64b, 75, 95b, 110t, 122t, 126t, 149, 158, 166, 174, 175t, 191t, 198, 205b, 253b, 261, 277, 361r, 378, 390t, 448, 458b, 464, 479t, 479b, 512t, 517, 529t, 554, 569, 604b, 619, 641, 651t, AEF/Yves Debay 102, Archive Photos 634, /Joe Muroe 667t, Derek Berwin 87, Jeff Cadge 74b, Luis Castaneda 162, Wendy Chan 337, Steve Dunwell 105, Bob Elsdale 17, Grant V. Faint 245, Will & Deni McIntyre 54, Nickolas Muray/George Eastman House 232b, Kevin Schafer 129, Pete Steward 106b, Keren Su 131, Taxi 202, Time Life Pictures/James Keyser 410, /MAI/Sandy Schaeffer 82t, Joseph Van Os 113, 168, 336t, Art Wolfe 46

Heidelberg: 490
Hemera: 65c, 66t, 66b, 72b, 170, 182, 244, 282t, 296b, 372b, 406, 427b, 503, 522b, 527t, 538, 589
Honda: 508
The Hutchison Picture Library: 408, John Hart 596b, Ian R. Lloyd 375, Nairn 6, Trevor Page 418, Andrey Zvoznikov 497

Image Ideas Inc.: 475b, 481
ImageState: 35t, 89, 92, 135, 276b, 571, Peter Atkinson 330–331, Brian Lawrence 268, 440
Imaging Body.com: Eurolois/Igor Bertrand 302
Independence National Historic Park: 356
Inst. Costa Rica: 117l, 119t, 254

Jane Addams Collection: 3
John Foxx Images: 668

The Kobal Collection: 227l, Industrial Light & Magic 109

Lebrecht Music Collection: 412
Library of Congress: 8b, 31t, 71t, 134, 207b, 256, 269, 280, 310, 341, 528, 547, 645, 651b, 654, Carl Van Vechten 445
Life File: Jeff Greenberg 612
Luxembourg National Tourist Office: 432

Marconi Corporation plc: 494
Mary Evans Picture Library: 70, 76t, 85b, 101, 103, 108b, 126b, 128, 138, 145b, 178b, 223, 260, 359, 360, 362t, 362b, 377, 382, 422, 470t, 636, 653, 656t, Sigmund Freud Copyrights 492

NASA: 51tr, 73b, 74t, 165, 259, 273, 379, 518, 557t, 566,

709